# COUNSELING AND PSYCHOTHERAPY WITH CHILDREN AND ADOLESCENTS

# COUNSELING AND PSYCHOTHERAPY WITH CHILDREN AND ADOLESCENTS

## Theory and Practice for School and Clinical Settings

### THIRD EDITION

Edited by

*H. Thompson Prout and Douglas T. Brown*

**John Wiley & Sons, Inc.**

New York  •  Chichester  •  Weinheim  •  Brisbane  •  Singapore  •  Toronto

*Library of Congress Cataloging-in-Publication Data:*

Counseling and psychotherapy with children and adolescents: theory and
   practice for school and clinical settings / [edited by] H. Thompson
  Prout and Douglas T. Brown.
      p.   cm.
   Includes bibliographical references and index.
   ISBN 0-471-18236-2 (cloth : alk. paper)
    1. Child psychotherapy.   2. Adolescent psychotherapy.
  3. Children—Counseling of.   4. Teenagers—Counseling of.
  I. Prout, H. Thompson, 1947–    .  II. Brown, Douglas T.
  RJ504.C64    1999
  618.92′8914—dc21                  98-16412

Printed in the United States of America.

10  9  8  7  6  5  4  3  2  1

*To our children*
*Alex and Lauren, and Adam*
*Who continue to teach us things you*
*can't find in a textbook!*

# Contributors

Anne P. Cituk
Multidisciplinary Center
Florida State University
Tallahassee, Florida

Harriet C. Cobb
Department of Psychology
James Madison University
Harrisonburg, Virginia

Richard A. DeMartino
Ballston Lake, New York

Raymond DiGiuseppe
Department of Psychology
St. John's University
Jamaica, New York

Barbara L. Fisher
Rocky Mountain Marriage and
    Family Institute
Fort Collins, Colorado

Gerald B. and Diane L. Fuller
Professional Psychology Program
Walden University
Traverse City, Michigan

Leigh R. Graves
Multidisciplinary Center
Florida State University
Tallahassee, Florida

William B. Gunn, Jr.
Dartmouth Family Practice Residency
    Program
Concord, New Hampshire

F. Donald Kelly
Psychological Services in Education
Florida State University
Tallahassee, Florida

J. Edward McKee
Department of Psychology
James Madison University
Harrisonburg, Virginia

Scott P. Merydith
Department of Psychology
George Mason University
Fairfax, Virginia

Helen B. Moore
Department of Psychology
James Madison University
Harrisonburg, Virginia

Jack H. Presbury
Department of Psychology
James Madison University
Harrisonburg, Virginia

Susan M. Prout
Department of Special Education and
    Rehabilitation Counseling
University of Kentucky
Lexington, Kentucky

Laura W. Smith
Department of Psychology
James Madison University
Harrisonburg, Virginia

Antoinette Thomas
University of Virginia
Charlottesville, Virginia

Patricia J. Warner
Department of Psychology
James Madison University
Harrisonburg, Virginia

# *Preface*

With the third edition of this book, we have observed noticeable changes in the area of counseling and psychotherapy with children and adolescents. We noted in our first edition (1983) that there were few volumes addressing this topic. Since that time, techniques and theory have been refined to more specifically target the mental health needs of children and adolescents, services are more widely applied in more settings, and the empirical base for these interventions is stronger. Our purpose with this edition remains similar to that of the first and second editions. We provide comprehensive overviews of major theoretical perspectives in treating mental health problems of children and adolescents in a comparative format and we highlight specific issues relevant to conducting child and adolescent therapeutic interventions. Throughout the book, we have attempted to address both theoretical and practice issues related to these interventions.

As this work has evolved, we have added chapters that supplement the original material and have increased the comprehensiveness of the coverage. In this edition, we have added two chapters. One new chapter covers important issues in counseling children from a multicultural perspective—an area not adequately addressed in the earlier editions. A second new chapter details an array of other techniques and strategies that do not fall under the coverage of the major approaches we have identified.

Many individuals contributed to this third edition. First, we would like to thank all the chapter authors for their valuable professional contributions. Second, we want to acknowledge the staff of Clinical Psychology Publishing Company who were the publishers of the first two editions of this work. Last, we thank Kelly Franklin and Dorothy Lin of John Wiley & Sons for their support and patience (most of all) in the preparation of this revision. We are proud to join the Wiley family!

H. THOMPSON PROUT
DOUGLAS T. BROWN

# Contents

**Chapter 1** ————————————————————————

# COUNSELING AND PSYCHOTHERAPY WITH CHILDREN AND ADOLESCENTS: AN OVERVIEW

H. Thompson Prout

The psychological treatment of children's problems is the focus of several professions and is carried out in many settings and situations. While theoretical viewpoints are wide-ranging and essentially rooted in adult-based theories, the child or adolescent presents a unique challenge to the child mental health worker. Children are not simply "little adults." Their treatment cannot be viewed as scaled-down adult therapy; their developmental stages, environments, reasons for entering therapy, and other relevant factors necessitate a different, if not creative, approach to therapy. The child/adolescent therapist must have an expanded knowledge base of the human condition and a different perspective of what constitutes therapy or counseling.

This book is about psychotherapy and mental health counseling with children and adolescents. It brings together in a comparative format the major theoretical views of psychological treatment of children and highlights major issues in the area. A number of concerns, however, cut across the theories and are relevant to any provision of mental health services to children. This introductory chapter describes some of these issues. Historical perspectives, the mental health needs of children and adolescents and need for services, developmental issues, the adolescent phase, the unique aspects of child and adolescent therapy, psychotherapy with adolescents, a multimodal view of treatment, practitioner concerns and patterns of practice, and research/efficacy issues are discussed. Throughout this chapter, the terms *counseling* and *psychotherapy* are used interchangeably.

## HISTORICAL PERSPECTIVES ON THE MENTAL HEALTH NEEDS OF CHILDREN AND ADOLESCENTS

Many major advances in clinical mental health work can, in some way, be traced to Freud. Mental health work with children is no exception. Freud's classic case study of "Little Hans" in 1909 is generally viewed as the first reported attempt to psychologically explain

1

and treat a childhood disorder (Freud, 1955). Although Freud did not directly treat Little Hans's phobia, he offered a psychoanalytic explanation of the problems and guided the father in the treatment of Hans. This case study is recognized as providing the base for Freud's theories on the stages of psychosexual development. Freud's interest in childhood disorders apparently waned at this point, and it was not until 1926 that his daughter, Anna, presented a series of lectures entitled "Introduction to the Technique of Psycho-analysis of Children" to the Vienna Institute of Psychoanalysis. These lectures generated considerable interest and established Anna Freud as a pioneer in child psychotherapy (Erickson, 1978). Shortly thereafter, Melanie Klein (1932), emphasizing the symbolic importance of children's play, introduced free play with children as a substitute for the free association technique used with adults, thus inventing play therapy. While these two camps disagreed on many issues, they have remained the dominant voices in the child psychoanalytic field, with most analytic work being a spin-off of either Anna Freud or Klein.

At approximately the same time (the early twentieth century), other forces were beginning to put more emphasis on work with children. In France in 1905, Alfred Binet completed initial work on his intelligence test, which was used for making educational placement decisions in the Paris schools. This work provided the base for the psychometric study of individuals and had great impact on child study and applied psychology (Schwartz & Johnson, 1985). At the University of Pennsylvania in the United States, Witmer had established a clinic for children in 1896 that focused on school adjustment (M. Erickson, 1978), and in 1909 Healy founded what is now the Institute for Juvenile Research in Chicago (Schwartz & Johnson). These events provided the base for the child guidance movement, emphasizing a multidisciplinary team approach to the diagnosis and treatment of children's adjustment and psychological difficulties. The child guidance model involved treating both the child and his or her parents. The increased interest in clinical and research work on children's problems led to the founding of the American Orthopsychiatric Association in 1924, an organization of psychologists, social workers, and psychiatrists concerned with the mental health problems of children (Schwartz & Johnson).

Through the 1940s and into the 1950s, psychoanalytic psychotherapies were used almost exclusively in the treatment of children. In 1947, Virginia Axline published *Play Therapy,* describing a nondirective mode of treatment utilizing play. Nondirective play therapy was, in effect, a child version of Carl Rogers's adult-oriented client-centered therapy. Both nondirective play therapy and client-centered therapy represented the first major departures from psychoanalytic thought, differing in conceptualization of the therapeutic process and content in the role of the therapist. Rogers's impact on adult psychotherapy was paralleled and followed by Axline's impact on child therapy. The next major movement in psychotherapy was the rise of the behaviorally based approaches to treatment. While the principles and potential applications of behavioral psychology were long known, it was not until the 1960s that behavior modification and therapy began to be used frequently in clinical work with children (Graziano, 1975).

The mental health treatment of children and adolescents has also been affected by two policy and legislative mandates. First, the community mental health movement was strongly influenced by the passage in 1963 of the federal program to construct mental health centers in local communities and begin a move away from large institutional treatment. This movement grew not only because it was mandated by a federal program but because it represented a philosophy that mental health interventions are more likely to be successful when carried out in the community where the maladjustment is occurring. The new programs emphasized early intervention and prevention of mental disorders. The second mandate, with a similar philosophical base, involved the provision of special education services to all handicapped children, including emotionally disturbed and behavior-disordered children and adolescents. Exemplified initially by Public Law 94-142 [now the Individuals with Disabilities Education Act (IDEA)], this movement has not only expanded the role of public education in provision of services to these children but also allowed more children to remain in their home communities. Psychotherapy and mental health treatment, if deemed a part of the total educational program of a child, has become by law and policy an educational service.

## CHILD AND ADOLESCENT MENTAL HEALTH NEEDS: A CHRONIC PROBLEM

There are well-documented estimates of large and perhaps increasing numbers of children who are experiencing significant mental health problems. These needs have been apparent for some time. Studies in the 1960s and 1970s clearly showed the pervasiveness of problems at that time. In a study of children in public school, Bower (1969) estimated that at least three students in a typical classroom (i.e., 10% of school-age children and adolescents) suffered from moderate to severe mental health problems; many of these children were disturbed enough to warrant special educational services for the emotionally handicapped. In 1968, Nuffield, citing an estimate of 2.5 to 4.5 million children under the age of 14 in need of psychiatric treatment, found indices of only 300,000 receiving treatment services. This figure represented services to roughly 10% of those in need. Berlin estimated in 1975 that each year there would be 6 million school-age children with emotional problems serious enough to indicate the need for professional intervention. Cowen (1973) noted a smaller group (1.5 million) in need of immediate help but estimated that fewer than 30% of these children were receiving this help.

Current findings show little change in the reduction of problems. Kazdin and Johnson (1994) noted that incidence studies show between 17% and 22% of youth under the age of 18 have some type of emotional, behavioral, or developmental problem. This represented between 11 and 14 million of the 64 million youth in the United States with significant impairment. They noted that many of those with disorders are not referred for treatment and are not the focus of treatment in the schools. Kazdin and Johnson also noted that there are high and increasing rates of at-risk behaviors including antisocial and delinquent behaviors, and substance abuse. Doll (1996), in a synthesis of epidemiology studies, notes a similar rate of 18% to 22% with diagnosable disorders, translating this to the analogy of a school of 1,000 students with 180 to 220 students in the school having a disorder in the clinical ranges. Doll sees the need for broad-based policies at all levels (school, district, governmental) to address these significant needs. Regardless of the estimate of incidence, it is clear that many children and adolescents with problems are not identified by educational, mental health, and social service institutions as having emotional difficulties and thus are not referred for or provided treatment services.

Children and adolescents remain critically underserved populations, despite ample recognition of the problem based on nearly 30 years of research documenting needs. The mental health needs of children present an enormous service delivery shortfall; and with funding problems continuing in the human services, the gap between need and available services is likely to continue. Preventive services may be a cost- and resource-efficient mode for dealing with part of this problem, but the provision of quality counseling and psychotherapeutic services will be a crucial component in the total mental health system.

## DEVELOPMENTAL ISSUES

The child/adolescent mental health worker must be familiar with human development for a number of reasons. With the exception of severe psychopathology or extreme behaviors, much of what is presented as problematic in children may simply be normal developmental deviation. What is considered pathological behavior in adults may not be abnormal in children or adolescents. Knowledge of development and the normal behavioral ranges at different ages is crucial to discriminating between truly deviant behavior and minor developmental crises. Development in children and adolescents may follow sequences with expected orders for the appearance of certain behaviors and characteristics yet still tend to be highly variable. Children's personalities are quite unstable when compared with expectations of stability in adults. Related to this instability is the evidence that indicates normal development is often marked by a number of behavior problems. The classic developmental study by MacFarlane, Allen, and Honzik (1954) pointed to a number of behaviors that parents considered to be problems yet were normative at different age levels. Sroufe (1991) emphasizes this, noting that age is important in distinguishing normal versus abnormal behavior. The child/adolescent therapist must be able to sort out these "normal" problems from those that may represent more serious disorders.

Awareness of development will also aid the therapist in clinical decision making at various points in the treatment process. Appropriate goal setting is important to any therapeutic venture. It provides a direction for our work, allows us to monitor progress, and tells us when we are done. The child/adolescent therapist sets these goals within a developmental framework and does not expect an average 8-year-old to acquire, in the course of therapy, the problem-solving cognitive abilities or the moral judgment of a 10-year-old. To set goals above developmental expectations is almost ensuring that the intervention will fail. This knowledge of development also allows the therapist to choose appropriate content and to decide what level of therapeutic interaction is best suited for the child. Within these developmental age expectations, the therapist must also be sensitive to developmental delays in children. Not only do delays, particularly in cognition and language, dictate goal setting, but also they must be distinguished from behavioral or emotional disorders. These delays may also be major contributing factors in the development of disorders. For example, children with learning disabilities or mental retardation often display poor self-concepts and negative self-images as well as other socioemotional difficulties (Clarizio & McCoy, 1976). On the other end of the spectrum, we need to be cautious not to set limited goals for developmentally advanced children. Although we are not advocating psychological assessment as a prerequisite for treatment, in most cases, the child/adolescent therapist will need to assess developmental levels of their clients early in the intervention.

The study of development can be broken down into essentially two types of information that are relevant for counseling or psychotherapy. The first involves an understanding of the developmental stage theorists, with the works of Freud, Piaget, Kohlberg, and Erikson most notable. Freud's psychoanalytic view of human development emphasizes the psychosexual aspects and pleasure-seeking drives that affect the child and adolescent. Development is seen as a series of developmental crises resulting in psychosexual conflicts that must be resolved for the individual to move on the next phase (Neubauer, 1972). While obviously most consistent with the psychoanalytic approach to treatment, Freud's description of the developmental phases and parent-child relationships provides a useful base for assessing socioemotional development. Similarly, Piaget's theory of cognitive development provides a parallel base for assessing intellectual development. Piaget suggested that maturation, physical experience, social interaction, and equilibration (the internal self-regulating system) all combine to influence cognitive development. At different periods, the type of information that can be processed and the cognitive operations that can be performed vary. Cognitive development is a coherent and fixed sequence with certain cognitive abilities expected at certain ages (Wadsworth, 1996). Piaget allows us to select developmentally appropriate modes of interacting with the child and to set appropriate goals for cognitive change. For example, a child in the concrete operations stage solves problems involving real or observable objects or events. He or she has difficulty with problems that are hypothetical and entirely verbal, making verbally oriented or more abstract counseling interventions inappropriate at this developmental stage.

Kohlberg (1964, 1973) has focused on the development of the understanding of morality, or what the individual believes would be the morally correct response to problem situations. Moral judgment is seen as a developmental, age-bound variable similar to the cognitive and psychosexual stages. At different ages, the individual has certain beliefs about the reasons for displaying moral behavior, the value attached to a human life, and the reasons for conforming to moral standards. Awareness of the stages of moral development can provide insights into the behavior of the child, provide content for therapy sessions, and also allow therapy to be conducted at levels commensurate with current moral development levels. Lowered stages of moral development have been hypothesized to be related to child deviance, particularly delinquency (Quay, 1979).

Erikson's (1963) developmental theory is based in psychoanalytic theory and emphasizes a series of psychosocial crises. At each stage, the individual encounters a crisis that he or she must resolve by acquiring a new phase of social interaction. An unsuccessful resolution of a psychosocial crisis impedes further development and can have a negative effect on the individual's personality. Although psychoanalytically based, Erikson places more emphasis on socialization and the demands of society. Erikson's work, along with the classic work of Havighurst (1951), is viewed by many as being particularly useful in understanding adolescent development. Taken together, these developmental stage theories provide the therapist with a comprehensive framework to view the child's current developmental levels.

The other child development information relevant to the child/adolescent therapist comes from the study of personality factors that are essentially specific developmental variables. In many cases, these factors are components of the major personality theories. While the list of variables that have been studied is almost infinite, Clarizio and McCoy (1976) have described several that are particularly relevant for child and adolescent therapy because they are often the focus of a referral concern or interact with the problem. These developmental characteristics often follow developmental sequences similar to the stage theories. Certain periods will present behaviors that may be perceived as bothersome by parents or teachers but are, in actuality, part of the normal growth pattern.

Clarizio and McCoy (1976) cite dependency, anxiety and insecurity, aggressiveness, and achievement motivation as factors that are commonly involved in child and adolescent problems. In looking at each factor, one finds a developmental pattern, behavioral manifestations, contributing factors to problematic instances of the factor, and adaptive and maladaptive outcomes. For example, dependency may involve child-adult relationships in which the child is often seeking help and physical contact, engaging in attention-seeking behavior, and maintaining physical proximity to the adult. These behaviors are relatively normal and expected with young children and their parents. As children get older, both the intensity of the dependency and the object of emotional dependence change. Maturing children become less dependent on their parents, with a resulting decrease in the dependent behaviors, and become more dependent on peers for approval and attention.

Certain parental patterns (e.g., overpermissiveness, overprotection) are seen as contributing to a child's overdependence and interfering with the move toward greater independence. The child who makes adequate progress in this area develops a sense of trust, is responsive to social reinforcers, and is able to display warmth toward others. The overly dependent child is more likely to become a passively dependent individual, submissive, and mistrusting of others. For dependency and other personality factors, a normal developmental progression is viewed as important to successful adult adjustment. Knowledge of these variables can be used in treatment planning and goal setting, in determining whether excessive or pathological behaviors are occurring at different ages, and in assessing contributing factors to problematic behaviors.

# THE ADOLESCENT PHASE

Probably no single developmental period provides more confusion and consternation for parents, teachers, and clinicians than adolescence. It is characterized more by a developmental phase than by a set, sequenced series of stages. Mercurial behaviors, many of them disturbing, seem to "possess" the adolescent. Weiner (1992) notes that many people view normal adolescence as a disturbed state. He notes that normal adolescent development will be characterized by a range of distressing, turbulent, and unpredictable thoughts, feelings, and actions and that as a consequence of such storm and stress, adolescents will normatively display symptoms that in an adult would suggest definitive psychopathology. This view yields two important aspects of adolescent psychotherapeutic work. First, the adolescent therapist must be cautious not to overinterpret typical and, perhaps, seemingly bizarre behavior, thoughts, or feelings as indicating severe psychopathology. Second, the therapist should not be surprised or upset by a rocky, unpredictable, and frustrating course of treatment.

Adolescents are, in fact, at the crossroads of life. They are making the transition from childhood to adulthood. Havighurst's (1951) classic list of adolescent developmental tasks provides much insight into the pressures and demands faced by adolescents. According to Havighurst, the mastery of nine developmental tasks is critical to adolescent adjustment:

1. Accepting one's physique and sexual role.
2. Establishing new peer relationships with both sexes.
3. Achieving emotional independence of parents.
4. Achieving assurance of economic independence.
5. Selecting and preparing for an occupation.
6. Developing intellectual skills and concepts necessary for civic competence.
7. Acquiring socially responsible behavior patterns.
8. Preparing for marriage and family life.
9. Building conscious values that are harmonious with one's environment.

The adolescent's response to much of this developmental stress leads to a number of what Copeland (1974) has described as "adolescent idiosyncrasies" that are not necessarily indicative of any pathological process. Copeland describes both the characteristics of adolescent thinking and the characteristics of adolescent affect and behavior. The characteristics of adolescent thought include:

- *Preoccupation with Self.* The adolescent's thought represents an intense involvement with the self at this stage. This involvement may be narcissistic, but it may also be coupled with self-doubt and crises of self-confidence.
- *Preoccupations with Fantasy.* A rich fantasy life is a result of the intense drives and feelings the adolescent is experiencing. The fantasies provide a means of controlling these drives as well as some degree of gratification.

- *Preoccupation with the Need for Self-Expression.* "Doing your own thing," as Copeland calls it, reflects the adolescent's struggle to establish an independence free from parental supervision and consent. Being unique also is involved in the adolescent's attempts to develop a sense of identity.
- *Preoccupation with Philosophical Abstraction, Theories, and Ideals.* The adolescent is preoccupied with such philosophical questions as "absolute truth" and "ultimate reality." The adolescent develops his or her own theories and views about the world, often strongly rejecting the established ideas of those in authority. Copeland attributes this perspective to Piaget's work. Piaget saw egocentrism in adolescence as a normal stage of cognitive development, when the adolescent becomes possessed with his or her newly found powers of logical thought. The adolescent is unable to differentiate between his or her own idealistic thought and the "real" world (Wadsworth, 1996).
- *Preoccupation with Sexuality.* The adolescent is extremely interested in sexual matters, with initial heterosexual relationships often intense and overidealized. The adolescent may become overconcerned with appearance and dress, spending considerable time preening and grooming.
- *Hedonism and/or Asceticism.* Because of the intensity of drive states, the adolescent is virtually forced to respond to them. This response tends to be extreme— either hedonistic, with the adolescent fully pursuing instinctual gratification, or ascetic, where he or she renounces the drive out of fear and guilt.
- *Conformism.* The adolescent, as part of the struggle for independence, shifts his or her identity patterns from parents and family to a chosen peer group. The behaviors and characteristics, often shown through dress and other interests, usually are antithetical to and criticized by the adults from whom the adolescent is attempting to become independent.

According to Copeland, the adolescent also tends to display certain characteristic affective states and behaviors:

- *Heightened Sensitivity.* The adolescent experiences life intensely and passionately, sometimes overreacting. Minor concerns can become major issues, with the adolescent being indifferent to very little.
- *Mood Swings.* Emotional reactions of joy and sadness can occur suddenly, and almost concurrently. The shifts in affect are quick and intense.
- *Propensity to Act Out.* Impulsive behavior often causes trouble both for the adolescent and for others. Rebelliousness may be common, and in some extreme cases delinquency and other antisocial behavior may occur.
- *Inhibition of Behavior.* The adolescent may have episodes of inhibition and may withdraw socially at times.

The child/adolescent therapist will find much in theory and research in child and adolescent development that pertains to psychological interventions with these groups.

In fact, it is difficult to imagine developing and carrying out treatment plans without a firm grounding in these areas. Developmental theory and research provide us with a framework to systematically, if not scientifically, work with children and adolescents and more objectively gauge our therapeutic progress with them.

## UNIQUE ASPECTS OF PSYCHOTHERAPY WITH CHILDREN AND ADOLESCENTS

In addition to the developmental issues previously discussed, a number of other issues related to the child's development and situation have an impact on the psychotherapeutic relationship. These factors relate to the direct work with the child or adolescent and stem from some of the differences between child/adolescent psychotherapy and adult psychotherapy.

Clarizio and McCoy (1976) have offered an overview of some of the unique aspects of the child/adolescent therapeutic relationship. Children and adolescents bring a different motivation for treatment into the counseling situation. While the adult is usually aware that a personal problem exists, the child may not agree or recognize that there are problems or concerns. Although others may encourage an adult to seek professional help, in most cases, he or she will decide whether to enter treatment. The child is unlikely to voluntarily initiate entering into therapy. This decision is usually made by an adult within the child's environment, with some varying degree of acceptance/compliance/resistance from the child. The involuntary nature of the child/adolescent client in many cases may yield little or no motivation on the part of the client to engage in a relationship with the therapist or not even an admission that any change is necessary. Thus, the first step in many interventions may be simply to establish some type of relationship with the child and to come to some agreement that change is necessary. Without developing some motivation in the client to at least examine the current situation, even if done nonjudgmentally, it will be difficult to make significant progress.

An aspect related to motivation is the child/adolescent's lack of understanding of both the therapeutic process and the treatment objectives. The adult is likely to recognize the need to "get something out of therapy" and to have certain expectations of what is supposed to happen in the counseling situation. The adult usually will be able to verbalize some expectations and goals and to engage in some role-appropriate "client behaviors," (e.g., talking, reflecting, responding to questions). The child may have no clear view of what the therapy situation presents. This blurred view may range from having total misinformation to seeing the therapist as an agent of his or her parents, the school, the courts, or some other individual or institution that forced the initiation of treatment. The therapist may initially have to simply educate the child about therapy, explaining what it is and what it is not. Children may bring in very distorted or stereotyped ("Oh, so you're the shrink. Where's your couch?") perceptions of therapists. This author is reminded of one extremely anxious 12-year-old boy who failed to respond to the usual reassuring techniques in an initial therapy session. After some gentle probing, it was learned that the young man had watched one too many late-night horror movies in which the fiendish doctor had done bizarre things to his subjects. Somehow the boy had associated coming to the mental health clinic with the scenes in movies where the hero gets wired to a machine and is never the same again. When I reassured him that the use of electrodes was not part of my approach and that we were simply going to talk about problems he was having at home and school, he visibly relaxed and began to volunteer all sorts of information.

Even as therapy progresses, it is necessary to monitor these perceptions. The child who views the therapist as the person he plays games with once a week is unlikely to focus on the tasks necessary to facilitate change. Similarly, there may be little agreement as to what changes are needed and what mutually acceptable treatment objectives are to be established. The therapist is likely to be faced with the predicament of reconciling, on the one hand, the goals of those who initiated treatment (e.g., parents, teachers) and, on the other hand, the child or adolescent client's own view of what is needed. A parent-referred adolescent who has been arrested three times for shoplifting may verbalize a goal of having his parents "get off my case." Although this position may be a factor in the acting out, it is not likely to produce an appropriate therapy objective, given the referral problem. Thus, the therapist must negotiate with the client appropriate goals, objectives, and topics or content for the counseling. These goals may not necessarily be in total agreement with the aims of the referral source or the therapist, but they will provide a starting point. Objectives can always be renegotiated as the relationship develops. Further, the therapist needs to demonstrate to the child or adolescent client that the client will get something out of counseling. Initially, this demonstration may take a form as simple as providing an interesting format. This accomplishment can lead to the establishment of a more congruent set of objectives.

Another major difference between child and adult therapy is the child's more limited verbal and linguistic development, which is also related to the limitations in cognitive development. Children may be unable to think in more abstract terms and may have even more difficulty verbally describing and discussing their thoughts and emotions. This limited verbal ability is one of the main reasons play has been used as a medium of therapy. Play and other nonverbal techniques allow expression without creating anxiety or frustration for the child because of an inability to find the correct verbal description. Further, the child may not have the receptive vocabulary to fully understand what is being asked in the interview situation. This author once observed a psychiatric interview of a 7-year-old girl in which the resident asked the child if she ever had any hallucinations. The little girl, obviously not knowing what was meant by the word "hallucination," happily responded, "Oh, yes, all the time," whereupon the resident made note of this finding and continued the interview along other lines. Therapy must be geared at the appropriate developmental level for both the child's expressive and receptive language capabilities. While not deemphasizing the worth of "talk therapy," alternative modes of expression should be investigated for use in conjunction with verbal interactions. The therapist may also find it useful to teach the child labels and verbal mediators for emotional experiences. This course of action can involve using the traditionally accepted labels for feelings or using the child's own terminology. An 8-year-old girl once accurately described several symptoms consistent with "feeling depressed." The girl, however, felt more comfortable generally describing the state as one of "yuckiness."

Children also differ from adults in terms of their dependence on environmental forces and changes. Children are reactors to changes in their living situations rather than initiators of change. They have relatively little power to take action to eliminate or prevent environmental causes of stress. They react to parental divorces, family moves, and school and peer pressures. The child's disturbance may actually be a relatively normal reaction to upheaval or stress in the environment. Yet, the child cannot divorce his parents, change schools, or move at will. Because the child is dependent on the environment, it is more important for those in the environment to be involved in treatment. Where the adult is more likely to seek treatment independently, the child is less likely to be treated in isolation. Even if the child makes significant progress in individual therapy, he or she still does not have the options available to adults in dealing with the environment. In some cases, therapy may even proceed on the notion of helping the child cope with a stressful situation, rather than assuming that change will be forthcoming in the environment. For example, an 11-year-old can exert little impact on the drinking and resulting behavior of an alcoholic parent yet may be assisted in finding ways to deal with the problem that make the stress more manageable.

Another factor that contributes to the difference between child therapy and adult therapy is that the child's personality is less likely to be set than the adult's. The child, whose defenses are not as well established, is more pliable and amenable to therapeutic influence, once the relationship and cooperation are established. The personality is still developing and changing rapidly, yielding a greater potential for change. But at the same time, this situation presents a somewhat more labile client and can result in inconsistent responses in therapy session. The child has a greater range of normal emotional and behavioral responses as a result of the unformed nature of the personality. The therapist, therefore, can be more flexible and must anticipate and not be discouraged by seemingly broad swings of emotion and behavior in the course of treatment. The plasticity of the child's personality is also an asset in the working out of a preventive model that heads off disturbing patterns with appropriate intervention prior to the crystallization of the personality.

## PSYCHOTHERAPY WITH ADOLESCENTS

As unpredictable as the adolescent's behavior is to those in his or her environment, a similar unpredictability exists in the therapeutic relationship. Weiner (1992) notes that psychotherapy with disturbed adolescents is a demanding task that some clinicians seek out while others actively avoid. Adolescents entering the therapy situation are characteristically impatient, intolerant, and uncommunicative. They may fail to elaborate on any details of the current situation or difficulties presented. They may deny any responsibility for the current problems, preferring to place blame elsewhere, or may actually have almost no insight into the reasons they have been referred for treatment. This uncooperativeness is frustrating and anxiety-arousing for the therapist and may even discourage attempts to build a therapeutic relationship. Picture a 16-year-old male sitting in your office, slouched in a chair, a cap and long hair covering his averted eyes. His first words and only complete sentence for the next hour are: "I don't want to talk to no f—king shrink." A reflective statement on your part that he must be upset about something only brings a muffled grunt. A series of your best open-ended questions elicits only a series of unelaborated "Yes"s, "No"s, "I don't know"s, "Maybe"s, and "It's the damn teachers." Your feeble attempts to introduce humor or to discuss "safe" topics bring only more grunts, a few eye rolls, or no response at all. His posture throughout the seemingly never-ending hour remains essentially unchanged. This initial session represents the base on which you will build your therapeutic relationship with the young man. It is little wonder that many therapists avoid such interactions. Despite our best rationalizing that the adolescent is reacting to the situation and not to us, it is often difficult to come out of such an unproductive session feeling as though we made progress and that our skills are up to the task of helping the adolescent.

Although the adolescent may be a difficult client, Weiner (1992) feels that most disturbed adolescents are accessible to psychotherapeutic intervention. Depending on the level of development and maturity, work with the adolescent may range from gamelike approaches utilized with younger children to therapy that resembles interventions with an adult presenting similar problems. Most adolescents will not be candidates for insight-oriented, in-depth therapy involving the reworking of previous experiences. According to Weiner, defenses may be serving a relatively useful function during this period of personality development, and attempts to strip these defenses away may be unproductive or actually counterproductive to the overall therapeutic plan. Goals may range from better self-understanding with some personality reorganization to simple stabilization and improved functioning without major personality change.

Weiner (1992) notes that adolescents differ from both adults and children in their view of treatment. While most children are initially unaware of the significance of therapy and most adults have made the choice to begin treatment, adolescents are clearly aware that they have been brought to treatment by others who can force continual attendance as sessions. Commenting on the beginning of treatment, Weiner notes that a swift and incisive beginning of the treatment relationship is critical to successful psychotherapeutic work with adolescents, probably more so than with other age groups. Initially, the therapist must attempt to put the adolescent at ease, explaining what to expect and taking steps to suppress apprehensions. Unstructured probing, queries about deep personal feelings, or challenging the adolescent to explain his or her misbehavior will likely produce further uncooperativeness or yield a strong emotional response. Beginning with factual information in a nonjudgmental manner will help allay initial anxieties. The therapist needs to explain how the relationship will differ from those with parents, teachers, peers, and others. The goal at this level is to achieve engagement with the adolescent and then implant the initial seeds for establishing a motivation. The initial agreement from the adolescent may simply be to return to another session.

Weiner (1992) states that continuing to build the relationship involves maintaining a flow of communication, fostering a positive identification with the therapist, and dealing with the adolescent's concern about how therapy might affect his or her independence. The adolescent therapist will be more active in comparison with the adult therapist. Long silences, noncommittal responses, and long periods of formulating answers to the adolescent's concerns should be avoided. Adolescent therapists may find they talk with these clients relatively more than with adult clients. Explaining thoughts explicitly, phrasing questions concretely, and, in general, using a direct approach will facilitate work with the adolescent. Many of the interpretive leads and nondirective probes used with adults may be perceived by the adolescent as trickery and may add to resistance. Therapists need to present themselves as genuine. A spontaneous, conversational approach that is more akin to talking with a casual friend is recommended. The adolescent is likely to be curious about the therapist's "real life," and the therapist's responses to such questions should be matter-of-fact and nonevasive. While not attempting to influence values, the therapist should be willing to share personal opinions and attitudes with the adolescent. Acknowledgment of the adolescent's feelings about various issues and situations is helpful; the therapist should be particularly aware of the current teenage values, fads, slang, and so on, and be sensitive to the pressures related to adolescents' social and emotional developmental levels. The therapist needs to communicate a liking of and interest in the adolescent. This is best done indirectly because the adolescent will recognize the artificiality of an "I like you." A sincere commitment to engage with the adolescent in mutual problem solving, along with other concrete gestures and expressions of interest, is most helpful. Finally, the therapist must work at maintaining a balance along the continuum of independence-dependence. Adolescents should not be treated like children; yet they should not be given signals that they are entirely free to make all of their own life decisions.

Meeks (1971), in the classic text on the subject aptly entitled *The Fragile Alliance,* has also written about therapeutic work with adolescents. The important components in a successful therapeutic alliance with an adolescent involve: (1) the adolescent being genuinely concerned about some aspect of his or her psychological functioning, (2) the adolescent being able to accurately and honestly observe his or her own functioning and report it to the therapist, and (3) the extent to which the family will support the therapeutic endeavor. The key to establishing this alliance, according to Meeks (1979), involves the "careful and systematic interpretation of affective states" (p. 136) presented by the adolescent in therapy. Signals or cues of changes in affect from the adolescent may be masked or quite subtle, and the therapist must be sensitive to the implications of these changes. Copeland (1974) in a similar vein has provided a list of prognostic indicators for a favorable outcome of adolescent psychotherapy: (1) sincere self-referral, (2) acceptance of the concept of personal problems, (3) presence of psychological pain, (4) motivation for change, (5) economic independence, (6) history of accomplishments, (7) sense of responsibility, (8) ability to form a working relationship with the therapist, (9) acceptance of rules and other limits, and (10) positive relationships to family or other surrogates (p. 109). Motivation to change and a history of positive accomplishments are viewed as the two most important determiners of potential therapeutic success. While Copeland's list may be useful in developing a prognostic prediction or even deciding whether to attempt therapy with an adolescent, one wonders what an adolescent who presents all or most of these indicators would be doing in therapy. It is likely that most of those referred adolescents would not present a positive prognostic picture given these guidelines.

## A MULTIMODAL VIEW OF TREATMENT

This book borrows (and somewhat bastardizes) the term *multimodal* from Lazarus (1976) to describe the overall philosophy implicit in the subsequent chapters. Lazarus presented his BASIC ID, an acronym for seven interactive modalities that are investigated as potential points of intervention for problems. The modes are Behavior, Affect, Sensation, Imagery, Cognition, Interpersonal relationships, and Drugs-Diet. This approach presents a comprehensive method of identifying problems and then deciding the most effective way to intervene. Keat (1979, 1990, 1996) expanded on this approach with his own acronym, BASIC IDEAL, by adding E for Educational or school pursuits, A for Adults in the child's life (parents, teachers, relatives), and L for Learn the client's culture.

This book takes a broad view of what is "psychotherapeutic" for a child or an adolescent. By multimodal, we refer to the many types of interventions to help troubled children and adolescents. Kazdin (1988) lists over 250 terms that have been used in the research and case study literature to describe interventions with children and adolescents. This nearly exhaustive list points to the many interventions we have available to facilitate therapeutic change with children and adolescents. There also exists a range within each alternative. Educational measures, for example, can range from resource room help to a full-time structured placement. Parental interventions may involve parenting classes or perhaps therapy for the parents. In most cases, a multimodal, or combined, approach will be used. For example, a child may receive individual therapy, his or her parents may receive counseling, and the teacher may conduct a behavior management program. Although it is desirable to intervene in the most efficacious and cost-efficient manner, we do not make assumptions that one technique is preferable to or more therapeutic than others. At this point, neither research nor clinical experience is able to identify whether a child with a low self-concept, for example, is helped more by two hours a week of individual therapy or by having a teacher who is trained to consistently provide positive successful school experience. We do not know whether group social skills training is more beneficial than family therapy. What we do know is that several types of intervention have some benefit for children and adolescents. The more interventions and systems that can be combined—the more modalities that are involved in the treatment—the more likely it is we will realize our overall therapeutic goals. This approach is not a "let's try everything" plan. It involves careful assessment of problems, selection of appropriate interventions, and coordination and communication among those providing services. As long as our treatment programs are not excessively costly or time-consuming, interventions involving several modalities are indicated.

This multimodal view also implies two other basic assumptions. First, professionals with a variety of backgrounds are involved in child treatment. A teacher with a B.A. in Special Education may be working with a child who is receiving individual therapy from a psychiatrist who has completed a child psychiatry fellowship program. A high school guidance counselor may work individually with an adolescent whose family is in therapy with a Ph.D. psychologist. A further assumption here is that one does not have to be called a therapist to have therapeutic impact on a child. The second, related assumption involves the settings where treatment takes place. Troubled children and adolescents receive "treatment" in, among other places, classrooms, schools, agencies, clinics, group homes, and hospitals. In this book, we do not make the artificial distinction between counseling and psychotherapy. We assume that a similar core of principles and techniques can be adapted to many settings. While the presenting problems may differ depending on the setting, we believe, for example, that an Adlerian-trained school counselor will function in a manner relatively similar to an Adlerian-trained psychiatrist in an inpatient setting. The overriding concern is the development of effective, coordinated, and multifaceted interventions.

## THE PRACTICE OF CHILD AND ADOLESCENT COUNSELING AND PSYCHOTHERAPY

The practice of counseling and psychotherapy with children and adolescents has been examined in two surveys of practitioners. Kazdin, Siegel, and Bass (1990) surveyed psychologists and psychiatrists whose practices included the provision of child and adolescent treatment. Their group was predominately private practitioners, but also included those based in hospital, medical, and community mental health settings. Almost half of their time involved treatment-related activities. Respectively, conduct disorder, attention deficit disorder, affective disorders, adjustment disorders, and anxiety disorders were the most common diagnostic categories of their child and adolescent patients. The respondents rated the following theoretical approaches in terms of usefulness: Eclectic, psychodynamic, family, behavioral, and cognitive were the most useful approaches, with some differences noted between psychologists and psychiatrists. These professionals conducted treatments that averaged 27 sessions in length, with an average of approximately one session per week. In most cases, parents and school personnel were consulted or involved in treatment.

H. Prout, Alexander, Fletcher, Memis, and Miller (1993) surveyed a sample of psychologists practicing in the schools to assess the patterns of practice of therapeutic interventions in that setting. Their respondents spent considerably less time providing counseling or psychotherapy, with only 17% of their time devoted to these activities. Additionally, these professionals had briefer contacts with their clients, averaging 10 sessions for individual counseling cases and 11 for group interventions. Treatment sessions were also shorter than the typical 50-minute hour in clinical settings, with both individual and group sessions averaging less than 40 minutes. In theoretical orientation, the school practitioners rated behavioral, cognitive-behavioral, multimodal, reality, and family systems as the most useful approaches, and individual counseling, supportive/ relationship building, crisis intervention, contracting, and parent counseling as the most useful techniques or modalities. Family problems, learning/underachievement, motivation/attitude, attention deficit/hyperactivity, and divorce were rated as the more frequent problems addressed in their practices.

Taken together, these studies show the wide range of practice and issues encountered in the practice of child and adolescent counseling and psychotherapy. Some differences appear to exist across disciplines and settings, but approaches and problems also vary within disciplines and settings.

## RESEARCH AND EFFICACY

### Historical and Traditional Reviews

Since Eysenck's (1952) classic and much-debated study on the effectiveness of psychotherapy with adults, researchers and clinicians have pondered the question, "Does psychotherapy work?" Eysenck's study, generally recognized as having spawned considerable research in psychotherapy, reviewed a number of studies of psychotherapy outcome with neurotic adults. His evaluation concluded that the percentage of treated clients who improved was not substantially different from the spontaneous remission rate (i.e., those individuals who improved without psychotherapy). He found that roughly two-thirds of each group, treated and untreated, reported improvement. Eysenck concluded that there was little evidence to support the effectiveness of psychotherapy with adult neurotics. Eysenck's data and methodology have been cited, reanalyzed and reinterpreted, criticized and condemned ever since. Despite its controversiality, his study is important for the discussion, research, and examination of the therapeutic venture it has fostered.

Systematically and carefully studying the psychotherapy effectiveness question is one of the most difficult research areas in the behavioral sciences. Understanding the process of psychotherapy and its relationship to behavior change is an extremely complex proposition. The four volumes of the *Handbook of Psychotherapy and Behavior Change* (Bergin & Garfield, 1971, 1994; Garfield & Bergin, 1978, 1986), point to both the methodological complexity and the enormity of the issues. These volumes have attempted to bring together current empirical knowledge and data on psychotherapy. To utilize current research findings or to attempt research in this area, one must be aware of the problems facing the researcher:

- Psychotherapy represents a wide variety of techniques, in some ways preventing a clear, unambiguous definition of psychotherapy. Psychotherapy differs depending on the theoretical orientation of the therapist, the length of time of the treatment, and the format (i.e., individual, group, marital, parent, family consultation).

- The clinical definition of client populations may be ambiguous and thus limit generalizability. Clear definition of symptomatology and the client characteristics may vary in studies and be somewhat a result of the setting. Would two studies of treatment of anxious children produce similar results if one were conducted in a school and one at a clinic? Similarly, there are subgroups that might be studied separately (e.g., males vs. females, blacks vs. whites, the disadvantaged, children).

- Therapists vary in age, sex, training, orientation, competency, style, and personality characteristics. Outcome could be affected by any one of these. Some research has studied the client/therapist match issue, (i.e., whether a certain type of therapist works best with a certain type of client).

- Research can focus on process or content variables. Process studies examine what goes on in therapy, typically some client/therapist interaction variable. Outcome studies examine whether the person is improved or whether there is behavioral or affective change following intervention. While some studies attempt to relate process to outcome, both have been and continue to be studied extensively.

- In outcome studies, what represents appropriate measures to gauge "therapeutic change"? Do rating scales, personality tests, client report, therapist rating, or the reports of significant others validly and reliably reflect genuine change? What represents improvement?

- Other methodological issues exist. Are single-subject research designs appropriate for studying the general effectiveness of techniques? What represents an appropriate control group for those who receive treatment? Both those people on waiting lists for treatment and defectors (those who fail to return to the clinic for therapy) have been used in comparison studies. Do these groups represent ones that are clinically comparable to the experimental group?

- Psychotherapy does not occur in isolation. How do we account for other extraneous variables that may affect our results?

- What are the long-term effects of our interventions? Does a 1-year positive follow-up on clients treated for depression mean that these individuals will also suffer fewer problems with depression in the subsequent 5 or 10 years? Psychotherapy research with children and adolescents presents some special research problems. Levitt (1971) notes that because the child is a developing organism, many of the symptomatic manifestations of essentially normal children tend to disappear as a function of development. Some problems like temper tantrums, enuresis, specific fears, and sleep disturbance tend to go away in time. Levitt notes, "There is some reality in the common-sense notion that children 'grow out' of certain behavior problems" (p. 477). This makes it difficult to sort out the effects of therapy versus the effects of maturation. Similarly, some problems that are indicative of underlying emotional disturbance may disappear as a function of development yet reappear in another form that Levitt calls "developmental symptom substitution" (p. 477). For example, a child successfully treated for enuresis at 8 years of age might be classified, for research purposes, as "cured" or "improved" yet present serious problems as an adolescent. Extending this view somewhat, research on the effects of childhood psychological treatment on later adult adjustment is difficult to do, yet this issue is an important one. Levitt also notes that, although the child may be the identified patient in clinical studies, persons other than the child may actually be the direct focus of treatment, thus making the isolation of treatment effects difficult.

In reviewing psychotherapy research studies, one is left with certain impressions. Because of the difficulty in conducting research in this area, it is possible to critically examine almost any single study and dismiss its results or offer alternative explanations of the findings on methodological grounds. The orthodox experimental psychologist who spends the day in a rat laboratory might smirk at some of our research conclusions. But because we work with humans who have difficulties in living and because the alleviation of these difficulties is a complex process, we must take a somewhat softer view of the research. We must examine the literature with the understanding that few, if any, studies are going to answer absolutely the question, "Does psychotherapy work?" Rather, we must continue to critically examine the data and conclusions and to glean from the research those implications that relate most directly to our clinical work. This proposal is made not to support "sloppy" research or blanket acceptance or rejection of findings but to support a flexible and open-minded view of the current literature and status of the psychotherapy venture. The question of whether psychotherapy works remains essentially unanswered at this point.

The effectiveness of psychotherapy with children has been chronicled in reviews by Levitt in 1957, 1963, and 1971, and in a review by Barrett, Hampe, and Miller in 1978. Levitt's 1957 study was modeled after Eysenck's (1952) study of the effectiveness of adult psychotherapy. Surveying reports of evaluation at both the close of therapy and at follow-up and comparing them with similar evaluations of untreated children, Levitt found that two-thirds of the evaluations at close and three-fourths at follow-up showed improvement. Roughly the same percentages were found in the untreated control groups. Levitt wrote: "It now appears that Eysenck's conclusion concerning the data for adult psychotherapy is applicable to children as well; the results do not support the hypothesis that recovery from neurotic disorder is facilitated by psychotherapy" (p. 193). Levitt noted, however, that his evaluation "does not prove that psychotherapy (with children) is futile" (p. 194) and recommended "a cautious, tongue-in-cheek attitude toward child psychotherapy" (p. 194) until additional evidence became available. The 1963 study utilizes a similar methodology and again concluded that the hypothesis that psychotherapy facilitated recovery from emotional problems could not be supported. Some of the 1963 data did suggest that comparisons should be made within diagnostic categories. Levitt also found that improvement rates tended to be lowest for cases of antisocial acting out and delinquency and highest for identifiable behavioral symptoms like enuresis and school phobia. The 1971 review departed slightly from the previous reviews and looked at a wider range of modalities than just child psychopathology. These included the effects of inpatient versus outpatient treatment, drug therapy, type of special class placement, and the use of mothers as therapists. While individual studies showed some effectiveness, the overall conclusion again pointed to a lack of proof that these interventions are generally helpful. Levitt also focused on two identifiable diagnostic classifications, juvenile delinquency and school phobia, for further examination. School phobia tended to respond favorably to treatment, but Levitt questioned whether treatment was simply removing the symptoms of more serious underlying core problems which would surface in some other form later. Conventional psychotherapy with delinquents appeared to be generally ineffective, but some moderately positive results were found in examining more comprehensive treatment programs for delinquents. In addition to still questioning the effectiveness of child psychotherapy, Levitt was able to provide some preliminary conclusions. He noted that many of the principles on which traditional psychoanalytically based child guidance treatment have been based are now being challenged by research. The evidence at that time did not support the necessity of involving the mother in treatment, the relative insignificance of father involvement, the relationship of outcome to intensity of treatment, the desirability of encouraging the expression of negative feeling, ignoring undesirable behavior, or the notion that the home or family situation is likely to be more therapeutic than other child-care settings. In other words, many principles that had guided, and probably still do guide, much of traditional child treatment simply are not supported in the research. Rigid orthodoxies are not empirically supported, although few of the innovative treatments are definitely supported either. Levitt calls for more studies of treatment of specific diagnostic classifications and more long-range follow-up studies.

Barrett et al. (1978) present a historical and methodological review in which they focus more on the research issues than on providing clinical guides. Noting that their review found little progress in this area of research, they again indicate that the issue of efficacy of child treatment remains unresolved. They pose a number of important questions for both future research and clinical work. They recommend abandoning the research questions of whether psychotherapy works and asking the more appropriate question: "Which set of procedures is effective when applied to what kinds of patients with which sets of problems and practiced by which sort of therapists?" (p. 428). Although this specific question complicates the issue, the answer is likely to be more productive in the long run than the answer to the general question. Further, they found classification systems to be inadequate and better systems to be needed for classifying childhood disorders. The efficacy of the *Diagnostic and Statistical Manual of Mental Disorders (DSM-III)* and of *DSM-IV,* which more clearly delineates childhood disorders, is yet to be established. Finally, research and practice both must focus more closely on the child's developmental level and the systems with which the child must interface.

Two other reviews of treatment bear mentioning. First, Abramowitz (1976) reviewed efficacy studies of group psychotherapy with children, reaching a conclusion similar to the reviews of individual therapy. Definitive conclusions are not possible at this point, and, based on available data, favorable responses to group therapy are not indicated. However, if a group therapy approach is indicated, the feasibility of using a behavioral approach might be considered first. Second, Tramontana (1980) has reviewed psychotherapy outcome research with adolescents and offered conclusions not much different from other reviews. Noting a sparseness in the adolescent literature,

Tramontana found no clear evidence of effectiveness but found the area to be fraught with research methodology problems.

## Meta-Analyses

The reviews previously noted could all be classified as evaluating the child psychotherapy research literature through the traditional critical literature review approach. In the past several years, the systematic approach of meta-analysis has been used for summarizing the efficacy literature in psychotherapy as well as other areas. This approach combines the results of efficacy studies by evaluating the magnitude of the effect of treatments. Smith and Glass (1977) popularized this statistical approach in the psychotherapy literature. In a meta-analysis, each outcome result in a controlled study is treated as one unit of magnitude of effect or "effect size" *(ES)*. The effect size is calculated by subtracting the mean of the control group; $(M_c)$ from the mean of the treated group $(M_t)$ and then dividing the difference by the standard deviation of the control group $(SD_c)$: $ES = M_t - M_c/SD_c$. The effect sizes are averaged to determine average effects across and between treatments. The effect size is a standard score that indicates how many standard deviation units a treatment group differs from an untreated control group. A positive effect size indicates improvement or the beneficial effects of treatment. For example, an effect size of 1.00 indicates that an untreated subject at the mean of his or her group (i.e., the 50th percentile) would be expected, on average, to rise to the 84th percentile (i.e., a one standard deviation improvement) with treatment.

Evaluating across all types of counseling and psychotherapy, Smith and Glass (1977) found an average effect size of .68. Similar replications by Shapiro and Shapiro (1982) and Landman and Dawes (1982) found overall effect sizes of .93 and .78 respectively. All three of these meta-analyses utilized primarily adult intervention studies, but were all generally supportive of the effectiveness of psychotherapy. Smith and Glass' analysis suggested that behavioral and nonbehavioral treatments were roughly equal in effectiveness, while Shapiro and Shapiro's findings suggested that behavioral and cognitive therapies were somewhat more effective than other therapies. The meta-analysis approach remains somewhat controversial and has met with some harsh criticism (e.g., Eysenck, 1978). Nonetheless, it does provide an option for more systematically and objectively summarizing research findings.

Several meta-analyses have been completed on the effectiveness of child/adolescent counseling and psychotherapy. Casey and Berman (1985) analyzed studies done with primarily younger children (under age 13) who received some form of psychotherapy, while H. Prout and DeMartino (1986) evaluated studies of children and adolescents who received interventions for school-based or school-related problems. Respectively, they found effect sizes across treatments of .71 and .58. These overall effect sizes are generally consistent with the meta-analyses done primarily with adult subjects. Using a model for evaluating the relative size of treatment effects proposed by Schroeder and Dush (1987), these effect sizes fall into the "moderate" effect size category.

More specifically, Casey and Berman (1985) found that behavioral and cognitive therapies were more effective than nonbehavioral (client-centered and dynamic) therapies with respective effect sizes of .91 and .40. Individual therapies were somewhat more effective than group interventions, .82 to .50. Similarly, H. Prout and DeMartino (1986) found behaviorally based treatments somewhat more effective than other approaches, .65 to .40, but found that school-based group interventions were superior to individual interventions, .63 to .39. Prout and DeMartino found only small difference between interventions with elementary students versus secondary students, .52 versus .65. Both studies also found some differences in outcome related to the type of treatment targets and outcome measures. Casey and Berman (1985) note, however, that many of these comparisons are not meaningful since the categorizing schemes also break the outcome studies into other classifications. For example, despite the differences they found between behavior therapies and nonbehavioral therapies, the respective studies were often evaluating different problems with different targets and outcome measures. Thus, the treatment foci are frequently not equivalent and it is not possible to make direct efficacy comparisons. It is best to view the previously noted differences cautiously.

However, subsequent meta-analytic reviews have produced similar results showing the effectiveness of child therapeutic interventions. Weisz and his colleagues (Weisz, Weiss, Alicke, & Klotz, 1987; Weisz, Weiss, & Donenberg, 1992; Weisz, Weiss, Han, Granger, & Morton, 1995) have conducted a series of meta-analyses on studies from child therapeutic intervention sources. While using somewhat different methodology and weightings, their series of analyses yielded overall effect sizes ranging from .71 to .79. Broadly defined behavioral interventions seemed to yield the strongest effects. S. Prout and Prout (1998) updated the H. Prout and DeMartino (1986) study of school-based therapies and found an overall effect size of .97. Interestingly, almost all the studies in this update that met the criteria for inclusion in the meta-analysis assessed the effectiveness of group interventions. There were very few controlled studies of individual counseling or psychotherapy conducted in school settings.

In the initial meta-analysis of child therapy studies, Casey and Berman (1985) concluded that the evidence in their analysis indicated that psychotherapy with children was as effective as therapy with adults. Despite some shortcomings in the diagnostic and methodological areas, they felt that the available outcome studies demonstrated the efficacy of treatment across a range of therapeutic approaches and problems. They noted: "Clinicians and researchers need not be hesitant in defending the merits of psychotherapy with children" (p. 397). Similarly, H. Prout and DeMartino (1986) concluded that there is evidence to support counseling and psychotherapeutic efforts in the schools and for school-related problems. Those conclusions continue to be an adequate assessment of the status of efficacy research in this area. Across all these meta-analyses, there is evidence of at least moderate effectiveness of child therapeutic interventions.

In the first edition of this book, we noted that the outcome research on child and adolescent psychotherapy left one with an unclear and confusing impression (H. Prout, 1983). The available reviews at the time did not support effectiveness, nor did they prove the ineffectiveness of child/adolescent therapeutic interventions. Yet at the same time, they pointed to the complexity of the issue and the methodological problems in conducting research in this area. While there remain some unresolved questions concerning the efficacy of child and adolescent therapeutic interventions, the array of meta-analyses present systematic reviews indicating some degree of benefit to these interventions. The question of effectiveness is much more clearly answered at this point. Further, data appear to support the greater efficacy of certain types of interventions, notably those falling in the broad category of cognitive-behavioral interventions. There is now support that therapeutic interventions with children and adolescents are a viable clinical activity. Nonetheless, we continue to recommend a cautious, thoughtful, and examining approach to child and adolescent treatment.

## CONCLUSION

This chapter has provided an overview of the broad area of the psychological treatment of children and adolescents. Many issues are important to those who do clinical work with children. The mental health needs of children create enormous demands that the social services and mental health delivery system have not yet even closely met. The child/adolescent therapist must be aware of developmental factors and plan and conduct treatment accordingly. Further, the therapist must be aware of the unique aspects of the therapeutic relationship with children and adolescents. A multimodal, combined approach to treatment is advocated, necessitating a broad view of what may potentially be therapeutic for the child/adolescent client. Finally, the question of efficacy has become somewhat less debatable since the first edition of this book. There is now moderate, but clear support for the general effectiveness of child and adolescent therapeutic interventions.

## REFERENCES

Abramowitz, C. V. (1976). The effectiveness of group psychotherapy with children. *Archives of General Psychiatry, 33,* 320–326.

American Psychiatric Association. (1994). *Diagnostic and statistical manual of mental disorders* (4th ed.). Washington, DC: Author.

Axline, V. (1947). *Play therapy.* Boston: Houghton Mifflin.

Barrett, C. L., Hampe, I. E., & Miller, L. (1978). Research on psychotherapy with children. In S. L. Garfield & A. D. Bergin (Eds.), *Handbook of psychotherapy and behavior change* (2nd ed., pp. 411–436). New York: Wiley.

Bergin, A. E., & Garfield, S. L. (Eds.). (1971). *Handbook of psychotherapy and behavior change.* New York: Wiley.

Bergin, A. E., & Garfield, S. L. (Eds.). (1994). *Handbook of psychotherapy and behavior change* (4th ed.). New York: Wiley.

Berlin, I. M. (Ed.). (1975). *Advocacy for child mental health.* New York: Brunner/Mazel.

Bower, E. M. (1969). *The early identification of emotionally handicapped children in school* (2nd ed.). Springfield, IL: Thomas.

Casey, R. J., & Berman, J. S. (1985). The outcome of psychotherapy with children. *Psychological Bulletin, 98*, 388–400.

Clarizio, H. F. (1979). Primary prevention of behavioral disorders in the schools. *School Psychology Digest, 8*, 434–445.

Clarizio, H. F., & McCoy, G. F. (1976). *Behavior disorders in children* (2nd ed.). New York: Crowell.

Copeland, A. D. (1974). *Textbook of adolescent psychopathology and treatment.* Springfield, IL: Thomas.

Cowen, E. (1973). Social and community interventions. *Annual Review of Psychology, 24*, 243–271.

Doll, B. (1996). Prevalence of psychiatric disorders in children and youth: An agenda for advocacy by school psychology. *School Psychology Quarterly, 11*, 20–47.

Erickson, M. T. (1978). *Child psychopathology.* Englewood Cliffs, NJ: Prentice-Hall.

Erikson, E. H. (1963). *Childhood and society* (2nd ed.). New York: Norton.

Eysenck, H. J. (1952). The effects of psychotherapy: An evaluation. *Journal of Consulting Psychology, 16*, 319–324.

Eysenck, H. J. (1978). An exercise in meta silliness [Comment]. *American Psychologist, 33*, 517.

Freud, S. (1955). *Analysis of a phobia in a five year old boy.* London: Hogarth Press. (Original work published 1909)

Garfield, S. L., & Bergin, A. E. (1978). *Handbook of psychotherapy and behavior change* (2nd ed.). New York: Wiley.

Garfield, S. L., & Bergin, A. E. (Eds.). (1986). *Handbook of psychotherapy and behavior change* (3rd ed.). New York: Wiley.

Graziano, A. M. (Ed.). (1975). *Behavior therapy with children.* Chicago: Aldine.

Havighurst, R. J. (1951). *Developmental tasks and education.* New York: Longmans.

Kazdin, A. E. (1988). *Child psychotherapy: Developing and identifying effective treatments.* New York: Pergamon Press.

Kazdin, A. E., & Johnson, B. (1994). Advances in psychotherapy for children and adolescents: Interrelations of adjustment, development, and intervention. *Journal of School Psychology, 32*, 217–246.

Kazdin, A. E., Siegel, T. C., & Bass., D. (1990). Drawing on clinical practice to inform research on child and adolescent psychotherapy. *Professional Psychology: Research and Practice, 21*, 189–198.

Keat, D. B. (1979). *Multimodal therapy with children.* New York: Pergamon Press.

Keat, D. B. (1990). *Child multimodal therapy.* Norwood, NJ: ABLEX.

Keat, D. B. (1996). Multimodal therapy with children: Anxious Ashley. *Psychotherapy in Private Practice, 15*, 63–79.

Klein, M. (1932). *The psychoanalysis of children.* London: Hogarth Press.

Kohlberg, L. (1964). Development of moral character and moral ideology. In M. L. Hoffman & L. W. Hoffman (Eds.), *Review of child development research* (Vol. 1, pp. 211–233). New York: Russell-Sage Foundation.

Kohlberg, L. (1973). Continuities in childhood and adult moral development revisited. In P. B. Baltes & K. W. Schaie (Eds.), *Lifespan developmental psychology: Personality and socialization* (pp. 380–402). New York: Academic Press.

Landman, J. T., & Dawes, R. M. (1982). Psychotherapy outcome: Smith and Glass' conclusions stand up under scrutiny. *American Psychologist, 37,* 504–516.

Lazarus, A. A. (1976). *Multimodal behavior therapy.* New York: Springer.

Levitt, E. E. (1957). The results of psychotherapy with children: An evaluation. *Journal of Consulting Psychology, 21,* 186–189.

Levitt, E. E. (1963). Psychotherapy with children: A further evaluation. *Behavior Research and Therapy, 60,* 326–329.

Levitt, E. E. (1971). Research on psychotherapy with children. In A. E. Bergin & S. L. Garfield (Eds.), *Handbook of psychotherapy and behavior change* (pp. 474–494). New York: Wiley.

MacFarlane, J., Allen, L., & Honzik, M. (1954). *A developmental study of the behavior problems of normal children between twenty-one months and fourteen years.* Berkeley: University of California Press.

Meeks, J. E. (1971). *The fragile alliance: An orientation to the outpatient psychotherapy of the adolescent.* Baltimore: Williams & Wilkins.

Meeks, J. E. (1979). The therapeutic alliance in the psychotherapy of adolescents. In J. R. Novello (Ed.), *The short course in adolescent psychiatry* (pp. 127–148). New York: Brunner/Mazel.

Nathan, P. E. (1979). Diagnostic and treatment services for children: Introduction to the section. *American Psychologist, 34,* 967–968.

Neubauer, P. (1972). Normal development in childhood. In B. B. Wolman (Ed.), *Manual of child psychopathology* (pp. 33–57). New York: McGraw-Hill.

Nuffield, E. J. (1968). Child psychiatry limited: A conservative viewpoint. *Journal of the American Academy of Child Psychiatry, 7,* 210–212.

Prout, H. T. (1983). Counseling and psychotherapy with children and adolescents: An overview. In H. T. Prout & D. T. Brown (Eds.), *Counseling and psychotherapy with children and adolescents: Theory and practice for school and clinic settings* (pp. 3–34). Tampa, FL: Mariner.

Prout, H. T., Alexander, S. P., Fletcher, C. E. M., Memis, J. P., & Miller, D. W. (1993). Counseling and psychotherapy services provided by school psychologists: An analysis of patterns in practice. *Journal of School Psychology, 31,* 309–316.

Prout, H. T., & DeMartino, R. A. (1986). A meta-analysis of school-based studies of psychotherapy. *Journal of School Psychology, 24,* 285–292.

Prout, S. M., & Prout, H. T. (1998). A meta-analysis of school-based studies of counseling and psychotherapy: An update. *Journal of School Psychology, 36,* 121–136.

Quay, H. C. (1979). Classification. In H. D. Quay & J. S. Weery (Eds.), *Psychopathological disorders of childhood* (2nd ed., pp. 58–81). New York: Wiley.

Schecter, M. D., Toussieng, P. W., & Sternlof, R. E. (1972). Normal development in adolescence. In B. B. Wolman (Ed.), *Manual of child psychopathology* (pp. 108–126). New York: McGraw-Hill.

Schroeder, H. E., & Dush, D. M. (1987). Relinquishing the placebo: Alternative for psychotherapy outcome research. *American Psychologist, 41,* 1129–1130.

Schwartz, S., & Johnson, J. H. (1985). *Psychopathology of childhood.* New York: Pergamon Press.

Shapiro, D. A., & Shapiro, D. (1982). Meta-analysis of comparative therapy outcome studies: A replication and refinement. *Psychological Bulletin, 92,* 581–604.

Smith, M. L., & Glass, G. V. (1977). Meta-analysis of psychotherapy outcome studies. *American Psychologist, 32,* 752–760.

Sroufe, L. A. (1991). Considering normal and abnormal together: The essence of developmental psychopathology. *Development and Psychopathology, 2,* 335–347.

Tramontana, M. G. (1980). Critical review of research on psychotherapy with adolescents: 1967–1977. *Psychological Bulletin, 88,* 429–450.

Wadsworth, B. J. (1996). *Piaget's theory of cognitive and affective development.* White Plains, NY: Longman.

Weiner, I. B. (1992). *Psychological disturbance in adolescence* (3rd ed.). New York: Wiley.

Weisz, J. R., Weiss, B., Alicke, M. D., & Klotz, M. L. (1987). Effectiveness of psychotherapy with children and adolescents: A meta-analysis for clinicians. *Journal of Consulting and Clinical Psychology, 55,* 542–549.

Weisz, J. R., Weiss, B., & Donenberg, G. R. (1992). The lab versus the clinic: Effects of child and adolescent psychotherapy. *American Psychologist, 47,* 1578–1585.

Weisz, J. R., Weiss, B., Han, S. S., Granger, D. A., & Morton, T. (1995). Effects of psychotherapy with children and adolescents revisited: A meta-analysis of treatment outcome studies. *Psychological Bulletin, 117,* 450–468.

# Chapter 2

# ETHICAL AND LEGAL ISSUES IN PSYCHOLOGICAL INTERVENTIONS WITH CHILDREN AND ADOLESCENTS

Susan M. Prout, Richard A. DeMartino, and H. Thompson Prout

The practice of child therapy has been in existence for several decades but, unlike its adult counterpart, has had historically less research, development, and classification systems designed specifically for it (Johnson, Rasbury, & Siegel, 1986). Kazdin and Johnson (1994) note some progress in recent years in the refinement of techniques and in outcome research, but the area remains in a developmental phase. Similarly, the professional ethical and legal considerations, as they pertain to therapy services for children, have also been limited. The primary emphasis has been in adult psychotherapy and the therapist's role in relation to the adult client. However, different issues arise, both ethically and legally, when children are the recipients of therapeutic interventions. According to Ross (1980, p. 62), "The ethical implications of treating an individual's psychological problems increase in magnitude as an inverse function of that individual's freedom of choice."

Ethical considerations, by nature, do not have simple, straightforward, or black-and-white solutions; but they are nonetheless critical to child clinicians and mental health service providers. It is important that each therapist understand his or her role as it pertains to children's legal rights as well as the ramifications, both negative and positive, of therapeutic interventions with minors.

The purpose of this chapter is to discuss the legal and ethical considerations involved with the provision of therapeutic services to children and adolescents. A brief review of general ethical principles is followed by a discussion of special considerations in working with child/adolescent populations. Legal issues related to definitions of treatment, confidentiality and privileged communication, informed consent, records and privacy, and special considerations in schools are discussed. Legal cases and precedent are presented to provide a historical overview of issues.

# ETHICAL ISSUES

Virtually all human service, educational, and medical associations have an ethical code or set of ethical principles to guide the professional behavior of their practitioners. These codes provide a basis and reference point for decision making in general case situations as well as crisis situations (Jacob & Hartshorne, 1991). These codes or principles are not legally binding, although their foci may overlap with some statutes. This is perhaps one of the major distinctions between ethical and legal principles. A violation of an ethical principle, when a related statute does not exist, can result only in censure, probation, or expulsion by the respective professional organization. Evidence of unethical practice may support documentation in a legal case, but by itself has consequences only related to the professional organization.

The ethical guidelines of the major helping service professions (e.g., American Counseling Association, 1988; American Psychological Association, 1992; National Association of School Psychologists, 1992; National Association of Social Workers, 1993) provide codes that, in part, relate to ethical considerations in conducting psychological interventions with children and adolescents. There tends to be a number of similarities and consistent themes across these sets of ethical principles. Additionally, many of these principles are interrelated. Some general themes that are relevant to the practice of child/adolescent therapy are reviewed in this chapter. More focused sets of ethical guidelines also exist. Allen, Sampson, and Herlihy (1988) note that several of the divisions (e.g., school counseling, mental health, career development) of the American Association for Counseling and Development (now the American Counseling Association) have their own sets of professional codes.

The following section provides an overview of several ethical principles related to therapeutic intervention with children and adolescents. Not all the ethical principles of the pertinent associations can be presented here. The principles reviewed here include responsibility and client welfare, confidentiality, professional relationships, competence, public statements and presentations, and private practice issues.

*Responsibility and client welfare* refer to the general concept of professionals assuming responsibility for their position of influence with clients and recognizing the consequences of their actions and professional activities. In doing so, they promote foremost the welfare of their client or clients. With regard to psychological interventions, professionals use techniques that have the likelihood of promoting therapeutic gain in their clients and accept the responsibility of the consequences/results/changes from using these techniques. Professionals should avoid conflicts of interest about their clients, clarifying allegiances between their clients, employers, agencies, and other persons directly involved. Clients should be fully informed about the services offered by the professional. When a client is clearly not benefiting from services, the professional should alter or terminate the therapeutic relationship.

Professionals have the responsibility to protect the *confidentiality* of information gathered in the context of a therapeutic relationship. The ethical principle of confidentiality should be distinguished from the legal concept of confidentiality, which is discussed later in this chapter. Information should be released only with the permission of the client, with special provisions to protect those clients who cannot give informed consent. Professional cases should be discussed only with directly concerned colleagues. This information and the client's identity should be disguised if it is used in other contexts (teaching, training, case examples, etc.), or the client's consent should be obtained. Confidentiality also relates to the proper maintenance, storage, and disposal of notes or records of counseling or therapeutic interventions.

Issues related to *professional relationships* involve relationships with colleagues, clients, and other concerned parties. Professionals should develop and maintain relationships with other colleagues in the human service area. They should be aware of the traditions and practices of those in other professional disciplines and groups in order to cooperate with and use the resources of these other professionals. Therapeutic services should not be offered to a client who is receiving services from another professional. Professionals should be aware that multiple parties may be concerned about the welfare of a client. Again, allegiances of the professional should be clarified.

Professionals are obligated to practice within the limits of their *competence.* They should recognize the limits of their skills, the techniques they utilize, and the range of clinical problems they are equipped to deal with therapeutically. They should function within the sphere of their education, training, and professional experiences and accurately present their qualifications and backgrounds to clients. In conjunction with this ethic, it is incumbent on professionals to participate in continuing education and other forms of professional development to maintain and improve their level of competency. If personal problems, personal conflicts, or other factors interfere with their therapeutic effectiveness and competence, they should take steps to protect their clients' welfare.

Issues related to *public statements and presentations* concern the presentation of materials in advertising, public lectures, and the print and electronic media. Announcements of services should present accurate, factual information about professional background and services and should avoid testimonials or guarantees. Public presentations about psychological topics should focus on scientifically accurate information. Therapeutic and other professional services should not be conducted in a public forum, but rather in the context of a professional relationship.

The proliferation of professionals in *private practice* presents some provoking problems. These practitioners should fully inform their clients about financial requirements and considerations in these relationships. If also employed in another institution, it is unethical to use one's institutional affiliation to solicit clients. In some situations, clients should be informed of services available through public institutions (e.g., schools).

A report from the Ethics Committee of the American Psychological Association (1988) found a large increase both in the number of inquiries (with intent to file) about ethical violations and the number of formal complaints actually filed. Ethical violations are classified by the specific principle and section(s) of principles found to have been violated. In terms of actual adjudicated complaints, the largest numbers of violations involved the principles of dual relationships, adherence to professional standards, governmental laws and institutional regulations, and confidentiality. "Dual relationships" refers to any relationship a psychologist might have with a client that might impair professional judgment and/or present the risk of exploitation. This could include the assessment and treatment of friends, relatives, or employees, as well as sexually intimate relationships with clients. The majority of complaints in this area dealt with psychologists being sexually involved with their clients. Complaints regarding adherence to standards, laws, and regulations most often dealt with violation of a law or other formal legal (civil or criminal) adjudication. In particular, psychologists have had problems related to fee policies and practices, mostly involving fraudulent third-party billing practices. Problems in confidentiality have involved both breaking confidentiality in violation of the law *and* refusing to break confidentiality where required by law, as in the case of mandated reporting of child abuse. Failure to follow informed consent procedures has posed problems in this area.

## Special Considerations with Children and Adolescents

There are several ethical considerations with which all individuals in the helping professions must be concerned. However, there are also issues that are specific to those who provide services to children and adolescents. These issues include client identification (child, parent/family, agency/school) and concomitant therapist responsibilities, child and parental rights, confidentiality, and general professional ethics with respect to service delivery and retraining.

### Client Identification

A major issue confronting child/adolescent therapists is identification of the client: the child, the parent(s), and in the case of educational personnel, the school. Ideally, there is minimal if any conflict between the triad or any combination of it.

According to the *Principles for Professional Ethics* of the National Association of School Psychologists (1992), the student is the primary client. It is, therefore, the responsibility of the school psychologist to place the needs and rights of the child as the client first. However, it cannot always be assumed that professionals are necessarily child advocates or that they automatically recommend what is most appropriate for the child (Koocher & Keith-Spiegel, 1990). Koocher and Keith-Spiegel further state that a therapist is morally obligated to serve as a child advocate, since a child cannot serve as his or her own advocate due to psychological, physical, immaturity, or legal statute.

While in theory it makes sense that a clinician would relegate the child to the role of client, since it is the child who is being treated, practically and legally the role of the parent must also be considered. Since parents have legal responsibility for the well-being of their children under the age of 18 according to most state statutes, therapists have a responsibility to them. However, this factor can be confusing and conflictual at times for the service provider. Gumaer (1984) stated that since parents are legally responsible for their children, they need to be informed of and approve of any therapy or interventions. Most often, parents are the primary referral agents for their child, and children frequently become involved in therapy because of parental referral. Children do not personally request help, but instead are identified as having a "problem" based on adult perception (Ross, 1980). According to Koocher and Keith-Spiegel (1990), therapists infrequently refuse to consider a child as a client at the onset based on his or her unwillingness to participate. Therefore, an agreement of sorts has been made with the parents, regardless of the child's wishes, which identifies the parent(s) as also having some client characteristics. Parental input is also critical to the therapeutic process concerning background information, problem identification, and goal setting.

Koocher and Keith-Spiegel (1990) and Ross (1980) raise the issue of whether parental rights are stymied when a child refuses treatment and a therapist accepts this decision. Several factors should be considered by a therapist when making this decision. According to Johnson et al. (1986), the specific factors to be considered are age, level of cognitive development of the child, the child's degree of disturbance, the degree of disturbance noted in the parents, and the degree to which the therapist feels that treatment is warranted. Wagner (1981) suggests that the younger the child's age, the greater the responsibility a therapist has to the parents. It is the role and responsibility of a counselor to view the child and parent(s) as clients and ascertain the most appropriate means to meet the needs of both parties (Gelfand & Hartman, 1984; Ross, 1980).

Another potential client is the agency, particularly when counseling a child in a school setting. Since many school psychologists, counselors, and social workers have been hired by educational agencies to provide therapy and counseling services to children within the schools, they have subsequent employer responsibilities. According to Huey (1986), acceptance of a staff position in an educational setting implies general agreement with the institution's objectives and principles. He further states that a counselor should not be perceived as more concerned with school rules than child rights, but rather with seeking solutions to protect these rights in addition to advocating for school policies to further them. Parental rights are seen as a third part of the triad of child and school, in which a cooperative relationship among the three is critical, albeit difficult, conflictual, and ambiguous at times. However, Huey sees ambiguity and ethical conflicts among the triad components as an inherent part of the school counselor/psychologist's role. It is a role that requires professional decision making based on ethical values and legal restraints in conjunction with a willingness to accept responsibility for judgments made concerning a child.

*Child and Parental Rights*

The majority of the literature that discusses child and parental rights emphasizes that both are to be considered clients, but that it is the primary responsibility of the therapist to protect the rights of the child (Huey, 1986; Hughes, 1986; Koocher & Keith-Siegel, 1990; Ross, 1980). This statement of ethical values provides what on the surface is an appropriate goal. In reality, however, it is not necessarily easily obtained nor specific. Duncan and Moffett (1974) stated that ethical guidelines do not apply to all situations and their interpretation is affected by the therapist's values and attitudes. When protecting the rights of parents and children, the therapist must be careful not to allow personal beliefs to interfere, but rather to assist clients in making appropriate decisions (Huey, 1986).

Several authors in the ethics literature (Huey, 1986; Jacob & Hartshorne, 1991; Koocher & Keith-Siegel, 1990; Ross, 1980; Simmonds, 1976) describe key rights for children and parents.

*Children in therapy* have the:

- Right to be informed about the evaluation process and reasons and results in understandable terms.
- Right to be informed about therapeutic interventions and rationale in understandable terms.
- Right to be informed about confidentiality and its limitations.
- Right to control release of information.
- Right not to be involved in therapy if uncomfortable or unsuccessful (this is not always possible when it is mandated by court order or Individual Education Plan).
- Right to be treated with respect and told the truth.
- Right to participate with the therapist and/or parent(s) in decision making and goal setting.
- Right not to be labeled the scapegoat in a dysfunctional family.

*Parents' rights and responsibilities* include the:

- Legal responsibility to provide for their child's welfare.
- Right to access to information (educational, medical, therapeutic) that pertains to their child's welfare.
- Right to seek therapy and/or treatment services for their child.
- Right to be involved in therapeutic decision making and goal setting for their child—right to give permission for treatments.
- Right to release confidential information concerning their child.

It is evident from these lists of child and parental rights that there is overlap and interface between the two. The parental rights mentioned are for the most part also legal rights, unless legal guardianship has been removed by the courts. However, several of the child's rights are ethical values and not mandated or dictated by law. The previously cited authors have presented these recommendations to protect a child's rights during counseling or therapeutic interventions. A professional must make decisions and recommendations, particularly where the child's rights are concerned, depending on the variables of age and so on, as mentioned earlier.

A factor in child rights that bears ethical consideration involves children referred for therapy when the family is the presenting problem (Simmonds, 1976). For example, a child is referred for counseling and identified by his parents as "problematic," whereas interviews and so on reveal a family/parental dysfunction that would warrant a family counseling/systems approach (Simmonds). The child may be labeled as "dysfunctional" for insurance purposes because he or she has no recourse or legal rights. Such a procedure may be prejudicial to the child in later years according to Simmonds.

Additionally, a conflict in values may arise between parent and child over a treatment goal based on parental request although the behavior causes no personal difficulties for the child. Ross (1980) raises the issue whether parental rights are violated in such a situation if a child, particularly a young child, has the right to refuse treatment.

These rights for children and parents are again going to be affected by the situation and clients. Professional decisions will vary from client to client as a therapist strives to protect both child's and parents' rights, while advocating for the child.

## Confidentiality

Another ethical issue that regularly confronts therapists both in private practice or agency/school settings is confidentiality. The American Psychological Association guidelines (1992) state that client information is confidential unless the client gives permission to reveal or discuss it. However, as Johnson et al. (1986) state, it is common for professionals to share reports on children with other professionals involved with the child, such as teachers, private psychologists, and counselors. This is done with permission of the child's parent or legal guardian, rather than the child. It appears that the child's permission to share this information should ethically be obtained as a matter of routine.

There are also legal limitations to confidentiality such as the Family Educational Rights and Privacy Act and court-ordered evaluation and/or counseling. In these situations, information obtained specifically must be available to parents or judicial or social services personnel. These issues are discussed later in this chapter.

Additional confidentiality issues, which are less specifically defined, such as those that occur during individual or group counseling, should also be considered by mental health providers. Since parents, as a child's legal guardian, in many states have access to therapy records (Ehrenreich & Melton, 1983), it seems logical to search for a level of communication that is acceptable to both parents and the child. For example, a child should be told initially in therapy what information will be shared with parents (i.e., statements of a suicidal nature or those that involve danger to others) without the child's permission. Johnson et al. (1986) recommend that therapists seek a balance between a child's and parents' rights, such as discussing general topics that arise during therapy but not the specific details.

Counseling provided in a group setting also involves protection of a child's rights of confidentiality. Gumaer (1984) recommends that the term be explained to the children at the onset of the counseling session in understandable terms (i.e., "What is talked about in group is not talked about outside group." "You may talk to others about topics discussed, but do not mention names"). Problems of breaking the confidentiality agreement can be decided by group members. Groups in school settings may be particularly prone to difficulties with breaking confidentiality.

Although confidentiality is designed to protect the child's privacy, acceptable compromises are not always available. Therapists may find they must sometimes make decisions that alienate or upset either the child/client or parent.

### Professional Ethical Responsibilities

In addition to ethical considerations that are primarily concerned with child and parental rights, a major issue pertaining to the service provider is professional competence or expertise in the areas of treatment to be provided. For example, a therapist trained in adult psychopathology should not ethically treat children or vice versa, without specific training. According to Johnson et al. (1986), general training in "clinical psychology, psychiatry, or social work does not necessarily qualify one to offer psychological services to children, as many training programs do not provide didactic and clinical experience in working with younger age groups" (p. 94). Professional ethics would warrant a referral to another appropriately trained therapist under these circumstances.

A related concern involves obtaining a second professional opinion in situations where a treatment recommendation is controversial (i.e., aversive treatment) or unacceptable to parents (Koocher & Keith-Spiegel, 1990).

Continuing education and professional growth and development are also ethically critical, particularly to ensure that a therapist is providing up-to-date treatment and therapy recommendations for a child.

## LEGAL ISSUES

### Interventions: Searching for a Model

Historically, mental health professionals went relatively unchallenged in their ability to make wise and informed decisions about the treatment of institutionalized individuals (Binder, 1980). Two landmark cases on patients' rights, *Donaldson v. O'Connor* (1974) and *Wyatt v. Stickney* (1971/1972), have led to significant reforms in the processes applied to mental health practice. These cases involved the problem of defining minimum standards of care as well as the rights of patients to adequate treatment.

The definition of "treatment," "intrusiveness," or "intervention" has been a matter of considerable debate in the field. Several authors have sought to define criteria for "degree of intrusiveness" (Binder, 1980; Friedman, 1975; Shapiro, 1974; Spece, 1972). Spece applied a continuum model of mental health treatments from least to most intrusive. The corresponding list included milieu therapy, psychotherapy, drug therapy, behavior modification, aversive therapy, ECT, brain stimulation, lobotomy, and stereotactic psychosurgery. Obviously, the more severe of these interventions are beyond the scope of the typical practice of most mental health professionals.

Binder (1980) presents an integration of many authors' views delineating seven criteria that may be used to examine intervention approaches:

1. The extent to which the "new mental state is foreign or unnatural" to the person in question.
2. The extent to which the effects of the therapy are reversible.
3. Duration of change.
4. The rapidity with which the effects occur.

5. The extent of bodily invasion.

6. The nature of side effects.

7. The extent to which an "uncooperative" patient can avoid the effects of the treatment.

These criteria highlight that mental health practice continues to function largely from a medical model perspective (Szasz, 1974) where "degree of intrusiveness" is frequently discussed in the context of medical invasion of the body (Binder, 1980). Without considering theoretical orientation or the subjective nature of defining the wide variety of therapeutic interventions, a continuum ranking such as provided by Spece (1972) suggests, from a legal standpoint, that certain interventions should only be used after other less intrusive therapies have been tried and have failed (Binder, 1980).

As Binder proposes, there is agreement that psychological treatments cannot be easily ranked. The multitude of psychotherapies alone differ markedly in terms of definition, implementation, and general acceptance within the mental health community. Even given an agreed-on definition, the variety of behavioral techniques such as systematic desensitization, biofeedback, and relaxation therapies would be difficult to rank order from a "degree of intrusiveness" viewpoint. It appears, however, that child mental health practitioners should consider the potential legal implications of "degree of intrusiveness" in selecting interventions. For example, the possible use of aversive techniques with school-age children involves more complex legal and ethical principles than a traditional counseling or consultative intervention.

## Relevant Case Law

Three rather broad and interrelated domains of law are discussed in this section as they apply to interventions: Confidentiality/Privileged Communication; Informed Consent; and Access to Records.

### Confidentiality and Privileged Communication

Although frequently used interchangeably, important distinctions exist between the legal concepts of "confidentiality" and "privileged communication." Confidentiality refers to a general obligation of a professional to avoid disclosing information regarding the relationship with a client to any third party. Privileged communication is narrower in scope than confidentiality. As Jagim, Wittman, and Noll (1978) note, "Whereas confidentiality concerns matters of communication outside the courtroom, privilege protects clients from disclosure in judicial proceedings" (p. 459). Thus, while an obligation to preserve confidentiality constitutes a broad duty owed by a professional to a client, "Psychotherapist-patient privilege is a rule of evidence relevant only in court proceedings" (Hulteng & Goldman, 1987, p. 239).

The courts have generally held that mental health professionals have a common-law obligation to protect the confidentiality of the relationship with a client (Hulteng &

Goldman, 1987). In *Doe v. Roe* (1977), a New York psychiatrist was held to have invaded a former client's privacy when he published a book about the plaintiff's treatment and failed to sufficiently conceal personally identifiable information. In this case, the court leaned heavily on the notion that physicians implicitly agree to keep in confidence all disclosures made by the patient within the context of a contract to provide medical treatment. The court specified that these disclosures included the patient's physical and mental condition, and all matters discovered in the course of examination or treatment (*Doe v. Roe,* 1977, p. 210).

In a New York case, *MacDonald v. Clinger* (1982), the state court held that a psychiatrist breached his "fiduciary duty" when he disclosed information to the wife of a patient under his care. A fiduciary duty is described as that duty imposed in a relationship based on professional trust. The court also ruled that damages were recoverable.

There has been spirited debate about the therapeutic necessity of absolute confidentiality. The psychiatric community has historically expressed the belief that therapy would not be successful unless the client could freely and with security disclose personal information. In contrast, some forms of psychotherapy seem to quash the sentiment that there can be no therapy without complete confidentiality (Kandler, 1977; Langs, 1976). Further, as Wilson (1978) suggests, clients do not seem more reluctant to convey personal information in states that do not protect communications from legal scrutiny.

Regardless of one's therapeutic position on total versus limited confidentiality, two general reasons exist for the continued safeguard of client-counselor confidentiality. First, a confidential relationship serves to limit clients' concerns about the social stigma often associated with participation in therapy (Denkowski & Denkowski, 1982; Sloan & Klein, 1977). A U.S. Department of Health, Education and Welfare (1963) survey documented the basis for the stigmatization concern. It found that 60% of those surveyed "would not act or feel normally towards a former mental patient, even though they did not learn of his illness until they had known him for some time without noticing anything about him" (1963, p. 8). Second, as discussed earlier, a central ethical obligation for professionals is the assurance that a client's right to privacy and reputation is well preserved (Denkowski & Denkowski).

The notion of a "special relationship" forms the basis of privilege as it applies to disclosures in the courtroom. The laws of various states ultimately govern the scope of privileged communication but may include husband-wife, attorney-client, member of clergy-penitent, and physician-patient relationships (Fischer & Sorenson, 1996). Psychologist-client communications are privileged from disclosure in court in 41 (82%) of the 50 states (Herlihy & Sheeley, 1986). All 50 states have regulations that apply for "school counselors." Privileged communication statutes exist in 21 of these states, "providing protection from disclosure of school counselor/student communications" (Herlihy & Sheeley, 1986, p. 4). The privilege is strictly limited to those communications relating to student drug and alcohol concerns in 5 of these 21 states.

Even in states that have statutes regarding "privilege," this right is typically granted to clients of psychologists—not psychologists themselves (McDermott, 1972). Since the right to assert or waive the privilege to prevent disclosure in courtroom proceedings is granted to the client, issues of competency are often involved. Typically, the child mental health practitioner's client is a minor and is, therefore, considered legally incompetent to exercise the privilege. In this case, the privilege reverts to the minor's legal guardians (McDermott). Since privileged communication for school counselors most frequently pertains to clients who are legally considered minors, some statutes include provisions for involving parents in the decision to waive counselor privilege. In fact, in only two states are there statutes that allow almost complete unilateral control by the student in waiving the rights of nondisclosure (Herlihy & Sheeley, 1986).

In states protecting the relationship between clients and psychologists, the term *psychologist* usually refers to those who have been licensed, registered, or certified by a state board of examiners or similar body for the purpose of regulating the public and private practice of psychology. This, for example, frequently excludes "school psychologists" (McDermott, 1972) or others using similar titles, but who are not licensed. Privileged communication may apply, however, if a school psychologist also holds a license as a psychologist and if the licensing statute provides for privilege in that state (Knapp & VandeCreek, 1983).

The courts, while often supporting the concept of privilege, have at times insisted that a therapist divulge "confidential" client information (Denkowski & Denkowski, 1982). Judicial sentiment has found that confidential privilege for "therapists" did not apply in *State v. Bishop* (1969), *State v. Pyle* (1975), and *Stevens v. State* (1976). As Fischer and Sorenson (1996) note, even in long-recognized exemptions such as attorney/client relationships, courts have demanded that certain conditions be met:

- One party in the relationship must be legally certified as a lawyer, doctor, or minister.
- At the time of the communication in question, he or she must have been acting in a professional capacity.
- The person making the communication, if in possession of his or her faculties, must have regarded the professional person as his or her lawyer, doctor, or minister.

School-based professionals should note that once information is included in a school file, it cannot be considered potentially privileged communication but, in fact, falls under the provisions of the Family Educational Rights and Privacy Act (FERPA) which governs access and privacy. Privileged communication statutes, even when they do exist, do not represent absolute guarantees. Even when there is statutory support, extenuating circumstances could include client request, and clear and imminent danger to the client or others (Herlihy & Sheeley, 1986).

It is this final exception, otherwise known as the "duty to warn principle," that has represented the "harbinger of perceived doom, gloom and tremulousness for many mental health professionals" (George, 1985, p. 291). In the well-known case of *Tarasoff v. Regents* (1974/1976) the confidential relationship of a psychologist and his patient were the subject of a controversial ruling.

The *Tarasoff* case revolved around a suit filed by the parents of Tatiana Tarasoff, who was killed in 1969 by the patient of a University of California hospital psychologist. Two months prior to her death, during therapy sessions with the psychologist, the patient had confided his intention to kill Ms. Tarasoff. The Tarasoffs' suit claimed that there was a "duty to warn" their daughter of the impending danger. Although the psychologist notified the campus police, the California Supreme Court ruled that the psychologist did indeed have a duty to warn a known, intended victim directly. The court held that a special relationship existed between any therapist and patient and that the duty arising from the therapist's knowledge that his patient posed a serious threat of violence meant reasonable care must be taken to protect a foreseeable victim of potential violence (George, 1985).

The *Tarasoff* case and other similar cases (e.g., *Hedlund v. Superior Court,* 1983) have caused considerable furor among mental health professionals. In tempering the "paranoia" generated by these cases George (1985) states, "the determinative question remains whether the professional person failed to exercise that reasonable degree of skill, knowledge, and care ordinarily possessed and exercised by members of that professional speciality under similar circumstances" (p. 294). Although the controversy remains, several state legislatures have enacted laws that limit the potential liability to some degree. It is perhaps safest to assume that professionals have a duty to warn a known intended victim of his or her client's violent intent (Fischer & Sorenson, 1996).

In a California case, *Phillis P. v. Clairmont Unified School District* (1986), the state supreme court held that a principal, teacher, and school psychologist failed to comply with their duty to warn the mother of an 8-year-old girl that her daughter was being sexually molested by another student at the school. The student, Phyllis P., stated to her teacher that another student was "playing games" with her. The teacher told the school psychologist, and the school psychologist initiated counseling. The principal was also aware of the situation. The court noted that not only did the school fail to notify the mother that the assaults were taking place, but neglected to obtain informed consent for treatment and did not properly supervise the molesting student. Additionally, the court held that the mother could sue the district for this failure to warn. In another case *(Pesce v. J Sterling Morton High School District 201,* 1987), the courts ruled that a school psychologist could be disciplined for misconduct for failure to report child abuse in a timely manner.

Confidentiality and privileged communication are two distinct concepts and should not be used interchangeably. Though emerging case law supports a common-law obligation to preserve confidentiality, it is largely an ethical consideration. Privilege, on the other hand, deals with the admissibility of evidence into court. Although various states have enacted statutes that grant these exceptions beyond the historical relationships (e.g., lawyer-client, minister-penitent) to psychologist-client, some professionals may nonetheless have a legal duty to testify if ordered by a court (Fischer & Sorenson, 1996). Refusal to do so may lead to contempt citations, fines, or jail terms. Moreover, the privilege belongs to the client and not the therapist.

In circumstances where a client expresses violent or harmful intentions toward another individual, a therapist has the duty to warn potential victims who are the targets of such threats. Further, professionals may not only have the duty to warn but may also infer a duty to protect third parties from violent acts (Mills, 1985). It is also clear that most professionals are "mandated reporters" for suspected cases of child abuse discovered in the course of their practice. Failure to report as required by state statute can result in both civil and criminal liability (Hulteng & Goldman, 1987).

## Informed Consent

The term *informed consent* refers to the "receipt of specific permission to do something following a complete explanation of the nature, purpose and potential risks involved" (DeMers, 1986, p. 45). Informed consent is defined legally as involving three aspects: knowledge, competence/intelligence, and voluntariness (Arambula, DeKraai, & Sales, 1993; DeMers, 1986; Grisso & Vierling, 1978). Under the strictest of interpretations, the knowledge test requires that a professional *fully* inform the student/client/parent of all relevant information about a specific intervention approach so that the person becomes "aware" of what is being consented to (Waltz & Scheuneman, 1970). The intelligence or competence aspect of consent focuses on the ability of the child or parent to arrive at the consent rationally and independently. Within this concept are the notions of cognitive capacity and other mental health related abilities of a client. Voluntariness refers to consent occurring in the absence of undue coercion or misrepresentation (Sadoff, 1985). The question of willful granting of permission is the typical legal standard by which this is measured (DeMers, 1986; Lidz et al., 1984).

Bray, Shepherd, and Hays (1985) suggest that the following must be included for valid consent; (a) a complete explanation of the treatment, risks, discomforts, and benefits; (b) a description of other possible treatment alternatives; (c) an offer to discuss the procedures or answer any questions; and (d) information that the client is free to withdraw consent at any time and discontinue treatment. Consent obtained pursuant to these disclosures will be "express consent." "Apparent consent" and "consent implied by law" are two other types of consent. In "apparent consent," all parties act as if consent was given, when in actuality none was formally stated. "Consent implied by law" comes into play in questions of competency for clients most frequently seen by mental health professionals in hospital or inpatient settings (Slovenko, 1973).

One of the major controversies in this area is the age at which a person may legally consent to treatment (Bray et al., 1985; Grisso & Vierling, 1978; Sadoff, 1985). While Bersoff (1982) notes there has been a general trend for the courts to grant adolescents greater leeway in obtaining medical or psychological intervention without parental permission, there is no question that treatment of preadolescents should involve the consent of parents or legal guardians (Reynolds, Gutkin, Elliot, & Witt, 1984).

Although some state legislatures have sought to institute parental consent as a prerequisite, the courts have generally found that a pregnant minor may obtain an abortion and/or purchase contraceptives without parental permission (e.g., *Carey v. Population Services International, Inc.,* 1977; *Planned Parenthood of Central Missouri v. Danforth,* 1976). These decisions have been based on the belief that a requirement for parental consent might inhibit minors seeking such treatments—contrary to the individual's and society's best interest (Bray et al., 1985). To infer that adolescents thus have the right to seek the broad range of therapies without parental consent may not be prudent for the practitioner, however. Bersoff (1982), for example, reports, "It is presently very risky for school psychologists to agree to see children for any kind of therapeutic purpose without their parents' consent" (p. 1068). Unless parents are clearly endangering their children as in the case of child abuse, the courts are decidedly "pro parents" with respect to consent (Reynolds et al., 1984). As an ethical and therapeutic consideration, the importance of parental permission for most psychological interventions is warranted. As a practical matter, it must be balanced by the issue of concern, the age of the child, and the child's legal status (e.g., minor, emancipated minor, adult). The assent of the child should clearly be obtained because cooperation with any procedure affects treatment and its outcome (Schectman, Hays, Schuham, & Smith, 1982).

### Access to Records/Right to Privacy

An analogous concern to the confidentiality/privilege issue is the privacy right granted by the federal Family Educational Rights and Privacy Act (FERPA), popularly known as the Buckley Amendment. While privilege was previously referred to as the protection of testimony or professional opinion about a client, the "data privacy" notion discussed in this section is more concerned with the release and storage of information (Lombard, 1981).

The Buckley Amendment essentially mandates the withholding of federal funds to schools or other educational agencies that fail to require parental consent or a court order for the release of records for other than defined educational purposes. With the increasing use of courts to resolve custody, child abuse/neglect, juvenile delinquency, and status offenses, the records of school-based professionals are often subpoenaed by clients, states, and adversarial parties. A subpoena may require the production of records, including notes, tape recordings, videotapes, memoranda, letters, and any other written material (Schrier, 1980). Though a detailed listing of all the provisions contained in FERPA is beyond the scope of this chapter, important requirements include that (a) parents or students 18 years or older be told the reasons for release and be given a copy of any released records, (b) parents be notified of any court order in advance of any release in order to have an opportunity to contest the contents of school records, and (c) parents can insert modifications into the record and challenge the contents. Parental consent must be obtained for release of information for children under age 18. For students 18 years of age or over, or those attending postsecondary education, the rights for permission or consent shift from the parents to the student.

The Buckley Amendment does contain an exclusory clause regarding the personal records of psychologists and counselors if these files are entirely private and not available to other individuals. This "memory aids" exception makes clear that private files of this type shall not be shared with or passed on to any other school personnel. They can be shared with a "substitute" without thereby becoming "education records" subject to FERPA (Fischer & Sorenson, 1996).

FERPA also requires that a record be kept of all parties requesting and receiving student information and that this record be made available to parents or eligible students.

School districts may, however, develop policies to allow for undocumented exchanges between local district personnel by explicitly stating which school officials may have access without parental permission and noting the "legitimate educational interests" justifying the access.

With respect to the release of school records to noncustodial parents, both FERPA and *Page v. Rotterdam-Mohonasen Central School District* (1982) clearly entitle the noncustodial parent to the same access to the child's educational records as the custodial parent (Fischer & Sorenson, 1996). This assumes that no specific court order prohibits contact between the child and the noncustodial parent. The federal law indicates that school professionals may assume a noncustodial parent's right to information unless otherwise stipulated. In cases where a child has no parent or legal guardian, educational records must also be accessible to a guardian or "an individual acting as a parent" (Fischer & Sorenson, 1996).

In a case involving children abused by a school employee, the courts ruled in *Parents Against Abuse in School v. Williamsport Area School District* (1991) that interview notes of a school psychologist should be released to parents. After allegations and evidence of abuse became known, the school psychologist had interviewed the students to assess the nature of the abuse and potential emotional consequences, and to assist the parents in arranging for appropriate therapy for their children, if needed. The issue involved whether FERPA provisions covered these notes. The court ruled that FERPA provisions did apply and ordered the release of the interview notes. Thus, even more informal "clinical" notes do not avoid release to parents if requested.

## SCHOOL-BASED INTERVENTIONS

In this section, legal issues are presented within the context of school-based interventions including behavior modification, the use of aversive techniques, group treatment, liability, and libel/slander.

### Behavior Modification

Traditionally defined, "behavior modification" involves the application of learning principles designed to alleviate human suffering and enhance human functioning through behavior change. Behavior modification emphasizes systematic monitoring and evaluation of its techniques. Used appropriately, these techniques are intended to facilitate self-control and expand individual skills, abilities, and independence (Stolz, Wienckowski, & Brown, 1975).

The legal concepts that apply in this area are "due process," "equal protection," and a number of concepts from case law precedents. Constitutional due process provides that if government (e.g., school) activity affects a student in a way that deprives the student of "liberty" or "property," it must be with due process of law (Martin, 1975). Using behavioral approaches in schools could be construed as impinging on liberty. Thus, professionals in schools must be prepared to follow specific rules of due process and be able to justify therapeutic decisions in the forum of a fair hearing.

Broadly stated, "equal protection" under the Constitution suggests that a student cannot be treated in a way that differs substantially from treatment accorded others, unless there is some special justification. Therefore, any behavior change technique cannot unreasonably "single out" one group for treatment based, for example, on race or sex.

In *New York State Association for Retarded Children v. Rockefeller* (1973), the issue of inadequate or inappropriate treatment of handicapped persons was examined. In this case, the court found in favor of the plaintiff/clients whose condition was worsening after being involved in a state-run behavioral intervention program. Not only must therapy not worsen the client's condition, but persons cannot be placed in control groups for research purposes and be allowed to worsen for lack of treatment (Martin, 1975).

In the case of *Dickens v. Johnson County Board of Education* (1987), a time-out technique devised by a teacher and principal to temporarily isolate a disruptive sixth-grade student was ruled not a violation of procedural or substantive due process. In this case, the "time-out box" had three sides and contained a school desk. The student spent as long as four-and-a-half hours on six consecutive days in the box. The court noted that the judicious use of behavior modification techniques such as time-out are preferred over expulsion in disciplining disruptive students. The court also cautioned that the arbitrary "caging of students" for indeterminant lengths of time was prohibited.

## Use of Aversive Techniques

Though many debate its value and the effects on the physical and mental health of students, punishment and other aversive interventions continue to be sanctioned in America's public schools (Wood & Braaten, 1983). Physical restraint, physically enforced overcorrection, and time-out procedures are among the approaches that may be employed by school-based professionals, particularly in specialized school or institutional settings.

The Eighth Amendment prohibition against cruel and unusual punishment as it applies to behavioral interventions has been debated in the courts in a number of cases. In *Wheeler v. Glass* (1973) the court held that the restraint of two mentally retarded persons for 77.5 hours constituted cruel and unusual punishment. Restraint has similarly been viewed as cruel and unusual punishment in *Welsch v. Liking* (1974). *Wyatt v. Stickney* (1971/1972) produced a ruling which stated that while restraint could be used to prevent injury to others or self, it could not be used as punishment or as a substitute for habilitative programming or for the convenience of the staff.

However, in a landmark case, *Ingraham v. Wright* (1977), the U.S. Supreme Court ruled that the severe paddling of two students for disciplinary reasons did not constitute a violation of the Eighth Amendment. In this case, the court ruled that the Eighth Amendment applied to the protection of criminals and was not designed to protect students in this way. Further, the court suggested that traditional common-law remedies are adequate to afford due process in a constitutionally protected liberty interest involving corporal punishment in public schools (e.g., sue for damages, assault and battery).

Time-out procedures are frequently used with exceptional children (Barton, Brulle, & Repp, 1983). The courts have distinguished between "time-out" and "solitary confinement." *Morales v. Turman* (1973), stated that seclusion was sanctioned only when it might prevent immediate physical harm to others or to the student or to prevent behavior that substantially disrupts the institutional routine. A maximum of 50 minutes in seclusion was determined in this case. *Horacek v. Exon* (1975) noted that seclusion in a locked room is forbidden.

## Group Treatments

Meyer and Smith (1977) present four interrelated axioms regarding the efficacy of group therapy. The first two are useful to the discussion of legal issues. Meyer and Smith submit that (a) confidences divulged in group therapy have the same protection under statutes of privileged communication as do those revelations made in individual therapy; and (b) confidentiality is crucial to the effectiveness of group therapy (p. 638). Despite the inherent soundness of these statements, the courts have not agreed that the status of privileged communication applies to group treatments. As Fischer and Sorenson (1996) submit, this is rooted in the reluctance of courts to grant privilege or extend it to new types of relationships. Only the state of Colorado has statutes that recognize privilege for participants in group therapy. Thus, although the vast majority of group therapists and clients assume that the axiom of privilege is in effect (Meyer & Smith, 1977), there is little or no statutory or judicial assurance for this assumption.

## Liability

In today's litigious society, the fear many professionals may have of being sued in connection with their professional practice is a valid concern. In fact, Hendrickson (1982) argues that for counselors, liability/malpractice insurance is a must. Civil liability (when one commits a wrong against an individual) is considered in this domain. In general, civil liability for negligence occurs if one person causes damage to another through a breach of duty owed to that person. "Malpractice" refers to negligent practice in the rendering of professional services (Fischer & Sorenson, 1996).

The anxieties of many school professionals soar when they consider student health matters, drug use/abuse, sexuality, and suicide. The ability to act with confidence in these areas rests not only on professional skill but on the understanding of these legal principles. Counselors legally have a duty to use professionally accepted skills and care in working with counselees (Fischer & Sorenson, 1996).

In *Bogust v. Iverson* (1960), the suicide of a college-age woman was alleged to be the result of negligence on the part of a college counselor/teacher since (a) the educator failed to secure emergency psychiatric treatment after he was aware, or should have been aware, of the young women's incapacity; (b) he failed to advise her parents of her problems; and (c) he failed to provide proper student guidance (Fischer & Sorenson, 1996). The Wisconsin Supreme Court ruled against the parents, finding no duty to warn, since there was no clear causal relationship between failure to alert her parents or secure help and the suicide.

Similarly, the ruling in *Bellah v. Greenson* (1978) refused to affirm the "duty to warn" principle in a case involving a suicide. In its ruling, the court did not see suicide as an equivalent to impending danger of violence on members of society. The California court further noted that confidentiality is a crucial factor in the treatment of suicidal persons—that it outweighs a duty to warn the suicide victim's parents (Fischer & Sorenson, 1996).

### Libel/Slander

Talbutt (1983) and Eades (1986) present brief reviews of issues relating to libel and slander in the practice of school counseling and psychology. "Libel" refers to written defamation and "slander" refers to defamation expressed by word of mouth. Alexander, Corns, and McCann (1969) offer the necessary elements for a tort of libel or slander: (a) a false statement concerning another was published or communicated; (b) the statement brought hatred, disgrace, ridicule or contempt on another person; and (c) damages resulted from the statement (p. 325).

Fischer and Sorenson (1996) suggest that the school-based professional is protected if he acted *reasonably* in carrying out the duties of his or her assigned responsibilities. The notion of what is *reasonable practice* in the field is often the legal standard applied in courtroom proceedings. "Qualified privilege" is a legal principle which protects the counselor who may communicate, in a professional manner to relevant persons, information or evaluations that may be considered negative or damaging. Certainly, mere random gossip or communication of derogatory information beyond ethical/professional guidelines may lead to successful suits for damages.

## CONCLUSION

Conducting psychological treatments of children's and adolescents' social-emotional problems is indeed a complex and challenging task. The clinical concerns and questions are compounded by an array of ethical and legal issues. Clinical options and plans must necessarily take these issues into consideration. At a basic level, the ethical principles of the major helping professions provide an overall guide for professional behavior. Because of age and developmental levels and the concerns of others (e.g., parents, schools), the child client presents some special ethical considerations. Similarly, there are some general legal issues that apply to persons receiving mental health services, and these are made more complicated by the status of child and adolescent clients as minors. Both statutes and relevant case law provide further guides for professional behavior.

While some questions in the ethical and legal areas have relatively straightforward answers, many grey areas remain. Ethical principles and legal statutes and case law do not completely overlap. In some cases, ethical principles may come into conflict with legal guidelines. This chapter has highlighted some of the major issues when working with children and adolescents. Finally, we concur with the conclusion of Huey

(1986)—ethical codes do not supersede the law, but legal knowledge may not always be sufficient to determine the most appropriate course of action.

## REFERENCES

Alexander, K., Corns, R., & McCann, W. (1969). *Public school law.* St. Paul, MN: West.

Allen, V. B., Sampson, J. P., & Herlihy, B. (1988). Details of the 1988 AACD ethical standards. *Journal of Counseling and Development, 67,* 157-158.

American Counseling Association. (1988). *Ethical standards.* Washington, DC: Author.

American Psychological Association. (1988). Trends in ethics cases common pitfalls, and published resources. *American Psychologist, 43,* 564–572.

American Psychological Association. (1992). *Ethical principles of psychologists and code of conduct.* Washington, DC: Author.

Arambula, D., DeKraai, M., & Sales, B. (1993). Law, children, and therapists. In T. R. Krataochwill & R. J. Morris (Eds.), *Handbook of psychotherapy with children and adolescents* (pp. 583–619). Boston: Allyn & Bacon.

Barton, L. E., Brulle, A. R., & Repp, A. C. (1983). Aversive techniques and the doctrine of least restrictive alternative. *Exceptional Education Quarterly, 3,* 1–8.

Bellah v. Greenson, 181 Cal. App. 3d 614, 146 Cal. Rptr. 535 (Calif. App. 1978).

Bersoff, D. N. (1982). The legal regulation of school psychology. In C. Reynolds & T. Gutkin (Eds.), *The handbook of school psychology* (pp. 1043–1074). New York: Wiley.

Binder, V. L. (1980, May). *Legal vs. psychological aspects of intrusiveness.* Paper presented at the annual meeting of the Western Psychological Association, Honolulu, HI.

Bogust v. Iverson, 102 N.W. 2d 228 (Wisc. 1960).

Brakman, C. (1985). A human rights committee in a public school for severely and profoundly retarded students. *Education and Training of the Mentally Retarded, 20,* 139–147.

Bray, J. H., Shepherd, J. N., & Hays, J. R. (1985). Legal and ethical issues in informed consent to psychotherapy. *American Journal of Family Therapy, 13,* 50–60.

Carey v. Population Service International, Inc., 431 U.S. 678 (1977).

DeMers, S. T. (1986). Legal and ethical issues in child and adolescent personality assessment. In H. Knoff (Ed.), *The assessment of child and adolescent personality* (pp. 35–55). New York: Guilford Press.

Denkowski, K., & Denkowski, G. (1982). Client-counselor confidentiality: An update of rationale, legal status, and implications. *Personnel and Guidance Journal, 60,* 371–375.

Dickens v. Johnson County Board of Education. [661 F. Supp. 155, (E.D. Tenn. 1987)].

Doe v. Roe, 93 Misc. 2d 201, 400 N.Y.S. 2d 668 (N.Y. Sup. Ct. 1977).

Donaldson v. O'Connor, 493 F.2d 507 (5th Cir. 1974), *vacated and remanded,* 422 U.S. 563 (1975).

Duncan, J., & Moffett, C. (1974). Abortion counseling and the school counselor. *School Counselor, 21,* 188–195.

Eades, R. W. (1986). The school counselor or psychologist and problems of defamation. *Journal of Law and Education, 15,* 117–120.

Eberlein, L. (1977). Counselors beware! Clients have rights! *Personnel and Guidance Journal, 55,* 219–223.

Ehrenreich, N. S., & Melton, G. B. (1983). Ethical and legal issues in the treatment of children. In C. E. Walker & M. C. Roberts (Eds.), *Handbook of clinical child psychology* (pp. 1285–1305). New York: Wiley.

*Family Educational Rights and Privacy Act of 1974.* 20 U.S.C.A. Sec. 123g with accompanying regulations set down in 45 C.F.R. Part 99.5.

Fischer, L., & Sorenson, G. P. (1996). *School law for counselors, psychologists, and social workers.* New York: Longman.

Friedman, P. R. (1975). Legal regulation of applied behavior analysis in mental institutions and prisons. *Arizona Law Review, 17,* 39–105.

Gelfand, D. M., & Hartman, D. P. (1984). *Child behavior analysis and therapy* (2nd ed.). New York: Pergamon Press.

George, J. C. (1985). Hedlund paranoia. *Journal of Clinical Psychology, 41,* 291–294.

Grisso, T., & Vierling, L. (1978). Minors' consent to treatment: A developmental perspective. *Professional Psychology, 9,* 412–427.

Gumaer, J. (1984). *Counseling and therapy for children.* New York: Free Press.

Hedlund v. Superior Court, 34 Cal. 3d 695, 194 Cal. Rptr. 805 (1983).

Hendrickson, R. M. (1982). Counselor liability: Does the risk require insurance coverage? *Personnel and Guidance Journal, 61,* 205–207.

Herlihy, B., & Sheeley, V. L. (1986, April). *Privileged communications legal status and ethical issues.* Paper presented at the annual convention of American Association for Counseling and Development, Los Angeles.

Horacek v. Exon, CA No 72-L-299 (1975).

Huey, W. C. (1986). Ethical concerns in school counseling. *Journal of Counseling and Development, 64,* 321–322.

Hughes, J. N. (1986). Ethical issues in school consultation. *School Psychology Review, 15,* 489–499.

Hulteng, R. J., & Goldman, E. B. (1987). Potential liability in outpatient practice: A primer for psychotherapists. In P. A. Keller & S. R. Heyman (Eds.), *Innovations in clinical practice: A source book* (Vol. 6). Sarasota, FL: Professional Resource Exchange.

Ingraham v. Wright, 430 U.S. 651, 97 S. Ct. 1401, 51 L.ED.2d 711 (1977).

Jacob, S., & Hartshorne, T. (1991). *Ethics & law for school psychologists.* Brandon, VT: Clinical Psychology.

Jagim, R. D., Wittman, W. D., & Noll, J. O. (1978). Mental health professionals' attitudes toward confidentiality, privilege, and third-party disclosure. *Professional Psychology, 9,* 456–466.

Johnson, J. H., Rasbury, W. C., & Siegel, L. J. (1986). *Approaches to child treatment: Introduction to theory, research, and practice.* New York: Pergamon Press.

Kandler, H. O. (1977). *Issues of confidentiality in psychiatry* [Newsletter]. New York: Society of Adolescent Psychiatry.

Kazdin, A. E., & Johnson, B. (1994). Advances in psychotherapy for children and adolescents: Interrelations of adjustment, development and intervention. *Journal of School Psychology, 32,* 217–246.

Knapp, S., & VandeCreek, L. (1983). Privileged communications and the counselor. *Personnel and Guidance Journal, 62,* 83–85.

Koocher, G. P., & Keith-Spiegel, P. C. (1990). *Children, ethics, and the law.* Lincoln: University of Nebraska Press.

Langs, R. (1976). *The therapeutic interaction* (Vol. 2). New York: Aronson.

Lidz, C. W., Meisel, A., Zerubavel, E., Carter, M., Sestak, R. M., & Roth, L. H. (1984). *Informed consent: A study of decision making in psychiatry.* New York: Guilford Press.

Lombard, T. J. (1981, August). *Current legislative and policy issues related to school psychological services.* Paper presented at the annual meeting of the American Psychological Association, Los Angeles.

MacDonald v. Clinger, 84 A.D. 2d 482, 446 N.Y.S. 2d 801 (N.Y. App. Div. 1982).

Martin, R. (1975). *Legal challenges to behavior modification.* Champaign, IL: Research Press.

McDermott, P. A. (1972). Law, liability, and the school psychologist: System of law, privileged communication, and access to records. *Journal of School Psychology, 10,* 299–305.

Meyer, R. S., & Smith, S. R. (1977). A crisis in group therapy. *American Psychologist, 32,* 638–662.

Mills, M. J. (1985). Expanding the duties to protect third parties from violent acts. In S. Rachlin (Ed.), *Legal encroachment on psychiatric practice.* San Francisco: Jossey-Bass.

Morales v. Turman, 364 F. Supp. 166 (1973).

National Association of School Psychologists. (1992). *Principles for professional ethics.* Washington, DC: Author.

National Association of Social Workers. (1993). *Code of ethics*. Washington, DC: Author.

New York State Association for Retarded Children v. Rockefeller, 357 F. Supp. 752 (1973).

Page v. Rotterdam-Mohonasen Central School District, 441 N.Y.S.2dis. 323 (Sup. Ct. 1982).

Parents Against Abuse in Schools v. Williamsport Area School District, 594 A.2d 796 (Pa. Commw.Ct. 1991)

Pesce v. J. Sterling Morton High School, 830 F.2d 789 (7th Cir. 1987).

Phillis P. v. Clairmont Unified School District (86 Daily Journal D.A.R. 2795, July 30, 1986).

Planned Parenthood of Central Missouri v. Danforth, 428 U.S. 52 (1976).

Prasse, D. P. (1986). Litigation and special education: An introduction. *Exceptional Children, 52,* 311–312.

Rachlin, S. (Ed.). (1985). *Legal encroachment on psychiatric practice*. San Francisco: Jossey-Bass.

Reynolds, C. R., Gutkin, T. B., Elliot, S. N., & Witt, J. C. (1984). *School psychology: Essentials of theory and practice*. New York: Wiley.

Ross, A. O. (1980). *Psychological disorders of children: A behavioral approach to theory, research, and therapy* (2nd ed.). New York: McGraw-Hill.

Sadoff, R. L. (1985). Competence and informed consent. In S. Rachlin (Ed.), *Legal encroachment on psychiatric practice*. San Francisco: Jossey-Bass.

Sales, B. D., & Grisso, T. (1978). Law and professional psychology: An introduction. *Professional Psychology, 9,* 363–366.

Schectman, F., Hays, J. R., Schuham, A., & Smith, R. (1982). Accountability and confidentiality in psychotherapy, with special reference to child treatment. *Clinical Psychology Review, 2,* 201–211.

Schrier, C. J. (1980). Guidelines for record-keeping under privacy and open-access laws. *Social Work, 25,* 452–457.

Shapiro, M. H. (1974). Legislating the control of behavior control: Autonomy and the coercive use of organic therapies. *Southern California Law Review, 47,* 237–356.

Simmonds, D. W. (1976). Children's rights and family dysfunction: Daddy, why do I have to be the crazy one? In G. P. Koocher (Ed.), *Children's rights and the mental health professions*. New York: Wiley.

Slovenko, R. (1973). *Psychiatry and law*. Boston: Little, Brown.

Sloan, S., & Klein, C. (1977). Psychotherapeutic disclosure: A conflict between right and duty. *University of Toledo Law Review, 6,* 55–85.

Spece, R. G. (1972). Conditioning and other technologies used to "treat?" "rehabilitate?" "demolish?" prisoners and mental patients. *Southern California Law Review, 45,* 616–681.

State v. Bishop, 128 Vt., 227–228, 260, A. 2d, 393, 398, (1969).

State v. Pyle, Kan., 423, 442, 532, P.2d, 1309, 1323, (1975).

Stevens v. State, 354 N.E. 2d 727 (Ind. 1976).

Stolz, S. B., Wienckowski, L. A., & Brown, B. S. (1975). Behavior modification: A perspective on critical issues. *American Psychologist, 30,* 1027–1048.

Szasz, T. S. (1974). *The myth of mental illness* (Rev. ed.). New York: Harper & Row.

Talbutt, L. C. (1983). Libel and slander: A potential problem for the 1980's. *The School Counselor, 30,* 164–168.

Tarasoff v. Regents of the University of California, 13 Cal. 3d 177, 529 P.2d 553 (1974), *vacated,* 17 Cal. 3d 425, 551, P.2d 334 (1976).

Thomas, S. B. (1985). *Legal issues in special education.* Topeka, KS: National Organization on Legal Problems of Education.

United States Department of Health, Education and Welfare. (1963). *Public opinions and attitudes about mental health.* Washington, DC: U.S. Government Printing Office.

Wagner, C. A. (1981). Confidentiality and the school counselor. *Personnel and Guidance Journal, 59,* 305–310.

Waltz, J., & Scheuneman, T. (1970). Informed consent to therapy. *Northwestern University Law Review, 64,* 628–650.

Welsch v. Liking, 373 F. Supp. 487, *affirmed* 525 F. 2d 987 (1974).

Wheeler v. Glass, 473 F. 2d 983 (1973).

Wilson, J. P. (1978). *The rights of adolescents in the mental health system.* Lexington, MA: Lexington Books.

Wood, F. H., & Braaten, S. (1983). Developing guidelines for the use of punishing interventions in the schools. *Exceptional Education Quarterly, 3,* 68–75.

Wyatt v. Stickney, 325 F. Supp. 781 (1971); 334 F. Supp. 1341 (1971); 344 F. Supp. 373 (1972); 344 F. Supp. 387 (1972).

# Chapter 3

# CULTURALLY RESPONSIVE COUNSELING AND PSYCHOTHERAPY WITH CHILDREN AND ADOLESCENTS

Antoinette R. Thomas and Harriet C. Cobb

Increasing cultural pluralism and the changing population demographics of the United States mean that therapists working with children, adolescents, and families today and during the approaching 21st century will have clients from many racial, ethnic, and cultural backgrounds. The population rate for people of color is rapidly increasing, and it is estimated that over the next few decades Whites will become a numerical minority. These demographic changes are in part a result of increased immigration and higher births among people of non-European heritage, increased longevity of the minority populations, and lower birthrates among Whites (Gibbs & Huang, 1998). Additionally, projections suggest that by the year 2020 the majority of school-age children in the United States will be from ethnic minority groups (C. Lee, 1997). According to the Western Institute Commission for Higher Education and the College Board (1988), between 1985 and 1995 the enrollment trends of Asian Pacific Islanders in the nation's schools were expected to increase 70% more rapidly than any other group while the Latino/Hispanic enrollment was expected to increase by approximately 54%. African Americans were expected to be the second largest racial/ethnic group and Native Americans, while still the smallest group, would increase by 29%. It is imperative that mental health professionals recognize and accept these changing realities while gaining awareness, knowledge, skills, and sensitivity for the effective and competent delivery of services to a diverse clientele.

A prerequisite to dealing with diversity requires an accurate understanding of the concepts and terminology found in the literature and used by professionals. Terms such as "race," "ethnicity," "culture," and "minority" have different meanings to different people and are sometimes inappropriately used. Since these terms will be referred to throughout this chapter, a brief definition of each is offered. "Race" is a biological/anthropological classification, which is based on physical and genetic characteristics. The term typically carries with it significant social meaning, political implications, and stereotypes. The term "ethnicity" refers to a shared social and cultural heritage that is passed from one generation to the next (Johnson, 1993). "Race" and "ethnicity" are sometimes used interchangeably, but they are not synonymous. While "race" is a biological term "ethnicity" is a sociological term. "Culture" is a much broader term. It has been defined by Fairchild (1970) as "all behavioral patterns socially required and socially transmitted by means of symbols including customs, techniques, beliefs, institutions and material objects" (p. 80). Religious beliefs, geographic region, and socioeconomic status also contribute to differences that influence an individual's development. The primary method of transmitting culture is language, which enables people to learn, experience, and share their traditions and customs. Finally, the term "minority" not only is used as a numerical reference but is defined as "a group of people who, because of physical or cultural characteristics, are singled out from others in the society in which they live for differential and unequal treatment and who therefore regard themselves as objects of collective discrimination. Minority status carries with it the exclusion from full participation in the life of the society" (Wirth, 1945, p. 347 as cited in Brems, 1993). While ethnic and cultural status can overlap with minority status, this is not always the case.

With these definitions in mind, the remainder of this chapter will focus on issues that address the mental health and development of children, adolescents, and families who represent different ethnic and cultural backgrounds from those who trace their ethnic and cultural origins to Europe. These are the clients who have been the most misunderstood and whose needs have been overlooked or inadequately addressed for so long.

Many a therapist has been surprised when their services have not been sought out by culturally diverse clients or when these clients prematurely terminate therapy. There are many reasons why this might be the case. First, it has been fairly typical for a therapist to utilize a traditional model of counseling or therapy when working with minority clients. The therapist may employ one or more of the three main helping orientations (psychodynamic, existential-humanistic, and cognitive-behavioral) exclusively with the client, using a one-on-one, "talk therapy" approach in an office setting. Culturally diverse clients may find this situation to be ambiguous because they may not understand what therapy is about, how it is conducted, and what their role should be in the therapeutic process. Second, expectations about what should happen in therapy can also be perceived quite differently by the minority client. The one-on-one approach and office setting may seem too formal and alienating while the theoretical approaches used may be antagonistic to the worldview and life experience of the minority client. Third, potential clients of color may never seek therapy for fear they will not be understood, validated, and respected, or will be compared with one standard (based on a White middle-class norm) and any deviations from that norm may be viewed as deficiencies. Also for many people of color, it is culturally inappropriate to self-disclose to a "stranger."

Factors and incidences such as these are just a few of the aspects that might contribute to the underutilization of mental health services by culturally diverse clients. They suggest the need for mental health providers to raise their level of awareness and knowledge regarding the concerns and needs of minority clients.

## AWARENESS

To become culturally responsive, one must begin with self-awareness. Therapists are typically encouraged to "know thyself"; however, it is essential for counselors and clinicians who work with culturally diverse clients to have some awareness of their own cultural background, cultural heritage, and that which has contributed to their values, beliefs, attitudes, and opinions. To do this, one might explore answers to questions such as:

1. What is my cultural heritage? What was the culture of my parents and my grandparents? With what cultural group(s) do I identify? (Locke, 1992)
2. What are some of the traditions and customs practiced in my family? Where did they originate? (Locke, 1992)
3. Am I a member of any minority group? What has that experience been like for me?
4. What values, beliefs, opinions, and attitudes do I hold that are consistent with the European-American culture? Which are inconsistent? How did I learn these?

Next, it is important to take an introspective look at one's own personal cultural biases, prejudices, and stereotypes. This can be painful because it is not easy to admit to thoughts and feelings that might be viewed as prejudice or offensive by someone else. However, recognizing and acknowledging these perceptions and attitudes are the first steps toward increased sensitivity for others. For this type of awareness, one might ask:

1. What are my perceptions and beliefs about members of other ethnic groups?
2. What is the origin or source of most of my views toward members of other ethnic groups? What have I ever done to validate my beliefs?
3. How do my beliefs affect my behavior toward persons from other cultural backgrounds?
4. How do my attitudes help and/or hinder me in my interactions/relationships with children and adults who are culturally different from me?

To heighten awareness, pay attention to your behavior when interacting with someone who is culturally different from you and the level of comfort you experience. Notice your internal reactions and participation in a variety of situations. Doing so may facilitate your understanding of your own biases and prejudices. How do you react when others make ethnic jokes or stereotypical comments? To what degree do you engage in making generalizations about others? What words and phrases do you use in reference to members of culturally different groups or those with minority status?

Evaluate the degree to which you are exposed to or have contact with those who are culturally different from you. What is the extent to which your personal interactions are with people who are of the same or different culture as you? Do you live in the same neighborhood, worship with, socialize with, or have as friends, members from other cultural groups?

How aware are you of the cultural privileges that have been granted to European Americans and the consequential impact this lack of privilege has had on ethnic minorities? McIntosh (1989) refers to this as "White privilege" and describes it as "unearned assets" obtained by virtue of being White and enjoyed while being "conditioned into oblivion about its existence." Some examples of White privilege observed by McIntosh, who is White herself, include: "I can if I wish arrange to be in the company of people of my race most of the time." "I can go shopping most of the time, pretty well assured that I will not be followed or harassed," "I can be sure that my children will be given curricular materials that testify to the existence of their race." "I am never asked to speak for all the people of my race."

Lastly, therapists should be aware of their own worldview (how a person perceives his or her relationship with the world) and recognize that it may differ from the worldview of culturally diverse clients. Worldviews are influenced by our cultural heritage and life experiences; they affect our values, beliefs, and how we think, behave, and define events (D. W. Sue, 1981). Failure to recognize such differences can be a significant barrier to effective therapy or counseling. For example, a therapist whose worldview incorporates the belief that individuals are responsible for their own destiny and should be able to "pull themselves up by their bootstraps" may find it challenging to work with clients who blame their problems and misfortune on "the system."

## KNOWLEDGE

In addition to awareness, mental health professionals must have accurate and relevant cultural knowledge. This knowledge can be gained from formal study (i.e., courses, workshops, inservices) culturally sensitive supervision, readings from many fields of study, and more informal experiences such as those obtained from firsthand encounters. Knowledge can also be gained directly from the client or other members of a particular cultural group.

Of utmost importance to the therapist is the acquisition of culture-specific knowledge. However, one must be careful not to generalize such information to all members of any group and be willing to pursue the validity of such information with each individual encounter. Such knowledge might include information regarding history, family structure, traditions and customs, child-rearing practices, indigenous help-seeking practices, and communication patterns. It would also be important for the therapist to have some understanding of the oppression and racism experienced by ethnic minorities and their impact on psychological adjustment.

C. Lee (1997) has described a number of cultural dynamics that he suggests are important in culturally responsive counseling practice. Two of these are acculturation and ethnic identity. Ethnic identity is "an individual's sense of belonging to an ethnic group and the part of an individual's personality that is attributable to ethnic membership" (Rotheram & Phinney, 1987). Acculturation, within the context of contemporary society, refers to the degree to which an individual identifies with or conforms to the attitudes, lifestyles, and values of the European-American based macroculture (C. Lee, 1997). Ethnic group members can fall anywhere on a continuum ranging from strong to weak ethnic identity and high to low levels of acculturation. Someone who has a high level of acculturation and a strong ethnic identity would be viewed as "bicultural." These individuals have a strong sense of belonging to a particular ethnic group while being able to identify and function effectively in the macroculture. By contrast, someone with a low degree of acculturation, yet a strong ethnic identity would be marginal to the macroculture but hold firmly to the cultural customs of the "old country." Recent immigrants best represent this combination. Assessing where an individual may lie on each continuum and the relationship between the two positions provides the therapist with vital information that may be helpful in defining the problem, setting goals, and selecting appropriate interventions. Other cultural dynamics such as language, kinship influences, sex role socialization, religious spiritual influences, immigration experience, and historical hostility (negative feelings that ethnic minority members possess toward the White majority of the United States for their role in oppressive and racist acts) are salient influences in the psychosocial development of culturally diverse clients that should further assist the therapist in establishing an appropriate therapeutic framework.

Therapists will also want to have some knowledge of racial and ethnic identity development as it applies to both the therapist and the client. A number of models such as Helms (1995) and Cross (1995) have been developed and modified over the years to describe the development of people of color and Whites as racial beings. This development has typically been viewed as stagelike and eventually progresses to a point where the individual accepts him- or herself as a racial being while respecting and appreciating diversity among other groups. Research suggests that these models have diagnostic value (D. W. Sue & Sue, 1990). Determining the identity status of an ethnic minority client may reveal something about his or her reaction to the counselor and the counseling process. Likewise, the therapist can assess his or her own level of cultural identity. The benefits in doing this are twofold. First, the therapist can perhaps gain a better understanding of the client-therapist relationship. Second, this self-awareness will further enhance the therapist's level of cultural sensitivity.

The combination of knowledge, skills, awareness, and sensitivity results in the desired goal of becoming a culturally responsive therapist. This requires a commitment to develop new ways of practicing psychotherapy and modifying existing methods. Such practice is typically grounded in theory. After 30 years of research and clinical observations as well as dialogue among professionals on multiculturalism and diversity, a metatheory of multicultural counseling and therapy has evolved.

## OVERVIEW OF THEORY

### Basic Theory and Assumptions

A theory of multicultural counseling and therapy (MCT) has recently been proposed by D. Sue, Ivey, and Pedersen (1996) to address some of the limitations of current theories of counseling and psychotherapy. Theories such as those described in this text (i.e., psychoanalytic, behavioral, humanistic, or cognitive) have been conceptualized from a European American perspective and thus reflect the values, mores, customs, philosophies, and language of that culture (Ponterotto & Casas, 1991; D. W. Sue & Sue, 1990) and cannot be easily adapted to a wide range of cultures (Pedersen, 1991). D. W. Sue (1992) states that a major weakness in these theories is that they focus on one aspect of the human condition. For example, cognitive theory emphasizes the thinking self, and humanistic-existential theory emphasizes the feeling self, while behavioral therapy and family systems are centered around the behaving and social self respectively. However, people are all of these—feeling, behaving, thinking, and social beings and more (i.e., cultural and spiritual). Consequently, what is needed is a metatheory (Ivey, Ivey, & Simek-Morgan, 1993; D. W. Sue, 1995) that utilizes a more holistic and comprehensive approach addressing the integrated aspects of the self. This metatheory would be culture-centered (Pedersen & Ivey, 1993) and applicable to European American culture as well as other cultural groups. The basic assumptions of this theory of multicultural counseling and therapy are addressed in six propositions and a number of corollaries, that further delineate each proposition. The propositions are:

*Proposition 1.* MCT theory is a metatheory of counseling and psychotherapy. A theory about theories, it offers an organizational framework for understanding the numerous helping approaches that humankind has developed. It recognizes that both theories of counseling and psychotherapy developed in the Western world and those helping models indigenous to non-Western cultures are neither inherently right or wrong, good or bad. Each theory represents a different worldview.

*Proposition 2.* Both counselor and client identities are formed and embedded in multiple levels of experiences (individual, group, and universal) and contexts (individual, family, and cultural milieu). The totality and interrelationships of experiences and contexts must be the focus of treatment.

*Proposition 3.* Cultural identity development is a major determinant of counselor and client attitudes toward self, others of the same group, others of a different group and the dominant group. These attitudes, which may be manifested in affective and behavioral dimensions, are strongly influenced not only by cultural variables but also by the dynamics of dominant–subordinate relationships among culturally different groups. The level or stage of racial/cultural identity will both influence how clients and counselors define the problem and dictate what they believe to be appropriate counseling/therapy goals and processes.

*Proposition 4.* The effectiveness of MCT is most likely enhanced when the counselor uses modalities and defines goals consistent with the life experiences and cultural values of the client. No single approach is equally effective across all populations and life situations. The ultimate goal of multicultural counselor/therapist training is to expand the repertoire of helping responses available to the professional, regardless of theoretical orientation.

*Proposition 5.* MCT theory stresses the importance of multiple helping roles developed by many culturally different groups and societies. Besides the basic one-on-one encounter aimed at remediation in the individual, these roles often involve larger social units, systems intervention, and prevention. That is, the conventional roles of counseling and psychotherapy are only one of many others available to the helping professional.

*Proposition 6.* The liberation of consciousness is a basic goal of MCT theory. Whereas self-actualization, discovery of the role of the past in the present, or behavior change have been traditional goals of Western psychology and counseling, MCT emphasizes the importance of expanding personal, family, group, and organizational consciousness of the place of self-in-relation, family-in-relation, and organization-in-relation. This results in therapy that is not only ultimately contextual in orientation, but that also draws on traditional methods of healing from many cultures.

These assumptions of multicultural counseling and psychotherapy are the essence of the core philosophy of a culturally responsive therapist. Acquisition of this theoretical knowledge along with enhanced awareness and sensitivity provides the foundation for responsive therapeutic skill development.

## THERAPEUTIC APPROACHES

### Principles of Practice

Based on the literature and on our own clinical experience, we are advocating the conceptualization of culturally responsive psychotherapy with children as *interpersonal, multidimensional,* and *systemic.*

The *interpersonal* perspective emphasizes the importance of developing a good *relationship* with the client. The quality of the relationship (even a short-term relationship) is the therapist's most effective tool in facilitating positive change.

A *multidimensional* approach means possessing a repertoire of methods that have empirical and clinical support, including solution-focused, cognitive behavioral, and an overall active involvement on the part of the therapist. Flexibility is essential in that the culturally sensitive therapist must respond to each client as a unique individual, whose experiences emerge from a particular familial and cultural milieu (Teyber, 1997). Culturally responsive counseling is highly *ideographic.* It focuses on the developmental history, personal experience, and current circumstances of the individual client, utilizing a range of therapeutic approaches to fit the situation of that specific client. For example, while there are guidelines for practice, there is no one "right" approach for all African American children, all Asian American children, or all White rural children.

Working within a *systemic* framework assembles a number of potential resources in addressing the child's problems. This suggests involvement of extended family, schools, and community, medical, or social services. The role of the child therapist may have more of a "case manager" component than for children in mainstream cultures. Because of the mental health, educational, and medical needs of many minority children, the therapist may potentially communicate with a number of other individuals to acquire information or arrange for services. This investment of time and energy may go well beyond the actual therapy sessions.

Particularly for children who live in poverty, the individual, one-on-one model of therapy as an exclusive intervention will be woefully inadequate. Vraniak and Pickett (1993), refer to therapists as service delivery agents. Some children who are referred for primarily emotional or behavioral problems may need intensive special educational interventions more than psychotherapy. If the child has medical problems such as chronic ear infections, severe headaches, nutritional deficiencies, or uncorrected vision problems, the medical treatment must be obtained for any therapeutic intervention to be successful. The mental health professional must be competent in decision making and prioritizing which interventions are most feasible and most important. It may be that the most effective action the counselor can take will be to consult with the family and other service agencies. The culturally responsive child therapist cannot merely sit in the office and conduct therapy sessions. He or she must be willing to engage in outreach and facilitate the mobilization of other resources for any positive, meaningful change to occur in the child's life. This may mean encouraging the client and family to make use of indigenous support systems (e.g., the church, medicine men, respected community member) and not continue in regular, clinician-provided counseling. Alternatively, a selective combination of interventions and resources is the cornerstone of a comprehensive, multidimensional approach to therapy.

While there is no single "correct" therapeutic approach with children of culturally diverse backgrounds, the quality of the relationship between the client and therapist has long-standing empirical support for being considered the most important factor in successful outcomes (Ho, 1992). The core conditions of accurate *empathy, respect,* and *genuiness* provide the foundation for cultural sensitivity. Cultural responsiveness is essential for an effective therapeutic alliance with children from a cultural context different from the therapist. As Trotter (1993) reminds us, empathy is the ability to understand the child from his or her perspective. A child's understanding of the world emerges from parents and family who are members of a particular cultural environment. Therefore, awareness and knowledge of this cultural environment are necessary conditions for accurate empathy (Johnson, 1993).

Respect refers to valuing the child as a person of worth, someone who possesses strengths and competencies, and is deserving of help. Genuineness is communicated by a sincere desire to help the child and to serve in an advocacy role.

Traditional ways of creating these core conditions may need to be modified for minority children. Eye contact, facial expressions, touch, and verbal responses such as self-disclosure have different meanings in different cultures. Therapists should be aware that in some cultures, addressing clients by their first names is perceived as being overly familiar; formality may be expected throughout the relationship. Using slang from the client's ethnic group may be offensive. Keeping the client waiting may have particularly negative repercussions, as will having a patronizing or condescending manner. In some other cultures, being "on time" may be perceived differently; thus, the therapist would do better to make suitable arrangements, rather than to discuss the reasons for lateness or to interpret tardiness as resistance. Regardless of the client's cultural background or socioeconomic standing, most clients expect that the therapist will be well dressed, and the office attractive and nicely furnished, as a reflection of the therapist's success. Gibbs (1985) emphasize that clients may be more appreciative of therapists who demonstrate interpersonal skills than who show instrumental competence in the early sessions, although some improvement is expected to occur soon.

According to Vraniak and Pickett (1993), the therapist must be aware of the following five considerations to develop good interpersonal relationships with minority children and their families:

1. A history of deleterious relationships with those in power. This contributes to a deeper level of mistrust when forming new relationships. For example, this may mean more discomfort with self-disclosure for African Americans, reflecting a cultural pattern of disguising true feelings from Whites in positions of authority.

2. This history contributes to client behaviors that test the limits of the therapist's practical knowledge of the client's culture. Adolescent skepticism may be especially acute.

3. Clients will explore the clinician as a person, including his or her authority role as well as the clinician's ability to connect with the client.

4. Clients will question how much the clinician actually cares about them, and how much the clinician can be of help.

5. Clients must be taught the protocol of therapy; an understanding of the purpose, nature of the process, potential content of the sessions, and expected outcomes.

Paniagua (1994) makes suggestions for preventing attrition, which is an all too common consequence if the therapist does not establish an alliance within the first session. These suggestions include:

• Be certain that the child and family feels the therapist accepts their belief system.

• Communicate to the clients that some relief of symptoms and at least a partial resolution of problems is possible within a relatively short time frame.

• Include therapy modalities that are direct, active, and structured and that provide a potential solution to the primary problem within the first session.

• Be prepared to discuss racial differences with African American families. If the client does not bring up racial discrimination, it is desirable to ask the client if it is an issue that he or she experiences.

• Communicate respect for and be prepared to include religious support groups in the treatment when religion is an integral part of the family's life.

- For some cultures, such as Asian, discussing the potential role of medication is expected; for others, such as African American, immediately recommending an evaluation for medication would be perceived negatively.
- With Southeast Asian clients, in particular, do not insist on the child or family discussing traumatic experiences immediately; the stress ensued could lead to attrition.

Since many minority clients see therapists as experts, therapists should not hesitate to refer to their own educational background and clinical experience (E. Lee, 1982). This acts to reassure the child's family that they have come to the right person and diminishes the chances for dropout. Spurlock (1985) points out that meeting with the child and parents together for the initial session provides information about how the process works, allows time for questions and clarifications, and gives the family the opportunity to "check out" the therapist. The family may legitimately want to know how many families like them the therapist has worked with. Lower SES families may also wonder if the information they reveal has anything to do with financial or other assistance they may be receiving.

Children and families with limited proficiency in English pose special challenges. Generally speaking, using translators in providing psychotherapy should be avoided (Lopez, 1995). Of course, in some circumstances, translators will be necessary in working with children and families who have limited English proficiency, if the therapist is not fluent in the client's language.

If translators are used, the following guidelines are recommended (Paniagua, 1994):

- Clinicians should try to use translators who share the client's ethnic background.
- Translators should have some training in mental health problems.
- Clinicians should use a sequential mode of translation (i.e., the client speaks, it's translated; the clinician speaks, it's translated).
- The clinician should introduce the translator to the family and allow time for them to become acquainted.
- Clinicians should avoid using family friends or relations as translators. Additionally, bilingual children should not serve as translators, since it inappropriately interferes with adult/child hierarchy.
- Allow the inevitable extra time needed for a translated session.

Introducing a third person into the psychotherapy process can lead to misinterpretation and distortions of the client's verbalization. Some children and families will simply not like the translator's presence. Ideally, mental health professionals who work with clients who have limited English proficiency should be bilingual. Since this is not yet the norm within the field, translators are sometimes needed.

Among some groups, such as Asians, showing the child and family that the therapist cares may mean attending to the child's or parents' physical condition with a question such as, "How are your headaches?" (Hsu, 1983), instead of focusing solely on the client's emotional/psychological status. Attention to practical, real-world problems must accompany concern about internal, less tangible issues. Korean-born clients rated therapists as more effective when the therapist was more directive, rather than nondirective (Foley & Fuqua, 1988). This means merely "listening," even listening well, may be interpreted as too detached. According to LaFromboise and Low (1989), Native Indian youth expect some practical advice about their lives, not analysis of their feelings. Caring must be demonstrated more actively, with attention to what is important for the child and his family.

The therapist must be able to communicate respect for generational differences within the family, and mediate effectively when necessary. The therapist must be able to convince the family that he or she is a resource by actually being one. Again, this requires flexibility and resourcefulness on the part of the therapist. The burden is on the therapist to learn about and understand as much as possible about a child's culture, particularly when it differs from the therapist's own background. This does not mean that the therapist must know everything about the culture. Awareness of the limits of our knowledge and a genuine interest in understanding cultural characteristics will be important for culturally responsive counseling. Making mistakes related to culture, such as asking a naive question, is inevitable, especially early in the therapist's experience. Most therapeutic mistakes of any kind are forgivable if they are in the context of a good relationship (Teyber, 1997). The therapist needs to avoid the temptation to withdraw or give up. Instead, errors comprise opportunities to grow and develop as a therapist. The process may be uncomfortable, even painful at times; but the outcome will be increasing cultural responsiveness. Conversely, therapists may mistakenly assume that clients from their culture are just like themselves, which may interfere with a successful outcome as well (Pinderhughes, 1989). While there may be a natural affinity between the therapist and client from the same culture, the tendency to overidentify with the client may dilute therapeutic effectiveness (Giordano & Giordano, 1995). Therapists in this situation must do their homework to learn about cultural differences. In either case, therapists need to examine their own beliefs, attitudes, and emotions with regard to culture.

Since the universal principle of connectedness between children and their families is particularly strong in most minority cultures, it defines a "best practice" procedure to be used with children: Involve the family, including extended family, early in the process whenever possible.

For many children and their families, the initial session will "make it or break it." If this is the first contact with a mental health professional, the therapist should work from a psychoeducational framework, explaining in understandable terms what psychotherapy is and how, specifically, it can help the child. This educative component serves to prepare the client and family for psychotherapy and prevent premature termination due to misunderstanding or miscommunication. In some circumstances, a home visit is the best way to obtain parent/family contact; in others, a session at the child's school can work as well. Explaining the reasons for asking personal questions about family and medical history and psychosocial stressors is also important so the therapist is not perceived as overly intrusive (Tsui & Schultz, 1985, as cited in Canino

& Spurlock, 1994). Furthermore, in the Asian cultures in particular, shame and guilt may arise in the course of history taking.

It is crucial to recognize the importance of an aunt or grandmother, for example, whose influence on other family members can be a real asset in making progress. Giordano and Giordano (1995) describe guidelines to use in working with families. Three of them are summarized here:

1. *Assess the importance of ethnicity to the child and his or her family.* For one family, identity with an ethnic group may be essential to their lives; in another family, ethnic identity may be more in the background. There may be significant generational differences within a family. For example, either grandparents or adolescents may retain a strong cultural identity. Other family members may develop a value system and lifestyle that is different from the family norms.

2. *Learn about the family's support systems.* The family may need assistance in exploring community resources and services of which they may not be aware. If relationships with extended family have been problematic, assist the family in working through this stressor. This may mean listening empathetically to the mother of the child with whom you are working about the rift between her and her sister. Supportive psychotherapy for the mother in resolving some of her problems can enable her to take a more active role in parenting her child.

3. *The therapist may serve as a culture broker.* This may mean assisting the family in feeling acceptance and pride in their background, along with accepting and learning about aspects of the new culture. This will facilitate the journey to developing biculturalism when this is needed.

## Classroom/Educational Applications

Psychological interventions to minority children extend to the school and classroom. School psychologists, school counselors, and other mental health professionals can provide either direct individual counseling, group counseling, or parent education. Cole, Thomas, and Lee (1988) specifically discuss ways psychologists and counselors in schools can bridge the gap between minority families and schools. Additionally, clinicians can consult with teachers and other school personnel with the goal of making schools good places for culturally diverse populations. The research on effective schools seems to highlight a common theme: The most effective combination for success is high expectations for students within a caring context (Baruth & Manning, 1992). Mental health clinicians have a clear role in consulting in schools when cultural issues arise. Cross-cultural consultation is defined as "a consultation relationship in which two or more of the participants differ with respect to cultural or ethnic background" (Duncan, 1995, p. 129). As in the case of providing direct psychotherapy, the clinician must be culturally responsive when consulting. The principles of best practice—being interpersonal, multidimensional, and systemic—apply to good consultation as well.

Minority children (particularly those who have been referred for mental health services) need to be in classrooms with culturally responsive teachers who foster a climate of warmth, understanding, and tolerance among class members. The clinician who is counseling a minority child with self-esteem issues can facilitate the development of cultural responsiveness in the teacher by increasing awareness of minority identity development and its impact on children's emotional/social behavior and academic achievement. Furthermore, the clinician and teacher can discuss systemic factors that interfere with progress for minority group children. Finally, the clinician may provide professional development activities such as recommending readings or conducting experiential in-service training in an effort toward increasing knowledge of multicultural education and curriculum (Duncan, 1995). For example, an elementary school teacher may need a reminder to use culturally relevant readings, rather than only using stories from the dominant culture (Canino & Spurlock, 1994). Involving the family to learn about favorite folk tales and working with librarians and other media specialists can facilitate a successful consultation outcome.

The mental health professional can facilitate a number of actions that schools can take to assist minority children in schools. Pairing students with mentors such as a classmate, older student, or parent volunteer who is knowledgeable about the child's culture and the majority culture can help soften the culture shock that some new students experience. These "culture brokers" can teach students how to behave in social situations and understand the behavior of mainstream-culture children whose behavior seems mysterious or threatening (Grossman, 1995). Conducting group counseling sessions with a social skills and discussion component can foster this new learning and respond to the myriad feelings the children experience.

Recent immigrants and their families who are not yet bilingual often find the English as a second language (ESL), or bilingual teacher, a tremendous resource. The school counselor or psychologist should find opportunities to collaborate with this individual as a part of the network of resources for children who are not yet proficient in English.

Classrooms should have aspects of immigrant students' home cultures. For example, displaying pictures of the child's native country, and coordinating activities that show the food and customs of the child's place of birth can help in the transition from one culture to the next. It should be noted that coed activities, competitive games, or group showers may not be acceptable for some children, particularly when they are new to the United States (Grossman, 1995). The mental health professional working with a particular child may provide consultation to the teacher to facilitate sensitive handling of cultural assimilation.

Teachers who are new to the experience of having a recent immigrant in the class may not realize the impact of calling on students who don't volunteer, or critiquing their behavior in front of others. According to Wei (1980), Vietnamese children often find American teachers' informality difficult to accept. Asking questions in class seems aggressive and disrespectful. When this behavior is rewarded by the teacher, it is especially confusing. The language barrier can be particularly problematic for students when there may be none or only a few other students who speak the same language. The language barrier can cause a small misunderstanding to become a large discipline problem. For example, one 13-year-old Hispanic girl experienced significant emotional distress when her lack of English proficiency inhibited her from accepting a telephone invitation from an English-speaking child to a party. Consulting with the parents of both girls helped facilitate a friendship between the two families. Again, the clinician/consultant can have a major role in encouraging collaboration among professionals in a better understanding of the child.

When working with a child who is a recent immigrant, the clinician needs to be aware of the demands often placed on the child to act as translator for the entire family. He or she may have to interpret for the parents, and be responsible for speaking with the landlord or salesclerk. Such children have far more pressure on them to perform tasks than do children whose families are English proficient.

At the systemic level, the therapist may organize workshops or presentations to heighten awareness and implement educational practices that benefit the psychological well-being of minority children. A number of school-based programs have been developed to foster healthy psychological development in minority children, particularly those from lower socioeconomic backgrounds. Canino and Spurlock (1994) describe the School Development Program (SDP), which is designed to increase coping skills and decrease behavior problems in children. The program model utilizes a mental health team approach with extensive parental involvement and applies basic social/behavioral principles to every aspect of the curriculum.

Project Self-Esteem is a parent involvement program for preventing substance abuse (McDaniel & Bielen, 1990). Multicultural issues, gender issues, and positive discipline are introduced to teachers, while parents and children learn about communication skills, goal setting, and other relevant issues. A sequence of lessons is integrated into the regular school curriculum.

Some intervention programs based on the social learning model are designed to teach situation-specific social skills. It is not unusual for social skills learned in one culture to lack usefulness within another cultural context. There is no assumption that previously learned skills are "bad," just that there may be more appropriate skills for a different context. This type of program can be less culturally biased in an effort to develop bicultural competence (LaFromboise & Rowe, 1983). The skills learned can be applied to a variety of problems, enhancing the child's general coping abilities. The five-step problem-solving program, Stop, Options, Decision, Action, and Self-praise (SODAS) for American Indian youth was designed to help adolescents make better decisions about drug use. The program provides information that includes the historical review of alcohol use in American Indian communities, tribal and personal values, and peer resistance training. There is some outcome research to indicate that there were lowered rates of drug use after participation in this program (Gilchrist, Schinke, Trimble, & Cuetkovich, 1987, as cited in Canino & Spurlock, 1994).

Affective education programs or classroom guidance activities can also enhance social relationships and skills among mainstream culture children as well as minority children. They can assist students in developing positive self-concepts, increased social skills, and increased understandings of different cultural and ethnic groups. Exposing children to multicultural issues during the elementary school years increases awareness and tolerance of individual differences, according to a number of studies (Hilliard, 1991).

Omizo and D'Andrea (1995) describe multicultural guidance activities that highlight cultural uniqueness and similarities among children. They are experiential and include such activities as examining advertisements for cultural diversity, creating diverse "communities" with their own language and customs within a classroom, and representing cultural concepts through art media. One classroom activity, entitled "Labeling" begins by the counselor or teacher selecting a concept such as "boy or girl" or "tall or short," that is not revealed to the class. The children are divided into groups that reflect the specific concept, such as boys in one group, and all girls in another. The facilitator then labels each group as being "good" or "bad." The class then guesses the criteria by which the children in each group were labeled.

Rules are put into place that determine what "good" students are allowed to do, and what "bad" students are not permitted to do. For instance, "good" children get to go to lunch early, while "bad" children must wait at the end of a long line. The class must guess the criteria that determined who received privileges. The children then discuss what it felt like to be "bad" or "good," not knowing what the criteria were, and not being in control of things. This enables the children to explore the consequences of stereotyping, prejudice, and value judgments.

"Portrait Pluralism" assigns students the task of drawing pictures of themselves. The pictures (with corresponding names) are displayed around the classroom and each child is asked to write a positive comment about each of their classmates. The children are encouraged to find out positive attributes about each other for the entire week. The children are then divided into pairs to discuss their portraits and the written positive comments. The facilitator points out cultural factors that may influence the ways some people are viewed by others. The discussion is used to point out how some members of different cultural groups are viewed, and the importance of discovering positive characteristics of each individual. Clinicians can play a major role in advocating for a culturally responsive perspective in the school and classroom settings.

Goldstein (1994) has developed a prosocial behavior program specifically designed for low-income youth, expanding his earlier "skillstreaming" approach. As mentioned earlier, social class differences often mean cultural differences. Goldstein contrasts the differences in child-rearing characteristics between middle class and lower socioeconomic families. In the former context, a 12-year-old boy calling his sister names may be asked why he did so (motivation); how he thinks such behavior made his sister feel (empathy), and be reminded he is capable of more self-control. The lower SES parents may be more likely to take immediate action, such as physically punishing their son, without necessarily encouraging introspection or increased self-regulated behavior.

Social skills interventions for low-income youth need to follow a prescriptive approach that emphasizes modeling appropriate behavior, and providing opportunities for supervised practice, performance feedback, and transfer of training.

The Prepare Curriculum has a number of components including training in specific skills, anger management, moral reason, empathy, and stress management.

This focus on action, consequences, and outcomes has a stronger probability of being successful than a highly verbal, insight-oriented approach to teaching social skills. Early outcome studies of skillstreaming and anger control training indicate that skill transfer occurs in about half of participants. Preliminary studies of other aspects of the Prepare Curriculum are encouraging (Goldstein, 1994).

Other intervention programs exist that provide a developmental counseling experience targeting specific populations. For example, C. Lee (1996) has developed a multisession group counseling experience for young African American males that facilitates personal and social growth by helping them develop the attitudes and skills which are necessary in meeting environmental challenges that often lead to problems in school and elsewhere. More specifically, the experience stresses the development of strong Black men through a strengthening of body, mind, and soul. The strengthening is accomplished through understanding and appreciating the Black man in African and African American history and culture, developing achievement motivation, developing positive and responsible behavior, and modeling positive African American male images. There are two programs: "The Young Lions" for Black males in Grades 3–6 and "Black Manhood Training" for adolescent Black males. A significant feature of the experience provided by these programs is the use of selected African and African American art forms (e.g., music, poetry, and graphic expression) as well as culture-specific curriculum materials as educational aids in the counseling process. These forms of African American expressiveness and instruction are considered a fundamental part of the group intervention and assist in the process of empowering Black males.

## EFFICACY

As with psychotherapy outcome studies in general, methodological or conceptual shortcomings are often cited in the literature on assessing treatment effectiveness (S. Sue, 1988). However, a number of studies have been conducted assessing the perceived effectiveness of therapy with clients from diverse backgrounds.

Tangimara and McShane (1990) cited in Vraniak and Pickett (1993), surveyed mental health providers with American Indian clients and compared the perceptions of Indian versus non-Indian therapists. Both Indian and non-Indian respondents reported reality therapy, behavioral therapy, and cognitive approaches as the most effective approaches when compared with more insight-oriented methods.

Other studies of different ethnic minority groups have supported the use of behavioral and cognitive approaches within the context of a good therapeutic relationship. These treatments are authoritative, concrete, action oriented, and focus on short-term learning, characteristics of a process that is generally favored by these groups (Paniagua, 1994).

Racial match appears not to be a necessary nor sufficient condition for positive treatment outcomes. Based on empirical and clinical studies, therapists of different cultures than their clients can be effective as long as cultural sensitivity and cultural competence are present (Paniagua, 1994). The characteristics of the culturally responsive therapist (awareness, knowledge, skills, and sensitivity) are more important than matching cultural backgrounds.

## CONCLUSION

Working with children and families from culturally diverse backgrounds is increasingly common for mental health professionals. Multicultural counseling and therapy (MCT) provides a metaframework for conceptualizing interventions with a cultural context. The culturally responsive therapist is one who has integrated awareness, knowledge, skills, and sensitivity into a comprehensive way of approaching therapeutic work with all children. An ideographic approach taken by the culturally responsive therapist is most likely to result in positive outcomes for the child. A strong therapeutic relationship (interpersonal) that makes use of methods that are solution focused and action oriented (multidimensional) while drawing on a number of resources (systemic) provides the underpinning for best practice. Culturally responsive therapists are natural advocates for children, bringing energy and commitment to developing and implementing interventions that improve the quality of life for children in every culture.

### CASE STUDY 1 _____

Darius is an 11-year-old African American male in the 6th grade. His mother, Mrs. G, approached the school psychologist for help with Darius because of his increasing anger and lack of interest in school. In addition, Mrs. G indicated that she felt she was losing control of him because he "wasn't minding" her like he used to.

Mrs. G is a single parent with an older daughter aged 15. Darius never really knew his father because he died shortly after Darius was born. Recently, Mrs. G and her family moved from another state due to a better job opportunity. Mrs. G works as a computer programmer. Darius has been attending this new school for 3 months. In his previous school, Darius was considered an exceptional student. He had been receiving services for the gifted and talented for the past two years. No one had pursued such services for Darius.

After talking with Mrs. G, the school psychologist met with Darius. This first meeting was used to establish rapport with him and get his perception of the problem. Initially, Darius was quiet and somewhat reserved; however, he seemed to warm up after the school psychologist asked him about his interests and conveyed her genuine desire to understand what he viewed as the problem and her willingness to help him have a more rewarding school experience. Darius explained that he hates school "because it's boring" and "because they don't study Black people or other minorities." He further stated that whenever he asks his teacher, who is White, anything related to Blacks, she ignores him or tells him to "go look it up." When asked about how things were going at home, Darius stated that his mother treats him like a baby and "won't let [him] do anything." He also said that he was tired of women pushing him around.

Next, the school psychologist met with the teacher, Ms. B. She described Darius as "a know it all" who constantly challenges her and seems to get a kick out of "putting her on the spot." She viewed these behaviors as attention getting and disruptive. Ms. B stated that Darius doesn't pay attention in class and spends a lot of time talking to his peers. He often responds to her in a sassy tone and sometimes vents his anger by becoming physically aggressive with peers or destroying school property. However, Ms. B admitted that Darius is able to successfully participate in classroom discussions and accurately responds to questions when called on. His grades have been suffering primarily because he has not been completing assignments and has spent a considerable amount of class time in the assistant principal's office for disciplinary action. Ms. B was unaware that Darius had previously been identified as gifted.

To address Darius's problem and Mrs. G's concerns, the school psychologist continued to work with Darius individually to further establish a therapeutic alliance. At the same time, the school psychologist met with the classroom teacher and the coordinator of the program for gifted and talented students to discuss Darius's eligibility for the school's program. Further consultation with the teacher focused on increasing her awareness and knowledge of cultural dynamics and how these might be recognized within a cultural context. The school psychologist also consulted with Ms. B to assist her in understanding Darius's feelings regarding a lack of minority presence in the curriculum and how she might incorporate more diversity and multiculturalism in the curriculum.

After meeting with Darius two times individually, the school psychologist invited him to join a group that focused on anger management. This group consisted solely of males his age, and included both White and Black students. The school psychologist also sought out community services that might provide him with positive Black male role models and address his development as a maturing African American man. A local church was running such a program and Darius was eager to participate.

Finally, the school psychologist arranged to meet with Mrs. G. She was initially somewhat resistant to having any additional contact with the school psychologist because she felt that Darius was the one with the problem, not her. Additionally, the majority of her interactions with school personnel had been negative so she was somewhat suspicious about the school psychologist's intentions although she said she was willing to do whatever she could to help Darius. The school psychologist wanted to explore ways in which support could be provided to Mrs. G. (i.e., being available for consultation regarding parenting skills and/or providing information about services offered in the school and in the community). In Mrs. G's case, it was important to build a good working relationship and focus on the process rather than the outcome.

## Analysis

Elements of Darius's case are similar to that experienced by a number of young African American male students. He is experiencing a great deal of frustration, in part because he feels as though the school is not adequately addressing his academic needs nor is it validating him as a Black male. Efforts were made by the school psychologist to acknowledge and address the concerns not only by providing culturally responsive interventions directly to Darius but by utilizing community resources, consulting with both the teacher and other school personnel, and employing an interpersonal orientation when working with the parent.

## CASE STUDY 2

Sixteen-year-old Marisa, a Mexican American sophomore in high school was referred by her teacher, who was concerned about Marisa's recent drop in grades. Marisa was known to be regularly disappearing at night, "running around" with the wrong crowd, and drinking alcohol.

Both parents worked in a poultry factory. Marisa was the youngest of five children. One unmarried older sister, Angele, lived in the home with her 2-year-old son and an aunt. Her sister, who had not completed high school brought Marisa to her appointments. Marisa, her sister, and her aunt were English proficient, although her mother and father primarily spoke Spanish in the home.

Marisa had not been turning in homework assignments, although she was generally described as congenial and no trouble in class by her teachers. Marisa stated that she wanted to finish high school and become a secretary.

Marisa was willing to talk to the therapist, but not eager to change her behavior, despite the concern of her teacher and family. During the second counseling session, Marisa informed the therapist that she believed that she was pregnant. A pregnancy test confirmed that Marisa was 3 months pregnant by a 17-year-old boyfriend with whom she had broken up; she had no desire to attempt reconciliation with him. Given her religious background, it was evident that abortion was not an option. Marisa had little concern for any potential negative consequences of becoming a mother at her age. She asked the therapist for help in talking to her parents, especially her father. A home visit was arranged. A translator was not used; communication was facilitated by Marisa's aunt. Most of the discussion was led by Marisa's father since he was the head of the household. It was evident from the family session, with Marisa's parents, aunt, and Angele present that they were upset about the pregnancy and strongly desired Marisa to marry her boyfriend. When Marisa convinced them he was "bad" for her, they clearly assumed the baby would become part of the household, and began talking about such matters as where the baby would sleep. Marisa seemed pleased that this could mean leaving high school, although her older sister said she wished she had stayed in school. In assisting the family, speculating about Marisa and the baby's future, it was necessary to be direct, specific, and concrete.

Marisa's acting out diminished considerably, although the distraction of the pregnancy took a rather deleterious toll on her classroom performance. She was responsive to the idea of being a good mother and willingly attended classes for pregnant teens at the local high school. After the baby was born, Angele was very supportive of Marisa's returning to school.

Marisa was seen for a total of four sessions across a 2-month period of time, including the one session in her home. At the time of a 6-month follow-up telephone call, Marisa was in school; both she and Angele were practicing some of the childcare skills Marisa was learning in one of her classes. No longer interested in office work, Marisa thought that eventually taking care of other children in the home might be better for her. Her family saw this as additional potential income for the household.

## Analysis

Marisa was quickly engaged in the therapeutic process; however, her family had no previous exposure to a mental health professional outside the school, so they were quite suspicious of the therapist at first. Coming to the private practice office was simply not a serious option for them, but they were quite responsive to the visit in their home, where all the participants sat around the kitchen table to discuss family matters. Acknowledging Marisa's father as the head of the household and building a therapeutic relationship with him and other significant family members were necessary for any positive outcome. Extended family and sibling relationships are very important in this culture; Angele had considerable influence over Marisa. Like many adolescents from this community, Marisa was not seeking independence nor looking for a way "out"; she wanted to be with her family and friends. The primary attraction of returning to school for Marisa was seeing friends and secondarily learning some information to help her with parenting. This situation is in contrast to the goal driven, high aspiration values of middle-class America.

A multidimensional approach of blending reality therapy within a family systems context would best describe the therapy that took place. "Wanting to be a good mom" was the focus of Marisa's willingness to modify any dysfunctional behavior, such as consuming alcohol.

It was important to work within the context of the world in which Marisa lived. Understanding the family structure, respecting religious beliefs, involving the extended family, and making use of community resources (in this case, the health department sponsored a low-cost prenatal care clinic that Marisa attended) were essential in this intervention.

# ANNOTATED BIBLIOGRAPHY

Canino, I., & Spurlock, J. (1994). *Culturally diverse children and adolescents: Assessment, diagnosis, and treatment,* New York: Guilford Press.

Clinical guidelines are provided for conducting sensitive and appropriate assessments and developing effective treatment strategies when working with children and adolescents from culturally diverse backgrounds. Concrete suggestions are outlined for obtaining relevant history, appropriately using diagnostic criteria, and planning and carrying out an intervention.

Lee, C. C. (Ed.). (1997). *Multicultural issues in counseling: New approaches to diversity* (2nd ed.). Alexandria, VA: American Counseling Association.

The focus here is on the practice of multicultural counseling with selected racial/ethnic groups. The book offers guidelines for determining and implementing culturally responsive counseling intervention and is designed to assist counselors in applying their awareness and knowledge of cultural diversity toward the development of culturally responsive skills.

McGoldrick, M., Giordano, J., & Pearce, J. (Eds.). (1996). *Ethnicity and family therapy* (2nd ed.). New York: Guilford Press.

The selections in this edition not only provide a description of the cultural values and characteristics of families representing a variety of ethnic groups but also examine the influence factors such as gender, class, and politics have on these families. Emphasis is placed on the ways in which these values and patterns impact therapy. Ethnic groups discussed include people of color as well as families of European origin, Jewish, and Slavic families.

Paniagua, F. (1994). *Assessing and treating culturally diverse clients: A practical guide.* Thousand Oaks, CA: Sage.

This book describes cultural variables that are relevant in the assessment and therapeutic treatment of four major multicultural groups; African Americans, American Indians, Asians, and Hispanics. It provides guidelines for demonstrating cultural competence and ways to avoid discriminating practices in the assessment and treatment of clients from these racial/ethnic groups. Practical information regarding the development of a therapeutic relationship, conducting the first session, providing psychotherapy, and preventing attrition are also addressed.

Pedersen, P., & Carey, J. (Eds.). (1994). *Multicultural counseling in the schools.* Boston: Allyn & Bacon.

In this comprehensive examination of multicultural counseling in a K-12 school setting, chapter topics range from one-on-one counseling to multicultural career guidance and parent and teacher consultation. The text offers practical suggestions and pluralistic helping strategies for effective multicultural practice within the school environment.

Sue, D., Ivey, A., & Pedersen, P. (1996). *A theory of multicultural counseling and therapy.* Pacific Grove, CA: Brooks/Cole.

> Beginning with a description of the shortcomings in contemporary theories of counseling and therapy for diverse clients, the authors then set forth a conceptualization of a theory of multicultural counseling and therapy (MCT). Several chapters are dedicated to the application of MCT to specific populations. The implications of MCT on research, practice, and training are also discussed.

## REFERENCES

Banks, J. A. (1988). *Multiethnic education: Theory and practice* (2nd ed.). Boston: Allyn & Bacon.

Baruth, L. G., & Manning, M. L. (1992). *Multicultural education of children and adolescents.* Needham Heights, MA: Allyn & Bacon.

Brems, C. (1993). *A comprehensive guide to child psychotherapy.* Boston: Allyn & Bacon.

Canino, I., & Spurlock, J. (1994). *Culturally diverse children and adolescents: Assessment, diagnosis, and treatment.* New York: Guilford Press.

Carey, J. C., Boscandin, M. L., & Fontes., L. (1994). Improving the multicultural effectiveness of your school. In P. Pedersen & J. C. Carey (Eds.), *Multicultural counseling in the schools* (pp. 239–250). Boston: Allyn & Bacon.

Cole, S. M., Thomas, A. R., & Lee, C. C. (1988). School counselors and school psychologists: Partners in minority outreach. *Journal of Multicultural Counseling and Development, 16,* 110–116.

Cross, W. E. (1995). The psychology of nigrescence: Revising the cross model. In J. Ponterotto, J. M. Casas, L. A. Suzuki, & C. A. Alexander (Eds.), *Handbook of multicultural counseling* (pp. 93–122). Thousand Oaks, CA: Sage.

Duncan, C. F. (1995). Cross-cultural school consultation. In C. C. Lee (Ed.), *Counseling for diversity* (pp. 129–142). Boston: Allyn & Bacon.

Fairchild, H. P. (Ed.). (1970). *Dictionary of sociology and related sciences.* Totowa, NJ: Rowan & Allanheld.

Foley, J., & Fuqua, D. (1988). The effects of status configuration and counseling style on Korean perspectives of counseling. *Journal of Cross-Cultural Psychology, 19*(4), 464–480.

Gibbs, J. T. (1985). Treatment relationships with African American clients: Interpersonal *vs.* instrumental strategies. In G. Germain (Ed.), *Advances in clinical social work practice.* Silver Spring, MD: NASW.

Gibbs, J. T., Huang, L. N., and Associates. (Eds.). (1998). *Children of color: Psychological interventions with culturally diverse youth.* San Francisco: Jossey-Bass.

Giordano, J., & Giordano, M. A. (1995). Ethnic dimensions in family therapy. In R. Mikesell, K. Lusterman, & S. McDaniel (Eds.), *Integrating family therapy.* Washington, DC: American Psychological Association.

Goldstein, A. P. (1994). Teaching prosocial behavior to low-income youth. In P. Pedersen & J. C. Carey (Eds.), *Multicultural counseling in the schools* (pp. 157–176). Boston: Allyn & Bacon.

Grossman, H. (1995). *Classroom behavior management in a diverse society.* Mt. View, CA: Mayfield.

Helms, J. E. (1995). An update of Helms' white and people of color racial identity models. In J. G. Ponterotto, J. M. Casas, L. A. Suzuki, & C. M. Alexander (Eds.), *Handbook of multicultural counseling* (pp. 181–198). Thousand Oaks, CA: Sage.

Hilliard, A. G. (1991). Why we must pluralize the curriculum. *Educational Leadership, 49*(4), 12–16.

Ho, M. K. (1992). *Minority children and adolescents in therapy.* Newbury Park, CA: Sage.

Hsu, J. (1983). Asian family interaction patterns and their therapeutic implications. *Internation Journal of Family Psychiatry, 4,* 307–320.

Ivey, A. E., Ivey, D., & Simek-Morgan, L. (1993). *Counseling and psychotherapy: A multicultural perspective.* Boston: Allyn & Bacon.

Johnson, M. (1993). A culturally sensitive approach to therapy with children. In C. Brems (Ed.), *A comprehensive guide to child psychotherapy.* Boston: Allyn & Bacon.

LaFromboise, T. E., & Low, W. (1989). American Indian children and adolescents. In J. T. Gibbs & L. N. Huang (Eds.), *Children of color: Psychological interventions with minority youth* (pp. 114–147). San Francisco: Jossey-Bass.

LaFromboise, T. E., & Rowe, W. (1983). Skills training for bicultural competence: Rationale and application. *Journal of Counseling Psychology, 30*(4), 589–595.

Lee, C. C. (Ed.). (1995). *Counseling for diversity: A guide for school counselors and related professionals.* Boston: Allyn & Bacon.

Lee, C. C. (1996). *Saving the native son: Empowerment strategies for young Black males.* Greensboro, NC: ERIC Counseling and Student Services Clearinghouse.

Lee, C. C. (Ed.). (1997). *Multicultural issues in counseling: New approaches to diversity* (2nd ed.). Alexandria, VA: American Counseling Association.

Lee, E. (1982). A social systems approach to assessment and treatment for Chinese American families. In M. McGoldrick, J. Pearce, & J. Giordano (Eds.), *Ethnicity and family therapy* (pp. 527–551). New York: Guilford Press.

Locke, D. (1992). *Increasing multicultural understanding: A comprehensive model.* Newbury Park, CA: Sage.

Lopez, E. C. (1995). Best practices in working with bilingual children. In A. Thomas & J. Grimes (Eds.), *Best practices in school psychology* (Vol. 3). Washington, DC: National Association of School Psychologists.

McDaniel, S., & Bielen, P. (1990). Project Self Esteem: A parent involvement program for improving self esteem and preventing drug and alcohol abuse, K–6 *(Revised ED347442)*.

McGoldrick, M., Giordano, J., & Pearce, J. (Eds.). (1996). *Ethnicity and family therapy* (2nd ed.). New York: Guilford Press.

McIntosh, P. (1989). White privilege: Unpacking the invisible knapsack. *Peace and Freedom, 2,* 10–12.

Omizo, M., & D'Andrea, M. (1995). Multicultural classroom guidance. In C. Lee (Ed.), *Counseling for diversity.* Boston: Allyn & Bacon.

Paniagua, F. (1994). *Assessing and treating culturally diverse clients: A practical guide.* Thousand Oaks, CA: Sage.

Pedersen, P. B. (1991). Multiculturalism as a fourth force in counseling [Special issue]. *Journal of Counseling and Development, 70.*

Pedersen, P., & Carey, J. (1994). *Multicultural counseling in the schools.* Boston: Allyn & Bacon.

Pedersen, P., & Ivey, A. E. (1993). *Culture-centered counseling and interviewing skills.* Westport, CT: Greenwood/Praeger Press.

Pinderhughes, E. (1989). *Understanding race, ethnicity and power.* New York: Free Press.

Ponterotto, J. G., & Casas, J. M. (1991). *Handbook of racial/ethnic minority counseling research.* Springfield, IL: Thomas.

Ponterotto, J. G., Casas, J. M., Suzuki, L., & Alexander, C. (Eds.). (1995). *Handbook of multicultural counseling.* Thousand Oaks, CA: Sage.

Rotheram, M. J., & Phinney, J. S. (1987). Introduction: Definitions and perspectives in the study of children's ethnic socialization. In J. S. Phinney & M. J. Rotheram (Eds.), *Children's ethnic socialization.* Beverly Hills, CA: Sage.

Spurlock, J. (1985). Assessment and therapeutic intervention of black children. *Journal of the American Academy of Child Psychiatry, 24,* 168–174.

Sue, D., Ivey, A., & Pedersen, P. (1996). *A theory of multicultural counseling and therapy.* Pacific Grove, CA: Brooks/Cole.

Sue, D. W. (1981). *Counseling the culturally different: Theory and practice.* New York: Wiley.

Sue, D. W. (1992). The challenge of multiculturalism: The road less traveled. *American Counselor, 1,* 7–14.

Sue, D. W. (1995). Toward a theory of multicultural counseling and therapy. In J. A. Banks & C. A. McGee Banks (Eds.), *Handbook of research on multicultural education* (pp. 647-659). New York: Macmillan.

Sue, D. W., & Sue, D. (1990). *Counseling the culturally different: Theory and practice* (2nd ed.). New York: Wiley.

Sue, S. (1988). Psychotherapeutic services for ethnic minorities: Two decades of research findings. *American Psychologist, 43,* 301–398.

Tangimara, M., & McShane, D. A. (1990, March). Theoretical orientation and treatment modality preferences of degreed mental health providers working with American Indian clients. In T. Kratochwill & R. Morris (Eds.), *Handbook of psychotherapy with children and adolescents* (pp. 502–540). Boston: Allyn & Bacon.

Teyber, E. (1997). *Interpersonal process in psychotherapy: A guide for clinical training* (2nd ed.). Pacific Grove, CA: Brooks/Cole.

Trotter, T. V. (1993). Counseling with young multicultural clients. In A. Vernon (Ed.), *Counseling children and adolescents* (pp. 137–155). Denver, CO: Love.

Vraniak, D., & Pickett, S. (1993). Improving interventions with American ethnic minority children: Recurrent and recalcitrant challenges. In T. Kratochwill & R. Morris (Eds.), *Handbook of psychotherapy with children and adolescents* (pp. 502–540). Boston: Allyn & Bacon.

Wei, T. D. (1980). *Vietnamese refugee students: A handbook for school personnel* (2nd ed.) (ERIC Document Reproduction Service No. ED 208 109). Midwest Organization for Materials Development, National Assessment and Dissemination Center for Bilingual Education.

Western Institute Commission for Higher Education and the College Board. (1988). *The road to college: Educational progress by race and ethnicity.* Boulder, CO: Author.

# Chapter 4

# *PSYCHODYNAMIC APPROACHES*

Scott P. Merydith

Almost exclusively through the work of Sigmund Freud, psychoanalysis has rendered, what still remains today, the most comprehensive and coherent theory of motivation and psychopathology. Indeed, Freud's insights and analyses of psychic determinism, early childhood, and unconscious processes have left an indelible mark on psychology (Korchin, 1983). Concepts such as trauma, mourning, defense, object relations, separation anxiety, and sensitive periods in early childhood are crucial to the psychoanalytic way of thinking about a client's presenting problem. Yet only recently have these terms been given serious consideration by other types of psychotherapies and behavioral disciplines (Bowlby, 1982).

Psychoanalysis, furthermore, is more than just a type of psychotherapy, it is also a theory of human behavior and a method of observation, which are evident in S. Freud's (1923) general definition: "a procedure for the investigation of mental processes, especially unconscious phenomenon, a method of treatment based upon this procedure, and a set of observations and facts gathered together in this way which gives rise to a cohesive body of theory regarding human behavior" (Orgel, 1995, p. 523). As a theory of human behavior, psychoanalysis rests on two fundamental hypotheses: (a) psychic determinism—all mental events are caused, nothing happens by chance; and (b) a dynamic unconscious—many basic needs, wishes, and impulses lie outside of a person's awareness (Brenner, 1973). But as a therapeutic process, the goal of psychoanalysis is to assist individuals in the fulfillment of their development; chiefly by making the unconscious conscious and thereby strengthening the organization of psychic structures (the ego) that perceive and interact with reality, especially the world of interpersonal relations (Greenson, 1967).

The terms: psychoanalysis, psychoanalytic therapy, and psychodynamic therapy are often used interchangeably to refer to a specific set of therapeutic assumptions and techniques first developed through the writings of Freud. Essentially, these three approaches to psychotherapy view the client's symptoms as the result of interplay among conflicting mental forces (e.g., motives, desires, or impulses) that regulate and channel behaviors. Additionally, psychoanalysis, psychoanalytic therapy, and psychodynamic therapy take a historic approach to treatment and rely on interpretation as the basic technique to produce insight-oriented change in the client's behavior or way of thinking. An understanding of the client's childhood, especially his or her early relationships with parents, helps both the counselor and the client to identify central themes in the client's life as they apply to current relationships and attitudes toward family, school, and work (Usher, 1993).

These three approaches to psychotherapy, however, are not synonymous; they differ from one another regarding specific aspects of treatment, such as therapy duration and the necessary qualifications to be a therapist or counselor. Psychoanalysis necessitates multiweekly treatment sessions over the course of several years by an analyst who has received specialized training and has personally undergone analysis. Psychoanalytic therapy and psychodynamic therapy adhere to the basic theory and methods of psychoanalysis but alter the therapy process by (a) using general therapists, (b) attempting to secure a quicker relief of symptoms, and (c) modifying the use of the traditional techniques (Wallerstein, 1995). For example, in the Alexander and French (1946) approach to psychoanalytic therapy, the technique of the *corrective emotional experience* is applied whereby the therapist intentionally creates an attitude toward the client that is different from those of the authoritative persons of the client's past. The use of this technique is seen as an effective method for the client to gain new emotional experiences that can nullify the pathological effects of previously experienced negative emotional events, all within a relatively short time in treatment.

## HISTORY AND CURRENT STATUS

Working alone outside the established universities, medical, and psychiatric communities, S. Freud published his *Three Essays on the Theory of Sexuality* (1905) in which he advanced his theory of infantile sexuality based on psychosexual developmental stages. More specifically, Freud traced the roots of adult behaviors back to childhood impulses and showed how conflicts related to the development of sexuality in childhood subsequently resulted in adult psychopathology. The theory of infantile sexuality, however, shocked the Viennese public and was viewed as moral turpitude. Subsequently, Freud was forced to abandon his aspirations of academic teaching; although the official anti-Semitic polices rampant in central Europe at the time also contributed to Freud's imposed isolation.

Thus psychoanalytic theory and treatment methods flourished within the settings of private practices, primarily those of clinical neurologists similar to Freud, who attempted to diagnose and treat individuals with hysterical disorders, which all too often were dismissed by psychiatric hospitals and clinics. Psychoanalytic institutes, too, began as private evening classes or discussion groups in the major cities of central Europe—Berlin, Budapest, Vienna, and Zurich. By the end of the 1920s, however, psychoanalysis was widely accepted throughout the European continent, England, and, to a limited extent the United States, despite its divorce from organized medicine and academia.

With the Nazis' rise to power in Germany in the 1930s', the major psychoanalytic institutes of Europe were dismantled as Jewish psychoanalysts escaped to America and

England. Unlike Europe, however, the growth of psychoanalysis in the United States was raddled in American psychiatry and soon became the single psychological theory and therapeutics in medical schools and formal psychiatric training centers (Wallerstein, 1995). Its undisputed status in academic psychiatry, consequently, allowed psychoanalytic theory and techniques to be applied to a broad range of mental disorders seen in the patients of psychiatric clinics and hospital wards. Simultaneously, the training of individuals in the clinical practice of psychoanalysis became highly formalized and restrictive.

Clinical training in the practice of psychoanalysis is conducted at psychoanalytic institutes approved by the American Psychoanalytic Association. All candidates must undergo a complete personal analysis, use psychoanalysis with several clients under supervision, and complete an organized series of seminars in psychoanalytic theory and application, which lasts for approximately 4 years (Orgel, 1995). Furthermore, until rather recently, the American Psychoanalytic Association barred the training of non-medical candidates in clinical psychoanalysis. But as of 1991, the American Psychoanalytic Association amended its bylaw so that persons with a doctorate in psychology, mental health, and social work are eligible for training in psychoanalysis.

In contrast to the general development of psychoanalysis based on adult recollections of childhood events, child psychoanalysis emerged with S. Freud's (1909) *Analysis of a Phobia in a Five-Year-Old Boy,* the case report of Little Hans who had an extreme phobia of horses. The boy's father, a physician and adherent of Freud, successfully treated his son while Freud provided clinical supervision. Although Freud doubted the general applicability of this type of treatment, he continued to affirm the potential value of psychoanalysis with children (S. Freud, 1926). The psychoanalytic community, on the other hand, heralded the case of Little Hans: The findings confirmed Freud's theory on infantile sexuality and clinical techniques; it established the usefulness of direct observations of children; and, it placed importance on understanding the child's developmental process (Rexford, 1982; Tyson & Tyson, 1990).

What became almost immediately self-evident to psychoanalysts working with children, however, was the stark contrast between the adult and child client. The child represents a developing personality, who interacts with adults in a nonverbal, active, and aggressive fashion (Chused, 1988). Hug-Hellmuth (1920, 1921) is believed to be the first analyst who wrote about specific child analytic techniques including the concept of play therapy with an emphasis on an educational tone in the child therapy session. Anna Freud, educated as a preschool and kindergarten teacher, also embraced the educational quality of psychoanalysis with children, especially during the initial course of treatment (Dowling & Naegele, 1995). Both Hug-Hellmuth and A. Freud (1927) stipulated that child analysis required the analyst to be both responsive and pleasing to the child and that, unlike adult analysis, the analyst needed to actively encourage a positive attachment with the child.

Another significant change in child psychoanalytic techniques was from case studies presented by Bornstein (1935, 1945, 1949) who suggested that child analysis begin with a study of the child's defensive reactions to unpleasant affect followed by timely interpretations that aimed at increasing the child's emotional awareness. Anna Freud extended Bornstein's work by drawing on her own experiences with children at the Hampstead Clinic in London. Her work with war orphans and children separated from their parents allowed her to recognize the therapeutic power and theoretical value of interpreting ego defenses of children and adults, and is best presented in her important book, *The Ego and the Mechanisms of Defense* (A. Freud, 1936).

Perhaps the most significant early contributions in the application of psychoanalytic theory and methods to the treatment of children came from the distinguished works of both Anna Freud and Melanie Klein, specifically from the period of 1926 to 1946. Although each differed from the other in terms of theoretical and clinical positions, taken together, their works brought an increased understanding of infants' and toddlers' psychological complexities (Dowling & Naegele, 1995; Hughes, 1989; Kessler, 1988; Tuma & Russ, 1993). Yet, fundamental differences between their positions had the unintended effect of dividing the psychoanalytic community into opposing camps: The London School adopted Kleinian thought with its set of a priori theoretical beliefs, and the Vienna School adhered to A. Freud's empirical and observational methods (King & Steiner, 1991). Anna Freud's approach to child psychoanalysis became pervasive in the United States while Melanie Klein's theory has held a powerful effect on European psychoanalytic thought.

In contrast to the educational aspect of child analysis espoused by Hug-Hellmuth and A. Freud, Melanie Klein (1921) took a noneducational view to the treatment of children. For Klein, the child in analysis presents with meaningful verbalizations and behaviors that are immediately interpretable (Klein, 1927, 1932). She placed special importance on the significance of play activities of the child during treatment. The infant enters the world with a complex of fantasies due to innately determined instinctual conflicts it has with its parents and will subsequently experience periods of abnormality. Klein's theory and child analytic treatment methods, however, derived from her work with severely disturbed children, whom she believed to be schizophrenic. Nevertheless much of Klein's theory is based on hypothetical-deductive reasoning rather than clinical observations. For example, if the death instinct is innate, then it follows that its destructiveness must be directed toward an external object to avoid self-destruction. The infant enters the world, therefore, predetermined to seek relations with others (object relations) that can have a destructive quality (Dowling & Naegele, 1995; MacKay, 1981).

Anna Freud, on the other hand, started her analytic work with children by closely observing them in the hospitals of Vienna and later in London. She presented her findings on child analytic techniques in a series of lectures given at the Vienna Institute of Psychoanalysis (A. Freud, 1927). Later, in collaboration with Dorothy Burlingham, she established an experimental preschool for the children of the poorest families in Vienna and subsequently published detailed and systematic observations on the effects that early mother-child separation has on the child (A. Freud & Burlingham, 1973). By combining her knowledge of psychoanalytic theory with systematic observations of children, Anna Freud has made several original contributions to child psychoanalytic techniques: (a) She developed the diagnostic profile, a method to arrange the information gathered from parent and child interviews; (b) she advanced the idea of developmental lines, how drives are expressed in different periods and aspects of the child's development (such as gender development); and (c) she developed a taxonomy for which to describe childhood disturbances in terms of causes and treatment goals.

More recent advances in psychoanalytic theory, applicable to both children and adults, have been derived from a synthesis of Klein and A. Freud. Winnicott (1960, 1962) made an original contribution to psychoanalysis in the area of mother-infant relationships. By using Klein's thoughts about object relations and A. Freud's developmental approach and method of systematic observations, he described the prime importance that "good enough mothering" has in the development of a confident and creative child. Spitz (1946, 1965) studied the development of hospitalized infants and carefully documented how a lack of human/infant interactions is tantamount to psychological malnutrition, which can result in infant anaclitic depression and mortality.

Finally, psychoanalysts have made lasting contributions to the psychology of personality theory. Bowlby's (1982) widely accepted attachment theory derives from his psychoanalytic underpinning. Erikson (1968) almost single-handedly reshaped our understanding of adolescence by augmenting Freud's psychosexual development with a psychosocial emphasis. Blos' (1962, 1967) clinical work with adolescents established treatment effectiveness, despite adolescent vicissitudes, and remains unmatched, as is Fraiberg's (1959) understanding of the emotional development of children. Present day psychoanalysis, therefore, continues to prove itself to be highly relevant to psychological theory building, research, and practice.

## OVERVIEW OF THEORY

### Basic Theory and Assumptions

Psychoanalytic theory is marked with a rich history and vicissitudes. Soon after Freud's inaugural writings on psychoanalysis (e.g., S. Freud, 1894, 1895, 1896, 1898, 1900, 1905), Jung and Adler broke with him and advanced their own psychodynamic theories, which respectively stressed the importance of a collective unconscious and social interest. The theoretical writings from "neo-Freudians," such as Sullivan and Horney emerged in the 1920s and 1930s and emphasized the interlace between psychic development and interpersonal relationships. Even within the orthodox psychoanalytic circles that embraced Freudian thought, basic constructs were altered and highlighted, such as evidenced in the work of Anna Freud and Melanie Klein, who revealed a far greater extensiveness of ego defense mechanisms than hitherto had been recognized. However, if one were to seek a commonality among these theoretical diversities, it is that all psychoanalytic theories attempt to account for the difficulties people have in their interpersonal relations; this unifying overlap is properly known as the problem of object relations (Greenberg & Mitchell, 1983).

Present-day psychoanalysis is best conceptualized as an interpretive discipline rather than a biological theory of mental activity. The thrust of Freud's theorizing was to understand human behavior by clarifying the biological source of mental activity, and hence he emphasized the concepts of drives, impulse gratification, and mental energy. This is not to say, however, that Freud didn't address interpersonal relations, for he did—but only within the context of overt expressions of unconscious mental forces. Greenberg and Mitchell (1983) have referenced Freud's approach to psychoanalytic theory as a drive/structure model and contrasted it with more recent psychoanalytic theorists who explicitly underscore object relations or a relationship/structure model of psychoanalysis. The Greenberg and Mitchell classification schema of psychoanalytic theory will be maintained throughout this overview.

## Drive/Structure Model

A fundamental idea in Freud's theory is that of drive or as the German word *Tribe* is sometimes translated into English, instinct. But since the concept of instinct is all too often associated with the notion of fixed-action patterns in animals, the word drive is less ambiguous. S. Freud (1905) thought of drive as an endogenous source of mental stimulation that starts the mind working. Yet the purpose of all mental activity, for Freud, is to reduce tension and eliminate stimulation, or in other words, to keep a constant steady state.

Greenberg and Mitchell (1983) cite this primary function of drive in Freudian theory as the *constancy principle,* which S. Freud (1911) later replaced with the term, *pleasure principle.* Critical features of life, however, negate the individual's achieving a state of constancy or low excitation. Primary sources of stimulation arise from somatic needs, such as hunger and thirst, which create tension until temporarily eliminated by some specific type of motor activity, such as eating and drinking. This produces a state of satisfaction or pleasure until the next stimulation occurs. Thus psychic tension arises from constant internal stimulation that motivates cognitive and affective mental states, which influence behavior. Unconscious mental events or thoughts occur, therefore, after somatic stimulation disrupts quiescence and the individual actively recollects a situation that resulted in contentment, which for Freud takes the form of a wish. Hence, every human action can be linked to a specific drive *source,* the most primary being somatic stimulation.

All drive motivation for Freud is unconscious mental activity that culminates in a variety of behaviors. Since we can only directly know observable behaviors and conscious thoughts experienced by ourselves or those reported by others, we must carefully deduce underlying motives of behavior, which in Freudian theory emanates from drives. According to S. Freud (1915) a drive has a biological source of energy, thus creating a force, or *impetus,* which characterizes the strength of the drive put forth toward activity. A drive also has an aim and an object. The *aim* of a drive is always to achieve satisfaction. Yet drive satisfaction can be immediate or delayed, inhibited, or deflected, with the latter resulting in only partially achieved satisfaction. By listing a wide array of aim outcomes, Freud attempted to account for a greater diversity of behaviors under the control of a single drive expressed within various external conditions. Lastly, the *object* of a drive is the thing or person used as a mean to achieve the aim, that is, satisfaction. As an example, a mother's breast can be the object used to satisfy hunger.

Freud adhered to a dualistic drive theory: sexual and aggressive. Although other drives exist, for Freud the sexual and aggressive drives are the only ones that are both primary and irreducible. Hence specific demands placed on the mind for work, that is unconscious mental stimulation, are derived from the sex drive, the libido, and aggression, that is self-preservation (S. Freud, 1915). Sexuality, then, is an internally arising force through somatic stimulation of an *erotogenic zone,* or pleasure-producing area, that underlies human activity. Despite the primary importance of the sexual and aggressive drives, which can operate alongside or in opposition to one another, only the sexual drive has developmental phases.

As the child matures and develops, the sexual drive, or *libido,* is modified and discharged in systematic ways. The developmental progression of the libido is a pattern of tension buildup and discharge from infancy through adulthood, which organizes experiences in a hierarchical fashion (Ritvo & Solnit, 1995). The developmental phases of organized experience, in turn, correspond to the maturation of the individual and derive from the influence of the libido. Freud specified this process as *psychosexual development* and described it in terms of oral, anal, phallic, latency, and genital stages. This does not mean, however, that the libido arises from the mouth, anus, or genitals; but rather, these erotogenic zones capture the dominant way conscious experience and attitudes are organized to achieve unconscious satisfaction, the quiescence of mental stimulation and, therefore, experienced as pleasure.

The *Oral Stage* (ages 0–2) is the first erotogenic phase that involves the infant's taking in nutrition. Pleasure, therefore, is achieved by the reduction of tension that occurs through the use of the mouth, such as when the infant sucks for the intake of food from its mother's breast. However, since sucking produced satisfaction, the act of sucking itself or stimulation of the lips becomes associated with pleasure. The *Anal Stage* (ages 2–4) characterizes the infant's derived pleasure from the elimination of urine and feces. These activities concomitantly stimulate the mucous membranes of the rectum, and hence are experienced as pleasurable due to their association with drive discharge (S. Freud, 1915). Anality patterns of behaviors, therefore, accentuate activities of absorption, retention, and expulsion that have distinct periods of buildup and discharge of drive tension.

The *Phallic Stage* of development (ages 4–6) highlights pleasure derived from manual stimulation of the child's genitals, most likely by the child's act of touch. The child discovers the genitals, in a sense, for the first time, even though sexual excitement does not become concentrated in the genitals until the child reaches puberty. Awareness of sex differences between boys and girls also occurs as do gratifications related to fantasies of penetration and being penetrated. Now drive-tension discharge can be experienced actively or passively, which increases the flexibility of drive activity. During the *Latency Stage* (ages 6–11) there is a reduction in libido due to a consolidation of previously acquired drive functions. This quiescence in sexual drive is necessary to prepare for the demands of puberty, the beginning of the *Genital Stage* (age 11 and continuing on through adulthood) where all sexual pleasure is hierarchically subsumed under the stimulation of the genitals for intercourse and adult sexuality.

An unconscious drive, libidinal or aggressive, expressed as a wish or an impulse pursues satisfaction. Temporary drive satisfaction is achieved by recathexing (re-invoking) the memory of a previously established association between the discharge of psychic tension with that of the drive object by means of a hallucination. The ensuing disappointment experienced from the failure of hallucinations to produce drive gratification, has the effect of expanding mental functioning so as to form conceptions of the external world, the *reality principle,* which for S. Freud, "proved to be a momentous step" (1911, p. 219). Freud introduced several models based on a priori assumptions to provide an overall view of how unconscious and conscious thinking interacts with reality, which are typically referenced as his metapsychology. The two models that he gave prime importance to throughout his work are the *Topographical model and Structural model.*

In the topographical model, the mind is a system comprising three areas, the *unconscious,* the *conscious,* and the *preconscious.* The conscious aspect of mind is governed by *secondary process thinking* (the cognitive and perceptual systems) and interacts with reality, which includes the person's awareness of reality. The unconscious part of the mind is regulated by *primary process thinking,* that is wishes and impulses derived from the urgency of drive discharge. The preconscious is composed of thoughts capable of becoming conscious through recollection.

Freud's structural model, on the other hand, divides the mind into three components on the basis of mental functioning: the *id, ego,* and *superego.* The operations of the id pertain to gratifying basic needs (i.e., pleasure seeking) related to the unconscious pressures that stem from the sexual and aggressive drives. Id functions, therefore, are a primary process of the mind; they emanate from within the body and are determined to seek drive discharge, irrespective of the external world. The ego is a "coherent organization of mental processes" that allow for reality testing, language, and adaptation to reality (S. Freud, 1923). The ego is also that part of the id that is in contact with reality and so, consequently, is inevitably motivated by the unconscious tension reduction forces of the sexual and aggressive drives. However, since the ego is also in contact with reality, its selection of drive objects to bring about pleasure will depend upon the external situation. The superego, finally, is the group of mental functions with inhibitory qualities. They relate to the ego with respect to the development of a conscience, which is emotionally experienced by the ego as guilt. The superego is formed through identification with parents.

By introducing the reality principle and the structural model of the mind, Freud was able to articulate to a greater extent the conditions that thwart drive satisfaction and result in frustration or disappointment, both consciously and unconsciously. The wishes and sexual impulses that seek satisfaction are often at odds with the external interpersonal situations that we may presently be in. Our sexual advances, so to speak, may offend the other. This leads to conflict between id impulses and the ego's perceptions of reality. The ego, therefore, tries to negotiate a compromise between drive discharge and the interpersonal situation. Often this entails a defensive reaction by the ego, such as that of *repression* whereby the tension for drive discharge is actively blocked from awareness until the social situation is changed.

Another type of conflict occurs intrapsychically between the ego and superego. Here the threat is not the expression of sexual impulses with external others, but the disapproval or inhibitory factors of the superego. The most noted conflict of this type is the *oedipal complex.* During the phallic stage, with the male child's discovery of his penis, there is an unconscious sexual wish to possess his mother in the way that his father does. However, the child has ambivalent feelings toward the father: The father has provided love, yet is also a rival for the mother's affection. The conflict occurs between the ego's selection of a drive with that of the moral imperatives of the superego. To eliminate the painful affect associated with such a conflict, an unconscious compromise is enacted whereby the child identifies with the same-sex parent and develops a conscience or sense of guilt that leads to further repression of such sexual drive expressions.

A cornerstone of psychoanalytic theory is the concept of *defense* that S. Freud (1894) first introduced to describe unconscious mental processes initiated by the ego to ward off painful affects such as anxiety and depression. The defenses are the ways in which ideas are kept out of consciousness and require a considerable amount of energy to block the expression of the sexual or aggressive drives. As noted previously, the unconscious defense process Freud wrote most extensively about was repression, which is initiated by anxiety. Anna Freud (1936), however, further elaborated on, refined, and clarified the concept of defense in her book, *The Ego and the Mechanisms of Defense.* She proposed the notion that the types of defenses used by the ego are far more extensive than previously thought. The client undergoing psychoanalysis needs to become consciously aware of the types of defenses he or she uses in order for unconscious wishes to emerge, and hence achieve a more complete understanding of the motives behind the behaviors.

## Relationship/Structure Model

Object relations theory has become the governing theoretical position within psychoanalysis over the past 20 to 30 years (Murray, 1995). Freud used the term *object* to represent the person or thing used in the satisfaction of sexual or aggressive drive discharge; the object is nothing more than a means to an end. Object relations theorists, however, have elevated the importance of the object in psychic functioning and emphasize the importance of the individual's relationship to that object. Greenberg and Mitchell's (1983) comprehensive synthesis of object relations theory defines object in terms of a "dual connotation" that describes both internal representations and real people in the external world. The object is an actual entity, but more importantly, the object and the person are related to each other in a meaningful way, and hence it becomes internalized in the person's psychic structure. In the Freudian Drive/Structure model of psychoanalysis, personality is formed essentially as a result of the pressures from the sexual and aggressive drives. But for object relations theorists (e.g.,

Klein, Fairbairn, Sullivan, and Winnicott) the relationship with the object is a powerful external force that shapes personality. Consequently, we are just as motivated by our emotional investments with others as we are by our primitive wishes and fears.

A fundamental premise of object relations theory is that the individual is in need of relationships. Given that the human infant enters the world in a state of extreme dependency, its physiological survival and subsequent psychological health demands interactions with others. There is no such thing as "just an infant," rather there is an inseparable mother-infant unit (Winnicott, 1960). Personality, then, is formed by how dependency needs are addressed in interpersonal relations. For Winnicott, the emergence of a healthy, creative person is dependent on "good-enough mothering." This relationship creates a *holding environment* whereby the infant experiences reality in graduated doses. The caretaker, or mother, permits greater amounts of separation to emerge as the infant develops. All of personality development reverberates on the movement from immature dependency to mature dependency.

Sullivan's (1953) theory of *Interpersonal Psychoanalysis,* a type of object relations theory, outlines developmental periods that are marked by types of interpersonal relatedness that are most desired: tenderness—the infant's requirement for bodily contact; attention—the toddler's desire for adults' participation in play; achievement and equality—the childhood request to compete with and be accepted by peers; intimacy—the adolescent's wishes for a close loving relationship with one other. For Sullivan, a failure to satisfy these relationships results in loneliness, the most painful of human experiences (Greenberg & Michell, 1983). Fairbairn (1952) also provides a comprehensive view of a relational/structure theory of personality development by arguing that the libido is fundamentally relationship seeking. Psychological health is determined by our efforts at connecting with others. Our essential struggle is not with negotiating conflicts between id impulses and reality, but rather we are conflicted over reconciling contradictory features of significant others. A mother can be both tender and harsh. With our greater tolerance for relationships marked with ambivalence, we develop an independent self as we relate to others.

## VIEW OF PSYCHOPATHOLOGY

In orthodox psychoanalysis, that is Freud's Drive/Structure model, psychopathology is the result of a *neurotic conflict*—an unconscious conflict between id impulses for drive discharge and that of the ego's defense against either the expression or emergence of id impulses into consciousness. Since the id never ceases its demands for drive discharge, intrapsychic conflicts create heightened somatic tension from the sexual and aggressive drives. This situation requires more and more effort on behalf of the ego to keep unconscious sexual and aggressive urges under control. Eventually the ego is unable to cope, becomes overwhelmed, and the sexual and aggressive drives are released in the form of neurotic symptoms, such as unexplained sadness, guilt, anger, or anxiety. The symptoms of psychopathology, therefore, are never due to happenstance; but rather they represent the neurotic conflict. Take for example, a young child who is oppositionally defiant at preschool and expresses considerable anger toward the teacher when requested to comply with group activities. The child's expression of anger toward the teacher may be linked to a buildup of drive pressure related to unfulfilled oral needs due to an unresponsive caretaker. The subsequent demands placed on the child at school to give up self-interest activities for group conformity may have overwhelmed the ego. The angry outburst and defiance expressed toward the teacher may actually be the discharge of id impulses from the oral stage that have now taken on the form of symptoms of an oppositional defiant disorder.

Although real-world situations can conflict with id impulses, this does not necessarily result in a neurotic conflict. For the conflict to be neurotic, it must be experienced as a struggle between the ego and id (Greenson, 1967). Real-world situations can galvanize sexual urges, which need to be avoided for fear of punishment; but the drive urges may dissipate by removing oneself from the situation. However, if sexual urges need to be blocked from consciousness, the ego and id will conflict, and hence the conflict will be neurotic. Anxiety is a signal that one is about to enter into a perceived dangerous situation without conscious awareness of the drive urges seeking discharge (S. Freud, 1926).

The superego, too, can produce a neurotic conflict with the ego. Since it serves as the center of moral imperatives, it can overwhelm the ego with guilt and shame at the ego's efforts to permit drive discharge through symbolic distortions. The key to understanding all neurotic conflicts, however, is that the ego needs to use energy to block the expression of drives that are deemed dangerous by the ego. This weakens the ego, making it more susceptible to becoming overwhelmed in the future by other threatening drive discharges; eventually the ego becomes traumatized and the person neurotic (Fenichel, 1945; Greenson, 1967).

In Freudian psychoanalysis, the core of human existence is that the individual is driven to seek pleasure through a reduction in endogenous arising tension. All psychopathology is to be understood in terms of difficulties associated with the discharge of id impulses. From an object relations perspective, however, the core of human existence resonates within interpersonal relationships. Psychopathology arises from the conflict people have in establishing and maintaining interpersonal relationships, from early relationships with parents marked with vulnerability to mature relationships with adults in a quest for intimacy.

For Winnicott (1958, 1965), suitable parental care is both a necessary and sufficient condition for the child's mental health. Psychopathology, therefore, is the result of poor parenting practices. Since the child resides within the shadow of the parents' personalities and their adopted parenting styles, these parental qualities have a vast impact on the child's development. Parenting styles that interfere with the nurturance and adequate care of the infant produce psychopathology within the child. A young child's need for attachment and relatedness is met principally through the parents, who makeup almost entirely the child's interpersonal world. Parents who are emotionally absent, intrusive, or chaotic present interpersonal difficulties to the child and, therefore, interfere with maturational development (Fairbairn, 1952). Psychopathology does not, however, correspond in a one-to-one fashion with the actual events that have happened to the child; rather, the child's development with respect to perceptual and cognitive organization abilities transforms the experienced events into an internalized representation. Previous attachments and loyalties to the parents have also become internalized and therefore color subsequent internalized events. The child brings unconscious expectations to the present interpersonal situation, which imbue the processing of the present parent-child interactions. The meaningfulness of the child's current object relational experiences is due in part to the child's developmental level and internalization of past object relations.

## General Therapeutic Goals and Techniques

In his paper, *Recommendations to Physicians Practicing Psychoanalysis,* S. Freud (1912) presented a set of technical rules on how psychoanalysis should be conducted. Psychoanalytic treatment is dependent on a fundamental rule, which is applicable to both the client and the analyst. For the client, all thoughts that one is aware of during the session must be communicated to the analyst without selecting certain ones over others because of some rational or emotional objections to them. Everything should be verbally expressed without self-censorship. The counterpart of this rule for the analyst is that the analyst must carefully refrain from intentionally concentrating on some preferred aspect of the material presented by the client. The analyst is to maintain an "evenly-suspended" attention to all that he or she hears. The meaning of the client's thoughts will be recognized only later on in treatment; consequently, attention must be given to all that one hears in order to avoid prematurely disregarding important material.

Freud also cautioned against the analyst taking notes during the session, using self-disclosure, and expressing sympathy toward the client. It is better to complete case notes from memory after the session, to behave opaque and mirrorlike by showing only that which the client shows, and to maintain an emotional coldness toward the client. By adhering to these technical rules, the analyst will be able to attend more fully to all of the material that the client brings to the sessions and, perhaps even more importantly, avoid interfering with the client's ability to express everything that occurs to him or her. In this way, psychoanalysis proceeds in achieving its goals; that is, disclosing the client's unconscious wishes and impulses. Psychoanalytic treatment outcomes, however, are modest. The analyst is to have considered the analysis successful if the client regains to some degree his or her capacity to work and to enjoy life (S. Freud, 1912).

Classical or orthodox psychoanalysis, as practiced today, still adheres closely to Freud's fundamental rule by having clients freely associate about their fantasies or things that just come up, irrespective of logic or content, in order to communicate about drive derivatives. A client also is often asked to report about dreams and other daily life events. The analyst attempts to be as unintrusive as possible by remaining silent and out of eyesight of the client so as not to contaminate any of the material that the client brings forth. Through this method, the unconscious enters preconscious and the analyst offers an interpretation whereby the neurotic conflict is exposed. Consequently, the ego is strengthened by no longer having to repress id and superego impulses. The ultimate aim of psychoanalysis, therefore, is to increase the ego's orga-nization so that it can deal more effectively with id demands in the face of reality (Greenson, 1967).

Object relations psychoanalysis, however, permits greater degrees of freedom be-tween the analyst and the client. The aim of treatment is for the relationship between the client and the analyst to be healthier than were the client's past relationships. The analyst is seen as a coparticipant with the client under analysis in order to produce a corrective emotional experience. In this regard, the therapeutic goal is to repair the client's object-relatedness functioning (Lasky, 1993). The analyst's interpretations of the client's material are a sign of the analyst's empathy and understanding of the client, and not that of emotional disinterest (Modell, 1981).

In contrast to more customary interpersonal situations, the psychoanalytic situation seems rather stilted. Typically when two people are in a room conversing, there is re-ciprocal social interaction. There is a give-and-take to the conversation. The person not talking is expected to listen to what is being said and ask questions of the other for the sake of clarity, or at least for the appearance of social niceties. This is exactly what does not occur in the psychoanalytic situation. The analyst attempts to remain neutral in the client's conflict and abstains from interfering with the client's associations by adopting, metaphorically, the position of a blank screen. This stance in itself can cause the client to become anxious and frustrated.

Not all clients, consequently, will benefit from psychoanalysis. Characteristics of clients who are good candidates for psychoanalysis are as follows: (a) have at least av-erage intelligence and do not presently experience hallucinations and paranoid thoughts; (b) be able to delay impulses and have at least some awareness of their affec-tive state; (c) show the capacity to form close relationships and have had at least one close relationship in the past, (d) express a willingness to cooperate with treatment; and (e) presently are not engaged in alcohol or substance abuse (Usher, 1993). Psycho-analysis becomes more problematical for children to the extent that they may lack these characteristics on their entering psychotherapy. In general though, children with inter-nalizing disorders (are overcontrolled with internal constraints) do better in psycho-analysis than those who have externalizing disorders (are undercontrolled and lack internal constraints).

Irrespective of either a classical or object relations orientation to psychoanalysis, both approaches contain the following components, which must carefully be addressed by the analyst throughout the course of treatment (Greenson, 1967):

- *Transference Reactions*. The client's experiencing of emotions, attitudes, fan-tasies, and defenses toward the analyst that arose from interactions with signifi-cant others during early childhood.
- *Transference Neurosis.* A synthesis of transference reactions in which the analyst and the analytic situation are now the primary focus of the client's emotional life while the neurotic conflict is currently being reexperienced in the treatment sessions.

- *Resistances.* The maintaining of the neurotic conflict by a repetition of all the ego defenses the client has used in the past.
- *Analyzing.* A term used to indicate the use of insight-enhancing techniques that include four different procedures: confrontation, clarification, interpretation, and working-through, of which interpretation is the most important technique.
- *Working Alliance.* A partnership is formed between the client's reasonable ego and the analyst's analyzing ego in which the two work together to help relieve the client of his or her psychopathology.

Although anti-analytic techniques can be used in psychoanalysis, such as abreaction, suggestion, and other ego-supportive techniques that are typically employed in covering-up types of psychotherapy, the hallmark of psychoanalysis is to uncover, to produce insight-oriented change in the client. By insight, however, is meant "emotional insight"; that is, cognitive understanding coupled with the ability to reexperience the emotions surrounding the buried memories (Pulver, 1995). Insight, then, is a process whereby both affect and awareness are required. The affect pertains to the emotional reliving of the significant events, whereas expanded awareness relates to understanding the meaning of previous events in terms of current ego organization and strengths (Neubauer, 1980).

Interpretations offered by the analyst to facilitate the client's insight are made only on ego defense mechanisms and unconscious thoughts that are in the preconscious. These are thoughts that are out of the client's current awareness but are capable of becoming conscious; such as the case when the client provides an "Aha" response. For the analyst to interpret id wishes directly (that is unconscious thoughts that are not ready to be transformed by the ego for the preconscious) runs the risk of conducting "Wild Analysis;" a term Freud used to indicate an interpretation that made the client worse by causing anxiety or depression.

## INDIVIDUAL PSYCHOTHERAPY WITH CHILDREN

Psychoanalysis with children is a lengthy process that requires a serious time commitment from the child and parents. Therapy typically lasts for several years, requiring frequent contacts with the child (three to five sessions weekly lasting 45 to 50 minutes) and working with the parents. Yet, several issues involved with providing therapy to children, makes psychoanalysis with them problematic.

Anna Freud (1980) observed that children are unaware that their suffering is due to their own internal conditions. Usually parents bring a child into treatment because they are the ones who have concerns about the child (e.g., school refusal or academic difficulties). The child lacks *krankheitseinsicht,* awareness of one's illness. For example, an adult who says, "I know that I am an alcoholic" has self-awareness of his or her disorder. Children, on the other hand, attribute their suffering to external causes, or else accept their symptoms as a part of their living. Their motivation to change reflects the intensity of the pain they feel. If the perceived discomfort associated with treatment surpasses their present discomfort, as is often the case with neurotic children, then their commitment to a time-intense analysis is severely lessened. This condition also questions whether insight-oriented change is possible with children. To the extent that children can tolerate painful emotions and engage in self-observations, however, does suggest that insight can be achieved with children, even if only to a limited degree (Kennedy, 1980).

Interpersonal psychoanalysts, on the other hand, argue that premature insight introduces thoughts and fantasies that are not part of the child's normal developmental process. Using interpretation with children to elicit insight, therefore, may actually thwart their psychosexual development (Gaines, 1995). Child analysis conducted by interpersonal psychoanalysts use modified analytic techniques including only "indirect interpretations" such as stories and metaphors, that can result in age-appropriate self-awareness.

Compared with adults, children are cognitively immature, with inadequate abstract thinking. They are prone to act rather than verbalize their thoughts and feelings. Consequently, children may not respond well to the analytic stance where the analyst is reserved and nonintrusive. Object relations psychoanalysts, hence, have modified child analysis so that the analyst participates more with the child in exploration of the child's fantasy themes (Altman, 1994).

Another problematic issue regarding the use of psychoanalysis with children is that children are overly dependent on their parents. The analytic process of the client establishing a transference and a transference neurosis with the analyst may be the exception rather than the rule with children. The child's parental-dependency results in the child's continuous libidinal investment with the parents; that is, since the parents are a primary source of love for the child, the child sustains an emotional commitment to them. The problem is that the child is less likely to become invested with the analyst. The analyst, therefore, is likely to include the parents in treatment as either allies to assist in the child's development, or as a recognition that the child's psychopathology resulted from a disturbed interpersonal relationship with them. However, even if a transference relationship occurs between the analyst and the child, the actual relationship the analyst has with the child's parents interferes with the child transference of fantasies to the therapeutic situation. This, in turn, makes the transference neurosis unattainable and in all probability the child's fantasies unanalyzable. Therefore, all child analysis, whether classical or object relations, includes the parents to some degree in treatment to compensate for the attainment of a transference neurosis.

As stated previously, children's cognitions are concrete and nonabstract. They do not verbally express themselves as adults do. With only limited verbalization, the analyst is restricted from using free association. Play, on the other hand, is a child's natural form of interpersonal expression. The emotions a child is currently feeling are apt to be indicated through play activities. In child analysis, therefore, play therapy is the primary method used to access the child's current emotions and in which to analyze both primary and secondary process thinking (Kessler, 1966).

A major consideration in providing individual psychoanalysis with children, however, is that the therapist must acknowledge and work with the child's developmental process. The primary goal of child analysis is to alleviate the child's developmental arrest and to assist in normal development. Yet the therapist must do so within the context of the stresses of normal development. The child is rapidly developing enhanced ego functions, new language skills, an expanded repertoire of ego defenses and coping skills, as well as establishing a personality identity (Chetnik, 1989). Therefore, the therapist must not only help the child understand the neurotic conflict but normal developmental changes as well.

Lastly, child analysis depends on there being a good relationship between the therapist and the child client. To this extent, Kessler provides a list of eight basic principles for the therapist to keep in mind while conducting analysis with children (1966, p. 376). The therapist should (a) develop a warm, friendly relationship with the child; (b) accept the child exactly as he or she is; (c) create an atmosphere of permissiveness in the relationship; (d) be keen to recognize the child's feelings and reflect them back to him or her; (e) maintain a deep respect for the child's ability to solve his or her own problems; (f) allow the child to lead and the therapist to follow that lead; (g) not attempt to hurry the therapy along; (h) impose only limitations that are necessary to ground the therapy to reality and make the child aware of his or her responsibility in therapy.

## Techniques Specific to Children

Children rarely request undergoing psychotherapy; rather, parents are the ones most likely to contact the therapist to initiate treatment. The child's parents, therefore, are typically seen first and interviewed. The interview should elicit their concerns about their child and gather additional information about the child's psychosocial history and current environment. Since the child's emotional problems are likely to be the result of difficulties in the parent-child relationship, or from poor parenting practices, parents can be both anxious and defensive when being interviewed. The therapist must take care in establishing a good relationship with the child's parents, reassuring them that they are allies in the treatment process.

After the initial interview with the child's parents, the therapist must make a decision whether to see the child alone or together with the parents. If the child is seen alone, then the parents are seen individually on a consistent, but less frequent basis. Typically, parents provide valuable information about the child's functioning at home and at school, but also want the therapist to report about their child's progress. However, confidentiality between the therapist and the child must be maintained. Parents should be provided with only general information. Gardner (1973) stipulates that children under the age of 10 do not need to be seen alone since they really don't have secrets from their parents at that age. But this is a clinical judgment call.

The child is seen in either the traditional conference room, or a play therapy room. Materials selected for play therapy should allow the child considerable latitude for self-expression in both verbal and nonverbal ways. Such equipment includes but is not necessarily limited to art material (clay, crayons, finger and water paints, and drawing materials), animation objects (dolls, figurines of people and animals, houses, cars and trucks), and interactive objects (balloons and Frisbees, sand and water, cards and poker chips). These materials provide the means for the child to describe his or her fantasies.

With the prelatency-age child, the analyst is expected to participate in the child's play and gently urges the child to describe his or her thoughts and feelings, which are carefully noted for primary and secondary process thinking. Ego defense mechanisms are interpreted first followed by a description of the neurotic conflict. However, with very young children (under the age of 5) the analyst also consults with the parents once weekly to discuss the child's behaviors at home. Interpretations are provided only to the parents; yet, more importantly, the analyst teaches them how to communicate this to their child (O'Conner, Lee, & Schaefer, 1983). Older children of latency age, nevertheless, are likely to be more interactive in their play with the therapist, or else feel comfortable with just verbalizing their thoughts and feelings. In play, the therapist makes connections between the child's past and present and verbally provides running comments (summarizes what the child is doing) and confrontations (points out that an ego defense is being used).

Only nondirect interpretations are offered to children, commonly through the use of metaphors (Spiegel, 1989), waking transformation of dreams (Lewis & O'Brien, 1991) and the Mutual Story Telling Technique (Gardner, 1968). Through the use of a metaphor, the therapist symbolically imparts a thought or feeling that relates to the child's neurotic conflict, but allows him or her to discover the connection. In the waking transformation of dreams, the child's dreams reported to the therapist in earlier sessions are incorporated into the child's play in an adaptive way. With the Mutual Story Telling Technique, the therapist encourages the child to initiate the telling of a story. The therapist, in turn, provides a story closely resembling the child's story, but has an alternate way to view the situation.

## INDIVIDUAL PSYCHOTHERAPY WITH ADOLESCENTS

### Treatment Process and Goals

Adolescents differ in striking ways from both children and adults. Compared with the relative quiescence of childhood and adulthood, adolescence is a developmental phase that features a continuous metamorphosis. Teenagers experience dramatic changes in their cognitions, affect, and physical growth. They can obsess over their body image and emotional reactions, while simultaneously be driven to search out new peer relationships. There seems to be an unmitigated quest for independence and acknowledged maturity, yet also a mourning over the inevitable loss of childhood dependency and parental attachments. Teenagers also have a low frustration tolerance and a heightened sense of anxiety, which propels them toward action rather than talking (Kantor, 1995).

Throughout adolescence, youth are given greater and greater freedom in making choices that were previously made for them during childhood. They face decisions about choosing a career, dealing with sexual urges, establishing personal moral and ethical values, evaluating the values of their friends, and indeed judging the values of their own families. The stresses that stem from having to make these choices are enormous even to adults who have acquired far greater ego supports and defenses. One of the goals of psychoanalysis with adolescents, then, is to help them see alternatives to the problems with which they are confronted. Through analysis, adolescents can learn to accept more easily their responsibility of having to choose their life, and abandon the wish to regress back to childhood where decisions were made for them (Spiegel, 1989). In other words, a principal goal of therapy for adolescents is helping them achieve identity formation.

Historically, the analysis of adolescents was fraught with difficulty and was questioned whether it was even appropriate for this age. S. Freud's published case study of an adolescent girl, Dora (1905), revealed how difficult it was for an adolescent to accept interpretations about the neurotic conflict (Dora never returned for a second session). Anna Freud, too, doubted the suitability of analysis with adolescents since this is a period of such extreme emotional volatility where attachments to parents are being severed. It seemed highly unlikely that the adolescent could develop a transference relationship with the analyst. Yet several classical psychoanalysts (e.g., Blos, 1962; Fraiberg, 1955) successfully demonstrated effective treatment outcomes with adolescents. However, these analysts recognized the need to engage the adolescent in a more interactive relationship, which is typically the method employed by modern Interpersonal psychoanalysts.

From a classical psychoanalytic perspective, a major portion of the analysis focuses on increasing the ego's tolerance for drive impulses since the adolescent commonly experiences an intense reawakening of sexuality. Given also the adolescent's role of reassessing values, the ego must also be equipped to handle harsh restrictions from the super ego and ego ideal as well. Interpersonal therapists, gear the analysis toward the adolescent exploring difficulties with real-life events. By focusing the therapy on current issues confronting the adolescent, this strategy also facilitates the establishing of the working alliance; the adolescent's rational ego is more likely to be engaged in a process in which it senses it will be strengthened. In this way, the adolescent gains an expanded experience of him- or herself in relationship with others so as to relate to them in more satisfying ways. The overriding goals, therefore, of therapy with adolescents is to help move them along their unique developmental maturation. This is made easier by helping them to understand better the complexities of their interpersonal relationships and then allowing them gradually to gain acceptance of the necessary connection between their affect and action (Kantor, 1995).

## Techniques

There must be an adaptation of the analytic techniques for analysis with adolescents. Because of the adolescent's low frustration tolerance, extended periods of silence should be avoided. Yet the adolescent often feels too young to talk, but too old to play. Thus, there should be considerable flexibility between playing and talking activities. Play activities can require greater concentration, such as model building, which can be accompanied by dialogue. However, the adolescent is likely to test the therapist by being resistant to participate in therapy. A technique to employ with this situation is for the therapist to go with the resistance by acknowledging that it is an expression of the adolescent's new freedom to make choices. By communicating respect to the adolescent, the therapist enhances the ego, acknowledges the adolescent's ability to make choices, and more importantly enables the adolescent to view the therapist as a new object, which opens up the possibility of the adolescent achieving a corrective emotional experience. The likelihood of the latter outcome, nonetheless, directly relates to helping the adolescent work through his or her present difficulties.

The use of a couch for the adolescent to free associate is considered far too threatening, as are the use of direct interpretations. Material generated from free associations are more likely to occur from within the context of play activities. Direct interpretation of conflict material can have the unintended effect of the adolescent viewing it as evidence of personal failure; that is, it reflects inadequacies in ego functioning. Therefore, it appears to be far better to communicate only indirect interpretations. Metaphors that can serve as a means for indirect interpretations can be that of relating film plots of current movies, animal metaphors, and stories about other people (Spiegel, 1989). These techniques are designed for the adolescent to draw a parallel between real-world difficulties he or she is currently facing while providing an alternative way to think about the situation. With these techniques, therefore, the adolescent's current ego defense mechanisms are likely to be modified and increased in appropriateness or adaptability.

## GROUP PROCEDURES

In his paper *Group Psychology and the Analysis of the Ego,* S. Freud (1921) points out that there is no sharp distinction between individual psychology and group psychology because we come to understand the individual as he or she is in relationships with others. Group psychology is concerned with the individual as a member of a family, an intimate dyadic relationship, a community, a country, an institution, or even as a member of a crowd. Yet the individual is in conflict with the group and with the aspect of self that creates the connectedness with the group (Bion, 1980). The ego represses those id impulses that are deemed dangerous to express in the external world, that is, in interpersonal relationships. The perceived danger is derived from the ego's perception of how relationship objects will respond to sexual or aggressive drive discharge. However, that aspect of the psychic structure that anticipates reactions from objects is also in conflict with that part of the structure that only seeks drive expression. The neurotic conflict, therefore, arises from intrapsychic conflict, which in turn is derived from relations with others.

For Freud, analysis of group behaviors or motivation is from a sociological perspective, the individual as a herd animal. An analysis of children and adolescents, then, is an analysis of how they develop in social relationships. As children move from a state of immature dependency to mature dependency they develop ego defenses to cope with drive discharge. This is not to say, however, that children develop a social instinct; rather, there is a qualitative difference in the expression of the sexual and aggressive drives as modified by ego defenses. The different types of ego defenses used by the child throughout development, then, is a reflection of the child's state of dependency; as the dependency changes, so do the defense mechanisms. This is why the neurotic conflict thwarts development. Ego defenses become fixated and no longer represent the child's condition of dependency. During adolescence, however, there is a radical shift in object relations. The family is replaced by peer cohorts and by the search for intimacy with one significant other. The ego's perception of dangerous drive discharge modifies to conform to these new object relations.

Psychoanalytic group therapy rests on a psychoanalytic understanding of the interaction of the unconscious motivation for drive discharge and the ego's executive functioning, both within the individual and within the treatment group (Day, 1982). In treatment groups, the interaction among group members is unconstrained yet socially suitable. Sexual and aggressive impulses are elicited from the individual group members, but they become transformed into socially acceptable expressions by the ego defenses and superego values. Through this type of interaction, the relationships among the group members and the therapist deepen and are then analyzed by the therapist in terms of their realistic and unrealistic sources in the past and present (Day). The therapist will clarify, summarize, confront, and interpret the unconscious material as it is expressed within the group, and insight is achieved for the group members by showing how their past manifests itself in the present. The therapeutic alliance is at a group level. The individuals must sense that their rational egos are working with one another and with the therapist to help solve their mutual problems; that is, their mutual reason for coming to group therapy.

According to Day (1982) there are principally three reasons why clients seek out psychoanalytic treatment groups:

1. *Loss or relative loss.* A gratifying object is now gone from the life of the client or else the function of a love object has changed for the client.
2. *Chronic frustration and defeat.* Repeated losses have occurred over the years.
3. *Life-cycle stresses.* These are events associated with developmental changes, such as the birth of a sibling, the onset of puberty, the end of adolescence without having achieved a personal identity.

Psychoanalytic group treatment goals pertain to the following: facilitating the client's return to a previous level of functioning before a known breakdown occurred; working out grief reactions; resuming daily life functioning; making changes in interpersonal relationships by helping the client to act differently in those relationships.

The extent to which children and adolescents are capable and motivated to work on these outcomes indicates the appropriateness of using group psychoanalytic therapy with them.

## CLASSROOM AND EDUCATIONAL APPLICATIONS

S. Freud (1933) was interested in the application of psychoanalysis to the education of children. He felt that psychoanalytic theory would prove useful in the schools and issued a challenge to psychoanalysts: "Perhaps the most important of all the activities of which I am thinking of is the application of psychoanalysis to education, to the upbringing of the next generation. It is time for us as psychoanalysts to concern ourselves with this goal" (p. 146). Anna Freud (1952), thereafter, published a series of papers designed to educate parents and teachers on how best to handle children's anxieties and psychic conflicts. She recommended that the principles of psychoanalytic treatment be applied to teaching. According to Anna Freud, teachers should try to understand their students from the perspective of the entire process of childhood, and not from just the particular age group they were currently teaching. Teachers also need to maintain their adult values when teaching children and be careful of countertransference issues. Lastly, Anna Freud cautioned teachers not to become overly attached to the children they were teaching to the extent that they saw them as their own; rather, they must sustain a genuine interest in the children's progress, yet remain objective.

Classical psychoanalysts' interest in education, however, mostly has pertained to the problems of learning in school, which reflect a reenactment of the nucleus of the neurotic conflict; that is, the oedipal complex (Cohler, 1989). For example, Melanie Klein (1932) considers that the child's problems of learning in school are due to the emotions that arise from the earlier experienced rivalry with parents. On the other hand, Kohut's (1977) reformulated version of the neurotic conflict in terms of the development of self, conceptualizes it as a deficit in self-esteem. Problems in learning, such as those manifested in having difficulties in writing papers, doing poorly on examinations, not performing in terms of talents and ideals, reflect a lowering of self-esteem. Psychoanalytic investigations of students who have had difficulty producing schoolwork showed that they felt inadequate in comparison to their fathers or felt guilt that they would outperform them, hence a rekindling of the original rivalry with parents (Cohler). By working through the original neurotic conflict, then, school problems will dissipate.

Psychoanalysis has also been useful in the classroom by highlighting the emotional aspect of learning. Bettelheim (1955) described ways to teach emotionally disturbed children that centered on the teacher developing an empathic approach to teaching. Jones (1968) showed how students were better able to comprehend the meaning of a social science curriculum by working with them in groups and having them discuss their feelings related to the topic. The intent of Jones's discussion groups was for the students to develop empathy. Taken together, the work of Bettelheim and Jones demonstrates that both teaching and learning depends on an emotional aspect.

A criticism of psychoanalysis, however, is that due to its lengthy, time-protracted methods has remained extremely costly and out of reach for most teachers and students to benefit from it; in a sense it has maintained an elitist stance (Barbanel, 1994). Psychoanalytic methods need to be shorter in time duration and more affordable to be of relevance to the schools. However, there appears to be a reemergence of psychoanalysts' interest in learning and education. In 1982, the Chicago Institute of Psychoanalysis held a conference whose theme was the motive and meaning of learning (Pollock, 1989).

More recently, psychoanalytic perspectives have been applied to curriculum assignments to increase the learner's meaning of the material. If the teacher's assignments hold a greater personal meaning to the student, then the learning objectives are more likely to be met. Grumet (1994) provides an example where students are asked to write autobiographical narratives of educational experiences. They are able to rediscover the learning experience and see their relationship to it. Through an object relations perspective, the students gain insight into their relationship with knowing and the motives they have for learning.

Psychoanalysis is also being applied to understanding learning disorders from the perspective of the disabled learner. Garber (1989) analyzes learning disabilities from the perspective that these children have limited empathic capacity. The learning disability itself contributes both directly and indirectly to the lack of empathy. An absence of cognitive integrative skills interferes with the accuracy of an immediate empathic response. But conversely, a tremendous amount of intellectual and emotional effort must be expended on maintaining a sense of self-intactness and stability to the extent that little psychic energy is left over for sensitivities toward others. The education of children with learning disabilities, therefore, must teach the range of human emotions and how to take the perspective on another.

However, a schism between the foci of education and psychoanalysis needs to be bridged if the two disciplines are to benefit from each other. Education has focused on the cognitive aspect of learning, the intellectual potential and necessary cognitive skills to master the curriculum. The emotional side of the learner has been ignored. Psychoanalysis, on the other hand, has focused on the emotional component of learning and learning difficulties while ignoring the intellectual side. For psychoanalysis to be useful to the schools, it must incorporate the cognitive domain as well as the emotional.

## PARENT INVOLVEMENT

A fundamental premise in psychoanalytic treatment is that parents' relationship with their child influences the child's mental health. Children do not live independently from caregivers. Practitioners of psychoanalytic therapy, therefore, have long recognized that part of the treatment process must aim at altering the parents' behaviors. This has been accomplished through two avenues: parent education and involving the parents in the treatment of their child (Kessler, 1966).

Parent education has had a long history in the United States. The National Council for Parent Education was founded in 1929. Additionally, several journals publish annual issues devoted to parent education and research on parenting practices. Parent education, furthermore, is an interdisciplinary field and is comprised of professionals from diverse backgrounds, such as home economics, medicine, nursing, psychology, public health, and social work. All these diverse professions attempt to provide parents with information about child-rearing practices from the viewpoint of their respective discipline in a suitable and simplified way. That is to say, disciplinary research is translated into a language that is easily understandable to parents.

Anna Freud (1956), however, wrote extensively about the misuse of psychoanalytic information to parents. Parents and teachers who were eager for advice on how to raise children attempted to apply psychoanalytic theory without fully understanding its approach. For example, psychoanalytic knowledge regarding the sexual enlightenment of children was translated by parents into permitting their child to become physically indulged for the sake of achieving gratification. Thumb-sucking, bed-wetting, and soiling of clothes were seen as acceptable. Parents' knowledge of the neurotic conflict and the oedipal complex was translated by parents into adopting a permissive, non-authoritarian parenting style. The outcome of this approach produced children who lacked internal controls and seemed to be overly self-centered. The outcome of this approach was that both parents and children were unhappy. In fact, an impetus for Benjamin Spock's famous book, *Baby and Child Care* (1946) was the state of affairs caused by the misuse of psychoanalytic principles. Spock wrote that parents had a right to expect politeness and cooperation from their children. According to Kessler (1966), there are five aims of parent education:

1. *Sharing of Information.* Parents communicate with one another about their parenting experiences.
2. *Study Groups.* Parents learn new parenting skills.
3. *Factual Information about Behaviors at Different Ages.* Parents gain an understanding of normal development.
4. *Interpretative Information.* Parents are provided with the "whys" of children's behaviors.
5. *Recommendations.* Parents receive useful advice on how they can handle specific child-rearing problems.

Involving parents in psychoanalytic treatment is the other avenue used to change the behaviors of parents that will impact their child's mental health. Parents involvement in treatment varies inversely with the age of their child. Consultations with parents of adolescents are held independently from their child in session. Parents may seek advice from the therapist or provide the therapist with information about their teenager's school and home performance. But the therapist provides no detailed information to the parents about what the child has talked about in session. Children under the age of

10, however, can be seen with their parents in session if the therapist chooses. At the very least, the therapist will elicit from the parents of the school-age child detailed information regarding the child's behaviors.

Parent involvement in their child's therapy is the most extensive with preschoolers. In this situation, it is actually the parents who are providing the treatment. The therapist may observe the parent-child interactions then provide the parents with recommendations. Or, the therapist and parents will collaborate and jointly analyze the child's behaviors. The therapist will, in turn, attempt to teach the parents how to communicate their derived interpretations to their child.

## EFFICACY OF TREATMENT STRATEGIES

Psychoanalysis has been researched as it applies to a method of study, a theory, and a clinical process. As a method of study, psychoanalysis employs naturalistic methods, that is, observations. Freud's early observations of children has been followed by increasingly sophisticated child observation studies. For example, Spitz observed hospitalized children and Bowlby conducted extensive observations regarding parent-child interactions. What was missing from these research endeavors, however, was formal experimental research. The findings from Spitz and Bowlby needed empirical confirmation as did other tenets of psychoanalytic theory. For theoretical confirmation, psychoanalytic theory has relied mostly on experimental research that has investigated mental functioning. For example, the outcome from studies investigating memory, dreams, mental representations, hypnosis, and cognitive styles that are consistent with psychoanalytic assumptions are cited as confirming evidence (Mayer, 1995). The problem that psychoanalytic theory faces is that the terminology developed by Freud was to serve the purpose of a metaphor. There is no ego; rather Freud used this term to indicate the psychic apparatus responsible for perceptions, language, and logic. Consequently, conducting a research study to investigate the ego directly is an impossibility. Therefore, psychoanalysis has had to rely on the outcome of studies that have directly investigated mental phenomenon to confirm or disconfirm its theoretical propositions.

Psychoanalytic outcome research regarding treatment efficacy is still in its infancy. The Menninger Project, however, was established to determine the effectiveness of psychoanalysis. This project pertained to long-term studies. A major finding from the Menninger Project was that clients with high ego strength are likely to do well in any treatment modality; however, psychoanalysis brought about the highest degree of improvement. Conversely, clients with low ego strengths benefited most from supportive type therapies (Mayer, 1995). But the results from the Menninger project are not too surprising. What the outcomes indicate is that insight-oriented change is best suited for those individuals who have the capacity to self-explore. To the extent that that capacity is limited, insight will not occur. Consequently, other treatment methods are more appropriate. For psychoanalysis to continue to prove useful, however, more research projects like the Menninger Project need to get underway.

## CONCLUSION

The importance of psychoanalysis for children and adolescents is that it offers a thorough description of child development in terms of cognitions, emotions, and interpersonal relationships. Psychoanalytic theory, too, has proven itself to be highly adaptive. It has changed from providing a description of the individual in terms of endogenous arising personality structures to that of giving a detailed explanation of the effects of personality due to interpersonal relationships. A difficulty with psychoanalytic theory, however, is the terminology it employs. Its terms, such as "object relations," seem foreign to the layperson. Consequently, it is often equated with mysticism instead of the science that it really is. The fundamental limitation to psychoanalysis, however, is that its treatment procedures aren't applicable to many settings. It is highly unlikely that psychoanalysis can be applied in the school setting. Given time constraints and the lack of resources that most schools and mental health centers face, other treatment methods may be more suitable. Psychoanalysis, therefore, must move in the direction of finding short-term approaches to treatment. If it is successful in this effort, then there will be a wider acceptance of psychoanalytic theory in general.

## CASE STUDY[1]

The case study concerns the analysis of a preadolescent boy, which emphasizes superego and defense analysis. This technique allowed the boy to become curious about and then attempt to understand the nature of his internal conflicts.

Lawrence was an 11-year-old boy whose parents brought him to treatment because of his inordinate oppositionalism and argumentativeness, which was interfering with his school performance, peer relations, and familial harmony. A prolonged consultation revealed a surprisingly and prematurely rigidified anal character structure. In contrast to his argumentativeness at home, Lawrence's behavior and words during the consultation revealed a boy almost lacking in emotional spontaneity. Excessive politeness and an inability to discuss topics of his own choosing seemed to indicate severe superego conflicts that were being externalized into the environment. Intense conflicts over aggression made life a laborious struggle to do right and maintain control for Lawrence. What seemed like willfulness and poor impulse control was in reality a defense against the dictates of his harsh superego. It appeared that Lawrence needed psychoanalysis to overcome the severe conflicts that were already beginning to compromise important ego functions such as intelligence and object relations. The repeated power struggles in which he engaged his parents seemed best understood as a defensive externalization of his excessively demanding and critical superego id an unconscious attempt to be controlled and punished.

---

[1] Adapted from "Toward helping child analysands observe mental functioning," by A. Sugarman (1994). *Psychoanalytic Psychology, 11*, 329–339. Copyright by Lawrence Erlbaum Associates, Inc. Reprinted by permission.

Lawrence's need to inhibit potential expressions of affect and impulse made the early stages of treatment slow and tedious. His refusal to play combined with his emphasis on emotionally shallow, external events (even beyond what is typical for most latency-age children) proved a formidable resistance. Interpretations of affect or impulse inevitably provoked negation. Consequently, Lawrence's refusal to play directly was confronted and interpreted as his inordinate need to maintain control. During an early play session, the analyst drew a picture depicting Lawrence's "conscience" waging war against his feelings, thoughts, and fantasies and pushing them into his "unconscience," based on the idea of drawing a variation on Freud's rendering of the mind. With this explanation of intrapsychic conflict in mind, Lawrence's refusal to play because it was "not appropriate" was interpreted as a manifestation of his conscience's dictate that his inner world be suppressed. Such a concrete approach to superego interpretation seemed necessary because of Lawrence's developmental limitations and dynamic inhibitions. It was not an attempt to suggest away his punitive introjects; rather, if the motivations for his superego injunctions could be understood, the analyst could gradually illustrate Lawrence's resistance to elaborating the fantasies of authority. Because these fantasies were reexternalized onto the analyst in the transference, they contributed to Lawrence's inhibition during sessions. These externalizations were also enacted at home in battles with his parents.

In fact, Lawrence's reaction to such a direct and concrete interpretation showed no evidence of perfunctory compliance. Instead, this approach drew Lawrence's interest, and he began to ask questions about the workings of the mind. To be sure, some of its attraction to Lawrence involved his defensive intellectualization. But this defense was easy to interpret as a manifestation of his conscience, also. And, in fact, Lawrence did not use this explanation of intrapsychic conflict to further distance himself from affect and impulse or to suddenly give vent. Instead, his curiosity allowed the analyst to slowly point out superego manifestations whenever they occurred and to gradually explore the nature of his superego prohibitions, their motives, and, at times, their genetic origins.

Maintaining the focus on superego conflict as it became manifested between Lawrence and the analyst was of particular help. For example, in one session after this intervention, Lawrence complained about the annoying behavior of some peers at school. He said that he would call them a name, even to his parents, but that he did not believe that swearing was acceptable in analysis. Thus, he showed the externalization of superego authority into the transference. Looking at his inhibitions as expressions of his strict conscience, his defensive externalizations were interpreted as Lawrence seeing the analyst as his own conscience. More working through was necessary before Lawrence began to feel comfortable with profanity during the sessions. But drawing attention to his own internal conflicts via the projection of his superego onto the analyst ultimately was successful in allowing him to be spontaneous in this way.

Lawrence slowly became more comfortable with expressions of affect, particularly aggressive derivatives. Anger toward his father was the affect that first became available in the sessions. Lawrence began to complain about what he experienced to be his father's excessive criticality, withholding, and control. For example, Lawrence complained that his father had no right to criticize his handwriting because his father's own handwriting was so bad. He also felt angry that his father would not let him turn up the thermostat in the house when he felt cold because his father felt that the house was warm. These tentative expressions of seemingly oedipal anger were often followed by silence or undoing. When the analyst would try to expand on Lawrence's feelings of anger toward his father, Lawrence would often say that he was not angry and that the analyst had misunderstood him. This denial and his silences after expression of anger were interpreted as further manifestations of his conscience. First on the list was "Thou shalt not be angry!"

Interpretations of Lawrence's ego's defensive use of superego functions aroused further curiosity and led him to ask questions such as, "In what part of the brain is the conscience?" Very effective in promoting insight into conflict were the opportunities to demonstrate resistances within the transference. Working with Lawrence's frequent and persistent questions proved a most fruitful arena for interpretive work. Lawrence found any refusal to answer questions and attempt to understand the motives behind them particularly frustrating. For instance, around one separation, Lawrence wanted to know where his therapist was going on vacation. Efforts to explore his fantasies led to silence. It was pointed out to Lawrence that this sequence wherein his questions were not answered subsequently resulted in his becoming silent. But he would not offer a possible explanation for the interchange. The possibility that Lawrence remained silent because his conscience had told him that he should not have asked was explored. Lawrence, however, replied that no, he know that it was acceptable to ask questions because he had been told so in the past. Consequently, the analyst asked if Lawrence felt angry at the refusal to answer and was silent to control his anger. Lawrence remained silent, not answering the question. His silence was taken as a confirmation and the analyst pointed out that Lawrence's conscience was once again telling him that he should not be angry. Working through various expressions of conflicts around anger allowed Lawrence gradually to acknowledge anger at the analyst's refusal to answer questions. Acknowledgment of disavowed affect occurred first with Lawrence saying that he felt "frustrated"; later in the analysis, he admitted to being "irritated" or "annoyed," and finally, he talked of being "pissed off" while he ridiculed what he perceived to be the analyst's "weird" way of relating through refusing to answer questions.

Other exchanges in the sessions allowed further interpretations of the defensive superego manifestations of his conflicts. Thus, Lawrence's continued need to ask permission to take a Kleenex when his nose was running was interpreted as a manifestation of his conscience's dictate that "Thou must be polite to adults at all times!" During yet another session, Lawrence asked if the analyst thought it acceptable to give his brother a bottle of soy sauce as a birthday present because his brother liked to drink soy sauce, something that Lawrence thought to be "disgusting." This need to ask the analyst's opinion was interpreted as another manifestation of his conscience, which seemed to be saying that it was not acceptable to give a joke present. Lawrence denied the interpretation and hastened to clarify that he intended to buy his brother a "real" present also. His reaction led the analyst to draw attention to his negation and clarification and to invite him to understand why he had done it. When Lawrence could not get beyond his own guilt to reflect on himself, the analyst interpreted his knee-jerk reflex that he would buy a real present as a further example of his own conscience and his fear that the analyst was as critical of his impulses as was his own conscience.

Such work evolved gradually, and Lawrence began to explore the nature of the anxiety situations prompting his superego deployment. Not surprisingly, this exploration first led to fears of losing control of his impulses. Insight into this fear was heralded during a session halfway through the second year of Lawrence's analysis when he noticed a new picture hanging on the office wall. The picture was so dark and detailed that he could not see what it represented. Consequently, Lawrence asked what it portrayed. This request was interpreted as another manifestation of his conscience; this time it told him that he was not allowed to walk over and look at the picture. Lawrence acknowledged that he felt to do so would be "rude." Furthermore, he would not be able to answer any questions that the analyst might ask him in as thoughtful and thorough a manner as he felt he should do while he was looking. After all, he could never behave that way in his classroom. The analyst replied that Lawrence continued to see him as demanding, controlling, and critical, just as he perceived his teachers to be. Once again, it was interpreted that Lawrence did so because he thought that the analyst was as disapproving as his own conscience.

This interpretation and its subsequent working through allowed Lawrence to explain that he felt that he needed his conscience to keep him in control. Otherwise, he feared that he would be rude far too often. At that point, Lawrence could not elaborate his fantasies about what his rudeness might entail or what repercussion it might precipitate. But he was able to stop and to stare at the picture as he entered the office for the next session, indicating some resolution of this particular conflict.

Within days, Lawrence expanded this exploration of his superego when he asked what people do if they lacked a conscience. But he was unwilling to speculate about what could ensue. Consequently, this was interpreted as his fear that he might lose his conscience completely were he to modify it. Lawrence acknowledged this fear and wondered out loud what might happen if he lost his conscience. He explained that he feared what he might do less than what he might not do if he stopped being so critical of himself. Specifically, Lawrence feared that he might not study as thoroughly in school without his conscience. Often he found himself rationalizing to friends that the reason he spent so much time studying was because his teachers wanted him to do so. But Lawrence admitted that he knew this was only an excuse. It was his own conscience that required it. If he did not study so much, he might get only Cs. Thus, Lawrence showed dawning insight into his defensive externalization of his superego as well as its excessive demands on him.

Gradually, insight into the defensive workings of his superego allowed Lawrence to become increasingly comfortable with the expression of intense affects and fantasies. Aggressive fantasies became increasingly comfortable for him as he worked through anger toward both his siblings and his parents. Greater comfort with such impulses reduced his provocative externalizations, and peer relations improved. As Lawrence engaged in the developmental tasks of early adolescence, he began to individuate from his parents in a way that seemed quite "adolescent" without being excessively provocative. Challenges to his parents' authority were negotiated in a way that allowed them to accede to his developmentally appropriate wishes rather than to limit him.

## ANNOTATED BIBLIOGRAPHY

Greenberg, J. R., & Mitchell, S. A. (1983). *Object relations in psychoanalytic theory.* Cambridge, MA: Harvard University Press.

This is comprehensive reference on object relations theory. Greenberg and Mitchell carefully describe classical psychoanalysis and how object relations theory developed from it.

Greenson, R. R. (1967). *The technique and practice of psychoanalysis.* Madison CT: International Universities Press.

Greenson provides a comprehensive approach to understanding the process of psychoanalysis. He describes in detail how psychoanalytic procedures work in therapy and specifically highlights the importance of the working alliance.

Usher, S. F. (1993). *Introduction to psychodynamic psychotherapy technique.* Madison, CT: International Universities Press.

Usher shows how the basic fundamentals of psychoanalysis can be applied in short-term therapy. She gives a detail description of how to conduct therapy that ranges from history taking to terminating treatment.

## REFERENCES

Alexander, F., & French, T. M. (1946). *Psychoanalytic therapy.* New York: Ronald Press.

Altman, N. (1994). A perspective on child psychoanalysis 1994: Recognition of relational theory and technique in child treatment. *Psychoanalytic Psychology, 11*(3), 397–400.

Barbanel, L. (1994). Psychoanalysis and school psychology. *Psychoanalytic Psychology, 11*(2), 275–284.

Bettelheim, B. (1955). *Truants from life.* New York: Free Press/Macmillan.

Bion, W. R. (1980). Group dynamics: A review. In S. Scheidlinger (Ed.), *Psychoanalytic group dynamics: Basic readings* (pp. 77–108). New York: International Universities Press.

Blos, P. (1962). *On adolescence*. New York: Free Press.

Blos, P. (1967). The second individuation process of adolescence. *Psychoanalytic Study of the Child, 22,* 162–187.

Bornstein, B. (1935). Phobia in a two-and-a-half-year-old child. *Psychoanalytic Quarterly, 4,* 93–119.

Bornstein, B. (1945). Clinical notes on child analysis. *Psychoanalytic Study of the Child, 1,* 151–166.

Bornstein, B. (1949). The analysis of a phobic child. *Psychoanalytic Study of the Child, 3–4,* 181–226.

Bowlby, J. (1982). *Attachment and loss* (2nd ed., Vols. 1–3). London: HarperCollins.

Brenner, C. (1973). *An elementary textbook of psychoanalysis*. New York: Doubleday.

Chetnik, M. (1989). *Techniques of child therapy: Psychodynamic strategies*. New York: Guilford Press.

Chused, J. (1988). The transference neurosis in child analysis. *Psychoanalytic Study of the Child, 43,* 51–81.

Cohler, B. J. (1989). Psychoanalysis and education: Motive, meaning and self. In K. Field, B. Cohler, & G. Wool (Eds.), *Learning and education: Psychoanalystic explorations* (pp. 11–71). Madison, CT: International Universities Press.

Day, M. (1982). Psychoanalytic group psychotherapy. In A. Jacobson & D. Parmelee (Eds.), *Psychoanalysis: Critical explorations in contemporary theory and practice* (pp. 139–161). New York: Brunner/Mazel.

Dowling, A. S., & Naegele, J. (1995). Child and adolescent psychoanalysis. In B. E. Moore & B. D. Fine (Eds.), *Psychoanalysis: The major concepts* (pp. 26–45). London: Yale University Press.

Erikson, E. (1968). *Identity: Youth and crisis*. New York: Norton.

Ezriel, H. (1980). A psychoanalytic approach to group treatment. In S. Scheidlinger (Ed.), *Psychoanalytic group dynamics: Basic readings* (pp. 109–146). New York: International Universities Press.

Fairbairn, W. R. D. (1952). *An object-relations theory of the personality*. New York: Basic Books.

Fenichel, O. (1945). *The psychoanalytic theory of neurosis*. New York: Norton.

Fraiberg, S. (1955). Some considerations in the introduction to therapy in puberty. *Psychoanalytic Study of the Child, 10,* 264–268.

Fraiberg, S. (1959). *The magic years*. New York: Scribner.

Freud, A. (1927). Four lectures on child analysis. In *The writings of Anna Freud* (Vol. 1, pp. 3–69). New York: International Universities Press.

Freud, A. (1936). *The ego and mechanisms of defense*. New York: International Universities Press.

Freud, A. (1952). Answering teachers questions. In *The writings of Anna Freud* (Vol. 4, pp. 560–569). New York: International Universities Press.

Freud, A. (1980). The role of insight in psychoanalysis and psychotherapy: Introduction. In H. P. Blum (Ed.), *Psychoanalytic explorations of technique: Discourse on the theory of therapy* (pp. 3–8). New York: International Universities Press.

Freud, A., & Burlingham, D. B. (1973). Infants without families. In *The writings of Anna Freud* (Vol. 3, pp. 1–664). New York: International Universities Press.

Freud, S. (1894). The neuro-psychoses of defense. In J. Strachey (Ed. and Trans.), *Standard edition of the works of Sigmund Freud* (Vol. 3, pp. 43–61). London: Hogarth Press.

Freud, S. (1895). Project for a scientific psychology. In J. Strachey (Ed. and Trans.), *Standard edition of the works of Sigmund Freud* (Vol. 1, pp. 283–387). London: Hogarth Press.

Freud, S. (1896). Further remarks o the neuro-psychoses of defense. In J. Strachey (Ed. and Trans.), *Standard edition of the works of Sigmund Freud* (Vol. 3, pp. 159–185). London: Hogarth Press.

Freud, S. (1898). Sexuality in the aetiology of the neuroses. In J. Strachey (Ed. and Trans.), *Standard edition of the works of Sigmund Freud* (Vol. 3, pp. 259–285). London: Hogarth Press.

Freud, S. (1900). The interpretation of dreams. In J. Strachey (Ed. and Trans.), *Standard edition of the works of Sigmund Freud* (Vols. 4 and 5). London: Hogarth Press.

Freud, S. (1905). Three essays on the theory of sexuality. In J. Strachey (Ed. and Trans.), *Standard edition of the works of Sigmund Freud* (Vol. 7, pp. 125–243). London: Hogarth Press.

Freud, S. (1909). Analysis of a phobia in a five-year-old boy. In J. Strachey (Ed. and Trans.), *Standard edition of the works of Sigmund Freud* (Vol. 10, pp. 3–149). London: Hogarth Press.

Freud, S. (1911). Formulations on the two principles of mental functioning. In J. Strachey (Ed. and Trans.), *Standard edition of the works of Sigmund Freud* (Vol. 12, pp. 218–226). London: Hogarth Press.

Freud, S. (1912). Recommendations to physicians practicing psychoanalysis. In J. Strachey (Ed. and Trans.), *Standard edition of the works of Sigmund Freud* (Vol. 12, pp. 111–120). London: Hogarth Press.

Freud, S. (1915). Instincts and their vicissitudes. In J. Strachey (Ed. and Trans.), *Standard edition of the works of Sigmund Freud* (Vol. 14, pp. 117–140). London: Hogarth Press.

Freud, S. (1921). Group psychology and the analysis of the ego. In J. Strachey (Ed. and Trans.), *Standard edition of the works of Sigmund Freud* (Vol, 18, pp. 67–143). London: Hogarth Press.

Freud, S. (1923). The infantile genital organization. In J. Strachey (Ed. and Trans.), *Standard edition of the works of Sigmund Freud* (Vol. 19, pp. 141–145). London: Hogarth Press.

Freud, S. (1926). The question of lay analysis. In J. Strachey (Ed. and Trans.), *Standard edition of the works of Sigmund Freud* (Vol. 20, pp. 183–258). London: Hogarth Press.

Freud, S. (1933). New introductory lectures on psychoanalysis. In J. Strachey (Ed. and Trans.), *Standard edition of the works of Sigmund Freud* (Vol. 22, pp. 136–156). London: Hogarth Press.

Garber, B. (1989). Deficits in empathy in the learning disabled child. In K. Field, B. Cohler, & G. Wool (Eds.), *Learning and education: Psychoanalytic explorations* (pp. 617–633). Madison, CT: International Universities Press.

Gaines, R. (1995). The treatment of children. In M. Lionells, J. Fiscalini, C. H. Mann, & D. B. Stern (Eds.), *Handbook of interpersonal psychoanalysis* (pp. 751–770). Hillsdale, NJ: Analytic Press.

Gardner, R. (1968). The mutual storytelling technique: Use in alleviating childhood oedipal problems. *Contemporary Psychoanalysis, 4,* 161–177.

Gardner, R. (1973). *Psychotherapeutic approaches to the resistant child.* New York: Aronson.

Gartner, R. B. (1995). The relationship between interpersonal psychoanalysis and family therapy. In M. Lionells, J. Fiscalini, C. H. Mann, & D. B. Stern (Eds.), *Handbook of interpersonal psychoanalysis* (pp. 793–822). Hillsdale, NJ: Analytic Press.

Greenberg, J. R., & Mitchell, S. A. (1983). *Object relations in psychoanalytic theory.* Cambridge, MA: Harvard University Press.

Greenson, R. (1967). *The technique and practice of psychoanalysis.* New York: International Universities Press.

Grumet, M. R. (1994). Reading and the relations of teaching. *Psychoanalytic Psychology, 11*(2), 253–264.

Hug-Hellmuth, H. (1920). Child psychology and education. *International Journal of Psychoanalysis, 1,* 316–323.

Hug-Hellmuth, H. (1921). On the technique of child analysis. *International Journal of Psychoanalysis, 2,* 287–303.

Hughes, J. M. (1989). *Reshaping the psychoanalytic domain: The work of Melanie Klein, W. R. D. Fairbairn, and D. W. Winnicott.* Berkeley: University of California Press.

Jones, E. (1968). *Fantasy and feeling in education.* New York: New York University Press.

Kantor, S. (1995). Interpersonal treatment of adolescents. In M. Lionells, J. Fiscalini, C. H. Mann, & D. B. Stern (Eds.), *Handbook of interpersonal psychoanalysis* (pp. 771–792). Hillsdale, NJ: Analytic Press.

Kennedy, H. (1980). The role of insight in child analysis: A developmental viewpoint. In H. P. Blum (Ed.), *Psychoanalytic explorations of technique: Discourse on the theory of therapy* (pp. 9–28). New York: International Universities Press.

Kessler, J. (1966). *Psychopathology of childhood.* Englewood Cliffs, NJ: Prentice-Hall.

Kessler, J. (1988). *Psychopathology of childhood* (2nd ed.). Englewood Cliffs, NJ: Prentice-Hall.

King, P., & Steiner, R. (Eds.). (1991). *The Freud-Klein controversies 1941–1945.* London: Routledge & Kegan Paul.

Klein, M. (1921). The development of a child. *International Journal of Psychoanalysis, 4,* 419–474.

Klein, M. (1927). Symposium on child analysis. *International Journal of Psychoanalysis, 8,* 339–370.

Klein, M. (1932). *The psychoanalysis of children.* London: Hogarth Press.

Kohut, H. (1977). *The restoration of the self.* New York: International Universities Press.

Korchin, S. (1983). The history of clinical psychology: A personal view. In M. Hersen, A. Kazdin, & A. Bellack (Eds.), *The clinical psychology handbook* (pp. 5–20). New York: Pergamon Press.

Lasky, R. (1993). *Dynamics of development and the therapeutic process.* Northvale, NJ: Aronson.

Lewis, O., & O'Brien, J. (1991). Clinical use of dreams with latency age children. *American Journal of Psychotherapy, 45,* 527–543.

MacKay, N. (1981). Melanie Klein's metapsychology: Phenomenological and mechanistic perspective. *International Journal of Psychoanalysis, 62,* 187–198.

Mayer, E. L. (1995). Psychoanalysis and research. In B. E. Moore & B. D. Fine (Eds.), *Psychoanalysis: The major concepts* (pp. 529–536). London: Yale University Press.

Modell, A. H. (1981). "The holding environment" and the therapeutic action of psychoanalysis. In R. Langs (Ed.), *Classics in psychoanalytic technique* (pp. 489–498). New York: Aronson.

Murray, J. F. (1995). On objects, transference, and two-person psychology: A critique of the new seduction theory. *Psychoanalytic Psychology, 12*(1), 31–41.

Neubauer, P. B. (1980). The role of insight in psychoanalysis. In H. P. Blum (Ed.), *Psychoanalytic explorations of technique: Discourse on the theory of therapy* (pp. 29–40). New York: International Universities Press.

O'Conner, K., Lee, A. C., & Schaefer, C. E. (1983). Psychoanalytic psychotherapy with children. In M. Hersen, A. Kazdin, & A. Bellack (Eds.), *The clinical psychology handbook* (pp. 543–564). New York: Pergamon Press.

Orgel, S. (1995). Education and training in psychoanalysis. In B. E. Moore & B. D. Fine (Eds.), *Psychoanalysis: The major concepts* (pp. 523–528). London: Yale University Press.

Pollock, G. H. (1989). Forward. In K. Field, B. Cohler, & G. Wool (Eds.), *Learning and education: Psychoanalytic perspectives* (pp. xvii–xix). Madison, CT: International Universities Press.

Pulver, S. E. (1995). The psychoanalytic process and mechanisms of therapeutic change. In B. E. Moore & B. D. Fine (Eds.), *Psychoanalysis: The major concepts* (pp. 81–94). London: Yale University Press.

Rexford, E. N. (1982). Psychoanalysis: A basis for child psychotherapy. In A. M. Jacobson & D. X. Parmelee (Eds.), *Psychoanalysis: Critical explorations in contemporary theory and practice* (pp. 118–138). New York: Brunner/Mazel.

Ritvo, S., & Solnit, A. J. (1995). Instinct theory. In B. E. Moore & B. D. Fine (Eds.), *Psychoanalysis: The major concepts* (pp. 327–333). London: Yale University Press.

Saravay, S. M. (1980). Group psychology and the structural theory: A revised psychoanalysis model of group psychology. In S. Scheidlinger (Ed.), *Psychoanalytic group dynamics: Basic readings* (pp. 255–284). New York: International Universities Press.

Scheidlinger, S. (1980). Current psychoanalytic group therapy. In S. Scheidlinger (Ed.), *Psychoanalytic group dynamics: Basic readings* (pp. 285–300). New York: International Universities Press.

Spiegel, S. (1989). *An interpersonal approach to child therapy: The treatment of children and adolescents from an interpersonal point of view.* New York: Columbia University Press.

Spitz, R. (1946). Hospitalism. *Psychoanalytic Study of the Child, 2,* 113–118.

Spitz, R. (1965). *The first year of life.* New York: International Universities Press.

Spock, B. (1946). *Baby and child care.* New York: Pocket Books.

Sugarman, A. (1994). Toward helping child analysands observe mental functioning. *Psychoanalytic Psychology, 11,* 329–339.

Sullivan, H. (1953). *The interpersonal theory of psychiatry.* New York: Norton.

Tuma, J. M., & Russ, S. W. (1993). Psychoanalytic psychotherapy with children. In T. R. Kratochwill & R. J. Morris (Eds.), *Handbook of psychotherapy with children and adolescents* (pp. 131–161). Boston: Allyn & Bacon.

Tyson, P., & Tyson, R. L. (1990). *Psychoanalytic theories of development: An integration.* New Haven, CT: Yale University Press.

Usher, S. F. (1993). *Introduction to psychodynamic psychotherapy technique.* Madison, CT: International Universities Press.

Wallerstein, R. S. (1995). *The talking cures.* London: Yale University Press.

Winnicott, D. W. (1958). *Through pediatrics to psychoanalysis.* London: Hogarth Press.

Winnicott, D. W. (1960). The theory of the parent-infant relationship. *International Journal of Psychoanalysis, 41,* 585–595.

Winnicott, D. W. (1962). The theory of the parent-infant relationship: Further remarks. *International Journal of Psychoanalysis, 43,* 238–239.

Winnicott, D. W. (1965). *The maturational process and the facilitating environment.* New York: International Universities Press.

# Chapter 5

# *ADLERIAN APPROACHES TO COUNSELING WITH CHILDREN AND ADOLESCENTS*

F. Donald Kelly

Alfred Adler identified his approach to understanding and treating emotional and behavioral problems with the term *Individual Psychology*. His theoretical formulations have been organized into a systematic and integrated presentation in *The Individual Psychology of Alfred Adler* (Ansbacher & Ansbacher, 1956). This approach represents (a) a theory of personality, (b) a system of psychotherapy, and (c) a philosophy of life.

The term Individual Psychology reflects Adler's belief in the value, worth, and dignity of each human being. He viewed each individual as creative, responsible, self-determined, and possessing the potential for both constructive as well as destructive approaches to life and its challenges. This approach, or life style, is designed to assist the individual in moving toward personal, self-created goals that represent his or her answer to the questions of significance, social acceptance, and survival in life. Unlike Freud, Adler believed in holism and the dynamic unity of personality. He theorized that cognition, emotion, and behavior function in a unified and integrated fashion to move individuals toward the realization of their self-created goals.

Adler's theory of Individual Psychology favored a psychology of "use" rather than a psychology of "possession." He recognized the significance of heredity and environment in providing the raw materials, or building blocks of life. However, these factors, according to Adler, served only as parameters, or constraints, within which individual development would unfold. They were not hard and invariant determinants of future development. He emphasized the unique and idiosyncratic manner in which individuals perceive and make use of their aptitudes, abilities, and experiences. For example, a child with a measured Intelligence Quotient (IQ) of 120 may or may not be successful in school-related pursuits. How the child views his or her intellectual ability and cultivates it through effort, practice, and persistence will affect subsequent performance and achievement more than the IQ itself.

Psychopathology, in the Adlerian view, is a reflection of "discouragement" rather than sickness. When individuals cannot cope effectively and constructively with feelings of inferiority, they become discouraged and, as a consequence, develop disordered beliefs, emotions, and behaviors in their efforts to manage the difficulties of life. Psychotherapy is essentially a process of encouragement and reeducation. The aim is to help clients develop the courage to face life's tasks and challenges directly, and to awaken their social interest. The primary ingredient in therapy is the encouraging relationship between therapist and client. The analytical phase of the process focuses on the goals of the client which, typically, are mistaken, distorted, or exaggerated. It also addresses the useful and useless aspects of the behavioral style that the individual has chosen to achieve his or her goals.

## HISTORY AND STATUS

Alfred Adler was born in 1870, in Vienna, Austria. He was the second of six children. His ordinal position among his siblings and serious health problems experienced during childhood had a significant impact on the development of his theoretical formulations. For example, he believed that position in the family constellation served as an important shaping influence on the personality development of the emerging child. In addition, his belief in compensatory striving to overcome felt inferiority can be traced to his experience of fragile health. Adler graduated from the University of Vienna in 1895 where he received his medical degree and subsequently entered practice as an opthalomologist. He shifted to general practice eventually, then to neurology and psychiatry.

In 1902, Adler was invited by Sigmund Freud to attend the Wednesday evening discussions of the Vienna Psychoanalytic Society. He was elected president of the society in 1910. However, growing differences between these pioneering theoreticians brought a strain to their relationship. In particular, they disagreed more and more on the (a) role of the unconscious, (b) importance of sexual instincts, (c) defensive role of the ego, and (d) unity of the neuroses. In 1911, Adler resigned as president of the Psychoanalytic Society and formed the Society for Free Psychoanalytic Research. In time, he changed the name to Individual Psychology, by which name it is referred to today.

One of Adler's most significant practical contributions was the establishment of numerous child guidance clinics in Vienna. He envisioned these clinics as serving the treatment needs of children, adolescents, and their families. In addition, they were to serve as vehicles for training physicians, social workers, teachers, and parents. In the context of these clinics, psychological education was equally available to the professional and layperson alike. During the 1920s, there were 22 Adlerian-based child guidance clinics in Vienna. The movement spread rapidly and at one point there were close to 50 clinics spread throughout Europe.

Adler's principal approach in teaching his theory and methods at these clinics was demonstration. He would conduct public demonstration sessions with individual patients and their families in front of an assembled group of professionals and interested laypeople. This was a controversial approach that had never been used. Some of his detractors believed that such psychological treatment should be reserved for the privacy of the consultation office. Adler, on the other hand, believed that the behavior of the child and the family was of public concern and not solely a private issue. In addition, he felt that this public counseling/consultation format helped reduce the mystique surrounding the counseling process. In this regard, he framed the presentation of his published papers and public lectures in down-to-earth, commonsense language that could be understood by the professional and layperson alike.

In 1926, Adler was invited to the United States to lecture and demonstrate his approaches. These visits became more and more frequent over the next 8 years. He finally fled Austria in advance of the Nazi domination of Europe and settled in the United States in 1934. He served on the medical faculty of the Long Island (NY) College of Medicine and lectured extensively in the United States and abroad. Adler died in 1937 while on a lecture tour in Scotland.

One of Adler's students and subsequent colleagues, Rudolph Dreikurs, assumed leadership of the Individual Psychology movement after Adler's death. He promoted the development of child guidance clinics and family education centers here in the United States and continued the public forum counseling/consultation process begun by Adler in Vienna. Dreikurs founded the Alfred Adler Institute of Chicago which is the largest training center for practitioners of Individual Psychology in the United States.

He made numerous contributions to both the theory and practice of Individual Psychology. One of his most useful theoretical contributions related to the understanding of children's misbehavior. From his clinical observations, he identified four common goals, or purposes, of misbehavior: attention seeking, power, revenge, and assumed disability. This concept serves as the centerpiece of most Adlerian-based parent and family education programs. Dreikurs was a prolific lecturer and writer. Among his most notable contributions were the following: *Children: The Challenge* (Dreikurs & Soltz, 1964), *Logical Consequences* (Dreikurs & Grey, 1968), and *Psychology in the Classroom* (Dreikurs, 1957).

Adlerian Psychology is currently supported by the North American Society of Adlerian Psychology (NASAP), which holds an annual convention. There are also numerous state and provincial associations throughout the United States and Canada. The University of Texas Press publishes a quarterly periodical, *The Journal of Individual Psychology*. This is the principal organ devoted to the examination and dissemination of ideas related to this theoretical school. In addition, the International Association of Individual Psychology publishes the *Individual Psychology Newsletter* and sponsors a quadriennial International Congress of Individual Psychology.

Institutes that offer advanced training and certification in Adlerian approaches to individual, family, and group psychotherapy, as well as family education, can be found in Berkeley, Chicago, Cincinnati, Cleveland, Dayton, Fort Wayne, Minneapolis, Montreal, New York, St. Louis, Toronto, and Vancouver. The Adler School of Professional Psychology in Chicago offers the doctoral degree (Psy.D.) in Clinical Psychology.

## OVERVIEW OF THEORY

### Basic Theory and Assumptions

The general assumptions underlying Adler's theory of personality are that people are responsible, creative, unified, social beings whose behavior is purposive and goal directed. While antecedent conditions and environmental contingencies (or consequences) can exert a strong influence on behavior, Adler believed that self-created goals and purposes explain the greatest proportion of variance in individual behavior. The individual's life style represents his or her unique and characteristic mode of thinking, feeling, and behaving in response to life's challenges. The lifestyle may be faulty and, therefore, dysfunctional, because of strong feelings of inferiority and diminished social interest. An individual with such a faulty lifestyle is considered to be "discouraged." The six primary propositions of the theory follow:

1. *The fundamental motivational force underlying all behavior is a striving from a felt minus to a felt plus, from a feeling of inferiority to a feeling of significance, completion, and perfection.* The condition of the human infant at birth is essentially one of helpless dependence on its caretakers for survival. Adler theorized that this condition of helplessness (felt minus) stimulated a compensatory striving to overcome and move eventually toward a felt plus. In some individuals, the direction of their striving to overcome will take a constructive and socially useful path. For example, they may overcome their early feelings of inadequacy by developing successful relationships, making solid and lasting friendships, or becoming competent workers and providers. Others, however, may take a destructive or socially useless path in their striving to overcome. These individuals may cope with their perceived inadequacies by dominating, controlling or bullying other people. Some, on the other hand, may become adept and skilled criminals. Still others, may compensate for their felt inadequacy by manipulating others into their service through failure, assumed disability, depression, or anxiety.

2. *Human behavior is purposive and goal directed.* While not denying the significant impact of antecedent factors on personality development and human behavior, Adler eschewed the linear cause-and-effect relationship that so dominated the empiricist tradition of American psychology at the time. He believed that behavior could be best understood and explained by virtue of the goal or purpose it served. At the simple biological level, he would view sneezing from the standpoint of purpose: to expel an irritant from the nose or nasal passages. Similarly, depression would not be conceptualized as being "caused" by a loss or a defeat in a person's life. It would be viewed as a creation of the individual to exempt him or her from responsibilities and obligations of life perceived as overwhelming, threatening, or impossible. According to Adler, the individual's goal was the ultimate "cause" or independent variable underlying behavior:

> If we know the goal of a person, we can undertake to explain and to understand what the psychological phenomena want to tell us, why they were created, what the person has

made of his innate material, why he has made it just so and not differently, how his character traits, his feelings and emotions, his logic, his morals, and his aesthetics must be constituted in order that he may arrive at his goal. (Ansbacher & Ansbacher, 1956, p. 196)

Goals are not necessarily understood by the individual who is motivated by them. A 6-year-old boy who displays symptoms of fear and anxiety over going to bed by himself is not consciously aware that the purpose of the symptom is to keep his parents involved and be at the center of their attention. However, an analysis of the behavior in terms of its "effects" often shows the result is intense parental involvement in a task that the child could and should be able to handle without parental assistance. Further assessment may reveal that the child is not receiving sufficient parental attention at legitimate and appropriate times. On the other hand, it may also reveal that this child has developed an exaggerated goal to be at the center of parental attention even though sufficient attention has been provided.

3. *Personality is organized in a unified, holistic, and self-consistent fashion.* All psychological processes such a perception, cognition, memory, and emotion are organized in a unified fashion from the standpoint of the individual's dominant goal. For example, a child whose goal is to be the center of adult attention, will perceive situations, encode them into memory, and recall the past in terms of this priority. The child will generate emotions and select behaviors that serve the functional purpose of goal attainment. Adler referred to this unified organization of personality as the "Life Style" (Adler, 1963b). More specifically, this concept of lifestyle represents the cognitive organization of the personality in terms of attitudes, beliefs, convictions, and conclusions about self and the world. It is this cognitive organization that allows the individual to order, understand, predict, and control life's experiences. The dominant goals and supporting cognitive schemas of the lifestyle are firmly established at an early age. Subsequently, one's approach to life is geared more toward seeking confirmation than toward disconfirmation of existing convictions and conclusions. In this fashion, the individual stabilizes and strengthens his or her existing cognitive representational system or lifestyle.

4. *Behavior occurs in a social context and therefore has social meaning.* Adler believed in the social embeddedness of each individual and the adaptive value of social relationships for individual survival as well as for the survival and advancement of the species. Thus the desire to attach to other humans and belong to one's family, peer, and social group is one of the ways in which humans strive to overcome their insufficiencies in the face of a complex world. Individual Psychology posits that each individual is born with an innate disposition toward *Gemeinschaftsgefuhl,* or social interest. This is a feeling of connection with one's fellow humans and a willingness to contribute to the common good of society. For this disposition to flourish, however, it must be cultivated and developed by the child's caretakers. This tendency is represented in the newborn child by the sucking, grasping, and orienting reflexes that naturally connect him or her to the social environment. Through healthy parenting and constructive modeling experiences, the innate disposition for social interest becomes

socialized into complex phenomena characterized by empathy, compassion, and cooperation. Gemeinschaftsgefuhl is a primary criterion for mental health.

5. *Behavior is assessed and evaluated within the social system.* Given the theoretical assumption regarding the social nature of behavior, any assessment or evaluation of individual behavior would involve an examination of the social context, or system within which it occurred. Thus, the nuclear family, extended family, peer group, classroom, and any other significant individuals whose presence or absence may impact the child in question are included in the evaluation. Most of the significant challenges and difficulties of life are social in nature. Alder identified three major life tasks that confront each of us: friends/social relationships, work/occupation, and love/intimacy. Each of these tasks requires the individual to cooperate, negotiate, share, and form constructive relationships to achieve satisfactory outcomes. The task of work and occupation for children and adolescents is school. While this may appear on the surface to be more of an individual versus a social task, some of the most troublesome and pernicious school problems are interpersonal. Fighting, opposition to authority, destructive competition and passive-aggressive resistence are typically more problematic than children's inability to master particular subject matter.

6. *The actions of an individual are best understood by the application of idiographic laws.* Nomothetic laws are those that explain human behavior in terms of universal principles that apply to most people, most of the time. For example, Thorndike's (1913) "Law of Effect" or the phenomenon of attraction between the sexes could be considered nomothetic laws. While these laws may be helpful in understanding the behavior of people in general, they are not useful in understanding the behavior of a particular individual. Individual Psychology emphasizes the lawful nature of individual behavior and attempts to identify those idiographic laws that explain specific behavioral acts of a particular individual in a particular situation.

The statement "Children become angry when they experience frustration" is a fairly common observation that represents a nomothetic law about behavior. "Billy becomes angry and aggressive when his teacher, Mrs. Reynolds, denies his request to go to the bathroom" may characterize a consistent and predictable pattern of behavior that represents an idiographic law for one particular child, during a particular circumstance. His emotional and behavioral response may not be the same with Mr. Jones, the physical education teacher. The nomothetic law gives a general frame of reference without which the idiographic statement has little meaning. However, without the idiographic law, the nomothetic rule is only an abstraction that fails to help in understanding this particular child and his behavior.

Idiographic laws can be discerned by observing patterns of behavior that remain consistent over time and are within particular contexts. They are regularly employed by the individual to achieve a particular goal. Billy, in the preceding example, may become angry and aggressive when any adult says "no," or thwarts his desires. He may persist in this behavior despite aversive consequences. It would be reasonable to hypothesize an idiographic law for Billy that is characterized by a generalized *belief* of entitlement ("I deserve to have my way"), an interpersonal *goal* ("I will overpower anyone who gets in my way"), a characteristic style of *behavior* (aggression), and an *emotion* that fuels and gives force to the behavior (anger). Thus, the principle of idiography provides a frame of reference for understanding the lawful, and therefore, predictable nature of Billy's behavior.

## ADDITIONAL THEORETICAL CONCEPTS

### Lifestyle

In the process of growing and developing during the early years of life, children gradually form conceptions of life and the experiences they encounter. These conceptions may be thought of as "rules" or generalizations. These rules are limited by the child's age and cognitive development, yet, they are necessary to aid the child in organizing and bringing stability to a complex and fluid world. These convictions, conclusions, and generalizations, are the beginnings of a cognitive map or schema. This cognitive map is what Adlerians refer to as the Style of Life. According to Mosak (1989) the lifestyle includes the aspirations and goals selected by the individual to ensure security and survival in the world (e.g., I must be the center of attention, I must avoid difficult challenges where I might not succeed, I must have the service and support of strong, competent others). In addition, it encompasses (a) a conception of self (I am . . . good, bad, competent, lovable, etc.), (b) a self-ideal (I should be . . . first, best, worst, helpful, etc.), (c) a view of the physical and social world (Life is . . . exciting, confusing, dangerous; People are . . . trustworthy, caring, competitive, etc.), and (d) a set of ethical convictions (the individual's personal standards of right and wrong). As the child matures, the lifestyle solidifies. It seeks confirmation and reinforcement. It is less and less open to information that may dispute its essential "truths." Stability and reliability of one's reality is chosen in favor of validity. Thus, dissonant information is typically resolved in the direction of maintaining cognitive consistency. Much of this information about self and the world can be considered tacit knowledge (Guidano & Liotti, 1983) and therefore unavailable for conscious, reflective examination. It was developed during a period when the child possessed limited verbal skills. It was coded and stored anologically in contrast to the analytical processes available to adolescents and adults that result in knowledge being more conscious and explicit. Once it forms a stable core, the lifestyle subsequently directs all other cognitive, emotional and behavioral processes. Thus, selectivity of perception and memory are guided by the truths embodied in the person's convictions about self, others and the world. For example, if my lifestyle convictions schematize the world as predatory and dangerous, I will tend to see danger where there is none and to exaggerate the threat of danger where it does exist.

### The Four (4) Goals of Children's Misbehavior

Clinical observation of children in many settings led Dreikurs (1948) to speculate that four basic goals were at the root of most childhood misbehavior:

1. Attention seeking.
2. Power.
3. Revenge.
4. Assumed disability.

He also noted that behaviors reflecting these goals were primarily directed at the significant adults (parents, teachers, coaches, extended family) in the child's life. The child who is *attention seeking* (Goal 1) believes that he or she is insignificant and unimportant unless at the center of adult attention. The child may use constructive behavior (success, charm, cute, and precocious remarks) or useless behavior (class clown, show-off, bashfulness, fearfulness) to accomplish the goal. The more uncertain the child is about his or her place of significance in the social environment, the more intense will be the goal of attention seeking and the behavior that supports the goal. Young children typically demonstrate a good deal of attention-seeking behavior; and parents need to provide much positive attention to satisfy basic needs for food, skin contact, and psychological nourishment. As children get older, however, they must be trained to accommodate to the social reality that attention can't be constant and, at times, must be shared with others. Too much or too little attention by parents may leave a child overemphasizing or questioning his or her value as an individual or place of importance in the family. Under these circumstances, then, the goal of excessive attention seeking may develop.

Children dominated by the goal of *power* (Goal 2) demonstrate an aversion to control by adults and other authority figures. They may display openly rebellious behavior such as arguing, contradicting, temper tantrums, and oppositional acts. On the other hand, they may respond in a more passive-aggressive manner with laziness, forgetting, and stubborness. These children gain a sense of significance and self-importance by showing adults that they will not be constricted by their rules, nor will they be overpowered by threats of punishment. Goal 2 children will often lure adults into power struggles to demonstrate their strength and adults' impotence in controlling them. For example, Reggie, a 13-year-old eighth grader would get out of his seat in language arts class without permission. Reggie would walk slowly, with a cocky swagger, to the pencil sharpener at the front of the classroom. When the teacher, Mrs. Adams, would remind Reggie of the "requesting permission" rule, and ask him to return to his seat, Reggie would ignore her and begin sharpening his pencil. A power struggle had been established. This goal, and the behavior that supports it, may develop as a result of inappropriate modeling. Parents, television, and movie heros as well as teachers often model the use of power, control, threats, and domination as a method of dealing with interpersonal problems. In addition, parents and teachers who acquiese and give in to children who use power to "get their way" are simply reinforcing the power goal and the particular behaviors that the child employs to attain that goal.

Typically, power struggles result in an escalating cycle of conflict between the child and adult. Neither wishes to give in, for this means "losing" the fight, and more significantly, losing self-esteem and a sense of personal autonomy. Consequently, as the struggles become more intense, the likelihood of adults trying to subdue the child through the use of threats (You'll be grounded for the next month), humiliation (You're a selfish little brat; you make my life miserable), or physical punishment (hitting, slapping) dramatically increase. These actions may subdue the child and end the immediate struggle. However, they typically result in the child feeling unimportant, badly about self, and hurt. In response, children sometimes want to retaliate or get back for the real or imagined hurts that have been inflicted on them. This desire represents the goal of *revenge* (Goal 3).

This goal is characterized by behavior that is designed to inflict hurt back onto adults or onto the society that those adults represent. Thus, lying, stealing, cheating, cursing at teachers and parents, and destructive and violent acts become the favored behavioral style of the revenge-driven individual. Children are perceptive of the important values and vulnerabilities of parents. Thus, if they feel that a hurtful action has been taken against them, they will often strike back in an area of parental vulnerability. For example, it is not uncommon for Goal 3 children of teachers to do poorly in school, for the daughter of a minister to become pregnant, or for the son of a counselor to strike back through substance abuse. They choose the problem area that will have maximum retaliatory impact on the parents who have hurt them. If these actions fail to prop up the child's deteriorating sense of personal significance, he or she may eventually sink into the final goal, *assumed disability* (Goal 4).

At this point, the child ceases to be an *active* behavior problem for parents and teachers. There is a significant reduction in conflict and acting-out behavior. This is replaced with a level of inactivity and passivity that reflects an attitude of giving up and not caring about school, family, or friends. These children sleep or daydream in the classroom. They do little or no academic work. Their involvement in hobbies, extracurricular activities, and social activities plummets. Much of their time at home is spent isolated in their bedroom, watching television or listening to music. The goal of the child here is to get people to give up on him or her. Why? For this child, life has become a series of defeats, failures, humiliations, and hurts. So, if he can get parents and teachers to give up on him, he can then escape the countless day-to-day occasions where his insignificance, incompetence, and helplessness are reaffirmed. This child is the most discouraged of all misbehaving children. Depression and the risk of suicide dramatically increase for these children.

## Birth Order and Family Constellation

The child's family of origin is one of the strongest and most significant influences on subsequent personality development. Every child strives to establish a position of importance within this environment. One might be the "boss," another the "clown," while still another might be the "helper." The child actively participates with parents and other family members in shaping, and developing his or her own unique personality. The family, however, establishes the initial coordinates that help frame the child's perception of social reality. In particular, Adler noted the birth-order positions in the constellation of siblings as a variable influencing development:

It is a common fallacy to imagine that children of the same family are formed in the same environment. Of course, there is much which is the same for all children in the same home, but the psychological situation of each child is individual and differs from that of the others, because of the order of their succession. (Adler, 1929, p. 96)

The term "family constellation" encompasses all significant members who will interact with and have an influence on the child. Thus, parents, siblings, grandparents, stepparents, aunts, uncles, and even deceased family members can be a part of the family constellation. However, the constellation of siblings in the nuclear family has an exceedingly strong impact on development. The psychological position of the child within this constellation is more important than the ordinal position of birth. For example, a secondborn child whose firstborn sibling suffers from a physical or mental disability may strive for and capture the psychological position of "first." A "change of life" baby, whose next oldest sibling is 8 years older, would be an ordinal youngest, but a psychological "only." Furthermore, psychological position is determined not only by objective factors, but also by the subjective perception of the child and the interpretation that he or she makes of a given situation. For example, an only child may revel in the attention provided by two conscientious parents. On the other hand, this child may feel deprived and disadvantaged at not having a sibling who might be a ready-made playmate.

Despite the variability attributed to individual differences in responding, Adler (1931) observed some typical characteristics and problems associated with specific ordinal positions. The firstborn is the initial receptacle for parents' expectations, aspirations, and ambitions. Consequently, this child often experiences the pressure of these expectations and the anxiety of living up to parental dreams. The firstborn is also typically impressed with the prestige and power associated with being number one. He or she is the biggest, fastest, strongest and possesses greater verbal fluency than his or her siblings for quite a few years. These children are impressed, therefore, with the importance of being number one and often conclude that their place of significance is tied to being the first or best. This tendency may find a useful expression through responsible behavior, high achievement motivation and caretaking of younger siblings. On the other hand, it may find a socially useless expression through control, domination, bullying, and the drive to be number one regardless of personal or social consequences.

The firstborn child is generally given a great deal of parental attention and may become comfortably accustomed to this prized and special position. When a second child is born into the family, the parental focus of attention shifts rather abruptly to the newborn. It is not uncommon for the firstborn to suffer what Adler called "dethronement" (Ansbacher & Ansbacher, 1956). If parents have not adequately prepared their child for the arrival of a new family member, the oldest may become negative, competitive, exhibit regressive behavior, and misbehave in an effort to regain "paradise lost." Inappropriate and negative responses (punishment, criticism, ignoring) on the part of parents to this rather typical scenario can contribute to the firstborn losing confidence, becoming discouraged, and adopting a negative perspective on self, life, and relationships.

The *secondborn* child, in an effort to carve out a unique position of significance for him- or herself, often develops personality traits and a behavioral style that are very different from, if not opposite to, the first child. Thus, if the firstborn is quiet, calm, helpful, and obedient, the second is likely to be more loud, rambunctious, and oppositional. The differences in personality are usually accentuated when adjacent siblings are close in age (2–4 years) and of the same sex. When a third child arrives on the scene, the secondborn often feels squeezed out and excluded as parents shift their attentional and emotional energy to the youngest and newest family member. This "squeezed" middle child often reacts with anger toward parents, resentment toward siblings, and an increase in oppositional and disruptive behavior.

By the time the *youngest* child has arrived, parents have typically become more comfortable with the parental role, and are less anxious about the day-to-day problems of child-rearing. Thus, the lastborn experiences a family atmosphere that is usually more relaxed and less rigid. With parents and older brothers and sisters in a caretaking role, however, the youngest is sometimes pampered. Too much is done for the child and too little is expected in return. Thus, the youngest may come to expect special service and treatment, and an exemption from the usual chores and responsibilities of life as a result of being the "baby." The youngest may cultivate this role of entitlement and privilege. On the other hand, he or she might strive to compete with and eventually overtake older siblings in one or more of their areas of strength.

## VIEW OF PSYCHOPATHOLOGY

The very term "psychopathology" presents a curious dilemma for the Adlerian therapist. While a medical practitioner himself, Alder avoided the application of the traditional disease model to the understanding and treatment of psychological/behavioral disorders, unless there happened to be an organic basis or involvement in the problem. Adler (1963a) viewed behaviorally and emotionally disordered individuals as discouraged rather than sick. More specifically, discouraged persons perceived themselves to be inadequate in the face of life's day-to-day challenges. The root of this discouragement appears to lie in three basic factors: (a) overambition ("I must be better than others"), (b) lack of courage ("I'm not up to the challenge"), and (c) pessimistic attitude ("Things won't work out well for me") (Dinkmeyer, Pew, & Dinkmeyer, 1979). The main life challenges facing the typical child or adolescent revolve around school, friends, and family. Solving the problems raised by these challenges requires a considerable measure of courage, optimism, cooperation, and social feeling (Gemeinschaftsgefuhl).

> Confronted with any of these problems, the individual who does not possess a sufficient amount of social feeling will be emotionally unprepared for these tasks, will fear failure, will shrink away from contact and feel excessively inadequate (inferior). (Adler, 1963b, p. v)

In the face of this felt inferiority, children will attempt to protect their self-esteem and self-worth by mobilizing what Adler (1963b) referred to"safe-guarding devices." Shulman and Mosak (1967) identified four different styles of safeguarding self-esteem through various "distancing" methods:

> "Moving backward" which includes suicide, agoraphobia, compulsive blushing, migraine, anorexia nervosa; "standing still" as in psychic impotence, psychogenic asthma, anxiety attacks . . . ; "hesitation and back and forth" as in all methods of killing time such as procrastination, compulsions, pathological pedantry; and "construction of obstacles," primarily psychosomatic symptoms. (p. 80)

Depression, fears, anxieties, rebellion, delinquency, as well as thought disorders, are all methods which the discouraged child may use to compensate for his or her inferiority feelings and lack of social interest. In a way, these problems may be considered "sideshows" that distract them and others from failures and inadequacies in the "main events" of life. The depressed, fearful, or anxious child may secure close emotional and physical support from parents and/or teachers while being exempted from the same rigors of social and academic life required of his or her peers. The oppositional or conduct-disordered child may defeat parents and teachers in their efforts to control and manage his behavior. Thus, he is allowed to operate by a different set of rules, and conventions than typically apply to the social situation. Such children pay a significant price for their psychopathology. However, the payoff in terms of special treatment, exemption from normal expectations, and avoidance of responsibilities is more than sufficient to sustain these psychopathological conditions. These distracting sideshows are not consciously contrived by the child. However, they are most definitely self-selected creations of the discouraged individual who deems him- or herself inadequate to face the direct tests of reality.

One of the primary tenets of Individual Psychology, that all behavior is purposive and goal directed, applies equally to both healthy and pathological behavior. In an effort to understand what the child is trying to achieve with the symptomatic behavior, the therapist would examine its effects or results. As stated earlier, most childhood misbehavior can be understood by the four goals of attention-seeking, power, revenge, and assumed disability. The choice of a particular style of symptomatic behavior depends, in part, on the goal that the behavior is designed to serve (Shulman & Mosak, 1967). For example, the cluster of behaviors descriptive of Oppositional Defiant Disorder (American Psychiatric Association, 1994) appears particularly well suited to the goal of power. The child who frequently loses his temper, argues with adults, refuses adult requests and deliberately annoys others is opposing the adult world and its demands. By employing this style, the child or adolescent provokes power struggles with parents and teachers. Most untrained adults are easily engaged by these power tactics. They attempt to reassert their authority and control. But seldom do they win the battle. Thus, the child demonstrates his objective: "You can't control me. I can and will do as I please." Some of these behaviors represent developmentally appropriate attempts on the part of adolescents to experiment with their emerging sense of autonomy as they begin the process of disengagement from parents and the world of traditional authority. Inappropriate responses by authority figures to dominate and control the child however, may stimulate all-out war where the frequency, intensity, and range of oppositional behaviors warrants the diagnosis of Oppositional Defiant Disorder.

Similarly, affective disorders such as Generalized Anxiety Disorder, and Social Phobia (Social Anxiety Disorder), thrust the child into the forefront of adult attention. Excessive anxiety and worry, crying, freezing, avoidance, and intense distress on the part of children are symptoms that most adults take seriously. The attention is typically sympathetic and solicitous, and often results in the child being elevated to a special role usually accorded to sick people. Special accommodation is often allowed to the anxious child, as well as exemption from environmental stressors (e.g., chores, difficult school assignments) that some adults may theorize to be the cause of the child's anxiety. Many of these adult responses provide the special attention that the child is convinced he or she must have to be happy and to feel secure. Thus, the goal of attention seeking and the particular behavioral style (anxiety/fear) employed by the child is reinforced. It is now likely that when this child's lifestyle clashes with the demands of reality in the future, an anxiety or phobic reaction will ensue as a preferred problem-solving approach.

Adlerian psychology proposes that the origin of behavioral and emotional disorders can be linked to some common underlying childhood conditions and experiences. These conditions are not causal in a hard, deterministic sense, yet they provide a fertile breeding ground for the development of the "neurotic disposition" (Adler, 1972). First, children born sickly, with infirmities, chronic illness, and developmental disabilities begin life at a significant disadvantage. They often experience their own bodies as a liability, and life as a continuous chore to be endured. Such children, quite naturally, may be overfocused on their own sensations, feelings, and limitations. They may overanticipate the difficulty that life presents, rather than the excitement of opportunity that it offers. Finally, the focus on self that naturally emerges may inhibit the development of social feeling and the spirit of cooperation that is so essential for social problem-solving.

The second condition that contributes to the development of psychopathology is characterized by neglect, ridicule, and abuse. Physical beatings, verbal put-downs and humiliation, ignoring and investing little time into children are so common in our society that we have become immune to the acts themselves and to their effects on children. According to Adler:

> Such a child has never known what love and cooperation can be; his interpretation of life does not include these friendly forces. . . . He has found society cold to him and will expect it always to be cold. . . . He will thus be suspicious of others and unable to trust himself. (Ansbacher & Ansbacher, 1956, pp. 370–371)

These children will find it difficult to experience empathy, compassion or tenderness toward others because fundamentally they dislike or even hate themselves. Interactions with parents and caretakers have communicated a message that the children are bad, inappropriate, and a burden. Thus, they do not feel worthy of love or affection. They may, therefore, adopt neglect, ridicule and abuse in their own interpersonal relationships because it was modeled for them.

The third condition that interferes with healthy development is pampering and spoiling. This represents doing for children what they can and should do for themselves, and shielding them too much from the normal stresses of life. It is not uncommon, in middle-class families in our society, for parents to do too much for their children with the mistaken belief that they are being good parents. A few common examples of pampering are completing the child's homework assignments, doing the bulk of the work on a "science fair" project, cleaning the child's room, or preparing a special meal when the child expresses displeasure over the meal being served to the rest of the family. Such indulgence establishes in these children the expectation of immediate success while bypassing the required effort. It produces a self-ideal ("I should be successful"), while simultaneously undermining the confidence and strength of the child to produce the outcomes and results without external assistance. In addition, pampering produces a dependency on others. These children come to be more reliant on strong, competent others than on a strong, competent self. Finally, pampering seems to result in an exaggerated attitude of specialness and entitlement that interferes with healthy social adjustment and cooperative peer relationships.

Finally, the fourth condition is a general societal climate of competition that exaggerates and intensifies the tendency of children and adolescents to strive toward self-serving goals and accomplishments at the expense of others and to the detriment of cooperative, social living. Competition can be fueled by adults "playing favorites" with children, unfair and unequal distribution of resources and reinforcers, too much praising of children in the presence of their peers, and comparing children to their peers or classmates. Problematic behaviors such as stealing, cheating, lying, criticizing, and bragging are stimulated by highly competitive environments. Lifestyle goals (Nikelly, 1971) associated with this condition are (a) superiority and self-aggrandizement coupled with the depreciation of others, (b) getting and acquiring (material, wealth, recognition) at the expense of others, (c) being "right" or correct by emphasizing the mistakes and weaknesses of others.

Given the view that the lifestyle is less stable and more open to influence during childhood and adolescence, psychological intervention during this time period has a greater probability of affecting positive change than in later life. Thus, distorted beliefs, problematic emotions, and self-defeating/uncooperative behaviors are responsive to a range of counseling and psychotherapeutic interventions.

## GENERAL THERAPEUTIC GOALS AND TECHNIQUES

The Adlerian perspective views psychotherapy as a collaborative educational process between therapist and client. It is designed to be a "corrective learning experience" where the client, hopefully, comes to understand and correct distortions, exaggerations, and mistakes in the cognitive schema. It is similar to the "collaborative empiricism" described by Guidano and Liotti (1983) in their discussion of the relationship between therapist and client from a cognitive therapy orientation. In addition, useless and counterproductive behaviors that contribute to ineffectiveness and unhappiness are targeted for alteration. Fundamentally, however, the Adlerian approach is more strongly oriented to a modification of the client's fundamental beliefs and "motives" as opposed to the behaviors that spring from these motives.

Mosak (1989) outlined six principal goals of the therapeutic process:

1. Strengthen the client's Gemeinschaftsgefuhl, or social interest.
2. Diminish the client's feeling of weakness, inability, and inferiority.
3. Recognize the client's strengths and resources; develop courage.
4. Alter the client's lifestyle; change faulty assumptions and beliefs; replace big distortions with relatively smaller distortions.
5. Change mistaken goals (motivation).
6. Help the client to become more cooperative and contributing in social relationships, and adopt an attitude of social equality.

Adlerian theory predicts that clients who attain these goals will develop closer and more fulfilling relationships with friends and work colleagues; they will be more effective social problem-solvers; they will be more accepting of self and others, and more courageous. Thus, they will be able to face the difficulties and challenges of life directly without the sideshows, distancing techniques, and distracting psychological/behavioral symptoms that previously characterized their approach to life.

The therapeutic outcomes identified in the preceding list are facilitated by four main process goals that coincide with the four phases of counseling or therapy.

## Phase 1. Establishment of a Cooperative and Collaborative Therapeutic Relationship

Adler believed that the key to establishing a "good" therapeutic relationship lay in the therapist's ability to enter the client's subjective, phenomenological world (Ansbacher & Ansbacher, 1956). To do this, the therapist must possess and demonstrate empathy. According to Adler, empathy was achieved in the following fashion: "We must be able to see with his eyes and listen with his ears" (1931, p. 72). Thus, the counselor listens carefully, respectfully, and nonjudgementally in an effort to communicate an understanding of the client's feeling and experiences, as well as a belief in the client's ability to change. During this phase, according to Mosak (1987), the counselor must convey *faith* in self, the client, and the therapy process, *hopefulness* that progress will result from the therapeutic collaboration, and *love* by treating the client with dignity, worth, and caring.

Goal alignment between the therapist and client is an important aspect of relationship building. Here, expectations and goals are explicitly examined and agreed on. If goal alignment is not achieved at the outset and continually monitored, the process is likely not to get started or to break down in midstream. For example, many adolescents initially enter therapy because they were "sent" by parents or other adult authority figures. Until the therapist and client can agree on a goal to which the teen is willing to commit, little or no progress will occur. Some clients who perceive themselves as continually being dumped on by others may be committed to having the therapist play the role of sympathetic supporter of "poor little me." It may not be part of these clients' agenda to examine and come to grips with their goal of securing sympathy through assuming the lifestyle of the "victim." The counselor must avoid this trap and turn the conversation to the issue of therapeutic goals.

It is believed that a more positive therapeutic connection can be made through focusing on client strengths and through the use of *encouragement* than by continually concentrating on client deficiencies. Thus, the counselor may spend some time examining the client's interests, successes, and perceived assets. In addition, clients reveal many characteristics and traits in a negative, pejorative fashion and may not be aware that the same qualities have an upside. For example, traits such as emotional, compulsive, and paranoid may be reframed as sensitive, organized and vigilant.

The relationship is the vehicle for change. It provides the occasion for self-reflection in the presence of a caring and (hopefully) skilled collaborator. Rather than allowing the child or adolescent to recreate the problematic relationship patterns that characterize his or her interactions with other adults (parents and teachers, etc.), the therapist recognizes, then foils these negative interpersonal scripts.The client is then invited to examine what just occurred in the relationship.

### Phase 2. Analysis and Assessment: Uncovering the Beliefs, Goals, and Behaviors That Make Up and Reflect the Client's Lifestyle

This phase actually begins with the first contact between the therapist and the client. Even though relationship building is the primary objective in Phase 1, the therapist is already observing the verbal and behavioral data which reflect the client's underlying convictions, values and goals. Phase 2 is characterized by (a) understanding the client's lifestyle, and (b) determining how this lifestyle affects client functioning in terms of the major life tasks. The lifestyle of the client emerges in bits and pieces through explicit and implicit verbal communications, overt actions, and subtle facial and bodily expressions. Gradually, these pieces begin to reveal patterns and themes that characterize the motif or style of the client's approach to life. Thus, the therapist is somewhat like a detective during this phase as he or she observes, explores, develops tentative hypotheses, retains those which are validated through confirmatory data, and discards or revises others. Eventually, the puzzle of the client's dynamics and why he or she is experiencing problems begins to emerge.

While the analysis may be conducted in an open-ended fashion with clients leading into their areas of concern, the therapist may also ask specific questions to zero in on unique issues. Some areas of inquiry and questions are as follows:

- *Self.* How would you describe yourself? What do you like about yourself? What do you dislike about yourself?

- *Social Relationships*. Who are your friends? How would you describe them? How do you feel about your friends? Describe the kids that you don't like.
- *School/Work.* What do you like about school/work? What do you dislike about school/work? In what areas are you successful. In what areas are you not successful?
- *Sexuality/Love (Adolescence).* How do you feel about being a boy/girl? Have you ever wished that you were the opposite sex? What kinds of relationships do you have with girls/boys?

A useful assessment strategy that can be employed in counseling both children and adolescents is an assessment of a typical day in the life of the family. This technique provides an ecological assessment of one of the most important social environments that impacts child and adolescent development as well as current behavior. Based on the theoretical premise (introduced earlier) that all behavior occurs in a social context and thus should be assessed in those contexts, Adlerians have a bias toward including the family in the treatment of children and adolescents. Information about the "typical day" is customarily elicited from the parents or primary caretakers. The focus is usually a school day rather than a weekend day. The assessment begins with a step-by-step description of the first person in the family to get up in the morning, and the pattern followed. This person is tracked, as well as each subsequent family member as he or she awakens and moves through the day. Of particular diagnostic significance are the "critical incidents" where the therapist elicits a description of each family member's approach to the daily challenges of living and the responses of other family members to that individual. Some of these critical incidents are as follows: **[Morning]** getting one's self up; getting dressed; taking care of personal hygiene; cleaning/straightening one's bedroom/bathroom; preparing, eating and cleaning up after breakfast; getting organized for school/work; leaving on time for school/work; **[Afternoon/Evening]** getting home from school/work; time spent between getting home and dinner; preparing, eating and cleaning up after dinner; time spent between dinner and bedtime; bedtime routine. These critical incidents represent situations for constructive action or socially useless behavior. In addition, they represent occasions for interpersonal interaction between and among family members. An examination of the typical day often gives the therapist a picture of the family lifestyle.

For example, 10-year-old Steve, the only child of dual career parents, was referred by the school counselor because of poor school performance (although possessing above-average ability) and passive-resistant behavior toward teachers. He was very forgetful as he lost books and assignments; he seldom had the required pencils and notebooks. Teachers described him as in "outer space" because he did not pay attention; he was always doodling or daydreaming. An assessment of a "typical day" in the family found dad awakening at 5:00 A.M., showering, dressing quickly, and leaving for work before the others even stirred. Mother awakened at 6:00 A.M., showered, dressed, and then gave Steve a wake-up call at 6:30. Steve would grunt and roll over while Mom went to the kitchen to prepare breakfast. At 6:45, another gentle/pleasant prompt by Mom would result in grumbling, complaining of being tired and not wanting to go to school. Mom's response? She would sit on the side of the bed, give Steve a back massage and explain to him the importance of going to school. Eventually, with a good deal of coaxing, she would get Steve on his feet, guide him into the bathroom, lay out his clothes, and organize his book-bag, school supplies, and lunch. With great effort, she would maneuver him through breakfast and at 7:40 drive him two blocks to the bus stop so that he wouldn't miss the bus. Then she would head to work already half-exhausted from the struggles of the morning. She described his bedroom and bathroom as "disaster areas," which she cleaned up on a regular basis as it was easier than "hassling" Steve. The same pattern revealed itself during the afternoon and evening. Steve's emerging lifestyle as the dependent, comfort-seeker who needed a private secretary and valet service at his disposal to function in life emerged very clearly from the assessment. In addition, Mom's role in promoting and reinforcing Steve's helpless/dependent style became evident, as well as Dad's absence. Given this pattern at home, it is not surprising that Steve was performing poorly at school. An examination of the typical day revealed numerous points for intervention that would provide both parents and Steve with opportunities for corrective learning experiences.

The use of "Early Childhood Memories" (ECM) as a projective assessment technique (Mosak, 1958) is used with adolescents and adults, through not typically employed with children. The usefulness of ECMs rests on the selectivity hypothesis. As postulated by Edwards "Experiences which harmonize with an existing frame of reference will tend to be learned and remembered better than experiences which conflict with the same frame of reference" (1942, p. 36). Thus, individuals will choose to recollect those memories from early childhood that are consonant with and reflective of their lifestyles. If the therapist can discern the meaning embedded in the ECM, it can reveal the "story" of the client's life. An ECM is the recollection of a single, one-time incident that occurred typically before the age of six or seven.

The following ECM of a troubled adolescent was reported by Adler (Ansbacher & Ansbacher, 1956) as an example of the utility of early memories in revealing a delinquent's uncooperative approach to life: "I was helping with the wash, when I saw a piece of money on the table; so I took it. That was when I was six years old . . ." (p. 421). This recollection reveals this boy's self-centered approach to life situations and his tendency to make choices that serve his own self-interest at the expense of others. The next ECM, reported by a well-adjusted 16-year-old female, is reflective of her attitude toward self and new challenges:

> I remember starting school for the first time when I was five. It was the first day of school and I was excited. My mother wanted to walk me to the school bus but I asked her not to because I felt I was big enough to do it by myself. She was a little disappointed and I felt independent.

This girl finds new challenges exciting. She possesses a positive sense of anticipation, and has the confidence that she can handle new challenges without outside help. Finally, she probably will not acquiese to others, but will stand up for her own positions even though her actions might disappoint others. Independence is an important psychological priority for her.

Some Adlerian clinicians evaluate ECMs from the perspective of specified constructs. Sweeny (1975) for example suggested the following categories:

- Is the individual active or passive?
- Is he/she an observer or participant?
- Is he/she giving or taking?
- Does he/she go forth or withdraw?
- Is he/she alone or with others?
- Is his/her concern with people, things or ideas? (p. 49)

## Phase 3. Insight through Interpretation

From an Adlerian perspective, insight is:

> Understanding translated into constructive action. It reflects the patient's understanding of the purposive nature of behavior and mistaken apperceptions as well as an understanding of the role both play in life movement. So called intellectual insight merely reflects the patient's desire to play the game of therapy rather than the game of life. (Mosak, 1989, p. 89)

Since many of the convictions, assumptions, and goals that compose the lifestyle are automatic, they are not subject to conscious, reflective observation. The therapist's role in Phase 3 is to raise the client's consciousness about self and to bring to an explicit level these implicit aspects of self, which can then be examined logically and rationally. In accomplishing this, the Adlerian therapist is an active, participating partner. He or she may employ a "Socratic" dialogue, leading clients, through a series of questions, to develop hypotheses about their own goals or purposes. For example, the therapist might inquire of the oppositional, power-oriented, 10-year-old child: "You don't like Mom telling you when to go to bed . . . even if it's 10 P.M. on a school night, do you? Do you have any idea why you react so strongly to her at times like this?" An answer such as: "All the other kids in my class stay up 'til way past 10:00 . . . she's so unfair," reveals little insight into his own motivation. He is still at the level of looking for and finding justifications for "his way." On the other hand, if he were to reply "It feels like she's bossing me around . . . and I don't like being bossed," it would show that this child is close to an awareness of his or her interpersonal goal of power.

The classic tool employed to facilitate insight is interpretation. However, Adlerian interpretation focuses not on causes, or where the client has been. It concentrates on goals, or where the client is heading and what methods are being used to get there. In addition, it stimulates an examination of the consequences (both advantages and disadvantages) associated with the particular goal and behavioral style the client is using. Since the past is often used to justify inappropriate and socially useless behavior in the present, Adlerians minimize the past in favor of the present and the future. A discussion of the past may be used to demonstrate the enduring consistency and pattern of the lifestyle over time and across situations. Adlerians typically frame a psychological interpretation as a "tentative hypothesis." They might say: "I have a hunch about why you do that. . . . Would you like to hear it? Could it be that you are trying to make others like you and approve of you?" During a recent conjoint counseling session with a single mother and her 12-year-old daughter who were thoroughly embroiled in nonstop power struggles, I offered the following interpretation: "Could it be that you are both playing the game of 'Who's Boss?'" With that comment, the daughter broke into a big grin. This nonverbal response, sometimes referred to as a "recognition reflex," revealed the daughter's acknowledgment of her own motivation in the battle for power and control in the family. It also permitted therapy to shift to a rational discussion of the important issues of control, boundaries, and limits and who was in charge of what.

## Phase 4. Reorientation

During this phase, the counselor and client work together to establish alternative frames of reference in terms of thinking, feeling, and behaving. It is the point when an active commitment to change is secured. It is the time when self-defeating perceptions ("Life is unfair"), faulty values ("Look out for number one"), exaggerated goals ("I must please everyone"), cognitive distortions ("You can't trust anybody"), and useless behavior patterns (overcontrol, excessive opposition) are targeted for change.

Therapist-client goal alignment must be revisited again in this reorientation phase of therapy. Many adult clients, as well as children and adolescents, hold on to the belief that life, circumstances, and other people should change in order for them to be happy. Such is not a very functional belief. Reorienting the client to a reality-based perception of life and other people as sometimes being difficult, unfair, and unpredicable is more adaptive and workable. Once these reality-based premises are accepted, then the business of learning how better to deal with life's difficulties can begin.

One therapeutic strategy used to translate insight into action is the recommendation to the client to *act "as if"* (Mosak, 1989). It is based on the common observation that people typically act on the basis of their beliefs or convictions. For example, a teenager who believes that she is weak and helpless will act "as if" she were weak and helpless. Thus, her behavior reflects the fundamental belief she holds about herself. Presuming that the therapist has exposed this self-perception to be an overgeneralization that has blinded her to some of her strengths and assets, the client is asked to act "as if" she were strong, capable and assertive. First, the therapist and client together would generate a descriptive list of these behaviors. Next, the client might role-play strong, capable and assertive behavior during the therapy session. Finally, she would identify two or three real-life situations where she will experiment with these new behaviors. During this process, the therapist uses support, encouragement, and challenge. Through this systematic approach to change, the client may gradually become comfortable with assertive and stronger styles of behavior and come to believe in herself as a strong and capable person. Thus, her lifestyle schema will have changed.

## Applications with Children

Much of children's behavior, as well as misbehavior, is directed toward parents, teachers, and other significant adults in their lives because questions of safety, security, and survival are generally answered through those relationships. Given these assumptions, Adlerians typically work with children's behavioral and emotional problems (up to the age of 12) through parent and teacher consultation as well as variants of family counseling. This is not to imply that children do not posses the faculties to engage in and benefit from individual counseling. However, it recognizes the reality that the home and school environments are still exerting a strong influence on the behavior and the development of the child. Thus, interventions that focus more on environmental change (parent-child relationship, family environment, classroom interaction, etc.) are generally more efficient and cost-effective than individual child counseling. Some individual sessions may be held with the "problem child." However, these sessions are usually directed toward making the child comfortable, winning his or her cooperation, and conducting an assessment.

## TECHNIQUES

Most children over the age of 5 or 6 possess sufficient verbal fluency to have a meaningful verbal interaction with the counselor. Thus, the counselor may use a modified version of the lifestyle assessment to gain some insight into the child's motives, goals, perceptions, and emerging style of fitting into his or her environment. Dinkmeyer and Dinkmeyer (1977) developed the Children's Life-Style Guide (CLSG) as a structured format for eliciting pertinent information to make this assessment. Shulman and Mosak (1988) also developed a *Manual for Life Style Assessment* that serves as a systematic approach to eliciting and interpreting the lifestyle of the individual. Two components of the lifestyle assessment will be addressed in this section: Family Constellation and Family Atmosphere. The appropriateness of using Early Childhood Memories with children will be discussed briefly.

### Family Constellation

Adler (Ansbacher & Ansbacher, 1956) theorized that individuals will attempt to carve out positions of significance and uniqueness in their primary social environments and that these positions will serve as the prototypes for future social interaction. It is presumed that no two people can occupy the same psychological position. Thus, children are continually defining themselves in contrast to other close and significant members of their social unit. This "jockeying for position" can be observed among children in their families and students in school, as well as among adults in various work and social groups. The family constellation assessment attempts to understand how the child is defining him- or herself in relation to the other sibling members. Adlerians believe that siblings affect the personality development of one another, just as much as parents influence development. Thus, rating self as well as brothers and sisters on a series of descriptive adjectives (intelligent, obedient, selfish, considerate, etc.) develops a profile of self and the position of self in the social milieu. It also produces an identification of allies (those most similar) and competitors (those most different). If the firstborn child in the family is described as "responsible, cooperative, highest grades, and hardest worker," we would expect the second child (especially if close in age and the same sex) to choose an alternative, and perhaps less constructive, path to significance. According to Shulman, "divergence in behavior between siblings is partly due to competition between them for a place in the sun; the second avoids the territory of the first and goes elsewhere to seek his fortune" (1973, p. 49). Such a divergence is often actively promoted by the responsible firstborn who might innocently point out the mistakes, failures, and rebelliousness of his or her competitor. Parents, too, often unwittingly contribute to the second being in the "bad child" role by comparing siblings and using the firstborn as the model to which all should aspire. This tactic usually backfires. It generates animosity among siblings, and strengthens the commitment of the rebellious child to his or her chosen role in the family.

Typically, with younger and less verbal, preadolescent children, some of the family constellation data may be elicited from parents. Shulman and Mosak (1988) provide a concrete and detailed approach to the collection and interpretation of family constellation data (pp. 75–178).

As part of this assessment, parents are asked to rate each child (most to least) on a series of descriptive adjectives. Generally, adjectives representing traits associated with general domains of behavior are included. For example, domains such as academic ability, cooperation, ambition, compliance/opposition, sociability, personal dominance, and independence/dependence are covered. Table 5.1 presents a sample of descriptive traits associated with these domains.

**Table 5.1.   Behavioral domains and sibling traits**

| Domains | Traits |
| --- | --- |
| Academic ability | Intelligence |
|  | Grades |
| Cooperation | Helpful at home |
|  | Considerate |
| Ambition | Industrious |
|  | Achieving (School) |
| Compliance/opposition | Obedient |
|  | Rebellious |
| Sociability | Pleasing |
|  | Charming |
| Personal dominance | Bossy |
|  | Demanding |
| Independence/dependence | Self-reliant |
|  | Helpless |

*Source:* The format for this chart is based on a table in B. H. Shulman and H. H. Mosak's (1988), *Manual for Life Style Assessment* (pp. 124–126), Muncie, IN: Accelerated Development, Inc.

The use of the family constellation sibling ratings procedure can be illustrated by examining the ratings given the three children in the Kraft family. An "M" (Most) was assigned to the child who most strongly demonstrated a particular trait. An "L" (Least) was assigned to the child who was the weakest on that particular trait. Plus (+) and minus (−) ratings are also employed to note siblings who, while not the most or least on a trait, demonstrated either a strength or a deficiency on that quality. Table 5.2 provides a condensed version of the full assessment.

In this abbreviated survey of sibling ratings for Brett, James, and Wendy Kraft, it is apparent that personal territories have already been established as each child strives to carve out a position of significance for him- and herself in the family. The firstborn, Brett has chosen and cultivated the position of the industrious, academically achieving, responsible, take-charge sibling. His "bossy" style of leadership probably does not endear him to his younger brother. Thus, conflict between the two boys would be expected. The youngest, Wendy, seems to have adopted a helpful, obedient, and conforming personality. She is most likely charming and eager to please adults and other authority figures in her life. The middle son, James, is the identified patient in the Kraft family and the reason for their referral for family counseling. As often occurs, James seems to have contrasted himself in opposition to his older brother Brett. So, in areas where Brett expresses a strength (responsible, good grades, industrious), James seems to have either given up or cultivated opposing characteristics. On the other hand, on traits where Brett is weak (easygoing, mischevious, rebellious), James walked through the door of opportunity and has developed these traits into his strengths.

James's position is made somewhat more difficult because he is squeezed between a responsible oldest and a charming, obedient youngest. Most of the recognition and positive reinforcement in the Kraft family is probably directed toward Brett for his successes and to Wendy for her charm. Thus, James is probably on the short end of the recognition stick, unless he can achieve it through rebellion, mischief, and poor school performance. These were the primary reasons for the Kraft family's referral to family counseling. Teachers reported that James clowned around in class, did not complete class assignments, and did not turn in homework assignments. Furthermore, at home,

**Table 5.2.   Siblings ratings for the Kraft children**

| Trait | Brett 12 | James 10 | Wendy 6 |
|---|---|---|---|
| Responsible | M | L | + |
| Grades | M | L | + |
| Helpful | + | L | M |
| Industrious | M | L | + |
| Obedient | + | L | M |
| Rebellious | − | M | L |
| Independent | + | M | L |
| Bossy | M | − | L |
| Easygoing | L | M | + |
| Mischievous | L | M | + |

parents reported verbal and physical conflict between the two boys, as well as resistence on James's part to performing and completing family chores.

James' position as the "Problem Child" in the family was one possible role available to him. This was a "high probability" role, however, considering that he was flanked by two, high-profile, "good" siblings. Competing with Brett or Wendy in their chosen territories was not perceived as a viable option for James. Such competition most likely would have resulted in a second-best standing and might have left him enveloped in a cloud of anonymity. At least as the problem child, he can be "first best." Brett had a 2-year head start on James and thus has a developmental age advantage that lasts until late adolescence. So too would it be difficult for him to compete with the only girl and youngest for the position of charming "baby" of the family. Thus, Brett, James, and Wendy (with cooperation of parents) have unwittingly participated in the creation and development of positions of significance for themselves within this three-child sibling constellation.

## Family Atmosphere

The Family Atmosphere represents the tone of the family which is set by the parents. Thus, questions about mother, father, their relationship, parental expectations, and their methods of discipline provide insight into the child's perception of the role models who are illustrating the family's values. In addition, the counselor is able to gain an understanding of important family dynamics such as boundaries and limits, expectations, style of discipline, methods of problem-solving, and degree of cooperation versus competition.

Shulman and Mosak (1988) identified three qualities that represent the family atmosphere: mood, order, and relationships. *Mood* represents the emotional style of the family and is typically set by the parents. If parents are depressed, anxious, or angry on a regular basis, children will typically experience tension and insecurity. This insecurity may express itself in some children through internalizing problems such as fearfulness and withdrawal. Other children, however, may respond to these same conditions by externalizing and acting out through temper tantrums, rebellion, or even destructive acts.

*Order* refers to the stability and structure of relationships and activity patterns that exist within the family. The structure of relationships may run the gamut from too strict (autocratic) to too loose (laissez-faire). The autocratic environment is headed by a strong leader whose authority is not questioned. This parent creates the rules, and delivers them precisely to the children. When rules are broken, discipline is usually immediate, firm, and overt. Such an autocratic style often invites rebellion when children reach adolescence. In terms of activity patterns, the family style may range from highly rigid to chaotic. In the overly rigid environment, everything runs by the clock. Morning wake-up, mealtimes, study times, and bedtime are set and fixed. No deviations are allowed. In the chaotic environment, everyone "does their own thing," in their own time. There are no predictable schedules, and children are often left on their own. Thus, children may be up until late at night watching television, eating snacks, or wandering around the neighborhood. These children often have difficulty with self-discipline. Consequently, experimentation with deviant behavior, poor school performance, and an insensitivity to the needs and feelings of others may result.

*Relationships* are reflected in the patterns of interaction that exist between and among family members. For example, the parents may display a dominant-submissive model for their children rather than one of mutual respect and cooperation. So too, parents may behave in ways that are consistently accepting or rejecting, warm or cold, controlling or neglecting. It is not uncommon to see the "Persecutor-Victim-Rescuer" relationship triangle manifesting itself in troubled families where the autocratic father is the persecutor, the underperforming child is the victim of a constant barrage of criticism, and the mother is the rescuer who feels she must protect and defend her helpless son.

Whatever relationship patterns are consistently displayed by parents for their children become the prototypical models for all human interaction. It is these models that children will carry with them into adolescence and adulthood as "the way" to relate to the world and the people in it. Table 5.3 presents a list of mood, order, and relationship indicators that can be assessed by the therapist to determine the quality of the family atmosphere.

The use of *early childhood memories,* or early recollections, with preadolescent children is open to some controversy among clinicians. Some feel that the projective value of early memories is seriously restricted with younger clients whose limited language

**Table 5.3.   Family atmosphere indicators**

| Mood | |
| --- | --- |
| Sad | Happy |
| Cold | Warm |
| Tense | Relaxed |
| Pessimistic | Optimistic |

| Order | |
| --- | --- |
| Predictable | Unpredictable |
| Rigid | Flexible |
| Arbitrary | Rational |
| Confusing | Clear |

| Relationships | |
| --- | --- |
| Dominant | Submissive |
| Superior | Inferior |
| Distant | Close |
| Accepting | Rejecting |

*Source:* The format for this chart is based on a table in B. H. Shulman and H. H. Mosak's (1988), *Manual for Life Style Assessment* (p. 44), Muncie, IN: Accelerated Development, Inc.

development constrains their ability to move backward in time. Children are, for the most part, here-and-now beings. Also, there may not be a sufficient length of time between the actual incident and the time of recall to allow the projective effect to color and shape the memory. On the other hand, children seem to enjoy the exercise and typically have no difficulty producing memories. Thus, the effect on motivation and building a positive bond with the counselor, apart from the diagnostic value, may make this intervention a useful part of the counseling process with children.

From the data elicited from the lifestyle assessment, the counselor should be able to develop a summary of the client that covers three main issues:

1. Convictions and beliefs about self, others, and the world.
2. Goals, purposes, and intentions.
3. Methods of operation to reach one's goals and to solve life's problems.

## APPLICATIONS WITH ADOLESCENTS

The advent of adolescence presents an interesting and often difficult challenge for children, their parents, and the counselor. It is a time of significant bodily and hormonal changes which often result in dramatic changes in emotionality and behavior. Psychologically and socially, there is a shift in emphasis and alliance from family to peer group as teenagers begin to assert themselves in a search for an identity separate from their parents. Behaviorally, we often observe a dramatic shift from a comfortable compliance during childhood to a suspicious and oppositional stance toward adults during adolescence. Teens are intensely preoccupied with their physical bodies, social relationships, and with love and sex. The developmental challenge of overcoming loneliness through the establishment of close and intimate relationships is a major concern at this time. Often, this new challenge is undertaken at the expense of academic achievement and previously established extracurricular and athletic interests. During these years, adolescents can be expected to demonstrate errors in judgment, impulsive behavior, lowered tolerance for frustration, and rebellion toward authority. It is not uncommon for students who were helpful, cooperative, achieving, and well behaved during childhood to become rebellious, disrespectful, and critical of adult values. Despite the oppositional stance struck by so many adolescents in relation to the adult world, they still need support, structure, and guidance from the significant adults in their lives.

The role of the counselor as an instrument of change in working with teenagers and their families is a difficult one. The Adlerian counselor realizes that typical adolescent behavior is motivated by the desire to prove that he or she is no longer a child (Adler, 1931). This desire converts into the goal of "power" where numerous skirmishes are fought over limits, rules, restrictions, and control. Through these skirmishes, the adolescent is struggling for individuation, autonomy, and independence. Similarly, in therapy the typical teenager will "test" the counselor's fairness, impartiality and need to control. The counselor who is skilled at recognizing and sidestepping power struggles, acknowledging client strengths/assets, and communicating respect has a higher probability of forming an alliance with the adolescent client.


## TECHNIQUES

### Private Logic

Several approaches have been found to be particularly useful in working with the oppositional adolescent. Using the client's "private logic" is one of these. "Private logic is a term used to denote the personal convictions and value system of an individual by which he judges how to think, feel and act about events" (Shulman, 1973, p. 7). Among behaviorally and emotionally disordered individuals, private logic is often at variance with common sense. The greater the variance, the greater the difficulty in understanding and solving life's problems. The private logic of a conduct-disordered adolescent is revealed in the following incident: "I saw this really cool Swiss watch while I was walking through the department store. I didn't have a watch; I just had to have it! So, I reached around the counter when no one was watching and put it in my pocket. It was so easy!" If we accept this youngster's premises that he "had to have it" (attitude of entitlement), and "It was so easy!" (I won't get caught) then it would logically follow that he would act on this conviction and steal the watch. His private logic took precedence over the commonsense conventions that guide everyday behavior for most people.

The advantage of understanding this teenager's private logic is that it helps the counselor to avoid responses or interventions that might build more resistance and opposition (Mozdzierz, Murphy, & Greenblatt, 1986). Many adults (counselors included) might be tempted to point out the inappropriateness of this behavior and recite a litany of consequences that might have occurred had he been caught. This tactic would most certainly build resistance on the part of the client because it attacks his private logic. On the other hand, the counselor can remain within the client's private logic and point out the attitude of entitlement (I deserve to have what I want, even if I must steal) implied by the behavior. In this way, the counselor is not moralizing or preaching, but simply describing the client's beliefs and assumptions. Dinkmeyer et al. (1979) suggested a series of exploratory questions that might prove useful in helping the client to understand his or her private logic: "What were you thinking about at the moment you took the action? What reason did you give yourself for doing it? What did you tell yourself?"


### Reframing

Reframing or redefining the client's actions within a new meaning system may help to alter the client's private logic. According to Mozdzierz et al. (1986), reframing "involved an interpretation of a patient's behavior . . . in such a way that a positive aspect of a situation becomes manifest" (p. 345). In the case of the young wristwatch thief, the therapist might reframe the stealing behavior as an attempt to get peer attention. On the other hand, the counselor might decide to redefine the motivation behind the behavior in more negative terms. Let's assume that the adolescent's goal in stealing was to "prove" to himself and to his friends his manliness, daring, and courage. The counselor might "spit-in-the-soup" (Dreikurs, 1967) of this mistaken thinking by characterizing the behavior as a rather cowardly act that required little skill and no courage. In taking this tack, the counselor attempts to thwart the achievement of the goal (feeling tough and macho) by spoiling the "soup" of the client's irrational thinking. This client may choose to continue the behavior; however, the payoff may not be quite so satisfying.

## Paradoxical Intention

Adler was one of the first practitioners to introduce the strategy of antisuggestion, or paradoxical intention, in the treatment of resistant clients (Mosak, 1989). In using this strategy, the therapist suggests that the client pay attention to and even exaggerate some of the very behaviors that have been presented as problems. Adler (Ansbacher & Ansbacher, 1956) describes the case of an 11-year-old girl who dominated her family by complaining incessantly about all her problems and travails at school. In addition, while at school she would brag of her accomplishments and show off before her peers. Adler recommended the following to this young client: "If I were you, I would make even a greater fuss about it . . . you have to be continually kicking up a fuss in order to stress your accomplishments and your own importance. Write in capital letters over your bed: 'Every morning I must torment my family as much as possible'" (Ansbacher & Ansbacher, 1956, p. 398). Adler footnoted this strategy with the observation that his clients never followed his paradoxical advice.

The rationale for the use of this strategy lies in the tendency for adolescent clients to resist and fight against the expectations of adults. So, rather than engaging in the futile task of persuading the adolescent to cease his or her inappropriate behavior, the therapist "joins" the client and the symptom by prescribing the inappropriate behavior. Most clients find this tactic to be very disarming because the therapist has done the unexpected. They were prepared to resist this presumed agent of parents and society, and suddenly they discover that there is nothing to fight against. Consequently, they are often intrigued by the novelty of the unexpected behavior, and thus, tune in more carefully to the therapist's words and actions rather than tune out, as so many adolescents do. Finally, when the client is confronted with the problem behavior in such a magnified way, these actions often begin to appear foolish and silly.

## GROUP PROCEDURES WITH CHILDREN AND ADOLESCENTS

The use of group counseling approaches in dealing with children and adolescents is a natural expression of the theoretical assumptions that underlie Adler's theory of Individual Psychology:

> Humans are social beings. Human behavior has social meaning . Everyone strives to be-
> long by establishing a position of importance and significance within his or her social
> milieu. A feeling of social interest stimulates active, cooperative social participation.

Given these assumptions it would appear quite natural that Adlerian practitioners would employ group approaches in counseling and therapy.

Adler first used group approaches for preventive and educational purposes in the local schools in Vienna as well as in the Child Guidance Clinics that he and his follow-ers established. His initial approach to group counseling included various contexts: (a) the family group including parents, problem child, and all siblings, (b) a children's group, (c) a parent group composed of parents seeking help for child rearing and be-havior management concerns, and (d) a community group of parents, teachers, and stu-dents (Sonstegard & Dreikurs, 1975). Each group presented unique issues and dynamics. However, the common goals for all the groups were assisting the partici-pants in (a) understanding their own and other's behavior, (b) developing an attitude of social equality, (c) facilitating democratic problem-solving, and (d) building social interest.

Contemporary applications of Adlerian group counseling with children and adoles-cents are most commonly seen in school settings. The preventive and educational phi-losophy inherent in this approach targets group work as an ideal vehicle to promote psychological and social development of children in parallel with cognitive and aca-demic development. Thus, as part of the developmental guidance curriculum, the ele-mentary school counselor would provide group counseling/guidance experiences that focus on communication, cooperation, problem-solving and conflict resolution. These skills are necessary for the child to face successfully the life tasks of school, friends, and family. In addition, there may be occasions where counseling groups are formed to deal with particular problems facing children. Some of these might include death and dying, divorce, weight loss, abusive relationships, and bullying.

Regardless of the particular content focus of the group, it is assumed that the group process will invariably lead to the creation of a social microcosm of individual mem-bers' experiences. Thus, it can be expected that group members will come to behave in ways that reflect their real-life interpersonal styles. Behavior in the group will express the individual's belief about self, attitude toward others, social values, convictions about how to achieve belonging, and methods of social problem-solving. Each mem-ber's lifestyle will reveal itself as he or she interacts with fellow group members. Thus, the role of the counselor is to observe carefully members' behavior (more so than their words), and to facilitate members' awareness of their distorted perceptions, mis-taken beliefs, and faulty problem-solving approaches.

These goals are accomplished in the group by the counselor's utilizing the four phases of the counseling process described earlier:

1. *Relationship.* In this case, it is not just the relationship between the counselor and the members, but between and among members themselves. Group cohe-siveness must be achieved.

2. *Analysis.* Formal assessment procedures are not typically employed in group counseling as members' faulty styles of thinking and behaving quickly become apparent during intrapersonal interaction.

3. *Insight.* Feedback from fellow group members, rather than interpretation by the counselor, becomes the primary vehicle to promote insight.

4. *Reorientation.* The group environment provides immediate corrective learning experiences as well as opportunities to experiment safely with novel perspectives and problem-solving approaches.

Dinkmeyer et al. (1979) describe the Adlerian approach to group counseling as a cycle that progresses through a series of steps:

(a) Perceptions and beliefs change, (b) courage and belonging enable one to try new behavior, (c) involvement and risking are rewarded by acceptance and belonging, (d) fear of making a mistake is replaced by the courage to be imperfect, which reduces anxiety and insecurity, and (e) as self-esteem and feelings of worth develop, the person is able to try additional change. (p. 141)

The criterion for the effectiveness of group counseling is the demonstrated ability of the member to participate in the give-and-take of social life, to successfully confront the life tasks facing him or her, and to engage in effective social problem-solving.

## Therapeutic Mechanisms

A number of mechanisms or forces related to group dynamics account for the effectiveness of this approach in promoting behavior and attitudinal change. An awareness of these mechanisms allows the counselor to maximize the power of the group in achieving therapeutic goals. While some of these may emerge spontaneously as the group evolves, typically, the leader must create situations and occasions that will mobilize these forces. Corsini (1964) identified nine emotional, intellectual, and action factors that account for the power of group counseling:

### Emotional Factors

1. *Acceptance.* A nonjudgmental atmosphere, cohesiveness, supportive relationships.
2. *Altruism.* Active support and encouragement, of fellow group members through challenge, positive feedback, and suggestions.
3. *Transference.* Identification with other group members and the group; mutual liking, attraction, and empathy.

### Intellectual Factors

4. *Spectator Therapy.* Vicarious learning through the observation of others in the group.

5. *Universalization.* Discovery that one is not alone in experiencing particular problems.

6. *Intellectualization.* Acquiring insight into oneself; understanding aspects of self that previously had not been known, or had been confusing or puzzling.

## Action Factors

7. *Reality Testing.* Experimenting with one's ideas, feelings, and behavior in the real interpersonal environment of the group; the group provides a here-and-now experience.

8. *Ventilation.* Freedom of expression (within limits) allows an expression of beliefs, feelings, and behavior that may be bottled up, and thus remain unexamined.

9. *Interaction.* Communication and sharing of common fears, anxieties, and problems. The degree to which the counselor can mobilize these forces of affection/caring, understanding, and action will be the key to the potency of the group counseling experience in promoting positive growth and development in its members.

# TECHNIQUES

A variety of group methods, applying Adlerian theoretical principles, have been developed. Each of these focus on the social nature of behavior and deal primarily with interpersonal problems.

## Lifestyle Groups

The focus in these groups is on the members' lifestyles and the manner in which each person handles the tasks of life. Members present enough data about themselves and their development for a brief lifestyle assessment to be conducted and presented. Walton (1975) developed a structured format to facilitate the disclosure and sharing of this information in adolescent groups. The following are brief excerpts from his four-part guide:

*Part I. Presenting Self to the Group:* What kinds of friends have you made? What kind of worker are you? What kinds of problems have you had over loving and being loved? How do people treat you generally?

*Part II. Sharing Responses:* What did you hear the other person sharing? Did you recognize things in yourselves that were similar to what was just shared? How do you feel toward the person who just shared?

*Part III. Describing Your Family Constellation:* How were you different from your siblings, and how were you like them? What were mothers/fathers expectations; how did you feel about them? In your family, what did it mean to "be a man/woman?"

*Part IV. Discussing a Family Constellation:* Can you see any similarities between the role people played in their families, and the roles they have assumed in the group? These roles reflect social goals; what goals are people in the group pursuing? (pp. 27–28)

According to Walton (1975), the group leader would cover Parts I and II with each group member in succession. This generates personal data that serve as the springboard for reflection and discussion that occur in Parts III and IV. It is anticipated that participants will better understand the patterns and themes of their interpersonal behavior, and be challenged by fellow group members to develop alternatives to troublesome and inappropriate aspects of their styles.

## Action Therapy

This method was developed using the theoretical principles of Individual Psychology and some of the psychodramatic techniques described by Moreno (1959). According to O'Connell (1975), "Action therapy is a form of group therapy which is focused on what the patient can do for others, rather than on the patient as such" (p. 36). It includes some didactic material in the form of "lecturettes" on such topics as mistaken goals, self-defeating beliefs, errors in living, and liabilities of low self-esteem. Action-oriented strategies include the "mirror" (enacting the subject's behavioral and verbal responses for him or her to observe), the "double" (group member stands behind the subject, verbalizing unspoken thoughts and feelings), and "role-reversal" (during an interaction, two subjects reverse roles, and resume the interaction from the opposing point of view).

Other group techniques described in the literature include the Midas Technique (Shulman, 1973), the Marshmallow (Dinkmeyer et al., 1979), Social Therapy (Schoenaker & Schoenaker, 1976), and the Encouragement Labs (O'Connell, 1975).

## CLASSROOM AND EDUCATIONAL APPLICATIONS

Adlerian principles and techniques have been applied to school and educational settings since the 1920s. His emphasis on prevention led Adler to establish Child Guidance Clinics in the community and the schools where parents and teachers could learn to better understand and manage the behavior of children and adolescents. Contemporary applications of Adlerian psychology to school and classroom settings seem to focus on two principal areas; (a) social skills training and affective education, and (b) classroom discipline and teacher consultation.

### Social Skills Training and Affective Education

Raymond Corsini, a student and colleague of Rudolph Driekurs, established a comprehensive approach to the application of Individual Psychology to the organization and operation of an entire school. His approach has been identified as Individual Education (Corsini, 1977), and more recently as IE/4R (Pierce, 1987). The four R's stand for respect, responsibility, resourcefulness, and responsiveness. In these schools, students, teachers, and administrators as well as parents are expected to participate in the program's components. A social skills curriculum focusing on the four R's is addressed alongside the standard academic curriculum. Teachers and school staff are provided training in discipline, classroom management, and encouragement skills. Parents are introduced to the IE system through workshops and parent education classes.

Developing Understanding of Self and Others (DUSO-1, DUSO-2) is an affective education program developed by Dinkmeyer and Dinkmeyer (1982) for use in prekindergarten through fourth-grade classrooms. Each program contains a series of structured activities through which 42 life-skill and developmental goals are delivered. The teacher or group leader employs various communication, relaxation, fantasy, and interactional exercises during DUSO sessions.

More recently, Clark (1995) has proposed a Social Interest Program in schools to promote a sense of belonging, skills of cooperation, and an attitude of empathy and sensitivity toward others. While he notes that there is a long history of such personal and social development programs, their impact seems limited to restricted samples of children and adolescents within the total student population. The Social Interest Program goal should be a daily focus that is integrated within the entire academic, social, and extracurricular fabric of the school. He identifies a series of component activities that have proven useful in promoting the program goals:

- *Class Discussions.* Regularly scheduled student meetings led by a teacher emphasizing mutual support, encouragement, decision making, and effective communication.
- *Community Service.* Students volunteer services through a club or organization.
- *Conflict Resolution.* Managing disputes between students through the intervention of trained student mediators.
- *Cooperative Learning.* Heterogeneous small groups of students assist one another in learning activities in the classroom with accountability for individual and group progress.
- *Group Problem-Solving.* Organized student teams creatively solve challenging issues. Innovative planning and performance of tasks is emphasized.
- *Peer Tutoring.* Students tutor other students in various subjects on a scheduled basis within the classroom or across grade levels. (Clark, 1995, p. 320)

## Classroom Discipline and Teacher Consultation

Since the publication of *Psychology in the Classroom* by Dreikurs (1957), Adlerian principles have become a frequent staple of classroom discipline and behavior management practices of teachers. The use of the four goals of misbehavior (Dreikurs, Grunwald, & Pepper, 1982), natural and logical consequences as an alternative to punishment (Dreikurs & Grey, 1968) and encouragement practices (Dinkmeyer & Dreikurs, 1963) have had a significant and positive impact on teacher behavior and student performance.

Many teachers find themselves poorly trained in understanding the actions of children and adolescents and inadequate to the difficult task of managing the behavior of 25 to 30 students in a classroom. The Adlerian approach provides a framework for the teacher to create a relatively democratic environment where responsibility and control is shared. It clarifies the issue of "Who is responsible for what?" thus reducing the occasion of power struggles and minimizing the role of the teacher as the sole enforcer of authority. Finally, it specifies an approach to discipline based on natural and social order that minimizes arbitrary and punitive teacher responses in favor of logical consequences designed to be corrective learning experiences.

Dinkmeyer, McKay, and Dinkmeyer (1980), developed an in-service training program for teachers based on Adlerian principles. Systematic Training for Effective Teaching (STET) is a 14-session program designed to enhance teachers' knowledge of child and adolescent behavior as well as develop effective behavior management and motivational skills. Components of the program include sections on goals of misbehavior, effective discipline, the encouraging and motivating of positive behavior, and the use of group processes in the classroom. STET encourages teachers to use themselves as well as the peer group as the agents of intervention and change when problems arise in the classroom.

## PARENTING SKILLS

The Adlerian approach assumes that much child and adolescent misbehavior originated within the context of the home and family environment and is maintained by that environment. Thus, it follows that intervention within this context would present an ideal approach to both prevention as well as remediation. It has also been apparent to practitioners from many theoretical orientations that the biological reality of parenthood does not automatically confer effective child-rearing skills. The increasing frequency of single-parent homes, blended families, and dual-career families makes the task of creating a stable family environment and raising psychologically healthy children a formidable task. Adlerians believe that personal intuition and past experiences are insufficient bases for the complex challenge of raising children. Parents need to be provided with (a) a knowledge base that enables them to understand the behavior of children and adolescents, and (b) skills and techniques that equip them to be effective behavior managers.

Several approaches to parent education using this theoretical framework have been implemented. The parent study group format is most popular. It comprises a group of 8 to 12 parents along with a professional or paraprofessional group leader. Most of these groups use *Children: The Challenge* (Dreikurs & Soltz, 1964) as the common reading source that introduces group participants to a philosophy of child rearing, a theory of human behavior, and a pragmatic approach to effective parenting. Soltz (1967) developed a *Study Group Leader's Manual* as a companion to the text. In the manual, she outlines a week-by-week format for presenting concepts and ideas, as well as suggestions for facilitating group discussion and applying the material to common child-rearing problems. Adlerian parent study groups have also used *Raising a Responsible Child* (Dinkmeyer & McKay, 1982), and *The Practical Parent* (Corsini & Painter, 1975). Most parent study groups include 7 to 10 weekly sessions. Each week, a specific topic from the readings is assigned and subsequently discussed. The group leader will attempt to direct the focus to an application of the weekly readings to specific family and child-rearing problems. A practice exercise, including role playing, helps parents bridge the gap from theory to application by practicing a specific concept, skill, or strategy. Finally, a homework assignment of reading and experimenting with a new skill/concept is specified for the next meeting.

Systematic Training for Effective Parenting (STEP) is a standardized parent education program developed by Dinkmeyer and McKay (1976, 1989). Subsequently, these same authors developed a version of this program specifically designed to assist parents of adolescents: STEP/Teen (Dinkmeyer & McKay, 1983). These structured programs provide a leader's manual, participant reading manual, charts, and (in the 1989 edition) video-based training scenarios. The STEP program addresses such critical parenting issues as (a) understanding the goals of misbehavior, (b) providing encouragement, (c) improving communication, (d) using natural and logical consequences, and (e) conducting a family council.

## FAMILY THERAPY

Adlerian practitioners have emphasized interpersonal behavior, family dynamics, and parent-child interactions since the first Child Guidance Clinics were established in Vienna during the 1920s. The theory of Individual Psychology emphasizes interpersonal processes as a more significant unit of focus than intrapsychic mechanisms. Family therapy, from this perspective, assumes that chronic conflict and recurrent behavior/emotional problems of any one family member affect all family members. In addition, each family member contributes to the problems and, thus, shares a responsibility to contribute to the solutions. The broad goal of family therapy is for members to live together in an atmosphere of social equality, where problems are resolved in a spirit of cooperative social problem-solving. For this goal to be realized, the therapist must assist the family in accomplishing the following tasks:

1. *Demonstrating Mutual Respect.* So many contemporary families are plagued by forces of competition, one-upsmanship, and feuding coalitions that healthy family processes are overwhelmed. These conditions often lead to scapegoating, where family members unconsciously select a member to be the "identified patient" or symptom bearer of the family's dysfunction. Selecting a scapegoat effectively relieves other family members from examining their own complicity in creating and maintaining family problems, and from actively participating in their resolution. Challenging family members to be appreciative of one another's strengths, and accepting of one another's weaknesses creates the environment for mutual respect and reduces

the tendency toward scapegoating. It allows family members, especially the children, the freedom to be imperfect and to make mistakes without subsequent humiliation and loss of self-worth.

2. *Pinpointing the Problems for Resolution.* Identification of salient issues for examination and subsequent resolution is an important and sometimes difficult task for the therapist. Potential problem areas for many families are: (a) dysfunctional beliefs (unrealistic expectations of parents/children), (b) dysfunctional roles (rebel, enforcer, family spokesperson, enabler), (c) weak boundaries (between parent and child generations), (d) poor communication patterns (unclear messages, vague directives, nagging, double messages), (e) chaotic organization (lack of routine, poor division of labor, lack of shared responsibility). Weaknesses in these five areas will typically contribute to symptomatic behavior on the part of one or more of the family members. However, rather than addressing simply the symptoms, the therapist must be alert to some of the underlying issues.

3. *Developing Alternative Perspectives.* Once problem areas have been pinpointed, the therapeutic task is to facilitate family members' development of options or alternatives to their current style of operating. The therapist might employ indirect methods such as modeling (clear communication), introduce structure/organization (during the therapy hour), Socratic questioning (to draw out ideas and suggestions), and visualization/imagination (to elicit alternative images of family functioning). More direct methods might also be used. Giving direct instruction or having the parents/children enroll in particular psychoeducational programs could be useful when there is a specific knowledge or skill deficit. In addition, role playing and coaching family members during structured problem-solving activities can have the effect of breaking old, destructive patterns of interaction and replacing them with more adaptive methods.

4. *Participating in Decision Making and Reaching New Agreements.* This last step involves securing a commitment to change. Active participation in the decision-making process will be influenced by the degree to which members perceive that their interests and the overall family interests are served by the agreements, and the degree to which they can affect the agreements made. Sherman, Oresky, and Rountree (1991) suggest a series of tactics that can be employed to promote a feeling of optimism and a sense of empowerment among family members:

(a) Affirm the family and each member, (b) Identify and recognize family strengths, (c) Emphasize positive change and movement, (d) Recall incidents that worked successfully in the past, (e) Promote assertion and negotiation rather than aggression. (pp. 14–15)

## EFFICACY

Adlerian psychology, by virtue of its origin in and strong ties to the European philosophical tradition, has not taken an assertive stance on the assessment and evaluation of therapeutic outcomes. Thus, the research available to support the efficacy of its proposed intervention models and approaches is limited. On the other hand, the relatively recent development of structured intervention programs (STEP and DUSO), as well as methodological advances in single-subject case study designs have led to a variety of evaluation/research studies over the past 20 years.

The most thoroughly researched aspect of Adlerian-based interventions is that of parenting programs. Burnett (1988) reviewed a series of 21 studies conducted between 1971 and 1984 on the efficacy of traditional Adlerian parent study groups, as well as parenting groups using the Systematic Training for Effective Parenting (STEP). Burnett notes that "Changes in a positive direction were noted on measures of children's behavior, children's self-concept, parental behavior, and parental attitudes. The studies were, on the whole, methodologically sound" (p. 74). He noted that two longitudinal follow-up studies of Adlerian parenting programs (3 months and 12 months) produced inconsistent results regarding the maintenance of gains immediately following treatment. Moore and Dean-Zubritsky (1979) evaluated pre- and posttreatment videotaped interactions between parents and their children. They found that parents who had participated in the group using the book, *Children: The Challenge* (Dreikurs, 1964) demonstrated significantly more contact with their children, used more encouragement, and also became more directive compared with controls.

Morse and Brokoven (1987) summarized the research on the efficacy of Dinkmeyer and Dinkmeyer's (1982) psychoeducational program for children in elementary school: Developing Understanding of Self and Others (DUSO & DUSO-R). They reported that the results generally support the effectiveness of this program in promoting self-reliance, self-esteem, and an awareness of social standards. However, caution was recommended because of methodological weaknesses of some of the studies.

A modest literature base exists on Adlerian approaches to such emotional and behavioral disorders as depression (Croake, 1982), anxiety (Adler, 1963b), enuresis (Rister, 1983), oppositional defiant disorder (Morrow & Kopp, 1988), conduct disorder (Croake, 1986), and delinquency (Hirschorn, 1982). This literature consists primarily of programmatic interventions and naturalistic case studies that are descriptive and anecdotal in nature. The case studies thoroughly describe the theoretical bases for the interventions and clearly articulate the specific interventions employed. However, for the most part, treatment outcomes are related in narrative fashion with little attempt to quantify the results. Exceptions to this trend, in the form of empirical case studies have demonstrated successful treatment of such problems as school phobia (Kelly & Croake, 1978), sibling rivalry (Kelly & Main, 1979), depression (Kelly, Dowd, & Duffy, 1983), and disruptive in-school behavior (Kelly, 1978). Furthermore, controlled group studies testing the efficacy of such interventions as goal disclosure (Porter & Hoedt, 1985), Adlerian group counseling (Kern & Hankins, 1977), and Adlerian individual counseling (West, Sonstegard, & Hagerman, 1980) have demonstrated promising results.

Kern, Matheny, and Patterson (1978) conducted a broad and comprehensive review of research into Adlerian-based interventions. Their review covered a 26-year period and revealed that evaluation studies with child and adolescent populations composed one of the most popular and successful areas of research. Most of these studies focused on behavior problems manifested in school and home situations. Overall, their review builds a strong case for the efficacy of Adlerian-based interventions in ameliorating the behavioral and emotional problems of children and adolescents.

## CONCLUSION

Adlerian psychology provides a comprehensive theoretical basis for understanding the behavioral and emotional problems of children and adolescents. In addition, it provides a pragmatic approach to intervention. For the most part, the theoretical concepts as well as the approaches to treatment are framed in commonsense, practical language that parents, teachers and counselors find uncomplicated and relatively easy to apply.

Counselors using the Adlerian approach believe that children and adolescents are responsible, decision-making individuals who create their own personal goals in answer to the questions of safety, security, and survival in this world. Some of these goals may be adaptive (cooperation, achievement), while others may be maladaptive (power, revenge). In facilitating the development of healthy goals in children, adults must provide nurturance, encouragement, structure, and discipline. The Adlerian counselor provides opportunities for reeducation and attempts to shift children away from a competitive, self-serving approach to life to a cooperative, socially useful orientation. The various interventions of encouragement, natural and logical consequences, paradoxical intention, and democratic problem-solving are applied primarily in the home and school environments where children interact with peers and significant adults on a day-to-day basis. Thus, consultation with parents and teachers is a significant component of any intervention program with an emotionally or behaviorally disordered child or adolescent.

Adlerian practitioners have taken a strong initiative in the development of preventive mental health programs. Individual Education and Developing Understanding of Self and Others (DUSO) attempt to promote development of healthy psychological processes. In addition, parent education groups (e.g., Systematic Training for Effective Parenting) and teacher education groups (e.g., Systematic Training for Effective Teaching) provide a sound and practical approach to the constructive management of behavior in home and school settings.

Finally, the efficacy research in the Adlerain approach is encouraging and promising. It tends to indicate that the preventive parent education programs are successful in changing parent attitudes and behaviors, as well as children's behavior. The dearth, however, of applied clinical research into specific interventions for specific behavioral and emotional disorders needs to be addressed. The anecdotal case studies indicate that this approach has much to offer the counselor, the teacher, and the parent. Well-designed studies, using current methodologies, will provide an empirical test of the promise of this approach.

## CASE STUDY _____

Michael was a 10-year-old White male who was referred for counseling because of a severe phobic reaction to school. He came from an intact nuclear family and had one sister, aged 8. He tested within the average ranges of intellectual ability. At the time of referral, Michael's family had recently moved to a new town because of his father's job change. He was initially enrolled in a local public school, but soon experienced adjustment problems. He complained about other kids "not liking him," and the public school being "inferior" to his previous school. He felt that he didn't "fit in" with the other children. Despite economic hardships, Mike's parents transferred him to a private school. After the first day at this new school, Mike resisted returning. He expressed fears of getting lost on the campus, felt that teachers did not like him, and believed that other students were "out to get him." For the remainder of that first week, Mike would sometimes have to be carried to the school office where the assistant principal would restrain him while his mother escaped to the car and drove home. At school, he would have lengthy conversations with the principal, the school counselor, office secretaries, and anyone else who would listen to his fears and apprehensions. All of their reassurance, however, proved futile in getting Mike into the classroom. Eventually, he would be permitted to call home to talk to his mother. These conversations would typically end in Mike sobbing and pleading with mother to come back to school to get him, promising that the next day would be different. Mom would relent. Each succeeding day, however, proved to be a repeat of the day before. Finally, Mike's accusations that mother did not love him, and threats to "run away from home" if parents made him go to that school prompted a referral for psychological intervention.

### Analysis

It is not uncommon for firstborn children to be pampered and spoiled before the arrival of the second child. An evaluation of the family history revealed that Michael was pampered and subsequently suffered "dethronement" shortly after his sister arrived on the scene. Dethronement entails the loss of a favored position or status within the family to another sibling. No longer is the first child the center of attention. Consequently, the child feels rejected and is resentful of the younger sibling and angry toward parents. At the same time, there are often strong parental expectations that the oldest child should be strong, independent, successful, and responsible. The pampered child typically responds to these expectations as unfair burdens. This lack of security (felt rejection) and the high levels of parental expectation do not bode well for adjustment.

Pampering and dethronement can result in attempts to pull mother back with strong efforts to regain the favored position. Sometimes these efforts can be positive in the form of becoming the "model child." On the other hand, the child may choose the path of disability, inferiority, weakness, and demands for help. This latter path was Michael's choice.

Mike displayed paranoid-type behavior with his sensitivity to the loss of his desired special position by feeling that others were "out to get him." This was a pattern he had repeated since his sister's birth: "People are unfair to me." It was accompanied by an exaggerated sense of his importance. Hence, he simultaneously felt that he was special and didn't belong: "I don't fit with the other kids." Teachers, principal, secretaries, counselor were all very involved with him. Their involvement confirmed his importance. This was a sign of Mike's discouragement. He was not a part of the regular peer group. Rather, he behaved as the pampered child who must have continual reassurance from adults of being special and worthy of attention.

An exploration of the parent-child relationships revealed several issues that seemed to have a significant bearing on the presenting problem. Mike's father suffered from a progressively disabling illness and had little energy to give either child. It was apparent that he had never been very involved with his children or the child-rearing enterprise. Mother "made up" for father's lack of interest by devoting herself to the children. In an effort to compensate for father's inattention, she was overly lenient and permissive, and held few expectations for either child. She reported feeling sorry for the children, especially Mike, because father wouldn't take an interest.

Mike's mom evidences the "good mother" syndrome. These parents feel that they must continually watch out for, take care of, and protect their children. This results in pampering, which is a major cause of maladjustment in children. In particular, pampering is defined as doing for children what they can do for themselves. Adlerians believe that the child's opportunity for self-confidence is attenuated when the parent expects too little, overindulges, or gives into unreasonable demands. This is the pampering process. For example, when confronted with Mike's sobbing calls from school, mother reported: "My heart would just break for him." When he came home from school early, Mike would spend the remainder of the day as mother's little companion. They would go shopping together, have lunch, and bake cookies. Then Mike would settle down in front of the television until 3:30 when the other children in the neighborhood would return home from school.

From an Adlerian perspective, all behavior is purposive and goal directed. It may be speculated that Mike's fears served as an excuse that justified his retreat from a new challenge that he did not feel able to handle. His school phobia protects him from the life task of school work for which he feels unprepared. Success at school requires problem solving. The pampered child continues to manipulate others (parents, teachers) into solving his problems for him. In this way he is spared the potential humiliation of defeat and failure. Mike's phobia removed him from school and placed him in the desired and favored position with his mother where he could press her into his service. Thus, the particular goals of Mike's symptomatic behavior were (a) attention getting, as he secured sympathy and concern from the adults in his life, and (b) power, as he defeated adults in their efforts to "make" him go to school.

## Treatment Program

As a result of the preceeding analysis and conceptualization of Mike's school phobia, it was determined that the most productive and efficacious approach to dealing with this problem was primarily through intervening with the parents. Thus, mother and father were seen on a twice-a-week basis for 4 weeks and once per week for the following 3 weeks. Mike was seen individually for 30 minutes each week over the first 4 weeks. During the parent sessions, the attention-getting and power dynamics of Mike's behavior were explained. It was pointed out that the fearfulness brought sympathy and short-term nurturance from mother and considerable attention from school personnel. In addition, Mike's fears served as a passive, yet powerful, means of defeating adults in their attempts to force school attendance. It was suggested that the more force they exerted, the more powerful resistence he would display. Consequently, the first recommendation was for parents to withdraw from the power struggle.

In executing this withdrawal strategy, parents would allow Mike the choice of school attendance each day. He would have to decide by 8:30 A.M. Arrival after the start of the school day was not an option. Parents were instructed to act "disinterested" and to avoid all prodding. It was explained to Mike (in a family session) that if he chose to stay home, he would have to remain in his room without any contact with mother until 3:30 P.M. The rationale provided to him was that mother needed "her" time to wash, cook, clean the house, and do errands. This was her job and she needed the day for it. His job was to go to school. However, if he felt too fearful to tackle his job and chose not to attend school, then he could not interfere with Mom's day. Mike was told that he could rest, sleep, read, play in his room, or do school work. Interacting with mother and watching television were off limits. If Mike were to come out of his room and engage her, Mother was instructed to go to her room, take a walk outside or get into her car and go shopping. She was asked not to coax or force him back into his room. Early in the intervention program, mother discovered Mike in the family room watching TV. She was shown how to temporarily disable the television.

The objectives of this strategy were (a) to sidestep the power struggle and minimize attention paid to the maladaptive behavior, (b) to place choice and responsibility with Mike, (c) to display a positive attitude toward the work task and its importance (i.e., Mother went about her chores for the day rather than attending to Mike), and (d) to employ a logical consequence as a form of discipline (i.e., if Mike chose to stay home he must suffer the boredom that inactivity would inevitably bring). It was hypothesized that the challenge of school, even with its uncertainties, would eventually begin to look positive and interesting compared with the boredom and nonattention at home.

In addition to the preceding strategy, it was determined that parents needed to be encouraging and attentive to their son at appropriate times. Thus, parents were instructed to be warm, receptive, and communicative until 8:30 A.M. and from 3:30 P.M. until bedtime. However, it was suggested that they retreat from any verbal complaints about the intervention strategy or his statements about feeling unloved. Another intervention strategy, considered to be a form of encouragement was a "special time" (Main, 1987) between Mike and his father, who would be available for a designated period of a half-hour each evening. During this time, Mike could decide on an activity of his choice. By providing a consistent and reliable special time, the parent is showing behaviorally that Mike is loved and accepted as he is.

Parents were cautioned not to expect immediate results because of the intensity and strength of the symptoms. Simultaneously, cooperation of school personnel was secured to avoid school attendance pressure on the parents or on Mike.

## *Evaluation*

The ultimate outcome of this intervention was defined as the frequency and regularity of school attendance. For the purposes of assessment, three separate attendance categories were developed: (a) nonattendance (did not attend classes during any part of the school day), (b) partial attendance (attended classes for some fraction of the school day), and (c) full attendance (attended classes for the full day).

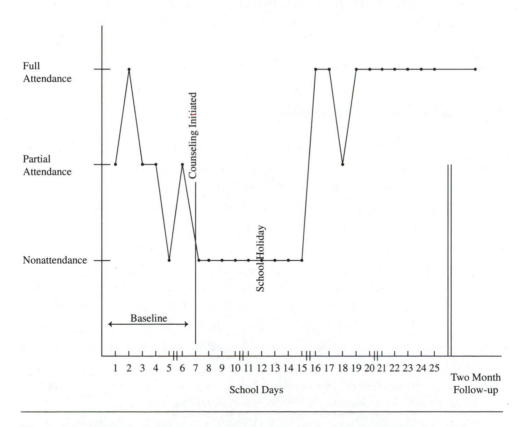

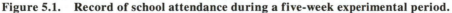

**Figure 5.1.    Record of school attendance during a five-week experimental period.**

During a pretreatment baseline period during which the initial assessment and evaluation were being conducted, Mike had 1 day of full attendance, 1 day of nonattendance and 4 days of partial attendance (see Figure 5.1). Even the days of partial attendance, however, were of questionable value educationally for Mike because of the conflict and emotional intensity of his fears. Once the intervention was initiated, the choice of attending school was immediately given to Mike. The 9 consecutive days of school absence represented a testing period for Mike. During that time he sought sympathy, threatened to run away from home, and accused parents of not loving him. However, Mike also experienced the boredom of staying home day after day, and learned that parents, mother in particular, would not be impressed with his fears, nor manipulated by his threats. Mike's holdout was longer than anticipated, therefore, a great deal of encouragement was necessary for parents. On the 16 day, Mike decided to go to school. He had come close on previous days, but changed his mind at the last minute. It can be speculated that this ambivalence may have been a subtle test of his parents' reaction, possibly to see if he could elicit their prodding and coaxing. On day 18 of the experimental period, Mike was caught misbehaving in class and given a detention. He left school at midday, however, returned the next day and served his detention. School attendance since that incident was found to be regular and consistent for the duration of the experimental period (25 days). A 2-month follow-up of this case showed a maintenance of regular school attendance. In addition, parents reported a significant reduction in Mike's verbal expression of fears, anxieties, and complaints about school.

---

## ANNOTATED BIBLIOGRAPHY

Adler, A. (1963). *The problem child.* New York: Capricorn Books.

Using specific clinical cases, Adler analyzes the lifestyles of emotionally and behaviorally disordered children. He discusses children and adolescents with such problems as stealing, lying, enuresis, and academic underachievement.

Ansbacher, H. L., & Ansbacher, R. R. (1956). *The individual psychology of Alfred Adler.* New York: Harper & Row.

The Ansbachers offer a systematic presentation of Alfred Adler's theoretical and clinical formulations. They cover the philosophical underpinnings, theory of personality, psychopathology, and approach to treatment. It represents the best and most complete presentation of Adler's original work with excellent commentary.

Dinkmeyer, D., Dinkmeyer, D., Jr., & Sperry, L. (1987). *Adlerian counseling and psychotherapy* (2nd ed.). Columbus, OH: Merrill.

This comprehensive overview of Adlerian counseling and psychotherapy covers theoretical foundations, personality development, psychopathology, phases of the therapeutic process, assessment, counseling strategies, and applications to children and adolescents as well as adults.

Dreikurs, R., & Soltz, V. (1964). *Children: The challenge.* New York: Hawthorn Books.

This is the most widely used book for Adlerian oriented parent study groups. It is practical and written in a style easily understood by parents. The book presents an orientation to the philosophy of child rearing exposed by Dreikurs and then covers myriad typical problems and critical incidents encountered by parents.

Dreikurs, R., Grunwald, B., & Pepper, F. (1982). *Maintaining sanity in the classroom: Illustrated teaching techniques* (2nd ed.). New York: Harper & Row.

Application of the Adlerian approach to school and classroom situations is the central focus of this book. Fundamentals of Adlerian psychology are covered. Then, practical applications to teaching, classroom management, and school-related behavior problems are introduced. This is a useful text for the classroom teacher or for the school guidance counselor.

Shulman, B., & Mosak, H. (1988). *Manual for life style assessment.* Muncie, IN: Accelerated Development.

These authors are two of the most eminent Adlerian practitioners today. They provide a clear conceptual explanation of lifestyle as well as a systematic approach to its assessment. Their structured methods of using early childhood memories and the family constellation prove useful in illuminating the personality or lifestyle of the client.

# REFERENCES

Adler, A. (1929). *Problems of neurosis.* London: Kegan, Paul, Trench, Truebner.

Adler, A. (1931). *What life should mean to you.* Boston: Little, Brown.

Adler, A. (1963a). *The practice and theory of individual psychology.* Patterson, NJ: Littlefield, Adams.

Adler, A. (1963b). *The problem child.* New York: Capricorn Books.

Adler, A. (1972). *The neurotic constitution.* New York: Arno.

American Psychiatric Association. (1994). *Diagnostic and statistical manual of mental disorders* (4th ed.). Washington, DC: Author.

Ansbacher, H. L., & Ansbacher, R. R. (1956). *The individual psychology of Alfred Adler.* New York: Harper & Row.

Burnett, P. C. (1988). Evaluation of Adlerian parenting programs, *Individual Psychology, 44,* 63–76.

Clark, A. (1995). The organization and implementation of a social interest program in the schools. *Individual Psychology, 51,* 317–331.

Corsini, R. (1964). *Methods of group psychotherapy.* Chicago: William James Press.

Corsini, R. (1977). Individual education. *Journal of Individual Psychology, 33,* 295–349.

Corsini, R., & Painter, G. (1975). *The practical parent.* New York: Harper & Row.

Croake, J. W. (1982). Adolescent depression: Identification and intervention. *Individual Psychology, 38,* 123–128.

Croake, J. W. (1986). Treating conduct disorder in adolescents. *Individual Psychology, 42,* 270–273.

Dinkmeyer, D., & Dinkmeyer, D., Jr. (1977). Concise counseling assessment: The children's life-style guide. *Elementary School Guidance and Counseling, 12,* 117–126.

Dinkmeyer, D., & Dinkmeyer, D., Jr. (1982). *Developing understanding of self and others, D-1 & D-2* (revised). Circle Pines, MN: American Guidance Service.

Dinkmeyer, D., & Dreikurs, R. (1963). *Encouraging children to learn: The encouragement process.* Englewood Cliffs, NJ: Prentice-Hall.

Dinkmeyer, D., & McKay, G. (1982). *Raising a responsible child.* New York: Simon & Schuster.

Dinkmeyer, D., & McKay, G. (1976). *Systematic training for effective parenting (STEP).* Circle Pines, MN: American Guidance Service.

Dinkmeyer, D., & McKay, G. (1983). *Systematic training for effective parenting of teens (STEP/Teen).* Circle Pines, MN: American Guidance Service.

Dinkmeyer, D., & McKay, G. (1989). *STEP: A new look.* Circle Pines, MN: American Guidance Service.

Dinkmeyer, D., McKay, G., & Dinkmeyer, D., Jr. (1980). *Systematic training for effective teaching (STET).* Circle Pines, MN: American Guidance Service.

Dinkmeyer, D., Pew, W., & Dinkmeyer, D., Jr. (1979). *Adlerian counseling and psychotherapy.* Monterey, CA: Brooks/Cole.

Dreikurs, R. (1948). *The challenge of parenthood.* New York: Duell, Sloan & Pearch.

Dreikurs, R. (1957). *Psychology in the classroom.* New York: Harper & Row.

Dreikurs, R. (1967). *Psychodynamics, psychotherapy and counseling: Collected papers.* Chicago: Alfred Adler Institute.

Dreikurs, R., & Grey, L. (1968). *Logical consequences.* New York: Meredith.

Dreikurs, R., Grunwald, B., & Pepper, F. (1982). *Maintaining sanity in the classroom* (2nd ed.). New York: Harper & Row.

Dreikurs, R., & Soltz, V. (1964). *Children: The challenge.* New York: Hawthorn Books.

Edwards, A. (1942). The retention of affective experiences: A criticism and restatement of the problem. *Psychological Review, 49,* 43–53.

Guidoan, V., & Liotti, G. (1983). *Cognitive processes and emotional disorders.* New York: Guilford Press.

Hirschorn, S. (1982). Pensacola new pride: An Adlerian-based alternative for juvenile delinquents. *Individual Psychology, 38,* 129–137.

Kelly, F. (1978). Modifying disruptive in-school behavior through parent consultation: A case study. In R. Kern, L. Matheny, & D. Patterson (Eds.), *A case for Adlerian counseling: Theory techniques and research evidence.* Chicago: Alfred Adler Institute.

Kelly, F., & Croake, J. (1978). Application of Adlerian theory to school phobia. *Individual Psychologist, 15,* 73–81.

Kelly, F., Dowd, E., & Duffy, D. (1983). A comparison of cognitive and behavioral intervention strategies in the treatment of depression. *British Journal of Cognitive Psychotherapy, 1,* 51–58.

Kelly, F., & Main, F. (1979). Sibling conflict in a single-parent family. *American Journal of Family Therapy,* 39–47.

Kern, R., & Hankins, E. (1977). Adlerian group counseling with contracted homework. *Elementary School Guidance and Counseling, 6,* 70–75.

Kern, R., Matheny, L., & Patterson, D. (Eds.). (1978). *A case for Adlerian counseling: Theory, techniques, and research evidence.* Chicago, IL: Alfred Adler Institute.

Main, F. (1987). Special time: A necessary but underrated strategy. *The Individual Psychologist, 15,* 40–47.

Moore, M. H., & Dean-Zubritsky, C. (1979). Adlerian parent study groups: An assessment of attitude and behavior change. *Journal of Individual Psychology, 35,* 225–234.

Moreno, Z. (1959). A survey of psychodramatic techniques. *Group Psychotherapy, 12,* 5–14.

Morrow, J. S., & Kopp, R. R. (1988). Stimulating social interest in oppositional teenagers: A psychotherapeutic application of Kopp's life-style typology. *Individual Psychology, 44,* 217–223.

Morse, C., & Brokoven, J. (1987). The Oregon DUSO-R research studies series: Integrating a children's social skills curriculum in a family education/counseling center. *Individual Psychology, 43,* 101–114.

Mosak, H. (1958). Early recollections as a projective technique. *Journal of Projective Techniques, 22,* 302–311.

Mosak, H. (1987). Religious allusions in psychotherapy. *Individual Psychology, 43,* 496–501.

Mosak, H. (1989). Adlerian psychotherapy. In R. J. Corsini (Ed.), *Current psychotherapies.* Itaska, IL: Peacock.

Mozdzierz, G., Murphy, T., & Greenblatt, R. (1986). Private logic and the strategy of psychotherapy. *Individual Psychology, 42,* 339–349.

Nikelly, A. (1971). Basic processes in psychotherapy. In A. Nikelly (Ed.), *Techniques for behavior change.* Springfield, IL: Thomas.

O'Connell, W. (1975). *Action therapy and Adlerian theory.* Chicago: Alfred Adler Institute.

Pierce, K. (1987). Individual education/Corsini's 4/R schools: Another look. *Individual Psychology, 43,* 370–377.

Porter, B., & Hoedt, K. (1985). Differential effects of an Adlerian counseling approach with preadolescent children. *Individual Psychology, 41,* 372–385.

Rister, E. S. (1983). Understanding enuresis as a defecit in mental imagery: The case of Larry. *Individual Psychology, 39,* 83–91.

Schoenaker, T., & Schoenaker, T. (1976). *Adlerian social therapy.* St. Paul, MN: Green Bough.

Sherman, R., Oresky, P., & Rountree, Y. (1991). *Solving problems in couples and family therapy.* New York: Brunner/Mazel.

Shulman B. (1973). Confrontation techniques in Adlerian psychotherapy. In B. Shulman (Ed.), *Contributions to individual psychology.* Chicago: Alfred Adler Institute.

Shulman, B., & Mosak, H. (1967). The various purposes of symptoms. *Journal of Individual Psychology, 23,* 79–87.

Shulman, B., & Mosak, H. (1988). *Manual for life style assessment.* Muncie, IN: Accelerated Development.

Soltz, V. (1967). *Study group leader's manual.* Chicago: Alfred Adler Institute.

Sonstegard, M., & Dreikurs, R. (1975). The teleoanalytic group counseling approach. In G. Gazda (Ed.), *Basic approaches to group psychotherapy and group counseling.* Springfield, IL: Thomas.

Sweeny, T. (1975). *Adlerian counseling.* Boston: Houghton Mifflin.

Thorndike, E. L. (1913). *Educational psychology* (Vol. 2). New York: Teachers College.

Walton, F. (1975). Group workshop with adolescents. *The Individual Psychologist, 12,* 26–28.

West, J., Sonstegard, M., & Hagerman, H. (1980). A study of counseling and consulting in Appalachia. *Elementary School Guidance and Counseling, 15,* 5–13.

# Chapter 6

# *PERSON-CENTERED APPROACHES*

Helen B. Moore, Jack H. Presbury, Laura W. Smith, and J. Edward McKee

*Person-centered therapy* is the term given by Carl Rogers and his associates in 1974 to the primary theme which expressed Rogers' professional life. Rogers considered "person-centered approach" to be most descriptive of his value framework, given the variety and increasing number of fields of application (Rogers, 1980). At the same time, he believed the term "client-centered" was still accurate when applied specifically to counseling and psychotherapy (Bohart & Todd, 1988). This chapter will use "person-centered" for consistency and as a means of incorporating modifications and extensions of Rogers' work.

Person-centered therapy assumes that, given a particular therapeutic climate, individuals can be trusted to choose for themselves a growth-producing and psychologically healthy direction for their lives. Historically, person-centered therapy grew out of the Rogerian revolution (Ivey & Simek-Downing, 1980) in the 1940s and 1950s. As the first distinctly indigenous school of therapy in the United States (Belkin, 1980), it was originally called *nondirective* in revolt against the diagnostic, interpretive, past-oriented methods and mystique of the psychoanalytic school and the directive vocational counseling methods. Rogers' book, *Client-Centered Therapy* (1951), ushered in both a new term and a wave of humanistically oriented therapists. The effects have been felt not only in counseling and therapy, but also in education, social work, business, pastoral training, group process, human relations skills programs, race relations, conflict resolution, and politics. This chapter is concerned with the current status, extensions, innovations, and applications of the person-centered approach to therapy with children and adolescents.

## HISTORY AND STATUS

In the preface to a book that he published at the age of 75, Carl Rogers spoke of a time when the sentence, "I walk softly through life," flashed into his mind (Rogers, 1977). As he speculated later on this experience, he saw how it described his professional life. His associations took him back to his childhood reading of Indians and frontiersmen who would "glide noiselessly through the forest without stepping on a dead twig or disturbing the foliage. No one knew their whereabouts until they had reached their destination or accomplished their mission" (p. xi). Viewed with suspicion by the therapeutic establishment, despite prestigious academic appointments, Rogers persistently broke new ground during his long career and often did not realize his impact on the field. A tribute to his pioneering accomplishments and to the open and growing person he continued to be, was in seeing his colleagues, his students, and their students over several decades take off from his own theoretical and process orientation, expanding his work to new areas and developing their own models and theories. "One of the facts that has always given me great satisfaction is that client-centered therapy, by its very nature, has always provided a congenial home for the development of creative hunches" (Rogers, 1970a, p. viii).

The years between 1928 and 1939 were times of experimentation for Rogers. After completing his education at Columbia Teacher's College in New York City, he moved to Rochester, New York, to work for the Child Study Department of the Society for Prevention of Cruelty to Children. At Rochester, he was influenced by the social workers of the Rankian school, especially Dr. Jesse Taft, to value the therapeutic relationship and to emphasize the present rather than the past. Rogers was also growing away from the therapist behaviors of coercion, advice giving, judging, and questioning, seeing these as unfruitful. Gradually, he relied more and more on the client providing the direction in therapy, trusting the client's wisdom and experience. His first major book, *The Clinical Treatment of the Problem Child* (1939), was written before he left Rochester.

In 1940, Rogers accepted a full professorship at Ohio State University. His book *Counseling and Psychotherapy* (1942) was written shortly thereafter. It was heavy on technique, characterizing the nondirective phase in his thinking. Although it was not a popular book, attacking as it did the time-honored ways of most therapists of the time, students began to flock to Ohio State to study with him.

One of his greatest contributions to the training and supervision of counselors and therapists was his use, for the first time, of electronically recorded interviews that could become actual case transcripts. This greatly demystified the process of psychotherapy. Rogers exposed his own counseling sessions to the scrutiny of colleagues and students, gave his own critical feedback, and welcomed the same from others.

During the 1940s and 1950s while at the University of Chicago, he and his students, many of whom later established their own reputations, turned out more research on psychotherapy than had ever before existed (Kirschenbaum, 1979). In 1951, his third major book, *Client-Centered Therapy,* was published. The establishment virtually ignored it; it was challenging and controversial, yet students and practitioners applauded it.

Rogers went to the University of Wisconsin between 1957 and 1963 with a joint appointment in psychology and psychiatry and a dream of working together with professionals of both disciplines on cooperative training and research projects. He made a valuable contribution through his work with chronic patients and collaborated on the book *The Therapeutic Relationship and Its Impact: A Study of Psychotherapy with Schizophrenics* with several authors who became famous in their own right in subsequent years (Rogers, Gendlin, Kiesler, & Truax, 1967). His most successful publication during this time was the book *On Becoming a Person: A Therapist's View of Psychotherapy,* a collection of essays that synthesized his work and applied his principles to many different kinds of relationships.

Rogers moved to California in 1964 at a time when humanistic psychology was having an impact on education, counseling, pastoral studies, group process, and other areas. The popularity of group work at that time gave him an opportunity to be with "normal" people and test out his hypothesis that, given the same therapeutic conditions, all people could be helped. He made tapes and films of his work and wrote a popular book called *Carl Rogers on Encounter Groups* (1970b). Again, he demystified what happens in counseling, this time in groups, by describing his own behavior as a facilitator, letting it be viewed on film and heard on tape.

In 1978, Rogers and some of his associates formed the Center for Studies of the Person, where members carried out their own projects, from drug education to interracial encounters, to helping unskilled people into the working world. Rogers himself became actively involved in applying his insights to the field of education, working with school systems and publishing the book *Freedom to Learn: A View of What Education Might Become* (1969) and *Freedom to Learn for the 1980s* (1983).

Rogers remained active during the 1970s, with his books on marriage and its alternatives (1972), personal power (1977), and his personal reflections, experiences, and future perspectives (1980) reflecting his range of interests. On his 80th birthday, Rogers announced his intention to devote the remainder of his life to working toward world peace. At the time of his death on February 4, 1987, at the age of 85, he had been focusing his energies on conflict resolution and on applying his methods to politics and international relations. To this end, he traveled widely, working with Catholics and Protestants in Ireland, with Blacks and Whites in South Africa, with Soviet leaders, and with Central American leaders. The Carl Rogers Institute for Peace was founded in 1983 at La Jolla with the purpose of providing occasions for political and lay leaders to meet person-to-person in informal, intensive, and spontaneous dialogues, using profound listening and nonjudgmental valuing as a means of resolving differences and reaching understandings.

During his long professional life, Rogers was a leader in many prestigious professional groups and received numerous awards including the American Psychological Association's first Distinguished Professional Contribution Award in 1972. Rogers has had a tremendous impact on the field of counseling and therapy.

## OVERVIEW OF THEORY

### Basic Theory and Assumptions

From his therapeutic work, Rogers developed a view of people at variance with the more pessimistic, deterministic theory of the psychoanalytic school and the tabula rasa orientation of the behaviorists. He believed it was in the nature of people to strive toward self-fulfillment or self-actualization. The self-actualization tendency is the "inherent tendency of the organism to develop all its capacities in ways which serve to maintain or enhance the organism" (Rogers, 1959, p. 196). This is the viewpoint of the school of humanistic psychology, the diverse "third force" group that Carl Rogers, Abraham Maslow, and others are credited with pioneering and popularizing during the 1950s. Humanistic psychologists view people as being rational and basically trustworthy and as having dignity and worth, striving to grow and enhance their potentialities and to become socialized in harmony with others in their environment (Gelso & Fretz, 1992).

Person-centered counselors and therapists are usually referred to as *self-theorists* or *phenomenologists*. Self-theory holds that individuals exist at the center of a changing world of experience, termed the *phenomenological field*. This perceptual field is, for the individual, "reality," and it is the understanding of this subjective world that is of concern to the counselor (Gelso & Fretz, 1992). This stance is in opposition to science-oriented positions, which assert that "clients must relate to the real world not just in accord with their perceptions but how it actually is" (Byrne, 1995, p. 191). More recently, the "constructivist" point of view has called our ability to know an objective real world into question, and has seemingly vindicated the Rogerian point of view (Neimeyer & Mahoney, 1995). The best vantage point for understanding the behavior of others is from their internal frame of reference, as only they can know how they perceive their private world. Much is unconscious, yet more is available to consciousness. People react as organized wholes to their unique perceptions and experiences (Hansen, Rossberg, & Cramer, 1994). Pain, struggle, and emotion accompany growth as individuals try to satisfy their needs and move toward greater socialization, independence, and integration. The basic motivational force is the drive toward self-actualization, which means that people try to meet not only their physiological needs but also their needs to relate to others, to feel self-esteem, and to become productive and self-regulated.

As children develop, a part of their perceptual field becomes differentiated as the self—the "I," the "me." This sense of self becomes the self-concept and is made up of children's internal experiences and environmental perceptions, especially how others respond to and interact with them. The needs of children for the positive regard of others, their needs to be prized, to be accepted, to be loved, are so addictive that they become the most potent of all needs (J. O. Prochaska, 1979; J. C. Prochaska & Norcross, 1994). Children who receive positive regard develop a sense of self-worth. When parents and others give the impression that their love is dependent on whether children please them, children begin to doubt their own internal feelings and thoughts and then begin to act to satisfy those significant adults. The behavior of children comes to be guided, not by whether their experience feels good and right to them, but by whether it is likely to result in their receiving love. For example, if anger is frowned on in the home, children will deny their angry feelings despite their inner sensations and bodily reactions to the contrary. When children incorporate the values of others just to please the others and to receive regard, they have developed conditions of worth and feel good about themselves only when they live up to the expectations of others.

Theoretically, children could develop positive self-concepts if there was congruence between what they valued and prized in themselves and what was valued and prized by parents and others:

> If an individual should experience only unconditional positive regard, then no conditions of worth would develop, self-regard would be unconditional, the needs for positive regard and self regard would never be at variance with organismic evolution, and the individual would continue to be psychologically adjusted and would be fully functioning. (Rogers, 1959, p. 227)

## View of Psychopathology

Pathology develops from the reactions of children to conditional love. The core of maladjustment is the incongruence between self, on the one hand, and, on the other hand, experiences that occur as children try to please their parents and significant people to receive more self-regard. "Psychopathology reflects a divided personality, with tensions, defenses, and inadequate functioning that accompany such lack of wholeness" (J. O. Prochaska, 1979, p. 114). The individual develops defenses to deal with incongruities, to cope with threats to self-esteem, and to lessen anxiety. Defenses, however, distort and deny the reality of experiences and result in inaccurate perceptions. Sometimes all that happens is a cognitive rigidity; at other times personality disorganization occurs and anxiety becomes overwhelming. Hansen et al. (1994) list the following as aspects of a maladaptive personality: (a) *estrangement:* the experience that one has come to falsify parts of the self that are no longer experienced as real or owned; (b) *incongruity of behavior:* instead of acting to satisfy the organism, one acts to acquire approval; (c) *anxiety:* the person begins to experience threats to the self; (d) *defense mechanisms:* the person begins to distort or deny experiences that are not compatible with conditions of worth, and to project blame for anxiety outward (pp. 78–79). All these aspects produce a feeling of not being whole; of becoming stuck and without personal value. "Whether a person goes into therapy because of a breakdown, or because defensive symptoms are hurting too much, or because of a desire for greater actualization, the goal is the same—to increase the congruence between self and experience through a process of reintegration" (J. O. Prochaska, 1979, p. 116).

## General Therapeutic Goals and Techniques

Person-centered therapy can be understood as an evolution in the thinking of a group of humanistically oriented therapists influenced by the leadership of Carl Rogers. Emphasizing the striking change in this therapy over several decades, Hart and Tomlinson (1970) stated: "The professional therapist who knows only early versions of client-centered therapy has seen the seeds but not the pumpkins" (p. 3). Since then, some of the "pumpkins" have matured and others are still developing. "Over the years an increasingly broad range of techniques has been permitted. The bottom line theoretically is that the techniques be in synch with person-centered theory and philosophy" (Gelso & Fretz, 1992). As Rogers grew and developed new insights in his work with clients, groups, and institutions, so did his emphasis change in regard to the process of counseling. Despite evolutionary changes, however, the original attitudes from Rogers' earliest work remain the centerpiece of the person-centered approach (Thorne, 1992). Ivey and Simek-Downing (1980) charted identifiable stages that represent the development of person-centered theory:

*Stage 1: Nondirective (1940–1950).* This stage emphasizes the acceptance of the client, the establishment of a positive and nonjudgmental climate, trust in the client's wisdom, permissiveness, and uses clarification of the client's world as the main technique. His [Rogers'] writings give a central emphasis to skills in the counseling process.

*Stage 2: Client-Centered (1950–1961).* This stage centers on reflecting the feelings of the client, incorporates resolving incongruities between the ideal self and the real self, avoids personally threatening situations for the client, and uses reflection as the main technique. Skills are not emphasized; rather a major emphasis focusing on the counselor as a person is evolving.

*Stage 3: Increased Personal Involvement (1961–Present).* While maintaining consistency with all past work, Rogers moved increasingly to emphasizing present-tense experience, a more active and self-disclosing role for the counselor, group as well as individual counseling, and consideration of broader issues in society, such as cultural differences and the use of power. The emphasis on skills remained low as Rogers emphasized the counselor attitudes rather than interview skills. Coupled with this is an extensive emphasis on experiencing oneself as a person in relation to others. (p. 262)

During the 1940s, Rogers was developing his hypothesis about help-seekers as responsible clients rather than dependent patients and his hypothesis about therapy as assisting them to achieve their own insights through a permissive, accepting, and nonauthoritarian atmosphere. The caricature of a Rogerian therapist during this nondirective period was one of a passive, innocuous person addicted to "uh-huh's." As Hart and Tomlinson (1970) stated: "Such a stereotype has never been accurate, but it does convey, in a distorted way, one of the main features of the early approach" (p. 3). Perhaps in their attempts to keep from adopting traditional therapist behaviors such as analyzing, diagnosing, giving advice, judging, and asking questions, early practitioners erred in the direction of too much passivity and shallowness.

During the client-centered phase, Rogers began to focus on the therapeutic relationship as the most important variable in the counseling process. This emphasis on the *quality* of the therapeutic encounter has been widely accepted in generic therapeutic practice. In their refinement of client-centered counseling, Boy and Pine (1982) listed the following characteristics of the relationship:

- A face-to-face relationship.
- A person-in-person relationship.
- A human relationship.

- A relationship of reciprocity and commitment.
- A relationship in which the client is voluntarily involved.
- A relationship possessing mutual respect.
- A relationship possessing effective communication.
- A relationship possessing genuine acceptance of the client by the counselor.
- A relationship in which the counselor empathically focuses on the needs and feelings of the client.
- A relationship that is liberating.
- An open-ended relationship in which outcomes essentially emerge from the client, not from the counselor.
- A relationship in which the client's desire for confidentiality is respected.
- A professional service that calls for acquired attitudes and skills on the part of the counselor.
- A professional service based upon a substantive rationale reflecting philosophical and psychological principles emanating from theoretical and empirical considerations of the person, human behavior, and society.
- A relationship in which the counselor possesses a concept of the person.
- A relationship in which being precedes becoming. (p. 127)

Subsequently, Boy and Pine (in Capuzzi & Gross, 1995) have taken the person-centered approach a step further; stating that the counselor must adjust the relationship and the techniques to the specific preferred mode of the client. "Their view is that a true person-centered approach will have a consistent foundation, but that a full range of the relationship must be built upon the unique aspects of the counselor or therapist, the client, and their personalized relationship together" (pp. 254–255).

In an important essay, Rogers (1957) hypothesized from his clinical experience and from the research he and his students had conducted, six "necessary and sufficient" conditions that appeared to initiate client growth and personality change. He believed that these conditions worked for all types of clients in all settings and that they needed to exist and continue over a period of time. In the article, he suggested operational ways of defining and measuring them and advanced his belief that empirical studies would provide future refinements. The conditions are:

1. Two persons are in psychological contact.
2. The client is in a state of incongruence, being vulnerable or anxious.
3. The therapist is congruent and integrated in the relationship.
4. The therapist experiences unconditional positive regard for the client.
5. The therapist experiences an empathic understanding of the client's internal frame of reference and endeavors to communicate this experience to the client.
6. The communication to the client of the therapist's regard is to a minimal degree achieved.

Person-centered counselors and therapists extracted from the essay the term *core conditions,* which they have assigned to attitudes of empathic understanding, respect (unconditional positive regard), and genuineness (congruence). Following the lead of Rogers, they believe that all people have within themselves the potential to understand themselves; change their attitudes, thoughts, and behaviors; enhance their self-concepts; and become more self-directing in a therapeutic climate that provides the core conditions.

Empathic understanding means that the counselor is able to sense accurately the client's private world and internal frame of reference and communicate that understanding so that it is felt by the client. This type of communication is a process by which the counselor not only understands the clearly presented and explicit client meanings, but also accurately senses and conveys those of which the client may be only dimly aware.

Respect implies that there are no conditions of acceptance for clients; rather, the counselor feels warm, positive, and nonjudgmental toward whatever or wherever clients are at the moment and is able to grant permission for them to have their own feelings, both negative and positive. It is not possible for therapists to feel such caring at all times, but the attitude needs to be conveyed frequently for constructive change to take place. In addition, basic to the concept of respect is the viewpoint that people live in separate realities, and thus, one person is in no position to judge another's reality as incorrect, distorted, or inadequate (Rogers, 1980). At the same time, acceptance does not imply one's approval of or agreement with the actions of another.

Genuineness depends on the awareness of counselors of their own experiencing-in-relationships and the degree to which their behaviors, nonverbal and verbal, and their inner feelings match. This does not mean that counselors are perfectly integrated in all their life aspects, nor does it mean that all their feelings need to be expressed in counseling; but it does require that they be aware of any discrepant feelings and behaviors. Being genuine in a facilitative sense implies a basic honesty but stresses the responsibility of the counselor to continue providing a supportive, nonthreatening atmosphere in large measure.

A means of conveying the core conditions became the basic verbal tool of the counselor during this client-centered phase. "The most striking change in the actual practice of psychotherapy was the therapist's emphasis on responding sensitively to the affective rather than the semantic meaning of the client's expressions" (Hart & Tomlinson, 1970, p. 8). This skill became known as *reflection of feeling,* and became important in conveying the *active listening* or *empathic listening* behavior taught in training programs and endorsed by modern counselors and therapists of many persuasions. More recently, the idea of responding to the meaning of the client has been reinstated.

> Reflecting meaning denotes counselor attempts to restate the personal impact of the event the client is describing . . . The formula for a good reflective response is "You feel ( ) because (  )" . . . the first blank is filled with a feeling or content plus feeling and the second blank with the meaning it holds for the individual. (Young, 1992, p. 47)

Sometimes the counselor draws on intuition or hunches to supply the meaning (Cark-huff, 1987; Egan, 1990).

The third, and present, period of person-centered therapy has also been termed *experiential* (Hart & Tomlinson, 1970). Therapists are process-oriented and interested in the ongoing experience of their clients. The goal of therapy is to help clients become able to experience feelings and to listen to their experience (Bohart & Todd, 1988, p. 132). Person-centered counselors and therapists today are more expressive and out-going with their clients and share moment-to-moment experiencing, personal mean-ings, and feelings. When therapists respond to clients by openly conveying their own immediate experiencing, they respond to clients as persons. Clients are free to accept or reject the therapist's communications but may eventually be touched and changed by them (Hart & Tomlinson, 1970).

This concept of genuineness has taken on new significance. In Rogers' (1977) words:

> The more the therapist is herself in the relationship, putting up no professional front or personal facade, the greater is the likelihood that the client will change and grow in a constructive manner. It means the therapist is openly being the feelings and attitudes that are flowing within the moment. The term transparent catches the flavor of this ele-ment—the therapist makes herself transparent to the client. The client can see right through what the therapist is in the relationship; the client experiences no holding back on the part of the therapist. As for the therapist, what she is experiencing is available to consciousness, can be lived in the relationship, and can be communicated if appropriate. (p. 9)

Gendlin (1974) represented the thinking of many modern-day person-centered counselors and therapists with his endorsement of the use of any skills and techniques which seem helpful, his emphasis on the experiential aspects and honesty of the thera-peutic encounter, and, especially, his focus on continuous empathic listening:

> Listening, therefore, is never a one-shot response, but involves at least a few steps; a lis-tening response, then again hearing, then again responding. When that first thing is re-ally heard, wait. Let the person see what now arises. Respond to that. Several such steps, not just one turn, are listening in this sense of the word. (p. 221)

Responding should take off from and return to client-centered reflection of feeling as a necessary baseline for all other responses: "Only in this way can the therapist stay constantly in touch with what is occurring in the person, and thus know and help make good use of whatever beneficial results other therapeutic procedures may have" (Gendlin, 1974, p. 216).

A hallmark of person-centered counselors in recent years has been their eclecticism (Boy & Pine, 1990). Person-centered counselors work in diverse ways and use a vari-ety of skills to enhance the counseling process. Their commonality is a trust in the therapeutic process and the belief that the growth potential of individuals of all ages and conditions tends to be released in a relationship in which the counselor feels and communicates genuineness, respect, a nonjudgmental attitude, and a deep empathic understanding toward the client. Counselors seek to fully understand their clients' phenomenological world and how it is affecting their present thinking and feeling. As authentic beings, counselors express their own thoughts, feelings, and experiences with their clients when appropriate. The therapeutic climate is one of openness, safety, and freedom for clients to be as they are at the time and to become what they would like to be. Problem-solving and making value judgments is primarily the job of the client, who can be trusted to act responsibly, given such a climate.

Therapist skills and techniques are valuable only to the extent that they enhance the therapeutic process and enrich the relationship. How something is said or what is said is less important than what is going on between the counselor and client and the feelings shared. It has become apparent that focusing on the counselor's ability to create facilitative conditions is not the whole story: "Qualities of the therapist are, in fact qualities of both the client and the relationship as well. . . . Rogers' facilitative conditions are very similar to contemporary, psychodynamic conceptualizations of the 'working,' 'helping,' or 'therapeutic' alliance" (Bergin & Garfield, 1994, p. 243). The process of effective counseling, however, is undergirded by a foundation of skills possessed by the counselor that help to communicate empathy, respect, genuineness, and faith in the client's drive toward self-actualization.

## Systematic Skills Training

The influence of person-centered theory has been felt in many training programs for counselors and therapists. Regardless of the theoretical stance of trainers or trainees, person-centered attitudes and concepts remain the foundation for relationship building with the development of trust and a facilitative working alliance. Most process work in therapy and counseling, at the least, begins from a person-centered framework.

Students today are taught in an experiential manner and through some method of systematic skills training. In experiential training, cognitive learning is not ignored, but there is an emphasis on helping trainees get in touch with their own experience and feelings, while working either in simulated or actual counseling situations. Experiential training is thought to foster congruence, genuineness, and self-understanding in future counselors, which in turn will better enable them to build relationships of trust, openness, and mutuality with clients.

Systematic skills models have roots in the research attempts of Rogers and his associates to quantify and demonstrate the effectiveness of the core conditions of empathy, respect, and genuineness. A great part of the effectiveness of any one orientation to counseling can be accounted for by the central core of facilitative conditions that each of these orientations holds in common (Carkhuff, 1969; Truax & Carkhuff, 1967). Carkhuff and Berenson (1967) demonstrated that those who possess academic knowledge and credentials may not be the best helpers and that, indeed, helping can be for better or worse. Egan (1975) suggests that overly cognitive, nonsystematic training programs, run by individuals who themselves lack basic helping skills, can be a devastating combination.

The *Carkhuff Model* (1969) divides the counseling process into two parts: the initial or facilitating stage based largely on Rogers' core conditions, and the action stage, which extends Rogerian theory. According to Carkhuff, counselors who offer high levels of empathy, genuineness, respect, and concreteness (the direct expression of specific feelings and experiences), as judged on a 5-point scale, help clients move toward self-exploration and eventual behavioral change. Counselors who demonstrate low levels of these conditions may increase client defensiveness and actually block client growth. Low levels are associated with counselor behaviors such as judging, moralizing, giving advice, asking questions, changing the focus of the client, and attending only to content.

Egan's first edition of *The Skilled Helper* (1975) became a popular three-stage model in person-centered concepts, particular in Stage 1 and Stage 2. In Stage 1, the helper responds with empathy, respect, genuineness, and concreteness to the world of the client to aid that person's self-exploration. In Stage 2, the helper uses advanced skills of accurate empathy, self-disclosure, confrontation, and immediacy to help the client achieve more objectivity and realize a need to change. Helpers aid in the choosing and implementing of constructive action programs and support behavioral change in Stage 3.

Since these early efforts to train helpers systematically and from a largely person-centered foundation, educators have continued to emphasize the relationship, the communication of empathy, and skills such as active or reflective listening (Byrne, 1995; Egan, 1994; Thompson & Rudolph, 1996). Young (1992) refers to these as attending skills and Baker (1996) calls them "basic verbal counseling responses" (p. 61). Taxonomies for training therapists and counselors have been developed that list skills recognized as person-centered (Byrne, 1995; Cormier & Cormier, 1991; Ivey, 1988). They discourage counselor behaviors that are nonfacilitative, and they stress empathic listening and responding, entering the phenomenological world of the client and exploring it in a nonthreatening manner. In general, the attitudes toward clients, the emphasis on building a relationship, and empathic responding skills of the person-centered therapist are considered to be "givens" and foundational.

## INDIVIDUAL PSYCHOTHERAPY AND COUNSELING WITH CHILDREN

Person-centered counselors work with children who are experiencing developmental, remedial, and crisis concerns by providing a safe climate that encourages free and open expression of feelings and thoughts. The relationship established between adult and child is one of acceptance. The counselor conveys empathy, respect, genuineness, and honesty and believes in the child's capacity to become self-directing.

### The Counseling Process in Elementary Schools

Counselors in school settings work with children to enhance their learning and help them through developmental and situational concerns. They provide referrals to clinics or private practitioners when long-term or intensive therapy is indicated. A person-centered counselor helps the child understand the counseling process, its purposes and goals, and accepts the child's experience and attitudes in regard to the reason for referral. In school settings, time constraints and accountability issues often result in the person-centered counselor becoming more action oriented. In the context of a warm, caring, and nonjudgmental atmosphere, the counselor attempts to give the child honest feedback with regard to what is going on in the relationship between the two of them and what seems to be taking place in the child's life. Because of the dynamic, changing nature of counseling theory, school counselors extend their basic person-centered stance into areas of information giving, mutual goal setting and decision making with children. Undesirable counselor behaviors are those that cause a child to become more defensive or feel less self-worth, such as moralizing, judging, lecturing, and asking "why" questions.

In the actual counseling situation, the counselor's first job is relationship building, establishing an atmosphere where the child feels there are no conditions for acceptance. Person-centered counselors seek ways to understand the child's world and the child's perception of problem areas. As Baker (1996) states:

> Children . . . benefit from knowing that someone cares and is trying to understand their circumstances. They respond best to counselors who provide support and understanding by creative facilitative mutual relationships. (p. 61)

Inviting children to decide how to use their time with the counselor is one way to proceed. Although person-centered therapists have more recently deemphasized techniques in favor of emphasizing the attitudes of the counselor and the counseling relationship, some skills have been identified through research and practice as being helpful in getting children to express their feelings about themselves, their world, and others, and to understand these feelings and their experiences in relationship to their behaviors. These skills enrich the relationship and set the stage for change.

Nelson (1972) states that counseling transcripts with children have identified at least five characteristic client-centered skills: simple acceptance, reflection, clarification, summarization, and confrontation. These skills remain effective today along with five others: immediacy, self-disclosure, open-ended questions, silence, and reflection of deeper feelings. The skills are defined as follows:

1. *Simple Acceptance.* The counselor gives a minimal, encouraging verbal or nonverbal response such as a head nod.
2. *Reflection.* The counselor expresses in different words the feelings and attitudes expressed by the child. When children hear back what they have said, they feel understood and their feelings accepted.
3. *Clarification.* The counselor checks out what the child has said and what is meant. Clarification can "make clear" and concrete what a child may have difficulty expressing in words.
4. *Summarization.* The counselor summarizes in a few words the essence of what a child has said. Children often jump around in their expression of ideas, feelings,

and experiences and a summary from the counselor helps them tie things together. Summarization can also help maintain a counseling focus, especially when the child likes to engage in storytelling.

5. *Confrontation.* The counselor tentatively and gently confronts discrepancies, distortions, or game playing that the child reveals. Confrontation, when caring and gentle, invites children to examine their behavior and decide if they want to change.

6. *Immediacy.* The counselor responds with feedback about the relationship between the child and the counselor. The counselor shares honest feelings and thoughts in an attitude of helpfulness and genuineness.

7. *Self-Disclosure.* The counselor shares similar feelings, experiences, and thoughts in an effort to help the child gain more understanding. Self-disclosure is not an attempt to change the focus to the counselor's own problems but a means of deepening the relationship.

8. *Open-Ended Questions.* The counselor asks questions designed to get at the feelings of children and keep them exploring events, experiences, and thoughts. These questions are the opposite of fact-finding or a "20 questions" approach which usually results in brief and less thoughtful responses from children.

9. *Silence.* Silence is used to allow both counselor and child to think about what has been said. Using silence can also convey to children that they can really say what they want.

10. *Reflection of Deeper Feelings.* The counselor responds with a feeling that seems under the surface or implicit in what the child is saying. The response is used to help promote more understanding on the part of the child.

In capsulated form, the following transcript illustrates how these skills might be used:

Child: My daddy took me to see a movie about spaceships.

Counselor: [Nods head.] I see . . . [Minimal encouraging lead.]

Child: Yes, he bought me a new softball, and Barbara got books about cats, and he didn't bring Mommy a single present and she didn't go to the movie, either.

Counselor: Everybody but Mommy got a present and I guess you're wondering what that was all about . . . [Clarification.]

Child: Daddy doesn't live with us anymore. Mommy and Barbara cry a lot.

Counselor: What's the feeling like for you when you think about your daddy being gone? [Open-ended question.]

Child: Sad. He could come back.

Counselor: You feel sad when he's not home and you'd like him to live with you. [Reflection of feeling and content.] [Silence.]

Child: When he comes back home, he's gonna take me to lots of movies and the circus. I saw a circus once and there were elephants and horses and clowns and they all got into a little car and kept coming out. I counted them.

Counselor: You think your dad would do things with you if he lived with you again. [Summarizing to keep the counseling focus.]

Child: [Silence.]

Counselor: Johnny, from what you've told me, your daddy loves you and likes to do things with you. You really want him to live with you and Barbara and your mom. But maybe that's not going to happen any time soon. What do you think? [Gentle confrontation.]

Child: He could if he wanted to. I'd be real good all the time.

Counselor: When my father and mother got divorced, I used to think it was my fault and that if I'd been really good it wouldn't have happened. I wonder if that's a little bit how you might be feeling? [Self-disclosure.]

Child: Once I saw a circus on TV, and a lady got shot out of a cannon.

Counselor: I'm mixed up, Johnny. When I told you about my parents getting divorced, you talked about the circus on TV. I wonder if you just want to stop talking about your daddy right now. Is that maybe what you are feeling? [Immediacy.]

Child: I want to tell you about the circus.

Counselor: It's hard to talk about things that hurt. [Reflection of deeper feeling.]

With young children or those having trouble expressing themselves, person-centered counselors offer activities that build rapport and help them see into the child's world. The child may draw, respond to stimulus pictures, or listen to a story picked by the counselor as offering an opportunity to elicit feelings, thoughts, and experiences. As children begin to feel secure with the counselor, accepted, and understood, many open up and express frustrations, hurts, and ambivalent feelings. Children who see their problems as caused by others are confronted to further their tendencies toward responsibility and self-direction. This is done with respect for the child's right to deny or disagree with the counselor's assessment. As counseling progresses, person-centered counselors in the schools help children design and implement plans for working on their expressed concerns. At this point, counselors are pragmatic in using what works and fits with the needs and wishes of the children.

If there was one problem common to the many clients he had helped over the years, Rogers considered that problem to be that they did not accept themselves (Kirschenbaum, 1979). They believed they were not "okay"—not capable or good enough. Counselors working with children have found this problem central to other symptoms and behaviors, and have incorporated into counseling sessions experiences designed to identify and enhance the child's positive feelings and strengths. The child is encouraged in finding ways to feel good, accepted, and worthwhile. In this way, person-centered school counselors resist the role of "fixer" and offer something more fundamental to the growth and development of children, the creation of a positive environment for learning.

Elementary counselors are often asked by administrators, teachers, or parents to work with a child on a particular issue that disturbs or worries the adult. The person-centered counselor feels uncomfortable using indirect methods of getting at the problem issues since such hedging would violate the important attitude of counselor genuineness in a relationship. One solution is for the adult who feels a concern for a child to meet with the counselor and child and openly express the concern, perhaps with prior support and collaboration between the counselor and the adult. The following is an example of such an effort; here the teacher, the child, and the counselor come together:

Teacher:  Jimmy, I am bothered by seeing you pick on some of the smaller children on the playground. I noticed today that you pulled Mary's hair and made her cry, and later I saw you hit Billy pretty hard. I'd like you to talk with Mr. Jones about this.

Mr. Jones:  [To Jimmy.] Let's go to the counseling room so we can talk by ourselves for a while. I'd like to know how you feel about what happened today on the playground.

Mr. Jones:  [To Jimmy, in counseling room.] We can be comfortable in here and you can tell me what you want to. What we talk about here is between the two of us. Your teacher would like us to discuss what happened on the playground today. I'd like to hear you tell me about it.

## The Counseling Process in Clinic Settings

The person-centered counselor in a clinic setting may work with children who display disturbed behavior or deep-seated anxieties, requiring more time for the solution of the problem. "In general, relationship based treatment is advocated for an extremely broad range of child clinical problems" (Bergin & Garfield, 1994). The disturbance is often a matter of degree and depends to a large extent on how adults in the life of the child are being affected. Supervisors of counseling and therapy interns often hear their students express a belief that the parent, not the child, has the problem. As practitioners know, this may indeed be the case, and the parents may need to be consulted and involved in the treatment program.

In clinics, as in schools, the child's assessment of what is wrong is most important because the child is the client. Yet responses of adults shape behaviors, influence the self-concepts of children, color their expectations for how others will treat them, and are important in determining the nature of their disturbance (Reisman, 1973). In the decision-making procedure of whether to begin the lengthy and demanding process of psychotherapy, the professional's assessment, the parents' assessment, and the child's assessment of the problem are all needed. This does not contradict the belief of the person-centered therapist that, regardless of diagnosis, the core relational process of treatment is the same (Davison & Neal, 1994); it respects the child and the situation or context in which the questionable behavior is occurring and in which the child is living. With adequate assessment, therapy may not be indicated; rather, changes in the child's environment or in the attitude or responses of adults in the child's life may be required (Sarason & Sarason, 1993).

Reisman (1973) has set forth seven principles of psychotherapy with children, as follows:

1. The therapist assesses the client as a precondition to psychotherapy and as an integral part of the process of psychotherapy.

2. The therapist listens to the client and allows ample opportunity for the latter to express feelings and beliefs.

3. The therapist communicates his [or her] understanding of the client, his respect, and his wish to be of help.

4. The therapist negotiates with the client a purpose or goal for their meetings.

5. The therapist makes clear what is unusual or inconsistent in the client's behavior, feelings, and beliefs.

6. When dealing with behaviors that are supported within a given system, the therapist may modify the behaviors by negotiation within the system.

7. The therapist negotiates termination with the client when he or she believes that the advantages of ending the meetings outweigh what may be gained by their continuance.

As can be seen, person-centered beliefs are incorporated into these principles. It is assumed that the child is capable of reasonable behavior, so limits in therapy are mentioned only as the need arises. Therapists let children know the reason for referral and that they understand and want to help. In deciding on goals, the child and therapist seek a mutual agreement, which may not necessarily adhere to the goals of the referral source. The therapist respects the child's attempts at self-direction and points out ways in which there are inconsistencies in beliefs, actions, and feelings. When the behavior of the child is inappropriate and ineffective, the child receives honest feedback, but not in the context of a judgment or threat to the child's self-esteem. Whenever possible, the client selects the termination date. In terminations, the courage, faith, and confidence of both the client and the therapist are put to the test (Reisman, 1973).

## Play as a Therapeutic Medium with Children

Play techniques have been used with children in clinics and in private therapy for many years (Davison & Neal, 1994); its use in schools has been more recent and more limited. One of the author's (HM) earliest experiences with this approach occurred some years ago in an elementary school with Joey, a 7-year-old boy, referred by his teacher for lack of motivation and disturbing behavior in the classroom.

Joey arrived promptly at 9:30 A.M., twice a week, said little or nothing, often rocked in an old rocking chair for a time, and then accepted the ongoing invitation to play with any of the materials available. He usually chose clay as his medium. He made clay people, including his teacher and classmates, and he dropped clay bombs on them or pushed them aside with his hand. The counselor responded initially only to what seemed to be taking place: "That took care of them." Gradually, Joey decreased his aggressive play, and his clay teacher and students began doing things together. The time spent in counseling over several months was largely in silence, spotted by simple reflective statements and open questions. To this writer's amazement, the teacher continually gave feedback such as: "I don't know what you're doing with Joey, but I wish you saw him every day; he's so good when he comes back to class." In retrospect, it can be seen that the relationship made no demands on Joey; he was accepted and allowed to choose the direction of the sessions, and the counselor tried to communicate an understanding of his actions and feelings during the session.

Person-centered therapy assumes children can solve their own problems as they recreate their world and their relationship to it in play. It can be particularly useful for young children with short attention spans, or who have difficulty expressing themselves verbally, or with those who are emotionally or developmentally immature. Using play with such children provides them with freedom and reduced pressure. It facilitates communication and helps the counselor or therapist enter the world of the child.

Early client-centered counselors who wrote on the use of play therapy with children include Axline (1947), Dorfman (1951), and Moustakas (1953). Axline advocated play as a more natural medium for self-expression with children than verbalization and saw it as an opportunity for them to "play out" feelings and problems just as adults "talk out" their difficulties. She suggested eight principles to guide play sessions with individuals, groups, and classrooms:

1. The therapist must develop a warm, friendly relationship with the child, in which good rapport is established as soon as possible.

2. The therapist should establish a feeling of permissiveness in the relationship so that the child feels free to express his feelings completely.

3. The therapist should accept the child exactly as he or she is.

4. The therapist should be alert to recognize the feelings the child is expressing and reflect those feelings back to him or her in such a manner that the child will gain insight into his or her behavior.

5. The therapist should maintain a deep respect for the child's ability to solve his (or her) own problems if given an opportunity to do so. The responsibility to make choices and to institute change is the child's.

6. The therapist does not attempt to direct the child's actions or conversation in any manner. The child leads the way; the therapist follows.

7. The therapist does not attempt to hurry the therapy along. It is a gradual process and is recognized as such by the therapist.

8. The therapist should establish only those limitations that are necessary to anchor the therapy to the world of reality and to make the child aware of his (or her) responsibility in the relationship.

Nelson (1972) urges counselors "to treat play behavior as if it were verbalized—reflecting, summarizing, confronting, and so on—yet remaining true to 'the givens' of the situation rather than extending into the interpretive realm" (p. 215). In an initial play situation where a child is pounding a girl doll with a mother doll, the counselor's response: "I wonder how the girl doll feels when the mother doll hits her like that?" is much less threatening than "How do you feel when your mother hits you?"

In one of the currently popular books on play therapy, Landreth (1991) states that "Children are quite capable of teaching adults about themselves if the adults are willing, patient, and open to learning" (p. viii). He uses 16 principles found in his own experience to guide him in his work with children. Carl Rogers would find them all acceptable. Because of length, we shall not include all of them here. One important principle states that Landreth likes to be accepted as a person and therefore strives to appreciate the person of the child. In another, he states: "It feels good to be an authority, to provide answers, therefore I shall need to work hard to protect children from me" (pp. 5–6).

In the permissive atmosphere of the playroom, only realistic, necessary limits are set (e.g., no physical behavior toward the counselor or therapist; no destroying of toys), and the child begins to feel valued in the presence of an empathic adult. While early nondirective therapists advocated complete freedom for children to choose toys with which to play, counselors and therapists with elementary school children may maximize time by putting into view toys that have the potential to elicit feelings and thoughts concerning problem areas already identified. For example, a doll family and a few props may be all that is needed for productive sessions, as with Mary:

> Mary, age 6, had been deserted by her mother and began acting out in her highly structured first-grade classroom. The counselor observed Mary and asked to work with her. When Mary first saw the counselor, she looked at her with obvious suspicion and asked: "Whose mama are you?" The counselor worked with Mary 1/2 hour weekly. The first 3 weeks were spent virtually in silence while Mary played. After 3 weeks she began to talk, using the doll family. She buried the mother doll three times that day, and it remained buried for 2 weeks, after which Mary laid it in a "coffin." The counselor reflected what she observed Mary doing and created the permissive atmosphere for Mary's feelings to come to the surface.

In this example, it required time for the child to work through her feelings and cope with her school and home situation. Ideally, in such situations, the school and remaining family members cooperate in providing the needed support and security.

Some young children in school and clinic settings can best express their feelings through play activities, using puppets, art, media, games, and other materials. Person-centered counselors may choose unstructured or structured means of facilitating the counseling process as long as a climate of trust, acceptance, and empathy is consistently applied. Using play has been effective with both normal and troubled children. The process may be slow, but a modification in the child's attitude and behavior often results as the child begins to feel more okay and competent.

## INDIVIDUAL PSYCHOTHERAPY AND COUNSELING WITH ADOLESCENTS

### Counseling with Adolescents in School Settings

The high school counselor with a reputation for keeping confidences and for being accepting, nonjudgmental, and empathic is likely to be a busy person, whether an adolescent needs help with a personal concern or has a need for career exploration and information. Counselors in school settings must operate within institutional guidelines and policies and support the academic and vocational goals of education. Many educators today agree that physical, personal, social, emotional, academic, and vocational aspects are intertwined; and they focus on educating the student as a whole person. School counseling programs have become an integral part of the educational system in the United States with individual and group counseling as one of its primary components.

In a competitive, constantly changing society with confusing values and messages, adolescents struggle to grow and develop into responsible, cooperative, productive adults. Problems abound for them: peer pressures, eating disorders, violence and abuse, family disorganization, issues of sexuality, AIDS, drugs, academic worries, college and job decisions. Many lack confidence, not only in themselves but in the world outside school.

Counselors with a person-centered philosophy convey to these students their faith that they, the students, can become self-directing and capable of finding viable solutions and coping strategies. This communication of faith in the student is not a passive process of merely listening and waiting for the adolescent to take the initiative. The person-centered counselor provides a relationship with attitudes of empathy, respect, and genuineness (the core conditions) and incorporates the skills that are used with children, except in more sophisticated form as consistent with the increased cognitive and abstract thinking processes of youth. Listening in an accepting, empathic manner is still fundamental to the process of counseling with adolescents and cannot be rushed. Students are the best judges of their current experience and must be allowed sufficient opportunity to explore who they are and what they want. "The client must feel free enough to reveal his innermost feelings without fear of contradiction or reprisal from the counselor. . . . In a truly permissive atmosphere he can explore his inner-most feelings, sift them, accept them, or reject them" (Boy & Pine, 1963, p. 48). Adolescence is a time of contradictory thoughts, feelings, values, and behaviors; and the person-centered counselor may help students obtain more objectivity through empathically encountering and confronting them.

Despite time constrictions during the school day, the person-centered counselor will still refrain from falling into a pattern of advice giving (as opposed to information giving, which is often desirable and necessary). For example, the open-ended question, "What do you see as your options in this situation?" is more respectful than, "Here are your options . . ." Skilled counselors ask few questions, especially avoiding those that seem to be based on curiosity and fact-finding or that ask why. Teenagers often receive "why" questions with defensiveness or hostility.

Dimensions are added in counseling adolescents in accordance with the expressed needs and concerns of the adolescent. Counselors use vocational interest inventories and computer-based programs as tools for self-exploration, and are knowledgeable and helpful in career as well as personal, social, and emotional areas. In educational and vocational counseling, the person-centered counselor expects students to make the choices and contacts that will result in their feeling confident and responsible. In essence, the person-centered counseling relationship is primarily one of talking together and experiencing together; however, the school counselor uses skills, activities, materials, and interventions to enhance self-concept development, to aid in self-understanding, and to foster independence and decision making for young people.

School counselors may not have the option during school time to prolong exploration of students' deeper problems; yet frequently, the relationship provided and the attitudes given in a few sessions may help students define for themselves a direction. Sensitive and competent school counselors need to be knowledgeable concerning referral sources for students who have problems that are more appropriately handled in longer-term therapy.

## Counseling with Adolescents in Agency Settings

Agencies provide a regular, specified time for adolescents to receive help in a setting apart from their family, school, peers, and neighborhood. Agency counselors can often be more objective and able to see a broader picture of the adolescent's functioning than is possible in the structure of a school setting. Many adolescents prefer to disclose themselves to an individual not connected with their everyday lives. On the other hand, the agency counselor often needs parental and school collaboration in meeting specific adolescent needs in therapy.

In their discussion of the use of "nondirective and relationship-based therapy" with adolescents, Bergin and Garfield (1994) wrote:

> In current child and adolescent psychotherapy research, there are few efforts to test nondirective treatments as originally formulated. A more generic and integrated therapy is often used in practice and studied in research. This therapy adheres in principle to features of client-centered therapy in which emphasis is placed on the therapist-client relationship to provide a corrective emotional experience and encourage the expression of feeling and self-exploration. (p. 550)

Adolescents seen in counseling often find their thoughts, feelings, and behaviors confusing even to themselves. Depression and suicidal thoughts are not uncommon (Comer, 1995), and the astute counselor searches out these possibilities. Teenagers worry about their mood swings and unpredictability. Inferiority feelings plague them, and small failures in relationships loom as major obstacles in their lives. Parents and other authority figures become symbols of their lingering dependence and sometimes rebellion. A person-centered counselor tries to see into this experience of teenagers to help them sort out beliefs, feelings, values, and behaviors. The counselor reflects both the explicit and implicit expressions and personal meanings of youthful clients. Short summaries also help systematize the adolescent client's thinking. As adolescent clients feel understood and better focused on the core of their concerns, they often begin to explore in more depth. The counselor risks tentatively confronting any mixed messages, ambiguities, and discrepancies perceived in the relationships in order to help young people see their behavior more clearly, both with the counselor and with others in their lives. After sufficient exploration has taken place and understanding begins to occur, the modern-day, person-centered counselor is ready to help the adolescent assess alternatives, make decisions, and formulate action plans.

Counselors often find that therapy with teenagers occurs in ups and downs as the young people test them by throwing out roadblocks and other resistances: They are late, they "forget" appointments, they talk about inconsequential things. Person-centered counselors remain mindful of their own experiencing when adolescents are inconsistent and avoidant: They behave in spontaneous fashion, perhaps showing humor, perhaps displaying frustration. The attitude of genuineness is the most important posture they offer at such times. Use of the skill of immediacy (disclosing the therapist's immediate feelings about the relationship) lets the client know that the counselor can be relied on not to manipulate but to be honest and open and to give accurate feedback. Immediacy creates a "you and me in this together" feeling that many teenagers long for.

## GROUP PROCEDURES WITH CHILDREN AND ADOLESCENTS

The Rogerian influence remains strong in group work, as evidenced by the following quote from M. Corey and Corey in their recent book *Groups: Process and Practice* (1997):

> We value Carl Rogers's *[sic]* (1970b) emphasis on the "facilitative dimensions of the therapeutic relationship," and we see certain attitudes and actions as enhancing the level of trust in a group. (p. 142)

Rogers once stated that he believed the intensive group was "the most rapidly spreading social invention of the century, and probably the most potent" (Rogers, 1970b, p. 1). As he had done for the process of therapy with the introduction of recordings and transcripts of sessions, he opened up group process to public scrutiny with the use of tapes and films. He believed that groups were unique opportunities for "normal" people to have honest and open interactions, intimacy, and the freedom to drop their facades. He thought that the group climate of safety, openness, risk taking, and genuineness fostered a trust that helped members recognize and change their self-defeating behaviors, test out more innovative and constructive behaviors, and begin to relate in a more adequate and effective fashion in everyday life.

The group setting provided an opportunity for Rogers to continue his own personal growth as he entered the decade of his 60s. He had never been a very spontaneous person, despite his lifelong beliefs in openness to expression of feeling and genuineness of relationships. Now he developed the quality of spontaneity as he participated in and facilitated groups during the 1960s and 1970s. The Rogerian group was unstructured; participants were encouraged to express their immediate experience and feelings and to share whatever they wished.

The process evolved in stages: At first, there was confusion, awkwardness, an emphasis on past experience, and a resistance to personal exploration and sharing of feelings.

Gradually, negative feelings began to be expressed in the group and personally mean-ingful material began to be explored. Then facades cracked, and confrontation and feedback occurred. Finally, deeper feelings and personal meanings began to be ex-pressed and stirrings of self-acceptance and commitment to change would begin.

Rogers came to believe through his group work that people had tremendous capaci-ties to be therapeutic and healing with one another. Group workers with children and adolescents have seen these potentialities come to life as the participants show accept-ing and empathic attitudes toward one another and offer their personal help. Rogers, whose work with groups extended to people in many professions and of all ages, ranked the group relationship as more easily developed with children because of their greater spontaneity and openness.

Many texts and articles have described group processes and procedures in detail (Schmidt, 1996). Small group counseling is becoming a preferred counselor interven-tion in the schools. It allows counselors to see more students and use their time more efficiently (Boutwell & Myrick, 1992). The basic dynamics of group counseling for children in agency and community settings do not differ substantially from the basic process and structure of groups run in educational institutions. Group work with children is perhaps more likely to take place in a school setting than in an agency setting because of the greater possibilities school counselors have for getting chil-dren of an age group together with regularity. Borders and Drury (1992) reported that a number of studies have identified positive effects using group counseling with student populations.

The unstructured group is seldom used with younger children in schools; instead, counselors plan activities that enhance children's self-esteem as they identify, clarify, and understand their feelings, talk freely about their ideas and concerns, and experi-ence more rewarding relationships with peers. Even when misbehavior or lack of moti-vation is the presenting concern of teachers or parents, person-centered counselors believe that children's behavior changes for the better as they feel better about themselves (develop more positive self-concepts) and receive positive feedback from others.

Group counseling provides an opportunity to talk about common concerns such as developing friendships, getting along with siblings, and decision making. "Feelings" groups are especially popular with person-centered counselors working with young children. In these groups, a feeling vocabulary is developed, feelings are discussed, with examples from the students' lives, and often situations involving feeling states are role-played. Self-concept groups are also popular, and the counselor may decide to open each session with an activity designed to enhance positive self-assessments. If peer relations is the area for exploration, the counselor may provide initial structure by using an activity such as having members tell one thing about themselves or about an-other member that makes that person a good friend. Listening is encouraged, and sometimes the counselor may have one child repeat what another has said to reinforce their attentiveness.

M. Corey and Corey (1997) give guidelines for working with children and adoles-cents which include legal and practical considerations, leader tactics, and sample format of group rules, letters to parents, and additional sources for those conducting groups with children. Counselors working with young children must closely monitor the group process to be sure that all children are included and experience no threat. They also need to ensure that the purpose and content of the group is appropriate for the setting and to be conscious of confidentiality. Confidentiality can be a problem with child groups, and it is probably best for counselors to assume that children will talk about what they did in the group. On the other hand, group members should be encouraged not to reveal what others say. Because adolescents and youth may be initially more uncomfortable, embarrassed, and resistant in a group setting than children, person-centered counselors need patience, understanding and, above all, faith in the group process.

Person-centered counselors accept the mixed feelings of children and adolescents who are experiencing common problems such as alcoholism or family disorganization, helping them to explore and understand how they really feel and what is happening in their lives. Often knowing that others in the group have similar thoughts, feelings, and experiences is enough to stimulate coping strategies.

A more unstructured group can often be used with older children in upper elementary and middle school. In this type of "growth" group, children may choose topics for discussion and may even take turns being facilitators. Person-centered counselors may use the small group setting to help children learn the same facilitative conditions and skills in communication taught to adults; and, in fact, children can become "peer counselors" assisting others in and out of the group and even leading groups of younger children. Establishing and maintaining confidentiality is also easier with older children, but it needs to be continually reinforced.

G. Corey (1995) lists a set of general goals that might be shared by group members including children and adolescents. These goals are consistent with the person-centered groups for children and can also be applied in school or agency settings. These goals include trust, self-awareness, universality, self-acceptance, conflict resolution, autonomy/responsibility, decision making, behavior change, social skills, sensitivity to others, caring confrontation, and internal locus of evaluation.

When agency counselors can get together a small group of children or adolescents, they have fewer limitations on time and duration of sessions, the depth of explorations, and the issue of confidentiality. Children or teenagers who meet only once a week together in a clinic setting without seeing one another daily in school and knowing each other as friends or neighbors will usually feel freer to discuss the deeper problems they have at home or in school or their worries about their feelings and behaviors. The person-centered counselor works to provide the safety, permissiveness, and intimacy that make children and youth comfortable in exposing themselves and their problems. The counselor facilitates the process, modeling deep respect, empathy, and genuineness. As the process develops, children and teenagers become effective helpers for one another.

Groups in schools and agencies today are often organized around common needs of children and adolescents, such as coping with divorce or establishing appropriate independence. Person-centered counselors accept the mixed feelings of children and adolescents who are experiencing common problems such as alcoholism or family dis-organization, helping them to explore and understand how they really feel and what is happening in their lives. Often knowing that others in the group have similar thoughts, feelings, and experiences is enough to stimulate coping strategies. Parents of children need to be informed that such a group is offered and can be helpful. Their permission is needed for the child's inclusion.

Group procedures in schools and agencies offer the potential for children and adolescents to help one another and to grow together toward a better self-understanding, better relationships with others, and a better adjustment to their environment.

## CLASSROOM AND EDUCATIONAL APPLICATIONS

Rogers had been influenced, since his days at Columbia Teachers College (1924–1928), by the idea that people learn best through experience. He believed that his own personal experiences had provided for him the most meaningful and significant learnings in his life. In his own teaching, he applied insights, becoming a facilitator rather than an expert or authority. Students were not accustomed to his unstructured classes and methods, and they often experienced frustration, even trying to change him. He continued to believe that they were the best selectors and judges of their learning, and that if he provided a nonthreatening atmosphere of freedom, they could be trusted to learn and evaluate themselves. He defined the elements involved in significant or experiential learning as follows (Rogers, 1969):

> *It has a quality of personal involvement*—the whole person is both his feeling and cognitive aspects being in the learning event. *It is self-initiated.* Even when the impetus or stimulus comes from the outside, the sense of discovery, of reaching out, of grasping and comprehending, comes from within. *It is pervasive.* It makes a difference in the behavior, the attitudes, perhaps even the personality of the learner. *It is evaluated by the learner.* He knows whether it is meeting his need, whether it leads toward what he *wants* to know, whether it illuminates the dark area of ignorance he is experiencing. The locus of evaluation, we might say, resides definitely in the learner. *Its essence is meaning.* When such learning takes place, the element of meaning to the learner is built into the whole experience. (p. 5)

Rogers believed that teachers preferred to facilitate this type of learning but were locked into traditional, conventional approaches. "When we put together in one scheme such elements as a *prescribed curriculum, similar assignments for all students, lecturing* as almost the only mode of instruction, *standard tests* by which all students are externally evaluated, and *instructor-chosen grades* as the measure of learning, then we can almost guarantee that meaningful learning will be at an absolute minimum" (Rogers, 1969, p. 5).

In his book, *Freedom to Learn* (1969), Rogers emphasized the belief he had held for some years, which was that he was interested only in facilitating the process of learning for individuals, not in teaching or instructing them. Thus, students would set their own goals and decide how they wanted to reach them. For teachers who wanted to grant this freedom, he advocated: (a) providing many resources; (b) using learning contracts; (c) helping students conduct their own inquiries and make their own discoveries; (d) using simulation activities for experiential learning; (e) using programmed instruction when students wanted to learn more efficiently; and (f) having students evaluate themselves. The first chapter in *Freedom to Learn* is still of interest to educators of children; it describes the attempts of a sixth-grade teacher to apply many of Rogers' beliefs on education to her classroom.

During the 1960s and 1970s, views similar to Rogers', if not as radical, were advanced by humanistic, person-centered educators who were seeking more democratic learning climates for students consistent with their beliefs in the drive toward growth, health, and self-actualization in individuals. These educators believed that the curriculum should include an affective component and that students should be helped toward self-awareness, self-understanding, and self-responsibility. Fostering creativity, divergent thinking, inquiry learning, and problem-solving became goals of these teachers and educators. A respect for the uniqueness of student perceptions, values, feelings, and beliefs was promoted.

At the same time, education was being greatly influenced by the behavioral school of psychology, which emphasized programmed learning, specific behavioral objectives, contingency management, management by objectives, and accountability. Perhaps both schools of thought went to extremes. Today there appears to be a trend toward a "return to basics" in education; however, the humanistic, person-centered influence is too compelling in a democratic society to be discarded, and much of the earlier influence continues to be felt.

Person-centered educators work together today in school systems, not only in the cognitive domain, but in helping children and adolescents develop positive self-concepts through encouraging their accomplishments and personal strengths, helping them clarify their beliefs and values, and conveying a trust in the ability of students to make their own choices and assume responsibility for their actions.

Person-centered counselors, especially in the elementary and middle schools, have influenced the curriculum in at least four ways:

1. By encouraging teachers to incorporate regularly within the school day opportunities for students to explore their feelings, beliefs, values, and attitudes through planned activities or by taking advantage of spontaneous opportunities during regular content instruction.
2. By compiling and demonstrating affective programs and materials for use in the classroom to complement the cognitive learnings.
3. By actually conducting classroom guidance activities on a regular basis.
4. By helping teachers conduct classroom meetings such as advocated by Glasser (1969) where children can communicate openly and honestly and develop personal responsibility.

High school counselors have been directly involved in the curriculum through offering workshops on topics such as understanding relationships, making decisions, and resolving conflicts, in addition to their regular counseling and guidance functions.

Spurred by an apparent rise in school violence and discipline problems, schools from elementary to high school have become interested in conflict resolution programs and in training peer mediators. Such programs teach skills of communication and problem-solving that can lead to win-win solutions for both parties to a dispute. Anger is recognized as a natural emotion to be used responsibly and constructively. Students "learn to deal with differing opinions, to listen to and understand another's point of view, and to maintain respect for the dignity of each [person] with whom they have a conflict" (Benson & Benson, 1993). One comprehensive program used in schools today is the Peer Mediation: Conflict Resolution in Schools program (Schrumpf, Crawford, & Usadel, 1991). It is interesting to note that Carl Rogers spent the last years of his life actively pursuing ways of resolving international conflicts.

Person-centered counselors firmly believe that early and continued classroom guidance activities can serve a preventive as well as a growth-enhancing function and help in the future adjustment of adolescents and youth. There are many published materials today from a variety of sources that can guide the counselors work in classroom guidance. Modern counselors may be more apt to create their own guidance materials by building on their own experience, consulting with colleagues and attending professional development workshops. This trend allows counselors to tailor a guidance program to meet the specific needs of their student population. Topics covered by counselors are timely and include getting along with others, enhancing self-esteem, problem-solving and decision making, dealing with family issues, anger management, body image, cooperating, sharing, and being responsible. Today's person-centered counselor also works with students to educate them about drugs, abuse, suicide, depression, grief, and loss.

In addition, person-centered counselors may have access to prepackaged guidance programs consistent with their beliefs. Among older programs still in use in some elementary schools are DUSO (Dinkmeyer & Dinkmeyer, 1982), I Am Loveable and Capable [IALAC] (Simon, 1973), and My Friends and Me (Davis, 1977). Another valuable resource is the book, now in its 4th edition, Counseling Children (Thompson & Rudolph, 1996), which lists many interventions for use with specific problem areas of children. Modern mass-produced programs are too numerous to list; however, all schools receive catalogs of current resources appropriate for counselor needs and goals.

Person-centered approaches have had an impact on education by calling attention to learning climates for children and adolescents where they can explore their feelings, values, and beliefs, see themselves as capable and trustworthy, and experience their own power to make choices and take responsibility. Educators have been influenced to look at their own patterns of communication and methods of teaching to see if they are enhancing all aspects of student development. Counselors have helped to bring into the curriculum of elementary, middle, and high school guidance experiences that encourage continued personal, emotional, and social growth of students.

## PARENTING SKILLS

Person-centered counselors help parents individually, but the group approach has demonstrated the power of parents to help one another as they share their struggles and successes in developing more effective ways of raising responsible children. As in other forms of person-centered helping, counselors create a climate of psychological safety for parents based on attitudes of empathic understanding, respect, and genuineness. Trust in the resources of parents to develop and implement their own goals is conveyed by the group leader.

Group approaches range from the unstructured Rogerian type to structured training models. In the less structured group, the counselor serves as a facilitator, letting the group go through the expected initial feeling of lack of direction and frustration, and trusting the group process. The belief is, and experience confirms this, that as trust develops parents will drop their defenses and choose what is most significant for them to work on in the group. Person-centered counselors use self-disclosure and confrontation and give feedback when appropriate, always in the attitude of caring, respect, and challenge of the parents' resources. Counselors believe that as members feel safe and understood, they will develop insights that will motivate them to change ineffective attitudes and behaviors toward their children and adolescents.

Arguably the earliest and most influential, structured person-centered program for parents was developed by Thomas Gordon, a graduate student of Rogers. Gordon began to offer courses for parents in the 1960s, beginning in his own community in California. The success of his course is attested to by the number of people who received special training as instructors and the thousands of parents across the country who completed his Parent Effectiveness Training (P.E.T.) programs. The book *Parent Effectiveness Training* (Gordon, 1970) presented his insights to the public at large, consistent with a person-centered educational philosophy that individuals can and will learn what has meaning for them.

Gordon believed that parents were more often blamed than trained, that parenthood was a difficult, demanding job, and that the skills of more effective parenting could be taught. He demonstrated faith in the ability and willingness of parents to learn attitudes, methods, and skills used by professional counselors and therapists in establishing relationships and working with children.

Gordon (1970) stressed the importance of parents being congruent and sending clear and honest messages that match their true feelings:

> Real parents will inevitably feel both accepting and unaccepting toward their children; their attitudes toward the same behavior cannot be consistent; it must vary from time to time. They should not (and cannot) hide their true feelings; they should accept the fact that one parent may feel accepting and the other unaccepting of the same behavior; and they should realize that each will inevitably feel different degrees of acceptance toward each of their children. . . . While children undoubtedly *prefer* to be accepted, they can constructively handle their parents' unaccepting feelings when parents send clear and honest messages. (pp. 27–28)

A valuable and often-quoted contribution of Gordon's has been his list of twelve typical ways parents respond to the feelings and problems of their children. These are the verbal behaviors that person-centered counselors and therapists try to avoid. Sometimes dubbed "the dirty dozen," the categories are:

1. *Ordering, Directing, Commanding.* Telling the child to do something, giving him an order or a command.

2. *Warning, Admonishing, Threatening.* Telling the child what consequences will occur if he does something.

3. *Exhorting, Moralizing, Preaching.* Telling the child what he *should* or *ought* to do.

4. *Advising, Giving Solutions, or Suggestions.* Telling the child how to solve a problem, giving him advice or suggestions, providing answers or solutions for him.

5. *Lecturing, Teaching, Giving Logical Arguments.* Trying to influence the child with facts, counterarguments, logic, information, or your own opinions.

6. *Judging, Criticizing, Disagreeing, Blaming.* Making a negative judgment or evaluation of the child.

7. *Praising, Agreeing.* Offering a positive evaluation or judgment, agreeing.

8. *Name-Calling, Ridiculing, Shaming.* Making the child feel foolish, putting the child into a category, shaming him.

9. *Interpreting, Analyzing, Diagnosing.* Telling the child what his motives are or analyzing why he is doing or saying something; communicating that you have him figured out or have him diagnosed.

10. *Reassuring, Sympathizing, Consoling, Supporting.* Trying to make the child feel better, talking him out of his feelings, trying to make his feelings go away, denying the strength of his feelings.

11. *Probing, Questioning, Interrogating.* Trying to find reasons, motives, causes; searching for more information to help solve the problem.

12. *Withdrawing, Distracting, Humoring, Diverting.* Trying to get the child away from the problem; withdrawing from the problem yourself; distracting the child, kidding him out of it, pushing the problem aside.

In place of these 12 communication styles, Gordon advocates responding to children in ways that help the parent-child relationship and increase the likelihood that children will feel free to talk, feel less guilt or inadequacy, and reduce defensiveness and resentment. He popularized the term *active listening,* which is now used widely to describe Rogerian listening, or the empathic listening that involves entering the world of another and reflecting feelings and meanings. This manner of listening is especially useful when children have problems they recognize, when they "own" their problems and need to feel understood.

Gordon differentiates between the *you message* ("you're always late," "you're lazy," etc.) that parents send their children, which may make them feel resistant and unworthy, and the *I message,* which confronts children with their parents' feelings and places responsibility on the children to modify their behavior. *I messages* are essentially those employed by person-centered counselors using immediacy with their clients, expressing their own feelings and thoughts about the here-and-now counseling relationship. Parents are taught by Gordon to use this type of verbal message when they are feeling annoyed or frustrated by something that is occurring and, thus, own the problem. An example of *you* and *I messages* for the same situation is given by Gordon (1970):

Situation:  A child has just kicked his parent in the shin.

Parental "you" message:  That's being a very bad boy. Don't you ever kick anybody like that!

Parental "I" message: Ouch! That really hurt me—I don't like to be kicked. (p. 118)

Gordon has been concerned about the negative effects of parental power tactics on children and believes that parents continue to use power out of a lack of knowledge and experience with any other method of resolving conflicts. His own method for parents is called the *no lose* method and assumes a relatively equal power between those involved in a conflictual situation. As Gordon (1970) describes it:

Parent and child encounter a conflict-of-needs situation. The parent asks the child to participate with him in a joint search for some solution acceptable to both. One or both may offer possible solutions. They critically evaluate them and eventually make a decision on a final solution acceptable to both. No selling of the other is required after the solution has been selected, because both have already accepted it. No power is required to force compliance, because neither is resisting the decision. (p. 196)

The no-lose method of conflict resolution is considered successful by Gordon because:

1.  The child is motivated to carry out the solution.
2.  There is more chance of finding a high-quality solution.
3.  It develops thinking skills in children.
4.  It reduces hostility and generates warm feelings.
5.  It requires less effort.
6.  It eliminates the need for power.
7.  It gets to the *real* problem.
8.  It treats children as individuals who can be trusted to make responsible, mature choices.

The trust and goodwill offered by parents toward their children in the no-lose method is similar to the person-centered attitudes offered by counselors and therapists. Therapeutic changes often take place in children whose parents use the P.E.T. principles and philosophy.

Another early and popular program for parents emphasizing democratic and positive parenting is the Systematic Training for Effective Parenting, or STEP program (Dinkmeyer & McKay, 1976). While this program is based on the Adlerian family counseling model, it incorporates many person-centered attitudes, such as listening for feelings, offering acceptance and encouragement, and showing confidence and trust in children to make responsible choices. The program also advocates person-centered counseling skills such as reflective listening, open responses, and the use of *I* statements to express authentic parental feelings. STEP calls attention to ineffective styles of communication similar to Gordon's "dirty dozen." It emphasizes parental attitudes that relate closely to those conveyed by person-centered counselors and therapists in their relationships with clients. In place of the no-lose method of solving conflicts, STEP teaches the use of natural and logical consequences in helping children take responsibility for their behavior.

More recently, person-centered educators have developed *Child Relationship Enhancement Therapy* and the *Parenting Skills Training Program* based on Virginia Axline's child-centered play therapy model (L. Guerney & Guerney, 1989). These two programs are designed to improve parent-child skills and remediate child problems.

Helping parents has become a necessary part of the work of counselors and therapists in both school and agency settings. The desire and need of parents to become more effective in their communication with and discipline of their children have been satisfied by these professionals through systematic training programs as well as through individual and group counseling.

## FAMILY INTERVENTIONS

Person-centered counselors help families in the following ways: (a) counseling with children and adolescents; (b) establishing parent groups and parenting programs; (c) doing consultation with parents; (d) counseling with parents; (e) training parents as therapists for their own children; and (f) doing family therapy. Counseling with children and adolescents and parenting programs have been discussed in prior sections of this chapter. This section will address parent consultation, parent counseling, training parents as therapists, and family therapy.

### Consultation with Parents

Reisman (1973) defines consultation as "an interaction process between two individuals, one of whom has a specialized area of knowledge that is sought or valued by the other, who has a problem in this area" (p. 212). Parents often ask counselors and therapists for help in understanding their children's problems and behavior and in considering ways to cope more effectively as parents. In consultation, information and ideas are exchanged, and the counselor collaborates in meeting the specific goal as articulated by the parent. When parents desire consultation, the counselor does not assume therapy is needed or should be provided. As consultants, person-centered counselors believe that parents can achieve insights and solve their problems with their children in an atmosphere of empathy and respect and an open, genuine exchange of ideas and information.

In Reisman's definition of psychotherapy as a form of communication of person-related understanding, respect, and a wish to be of help, the distinction between consultation with parents about their children and psychotherapy with parents may become blurred. "Psychotherapy can be employed in consultation, and consultation can be employed in psychotherapy" (Reisman, 1973, pp. 220–221). The difference lies in the parents' goal which, in consultation, is to receive help related to their role as parents. The therapist-consultant accepts and understands what it is the parents want. It may become appropriate for the therapist to invite parents to join a parenting group for additional support and assistance. Should it become apparent that one or both parents desire more than consultation, and, in fact, want personal counseling, the therapist would need to either refer them or renegotiate for counseling services.

## Counseling with Parents

When a counselor is seeing a child or adolescent individually, it may not be advisable to see the parent or parents for personal therapy also. This is especially problematic when it is an older child or adolescent being seen by the counselor. These clients need to feel that their counselor is their own, is objective and impartial, and can be trusted to maintain confidentiality. When parents feel the need for more help than is given in the consultation process and desire to explore their marital relationship or their personality functioning, a referral can be made.

In the process of individual therapy, the families of clients often reap benefits. In his essay "The Implications of Client-Centered Therapy for Family Life" (Rogers, 1961a), Rogers discussed his observations of some of the ways clients changed in their family living as a consequence of counseling. Clients became more expressive of their true feelings with family members and became better at accepting their own real feelings without defensive pretenses. Communication improved and mutual understanding developed as clients began to listen empathically and to respond to their families with respect. Another dividend was a willingness on the part of clients to let other family members be separate persons with their own feelings, values, and beliefs, and to trust in the potential of these family members to become responsible and self-directing.

## Training Parents as Therapists

Possibly the first innovative person-centered approach for helping emotionally disturbed children up to age 10 was *filial therapy* (B. Guerney, 1964), which trained small groups of parents as play therapists for their children. The advocates of filial therapy regarded "the essence of the filial technique to be that of systematically tapping a relatively neglected but potentially powerful resource: the energy of parents in working for the betterment of their children" (Guerney, Guerney, & Andronico, 1966, p. 886). In filial therapy, parents were trusted and helped to effect change in their children in their homes, rather than in clinic settings. The training process for parents was extensive, combining didactic instruction with supervised experience in the methods of person-centered play therapy and a person-centered group experience. In group counseling, parents observed the modeling of communication skills and were helped to cope with feelings and difficulties as they emerged during the course of filial therapy (Andronico, Fidler, Guerney, & Guerney, 1967).

In learning the process, parents in the small groups watched demonstrations, role-played, observed one another conducting play sessions with their own children, and gave and received feedback. Parents were taught to encourage, accept, and reflect all feelings expressed by their children and to convey person-centered attitudes of empathy, acceptance, and understanding. After training, they continued sessions in their own homes, using a particular room, time, and group of toys. The direction of play was left to the child; the only limits were that children could not extend the time of the sessions, break expensive toys, or physically hurt the parents.

Another program focusing on adolescent-parent relationships was PARD, Parent-Adolescent Relationship Development (B. Guerney, 1977). PARD grew out of the filial therapy program and was begun to help dysfunctional parent-adolescent relationships. PARD used both didactic and experiential instruction, but differed from filial therapy in that the adolescents as well as their parents were trained in self-expressive and empathic skills. PARD therapists worked with both individual dyads and groups of youth and parents. Carkhuff (1971) first proposed the concept of "training as treatment," and following this lead, person-centered therapists and counselors explain the therapeutic process and help clients develop those skills that enhance any relationship. PARD is an example of this trend and has also been employed as a preventive and developmental program for use with normal families (Lavant, 1978a).

## FAMILY THERAPY

Rogerian therapy can be useful to families in the areas of helping family members to establish authentic contact with each other, helping family members express innermost feelings to each other, helping each member become fully individual within the family, and helping improve the listening and two-way communication in the family (Horne & Passmore, 1991). Person-centered family therapists find the family systems paradigm consistent with their beliefs in the inherent resources for growth and self-understanding of individuals: "To most effectively employ the person-centered approach with families, an expansion of traditional person-centered theory is required" (Fennell & Weinhold, 1997, p. 188). The family-as-client is offered respect, empathy, and a genuine therapist who is concerned with the family's movement toward wholeness. In fact, the spontaneity and humor of the experiential school of family therapy is made to order for person-centered therapists who value responding to the moment-to-moment experience of a family in therapy.

Person-centered family therapists do not begin with preconceived notions of family pathology, nor do they see themselves as skilled diagnosticians calling the shots (Raskin & Van deer Veen, 1970). The therapist interacts freely and genuinely with family members, responding empathically but leaving with the family members the locus of responsibility for interpretation and action.

While the person-centered family counselor is actively involved, expressive, and interested in facilitating a genuine, honest encounter among family members, the essential philosophy remains the same: Family members are trusted to assume responsibility for their own change and growth. While not reluctant to state a preference based on experience with families, the therapist respects their ability to make appropriate decisions for each member about all aspects of the therapy, such as, Who will participate and to what extent, what the significant areas for discussion will be, what meaning will be derived from the experience, and what action(s) will be taken, if any (Lavant, 1978b). The counselor trusts the group process, enters the phenomenological world of the family, communicates an empathic understanding of family experiences, and acts as a facilitator and model of therapeutic attitudes and behaviors.

Person-centered family therapy is an underdeveloped area in terms of theoretical and clinical writings and empirical research (Lavant, 1978a), but it is being used by individual practitioners who believe in the relationship conditions of empathy, respect, and genuineness. These therapists emphasize the experiencing of family members and trust the self-determination and drive of the family members toward healthy individual and family growth.

## THE LEGACY OF CARL ROGERS

In 1985, an observer on the humanistic movement in psychology pronounced it a failure: "Humanistic psychology was a great experiment, but it is basically a failed experiment in that there is no humanistic school of thought in psychology" (Cunningham, 1985, p. 18). Carl Rogers himself (in Schultz & Schultz, 1996) was quoted as saying, "Humanistic psychology has not had a significant impact on mainstream psychology. We are perceived as having relatively little importance" (p. 443). Schultz and Schultz, historians of psychology, display a time line for humanistic psychology in their text, which begins at the end of World War II and ends sometime in the 1980s. But this may be a situation similar to that of Mark Twain, who, on reading of his own demise in the newspaper, suggested that rumors of his death had been greatly exaggerated.

One reason for the suggested demise of humanistic psychology may be that the approach springs from concepts and values that are not easily systematized. Rogers was suggesting a new phenomenological method of understanding the person, he was not interested in founding an independent system of thought in psychology. Nor did he seek to promote a uniform application of his therapeutic ideas. Rogers believed that each person must find his or her own unique way of becoming person-centered (Thorne, 1992). He worried that people might try to make him into a guru figure, and he found that prospect repugnant:

> Rogers feared that the establishment of some kind of international association or society would inevitably lead to the development of doctrinal rigidity and the imposition of

accreditation or admission procedures, which he abhorred . . . He could not tolerate the thought of producing "clones" of himself and the adjective "Rogerian" was one he always rejected with deep distaste. (pp. 91–92)

Such an attitude does not make for the founding of a recognizable and lasting school of thought in psychology. Rogers preferred to infiltrate, influence, and to reform psychotherapy. This, he certainly did.

## ROGERIAN "EMBEDDEDNESS" IN PSYCHOANALYTIC, FAMILY, AND BRIEF THERAPY

It is not unusual for a person-centered therapist to attend a workshop or conference where people are speaking with great enthusiasm about a new attitude or technique that has been developed in their field, only to realize that it is right out of a Carl Rogers book. Often, without credit to Rogers, the new approach has been given a new name and declared a new discovery; much like Columbus "discovering" America, even though people already lived there.

It would be difficult to predict whether person-centered therapy will persist intact beyond the next century. One thing is certain, however: Rogers' ideas have become so pervasive that their influence is felt in nearly all the newer forms of therapy. What initially had seemed to be his simplistic, overly optimistic, and naive ideas, now are appreciated for their "profound beauty and importance" (Kahn, 1991, p. 35). Perhaps the legacy of Rogers will be that his ideas will become "embedded" in most therapies, even without the awareness or appreciation of their originators.

Heinz Kohut, known for his "self psychology" and its contribution to the post-Freudian tradition, merged the attitudes of Rogers' person-centered approach with psychoanalytic principles in his method of therapy (Kahn, 1991). Kohut, breaking with his analytic colleagues, made empathy the primary investigative method in the analytic relationship. It is the task of the therapist to provide a "corrective emotional experience," the main component of which is empathy (Kahn):

> Humanistic therapists and group leaders, led by Carl Rogers, have long insisted that the client was the expert on herself. Traditionally, this has been seen as the direct opposite of the psychoanalytic view, with its notions of the unconscious, resistance, and defense, all of which imply that clients know little about themselves. And now here is a psychoanalyst teaching that clients know what they need a good deal better than the therapist, and that the therapist would do well to listen carefully and attempt to empathically grasp the client's experience.
>
> The first task is understanding and conveying one's understanding to the client. Like Rogers before him, Kohut believed that this in itself is therapeutic. If you do nothing but strive for the deepest possible understanding of the client, and if you communicate that understanding, that experience will be life-changing. (pp. 102–103)

Although Kahn (1991) did not see Rogers' methods as sufficient for a complete therapy, he considered their relationship aspects to be indispensable. He wrote, "It seems to me that whatever view one holds of the human mind and however one chooses to conduct therapy, there is much to be learned by paying careful attention to Rogers' advice about the relationship between therapist and client" (pp. 35–36).

While Rogers has been criticized by some (Becvar & Becvar, 1993) as having a "hidden agenda," and therefore being less than honest when it came to his construct of "genuineness" or "transparency," Kahn (1991) attempted to clarify this point by stating that "genuineness does *not* mean blurting out every passing feeling" (p. 39), or revealing aspects of the counselor's agenda that the client does not need to know. Kahn contrasts the attitudes of Rogers with those of some traditional psychoanalytic views. In the new—Rogerian influenced—psychodynamic attitudes, he considers the old Freudian-influenced views to be incompatible with effective therapy. These incompatible attitudes include (a) the notion that people are "neither valuable nor nonvaluable; they are simply interesting to try to figure out"; (b) ". . . they furnish material for books and articles, which is to say for ideas, and ideas certainly are interesting"; (c) "the therapist soon learns all there is of interest to learn about the client. The rest of the work consists of getting the client to learn it"; (d) "the therapist's theory handles all the data . . . the client will fit the theory"; (e) "clients can't be trusted to find their own way"; and (f) "the therapist knows better than the client what is good for him and tries to figure out a way to influence them for their own good" (p. 48).

It has been said that it would be difficult to imagine 20th-century thought without Sigmund Freud (Schultz & Schultz, 1996). The psychoanalytic tradition has certainly influenced every nook and cranny of Western thinking. But it took Carl Rogers to humanize the psychoanalytic approach to therapy. Freud himself stated that he was not really interested in helping people, but, rather, saw himself as a researcher. He was described as impersonal, indifferent, and brisk in dealing with his patients. Freud admitted to a friend, "I lack that passion for helping" (quoted in Schultz & Schultz, p. 385). Freud's deficit was Rogers' greatest asset; the passion for helping seemed to be the driving force of his life. While most post-Freudian approaches still remain faithful to certain core aspects of Freud's theories, they have, for the most part, adopted the attitudes of Rogers in their approach to the counselor-client relationship and their respectful treatment of clients.

People whose theories are considered to be foundational in many areas of family and brief therapies, such as Virginia Satir, Gregory Bateson, Milton Erickson, and Carl Whitaker, have also borrowed liberally from Rogers. Experiential family therapy, for example, is a branch of family systems work that "emerged from the humanistic psychology of the 1960s, that, like the individual humanistic therapies, emphasized immediate, *here-and-now* experience. The quality of ongoing experience was both the criterion of psychological health and the focus of therapeutic interventions" (Nichols & Schwartz, 1991, p. 275). Among those included in this category was Virginia Satir, whose core assumptions contained the following familiar themes: "The natural movement of all individuals is toward positive growth and development . . . all individuals possess all of the resources necessary for positive growth and development . . . [and] . . . each person is in charge of himself or herself. Indeed each family member is to become as whole as possible, and therapy is merely to provide a support-ive context for such development" (Becvar & Becvar, 1993, pp. 220–221). Satir be-lieved that the key to positive change lay in the ability of the therapist to create a safe environment in which to allow client growth, encourage their expressions of congru-ence, and help clients explore themselves and experience their feelings. Likewise, Carl Whitaker (in Nichols & Schwartz, 1991) expressed "a deep respect for people's ability to discover their own directions in life" (p. 279).

Often, ideas that were seen as profound and revolutionary in family therapy, but which had been given different names, were notions that had previously been put forth by Rogers. One example is the concept of "joining." In a passage that would appear ob-vious to person-centered therapists, Nichols and Schwartz (1991) display the embed-dedness of Rogers' beliefs in family therapy:

> If people do not feel respect or caring from a therapist they will be more likely to resist. The process by which therapists convey these feelings to all family members has come to be known as **joining** with the family . . . To join with clients, therapists are taught to be themselves; that is, to relate in a friendly rather than stilted way. This freedom to be genuinely oneself is one of the qualities that initially attracts students to family therapy. (p. 127)

In another passage, an attitude attributed to Milton Erickson would appear directly parallel to that of Rogers: "Erickson's optimistic view of people—that they wanted to change and possessed the resources to do so—was, perhaps, his most important contri-bution to the family therapy movement" (p. 111). Erickson also stressed the impor-tance of cooperating with clients. He is credited with such metaphoric statements as: "The therapist should ride the horse in the direction it is going," "For the fisherman, it is not so much the quality of the equipment but knowledge of the ways of the fish that is important," and "It is better to channel a river than to dam it." All these utterances have a decided Rogerian flavor.

Likewise, in the solution-focused brief therapy approach (Cade & O'Hanlon, 1993; W. O'Hanlon & Weiner-Davis, 1989; W. O'Hanlon & Wilk, 1987), the following inter-ventions suggested have a Rogerian ring:

> "Speaking the client's language" describes the therapist's attempt to join by using as-pects of the client's language . . . so that the client may feel understood. . . .
> "Utilization" describes a process of accepting the client's perspective rather than rejecting, disagreeing, or resisting the client's views. (Becvar & Becvar, 1993, p. 298)

Sometimes one can find, in a new approach to psychotherapy, Rogerian principles adopted with credit given. Such is the case with B. O'Hanlon and Beadle's (1994) "Carl Rogers with a Twist" technique, and a recent book on solution-focused therapy that contains a chapter entitled: "On the shoulders of Carl Rogers" (Miller, Duncan, & Hubble, 1997). Also, in their book on a brief therapeutic approach called "possibility therapy," which directly proceeds from the "solution-oriented" method (W. O'Hanlon & Weiner-Davis, 1989), they state:

> Like Carl Rogers, we accept people where they are right now, and help them to accept themselves. But then we add a little twist. We communicate, "where you are now is a valid place to be, AND you can change." (p. 15)

Eugene Gendlin, a one-time close associate of Rogers, has the distinction of being the first to develop an alternative method based on the core ideas of "client-centered therapy" (Thorne, 1992). His "focusing" approach, however, goes beyond Rogers' original "necessary and sufficient" conditions of therapy:

> Focusing is a very deliberate way to touch something inside. I have seen that help the bigger process . . . focusing is a very deliberate thing where an "I" is attending to an "it." I think it is very valuable. But surely it is not therapy. Therapy is a relationship, therapy is a process of development. These focusing steps I described come in client centered therapy. That is where I learned them from, that is where I saw them. . . . (Gendlin, 1990, p. 222)

While "purists" decry the addition of more directive techniques to the core conditions of Rogers as heresy (Thorne, 1992), others declare the necessity for moving beyond the foundation that Rogers laid for the relationship in psychotherapy. But even while stating the need for more active interventions, most approaches today continue to emphasize the core conditions as the starting place. The requirements for the counselor to be authentic, respectful, and supportive remain the centerpiece of most of the brief approaches (Parsons & Wicks, 1994). Walter and Peller (1992) are solution-focused brief therapists who place little emphasis on building a trusting relationship with a client. They presume that trust simply exists. However, they specifically cite the basic techniques of Rogers as important to facilitating and maintaining a working relationship. "We have probably all received training at some time in our careers in what to do to help the client feel understood and supported. We have probably learned reflective listening and empathic listening, the restating what the client said, with the same affect and tone" (p. 42). This remains essential to communicating . . . "initial support of the client's position" (p. 43).

The embeddedness of Rogers' ideas in the more recent approaches to therapy may not necessarily ensure his continued name-recognition, but it certainly will ensure his continued influence. As J. C. Prochaska and Norcross (1994) put it, "Rogers' major contributions have been gratefully incorporated by most practitioners whose preferred orientations are not Rogerian. These lasting influences include the centrality of accurate empathy, the importance of the *person* of the therapist, and the healing context of the therapeutic relationship" (p. 154). While purists would attempt to maintain a Rogerian orthodoxy, others cite Rogers' pragmatic approach and concern with what works as evidence that he would approve of what has happened to his theory. This point was well stated by Thorne (1992):

> I had always considered myself to be somewhat of a "purist" until a member of the "purist camp" walked out of a video demonstration of my work when he witnessed what was clearly, for him, a directive response from me to my client, even if delivered with

extreme respect and tentativeness. At that moment, in his eyes, I had ceased to practice client-centered therapy. I sense that Carl Rogers would have stayed to see what happened next. (p. 94)

## EFFICACY

Rogers' emphasis on the therapeutic relationship has become almost universally adopted (Bohart & Todd, 1988). Person-centered attitudes and skills have become givens for therapists and counselors of many orientations. This is demonstrated by the wide acceptance and adoption of systematic skills training, which includes training in warmth, empathy, respect, and genuineness, in most current counselor training programs. Person-centered ideas thus become the process whereby therapists of differing theoretical bases can establish the type of relationship and attitudes that will help them proceed in fostering client change and development. Person-centered counselors hold beliefs that children, adolescents, and adults can become responsible and self-directing and thus actively help them set their own goals and find ways to achieve these goals. These counselors are involved and spontaneous as they seek to understand the feelings and attitudes of clients of all ages, using many skills and interventions in their desire to help and encourage client growth. Thus, "pure" person-centered counseling that can be subjected to rigorous research is hard to come by today. Studies that purport to compare or contrast client-centered counseling with children and adolescents to other therapeutic orientations still conceive the client-centered counselor as leaving out the "action" part of helping. Much of the efficacy of the person-centered approach lies in the counseling relationship; the use of core attitudes on the part of the counselor, which research has demonstrated to facilitate client growth; and in the flexibility and openness of the person-centered counselor to discover with clients what will best help them meet their goals.

A major contribution of Rogers to the field of psychotherapy was his willingness to state his formulations in testable hypotheses and submit them to research efforts. Rogers consistently modeled an unusual combination of a phenomenological understanding of clients and an empirical evaluation of therapy. He and his colleagues demonstrated that a humanistic approach to doing therapy and a scientific approach to evaluating it need not be incompatible (J. O. Prochaska, 1979). When he began his research attempts, there were few precedents, and his first significant contribution was in taping, transcribing, and publishing therapy sessions verbatim. Initial research efforts consisted of classifying responses from transcripts to see what happened in therapy. Later, researchers put their minds to the major goal of testing hypotheses that the *process* of therapy results in change and that the therapeutic conditions of empathy, unconditional positive regard, and congruence foster the process.

Rogers received large-scale grants while at Chicago and worked with 15 to 20 researchers over several years, about 10 of whom stayed involved the entire time. Designs were created to address earlier research problems of small population samples, lack of controls, and lack of instrumentation to measure changes in client attitudes.

Some of the research results were presented in *Psychotherapy and Personality Change* (Rogers & Dymond, 1954). Rogers and a colleague developed the 7-point Process Scale to demonstrate where individuals were at the beginning of therapy, at points during the process, at termination, at follow-up (Rogers & Rablen, 1958). The scale described behavior in the areas of feeling and personal meanings, manner of experiencing, degree of incongruence, communication of self, manner in which experience is construed, relationship to problems, and manner of relating (Corsini, 1979). The scale was used subsequently in many studies, including those with schizophrenics (Rogers et al., 1967). Reporting on validation studies, Rogers (1961b) wrote: "Studies with the Process Scale have reliably correlated process movement in therapy with outcome, as well as correlating positive process movement with the presence of the three therapist conditions: genuineness, caring, and understanding" (p. 33).

Research in person-centered therapy has demonstrated that certain skills used by counselors directly influence the degree to which clients will explore their concerns (Carkhuff, 1969; Rogers et al., 1967; Truax & Carkhuff, 1967). Carkhuff called these skills "responding skills" and "the core of facilitating dimensions." His 5-point scales (1969, Vol. II) have stimulated much research and are widely used in training and supervision. Truax and Carkhuff believe that from 20% to 50% of the variability of outcome indices may be accounted for by these primary core dimensions, essentially those which person-centered counselors convey in providing the "core conditions."

Rogers and Sanford (1984) summarized research done in foreign countries on psychotherapy, the student-teacher relationship, and the use of encounter groups. They reported the studies as demonstrating the efficacy of the person-centered approach. In general, research has supported the effectiveness of client-centered therapy (Smith, Glass, & Miller, 1980). As he neared the end of his long and productive life, Rogers was concerned about the lack of humanistically oriented research. In a significant article (Rogers, 1985), he reemphasized his call over the years for new models of science that would allow for research methodology more appropriate for person-centered, phenomenological and humanistically oriented concepts and beliefs. He believed that new models were beginning to appear and that there was "clearly no one best method for all investigations . . . one must choose the means or model best adapted to the particular questions being asked" (p. 7). Rogers' continued modeling of the artist/scientist by his own life is a legacy for all person-centered and relationship-oriented practitioners.

## CONCLUSION

Person-centered counselors seek to provide a therapeutic climate with attitudes of empathy, respect, and genuineness where clients of all ages and with a variety of concerns can be themselves and feel cared about and safe. In this atmosphere, counselors trust that the process will release the vast resources for growth and behavioral change that people possess.

Counselors with a person-centered orientation believe that children and adolescents are capable of self-direction and self-responsibility. In facilitating the development of children and youth, person-centered therapists listen with care and patience, apply skills that convey the core attitudes of empathy, respect and genuineness, and make use of interventions and materials to enhance the counseling process and relationship.

## CASE STUDY

The following account[1] demonstrates person-centered attitudes and skills in working with a 16-year-old adolescent male. In addition, the example offers a glimpse at person-centered supervision that helps counselor trainees keep in touch with their own feelings in counseling relationships.

"Donny" was referred to the clinic for psychoeducational evaluation by the juvenile court at the request of his father and stepmother who termed his behavior "incorrigible." One of the recommendations of the diagnostic evaluation was for counseling, and Donny was assigned to a counselor-trainee. Donny appeared resistant and reluctant during early sessions, and the counselor felt frustrated. In the counselor's own words:

> Donny was my first adolescent case, I knew my philosophical stance toward counseling was essentially a humanistic, Rogerian blend, but I had not yet developed a sense of my own "style" as a counselor. Words such as genuine, accepting, empathic, and so on, sounded good and made a lot of sense to me, but I had not had a real chance to see them work for me. This, coupled with the fear that Donny would perceive me as yet another judgmental authority figure in his life caused me to rely very heavily on technique. I felt like I was playing the role of counselor, I wasn't very effective, I wasn't very genuine, and most of all, I wasn't very comfortable.

Donny had not shown up for his second appointment. At the beginning of the next one, the counselor said, "I missed you last week." Donny replied, "Well, I had to talk with Mr. Jones, and I kinda forgot about it." While reviewing videotapes of the sessions, a supervisor helped the counselor develop insight into Donny's feeling by role-playing what Donny might like to be saying if he were honest and also what he might be revealing through his body language. The counselor was encouraged to role-play what he had experienced during the sessions, and, most importantly, what he wished he had said. An example is as follows:

Counselor: Donny, I was disappointed last week when you didn't show up or call me. What do you think it was like for me when you weren't here?

---

[1] This example was based on a case contributed by Duncan Adams while he was a counselor-trainee Child Case Study at the Human Development Center at James Madison University.

Supervisor [as Donny]: The other day when you said you missed me, that sounded phoney. What you just said about being disappointed made me feel bad but, at least you were being straight with me this time.

Another supervisory session went a step further. The clinic setting was fairly sterile and probably intimidating to Donny. It was decided that the two would begin meeting in a more natural setting—walking outdoors, going for a drive, and so on. The counselor reported that the binding "counselor-client" role was loosened, and he and Donny became closer. Donny was more at ease, talked more, and made substantially more eye contact.

During the next session, the counselor and client drove to the country to talk. The day before had been Donny's birthday. The following dialogue took place:

Counselor: Tell me about your birthday.

Donny: It was alright.

Counselor: Just alright?

Donny: Well, I mean . . . a birthday is a birthday. No big deal. Who cares?

Counselor: (Brief silence.)

Donny: (Tears come to Donny's eyes.) Well wouldn't it make you mad if nobody cared about you or your stupid birthday?

Counselor: You just said, "Nobody."

Donny: Well, I mean, nobody important.

Counselor: If somebody important to me forgot my birthday, it would really hurt my feelings.

Donny: He should have remembered. He is always doing something for somebody else. He's too busy being Mr. Nice Guy. Everybody tells me how lucky I am to have such a great dad. Everybody tells me I should be good. Why should I? Why doesn't he be a dad like he is supposed to? I mean really, when your own dad forgets your birthday . . .

The two talked more about Donny's anger, particularly toward his father, a taboo area before this time. Donny allowed himself to express his anger and went on to reveal more events in which he felt short-changed and unloved. In the counselor's words: "I felt like we were closer at this point than at any other time in our relationship."

## ANNOTATED BIBLIOGRAPHY

Hart, J. T., & Tomlinson, T. M. (Eds.). (1970). *New directions in client-centered therapy.* Boston: Houghton Mifflin.

Resulting from the collaboration of a number of distinguished authors, this book demonstrates the theoretical sophistication and complexity that has resulted from Rogers' original system. Areas of theory, practice, and research are explored. All the writers have practiced from a client-centered background and have done research related to therapy. The book includes sections on parenting, family therapy, filial therapy, and groups.

Rogers, C. R. (1951). *Client-centered therapy.* Boston: Houghton Mifflin.

Written in a personal rather than an academic style, Rogers describes changes in his thinking and practice and, for the first time, attempts to organize and systematize his insights to other fields such as education and counselor training. Colleagues contributed chapters on play therapy, group-centered psychotherapy, and group-centered leadership and administration.

Rogers, C. R. (1961). *On becoming a person: A therapist's view of psychotherapy.* Boston: Houghton Mifflin.

A collection of 21 of Rogers' essays, this book was, of all of his own books, his favorite. Not just a book on psychotherapy, it synthesizes the work of his career and applies his therapeutic principles to a variety of human relationships. The essay titled "The Characteristics of a Helping Relationship" has been reprinted in journals of many professions, and the questions Rogers asked at that time are still being asked by those who choose a person-centered approach toward helping.

Rogers, C. R. (1980). *A way of being.* Boston: Houghton Mifflin.

A compilation of personal experiences, thoughts, feelings, and beliefs, this book is a testament to Rogers' ever active mind, keen intellect, honesty, integrity, and faith in people and community. The book also provides final thoughts on person-centered theory and its extensions.

## REFERENCES

Andronico, M. P., Fidler, J., Guerney, B. J., Jr., & Guerney, L. F. (1967). The combination of didactic and dynamic elements in filial therapy. *International Journal of Group Psychotherapy, 17,* 10–17.

Axline, V. (1947). *Play therapy.* Boston: Houghton Mifflin.

Baker, S. B. (1996). *School counseling for the twenty-first century* (2nd ed.). Englewood Cliffs, NJ: Prentice-Hall.

Becvar, D. S., & Becvar, R. J. (1993). *Family therapy: A systemic integration* (2nd ed.). Boston: Allyn & Bacon.

Belkin, D. S. (1980). *Contemporary psychotherapies.* Chicago: Rand McNally.

Benson, A. J., & Benson, J. M. (1993). Peer mediation: Conflict resolution in the schools. *Journal of School Psychology, 31,* 427–430.

Bergin, A. E., & Garfield, S. L. (1994). *Handbook of psychotherapy and behavior change* (4th ed.). New York: Wiley.

Bohart, A. C., & Todd, J. (1988). *Foundations of clinical and counseling psychology.* New York: Harper & Row.

Borders, L. D., & Drury, S. M. (1992). Comprehensive school counseling programs: A review for policy makers and practitioners. *Journal of Counseling and Development, 70,* 487–498.

Boutwell, D. A., & Myrick, R. D. (1992). The go for it club. *Elementary Guidance and Counseling, 27,* 303–304.

Boy, A. V., & Pine, G. J. (1963). *Client-centered counseling in the secondary school.* Boston: Houghton Mifflin.

Boy, A. V., & Pine, G. J. (1982). *Client-centered counseling: A renewal.* Boston: Allyn & Bacon.

Boy, A. V., & Pine, G. J. (1990). *A person-centered foundation for counseling and psychotherapy.* Springfield, IL: Thomas.

Bruner, J. (1990). *An act of meaning.* Cambridge, MA: Harvard University Press.

Byrne, R. H. (1995). *Becoming a master counselor: Introduction to the profession.* Pacific Grove, CA: Brooks/Cole.

Cade, B., & O'Hanlon, W. H. (1993). *A brief guide to brief therapy.* New York: Norton.

Capuzzi, D., & Gross, D. R. (1995). *Counseling and psychotherapy: Theories and interventions.* Englewood Cliffs, NJ: Merrill.

Carkhuff, R. R. (1969). *Helping and human relations: A primer for lay and professional helpers* (Vols. 1 & 2). New York: Holt, Rinehart and Winston.

Carkhuff, R. R. (1971). Training as a preferred mode of treatment. *Journal of Counseling Psychology, 18,* 123–131.

Carkhuff, R. R. (1987). *The art of helping* (Vol. 6). Amherst, MA: Human Resource Development Press.

Carkhuff, R. R., & Berenson, B. G. (1967). *Beyond counseling and therapy* (1st ed.). New York: Holt, Rinehart and Winston.

Comer, R. J. (1995). *Abnormal psychology* (2nd ed.). New York: Freeman.

Corey, G. (1995). *Theory and practice of group counseling.* Pacific Grove, CA: Brooks/Cole.

Corey, M. S., & Corey, G. (1997). *Groups: Process and practice* (5th ed.). Pacific Grove, CA: Brooks/Cole.

Cormier, W. H., & Cormier, L. S. (1991). *Interviewing strategies for helpers: Fundamental skills and cognitive behavioral interventions* (3rd ed.). Pacific Grove, CA: Brooks/Cole.

Corsini, R. J. (1979). *Current psychotherapies* (2nd ed.). Itasca, IL: Peacock.

Cunningham, S. (1985, May). Humanists celebrate gains, goals. *APA Monitor,* pp. 16,18.

Damasio, A. (1994). *Descartes' error.* New York: Putnam.

Davis, D. E. (1977). *My friends and me.* Circle Pines, MN: American Guidance Service.

Davison, G. C., & Neal, J. M. (1994). *Abnormal psychology* (6th ed.). New York: Wiley.

Dinkmeyer, D., Sr., & Dinkmeyer, D., Jr. (1982). *Developing understanding of self and others (DUSO-1 [R] and DUSO-2 [R]).* Circle Pines, MN: American Guidance Service.

Dinkmeyer, D. C., & McKay, G. (1976). *Systematic training for effective parenting.* Circle Pines, MN: American Guidance Service.

Dorfman, E. (1951). Play therapy. In C. Rogers (Ed.), *Client-centered therapy.* Boston: Houghton Mifflin.

Egan, G. (1975). *The skilled helper: A model for systematic helping and interpersonal relating.* Monterey, CA: Brooks/Cole.

Egan, G. (1990). *The skilled helper* (4th ed.). Monterey, CA: Brooks/Cole.

Egan, G. (1994). *The skilled helper: A problem-management approach to helping.* Pacific Grove, CA: Brooks/Cole.

Fennell, D. L., & Weinhold, D. K. (1997). *Counseling families: An introduction to marriage and family therapy.* Denver. CO: Love.

Gelso, C. J. (1992). *Counseling psychology.* Fort Worth, TX: Harcourt Brace Jovanovich College.

Gelso, C. J., & Fretz, B. R. (1992). *Counseling psychology.* Fort Worth, TX: Harcourt Brace Javanovich College.

Gendlin, E. T. (1974). Client-centered and experiential psychotherapy. In D. Wexler & L. Rice (Eds.), *Innovations in client-centered therapy.* New York: Wiley.

Gendlin, E. T. (1990). The small steps of the therapy process: How they come and how to help them come. In G. Lietaer, J. Rombauts, & R. Van Balen (Eds.), *Client-centered and experiential psychotherapy in the nineties* (pp. 205–224). Leuven: Leuven University Press.

Gladding, S. T. (1995). *Group work: A counseling specialty.* Englewood Cliffs, NJ: Merrill.

Glasser, W. (1969). *Schools without failure.* New York: Harper & Row.

Goleman, D. (1995). *Emotional intelligence.* New York: Bantam Books.

Gordon, T. (1970). *Parent effectiveness training.* New York: Wyden.

Gordon, T. (1974). *Teacher effectiveness training.* New York: McKay.

Greenburg, L. S., Elliott, R. K., & Lietaer, G. (1994). Research on experiential therapies. In A. E. Bergin & S. L. Garfield (Eds.), *Handbook of psychotherapy and behavior change* (4th ed., pp. 509–539). New York: Wiley.

Guerney, B. G., Jr. (1964). Filial therapy: Discussion and rationale. *Journal of Consulting Psychology, 28,* 304–310.

Guerney, B. G., Jr., (1977). *Relationship enhancement.* San Francisco: Jossey-Bass.

Guerney, B. G., Jr., Guerney, L. F., & Andronico, M. P. (1966, March). Filial therapy. *Yale Scientific Magazine.*

Guerney, L. F., & Guerney, B. G. (1989). Child relationship enhancement: Family therapy and parent education. *Person-Centered Review, 4*(3), 344–357.

Hansen, J. C., Rossberg, R. H., & Cramer, S. H. (1994). *Counseling: Theory and process* (5th ed.). Boston: Allyn & Bacon.

Hart, J. T., & Tomlinson, T. M. (Eds.). (1970). *New directions in client-centered therapy.* Boston: Houghton Mifflin.

Hazler, R. J. (1995). Person-centered theory. In D. Capuzzi & D. R. Gross (Eds.), *Counseling and psychotherapy: Theories and interventions* (pp. 237–265). Englewood Cliffs, NJ: Merrill.

Horne, A. M., & Passmore, J. L. (1991). *Family counseling and therapy* (2nd ed.). Itasca, IL: Peacock.

Ivey, A. E. (1988). *Intentional interviewing and counseling: Facilitating client development.* Monterey, CA: Brooks/Cole.

Ivey, A., & Simek-Downing, L. (1980). *Counseling and psychotherapy: Skills, theories, and practice.* Englewood Cliffs, NJ: Prentice-Hall.

Jacobs, E. E., Harvill, R. L., & Masson, R. L. (1994). *Group counseling: Strategies and skills.* Pacific Grove, CA: Brooks/Cole.

Kahn, M. (1991). *Between therapist and client.* New York: Freeman.

Kirschenbaum, H. (1979). *On becoming Carl Rogers.* New York: Dell.

Kirschenbaum, H., & Henderson, V. L. (1989). *The Carl Rogers reader.* Boston: Houghton Mifflin.

Landreth, G. L. (1991). *Play therapy: The art of the relationship.* Bristol, PA: Accelerated Development.

Lavant, R. F. (1978a). Client-centered approaches to working with the family: An overview of new developments in therapeutic, educational, and preventive methods. *International Journal of Family Counseling, 6,* 31–44.

Lavant, R. F. (1978b). Family therapy: A client-centered perspective. *Journal of Marriage and Family Counseling, 40,* 35–42.

LeDoux, J. (1994, June). Emotion, memory and the brain. *Scientific American, 220,* 50–57.

Lerner, M. S., & Clum, G. A. (1990). Treatment of suicide ideators: A problem-solving approach. *Behavior Therapy, 21,* 403–411.

Miller, S. D., Duncan, B. L., & Hubble, M. A. (1997). *Escape from Babel.* New York: Norton.

Moustakas, C. (1953). *Children in play therapy.* New York: McGraw-Hill.

Neimeyer, R. A., & Mahoney, M. J. (1995). *Constructivism in psychotherapy.* Washington, DC: American Psychological Association.

Nelson, R. (1972). *Guidance and counseling in the elementary school.* New York: Holt, Rinehart and Winston.

Nichols, M. P., & Schwartz, R. C. (1991). *Family therapy: Concepts and methods* (2nd ed.). Boston: Allyn & Bacon.

Oatley, K., & Jenkins, J. M. (1996). *Understanding emotions.* Cambridge, MA: Blackwell.

O'Hanlon, B., & Beadle, S. (1994). *A field guide to possibilityland: Possibility therapy methods.* Omaha, NE: Possibility Press.

O'Hanlon, W. H., & Weiner-Davis, M. (1989). *In search of solutions: A new direction in psychotherapy.* New York: Norton.

O'Hanlon, W. H., & Wilk, J. (1987). *Shifting contexts: The generation of effective psychotherapy.* New York: Guilford Press.

Parsons, R. D., & Wicks, R. J. (1994). *Counseling strategies and intervention techniques for the human services.* Boston: Allyn & Bacon.

Prochaska, J. O. (1979). *Systems of psychotherapy: A transtheoretical analysis.* Homewood, IL: Dorsey Press.

Prochaska, J. O., & Norcross, J. C. (1994). *Systems of psychotherapy: A transtheoretical analysis.* Pacific Grove, CA: Brooks/Cole.

Raskin, N. J., & Van deer Veen, F. (1970). Client-centered family therapy: Some clinical and research perspectives. In J. T. Hart & T. M. Tomlinson (Eds.), *New directions in client-centered therapy.* Boston: Houghton Mifflin.

Reisman, J. M. (1973). *Principles of psychotherapy with children.* New York: Wiley.

Rogers, C. R. (1939). *The clinical treatment of the problem child.* Boston: Houghton Mifflin.

Rogers, C. R. (1942). *Counseling and psychotherapy.* Boston: Houghton Mifflin.

Rogers, C. R. (1951). *Client-centered therapy.* Boston: Houghton Mifflin.

Rogers, C. R. (1957). The necessary and sufficient conditions of therapeutic personality change. *Journal of Consulting Psychology, 21,* 95–103.

Rogers, C. R. (1959). A theory of therapy, personality, and interpersonal relationships as developed in the client-centered framework. In S. Koch (Ed.), *Psychology: A study of a science: Vol. 3. Formulations of the person and the social context.* New York: McGraw-Hill.

Rogers, C. R. (1961a). *On becoming a person: A therapist's view of psychotherapy.* Boston: Houghton Mifflin.

Rogers, C. R. (1961b). The process equation of psychotherapy. *American Journal of Psychotherapy, 15,* 27–45.

Rogers, C. R. (1969). *The freedom to learn: A view of what education might become.* Columbus, OH: Merrill.

Rogers, C. R. (1970a). Foreward. In J. T. Hart & T. M. Tomlinson (Eds.), *New directions in client-centered therapy.* Boston: Houghton Mifflin.

Rogers, C. R. (1970b). *Carl Rogers on encounter groups.* New York: Harper & Row.

Rogers, C. R. (1972). *Becoming partners: Marriage and its alternatives.* New York: Delacorte Press.

Rogers, C. R. (1977). *Carl Rogers on personal power.* New York: Delacorte Press.

Rogers, C. R. (1980). *A way of being.* Boston: Houghton Mifflin.

Rogers, C. R. (1983). *Freedom to learn for the 1980s.* Columbus, OH: Merrill.

Rogers, C. R. (1985). Toward a more human science of the person. *Journal of Humanistic Psychology, 25,* 7–24.

Rogers, C. R. (1986). A client-centered/person-centered approach to therapy. In I. Kutash & A. Wolf (Eds.), *Psychotherapist's casebook* (pp. 197–208). New York: Jossey-Bass.

Rogers, C. R., & Dymond, R. (1954). *Psychotherapy and personality change.* Chicago: University of Chicago Press.

Rogers, C. R., Gendlin, E. T., Kiesler, D. J., & Truax, C. B. (Eds.). (1967). *The therapeutic relationship and its impact: A study of psychotherapy with schizophrenics.* Madison: University of Wisconsin Press.

Rogers, C. R., & Rablen, R. (1958). *A scale of process on psychotherapy.* Unpublished manuscript, University of Wisconsin.

Rogers, C. R., & Sanford, R. C. (1984). Client-centered psychotherapy. In H. I. Kaplan & B. J. Sadock (Eds.), *Comprehensive textbook of psychiatry* (Vol. 4). Boston: Williams & Wilkins.

Sarason, I. G., & Sarason, B. R. (1993). *Abnormal psychology: The problem of maladaptive behavior* (7th ed.). Englewood Cliffs, NJ: Prentice-Hall.

Schmidt, J. J. (1996). *Counseling in schools.* Needham Heights, MA: Allyn & Bacon.

Schrumpf, F., Crawford, D., & Usadel, H. C. (1991). *Peer mediation: Conflict resolution in schools.* Champaign, IL: Research Press.

Schultz, D. P., & Schultz, S. E. (1996). *A history of modern psychology* (6th ed.). Fort Worth, TX: Harcourt Brace College.

Sharf, R. S. (1996). *Theories of psychotherapy and counseling: Concepts and cases.* Pacific Grove, CA: Brooks/Cole.

Simon, S. (1973). *I am loveable and capable: A modern allegory on the classical putdown.* Niles, IL: Argus Communications.

Smith, M. L., Glass, G. V., & Miller, T. I. (1980). *The benefits of psychotherapy.* Baltimore: Johns Hopkins University Press.

Thompson, C. L., & Rudolph, L. B. (1996). *Counseling children* (4th ed.). Pacific Grove, CA: Brooks/Cole.

Thorne, B. (1992). *Carl Rogers.* London: Sage.

Truax, C. B. (1966). Reinforcement and nonreinforcement in Rogerian psychotherapy. *Journal of Abnormal Psychology, 71,* 1–9.

Truax, C. B., & Carkhuff, R. R. (1967). *Toward effective counseling and psychotherapy.* Chicago: Aldine Press.

Truax, C. B., & Mitchell, K. M. (1971). Research on certain therapist interpersonal skills in relation to process and outcome. In A. E. Bergin & S. L. Garfield (Eds.), *Handbook of psychotherapy and behavior change: An empirical analysis* (pp. 299–344). New York: Wiley.

Walter, J. L., & Peller, J. L. (1992). *Becoming solution-focused in brief therapy.* New York: Brunner/Mazel.

Wexler, D., & Rice, L. (Eds.). (1974). *Innovations in client-centered therapy.* New York: Wiley.

Young, M. E. (1992). *Counseling methods and techniques: An eclectic approach.* New York: Merrill.

# Chapter 7

# *BEHAVIORAL APPROACHES*

Douglas T. Brown and H. Thompson Prout

The behavioral approach to therapeutic change is rooted in learning theory concepts, originally formulated in experimental psychology laboratories. The terms *behavior modification, behavior therapy,* and *cognitive behavior therapy* refer to the interventions utilized by behaviorally oriented practitioners. Although the terms are often used interchangeably, behavior modification refers to operant procedures, whereas behavior therapy is typically associated with classical conditioning procedures. The entire field of behavior therapy represents a wide range of techniques based on learning theory. Much of the terminology and basic concepts used by behavior therapists in conducting interventions are borrowed from learning principles first demonstrated by psychologists doing research with animals and humans in well-controlled experimental settings. In fact, the methodology and procedures of behavior therapy were well known before they were widely applied to clinical problems.

The behavioral view of human functioning is based on the assumption that most behaviors, abnormal or undesirable and normal or desirable, are the result of learning. Environmental influences and factors, which include how people respond to our behaviors, are seen as the key etiological factor in most psychological disorders. Relying heavily on the scientific approach to problem-solving, the behavioral therapist uses a systematic, objective, and data-based approach to developing interventions. Behavioral treatment involves the application of learning principles to help the client eliminate maladaptive behaviors or learn more adaptive modes of functioning.

## HISTORY AND STATUS

John Watson (Watson & Raynor, 1920) is generally viewed as the father of behaviorism as a result of the now-classic experiment with a child known as "little Albert." Albert was a child who had previously not demonstrated any fear when presented with white, furry, animal-like objects. In the experiment, Albert was exposed to a white rat and, at the same time, a loud noise. After several trials of pairing the rat with the noise, Albert showed a strong fear response when presented with the rat alone. The fear response also generalized to other white, furry objects (e.g., cotton, rabbits). This experiment was significant because it demonstrated that human emotional responses could be developed through a learning paradigm. This circumstance was in contrast to the dominant psychoanalytic views of the time, which focused on intrapsychic and unconscious drives that allegedly accounted for most significant human emotions. Shortly after the "little Albert" experiment, Mary Cover Jones (1924) reported a case study of a rabbit-phobic child. Jones, through a gradual, graded exposure of the child to a rabbit and the association of the exposure with food for the child, was able to eliminate the fear response to the point that the child was able to pet the rabbit at the end of the treatment. This case is recognized as one of the first applications of learning principles to a clinical problem and is viewed as a precursor of systematic desensitization and other fear- and anxiety-reducing procedures.

While experimental research continued, it was not until the 1950s that behaviorists began to look more closely at human problems. During this decade, three important works were published that essentially provided the theoretical base for most of the behavior therapy and behavior modification techniques used today. In 1950, Dollard and Miller published *Personality and Psychotherapy,* which attempted to integrate psychoanalytic theory and learning theory. They reformulated and translated the then popular psychoanalytic theory and concepts into learning theory, stimulus-response language. While this work did not refute or dismiss psychoanalytic theory, it offered an alternative behavioral view of interpreting personality and the psychotherapeutic process. B. F. Skinner's book, *Science and Human Behavior* (1953) extended the use of operant principles to solving human problems. Skinner's work provided the base of operant methodology, criticized the psychoanalytic view of human functioning, and strongly advocated a scientific approach to clinical work, emphasizing observable behavior as the focus of therapeutic change. Skinner did not deny the existence or importance of private, internal events but felt that these events were too subjective to deal with effectively in a scientific approach to changing human behavior. In 1958, Joseph Wolpe published *Psychotherapy by Reciprocal Inhibition,* which dealt with learning theory approaches for treating adult neurotic disorders. Utilizing a classical conditioning base and viewing anxiety as a key determinant in neurotic disorders, Wolpe developed the basic procedures for systematic desensitization.

Bandura (1969) is credited with recognizing the importance of observational learning in both the acquisition and change of behavior. Bandura (1977) has also developed a social learning theory that involves elements of operant, classical, and observational learning to explain behavior. This approach emphasizes multiple influences on behavior and the importance of the environment and social context and offers a comprehensive framework for explaining behavior in general (Kazdin, 1980). The social learning view probably best represents what would be the orientation of an eclectic behavior therapist. Lazarus's (1976) multimodal behavior therapy, which emphasizes a comprehensive behavioral view of problem definition and intervention, is compatible with the social learning view.

Meichenbaum (1977) is generally credited with developing the area of cognitive behavior modification. His procedures incorporate behavioral techniques for modifying thought patterns generally associated with dysfunctional or abnormal behavior. Meichenbaum believes that thought patterns and environmental influences are interactive in producing behaviors. Thus, behavioral interventions should concentrate on both areas to be effective.

From the late 1960s to the present, an enormous number of behavioral techniques have been developed, applied, and researched. Techniques have included systematic desensitization, relaxation training, anxiety management training, emotional flooding, self-control procedures, aversive procedures, token economies, behavioral contingency contracting, modeling, and cognitive behavior modification, to name a few. Behavioral approaches have been applied to problems of anxiety, depression, aggression, lack of assertiveness, psychosis, social skill difficulties, addiction, sexual dysfunction, eating disorders, psychosomatic disorders, academic difficulties, marital and family dysfunction, delinquency, withdrawal, enuresis, encopresis, and so on. With this array of techniques and applications, it is difficult to point to one set of procedures and say that they are representative of behavior therapy.

The explosion of behavior therapy in the past 20 years has yielded a number of journals that present almost exclusively articles on behavioral approaches to human problems. Among these journals are *Behavior Research and Therapy, Behavior Therapy, Journal of Applied Behavior Analysis, Cognitive Therapy and Research, Behavioral Assessment, Behavioral Counseling Quarterly,* and *Behavior Modification.* Many of the major professional groups have divisions or interest groups on behavioral approaches. The *Association for the Advancement of Behavior Therapy* (AABT), located in New York City, is the largest and most established organization dedicated to behavior therapy. It is a multidisciplinary organization that holds an annual convention, publishes journals and other publications, and sponsors training for those interested in behavior therapy.

## OVERVIEW OF THEORY

### Basic Theory and Assumptions

The behavioral approach to counseling and psychotherapy rests on six basic assumptions (Rimm & Masters, 1979):

1. *The behavioral approach tends to focus on specific behaviors rather than on presumed internal, underlying causes.* While other approaches view behaviors as symptoms of underlying psychopathology, the behaviorist sees the behaviors as the primary focus of intervention. Internal and unobservable events such as cognition, self-verbalizations, and physiological reactions (e.g., anxiety) are considered in treatment but only by virtue of how they mediate observable behaviors. The behavioral approach considers external stimuli or events as being the most influential of the behavioral determinants, rejecting the medical model or traditional psychodynamic view of internal stimuli or states as being primary factors. Further, behavior therapists do not accept the concept of psychological traits as primary behavioral determinants. More emphasis is placed on the situational aspects of behavior. The behavior therapist will not focus on changing these internal states as a goal of treatment. These internal states, compared with overt behaviors, are seen as less accessible and reliable and more subjective; and apparent changes

in these internal psychological states do not necessarily result in behavior change and improved functioning.

2. *Maladaptive behaviors are acquired through the same principles of learning as are "normal" behaviors.* The way an individual learns behaviors is a product of the environment and the individual's unique learning history. However, the basic learning mechanisms are same for normal and for abnormal behavior. Other theories view pathology as a result of a different psychological process. For example, behavioral research has shown that aggressive behaviors can be learned through observation of an adult mode. (Bandura, Ross, & Ross, 1963). Similarly, we know that more appropriate social behaviors (e.g., social skills) are also learned through modeling. Thus, the two behaviors, one undesirable and the other desirable, are learned through the same mechanism of learning—modeling.

3. *The behaviorist uses psychological and learning principles as the basis for developing interventions to modify maladaptive behavior.* Since the behavioral approach assumes that most behaviors are acquired via learning, the behaviorist further assumes that employing the learning principles can modify maladaptive behaviors. It is assumed that previous learning produced the maladaptive behavior. New learning can, therefore, be employed to modify the maladaptive behavior pattern.

4. *The behavioral approach involves setting specific, defined goals for intervention.* Goals of treatment are often stated in a form that allows for objective, preferably measurable, assessment of treatment progress. The alleviation of specific problems, the reduction of certain problem behaviors, or the acquisition of new, desirable behaviors would be appropriate goals. For example, the behavior therapist would attempt to identify specific situations and problem areas related to a client's reported generalized "unhappiness."

5. *The behavior therapist selects his or her intervention techniques to deal specifically with the client's unique problems.* Some forms of traditional counseling and psychotherapy utilize essentially the same approach, regardless of the client's presenting problems. For example, a nondirective play therapist might treat an anxious child and an aggressive child in a similar fashion. The behavior therapist, on the other hand, might provide desensitization for the anxious child and develop a reinforcement program for the aggressive child. These two sets of techniques are vastly different, yet both have a learning theory base.

6. *Behavior therapy focuses on present behavior and social contexts.* The notion of psychological insight as being curative is generally rejected by behaviorists. Individual historical data is seen as important only as it relates directly to the current problem behaviors from a learning theory standpoint. The behavior therapist will focus on present behaviors and current social context factors that seem to be maintaining problematic behaviors.

## LEARNING OR CONCEPTUAL BASES

As has been mentioned, the behavioral approach utilizes learning principles to assess problem behaviors and develop interventions. The four major types of learning or conceptual bases are classical conditioning, operant conditioning, observational learning, and cognitive learning.

## Classical Conditioning

Classical conditioning focuses on involuntary or reflex behaviors. Various stimuli in the environment automatically evoke or elicit reflex responses. Startle responses to loud noises and salivating with food in the mouth are respondents or unconditional responses. These are learned, automatic, or involuntary responses. However, respondents can also be learned through classical conditioning in which a previously neutral stimulus begins to yield a reflex response, usually through repeated associations of the stimulus with some unconditional stimulus. Phobias are often respondent behaviors. The famous "little Albert" case previously noted is an example of a classically conditioned fear response. In classical conditioning, the stimuli or events that precede the behavior are viewed as the controlling influence in behavior. Wolpe's (1958) systematic desensitization is a behavior therapy procedure based on classical conditioning principles (Kazdin, 1980).

## Operant Conditioning

Operant behaviors are viewed as voluntary behaviors that are spontaneously and freely emitted by the individual. These behaviors are developed and controlled by the consequences that follow them. Whether a behavior is strengthened (increased) or weakened (decreased) is a function of the consequences or events that follow the behavior. In general, behaviors that increase following a desirable consequence are strengthened by positive reinforcement. Behaviors that decrease following an undesirable consequence are weakened through punishment. Behaviors that decrease because reinforcement has ceased to occur are weakened by extinction. For example, children who receive teacher praise for homework completion and who increase their completion rate might be said to have had their academic behaviors strengthened by positive reinforcement. If, on the other hand, the teacher gives no praise for the desirable behavior (i.e., does not strengthen the behavior by positive reinforcement), the behavior would decrease. A comprehensive set of operant procedures and technology is available to the practitioner (see Kazdin, 1980, and Sulzer-Azaroff & Mayer, 1986). Most everyday behaviors are operants, and operantly based intervention programs are most often used in applied settings such as schools, institutions, and correctional facilities (Kazdin).

## Observational Learning

Observational learning is concerned with learning that occurs when an individual observes another person (i.e., a model) engaging in a certain behavior and then acquires and displays the same or similar behavior. The behavior is learned through the individual's watching the model, and the behavior is said to be imitated. The individual who acquires the new behavior does not have to receive any direct consequences of the behavior for learning to have taken place. For example, a small boy observes his father working with tools. Later, the boy is seen hammering on a piece of wood. The boy has imitated his father's (i.e., the model's) behavior. A variant of observational learning is vicarious reinforcement in which an individual observes a model receiving reinforcement for certain behaviors. The effects of the reinforcement "spread" to others in the environment. For example, a child sees an older sibling receive parental praise for doing household chores. An increase in the younger child's completion of chores would be attributed to vicarious reinforcement (Kazdin, 1980).

In reality, most behaviors are not attributable to a single type of learning. Most situations have elements of classical, operant, and observational learning, and most problem behaviors are probably acquired through several learning mechanisms. School phobia has been explained from all three learning viewpoints: From a classical view, a child acquires a fear response through associational learning; from an operant viewpoint, a child is not reinforced or is punished (e.g., peer taunting) for school attendance; finally, an observational view suggests a child observes other children's fear responses. Social learning theory (Bandura, 1977) utilizes elements of the three types of learning to explain behavior and emphasizes multiple influences on behavior that occur in most social contexts. This allows learning theory to account for a broader range of behaviors than the more simplistic explanations provided by any one type of learning alone.

## Cognitive Learning

The cognitive approach in behavior therapy represents one of the more recent developments in the field. The cognitive approach (e.g., Mahoney, 1974; Meichenbaum, 1977), is concerned with cognitions or thoughts, the thinking process, and how cognitions influence emotions and behavior. In part, the cognitive-behavioral view is behavior therapy's response to the criticism that behaviorists are concerned only with observable and measurable behaviors and that important internal events are ignored in treatment and planning. Behavior is viewed as being mediated by cognitions, and, thus, behavior can be modified by a change in thoughts. For example, an impulsive child hurries through his schoolwork and the resulting work is sloppy and full of errors. The child is then taught to self-verbalize or silently say to himself cues like "slow down" or "take your time," with the result being neater, more correct work. In this situation, the thought or self-verbalization yielded an observable behavior change. Other cognitive-behavioral approaches focus more on the thought process and how it contributes to maladaptive behaviors and emotions. These approaches are quite similar to rational-emotive therapy and Beck, Rush, Shaw, and Emery's (1979) cognitive therapy. Hughes (1988) has described the use of cognitive behavioral techniques with children and adolescents in school settings.

The behavioral approach in general has not focused much attention on developmental variables. Ross (1980) notes the importance of genetic-constitutional factors and temperamental characteristics in the development of behavior. Social learning theory offers a comprehensive framework for looking at how environmental and learning factors contribute to development. The behavioral approach, however, does not have a developmental age- and stage-bound theory similar to that offered by psychoanalytic theorists. Most behaviorists consider developmental variables in treatment planning but use them largely in determining the expected ranges of behavior for different age groups and in setting goals. For example, social skills training must be planned with consideration of cognitive and language development variables (Forehand & Wierson, 1993). We should not expect a 6-year-old to have the vocabulary to conduct a complex social interaction, although the strategies for teaching those skills are available. The behaviorist, lacking a specific developmental theory, must interface interventions with data from child and adolescent development.

## VIEW OF PSYCHOPATHOLOGY

Abnormal behavior or psychopathology is not considered as distinct from normal behavior in terms of how it develops and how it is maintained (Kazdin, 1980). It is not a disease process that overwhelms the normal personality. The behavior therapist will shy away from diagnostic labeling and a search for underlying causes for abnormal behavior. The same learning principles that explain normal behavior can also account for abnormal behavior. The determination of what is abnormal is often subjective and influenced by the social context of where the behavior occurs. Crying hysterically at a funeral might be considered normal behavior, but doing the same thing throughout a party might be looked on as abnormal behavior.

Erwin (1980) noted that the medical model concept of "mental illness" is rejected by behavior therapists, who prefer to substitute terms such as "abnormal behavior," "deviant behavior," "maladaptive behavior," and "problems in living." While Erwin notes problems with these terms, they convey meanings different from "mental illness." Abnormalcy and deviance connote a statistical difference as well as deviance from some social criterion or norm of acceptable behavior. Maladaptive implies that the behavior is preventing optimal functioning or interferes with the acquisition of certain desired goals. Problems in living refer to a similar concept, focusing more on behavior that impedes routine functioning. Erwin further notes that the term "maladaptive characteristics" probably comes closest to covering the concerns focused on by behavior therapists because it includes not only unwanted behaviors but also images, feelings, and thoughts.

Ross (1980) notes that there is no absolute definition of a psychological disorder. Children's behavior is considered normal when it conforms to the prevailing consensual norm, that is, a norm set by both peers and adults in the environment. Ross has proposed a definition of psychological disorders in children:

> A psychological disorder is said to be present when a child emits behavior that deviates from an arbitrary and relative social norm in that it occurs with a frequency or intensity that authoritative adults in the child's environment judge, under the circumstances, to be either too high or too low. (p. 9)

Implicit in this definition is the concept of viewing behaviors as either deficient or excessive. Rather than utilizing diagnostic labels or global descriptions, the behavior therapist may assess or classify behaviors into one of these categories. A deficit behavior occurs not at all or at too low a rate, with too little intensity, or too slowly. Conversely, an excess behavior occurs at too high a rate, with too much intensity, or for too long. A withdrawn child who fails to approach other children might be termed deficient in prosocial behavior. A hyperactive child might be considered as displaying excessive motor activity.

## General Therapeutic Goals and Techniques

Behavior therapy follows a systematic and databased model of intervention. The assessments of diagnostic phases are not seen as separate components, but as part of a total process. Gottman and Leiblum (1974) and J. Brown and Brown (1977) have both conceptualized counseling and psychotherapy in a systematic step-by-step process. In fact, both use flowchart models to assist the practitioner in systematically planning, developing, and making decisions about interventions. This allows looping back either to reassess a problem or to modify strategies. While their approaches are not totally intended for the behavior therapist, they are consistent with and based on behavioral intervention principles.

Step 1 in the intervention process involves deciding who is to be involved in the assessment and intervention phases. This decision is made by determining the settings where the problem is occurring and who are the significant individuals in those settings. For example, if a child is displaying problem behavior both at home and at school, it will be best to see both parents and teachers at some point. It is also important to determine who initiated the referral, how the decision was reached to seek treatment, and what the differing opinions are concerning the need for treatment based on whether a problem actually exists.

Step 2 involves definition and operationalization of the problem. This step may include formulation of target behavior definitions into measurable or observable terms. At this point, some general assessment will be made regarding whether the problem represents an excess or deficit behavior. However, the assertion that a problem exists as the result of a performance discrepancy may mean that the child's performance or behavior does not match the expectation of another individual. While the behavior can be objectively measured and quantified, expectations are more subjective and value based. The discrepancy can exist when, for example, a child's behavior is genuinely excessive or deficient, or when the expectation of the adult is too rigid. A child who receives a single *B* on a report card with all the rest of the grades being *A* would not generally be considered academically deficient. Yet, a parent with an expectation of all *A*'s might label this a problem. This would appear to be a problem of very high expectations, rather than a child behavior difficulty. Thus, the assessment at this phase focuses not only on the behaviors, but also on the norms of the referral sources.

Step 3 involves collecting baseline data on the problem or target behaviors. In behavioral therapies, this may range from direct observation with collection of frequency data to more subjective ratings of the intensity of a problem. This step has a goal of obtaining a representative sample of the current level of the problem behavior, with this level assessed in a quantifiable fashion. An overactive child's problem may be described by the number of times the child is out of his or her seat in school. An anxious high school student may report ratings from 0 to 10 to describe anxiety experienced at various times during the day. Related to this data collection phase may be an assessment of the environments the child is in to determine what environmental factors may be contributing to the problem and to determine what learning mechanisms may be operating.

Step 4 consists of negotiating a contract with the clients and setting treatment objectives or goals. The goals will ordinarily be stated in quantifiable form so that both client and therapist can agree that the goal has been met.

Step 5 is the beginning of the actual intervention. Depending on the results of the previous assessments, the therapist will choose from the behavioral techniques available. The intervention will be designed to meet the unique problems presented. The overactive child may respond to a reinforcement program while desensitization may help the anxious adolescent.

Step 6 involves the monitoring of the intervention. Data is collected periodically and systematically during the intervention phase. The process permits modifying the behavioral strategy if change does not occur, as well as determining when the goals have been met.

Finally, the behavior therapist plans strategies to ensure that desirable changes are maintained and that these changes are transferred to settings other than those where the treatment may have been focused. At this point, the therapist is concerned with ensuring that a reduction in overactive behavior in the classroom is generalized to the home and other environments. The therapist teaches coping skills to the adolescent who has become anxious about current problems so that he or she will be better able to handle anxious situations in the future.

The behavioral approach to therapy presents some distinct practices:

- It is systematic, objective, and orderly.
- Assessment and intervention are interrelated and interdependent functions.
- It focuses on monitoring of change and modifying of strategies if necessary (i.e., the flowchart conceptualization).
- It is databased emphasizing operationalization of problems.
- It emphasizes interventions that are based on learning principles but that are uniquely designed to deal with the specific problems presented.

## APPLICATIONS WITH CHILDREN

Children present a unique challenge to the applied behavior therapist. While most of the behavior of young children appears to be governed by operant conditions which are externally controlled, the rapid development of cognition changes the nature of therapeutic interventions across mental age levels. For the most part, however, behavior analysis with children is highly performance-based (Schloss & Smith, 1994; Sulzer-Azaroff & Reese, 1982). Thus, all the terminology used to define pathology is operationalized so that its rate and duration may be accurately measured. Intervention techniques are designed to provide experimental paradigms that result in the identification of the antecedents and consequences surrounding a given behavior. Thus, while a behavior therapist may look at the precipitating factors leading to a child's pathological behavior, the focus is on identifying specific procedures that will yield more acceptable behavior patterns. With younger children, the procedure utilized is usually highly "noncognitive." That is, little attempt is made to use intrinsic reinforcement systems and to modify behavior by modifying cognitive structures. A high degree of precision in controlling external environmental stimuli is thus required.

## Operant Techniques

In very young children, operant techniques have been utilized for modifying vocalization behavior such as crying and tantrums (Etzel & Gewirtz, 1967). It has been demonstrated that the level of vocalization in infants is dependent on specific patterns of adult reinforcement (Weisberg, 1963). It has also been established that social learning principles control a wide array of deviant behaviors in very young children, including uncontrolled crying, anxiety, regressed motor development, and delayed language.

Behavior therapy has been particularly successful in dealing with incontinence and toilet training in young children. Foxx and Azrin (1973a) have described a technique for the rapid toilet training of young children. Their technique requires that the child be able to respond to verbal instructions and to exhibit a minimal amount of social imitation skill. Generally, the technique requires implementing the following procedures:

1. Minimize distracting stimuli during the operant conditioning phase.
2. Produce a high number of urination trials by increased fluid intake in order to increase the number of positive reinforcements provided per unit time.
3. Provide precise delivery of operant reinforcement for correct toileting behavior. This includes exact timing of reinforcement so that it is delivered at the termination of the appropriate behavior.
4. Reinforce of all component skills such as raising of pants, flushing of toilet, and so on.
5. Use high-quality reinforcers such as food and physical contact.
6. Use a variety of reinforcers with a high level of frequency (continuous reinforcement).
7. Use a high degree of verbal instruction.
8. Provide negative reinforcement for "accidents," such as continuous reprimands, and so on.
9. Gradually fade all prompts and reinforcers.

Using this training technique, Foxx and Azrin have been able to demonstrate that children can be effectively toilet-trained in a short period of time. The behavior can usually be stabilized within one month. Physiological maturation and developmental age level are important factors, with children in the 26- to 48-month range being most responsive to this technique.

Generally, operant techniques have been very successful with overt behavior in very young children. At this age, however, most behaviors have readily identifiable antecedents. It is difficult to label a given behavior as "pathological" since few behaviors meet the criterion of being enduring personality characteristics. In addition, language per se is not necessary to implement a behavior therapy approach with young children. These techniques are also utilized primarily by adults in the child's ecological milieu rather than by professional therapists working in more restrictive environments. The relative susceptibility of young children to operant techniques significantly improves the likelihood of success using behavior therapy.

## Fears and Phobias

Fears and phobias have been studied more widely in adults than in children. It is only with the relatively recent realization that children suffer from anxiety disorders that childhood phobias have been investigated more intensely. In behavior therapy, Watson first described phobic reactions in the case of "little Albert" (Watson & Raynor, 1920) discussed earlier. Watson was able to demonstrate that nonfearful stimuli can be made fearful through association and that such phobic reactions tend to generalize to a number of similar stimuli. Thus, in the case of little Albert almost all furry objects produced phobic responses.

Longitudinal studies indicate that fears and phobias of children persist into adulthood and possibly worsen (Hughes, 1988; Ollendick, 1983; Ollendick & Cerny, 1981). Persistent maladaptive fears are present in an estimated 3% to 8% of children. In many cases, fears and phobias dramatically interfere with the child's academic and social development or play a role in the development of behavior problems that adversely affect the family and school systems. A number of studies (Fox & Houston, 1983; Werry & Wollershein, 1989) have shown that state anxiety, trait anxiety, and high stress in children are related to decrements in performance in a variety of settings. In addition, children with high cognitive state anxiety tend to exhibit somatic disorders either in childhood or in later life. Reynolds and Paget (1983) have suggested that self-esteem is also adversely affected by high states of stress and anxiety and in turn, stress and anxiety are affected by low levels of self-esteem.

Between the ages of 48 and 72 months, children develop fears of imaginary objects. Fears of this type are complex and tend to vary across a number of dimensions including health, race, socioeconomic status, and parental upbringing (Kennedy, 1971). Some of the more common phobias include fear of school, of bodily injury, of the dark, of animals, of other children, of adults, and of strange places. Phobias tend to be acquired along several dimensions. First, children tend to acquire many of their parents' fears. Second, learned fear of a given object tends to generalize easily to other similar objects. And finally, it appears that phobias can be conditioned and unconditioned with relative ease by using operant techniques.

A number of general approaches have been used with fears and phobic reactions in children. These approaches include systematic desensitization, emotive imagery, muscular relaxation, reciprocal inhibition, and reinforced practice. In addition, self-monitoring and self-control have been stressed in some studies (Ollendick, 1981; Ollendick & Cerny, 1981; O'Mara & Graziano, 1974). In this technique, children are taught to monitor and record their fear reactions and to utilize pleasant scenes to inhibit the fear.

Systematic desensitization involves teaching the child relaxation skills and then exposing the child to a hierarchy of fears beginning with the least emotionally arousing stimulus. This exposure can be "in vivo" or through the use of films or imagery. As the therapist progresses through the hierarchy of fears, the child is taught how to relax in the presence of fear-evoking stimuli. Some children have difficulty achieving deep muscle relaxation either through lack of attention, cooperation, or motor ability. They may also be unable to achieve vivid enough images to allow for deconditioning with relaxation. Other more concrete counterconditioning agents such as food, music, or play therapy may be necessary.

*School Phobia*

Children who are school phobic suffer extreme anxiety when faced with the prospect of going to school. They may be unable to eat, complain of somatic ailments (e.g., stomachaches, headaches, fatigue) and experience high rates of tardiness, absenteeism, and illness (Rhine & Spaner, 1983). Some children who are school phobic may also be depressed and withdrawn, frequently remaining at home, often without the parents' knowledge (Boyd, 1980; Trueman, 1984). Many school-phobic children exhibit anxieties regarding school performance. They constantly seek approval and worry excessively about their competence. Children with school phobia are also often in an enmeshed relationship with one or both parents, most often the mother.

Kennedy (1965) has suggested that two classes of school phobia exist: Type I and Type II. Type I school phobia is described as an actual school-related phobic reaction. Type II school phobia is a more generalized phobic reaction related to school and numerous other environments. Children exhibiting Type I school phobia have a number of characteristic behaviors including acute onset of the phobic reaction, lower grades in school, questionable physical health of their mother, and expressed concern about death. In general, Type I phobics have parents who have questionable health but are otherwise well adjusted. Type II phobics tend to be more chronic, are more likely to occur in the upper elementary grades, and come from families in which the communication patterns are poor and in which a more generalized disturbance is present.

Kennedy suggests that a number of conditions must be met in the behavioral treatment of school phobia to achieve success. These include:

• The establishment of good professional interaction between the school system and the behavior therapist.

- Enforced school attendance through the cooperation of the parents and behavior therapist.

- The amelioration of the child's somatic complaints by refusal to deal with them on the part of both parents and the behavior therapist.

- An intensively structured home-based program for the parents in order to give them the confidence necessary to deal with the child.

- A brief interview/interaction with the child by the behavior therapist to explain the contingencies of the treatment.

- Continuous follow-up with the parents by the behavior therapist and, if necessary, in-home intervention by the behavior therapist to provide modeling and instruction regarding appropriate parental behaviors.

Children with Type I phobias are more successfully treated by the preceding techniques than those with Type II phobias. It is often necessary to use more intensive anxiety desensitization procedures with children suffering from Type II phobias in order to treat them effectively.

### Direct Deconditioning of Childhood Phobias

Wish, Hasazi, and Jurgela (1975) have described a process for the direct deconditioning of childhood phobias. While deconditioning techniques have been utilized extensively with adults, it is only recently that they have been used with childhood phobic reactions. In this procedure, feared or phobic stimuli are paired with pleasant events. In addition, systematic desensitization is used. The first step in the procedure is to establish a fear hierarchy by having the child rate the level of fear associated with similar stimuli. In the second step, the child undergoes progressive relaxation utilizing a modified technique such as that described by Keat (1979). The third step of treatment involves the self-administration of the deconditioning procedure. Here the feared stimuli are paired in some meaningful way with pleasurable stimuli over successive trials. Wish et al. (1975) describe this procedure specifically for a child experiencing phobic reactions to loud sounds:

> The deconditioning procedure was accomplished in the following way. The record album, a pleasurable record album, which was forty minutes in length, was recorded on four tracks of an 8 track stereo tape. The remaining four tracks of the tape were used to superimpose the feared stimuli (sounds in the fear hierarchy) upon the ongoing music. Each sound was presented five times on the tape with an average of approximately 30 seconds between sounds. Order of sound presentation was based upon the subjective unit of disturbance ratings, with least feared sounds being presented earliest in the tape. Feared sounds were obtained from a series of professional sound effects recordings. After the tape was completed, it was transferred to an 8 track stereo tape cartridge and given to the child. (p. 298)

Utilizing this technique, it is possible to reduce most learned phobic reactions in a relatively short time. Basically, the success of systematic desensitization rests on the ability of the behavior therapist to passively recondition responses by associating them with other responses that are incompatible with anxiety (i.e., relaxation). As incompatible responses are paired with increasing levels of the phobic stimulus, they eventually displace the fear reaction. As will be discussed, this general technique is used to reduce a number of anxiety-related behaviors.

## Social Isolation and Withdrawal

Some children develop fears and phobias of being ignored, ridiculed, or attacked by other children. Such a child can be described as socially isolated (Ross, 1980). Like other phobias, this behavior tends to worsen over time with increases in withdrawn behaviors being observed. It is critical that intervention be undertaken as soon as possible to break this cycle. A number of techniques have been developed for this purpose including the teaching of social skills through modeling and other forms of therapy that maximize peer interaction. Strain, Shores, and Timm (1977) developed a social skills training procedure in which other children were used as confederates in increasing overt social behavior of isolated children. They asked their confederates to approach withdrawn children and solicit social contact. Gresham (1980) has described modeling techniques that can be used with withdrawn children. These include verbal, symbolic, and live modeling. He has described several procedures including symbolic modeling through videotapes, abstract modeling, covert modeling through imagery, participant modeling, and self-modeling. Lowenstein (1982) reduced general anxiety in withdrawn children by developing assertiveness in the child's behavior and promoting an improved ability to communicate effectively. Family patterns were investigated to determine factors in the environment that maintained the children's shy and withdrawn behavior. Lowenstein employed implosive therapy to prompt and reinforce emotions other than shyness and withdrawal in the presence of discriminative stimuli.

Research with withdrawn children indicates that substantial progress is possible through the consistent use of behavior therapy. As the level of withdrawal increases, however, the number of potential therapy sessions necessary to effect change increases. The presence of adequate language development is another critical variable in predicting the rate of success with these children since language is a key component of social interaction.

## Enuresis and Encopresis

Enuresis describes a condition in which urine is involuntarily discharged and in which no organic pathology is present. Nocturnal enuresis occurs in approximately 20% of young children and constitutes a serious violation of social folkways in the perception of most parents. Therefore, the stress experienced by a child who is enuretic is significant because of perceived social rejection and loss of parental love. This in turn can result in a generalized anxiety disorder. Common symptoms may include disturbances in sleep, eating, and social interactions.

Instrumental conditioning methods have been used with success in the treatment of enuresis (Mowrer & Mowrer, 1938). A number of commercially manufactured devices are available for this purpose. Generally, the devices consist of a urine-sensitive pad that is connected to some sort of auditory or tactile stimulus. When the device senses wetness, it responds with a bell, a mild shock, or a buzzer. It is then the child's responsibility to turn off the alarm.

The general procedure for instrumental conditioning of enuresis involves the gradual shaping of the desired behavior (bladder retention) followed by appropriate reinforcement. This process involves increasing the time frame in which bladder distention cues are present without urination occurring (Kimmel & Kimmel, 1973). The presence of an alarm provides feedback in this process. In the first day of training, the child is asked to refrain from urination for approximately 5 to 10 minutes. The child is promised a reinforcement if the task is accomplished. It is important that this first retention activity be a success and, therefore, be followed by a reward. The time demand is then gradually increased with appropriate reinforcements following successful trials. At night, the alarm device provides feedback and, therefore, reinforcement for retention. This process can be supplemented by direct social reinforcement from the parents.

Houts, Liebert, and Padawer, (1983) provide convincing experimental evidence on the effectiveness of the bell-and-pad method for training bladder retention control. Their study involving 60 enuretic children, ages 4–12, involved in one-hour group training sessions and treatment at home. Some subjects in the study were also treated with imipramine (a drug commonly used to control enuresis). An interesting finding of the study is that the subjects who later relapsed were more likely to have been treated with imipramine than subjects who showed long-term bladder control.

Cognitive control theory has also been used in conjunction with more traditional operant techniques in the treatment of enuresis. Cotugno (1987) reports a study in which children's "self talk" was successfully modified to help them achieve better bladder control.

The procedure for control of enuresis includes (a) teaching the child to hold urine for longer and longer periods before going to the bathroom; (b) introducing large amounts of fluids to increase the number of trials; (c) reinforcing the child after urination in an appropriate setting; (d) keeping a careful chart of progress and making the chart available to both the parent and the child; (e) having the child practice starting and stopping the urination stream; and (f) shaping toward independent practice trials on the part of the child.

Encopresis is a term that defines any disturbance of bowel evacuation or retention. This can include either soiling or constipation. In either of these cases, prior to the use of behavior therapy, the child should undergo a thorough physical examination. While the behavioral etiology is not well understood, it is assumed to be a stress reaction that falls in the general class of anxiety disorders. In some instances, it may be an attention-getting device on the part of younger children. Much of the early work of Mowrer and Mowrer (1938) relates directly to the treatment of encopresis. In encopretic children, the feedback mechanisms which signal the need to defecate are often dulled or missing. The child becomes unaware that his or her rectum is full. The normal response is that of evacuation, but this response occurs in inappropriate settings. The task of behavior therapy is to develop a stimulus-response link that is socially appropriate. Neale (1973) has described a method of treatment in which instrumental conditioning is used to cause decay of the anxiety response. This is done through reciprocal inhibition where the child is taken to the bathroom at least four times daily and permitted to void while simultaneously receiving positive reinforcement or associating other positive circumstances (e.g., candy). As soon as the child has become accustomed to using the bathroom four times a day, this procedure is gradually faded and the child is allowed to use the bathroom as needed. A careful record is kept of defecation, and both the behavior therapist and the child review this record.

Other researchers have used cathartics or suppositories in conjunction with behavior therapy. O'Brien, Ross, and Christophersen (1986) investigated a combination of cathartic and behavioral treated procedures for eliminating diurnal and nocturnal encopresis. They found that independent toiletings resulted after 8 to 39 weeks of treatment using a combination of suppositories, positive practice, time-out, and hourly toilet visits. Ultimately, for all subjects, the suppositories were systematically faded. B. Brown and Doolan (1983) emphasized the need for detailed analysis of the etiology of individual cases of encopresis and the need for sustained treatment approaches sometimes over lengthy time periods.

The general procedure for the treatment of encopresis includes: (a) complete physiological examination to determine any medical abnormalities; (b) correction of any physiological difficulties (i.e., constipation, impaction) by the use of appropriate suppositories or cathartics; (c) use of instrumental condition techniques for feedback and reinforcement during appropriate evacuation; (d) the systematic fading of treatment contingencies when bowel control is accomplished; and (e) the use of reciprocal inhibition techniques to associate positive circumstances with evacuation rather than punishment.

## Autism and Childhood Psychosis

Autism and childhood schizophrenia are serious child behavioral disturbances that have not been susceptible to traditional modes of therapy. Professionals do not agree on the etiology of these disorders. Thus, specific strategies for their treatment vary tremendously. While autism is considered a relatively rare disorder, it has several specific behavioral characteristics. Webster (1980) has described these characteristics, including affect isolation, unrelatedness to others, inconsistent developmental continuity, self-destructive behavior, temper tantrums, self-identity confusion, concrete thinking, perceptual inconsistencies, echolalia, physical uncoordination, and language deficits. Kanner (1945) describes autism as the inability of the child to relate to people in a natural way which is evident from the beginning of maturation. In addition, the autistic child shows an obsessive-compulsive desire for sameness coupled with perserverative activity.

Childhood schizophrenia is considered by most theorists to differ from autism. Ross (1980) lists seven defining characteristics:

1. Distorted interpersonal relationships.
2. A distorted concept of self and the relationship of one's body to the environment.
3. Preoccupation with specific objects without regard for their use.
4. Demand for consistency in the environment.
5. Use of speech to communicate bizarre and meaningless content.
6. Poor motor coordination and locomotion.
7. The appearance of retardation with occasional periods of "normality."

Interventions with autistic and other psychotic children are similar. Ferster (1961) has indicated that psychotic children experience a decrement in their developmental process that reduces the general efficiency of reinforcers. Thus, psychotic children do not produce behavior that solicits reinforcement from parents, and this reciprocally reduces the amount and variety of reinforcement that parents provide their children. In the case of autistic children, the absence of language eliminates totally the use of verbal interchange and reinforcement. With other psychotic children, bizarre language may severely limit the ability of the parent to provide verbal reinforcement. The primary focus of most behavioral interventions has been on the area of selective attention. Autistic children and some schizophrenic children develop overexclusive attention. Thus, these children attend in a perseverative manner to a limited array of stimuli within the environment. Other psychotic children exhibit overinclusive attention on a subset of environmental stimuli. Thus, a major goal for behavior therapy is to generalize attention span or make it more susceptible to specific environmental stimuli. This goal is accomplished through traditional operant discrimination training techniques.

Foxx and Azrin (1973b) have described a technique called positive practice overcorrection. It has the objective of interrupting self-stimulatory behavior evident in many psychotic children. By injecting an annoying or punishing consequence, we teach the child that self-stimulatory behavior is not rewarded. Positive reinforcement is provided for appropriate social interaction and behaviors that are directed to the outward environment of the child. Lovaas, Koegel, Simmons, and Long (1973) have delineated several of the most effective behavioral procedures for use with psychotic children. These include (a) use of food as a contingent primary reinforcer, (b) use of reinforcement withdrawal when necessary, (c) aversive stimulation for self-stimulatory and injurious behavior, (d) modeling or appropriate behaviors, (e) reinforcement of incompatible behaviors, and (f) use of socially reinforcing language experiences.

Brawley, Harris, Allen, Fleming, and Peterson (1973) have described procedures for intervention with autistic children. They first identify appropriate and inappropriate behaviors in a given child. The appropriate behaviors include verbalization of words and phrases, use of objects in their intended mode, and compliance with requests or commands. Inappropriate behaviors include self-stimulation such as hitting, slapping, random verbalizations, withdrawal, and temper tantrums. These behaviors are recorded for a sufficient period to develop an appropriate baseline. In the first reinforcement phase, a number of reinforcers are used to determine those that will be most effective. Next the therapist determines which behaviors the child is capable of imitating and reinforces all appropriate imitations performed by the child (i.e., mimicking of sounds and gestures). To encourage appropriate use of materials, the child is directed and reinforced in a number of activities including hopping, skipping, ball throwing, balance beam walking, and other similar tasks. Verbal commands are constantly paired with gestural stimuli. To determine whether reinforcements have been effective, a reversal period is used to elicit an extinction response. This is followed by a second reinforcement period for a total of 20 to 30 sessions. Brawley and his colleagues have demonstrated an average of 80% success using this methodology.

Autistic and schizophrenic behavior requires utilization of fundamental operant techniques. However, unlike other disorders, the array of reinforcers available to the behavior therapist is limited. These reinforcers tend to saturate rapidly and may or may not have potency on a given day. A major goal of behavior therapy is to establish fundamental language control of the child's behavior. Research has tended to show that relatively lengthy behavioral programming is necessary to effect permanent change in psychotic children (Werry & Wollershein, 1989). In any case, fundamental goals include establishing social reinforcers and basic language as well as functional adaptive behaviors.

## APPLICATIONS WITH ADOLESCENTS

Many anxiety-related disorders occur in adolescence. For behavior therapists, the term *anxiety* or *neurosis* refers to a dysfunctional behavior pattern that is under the control of a number of stimulus conditions, many of which are abstract. Some of these stimulus conditions may be totally unknown to the client. The task of the behavior therapist is to determine the environmental contingencies that are associated with the undesirable or dysfunctional behavior pattern. These stimuli may be both external (environmentally controlled) and internal (cognitively controlled). This fact has given rise to two kinds of behavior therapy: the traditional operant variety and cognitive behavior modification as proposed by Meichenbaum (1977).

### Anxiety and Phobic Disorders

Ross (1980) has suggested that anxiety may be viewed as a construct. It functions to maintain avoidance behavior in the absence of specific aversive stimuli. Thus, anxiety takes the place of previously associated aversive stimuli. Anxiety in the absence of these aversive stimuli produces physiological and psychological phenomena including heightened heart rate, blood pressure, and respiratory rate and a sense of distress. Mowrer (1947) has described anxiety as a classically conditioned autonomic arousal that is causally linked to instrumental avoidance behavior. Bandura

(1977) has provided a social learning context for anxiety-related disorders in which children and adolescents acquire, through modeling, characteristics associated with anxiety reactions and irrational behavior.

Many dysfunctional behavior patterns in adolescents are anxiety based. One of the major treatment interventions for these disorders is a procedure called systematic desensitization, which was developed by Wolpe (1958). Wolpe's principle of reciprocal inhibition states that anxiety-related stimuli could be neutralized if they were elicited contiguously with other stimuli antagonistic to anxiety reactions. Thus, if anxiety-evoking stimuli could be associated with relaxation-evoking stimuli, this would reduce the probability of a generalized anxiety response to a given stimulus. Wolpe's technique of progressive relaxation training is well known by many students of behavior therapy. This technique involves the training of the client to relax progressively various sets and subsets of muscles throughout the body and to experience simultaneously a feeling of psychological comfort and well-being. Since imaginary or cognitive stimuli are as effective in eliciting anxiety behavior as other environmental stimuli, Wolpe concluded that these cognitive stimuli could be replaced by other subjective feelings of well-being. A critical aspect of progressive relaxation is the creation of a hierarchy of responses. The client is asked to think of anxiety-producing stimuli ranging from mildly anxiety producing to very anxiety producing. This is done while the client is deeply relaxed over repeated sessions ranging across the anxiety hierarchy. Each level of the hierarchy is presented until the client can visualize the anxiety-producing experience without responding negatively. Wolpe's desensitization technique has been one of the most effective techniques for anxiety and phobic reduction in adolescents and adults.

Weiner (1973) investigated the deconditioning of neurotic anxiety in adolescents. Obsessive-compulsive neuroses in this group are quite common. In such disorders, elimination of the conditioned autonomic drives is critical in eliminating the neurotic behavior. Since compulsive disorders are focused on habits that control the neurosis, the task of the behavior therapist is to desensitize the person to these stimuli. Weiner described a 15-year-old boy with acute onset of obsessive-compulsive behaviors including washing, dressing, reading, and writing. The boy felt that if these behaviors were not executed something terrible would happen to him or his parents. The major treatment plan involved replacement of the obsessive, maladaptive rituals with a series of other, more delimited, rituals that would interfere only moderately with normal activity. In this regard, the adolescent was asked to think of numerous positive reasons for carrying out the obsessive behaviors. In addition, a time limit was devised for each obsessive behavior. Thus, an attempt was made to develop positive environmental stimuli for the obsessive responses. An alternative technique would have been to desensitize the boy to the stimulus conditions themselves. With obsessive-compulsive disorders, it is important to modify conditions so that the link between stimulus and response is broken.

Behavior therapy has also been utilized to treat depressive reactions in adolescents. Depressive reactions are a common response to anxiety. Symptoms of depressive reaction include loss of self-esteem, sleep disorders, lack of appetite, unresponsive social interaction, and substance abuse. Libert and Lewinsohn (1973) have demonstrated that clients with depressive reactions show considerably less social skill than their peers. Thus, depressive adolescents emit behaviors that are not positively socially reinforced. When these adolescents encounter traumatic experiences, they respond with depressive behavior. In addition, there is a tendency for prior depressive reactions to increase the future traumatic stimuli. Thus, depression tends to be a cyclical downward spiral in which the depressive behavior elicits nonsocial reinforcement on the part of adolescent peers.

The primary behavioral treatment for depressive behavior involves the reinforcement of socially appropriate behaviors and the heightening of the potency of satiated reinforcers (Beck, 1976; Lewinsohn, Munoz, Youngren, & Zeiss, 1986). Since the families of depressed adolescents tend to inadvertently reinforce passive and depressive behaviors, it is important to modify this pattern. Family and peer group members must be taught to elicit socially desirable behaviors and to reinforce them appropriately. In addition, the depressed adolescent must be taught to initiate social contact in a variety of situations and to receive reinforcement for this effort. Since many of the stimuli associated with depression are internal and self-generated, these cognitive mediators must also be modified. Cognitive theorists believe that distorted thinking is central to the development of depression in children and adolescents. Self-statement and self-management techniques are often used in cognitive restructuring to modify internal stimulus conditions that trigger depression and negative self-concept (Clarizio, 1985; Meichenbaum, 1977).

Many of these behavior therapy procedures can also be used with adolescents experiencing hysterical and psycho-physiological reactions. In most instances, a social learning framework is the most appropriate vehicle for understanding these disorders. Modification of the external social environment and reinforcement system is critical together with utilization of techniques such as desensitization, cognitive behavior modification (i.e., thought stopping, stimulus substitution) and, in some instance, aversion therapy.

## Treatment of Delinquent Behavior: Aggression and Social Maladjustment

The treatment of antisocial and delinquent behavior has become a major focus in U.S. society. Davidson and Seidman (1975) suggest that the treatment of juvenile delinquency through behavior modification is a relatively recent phenomenon. Behavioral interventions undertaken during the past two decades have shown promising results in modifying delinquent behaviors. However, since most of the research undertaken with delinquent populations has occurred under poorly controlled conditions, it is difficult to ascertain precisely the impact of behavioral intervention techniques. Davidson and Seidman conclude that more careful delineation of specific delinquent behaviors is needed.

Wright and James (1974) have delineated some of the behavioral content that characterizes delinquent children including (a) signs of early childhood behavior problems (e.g., excessive temper tantrums, enuresis, encopresis); (b) antisocial behaviors; (c) undisciplined or so-called delinquent behaviors such as school truancy, running away from home, and vandalizing property; and (d) eventual serious illegalities such as larceny, robbery, and assault. A number of environmental factors have been identified that promote delinquency. Families with delinquents typically have single parent guardianship. In addition, family members are often themselves involved in quasi-legal activities (e.g., prostitution, excessive drinking). This circumstance is coupled with economic insecurity and poor parental supervision. The delinquent is likely to have experienced a number of negative interactions with schools and school personnel. Teachers in school settings are likely to have used negative or aversive stimulation as a means of physical control when dealing with delinquents. In addition, delinquents are likely to have few friends and relatively limited social contacts. Thus, the instances for receiving social reinforcement for appropriate behavior are severely limited.

Sutherland and Cressey (1970) have formulated several hypotheses with regard to the learning patterns of delinquents. He indicates that criminal behavior is learned through operant techniques including direct social reinforcement and through social modeling. Delinquent behavior is often learned through the adolescent's peer group since this group provides the majority of social reinforcement. The specific group of delinquent behaviors that are learned is totally a function of the reinforcers available and the frequency of their occurrence. The atypical social norms acquired by most delinquents are a function of high rates of reinforcement for antisocial behavior in an environment of relative acceptance for these behaviors. Basically, the level of conditioning for a given delinquent behavior is directly contingent on the amount, frequency, and probability of reinforcement for that behavior. In this regard, Eysenck (1964) has suggested that certain personality traits lead to susceptibility in delinquents. These traits include a high degree of suggestibility, lack of emotional stability, and lack of perseverance.

Two behavioral etiologies are suggested for the acquisition of delinquent behavior. The first states that delinquents have an inferior ability for socialization. In effect, they are not able to acquire rapidly the conditioned fear responses present in most persons. In the second, social learning theory is used to explain the rapid acquisition of psychopathic behavior present in many delinquents. Bandura and Walters (1963) feel that delinquents have few prosocial models operating in their environments and that they receive greater reinforcement for antisocial behavior both in peer groups and through social learning. Since the dominant subculture stresses aggressive and antisocial behavior, the delinquent adolescent adopts this mode.

Several behavioral treatment approaches that have been utilized with delinquents seem to relate especially well to these populations. First, treatment should be directed toward reinforcement of achievement rather than toward obedience. The selection of positive reinforcers should be done carefully to minimize any satiation effects. When punishment is utilized, it should be on the basis of previously agreed on rules. It should be administered immediately and consistently when these rules are broken. After punishment, attention should be immediately refocused toward positive behavior with appropriate reinforcements. Generally, when dealing with delinquent populations, consistency is critical if unwanted behaviors are to be extinguished or counterconditioned.

Bandura (1973) has suggested that much of the aggressive behavior acquired by adolescents is modeled by their peer group. He hypothesizes that new types of aggressive responses can be acquired through observational learning. Further, Bandura feels that the level of aggression may also be influenced by other factors such as frustration and the cultural relativity of the particular aggressive act. If we consider what is known about aggression, several conditions would reduce the probability of its acquisition in adolescents. First, environmental conditions that promote social learning of aggressive behavior should be reduced or eliminated. Second, training should be undertaken to inform parents that permissive treatment, on their part, of aggressive behavior actually acts to reinforce this behavior. Third, reinforcement contingencies should be set up to maximize nonaggressive, cooperative play in children. And finally, parents themselves should be taught not to model aggressive behavior to their children.

A number of other theorists have developed behavioral techniques for dealing with aggressive behavior in children and adolescents (Frankel & Simmons, 1985; Kettlewell & Kausch, 1983; Saylor, Benson, & Einhaus, 1985). Treatment strategies employed include extinction, differential reinforcement of other behaviors, time-out, physical punishment, environmental manipulations, and arousal reduction. Stress inoculation has also been used including discussion of the components of anger, relaxation, modeling, and rehearsal of adaptive self-statements while in the presence of anger-provoking stimuli. Generally, the results of these studies indicate improved interpersonal problem-solving skills, decreases in fighting and aggressive behavior, and decreases in verbal aggression.

Behavioral contracting has been used extensively in working with delinquents. Contracting is simply a method for determining the exchange of positive reinforcement between two or more people. This is done by delineating the circumstances under which positive reinforcement will occur and, thereby, maximizing the probability that responses emitted by the delinquent will be socially acceptable. Phillips, Phillips, Wolf, and Fixsen (1975) describe a program that employs contracting in conjunction with a token system. The program, known as the *Achievement Place,* uses a three-pronged system: (a) Tasks are assigned, (b) performance is evaluated, and (c) consequences for performance are made explicit. Within the contracting framework, Phillips and his colleagues studied methods for assigning tasks including (a) individual versus group-assigned tasks, (b) consequences for individual performance versus consequences for group performance, and (c) a peer managership determined democratically by peers. Generally, their data show that as tasks and consequences are more individualized, they become more effective in producing the desired behavior. Group consequence conditions are not very effective when compared with individual consequence systems. No particular advantage was found to exist for democratically determined group leaders over those appointed on the basis of earned points. Generally though, adolescents in this project preferred an elected managerial system.

Wright and James (1974) have reviewed the array of behavioral programs available to delinquents. These include (a) residential programs in which point economies are used together with response cost systems, (b) part-time residential community-based programs in which point economies and contingency contracts are used in the programming effort, and (c) nonresidential community-based programs in which contingency contracts are used exclusively. Wright and James suggest that smaller, community-based programs provide the most efficacious solution for delinquent behavior because behavioral programming can be more closely controlled and related to more realistic settings available in a community. They present cost-benefit data indicating that community-based programs are considerably less expensive than their institutional counterparts. In another community-based study, Stuart (1973) asserts that behavioral contracting may be the major intervention technique that can be acquired by parents and paraprofessionals. Techniques that are effective in home settings must require comparatively small amounts of time and be able to influence a broad array of behaviors. Behavioral contracting meets these criteria. Since the family plays a crucial role in the development and maintenance of delinquent behavior, teaching parents effective behavior management strategies could have significant long-term gains. Stuart has listed four assumptions that underlie behavioral contracting in families:

1. The receipt of positive reinforcements and interpersonal exchanges is considered a privilege rather than a right.
2. Effective interpersonal agreements are governed by the norm of reciprocity.
3. The value of an interpersonal exchange is a direct function of the range, rate, and magnitude of positive reinforcements mediated by that exchange.
4. Rules create freedom in interpersonal exchanges.

All behavior contracts are governed by these rules, and as a result many points of family debate are removed since they are covered contractually.

## Eating Disorders

Obesity, bulimia nervosa, and anorexia nervosa are the major eating disorders associated with adolescent populations. Obesity appears to be familial in that multiple members of a given family are often overweight. A social learning model seems to be the best explanation for this behavior. Schacter (1971) suggests that obese people attend to external cues primarily for the triggering of eating behavior, whereas persons of normal weight attend primarily to internal cues. This suggests that the treatment of obesity should focus on the management of external behavioral factors while modifying internal factors such as self-talk. Treatment of obesity involves a considerable amount of client contracting and in some cases, family therapy. Successful weight control programs appear to include physical activity, contracting, maintenance strategies, and appropriate peer reinforcement for weight loss (Brownell, 1989). The treatment of obesity involves a considerable amount of client involvement in the development of goals and in measuring weight change. The primary target behaviors are those that act as discriminative stimuli for eating. The behavior therapist assists the obese client in identifying the range of these cues available in the environment. This range is then narrowed significantly by eliminating the discriminative stimuli. In addition, the array of response behaviors involved in eating itself is modified to reduce the amount of food consumed. For example, slower eating behavior is heavily reinforced together with delay of gratification in eating. Some behavior therapists have used aversive stimuli in modifying eating behavior. The most common aversive stimulus applied is social disapproval. In a study by Lansky and Vance (1983), obese high school students were treated in a behavior therapy program. In this program, behavior therapy resulted in significant weight reduction in the experimental group compared with the control group. Parental participation in the treatment was positively associated with increased weight loss.

Bulimia nervosa refers to an eating disorder in which there are recurrent episodes of binge eating of large amounts of food in relatively short periods of time (under two hours). These episodes are usually terminated by social interruption, sleep, or self-induced vomiting. Bulimics undergo repeated attempts to lose weight by severely restrictive diets, self-induced vomiting, or the use of cathartics. They have an awareness that the eating pattern is abnormal and suffer chronic anxiety regarding their inability to control it. Depressed mood and reduced self-concept are common correlates of this disorder. Cognitive behavior treatment has been shown to be effective in dealing with bulimia (Fairburn, 1984; Fairburn & Wilson, 1993). This treatment involves the following:

1. Control over eating patterns includes daily self-monitoring of all behaviors associated with bulimia.
2. Stimulus control techniques and behaviors incompatible with eating are used to counteract urges to binge.
3. Cognitive behavior therapy is employed to identify dysfunctional thoughts and beliefs and obsessive behaviors associated with bulimia.
4. A maintenance program is developed for self-monitoring of eating patterns.

Anorexia nervosa is a severe disorder characterized by restriction of food intake. Adolescents with this disorder have an intense fear of being obese. They also exhibit a distorted body image and refuse to maintain a weight near their ideal body weight. Social learning appears to be the determinant of this disorder (Crisp, 1984). Anorexics are often hospitalized because of severe malnutrition. Successful treatment of this disorder involves the use of reinforcement principles, social skills training, family therapy, and cognitive behavior therapy. The use of behavioral techniques has been shown to improve weight gain in anorexics (Agras, 1987). However, persons with anorexia are extremely resistant to treatment and often require many months or years of therapy to achieve permanent behavior change.

## GROUP PROCEDURES WITH CHILDREN AND ADOLESCENTS

By virtue of the group members coming together, sharing experiences and problems, and interacting, behavioral group therapy offers many of the same curative factors as other types of group therapy. Group approaches also provide social models, allow the individual a format in which to try out new behaviors, and present a less isolated and more realistic situation than does individual therapy. The group itself may represent a microcosm of society. Thus, working in a group may promote generalization more effectively than working on the same problems alone with a therapist. Several behavioral group therapies have been utilized with children and adolescents. Most techniques fall into one of four categories: (a) operant group therapy, (b) modeling and behavioral rehearsal, (c) social skills training, and (d) group procedures for reducing anxiety. In practice, it is likely that behavioral group therapy would employ more than one of these techniques.

Operant group therapy views the group as a microlaboratory of a social environment in which the appropriate behavior of individuals can be increased or the inappropriate behavior decreased through the application of operant techniques and principles (Walker, Hedberg, Clement, & Wright, 1981). The therapist selects certain behaviors that also usually represent problem behaviors in the child's natural environment. The group serves as an environment over which there is more control and in which the behaviors can be modified and eventually generalized to other settings. The therapist may employ the operant techniques of positive reinforcement, punishment, tokens, time-out from reinforcement, response cost, shaping, and chaining within the group to develop or increase adaptive behaviors or decrease maladaptive behaviors (Rose, 1972). For example, a withdrawn child may show little initiative in interacting with peers in the classroom. The larger classroom may also prevent the teacher from developing a systematic program to deal with the problem. In the small group situation, the therapist could use shaping techniques—first reinforcing any movement the child makes toward the group, then any attempt on the part of the child to interact with group members, gradually working toward normal peer interactions in the group. This would be paired and followed up with a classroom program to promote the transfer of these newly developed prosocial skills. Similarly, operant group procedures could be used to decrease aggressiveness in a group with the goal of reducing aggression in other settings.

Operant group techniques may also be used as an adjunct to other types of group procedures. Children, and adolescents to a lesser degree, may enter a group without the prerequisite skills necessary to benefit from group discussion. For example, a psychologist might want to run an affectively oriented group for 10-year-old children with learning disabilities. On beginning the group, the psychologist finds that the children have difficulty staying in their seats, tend to interrupt each other, and generally engage in horseplay. Through the application of operant techniques, the psychologist can increase behaviors that promote group functioning and decrease those that hinder desirable group interaction. The operant techniques may allow more rapid movement toward effective group interaction, even though the focus of the group is nonbehavioral.

Modeling and behavioral rehearsal are based on social learning theory and the laboratory research on modeling and imitation. Since the group already contains individuals who serve as models and potential models, the systematic use of modeling is especially well suited to the group context. Observational learning assumes that individuals can learn simply by observing behavior and its consequences. The therapist serves as a model for group members and the members serve as models to one another. The therapist, cognizant of the different variables that help determine whether someone is an effective model (e.g., see Bandura, 1969), systematically sets up situations for models to engage in desirable behaviors. Similarly, the therapist may selectively reinforce by praise certain desirable behaviors that other group members might develop via vicarious reinforcement. For example, in a group for adolescents, one individual may be admired or respected by most group members. This adolescent may be an effective model for other group members. The group may, for a session, be focusing on interviewing skills. The therapist may select the admired group member to be the focus of a role play for a hypothetical job interview. During the role play, the therapist could systematically reinforce selected behaviors appropriate for the situation. The other group members would learn from observing their peer and also be vicariously reinforced by the therapist's reinforcement of the model. The therapist may also model desired behaviors and may invite guest models to visit the group periodically.

Behavioral rehearsal is usually used in conjunction with modeling. Behavioral rehearsal requires group members to initiate (actually engage in) behaviors and receive feedback from the therapist and other group members. It is different from simple role playing in that someone else models the desired behaviors to show the client how the role should be played (Rose, 1972). It also allows the practicing of these behaviors, often relatively complex sequences, in a more protected and less anxiety-arousing situation. Behavioral rehearsal employs modeling and imitation, as well as direct reinforcement through feedback.

A typical modeling and behavioral rehearsal sequence might focus on asking a teacher for help and clarification on an assignment. Initially, the therapist or therapists (behavioral groups of this nature often utilize coleaders) and the group member set up the situation by describing the scene. The initial role play might involve one therapist playing the teacher and the other therapist playing the student. The therapist playing the student displays the desirable behaviors for that situation. A discussion follows in which group members comment on the situation and the behavior, with the therapists highlighting certain desirable aspects (e.g., eye contact, requesting rather than demanding) of the sequence. Next, a group member volunteers or is selected to engage in a similar role play, also followed by feedback and discussion period. Depending on time, each group member might engage in the role play in front of the entire group, or the group might break into dyads for further practice. The group would conclude with a summary discussion of the important aspects of the situation and the appropriate behaviors.

Social skills training can occur either in a classroom teaching situation or in a group context. In the classroom, the teacher is more likely to utilize operant techniques to selectively reinforce desirable social behaviors, while group procedures will tend to use modeling and behavioral rehearsal techniques. In fact, the preceding modeling and behavioral rehearsal sequence might be fairly typical of a social skills training group activity. The primary difference is that social skills programs often have a more structured, task-analyzed, sequential organization similar to a curriculum, whereas modeling and behavioral rehearsal groups might utilize group- or therapist-generated problem situations to a greater degree. Elksnin and Elksnin (1995) have developed a comprehensive framework for the assessment and teaching of social skills. Their curriculum contains specific interventions for children and adolescents including modifications in the curriculum depending on the moral/ethical development exhibited by the children.

Goldstein and McGinnis (1997), in their most recent social skills series, describe a structured group approach for teaching prosocial skills to children and adolescents. It provides the leader with instructions for beginning and continuing group sessions, a checklist for determining areas for needed skill work, and a skill checklist summary to record progress. Skills are broken into categories including beginning social skills (e.g., listening, asking a question), advanced social skills (e.g., asking for help, joining in), skills for dealing with feelings (e.g., knowing your feelings, expressing your feelings), skill alternatives to aggression (e.g., asking permission, sharing something), skills for dealing with stress (e.g., making a complaint, answering a complaint), and planning skills (setting a goal, making a decision). Each skill is outlined in behavioral steps. This type of format breaks down the specific skills into component parts and allows the teaching of the specific skill. A number of similar programs are available for adolescents as well as younger children.

A comprehensive review of the literature on cognitive behavior training for social skills in adolescents can be found in an article by Gresham (1990). Kazdin, Esveldt-Dawson, and Matson (1983) have also reviewed the effect of various instructional systems on the development of social skills.

## CLASSROOM AND EDUCATIONAL APPLICATIONS

Behavioral principles have been extensively applied in the schools since the 1960s. Lindsley (1968) has suggested that the teacher can be considered a behavioral engineer in the classroom provided he or she has the proper tools. If one adopts the behavioral viewpoint that human activities are controlled by their environmental consequences, then many aspects of the classroom can be arranged and rearranged to produce specific desired behaviors. In this model, the teacher becomes the major instrument for making use of the basic principles of behavior control to alter children's behavior. Fundamental reinforcement contingencies are examined and modified if necessary.

One of the more comprehensive methods for utilizing behavioral principles in the classroom was developed by Ogden Lindsley (1972). His method is known as *precision teaching,* and it utilizes operant techniques in the classroom. Precision teaching provides exact means for measuring performance on a continuous basis by clearly delineating the desirable behaviors required of students and measuring these behaviors over time with the aid of behavioral charts. Precision teaching stresses accountability on the part of teachers as well as students. The rate of production or efficiency is a critical variable to be measured in precision teaching. In dealing with exceptional children, precision teaching seeks to define operationally wanted and unwanted behaviors. Children are given considerable involvement and responsibility in the learning process. All assessment of child disorders is done through adaptive behavior measures in order to make intervention possible.

Proficiency is a key concept in precision teaching. Proficiency is the frequency per unit of time at which competency is achieved for a particular skill. The expectation is that proficiency increases over time and is, therefore, a measure of cost-effectiveness. If in a given programming effort proficiency begins to decline, then modifications must be made in the program to make it efficacious. For behavior to be measurable, it must contain movement cycles. Therefore, it must be observable and it must be repeatable and measurable in the scientific sense. For Lindsley, much of the current educational jargon (e.g., thinking, synthesizing, integrating, conceiving) does not lend itself to measurement. He suggests that output terminology (e.g., writing, saying, marking, doing, pointing) must be measurable for education to have accountability. Lindsley indicates that children go through four stages of learning. The first stage, *acquisition,* focuses on learning the information and skills necessary to perform a task. Performance at this level is characterized by a relatively high error rate and a relatively low rate of acquisition. In the second stage, *fluency building,* the child has acquired the basic skill but needs a variety of settings in which to practice that skill. At this stage, the performance level increases as the child generalizes the skill to various situations. In the third stage, *maintenance,* intermittent reinforcement is provided to maintain the skill over a long period of time. In the final stage, *application,* the emphasis is on practical application of the skill to everyday life experiences.

Since precision teaching provides predictable contracted rewards for performance, it tends to increase motivation in formerly unmotivated children. The emphasis on intrastudent performance further helps to increase the efficiency of individual students while maintaining relatively low anxiety levels. The system provides an overall evaluation of the educational process within a given classroom based on data and, therefore, aids in providing documentation regarding needs. The reciprocal reinforcement system inherent in precision teaching is a fundamental reason for its success. In this system, both teachers and students provide reinforcement for one another based on mutually agreed on behavioral contracts.

Another classroom application developed by Shure (1992) is a problem-solving curriculum *(I Can Problem Solve)* for young children, ages 4 to 11. Children are taught the basic concepts that allow them to choose alternative and more socially appropriate responses to conflicts. Through a completely scripted set of materials, teachers or group leaders can present specific lessons on concepts such as *same* and *different.* These concepts are then reintroduced within the instructional curriculum and reinforced through daily practice in real-life social settings. This curriculum very cleverly uses operant techniques, social learning theory, and cognitive learning theory to achieve concept development and generalization of skills.

Other operant principles have been employed for classroom management purposes. Morris (1980) has described the use of the Premack principle in classroom settings. This principle simply states that high-probability behaviors can be used to reinforce low-probability behaviors if the high-probability event is made contingent on the performance of the low-probability event. For example, recess (a high-probability event) can be used to reinforce completing an arithmetic assignment (a low-probability event). Morris has described a four-step process for implementing the Premack principle in the classroom:

1. Designing an observation session for measuring the frequency level of various behaviors.
2. Determining the amount of time the child will be allowed to engage in the high-frequency behavior.
3. Setting up a contingency program in which the child's access to the high-frequency behavior is clearly contingent on performance of the low-frequency behavior.
4. Evaluating whether the procedure is successful and modifying it if necessary using some other high-frequency behavior.

Andrews (1971) describes the use of the Premack principle with verbally aggressive and acting-out adolescents. In Andrew's research, these aggressive behaviors were occurring at the rate of 15 to 20 per hour. Andrews observed that when students were given free time, they spent much of that time working with tutors or watching television. During these free-time periods, the incidence of aggressive and unwanted behavior was half that previously reported. In order to implement the Premack principle, the students were asked to delineate 12 behaviors that were considered unacceptable. These behaviors included aggressive and destructive behaviors previously mentioned. A contract was drawn up in which the high probability behavior of meeting with tutors and watching television was made contingent on a decrease in the rate of aggressive behaviors from 15 to 20 per hour to no more than 3 per hour. Andrews' results showed significant success in extinguishing the unwanted behavior patterns.

A review of the literature indicates that differential reinforcement of other behavior (DRO) has been shown to be effective in decreasing a number of inappropriate behaviors (Bear, 1980). These behaviors include aggression, perseverative behaviors, self-injurious behavior, and a plethora of more minor disorders. Bear suggests that DRO is most effective in controlling serious disturbance when used in combination with other behavioral techniques. These techniques include punishment, response-cost, time-out, and overcorrection.

Meyers (1980) has described the use of time-out procedures in the classroom. Time-out is especially useful for disruptive and aggressive students. The procedure involves withdrawal of the student from reinforcing stimuli contingent on some response such as relaxation or calmness. The procedure can be put on a gradient ranging from total withdrawal of the student from the environment to simple removal of adult attention. Meyers details a number of considerations in the use of time-out. The child must be given a verbal explanation of why the time-out is necessary. A warning should be provided indicating that a time-out is imminent. The time-out should be administered in a nonemotional manner and in a location that has zero reinforcement valence. The success of time-out depends on the regular classroom setting being a reinforcing environment. If this is not the case, time-out will not have the desired effect. Furthermore, the skill with which the instructional staff performs the time-out procedure is critical. Thus, a relatively high degree of behavioral training is necessary to perform this procedure correctly, particularly with emotionally disturbed students.

Modeling has been shown to be effective in modifying disruptive and aggressive behaviors in children and adolescents (Bandura, 1969). For example, children in counseling groups can be asked to discuss and to fantasize about their aggressive behavior. Nonaggressive ways of behaving can then be modeled either by the behavior therapist or by peer models. This technique has been shown to be highly effective in modifying behavior patterns. Fears and phobias have been the focus of some modeling efforts (Graziano, DeGiovanni, & Garcia, 1979). Children are asked to observe a model who is successfully interacting with feared stimuli. In some cases, multiple models are used with varying degrees of the feared stimuli. Results have tended to indicate improvement through this modeling procedure.

Undoubtedly, operant techniques will continue to be used in the schools at an ever-increasing rate. The success with which they will be used will depend on the willingness of educators and psychologists to operationalize behaviors and measure the impact of a given program. Sulzer-Azaroff and Mayer (1986) provide an excellent review of operant techniques applied to educational settings.

## PARENTING SKILLS

The assumption of behavior therapists in training parents to implement behavioral programs is that children's maladaptive behaviors can best be controlled in the context of family and home. Maladaptive behaviors that develop in the home, but are treated in the clinic setting, may not change in the home environment. Berkowitz and Graziano (1972) point out that behavior therapists assume that it is important to teach their knowledge and techniques to others, including paraprofessionals. This is considerably discrepant from the attitudes of other more traditional therapists in which the basic technology is a closely held professional secret. Berkowitz and Graziano suggest that, since parents maintain a high degree of contact with their children and have the principal moral and ethical responsibility for their children's behavior, they are also responsible for the child's affective well-being. Thus the traditional dyadic model in which a professional provides direct services to the child has been replaced by a three-dimensional model where the behavior therapist acts as a mediator among family members. The general task of the therapist is to reduce or weaken dysfunctional behaviors and to set up reinforcement mechanisms for appropriate social behaviors.

Several models of behavioral parent training have been identified. The dyadic model (Patterson & Reed, 1970) examines faulty relationships between the child and primary persons in the home. This model postulates that problems in the home result from ineffective interactions between the child and parents. The parents may be providing little or no positive reinforcement for behavior while the child is providing predominantly negative stimulation to the parents. A reciprocal process occurs in which aversive stimulation provided by the child results in aversive stimulus patterns from the parents. This aversive pattern spirals downward until a family crisis occurs. In the dyadic model, treatment is focused on aiding parents in assessment of their behavioral interactions with their children. A number of traditional assessment techniques are used including behavioral observation and checklists. After these data are collected, formal parent training begins. Parents are taught the fundamental principles underlying social learning theory and behavior management. A second model of parent training involves an eclectic approach in which dysfunctional interactions are viewed in terms of the child's entire ecological environment. While parents are part of this ecology, other groups such as peers and teachers are also involved. In this model, dysfunctional relationships are examined in terms of behavioral interactions among all relevant groups. Factors that may interfere with parent training are examined. For example, in a given family the marriage relationship may be deteriorating. It will be necessary to deal with this factor to deal more effectively with the parent-child interaction pattern. A third model, the social systems model, postulates that a child's misbehavior is representative of conflict elsewhere in the family and that this conflict is often in the marriage relationship. The social system model is similar to the eclectic model except that it postulates faulty interactions between the parents as the main cause for childhood disturbance. Both the eclectic and social system models require that comprehensive ecological assessments be performed that detail the interactional nature of behaviors among family members. It is from this data that therapeutic behavioral techniques are designed.

Keefe, Kopel, and Gordon (1978) have designed a five-level model of behavioral assessment for use with families:

1. Problem identification and delineation.
2. Measurement of behavior together with a functional analysis.
3. Matching of client treatment to the functional analysis.
4. Assessment of progress during ongoing therapy.
5. Long-term assessment of therapy.

Keefe et al. believe that this model should be applied in all behavior therapy situations to maximize the probability of success. Behavior therapists typically neglect to perform adequate functional analysis of family behavior patterns prior to parent training. This omission results in questionable treatment decisions based on the identification of lower priority issues. For example, it must be determined whether the dysfunctional behavior in a given child is the result of faulty interactions between the parent and the child or faulty interactions between the parents themselves.

Berkowitz and Graziano (1972) have divided structured parent training techniques into respondent-based and operant-based categories. The majority of techniques have focused on operant procedures. Most respondent techniques involve the conditioning of enuretic and encopretic children. Parents use devices such as those described earlier in this chapter for control of enuresis. Using operant conditioning, parents have been trained to provide simple extinction of behavior, modeling, and the use of simple shaping procedures. Other programs have trained parents to modify autistic and schizophrenic behavior, aggressive and hyperactive behavior, and socially unacceptable behaviors. Berkowitz and Graziano conclude that research is needed to develop predictive measures of parental success and more specific measures of parental and child behavior change as a result of intervention. Engeln, Knutson, Laughy, and Garlington (1968) describe the use of systematic family programming in behavior therapy. In their case, a 6-year-old boy with extremely aggressive behavior toward other children was treated in a family context. The boy's behavior was so extreme that it left the family isolated from the community and the boy from his peer group. A behavioral program consisting of several contracts was devised with the following five steps:

1. Systematic reinforcing of eye contact and commanding compliance.
2. Training of the boy's mother in relevant behavioral principles through modeling of the therapist's behavior and through discussion.
3. Training of the mother in reinforcement and extinction techniques regarding her son's behavior.
4. Developing a home-based program of systematic reinforcement for both the boy and his siblings.
5. Using the Premack principle as a reinforcement technique.

The program resulted in a significant decrease in the boy's unwanted aggressive behavior.

In relation to structured parent training, Gordon, Learner, and Keefe (1979) have summarized the research and drawn a number of conclusions. They feel that in providing formal parent training, written materials and supervision should be the first service provided to parents. Those parents who need additional training should be provided with on-site performance instruction. The preferred training techniques include modeling, prompting, shaping, and behavioral rehearsal. Modeling has been found to be especially effective when compared with other, more extensive, behavioral interventions such as behavioral rehearsal and feedback. Gordon et al. conclude that the paucity of behavioral parent training materials requires that behavior therapists use their own clinical judgment in deciding what might or might not work with a given client family. An outline of a basic behavioral parent-training program should include at least the following:

1. Measuring and operationally defining behaviors, including instrumentation for observations.
2. Establishing behavioral baselines and making meaningful recordings of behavior (e.g., with graphs, charts).
3. Using various kinds of reinforcement to increase behavioral probability.
4. Identifying antecedents and consequences in the use of various reinforcement patterns.

5. Using the Premack principle: reinforcing low-rate behaviors with high-rate behaviors.

6. Using techniques for reducing unwanted behaviors: DRO, extinction, negative reinforcement.

7. Understanding the uses and misuses of punishment.

8. Understanding how body language affects behavior.

9. Recognizing the importance of parents being appropriate social models for their children.

10. Learning how to maintain behaviors once they are established.

Abidin (1996) has developed a parenting skills program for use by mental health professionals. This program includes a series of sessions designed to help parents understand the development of a child's self-concept, learn to manage behaviors, and learn to understand and recognize various emotions. This program can best be described as a combination of operant and cognitive behavior therapy techniques. Since the program was designed for mental health professionals, it requires a high degree of sophistication to use it effectively.

## FAMILY THERAPY

Behavior therapy does not provide a framework for conducting family therapy in the traditional sense (see Chapter 10 for further information on family therapy). That is, the behavioral family therapist is not likely to bring an entire family together and work on issues in joint sessions. The behavior therapist is more likely to focus on interactional or reinforcement patterns that exist in the family unit and occur in the natural setting. Although there is recognition of complex interdependencies in families, the behavior therapist is more prone to treat those specific dysfunctional patterns that appear to be creating most of the difficulties and does not necessarily treat the whole family. In fact, behavioral family therapy can best be described as a combination of behavioral approaches to parenting (previously described) and behavioral marital therapy.

Marital relationships may be viewed as interactive dyadic relationships in which there is sufficient potential for mutual reinforcement between marital partners. Marital relationships are satisfactory as long as each partner receives adequate amounts of reinforcement. However, when such reinforcement does not occur, negative interaction patterns may result. While these negative patterns may not directly involve the children in a family, marital problems can indirectly affect child behavior.

Hope (1976) has described a multifaceted approach for the treatment of marital problems. The first step in the process involves teaching couples to pinpoint behaviors that they wish to change in each other in order to determine precisely what behaviors are at issue. This teaching may include discrimination training to help an individual distinguish between behaviors that are actually positive and those that are really negative. A second facet of behavioral marital therapy is communication skills training. This step includes training in how to listen, how to share in a two-way dialogue, and how to reduce negative, aversive, and sidetracking verbal behaviors. How to reinforce one another or provide "positives" is an important part of the communication training. Couples are asked to practice these skills outside the therapy situation. In the next stage of therapy, couples are taught how to problem-solve and negotiate. Problem-solving is viewed as progressive and future-oriented. Changes in each other's behavior are considered negotiable, and compromises are a necessary component of problem solving. In the final stage, couples utilizing their new skills in communication, reinforcement, and problem-solving, are taught how to develop contingency contracts.

Social learning theory approaches (e.g., the work of Gerald Patterson at the University of Oregon) are probably the best examples of behavioral family applications (Hansen & L'Abate, 1982). Patterson has done numerous empirical studies in family interventions, focusing mostly on changes in child behavior. The family is seen as the center of learning for social behaviors, with the family consisting of a series of mutually interdependent dyads. In the dyad, both individuals (e.g., parent and child) influence the behavior of the other. The interactions in the dyad help determine which behaviors will be developed and which will persist. The social learning approach to family intervention places heavy emphasis on teaching parents behavioral (i.e., operant) principles, making the approach virtually indistinguishable from behavioral parenting approaches. Hansen and L'Abate (1982) criticize this approach because of this relatively narrow focus. They note that the approach fails to consider the family as a system, focusing almost solely on parenting styles. The approach does not recognize ineffective parenting styles as possibly resulting from a broader family system problem or family pathology. The approach also does not view the family as the client since the child's behavior is at odds with many of the traditionally accepted premises of family therapy.

## EFFICACY

Behavior therapy, with its ties to empirical and scientific psychology, is able to offer vast amounts of data to support its efficacy. The behaviorally oriented journals tend to present relatively well-designed studies that provide evidence of observable, measurable behavior change. Further, behavior therapy provides well-specified descriptions of the various therapeutic procedures and has demonstrated effectiveness with a wide variety of disorders. In fact, the efficacy literature of behavior therapy, compared with that of other types of therapy, is superior in terms of rigor and demonstrated uses.

Despite this superiority, one must read this literature with a somewhat critical view. Agras, Kazdin, and Wilson (1979) have commented on the status of research in behavior therapy and note numerous areas of concern. Behavior therapy suffers from the lack of good long-term follow-up studies, much as do other approaches. Further, some of the research has studied rather trivial concerns of questionable social significance, while other research studies, in an attempt to be scientific, have narrowly defined target behaviors without consideration of how the behavior change might relate to an individual's total functioning. In a similar vein, some behavioral research has not considered the generalization of behavior change to other settings. Allen, Tarnowski, Simonian, and Elliott (1991) provide an excellent review of generalization. This review suggests that generalization of behavior resulting from behavior therapy has been demonstrated in approximately 40% of the studies conducted. In general, while the literature of behavior therapy is impressive and significant progress has been made, the research is still in a developing state.

Ross (1978) and Kazdin (1980) have reviewed areas in which behavioral approaches have been shown to be effective interventions. Kazdin notes that behavioral techniques have been successfully applied with fear and avoidance reactions, social behavioral problems such as withdrawal and aggression, habit disorders, academic problems, conduct problems, delinquency, autism, childhood schizophrenia, mental retardation, and learning disabilities. Further, within each of those areas, various disorders have been treated with a variety of techniques. Ross also notes a similar set of applications but offers several cautions in viewing the research. The lack of follow-up data is also a problem with child behavior therapy research because children are followed only for a brief period after treatment. A related problem is that most research is focused on treatment of a single disorder or problem. In reality, many children present complex, multiple problems. The research generally has not dealt with the more complex problems; thus little is known about the effectiveness of behavior therapy with children with multiple problems. Still, despite limitations in the research, child behavior therapy presents one of the most comprehensive research bases on the psychological treatment of the child.

In the area of cognitive behavior therapy, Meador and Ollendick (1984) have reviewed the literature on efficacy. Generally, they have found that interventions with hyperactive/impulsive children have met with a degree of success. Cognitive therapies have also been shown to be effective in modifying academic and classroom-relevant behaviors with nonclinical children. Evidence pertaining to the effectiveness of cognitive behavior therapy in clinical samples is less common (e.g., institutionalized, anxiety disorders, or schizophrenics). McAdam (1986) presents a review on the research applying cognitive behavior therapy to adolescents. McAdam argues that cognitive behavior therapy has been more successful with this group than with younger children both in clinical and nonclinical populations.

Because it would be impossible even to begin to review all the research literature in child behavior therapy in this context, a review of behavioral treatments for school phobia will be presented as an example of the efficacy literature. School phobia has been treated with many techniques. It appears to have multiple behavioral explanations from a theoretical standpoint, and behavior therapy has been relatively successfully in treating it.

A number of desensitization and counterconditioning techniques have been successfully employed to treat school phobia. These techniques include systematic desensitization, implosive therapy, in vivo desensitization, emotive imagery, and anxiety-reducing stories. Lazarus (1960) described the application of systematic desensitization with a 9-year-old school-phobic girl. A seven-item hierarchy, based on the theme of separation from the mother, was administered to the girl in five treatment sessions over a 10-day period. At the conclusion of these sessions, the girl voluntarily returned to school. Miller (1972) reported a case study of a 10-year-old school-phobic boy who also displayed separation anxiety and fear of death. Relaxation training was followed by systematic desensitization, with reinforcement provided for participating in treatment. Because the boy reported the fear of death at bedtime, the therapist administered relaxation procedures over the telephone just before the child went to bed. Systematic desensitization was followed by in vivo desensitization. A final part of the training was anxiety management training (i.e., teaching the boy to relax when he experienced anxiety). This combined treatment took 6 weeks and resulted in the boy's return to school and elimination of the boy's fear of death.

Lazarus, Davison, and Polefka (1965) employed in vivo desensitization to treat a 9-year-old school-phobic boy. Because of the boy's inarticulate and acquiescent response style, an initial attempt at systematic desensitization was abandoned. The in vivo treatment involved 16 steps progressing from walking to school with the therapist on a Sunday afternoon to independent reentry into the classroom. Token reinforcement was also utilized to maintain attendance in this successful intervention. Garvey and Hegrenes (1966) also report a case study using in vivo desensitization. They began by having the subject simply ride to school and place his foot on the curb, with a gradual buildup to full resumption of class attendance. Van der Ploeg (1975) interspersed stories of a pleasant sailing experience with discussions of typical school scenes as part of treatment for a 14-year-old school-phobic boy. Successful applications of implosive therapy (Smith & Sharpe, 1970) and emotive imagery (Lazarus & Abramowitz, 1962) have also been reported. Implosive therapy, based on a respondent extinction model, involves high-intensity presentations of the anxiety-provoking stimuli. Emotive imagery involves the visualization of anxiety-producing scenes, with imagined successful outcomes.

Reinforcement-based programs have also been used successfully. Hersen (1970), noting that staying away from school may actually be reinforced at home, has used differential reinforcement of successive approximations of returning to school with positive reinforcement for school attendance. Tahmisian and McReynolds (1971) were unsuccessful in treating a school-phobic 13-year-old girl with systematic desensitization. They then developed a shaping program in which school-approach behaviors were reinforced with privileges, resulting in a return to full-time school attendance.

Kennedy (1965), using an approach described as consistent with Wolpe's approach, involved paid referral, parent involvement, removal of secondary gains in the home, and the abrupt desensitization approach of forced attendance. Kennedy reported successful treatment of 50 cases of what he called Type I school phobia, a nonchronic, neurotic maladjustment, usually seen in younger children and discussed in the school phobia section above. Stedman (1976) reported a case study that involved behavioral family counseling, systematic desensitization, and operant contingency contracting program to treat a 9-year-old school-phobic girl.

Although most of the reported efficacy literature is in the form of case studies, it suggests that school phobia responds positively to behavioral interventions. Both operant and respondent techniques have been successfully applied, often in combination. Prout and Harvey (1978), in a review of the application of desensitization procedures for school-related problems, found that approximately 80% of the studies reported the use of a combination of techniques. The research literature supports a multimodal behavioral assessment and intervention.

## CONCLUSION

Behavior therapy has been utilized with many populations in institutional and noninstitutional settings. It is applicable equally with children, adolescents, and adults and is perhaps the most widely used therapy with children. Prior to the development of behavior therapy, anxiety disorders and phobic reactions were difficult and sometimes impossible to treat. The pioneering work of behaviorists such as Wolpe established the ability of psychologists to condition autonomic behaviors. From the standpoint of dealing with some of the more complex anxiety-related disorders, this feature of behavior therapy has had robust success.

In school settings, school phobia and other behavior disorders have proved to be highly susceptible to behavior therapy. The treatment of enuresis in young children has been virtually revolutionized by the work of Foxx and Azrin. In addition, almost every classroom teacher in the United States has been exposed to and has attempted to use behavior-learning principles. Techniques such as precision teaching have been utilized in the classroom to maximize learning and affective harmony.

With the development of cognitive behavior therapy, new applications with adolescents have been made possible. Prior to cognitive behavior therapy, the application of operant principles with cognitively sophisticated adolescents and adults was questionable. It was felt that these principles did not attune themselves to developmental changes in cognition in adolescence and adulthood. Cognitive behavior modification addresses itself directly to internal thought patterns and their modification. Thus, the first step in linking operant theory to cognitive development has been made. The utilization of social learning theory principles with children and adolescents has also aided movement in this direction.

The efficacy research in behavior therapy is substantial and diverse. It tends to indicate that behavior therapy is successful in varied settings, especially those where the behaviors to be changed are well operationalized. Future research in behavior therapy will need to focus on the behavioral assessment of ecologically complex environments and the measurement of behaviors derived from these assessments. In addition, further work will be needed to relate learning in adolescence and adulthood to the methodology currently available in behavior therapy. Achieving this goal will undoubtedly mean the development of new methodology that will improve efficiency of treatment, particularly with more complex psychotic disorders.

## CASE STUDY

Jimmy, age 13, was referred for behavioral treatment following a comprehensive behavioral, medical, psychological, and educational evaluation at a children's diagnostic center. Jimmy consistently tested in the upper ranges of the mildly mentally retarded, or educable mentally retarded range (e.g., high 60s), and had been involved in special education programs through his entire educational career. At the time of referral, he was in a junior high school educable mentally retarded class. Although Jimmy was a relatively strong student academically, attempts at mainstreaming and other integration into regular school activities were unsuccessful because of behavior difficulties.

The presenting problems included extreme impulsiveness, socially inappropriate behaviors, and noncompliance. The school and home reports were relatively consistent with regard to these problems, although the noncompliance appeared to be more of a problem at home. These problems were long-standing, with the parents initiating the first of a series of mental health referrals when Jimmy was age 6 years. Trials of psychotropic medications (according to reports, eight different drugs had been attempted), loosely structured parent counseling, and individual play therapy had not yielded significant positive changes.

The initial evaluation indicated that there was a significant anxiety component contributing to the behavior difficulties. While it was felt that some of the impulsiveness was developmental or constitutional in nature, a generalized anxiety response seemed to exacerbate this condition and contributed to the inappropriate social responses and noncompliance. Further, the initial evaluation indicated that both parents, particularly the mother, were experiencing considerable stress and frustration related to management difficulties in the home.

### Behavioral Assessment

Prior to the beginning of treatment, behavioral data was collected over a 2-week period to further specify goals and concerns. Based on initial behavioral interview data from both parents and teachers, an individualized behavior rating form was constructed. This form asked the parents and teachers to rate on a daily basis the severity of several problem behaviors. Using the A-B-C format (i.e., Antecedent-Behavior-Consequence), parents and teachers were also asked to provide daily anecdotal reports on desirable and undesirable behaviors they observed in the two settings. Jimmy was observed twice at school by the therapist and was interviewed in an attempt to determine the generality or specificity of the anxiety.

These assessments resulted in a number of conclusions. No specific source of anxiety could be identified, and it appeared that the anxiety was relatively generalized across social situations in both settings. The social inappropriateness and impulsiveness were problems in both settings but seemed to increase in group situations or in situations where large numbers of people were present. For example, Jimmy's behavior became more problematic in the school cafeteria and also at large family gatherings in the home. The assessment also confirmed that noncompliance was essentially a problem at home and not at school.

## Treatment Program

A multimodal behavioral treatment program evolved over a period of several months. The program, which included periodic assessment of the problem behavior, had five components:

1. Relaxation training.
2. Individual behavioral counseling with Jimmy.
3. Behavioral parent counseling.
4. Behavioral programming in the home.
5. Referral to a community agency that was conducting social skills groups for mildly retarded adolescents.

The initial phase of treatment focused on the relaxation training. The goal of the relaxation training was to reduce the level of general anxiety based on the hypothesis that this would reduce impulsiveness and other apparently anxiety-related behaviors. Although relaxation programs for children are available, the relaxation script that was used in this case was a slightly modified version of a muscle relaxation script used with normal adults. The instructions were essentially the same except for modification of the vocabulary to make it appropriate for Jimmy's cognitive level. Jimmy was initially trained in a clinic setting with his parents observing through a two-way mirror. The parents were then instructed in the procedures and began to administer them to Jimmy at home on a daily or twice-daily basis. The therapist eventually tape-recorded the instructions and Jimmy was able to listen to the tape at home. The final part of the training involved instructing Jimmy on how to apply the relaxation techniques in stressful situations. Using key words from the script (e.g., "calm down") or slightly tensing certain muscle groups were the methods taught to cope with stress. From Jimmy's verbal report, he was able to use these techniques at various times.

The individual behavioral counseling sessions with Jimmy focused on discussions of situations in which he encountered difficulty. Jimmy was shown ways in which his responses might be maintaining poor relationships with others. Sessions also centered on alternative ways of responding and provided behavioral rehearsal of the alternative response. For example, Jimmy complained about a boy at school who always called him "pumpkin face." Jimmy's typical response was to get upset, make verbal threats, and usually go running off screaming, apparently much to the amusement of the other students. Initially, Jimmy was shown how the goal of the other boy's teasing might be to get Jimmy upset. A simplified explanation of reinforcement was provided, showing Jimmy how his getting upset might contribute to maintaining the other boy's teasing. Interestingly, the example that was most useful in conveying this concept was showing Jimmy how some of his own behaviors had a goal of getting his parents upset. It was decided in this situation to utilize an extinction procedure by teaching Jimmy to ignore the teasing. In the behavioral rehearsal, the therapist played a rather persistent teaser with Jimmy following instructions on how to ignore and how not to react to the teasing. Jimmy's "new" response was to not respond verbally to the teasing, to maintain a calm disposition and, if the teasing persisted, to walk quietly away from the situation. Anecdotal reports from the teachers indicated that Jimmy was able to employ the new behaviors in situations where he had been teased in the past, and, more importantly, the teasing from the other boy ceased to be a problem.

The parent counseling and behavioral programming in the home were simultaneous activities. The parents were asked to read Patterson's (1976) *Living with Children* at the beginning of treatment. (This book is one of several books written for parents that explain basic behavioral concepts and how they can be applied with children.) This book provided the parents with some insight into how their responses to Jimmy's behaviors might be contributing to the maintenance of his problem behaviors. In particular, Jimmy's mother realized that her "yelling" was not promoting behavior change and was probably contributing to the maintenance of certain problem behaviors. After a brief baseline, in which Jimmy's mother was allowed to yell normally, Jimmy's mother was instructed not to yell at him for a period of 2 weeks. She was instructed to provide corrective feedback in a calm voice and in a positive manner. This action resulted in a gradual decline of the specific problem behaviors over the 2-week period, with Jimmy reporting positively in the individual sessions that "Mom's acting different." During this period, a token point program was also initiated at home to deal with noncompliance. Jimmy's progress was monitored on a chart on his bedroom wall. Points were awarded for successful completion of household tasks and chores (e.g., doing dishes, cleaning room, doing homework) with small rewards available daily from a grab bag. A larger reward (e.g., going to a movie, going out for a pizza) was available at the end of each week if Jimmy met a specified weekly goal.

The social skills training, conducted by another community agency, consisted of a series of small group sessions. Other group members were of similar age and also students of special education classes. Sessions focused on discussions of common social situations and the appropriate behaviors expected for those situations. Group members then took turns rehearsing the appropriate behaviors and providing feedback to one another. Typical role plays included introducing oneself, asking for help, saying no to a peer.

### Evaluation

Improvements were seen on all measures administered prior to the beginning of treatment. Additional data (e.g., noncompliance) taken during treatment also showed positive behavior changes. In general, while Jimmy still displayed problem behaviors at times, these behaviors had been reduced to a more manageable and tolerable level. On the affective side, Jimmy also expressed more satisfaction and happiness with his own situation. His parents reported considerably less frustration and had more confidence in their ability to deal with him.

## ANNOTATED BIBLIOGRAPHY

Craighead, L. W., Craighead, W. E., Kazdin, A. E., & Mahoney, M. J. (1994). *Cognitive and behavioral interventions: An empirical approach to mental health problems.* Boston: Allyn & Bacon.

This comprehensive overview of cognitive and behavioral interventions with children and adults, covers topics ranging from eating disorders to autism. A substantial amount of research is reviewed throughout.

Elksnin, L. K., & Elksnin, N. (1995). *Assessment and instruction of social skills* (2nd ed.). San Diego: Singular Publishing Group.

This is a review of assessment and intervention techniques used with children and adolescents in developing or modifying social skills. Many interventions are discussed including operant techniques, social learning methods, and cognitive behavioral techniques. The role of the child's peer group and family constellation is considered when the authors discuss techniques.

Hughes, J. M. (1988). *Cognitive behavior therapy with children in the schools.* New York: Pergamon.

This overview of cognitive behavior assessment and intervention is school-focused, but the author provides a review of cognitive behavioral interventions with a variety of child disorders including both internalizing and externalizing problems. The book also includes guidelines for using cognitive behavioral approaches in the prevention and consultation framework.

Spiegler, M. D. (1993). *Contemporary behavior therapy* (2nd ed.). Palo Alto, CA: Mayfield Publishing Co.

In this general review of behavior therapy concepts and procedures, the author deals with interventions such as consequential therapies, substitution behavior therapies, token economies, modeling therapies, and self-control therapies. The book is oriented toward specific interventions and provides numerous detailed case studies.

Schloss, P. J., & Smith, M. A. (1994). *Applied behavior analysis in the classroom.* Boston: Allyn & Bacon.

The authors provide a comprehensive review of operant techniques that can be used in the classroom including information on behavior assessment and task analysis techniques. A wide variety of interventions are discussed, especially for socially inappropriate and aggressive behaviors.

# REFERENCES

Abidin, R. R. (1996). *Early childhood parenting skills: A program manual for the mental health professional.* Odessa, FL: Psychological Assessment Resources.

Agras, W. S. (1987). *Eating disorders: Management of obesity, bulimia, an anorexia.* New York: Pergamon Press.

Agras, W. S., Kazdin, A. E., & Wilson, G. T. (1979). *Behavior therapy: Toward and applied clinical science.* San Francisco: Freeman.

Allen, J. S., Tarnowski, K. J., Simonian, S. J., & Elliott, D. (1991). The generalization map revised: Assessment of generalized treatment effects in child and adolescent behavior therapy. *Behavior Therapy, 22*(3), 393–405.

Andrews, H. B. (1971). The systematic use of the Premack principle in modifying classroom behavior. *Child Study Journal, 2,* 74–79.

Bandura, A. (1969). *Principles of behavior modification.* New York: Holt, Rinehart and Winston.

Bandura, A. (1973). *Aggression: A social learning analysis.* Englewood Cliffs, NJ: Prentice-Hall.

Bandura, A. (1977). *Social learning theory.* Englewood Cliffs, NJ: Prentice-Hall.

Bandura, A., Ross, D., & Ross, S. A. (1963). Vicarious reinforcement and imitative learning. *Journal of Abnormal and Social Psychology, 67,* 601–607.

Bandura, A., & Walters, R. H. (1963). *Social learning and personality development.* New York: Holt, Rinehart and Winston.

Bear, G. G. (1980). Differential reinforcement of other behavior. In *Behavioral strategies for psychological intervention.* Des Moines: Iowa Department of Education.

Beck, A. (1976). *Cognitive therapy and the emotional disorders.* New York: International Universities Press.

Beck, A. T., Rush, A. J., Shaw, B. F., & Emery, G. (1979). *Cognitive therapy of depression.* New York: Guilford Press.

Berkowitz, B. P., & Graziano, A. M. (1972). Training parents as behavior therapists: A review. *Behavior Research and Therapy, 10,* 297–317.

Boyd, L. A. (1980). Emotive imagery in the behavioral management of adolescent school phobia: A case approach. *School Psychology Review, 9*(2), 186–189.

Brawley, E. R., Harris, F. R., Allen, E., Fleming, R. S., & Peterson, R. F. (1973). Behavior modification of an autistic child. In J. M. Stedman, W. G. Patton, & K. F. Walton (Eds.), *Clinical studies in behavior therapy with children, adolescents, and their families.* Springfield, IL: Thomas.

Brown, B., & Doolan, M. (1983). Behavioral treatment of faecal soiling: A case study. *Behavioral Psychotherapy, 11*(1), 18–24.

Brown, J. H., & Brown, C. S. (1977). *Systematic counseling.* Champaign, IL: Research Press.

Brownell, K. D. (1989). *Learn to eat.* Dallas, TX: Brownell & Hager.

Clarizio, H. (1985). Cognitive-behavioral treatment of childhood depression. *Psychology in the Schools, 22*(3), 308–322.

Cotugno, A. J. (1987). Cognitive control therapy in the treatment of an 8-year-old enuretic boy. *Journal of Child and Adolescent Psychotherapy, 4*(2), 101–106.

Crisp, A. H. (1984). The psychopathology of anorexia nervosa: Getting the "heat" out of the system. In A. J. Stunkard & E. P. Stellar (Eds.), *Eating and its disorders.* New York: Raven Press.

Davidson, W. S., & Seidman, E. (1975). Studies of behavior modification and juvenile delinquency: A review, methodological critique, and social perspective. In A. M. Graziano (Ed.), *Behavior therapy with children* (2nd ed.). Chicago: Aldine.

DiGiuseppe, R. (1986). Cognitive therapy for childhood depression. *Journal of Psychotherapy and the Family, 2*(3/4), 153–172.

Dollard, J., & Miller, N. E. (1950). *Personality and psychotherapy.* New York: McGraw-Hill.

Durlak, J. A., Furman, T., & Lampman, C. (1991). Effectiveness of cognitive behavior therapy for maladapting children: A meta-analysis. *Psychological Bulletin, 110*(2), 204–214.

Elksnin, L. K., & Elksnin, N. (1995). *Assessment and instruction of social skills* (2nd ed.). San Diego: Singular.

Engeln, R., Knutson, J., Laughy, L., & Garlington, W. (1968). Behavior modification techniques applied to a family unit: A case study. *Journal of Child Psychology and Psychiatry, 9,* 245–252.

Erwin, E. (1980). *Behavior therapy: Scientific, philosophical, and moral foundations.* England: Cambridge University Press.

Etzel, B. C., & Gewirtz, J. L. (1967). Experimental modification of caretaker-maintained high rate operant crying in a 20-week-old infant: Extinction of crying with reinforcement of eye contact and smiling. *Journal of Experimental Child Psychology, 5,* 363–377.

Eysenck, H. J. (1964). *Crime and personality.* London: Routledge & Kegan Paul.

Fairburn, C. G. (1984). Bulimia: Its epidemiology and management. In A. J. Stunkard & E. P. Stellar (Eds.), *Eating and its disorders.* New York: Raven Press.

Fairburn, C. G., & Wilson G. T. (Eds.). (1993). *Binge eating: Nature, assessment, and treatment.* New York: Guilford Press.

Ferster, C. B. (1961). Positive reinforcement and behavioral deficits of autistic children. *Child Development, 332,* 437–456.

Ferster, C. B., & DeMyer, M. K. (1962). A method for the experimental analysis of the behavior of autistic children. *American Journal of Orthopsychiatry, 32,* 89–98.

Forehand, R., & Wierson, M. (1993). The role of developmental factors in planning behavioral interventions for children: Disruptive behavior as an example. *Behavior Therapy, 24*(1), 117–141.

Fox, J. E., & Houston, B. K. (1983). Distinguishing between cognitive and somatic trait and state anxiety in children. *Journal of Personality and Social Psychology, 45,* 862–870.

Foxx, R. M., & Azrin, N. H. (1973a). *Behavior research therapy* (Vol. 2). New York: Pergamon Press.

Foxx, R. M., & Azrin, N. H. (1973b). The elimination of autistic self-stimulatory behavior by overcorrection. *Journal of Applied Behavior Analysis, 6,* 1–14.

Frankel, F., & Simmons, J. Q. (1985). Behavioral treatment approaches to pathological unsocialized physical aggression in young children. *Journal of Child Psychology and Psychiatry and Allied Disciplines, 26*(4), 525–551.

Garvey, W. P., & Hegrenes, J., Jr. (1966). Desensitization techniques in the treatment of school phobia. *American Journal of Orthopsychiatry, 36,* 147–152.

Goldstein, A. P., & McGinnis, E. (1997). *Skill streaming the adolescent* (Rev. ed.). Champaign, IL: Research Press.

Gordon, S. B., Learner, L. I., & Keefe, F. (1979). Responsive parenting: An approach to training parenting of problem children. *American Journal of Community Psychology, 7,* 45–56.

Gottman, J. M., & Leiblum, S. R. (1974). *How to do psychotherapy and how to evaluate it.* New York: Holt, Rinehart and Winston.

Graziano, A. M. (Ed.). (1975). *Behavior therapy with children* (2nd ed.). Chicago: Aldine.

Graziano, A. M., DeGiovanni, I. S., & Garcia, K. A. (1979). Behavioral treatment of children's fears: A review. *Psychological Bulletin, 86,* 804–830.

Gresham, F. M. (1980). Modeling based interventions with children. In *Behavioral strategies for psychological intervention.* Des Moines: Iowa Department of Public Instruction.

Gresham, F. M. (1990). Best practices in social skills training. In A. Thomas & J. Grimes (Eds.), *Best practices in school psychology* (Vol. 2, pp. 695–709). Washington, DC: The National Association of School Psychologists.

Hansen, J. C., & L'Abate, L. (1982). *Approaches to family therapy.* New York: Macmillan.

Hersen, M. (1970). Behavior modification approach to a school-phobic case. *Journal of Clinical Psychology, 20,* 395–402.

Houts, A. C., Liebert, R. M., & Padawer, W. (1983). A delivery system for the treatment of primary enuresis. *Journal of Abnormal Child Psychology, 11*(4), 513–519.

Hope, H. (1976). Behavioral treatment of marital problems. In W. E. Cragihead, A. E. Kaxein, & M. J. Mahoney (Eds.), *Behavior modification: Principles, issues, and applications.* Boston: Houghton Mifflin.

Hughes, J. M. (1988). *Cognitive behavior therapy with children in the schools.* New York: Pergamon Press.

Jones, M. C. (1924). The elimination children's fears. *Journal of Experimental Psychology, 7,* 383–390.

Kanfer, F. H., & Goldstein, A. P. (1980). *Helping people change* (2nd ed.). New York: Pergamon Press.

Kanner, L. (1945). Autistic disturbances of affective contact. *The Nervous Child, 2,* 217–250.

Kazdin, A. E. (1979). Advances in child behavior therapy: Applications and implications. *American Psychologist, 34,* 981–987.

Kazdin, A. E. (1980). *Behavior modification in applied settings* (2nd ed.). Homewood, IL: Dorsey Press.

Kazdin, A. E., Esveldt-Dawson, K., & Matson, J. L. (1983). The effects of instructional set on social skills performance among psychiatric inpatient children. *Behavior Therapy, 14*(3), 413–423.

Keat, D. B. (1979). *Multimodal therapy with children.* New York: Pergamon Press.

Keefe, F. S., Kopel, S. A., & Gordon, S. B. (1978). *A practical guide to behavioral assessment.* New York: Springer.

Kennedy, W. A. (1965). School phobia: Rapid treatment of fifty cases. *Journal of Abnormal Psychology, 70,* 285–289.

Kennedy, W. A. (1971). *Child psychology.* Englewood Cliffs, NJ: Prentice-Hall.

Kettlewell, P. W., & Kausch, D. F. (1983). The generalization of the effects of a cognitive-behavioral treatment program for aggressive children. *Journal of Abnormal Child Psychology, 11*(1), 101–114.

Kimmel, H. D., & Kimmel, E. (1973). An instrumental conditioning method for the treatment of enuresis. In J. M. Stedman, W. F. Patterson, & K. F. Walton (Eds.), *Clinical studies in behavior therapy with children, adolescents, and their families.* Springfield, IL: Thomas.

Krumboltz, J. D., & Thoreson, C. E. (Eds.). (1969). *Behavioral counseling: Cases and techniques.* New York: Holt, Rinehart and Winston.

Krumboltz, J. D., & Thoreson, C. E. (Eds.). (1976). *Counseling methods.* New York: Holt, Rinehart and Winston.

Lansky, D., & Vance, M. A. (1983). School-based intervention for adolescent obesity: Analysis of treatment, randomly selected control, and self-selected control subjects. *Journal of Consulting and Clinical Psychology, 51*(1), 147–148.

Lazarus, A. A. (1960). The elimination of children's phobias by deconditioning. In H. J. Eysenck (Ed.), *Behavior therapy and the neuroses.* New York: Pergamon Press.

Lazarus, A. A. (1976). *Multimodal behavior therapy.* New York: Springer.

Lazarus, A. A., & Abramowitz, A. (1962). The use of "emotive imagery" in the treatment of children's phobias. *Journal of Mental Science, 108,* 191–195.

Lazarus, A. A., Davison, G., & Polefka, D. (1965). Classical and operant factors in treatment of a school phobia. *Journal of Abnormal Psychology, 70,* 225–229.

Lewinsohn, P. M., Munoz, R. F., Youngren, M. A., & Zeiss, A. M. (1986). *Control your depression* (2nd ed.). Englewood Cliffs, NJ: Prentice-Hall.

Libert, J. M., & Lewinsohn, P. M. (1973). Concept of social skill with special reference to the behavior of depressed persons. *Journal of Consulting and Clinical Psychology, 40,* 304–312.

Lindsley, O. R. (1968). *Operant behavior management: Background and procedures.* Brecksville: Brecksville Ohio Institute.

Lindsley, O. R. (1972). From Skinner to precision teaching: The child knows best. In J. B. Jordon & L. S. Robbins (Eds.), *Let's try doing something else kind of thing: Behavioral principles and the exceptional child.* Arlington, VA: Council for Exceptional Children.

Lovaas, O. I., Koegel, R., Simmons, J. O., & Long, J. S. (1973). Some generalizations and follow-up measures on autistic children in behavior therapy. *Journal of Applied Behavior Analysis, 6,* 131–166.

Lowenstein, L. F. (1982). The treatment of extreme shyness in maladjusted children by implosive, counseling and conditioning approaches. *Acta Psychiatrica Scandinavica, 66*(3), 173–189.

Mahoney, M. J. (1974). *Cognitive and behavior modification.* Cambridge, MA: Ballinger.

McAdam, E. K. (1986). Cognitive behavior therapy and its application with adolescents. *Journal of Adolescence, 9*(1), 1–15.

McGinnis, E., & Goldstein, A. P. (1997). *Skill streaming the elementary school child* (Rev. ed.). Champaign, IL: Research Press.

Meador, A. E., & Ollendick, T. H. (1984). Cognitive behavior therapy with children: An evaluation of its efficacy and clinical utility. *Child and Family Behavior Therapy, 6*(3), 25–44.

Meichenbaum, D. H. (1977). *Cognitive-behavior modification.* New York: Plenum Press.

Meyers, J. (1980). Time-out: Guidelines for the school psychologist. In *Behavioral strategies for psychological intervention.* Des Moines: Iowa Department of Public Instruction.

Miller, P. M. (1972). The use of visual imagery and muscle relaxation in the counterconditioning of a phobic child: A case study. *Journal of Nervous and Mental Diseases. 154,* 457–460.

Morris, R. (1980). The Premack principle: How it can be applied to change behavior in educational settings. In *Behavioral strategies for psychological intervention.* Des Moines: Iowa Department of Public Instruction.

Mowrer, O. H. (1947). On the dual nature of learning: A reinterpretation of conditioning and problem solving. *Harvard Educational Review, 17,* 102–148.

Mowrer, O. H., & Mowrer, W. M. (1938). Enuresis: A method for its study and treatment. *American Journal of Orthopsychiatry, 8,* 436–469.

Neale, D. H. (1973). Behavior therapy and encopresis in children. In J. M. Stedman, W. F. Patton, & K. F. Walton (Eds.), *Clinical studies in behavior therapy with children, adolescents, and their families*. Springfield, IL: Thomas.

O'Brien, S., Ross, L. V., & Christophersen, E. R. (1986). Primary encopresis: Evaluation and treatment. *Journal of Applied Behavior Analysis, 19*(2), 137–145.

Ollendick, T. H. (1983). Reliability and validity in the Children's Fear Survey Schedule–Revised. *Behavior Research and Therapy, 21,* 685–692.

Ollendick, T. H., & Cerny, J. A. (1981). *Clinical behavior therapy with children*. New York: Plenum Press.

O'Mara, M. A., & Graziano, A. N. (1974). *Self monitoring by children to reduce fear of dark*. Unpublished manuscript, State University of New York–Buffalo.

Patterson, G. R. (1976). *Living with children*. Champaign, IL: Research Press.

Patterson, G. R., & Reed, J. (1970). Reciprocity and coercion: Two facets of social systems. In C. Neuringer & J. Michaels (Eds.), *Behavioral modification in clinical psychology*. New York: Appleton-Century-Crofts.

Phelan, T. W. (1995). *1-2-3 magic* (2nd ed.). Glen Ellyn, IL: Child Management.

Phillips, L., Phillips, E. A., Wolf, M. M., & Fixsen, D. L. (1975). Achievement place: Development of the elected manager system. In A. M. Graziano (Ed.), *Behavior therapy with children* (2nd ed.). Chicago: Aldine.

Prout, H. T., & Harvey, J. R. (1978). Applications of desensitization procedures for school-related problems: A review. *Psychology in the Schools, 15,* 533–541.

Reynolds, C. R., & Paget, K. D. (1983). National normative and reliability data for the Revised Children's Manifest Anxiety Scale. *School Psychology Review, 12*(3), 324–335.

Rhine, W. R., & Spaner, S. D. (1983). The structure of evaluating anxiety among children differing in socioeconomic status, ethnicity, and sex. *Journal of Psychology, 115,* 145–158.

Rimm, D. C., & Masters, J. C. (1979). *Behavior therapy: Techniques and empirical findings* (2nd ed.). New York: Academic Press.

Rose, S. D. (1972). *Treating children in groups*. San Francisco: Jossey-Bass.

Ross, A. O. (1978). Behavior therapy with children. In S. L. Garfield & A. E. Bergin (Eds.), *Handbook of psychotherapy and behavior change* (2nd ed.). New York: Wiley.

Ross, A. O. (1980). *Psychological disorders of children*. New York: McGraw-Hill.

Saylor, C. F., Benson, B., & Einhaus, L. (1985). Evaluation of an anger management program for aggressive boys in inpatient treatment. *Journal of Child and Adolescent Psychotherapy, 2*(1), 5–15.

Schacter, S. (1971). Some extraordinary facts about obese humans and rats. *American Psychologist, 26,* 129–144.

Schloss, P. J., & Smith, M. A. (1994). *Applied behavior analysis in the classroom.* Boston: Allyn & Bacon.

Shure, M. B. (1992). *I can problem-solve.* Champaign, IL: Research Press.

Skinner, B. F. (1953). *Science and human behavior.* New York: Macmillan.

Smith, R. G., & Sharpe, T. M. (1970). Treatment of school phobia with implosive therapy. *Journal of Consulting and Clinical Psychology, 35,* 239–243.

Stedman, J. M. (1976). Family counseling with a school-phobic child. In J. D. Krumboltz & C. E. Thoreson (Eds.), *Counseling methods.* New York: Holt, Rinehart and Winston.

Strain, P. S., Shores, R. E., & Timm, M. A. (1977). Effects of peer social imitations on the behavior of withdrawn preschool children. *Journal of Applied Behavior Analysis, 10,* 289–298.

Stuart, R. B. (1973). Behavioral contracting within the families of delinquents. In J. M. Stedman, W. F. Patton, & K. F. Walton (Eds.), *Clinical studies in behavior therapy with children, adolescents, and their families.* Springfield, IL: Thomas.

Sulzer-Azaroff, B., & Mayer, G. R. (1986). *Achieving educational excellence: Using behavioral strategies.* New York: Holt, Rinehart and Winston.

Sulzer-Azaroff, B., & Reese, E. P. (1982). *Applying behavior analysis: A program for developing professional competence.* New York: Holt, Rinehart and Winston.

Sutherland, E., & Cressey, D. (1970). *Criminology.* Philadelphia: Lippincott.

Tahmisian, J. A., & McReynolds, W. T. (1971). Use of parents as behavioral engineers in the treatment of a school-phobic girl. *Journal of Counseling Psychology, 18,* 225–228.

Trueman, D. (1984). What are the characteristics of school phobic children? *Psychological Reports, 54,* 191–202.

Van der Ploeg, H. M. (1975). Treatment of frequency of urination by stories competing with anxiety. *Journal of Behavior Therapy and Experimental Psychiatry, 6,* 165–166.

Walker, C. E., Hedberg, A. G., Clement, P. W., & Wright, L. (1981). *Clinical procedures for behavior therapy.* Englewood Cliffs, NJ: Prentice-Hall.

Watson, J. B., & Raynor, R. (1920). Conditioned emotional reactions. *Journal of Experimental Psychology, 3,* 1–14.

Webster, C. C. (1980). The characteristics of autism. In C. D. Webster, M. M. Konstantareas, J. Oxman, & J. E. Mack (Eds.), *Autism: New directions in research and education.* New York: Pergamon Press.

Weiner, I. B. (1973). Behavior therapy in obsessive-compulsive neurosis: Treatment of an adolescent boy. In J. M. Stedman, W. F. Patton, & K. F. Walton (Eds.), *Clinical studies in behavior therapy with children, adolescents, and their families.* Springfield, IL: Thomas.

Weisberg, P. (1963). Social and non-social conditioning of infant vocalizations. *Child Development, 34,* 177–388.

Werry, J. S., & Wollershein, J. P. (1989). Behavior therapy with children and adolescents: A twenty year overview. *Journal of the American Academy of Child and Adolescent Psychiatry, 28*(1), 1–18.

Wish, P. A., Hasazi, J. E., & Jurgela, A. R. (1975). Automated direct deconditioning of childhood phobia. In A. M. Graziano (Ed.), *Behavior therapy with children* (2nd ed.). Chicago: Aldine.

Wolpe, J. (1958). *Psychotherapy by reciprocal inhibition.* Stanford, CA: Stanford University Press.

Wright, J., & James, R. (1974). *A behavioral approach to preventing delinquency.* Springfield, IL: Thomas.

# Chapter 8

# *RATIONAL EMOTIVE BEHAVIOR THERAPY*

Raymond DiGiuseppe

Rational Emotive Behavior Therapy (REBT), one of the original cognitive-behavioral psychotherapies, was founded by Albert Ellis, a psychologist, psychotherapist, and philosopher. REBT is an active, direct, psychoeducational, philosophical, and multimodal form of cognitive behavior therapy. REBT is active because it recommends that therapists intervene early and often to help clients resolve their emotional difficulties. REBT is directive because the theory hypothesizes that certain types of cognitions cause disturbance and other types of cognitions lead to adjustment. It recommends that therapists focus on these cognitions rather than wait for clients to self-discover the reasons for their problems. REBT is psychoeducational because it maintains that people can be taught the skills of identifying, challenging, and replacing their dysfunctional beliefs. REBT is philosophical because it takes specific positions on epistemology and recommends a philosophy of life. REBT is multimodal because it recognizes that people learn to think, feel, and act differently through many methods. REBT recommends the use of cognitive, emotive, imaginal, behavioral, and systemic techniques.

The trademark of REBT is its emphasis on teaching people to learn their ABC's of emotional disturbance, identifying the Activating events, their Beliefs about those events, and the resulting Consequences. REBT teaches that disturbed emotional and behavioral Consequences result from irrational Beliefs individuals hold rather than from Activating events. REBT works to alleviate emotional disturbance by helping people to (a) identify their irrational beliefs, (b) recognize that the irrational beliefs are maladaptive, and (c) replace those dysfunctional cognitions with more adaptive beliefs.

Ellis's writings include his personal philosophy, a recommended philosophy of life, a theory of psychopathology, and a theory of psychotherapy. As one reads the REBT literature, it is helpful to keep in mind which of these elements is being discussed. One could agree with some aspects of Ellis's writings, such as his theory of psychopathology, and yet disagree with others aspects, such as his personal philosophy. For example, Ellis is an atheist. However, REBT is compatible with religious beliefs (DiGiuseppe, Robin, & Dryden, 1991; Johnson, 1996; Nielson, 1996), and research has demonstrated that secular REBT and religious versions of REBT are equally effective with religious clients (Johnson, Devries, Ridley, Pettorini, & Peterson, 1994; Johnson & Ridley, 1992).

## HISTORY AND STATUS

Before becoming a psychologist, Ellis supported himself as an accountant while he pursued his interests in music, literature, philosophy, and politics. He wrote operas and other musical scores, authored novels, and spent time as a political activist. During these years, Ellis was interested in romantic and sexual relationships and read voraciously on the topic, partly to overcome his own anxiety about dating. Friends frequently approached him for romantic advice, and on their recommendation, he enrolled in the doctoral program in clinical psychology at Columbia University at the age of 40.

After completing graduate school in the late 1940s, Ellis started psychoanalytic training and simultaneously started to practice marital and sex therapy. Ellis became discouraged with the efficiency and effectiveness of psychoanalysis in the early 1950s. He realized that he helped clients in his sex and marital therapy practice more than those he treated with psychoanalysis. Initially, Ellis thought that he needed to dig deeper into his patients' pasts before they would improve. Yet, after they gained more insight, they still failed to improve. Ellis thought that years of insight into childhood experiences did not make for healthier patients and concluded that insight, in and of itself, led to change in only a small percentage of individuals.

Ellis recognized that he behaved differently with clients in his marital and sex therapy practice. He actively taught these clients to change their attitudes. Ellis's interest in philosophy had led him to the works of great Asian and Greek thinkers including Confucius, Lao Tze, Marcus Aurelius, and Epictetus. He had been providing advice to clients based on these philosophical works. Ellis was intrigued by the philosophers' notion that people can choose whether or not they become disturbed, or in the words of Epictetus, "Men [and women] are not disturbed by things, but by the view which they take of them" (from the Enchiridion). Ellis utilized this philosophy as the foundation for his new therapy. In 1955, he formulated his theory in a paper delivered at the American Psychological Association. It was not until 1961 that he wrote his most influential self-help book with Robert Harper, A Guide for Rational Living, now in its third edition having sold over 2 million copies. The following year, Ellis (1962) published his first professional book, Reason and Emotion in Psychotherapy.

Ellis originally named his therapy "Rational Therapy" because he focused on the role of cognitions. He later realized that he had underemphasized the role of emotions in the title and renamed it "Rational Emotive Therapy." He finally changed the name to "Rational Emotive Behavior Therapy" (Ellis, 1994a) at the urging of Ray Corsini. Corsini was revising his psychotherapy text and noticed that Ellis almost always used behavioral interventions. He suggested that a new name was needed to better represent what Ellis actually did and recommended.

In 1965, Ellis founded The Institute for Advanced Study in Rational Psychotherapy for professional training in his form of therapy. It survives today as the Albert Ellis

*Institute.* Affiliated training centers that train mental health professionals exist in Australia, Canada, France, Germany, Israel, Italy, Mexico, and the Netherlands. Over 12,000 therapists throughout the world have been trained by the Institute or its affiliated centers. Ellis has been a prolific writer and he has published over 60 books and over 700 peer-reviewed journal articles. The Institute sponsors the *Journal of Rational Emotive and Cognitive Behavior Therapies* under the editorship of Dr. Michael Bernard.

## OVERVIEW AND THEORY

### Philosophical Assumptions

As mentioned, REBT contains some philosophical assumptions. The first of these is a commitment to the scientific method. Ellis believes that if one applies the scientific method to one's personal life, one will be more likely to give up dysfunctional, irrational beliefs that can lead to emotional disturbance and ineffectual behavior. Ellis's philosophy contains elements of constructivism, the philosophy of science and epistemology. Specifically, Ellis maintains that all humans would be better off if they recognized that they create images or constructions of how the world is or ought to be. Ellis directly built on George Kelly's (1955) famous work, *The Psychology of Personal Constructs.*

Second, Ellis believes that people would be better off if they recognized that all of their beliefs, schemata, perceptions, and cherished truths could be wrong. Testing one's assumptions, examining the validity and functionality of one's beliefs, and having a willingness to entertain alternative ideas is necessary for one to develop new beliefs and schemata to guide one's behavior. Rigid adherence to a belief or schema of the world prevents one from revising one's thinking, and thus dooms one to behave as if the world is as one hopes it will be, rather than the way it is. REBT differs from the Post Modernist philosophers and the constructivist cognitive therapists such as Mahoney (1991) and Neimeyer (1993) in two ways. First, the constructivist therapists believe that the sole criterion to assess beliefs is their utility or viability. Empirical reality is not a criterion because the extreme constructivist approach maintains there is no knowable reality. REBT posits that empirical reality is an important criterion and that one needs to assess the empirical veracity of one's beliefs along with their utility and logical consistency.

Second, modern constructivists believe that people should be allowed to find their own reality and the imposition of another's worldview is oppression. Constructivist therapists believe that therapists should not provide alternative beliefs for clients, but allow them to develop alternatives on their own. REBT posits that there are some rational alternative beliefs that will promote emotional adjustment.

REBT recommends (DiGiuseppe, 1986, 1990, 1991a; Ellis, 1962, 1994b) that humans would function best if they adopted the epistemology of the philosophy of science, specifically the positions of Popper (1962) and Bartley (1987). Popper noted that all people develop hypotheses. Preconceived hypotheses distort the data one collects and lead to a confirmatory bias in reasoning. This renders objectivity in inductive data collection an impossibility. As humans, we cannot stop ourselves from forming hypotheses. Therefore, the solution is to acknowledge our hypotheses and attempt to falsify them. Popper maintains that knowledge accumulates and advances quickest when people deduce predictions from their hypotheses and collect data to disprove them. Bartley's epistemology of comprehensive critical rationalism adds that people should use such empirical falsifiablity tests and any other argument one can muster to disprove one's thinking. Ellis believes that it is best to apply any and all means to challenge one's thinking as a theorist and as an individual. Accordingly, therapists would do best to challenge their ideas about their clients and to teach their clients to do the same to their beliefs.

REBT maintains that certain values promote emotional adjustment and mental health. These appear in Table 8.1. REBT practitioners attempt to develop attitudes and behaviors that reflect these values.

## Theoretical Assumptions

REBT assumptions about psychopathology and change appear in Table 8.2. These six principles can be summarized as follows:

1. Cognitions or beliefs are the most proximate and identifiable cause of human disturbance.
2. Irrational, illogical, and antiempirical beliefs lead to emotional disturbance. Rational beliefs will lead to emotional adjustment and mental health.
3. The best way to change our emotional disturbance is to change our thinking.
4. Humans have a biological predisposition to learn to think irrationally and get themselves upset. However, culture and family teach people the specific issues that they will become upset about.
5. Although nature and nurture influence how and whether people develop emotional disturbance, the reason people stay upset is because they rehearse their irrational beliefs and reindoctrinate themselves with what they were taught.
6. Change is difficult and people change only with repeated efforts to challenge their dysfunctional thoughts and rehearse new rational adaptive modes of thinking.

Many theorists and practitioners ascribing to generic cognitive behavior therapy (CBT) think in terms of cognitions causing emotions and behavior. REBT acknowledges that thinking, feeling, and behaving are interconnected elements, with each aspect of experience influencing the others. People think, feel, and behave, simultaneously. It follows then, that what people think affects the way they feel, that people rarely feel and/or act without thinking, and that the way people behave influences what they feel and think. There are two implications of these theoretical assumptions.

First, one can assess one element of experience by asking the person to focus on that element while experiencing another element. For example, one can assess irrational beliefs by asking people to focus on what they are thinking while they are performing

### Table 8.1.   Values of rational emotive behavior therapy

*Self-acceptance.*   Healthy people *choose* to accept themselves unconditionally, rather than measure themselves, rate themselves, or try to prove themselves.

*Risk-taking.*   Emotionally healthy people choose to take risks and have a spirit of adventurousness in trying to do what they want to do, without being foolhardy.

*Non-utopian.*   We are unlikely to get everything we want or to avoid everything we find painful. Healthy people do not waste time striving for the unattainable or for unrealistic perfection.

*High frustration tolerance.*   Paraphrasing St. Francis, healthy people recognize that there are only two sorts of problems they are likely to encounter: those they can do something about and those they cannot. Once this discrimination has been made, the goal is to modify those obnoxious conditions we can change, and accept—or lump—those we cannot change.

*Self-responsibility for disturbance.*   Rather than blaming others, the world, or the fates for their distress, healthy individuals accept a good deal of responsibility for their own thoughts, feelings, and behaviors.

*Self-interest.*   Emotionally healthy people tend to put their own interests at least *a little* above the interests of others. They sacrifice themselves *to some degree* for those for whom they care, but not overwhelmingly or completely.

*Social interest.*   Most people choose to live in social groups; and to do so most comfortably and happily, they would be wise to act morally, protect the rights of others, and aid in the survival of the society in which they live.

*Self-direction.*   We would do well to cooperate with others, but it would be better for us to assume primary *responsibility* for *our* own *lives* rather than to *demand* or *need* considerable support or nurturance from others.

*Tolerance.*   It is helpful to allow humans (the self and others) the right to be wrong. It is not appropriate to like obnoxious behavior, but it is not necessary to *damn* the human for doing it.

*Flexibility.*   Healthy individuals tend to be flexible thinkers. Rigid, bigoted, and invariant rules tend to minimize happiness.

*Acceptance of uncertainty.*   We live in a fascinating world of probability and chance; absolute certainties probably do not exist. The healthy individual strives for some degree of order, but does not demand perfect certainty.

*Commitment.*   Most people, especially bright and educated ones, tend to be happier when vitally absorbed in something outside themselves. At least one strong creative interest and some important human involvement seem to provide structure for a happy daily existence.

the target behavior or experiencing the target emotion. Second, one had better use cognitive, emotive, and behavioral interventions in therapy to achieve success. Cognitions may be the focal point of much discussion not because of their primacy but because of their utility. People often can describe what they are thinking and entertain challenges to their thoughts or new thoughts easier than they can "do" new behaviors or "feel" emotions.

**Table 8.2.   Basic principles of rational emotive behavior therapy**

*Principle 1*

Cognition is the most important proximal and accessible determinant of human emotion.
Simply stated, we feel what we think. Events and other people do not make us "feel good" or
"feel bad"; we do it ourselves, cognitively. It is as if we are writing the scripts for our
emotional reactions, although usually we are not conscious of doing so. Past or present
external events contribute to, but do not directly "cause" our emotions. Rather, our internal
events—our perceptions and our evaluations of those perceptions—are the more direct source
of our emotional responses.

*Principle 2*

Dysfunctional thinking is a major determinant of emotional distress. Dysfunctional emotional
states and many aspects of psychopathology are the result of dysfunctional thought processes.
These processes are over exaggeration, oversimplification, overgeneralization, illogic, use of
unvalidated assumptions, faulty deductions, and absolutistic rigid schema.

*Principle 3*

Since we feel what we think, to break out of an emotional problem, we would begin with an
analysis of thought. If distress is a product of irrational thinking, to conquer distress one
changes this thinking.

*Principle 4*

Multiple factors, including both genetic and environmental influences, cause irrational
thinking and psychopathology. Humans have a natural predisposition to think irrationally
(e.g., Ellis, 1976). Although we may have a tendency to easily learn irrational beliefs, as
witnessed by the fact that they are so widespread, the culture in which we live seems to
furnish the specific content that we learn.

*Principle 5*

Although heredity and environmental conditions are important in the *acquisition* of irrational
beliefs, people *maintain* their disturbance by *self-indoctrination,* or *rehearsal* of their
irrational beliefs. The contemporary *adherence* to irrational beliefs, rather than how they
were acquired, is the proximal cause of emotional distress. If individuals reevaluated their
thinking and abandoned it, their current functioning would be quite different.

*Principle 6*

Contemporary *beliefs can be changed,* although such change will not come about easily.
Irrational belief can be changed by active and persistent efforts to recognize, challenge, and
revise one's thinking.

## VIEW OF PSYCHOPATHOLOGY

### Adaptive and Maladaptive Emotions

REBT distinguishes between disturbed, dysfunctional emotions and normal, motivating, albeit negative emotions. The presence of negative emotions is not evidence of
psychopathology. If an activating event occurs (**A**) and one thinks irrationally (**B**), one
will experience a disturbed emotion such as anxiety or depression (**C**). If one then

challenges one's irrational belief and replaces it with a rational belief (a new **B**), what will cause a new emotional consequence (the new **C**)? If the unpleasant activating event is still present, it would be inappropriate or unrealistic to expect a person to feel neutral or good after the challenging of his or her irrational beliefs. What does one feel if the intervention is successful? The answer is a negative, nondisturbed, motivating emotion. Most psychotherapists conceptualize therapeutic improvement as a quantitative shift in the emotion. Often therapists ask clients to rate their emotion on the SUDS scale (subjective units of discomfort) developed by Wolpe (1990). Therapy is successful if the SUDS rating demonstrates much less of the emotion.

Emotions differ by their intensity of physiological arousal, phenomenological experience, means of social expression, and the behaviors that they elicit. Ellis (1962; Ellis & DiGiuseppe, 1993) proposed that when people think rational thoughts they actually experience a qualitatively different emotion rather than less intensity of the disturbed emotion. The emotions generated by rational thoughts will be in the same family of emotions as the disturbed emotion; but they differ in many aspects. Ellis posits that although irrational thinking leads to anxiety, depression, or anger; rational thinking will lead to concern, sadness, and annoyance, respectively. These emotions are not necessarily less intense but they may lead to qualitatively different phenomenological experiences, and to different forms of expression, and they will elicit different behavioral reactions. A good example of this principle is Dr. Martin Luther King Jr.'s emotional response to racism. Dr. King had an intense emotional reaction to racism, but it led to problem-solving, commitment, high frustration tolerance and goal-directed behavior. The English language often fails to provide a lexicon to label such emotions. Emotional disturbance may correlate with the intensity of the physiological arousal but this is different from the intensity of the phenomenological feeling. Disturbance may also be characterized as an emotion that results in dysfunctional behavior or alienating social expression. Nondisturbed emotion elicits problem-solving, coping, and social cohesion. REBT focuses on the qualitative differences in emotion and rejects the notion, implicit in many theories, that emotions differ only quantitatively. Rational beliefs elicit adaptive emotions that lead to adaptive responses and social communications. REBT has adopted the script theories of emotions (DiGiuseppe, 1995) and believes that clients need to learn adaptive emotional scripts, and not just change the intensity of their feelings. As a result, therapists are very careful in the words they use to describe emotions and to help clients to choose which emotions they might like to feel in place of their disturbed emotion. They help clients formulate a vocabulary to describe adaptive, albeit negative, affective states that they could feel instead of the disturbed emotions.

## Irrational Beliefs and Emotional Disturbance

Ellis originally identified 11 irrational beliefs that he thought led to emotional disturbance (Ellis, 1962; Ellis & Harper, 1961). Over the years, the list of irrational beliefs has dwindled to four and more recently (Ellis & Dryden, 1997) down to one demandingness. The major theoretical problems REBT needs to address are which cognitive processes or irrational beliefs lead to emotional disturbance and how does irrational thinking initiate strong, sustained emotional disturbance.

There are a number of cognitive-behavioral therapies, each of which posits some type of cognitive process or cognitive content that leads to emotional disturbance and that is remediated by the respective therapy. A number of types of cognitions have been proposed to mediate psychopathology, such as attributions (Seligman, 1991), negative erroneous automatic thoughts (Beck, 1972), behavior guiding self-statements (Meichenbaum, 1971), beliefs in self-efficacy (Bandura, 1986), and core schemata (Beck & Freeman, 1990; Persons, 1989). If therapists are to develop CBT treatment plans, it is important to understand all these constructs and how they may interact with each other and lead to psychopathology.

Originally, Ellis's theory presented irrational beliefs as ideas separate from these other constructs in a linear model of causation of emotional disturbance. Maultsby defined three criteria for irrational beliefs. To be irrational, a belief is either illogical, inconsistent with empirical reality, or inconsistent with accomplishing one's long-term goals. These criteria are similar to those that Thomas Kuhn (1970), the historian of science, proposes scientists use to evaluate theories: logical consistency, empirical predictability, and heuristic or functional value.

Irrational beliefs were originally conceptualized as being independent from the constructs of other cognitive theories because they were more evaluative in nature (Walen, DiGiuseppe, & Wessler, 1980; Wessler & Wessler, 1980). This distinction failed to be maintained because some of Ellis's original irrational beliefs are factual errors. Irrational beliefs actually have the same characteristics as rigid, inaccurate schemata (DiGiuseppe, 1986, 1991a, 1991b; Dryden & DiGiuseppe, 1990; Walen, DiGiuseppe, & Dryden, 1992). In fact, DiGiuseppe (1996) and Ellis (1996) have proposed that it may be more accurate to call them irrational schemata than irrational beliefs. REBT construes irrational beliefs as tacit, unconscious, broad-based schemata that operate on many levels. Schemata are sets of expectations about the way the world is, the way it ought to be and what is good or bad in what is and ought to be. Schemata help people organize their world by influencing (a) the information to which a person attends; (b) the perceptions the person is likely to draw from sensory data; (c) the inferences or automatic thoughts the person is likely to conclude from the data one perceives; (d) the beliefs one has in one's ability to complete tasks; (e) the evaluations a person makes of the actual or perceived world; and (f) the solutions that a person is likely to conceive to solve problems. Conceptualizing irrational beliefs as schemata means they are both factual and evaluative in nature. They predict what is and what is good. Irrational beliefs/schemata influence other hypothetical cognitive constructs that are mentioned in other forms of CBT. Figure 8.1 represents how irrational beliefs relate to other cognitive constructs and emotional disturbance. The model suggests that interventions aimed at the level of irrational beliefs/schemata will change other types of cognitions as well as emotional disturbance; and that interventions aimed at other cognitive processes may, but will not necessarily, influence the irrational schema.

According to current REBT theory, four types of irrational thinking lead to emotional disturbance: demandingness, awfulizing, frustration intolerance, and global

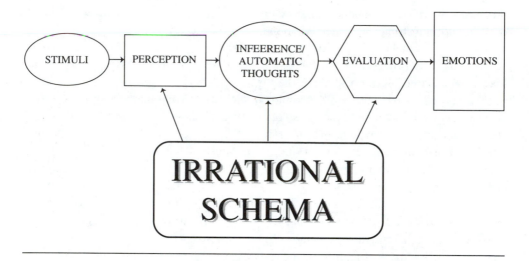

**Figure 8.1.    Schematic representation of the role of irrational schema on cognitions emotions.**

condemnation of human worth. Ellis (1994b) has revised his theory several times and now maintains that "demandingness," or absolutistic, rigid adherence to an idea, is the core of disturbance and that the other types of irrational thinking are less important and are psychologically deduced from or created from irrational demandingness.

*Demandingness*

Demandingness is represented in English by the words "must," "should," "ought," and "have to." These words reflect a demand on how oneself, others, or the world must be. REBT makes the distinction between preferences and demands. Preferences are neither rational or irrational, they just are. Therapists do not attempt to change a person's "wants." To quote Zajonc (1980), "Preferences need no inferences." REBT posits that it is okay to want anything and no desire is a sign of pathology or normalcy except in the statistical sense. People's desires do not cause disturbance. However, when people demand that their preferences are reality, they become disturbed. But how and why does demandingness lead to disturbance?

REBT believes people construct schemata of the way the world is. Research has demonstrated that when people hold a schema of the way the world is, and reality is discordant with their expectations, emotional upset occurs. The crucial event here is that our sensors detect information that is inconsistent with our expectations. When a reality-expectation discrepancy occurs, people become startled or upset. A well-adjusted person is motivated by this emotional arousal to seek out further information and will revise his or her schema. Piaget (1963) noted that people revise their schema by assimilation or accommodation. REBT maintains that disturbed individuals do neither of these. They continue to hold on to their existing schema and demand that the world be consistent with their conception of it. This results in increased emotional upset as their sensory information continues to supply information that the world is not complying. Thus, demandingness is actually believing and expecting that the world will be the way one prefers it to be.

For example, an adolescent girl might tell herself, "My parents must treat me fairly and let me do what I want." Not only does she want her parents to allow her to do as she desires, but she believes that because she wants it, they must comply. She may be shocked when they punish her for transgressions of their rules, and she may continue to behave against their rules despite all the feedback that they disapprove of the behavior and will initiate consequences for it. Also, she may conclude that "Since I must do what I want, I cannot stand it if they do not let me." Or "It is terrible and awful if my parents do not let me do what I want."

Some irrational beliefs include demands about what one must do to be a worthwhile, valued person. For example, a recent client, Melissa, age 11, believed that she must be liked by a certain "in group" of peers in her class to be a "good person." Melissa demanded that she be liked by this group of girls, and she recognized that they did not like her. Her demand was of her self-worth. She said "I must have their approval to be worthwhile." Her schema of human worth was rigidly linked to approval by certain others. No other characteristics counted. Attempts to demonstrate that she possessed other exemplar traits, and that she was esteemed by her family, teacher, and some peers outside the "in group" failed to change her self-worth. She neither assimilated nor accommodated her schema of her self-worth. Her demand was not on the way the world or others were, but on the criteria for her self-acceptance or worth.

Rational cognitions express preferential, flexible desires, whereas irrational cognitions express absolutistic, rigid needs. Rational thinking leads to happiness and enables individuals to attain their goals and strive toward their potential; irrational thinking causes people to be extremely disturbable and thwarts individuals' ability to attain their goals, leading to unhappiness.

### Awfulizing

These beliefs are characterized by exaggerated negative evaluations and thoughts that something about oneself, others, or the world is terrible, awful or catastropic. One might say that "It is awful if I do not have the approval of everyone around me." Rorer (1989) suggested that when people hold such a belief they are unable to define just what awful or terrible is, or what catastrophe will occur. They are, in fact, uncertain of the outcome and define it as extremely bad. Rorer believes awfulizing is definitional. People arbitrarily assign an extremely negative valence to an event and never test reality to see if the occurrence of the event brings such negative consequences. The empirical argument against awfulizing thinking is best summarized by Mark Twain who said, "I have survived many a catastrophe that never occurred." Rational thinking would acknowledge that some things are bad, but stress that they are survivable.

### Frustration Intolerance

Ellis (1979, 1980a) originally called this type of irrational belief low frustration tolerance, or LFT. Such beliefs imply that an individual can't stand something he or she finds frustrating or that the individual does not have the endurance to survive in its presence. For example, someone who is addicted to caffeine might say, "I cannot stand feeling the slightest bit tired when I have all this work to do; I must have some coffee." These beliefs are illogical as well, because, short of dying, one is actually tolerating whatever one claims one cannot stand. The term frustration intolerance (FI) appears more appropriate than Ellis's term low frustration tolerance. The Australian psychologist, Dr. Marie Joyce pointed out that the term LFT can invalidate clients' difficulties. While Dr. Joyce was working with parents of neurologically disabled children, she had difficulty getting these parents to follow behavior management strategies. The parents commented that it was too hard, and that they could not stand being so consistent with their children when they misbehaved. When Dr. Joyce challenged the parents' LFT, they felt misunderstood. Dr. Joyce admitted that these parents had more difficulty raising their children than most other parents. In fact, they had been tolerating more frustration than most parents. The problem was not that the parents had LFT, but that they did not have *sufficient* frustration tolerance. They needed to have greater frustration tolerance than the average parent if they wished to accomplish their goal of getting their children to behave better. Dr. Joyce suggests that the unwillingness to sustain or tolerate the degree of frustration necessary to achieve one's goals be labeled frustration intolerance. This prevents therapists from invalidating the difficulties of people who are intolerant of the frustration needed to accomplish their goals but who have experienced more frustration than most people.

### Global Condemnation of Human Worth

These beliefs consist of negative evaluations of oneself, others, or the world, such as "I must be worthless if I do not have the approval of everyone around me." Ellis (1962, 1976, 1994b) states that a person cannot be rated as either good or bad because it is not possible for one to be completely good or bad due to people's complexity. Instead, ratings should be restricted to people's behaviors. It is more logical, and certainly healthier to state that "I performed poorly on the math test," instead of saying in addition, "Therefore, I am a bad student." Ellis's position here is a philosophical one. He proposes that people take seriously the Preamble to the U.S. Constitution or the Judeo-Christian religious tradition, both of which state that all persons are created equal, the former by government and the latter by God. REBT tries to teach people to rate their deeds and not themselves. As the proverb goes, "Hate the sin, but love the sinner." Self-evaluations are replaced with what Ellis calls USA, unconditional self-acceptance.

REBT is very much against the self-esteem movement popular in education today. Self-esteem is a combination of two different cognitive processes. The first is self-efficacy, which is the belief that one can in fact adequately perform a task. If you search the items of self-esteem scales, you will notice that many items reflect this type of statement. The second is self-evaluation. This involves making conclusions about one's worth as a person. Humans often get these two confused and evaluate their worth, or lack of it, based on perceived self-efficacy or lack of it. For example, an adolescent recently seen in therapy concluded that because he could not read as well as other children, he was "no good" as a person. He had negative self-efficacy and negative self-evaluation.

The problem with many self-esteem programs is that they either teach children that they are special or good people because they are efficacious, or that they directly teach people unwarranted self-efficacy. REBT points out two difficulties with such programs. First, they teach the children that they have self-worth because of self-efficacy. This may be fine for the moment but what if their skills falter or they are surpassed by their peers to a great degree? The mental health of such children may be on a roller coaster; they feel good when they perform well and feel worthless when they perform badly. Second, it often teaches self-efficacy beyond the child's skills. They are likely to collapse emotionally when they can no longer get feedback that they are efficacious. Third, self-esteem programs fail to provide coping strategies for poor performance. Since most people fail on the way to success, or fail more often then they succeed, people need to cope with doing poorly.

Consider the case of an 8-year-old special education student originally referred for depression and social isolation. Another professional had taught him to play basketball and had taught him that he was special because he had done well at basketball. The boy was fine for several days, until he bragged about his athletic skills to some neighborhood peers. When they then trounced him in a game, he became depressed. Teaching children that they are worthwhile people even when others outperform them or when they perform poorly, is most important for working with many of the exceptional children we encounter.

As mentioned, each of the irrational beliefs can be applied to oneself, others, or the world. Ellis proposed that irrational beliefs directed toward the self often result in depression, anxiety, obsessiveness, self-hatred, and even suicide. Irrational beliefs directed toward others frequently lead to feelings such as anger, contempt, and rage. Moreover, irrational beliefs about the conditions of the world can lead to depression, anger, and dysfunctional behaviors such as procrastination and addiction (Bernard, 1995).

Table 8.3 presents examples of common referral problems of children and adolescents, their behavioral and emotional consequences, and corresponding irrational beliefs (Griger & Boyd, 1987).

### Research Support

Scores of studies have correlated irrational beliefs to measures of emotional disturbance. However, there has been little research to specifically test Ellis's revised theory, that demandingness is the core irrational belief from which all the others are derived and that emotional disturbance can be explained best by demands people put on themselves, others, and the world. The empirical evidence does not totally support the revised theory. It has been found that subscales of frustration intolerance (FI) and self-downing beliefs correlate more strongly with emotional disturbance than subscales of demandingness or awfulizing beliefs. Also, several factor analyses have indicated that there are two distinct categories of irrational beliefs. These studies have found that demandingness, awfulizing, and frustration intolerance items factor

**Table 8.3.  Referral problems, behavioral consequences, emotional consequences, and corresponding irrational beliefs**

| Problem | Behavioral "C" | Emotional "C" | Irrational Beliefs |
|---|---|---|---|
| Withdrawal, avoidance | Avoidance of people and tasks, shyness, and dependency | Anxiety and fears<br><br>Feelings of inferiority<br><br>Depression (secondarily) | I must do well and be approved of. I must avoid getting noticed at all costs, because if I try, I will fail and be disapproved of. That would be terrible and I would be worthless. So long as I can be left alone and nothing is demanded of me, my worthlessness will not be obvious and I won't feel worthless. |
| Perfectionism | Compulsiveness, over-achieving, overdriving to excel | Feeling okay when he or she succeeds<br><br>Anxiety before performance<br><br>Depression, guilt, self-downing when he or she fails | I must do well in order to get attention and be approved of or else I will be lost and worthless. I must always do my very best. My performance at school and everywhere else should always be competent.<br><br>It's terrible to do poorly and doing poorly shows what an incompetent person I am.<br><br>If I don't totally and always do well, then I'm totally and always a failure. |
| Attention seeking | Acting as the model child, cute, charming, acting as the class clown, showing off, pestiness, helpless-ness, dependency | Anxiety<br><br>Feelings of inferiority<br><br>Depression (secondarily) | I must be noticed at all costs or else I am lost and worthless. I must be loved and approved of, all the time. It's awful to be unnoticed or unacknowledged. |
| Power struggles | Disobedience, stubborn-ness, uncooperativness, argumentativeness, "Smart-mouthing," hos-tility toward students who do not agree | Anger<br><br>Jealousy | The only way I can feel like somebody is to defy pressure and do what I want. I must win, because if I don't I am a loser. People must acknowledge that I am right. I must be on top. People should give me attention and approval by making me No. 1. |
| Procrastination | Laziness, sloppiness, self-indulgence, grousing and griping, noncompliance with assignments | Frustration<br><br>Self-pity<br><br>Resentment | I shouldn't have to work so hard to get things done. I can't stand to do these boring things necessary to reach some goal. It's too hard and it takes too much work. I can't stand to delay pleasure. Because I don't like it and it's not fair, I shouldn't have to do it. It's easier and better to take one's pleasure now rather than deny oneself and get pleasure later. |
| Revenge | Bullying, passive/aggres-sive noncompliance, stealing, aggression | Anger<br><br>Resentment<br><br>Jealousy | People should/ought must do right by me. People who do wrong by me are wicked and blameworthy and deserve to be punished and to suffer. Those who do not give me attention deserve to be hurt. I must feel significant, and the only way I can feel significant is to hurt others as much as I feel hurt. |
| Depression | Lethargic behavior, exces-sive sleeping, significant loss or increase of appe-tite, withdrawing, verbal expressions of helpless-ness and hopelessness | Guilt<br><br>Depression | I did a bad thing and I'm a bad person for having done it. I must be totally competent and loved, or else I'm worthless. This is a hassle; it's too much of a hassle; I can't stand it. Poor me. |

together, as Ellis had assumed they would. Thus, demandingness, awfulizing, and FI may be different aspects of the same psychological construct. Items reflecting negative self-ratings loaded on as separate factors by themselves (Bernard, 1988; DiGiuseppe et al., 1988; see Kendall et al., 1995 for a review). There have been no direct tests of the idea that demandingness is the core from which the other irrational beliefs emerge.

### Primary and Secondary Disturbance

REBT posits two types of disturbances that can result from irrational thinking. Primary emotional-behavioral disturbance arises when one thinks irrationally about concrete activating events. Secondary emotional-behavioral disturbance occurs when one thinks irrationally about one's primary emotional-behavioral disturbance. That is, the emotional consequence of a primary ABC becomes an activating event for a new ABC. Since people not only think about events they experience but also reflect on their own cognitions, emotions, and behaviors, irrational beliefs about one's own thoughts, feelings, and actions often lead to secondary emotional disturbance. People can get depressed about being depressed, anxious about their anxiety, and angry at themselves for getting angry. Secondary emotional disturbance helps to maintain one's disturbed state. Considerable research exists to support the importance of this secondary emotional disturbance in the areas of anxiety disorder, and especially panic disorder. Barlow (1991) has gone so far as to state that all emotional disorders may be secondary disturbance. He believes that people often produce secondary disturbance after they experience nondisturbed emotions because of frustration intolerance over experiencing the nondisturbed emotions.

When a secondary disturbance does exists, attempts to intervene at the level of the primary disturbance usually fail. Whenever people think about how they upset themselves or what strategies they could use to overcome their primary disturbance, they elicit their catastrophic thinking or frustration intolerance and bring on the secondary disturbance. REBT suggests that therapists treat the secondary disturbance first, and when finished, treat the primary disturbance (Dryden & DiGiuseppe, 1990; Ellis & Dryden, 1987; Walen et al., 1992). Several other therapists have come to similar conclusions and recommend that clients learn to tolerate their emotional disturbance as a means of preventing further escalation of their problems (Hayes, McCurry, Afan, & Wilson, 1991; Jacobson, 1992).

## THERAPEUTIC STRATEGIES AND TECHNIQUES

### Unconditional Acceptance

In the early days of psychotherapy, Ellis and Rogers (Ellis, 1959, 1962, 1994b; Rogers, 1957) had many debates on the necessary and sufficient conditions for behavior change. Rogers believed that unconditional acceptance of the client by the therapists was *necessary and sufficient* for change to occur. Ellis (1959) disagreed. He believed that unconditional acceptance of the client was *neither necessary nor sufficient.* However, he believed that it was highly facilitative of change.

Ellis (1959, 1962) believed that unconditional acceptance is not necessary for change since many people change without it or even without therapy. People are capable of changing on their own by bibliotherapy, modeling, or other experiences. It is only recently that Prochaska, DiClemente, and Norcross (1992) have focused their work on how people change without therapy. They have found that a "relationship" is only one of many processes that can lead to change. Ellis believed that unconditional acceptance is not sufficient for change because people who are unconditionally accepted must draw some conclusions about themselves based on the experiences of being accepted. There are many disturbed people who experience unconditional acceptance and have not changed. Once people deduce something about themselves because they have received unconditional acceptance, they need to rehearse it, because they will still have the same old well-rehearsed belief that they are worthless. Some people develop self-acceptance without the help of others.

Many people have the misconception that REBT disregards the therapeutic relationship, and many books and chapters on REBT have spent little time discussing the issue. Ellis (1962, 1994b) did and has always acknowledged that unconditional acceptance of the client is a crucial part of therapy. Research indicates that therapists practicing REBT at Ellis's Institute establish excellent therapeutic relationships with their clients (DiGiuseppe & Leaf, 1993). Ellis's theory places a major emphasis on the role of self-devaluation as a cause of psychopathology, and attaining unconditional self-acceptance (USA) as a means of becoming emotionally adjusted. One place where clients can learn USA is from their therapists' acceptance of them.

REBT maintains that therapists' acceptance of their client is a crucial part of therapy for several reasons. First, it provides a model for clients that their worth as people is not linked to any specific behavior. Second, the therapists' acceptance of clients may be necessary if clients are to reveal their secret emotions, acts, or thoughts to the therapists. Also, clients are much more likely to listen to their therapists and follow their advice if they are accepted by their therapists. Third, therapists also coach their clients to practice new ways of thinking and feeling about themselves.

*All therapists, to be effective, need to learn how to communicate acceptance to their clients, and to develop an accepting attitude toward all humans, which will enable them to actually feel acceptance toward their clients.*

This behavioral and emotional skill is difficult to maintain when treating narcissistic, defiant, aggressive, or conduct-disordered children and adolescents. Often therapists are confronted by children and adolescents who do despicable acts. How do we accept them? Recently, I treated a 15-year-old sex offender who chose kindergartners as his victims. The client enjoys and desires sexual contact with these very young victims. Will accepting him lead him to falsely conclude that his therapist approves of his performing such behaviors? If the therapist takes a strong disapproving stand, will the boy reveal any of his thoughts and desires to the therapist again? These are the dilemmas that one faces daily in therapy. REBT (Walen et al., 1992) has adopted a view that has also been proposed in psychoanalytic therapy (Sherwood, 1990). It is important for therapists to acknowledge and accept clients with their aberrant desires. However, it is also important to express disapproval of acting on the desires, while accepting clients even though they have acted on such desires. Developing such attitudes toward humans may be a prerequisite for becoming an effective therapist.

## Practical versus Emotional Solutions

REBT makes a distinction between practical and emotional solutions (Ellis, 1994b; Walen et al., 1992). A practical solution involves a problem-solving or skill-development approach that helps the client change the activating event. An emotional solution attempts to change the client's emotional reaction to the activating event. Practical solutions try to change the A's; emotional solutions try to change the C's. For example, consider the case of a professional treating a middle school child, Serge, who was disrespectful and angry at a teacher. Serge thought the teacher disliked him because of the way he talked and the style of his clothes, which based on Serge's reports, seemed accurate. Serge regaled in "hip-hop" garb and slang, and the teacher made it clear that she found this unacceptable. The professional's strategy was to teach Serge to behave toward the teacher in a manner that would endear Serge to the teacher. This was a practical solution designed to change the activating event, the teacher's disapproval of Serge. REBT recommends that therapists seek an emotional solution first, for reasons that are apparent in the preceding case. Often there are not practical solutions, and clients must "bite-the-bullet" and learn to cope with harsh realities. Second, clients are more likely to learn problem-solving and behavioral skills after they have calmed down. In the case of Serge, REBT would have recommended an emotional solution for several reasons. First, Serge may never succeed in getting the teacher to like him and may always have to deal with her rejection of him. Second, it is hard to improve your relationship with someone at whom you are angry. Serge would be more likely to endear himself to the teacher if he gave up his anger.

Some trainees misinterpret REBT's strategy of seeking the emotional solution first to mean that REBT only works on the emotional solution. They think that helping clients achieve the practical solution is selling out the stoic philosophical roots of REBT. However, one of REBT's goals is to have clients lead happier lives. People can do this best if they can tolerate and handle hassle. It is not consistent with the theory that people should tolerate frustration when they don't have to. Helping clients change their A's is an acceptable goal of therapy. However, REBT recommends that this intervention be done after an emotional solution, in case there is no practical solution, and because clients are best able to pursue practical solutions when they are not disturbed.

## Philosophical/Elegant versus Inelegant Solutions

REBT believes that therapists will best achieve emotional solutions by changing clients' core irrational beliefs instead of changing clients' perceptions or automatic thoughts. Ellis refers to such interventions as "the elegant solution." Ellis' considers the philosophical/elegant solution preferable because it provides a coping strategy that clients can use to deal with a wide number of similar and possibly more negative activating events. Philosophical solutions promote more generalizable change across a wider array of situations.

REBT recommends that therapists avoid interventions focused at changing perception through reattributions or reframing, or correcting negative automatic thoughts. Ellis calls such interventions "inelegant." They are considered inelegant because they do not require a major philosophical change and may provide a coping strategy for a particular activating event but not for a wide range of situations. Also, the reattribution, reframing, or changing of the automatic thought may be inconsistent with reality. That is, clients' perceptions and inferences about reality may be accurate. Table 8.4 identifies the interventions for each type of hypothesized mediating cognition in the case of Serge, the angry middle school child mentioned earlier.

**Table 8.4.   Practical, emotional, inelegant and elegant solutions in the case of Serge**

| Construct | Example from the Case of Serge | Intervention | REBT Label |
|---|---|---|---|
| Social skills deficit to change the "A" | Serge's disrespectful speech to the teacher. | Model, coaching, and rehearsal of new skills | A practical solution |
| Social skills deficit to change the "A" | Serge's lack of prosocial speech to endear him to the teacher. | Model, coaching, and rehearsal of new skills | A practical solution |
| Reduce anger by reframing | Serge thinks, "She only acts that way because she dislikes me." | Change Serge's thinking to: "She is being tough with me to make me a better person." | An emotional solution but an inelegant solution |
| Reduce anger by reattribution | Serge thinks "This teacher hates everything about me and all kids like me. She's prejudiced and always will be." A global, stable, external attribution. | Change the attribution to a specific, or temporary attribution. "She is just having a bad time and is taking it out on me. She will get over it." | An emotional solution but an inelegant solution |
| Reduce anger by changing Serge's automatic thoughts | Serge thinks, "She hates me and thinks I am a trouble-maker. I can never please her!" | Challenge this belief by having Serge identify times he has not acted hatefully and times he has pleased her. | An emotional solution but an inelegant solution |
| Improve Serge's problem-solving skills. | Serge does not think that his behavior alienates his teacher; he is unaware of strategies that will get the teacher to like him. | Teach Serge to anticipate what the consequences of his actions will be and to generate alternative ways to achieve his goals | A practical solution, and an inelegant emotional solution |
| Reduce anger by changing Serge's core irrational beliefs. | Serge thinks. "People must always show me respect; and if they don't they are against me and must pay." | Change this to a rational belief such as "I would like to be respected by people but if they do not respect me, I can handle it and will not let them get me upset or get me out of control." | An emotional solution and an elegant solution |

The first three cognitive interventions, reframing, reattribution, and challenging the automatic thoughts are labeled as inelegant. In each of these, the cognitive intervention attempts to change Serge's thinking to believe that the teacher is not as negative toward him as he believes. The reframing ascribes positive motives to her actions. The reattribution presents the problem as temporary, and challenging the automatic thought gets him to reevaluate whether the teacher behaves as negatively toward him as he thinks. Each of these interventions assumes that Serge has overestimated the teacher's dislike of him. Each may work if Serge has overestimated the teacher's dislike of him. However, what if Serge is correct? Suppose the teacher does feels prejudiced against him because of his dress, his speech, his ethnic heritage, his taste in music, or for any other reason? These solutions could invalidate Serge's perception and will have failed to provide him with a coping strategy for the continuing disapproval from the teacher.

The social problem-solving intervention helps Serge achieve the practical solution, and we know will result in less emotional disturbance since Serge may entertain the idea that the "A" can change. However, the teacher may be so negative toward Serge that no actions will be successful. REBT almost always uses the elegant strategy. After Serge accepts that the teacher may never like him, the REBT hypothesis is that Serge will do even better problem-solving if he is less upset. He will also be able to cope if the alternative solutions fail.

If Serge has overestimated the teacher's dislike of him, the elegant solution will work. And according to REBT and Figure 8.1, a change in the core irrational beliefs will result in changing his perceptions, attributions, and automatic thoughts if they are in fact incorrect. It can also result in improved problem-solving skills.

REBT does not say that the inelegant cognitive interventions will not work. Rather, Ellis believes that they are not philosophical. They do not provide coping strategies across a wide range of stimuli. They could be incorrect and fail to acknowledge clients' negative reality, and thereby fail to provide clients with a coping strategy to their negative reality. REBT acknowledges that all clients may not achieve the philosophical solution, and advocates that the inelegant interventions be used in such cases (Ellis, 1977, 1980b, 1994b; Walen et al., 1992).

## The Three Insights

During therapy, therapists continually work at helping their clients develop three insights that will improve their adjustment (Dryden & DiGiuseppe, 1990; Ellis & Dryden, 1987).

**Insight 1.** Past or present activating events do not cause one's disturbance. It is beliefs one has about them that lead to disturbance.

**Insight 2.** Regardless of how one learned to think what one thinks, and regardless of how compelling these beliefs have been, one continues to believe in them now because of one's own reindoctrination, rehearsal, or acceptance of these beliefs.

**Insight 3.** Insight alone is usually not sufficient to change one's overrehearsed irrational thinking. People usually change irrational dysfunctional thinking through repeated, effortful attempts to challenge these beliefs, construct new ones, and re-hearse these new rational beliefs.

## The Thirteen Steps of REBT

Dryden and DiGiuseppe (1990) identified 13 steps that normally occur in a REBT psy-chotherapy session. They recommend that therapists new to the system learn and fol-low these steps to avoid mistakes and ensure they perform all the crucial aspects of the model. Some trainees keep a checklist to remind them of the steps and to guide them through a session. Table 8.5 presents the 13 steps in a session note format that can be copied from this book and used to record the specific information revealed at each step. All the steps apply to the treatment of children and adolescents, even if the tech-niques used to accomplish the step may differ across age groups.

The first step is to ask clients what problems they want to discuss in the session. Sometimes clients present problems that are unrelated to topics discussed in previous sessions, but mostly they present examples of the primary referral problem. The second step is to agree on the goal of the session. Clients may present entirely new issues un-related to the issues discussed in previous sessions; therapists may wish to continue with ongoing topics before switching to a new topic. As a result, there may not be agreement on what to cover in the session and, before continuing, agreement is needed. Also, clients often see the goal as changing the "A" and therapists see it as changing the "C." Because REBT recommends working on emotional problems first, the agree-ment on the goals aspect of the therapeutic alliance may break down. A consensus on what problem to tackle is crucial for the session to continue. Steps 3, 4, and 5 involve assessing the "C," assessing the "A" and assessing for secondary emotional distur-bance, respectively. At Step 6, the therapist teaches the client the "B→C" connection (see Vernon, 1989a, 1989b for techniques).

Step 7 is to assess a client's irrational beliefs. Remember that irrational beliefs are tacit, unconscious, schematic cognitions. They are not experienced in the stream of consciousness, although they are available to our consciousness. Most therapists ask clients, "What were you thinking when you got upset?" Such questions are likely to elicit automatic thoughts, not irrational beliefs. DiGiuseppe (1990, 1991a) suggests that there are two primary strategies to assess irrational beliefs. The first is "inference chaining." Automatic thoughts are inference that people draw from the perceptions they make, and which they are prepared to make by the core schema or irrational beliefs they hold. Follow the logic of the inferences and one can uncover the core irra-tional belief. Inference chaining involves a series of follow-up questions to the auto-matic thoughts. These questions ask clients to hypothesize that their automatic thought was true. If it were true, what would happen next, or what would it mean to them? Clients usually respond with other automatic thoughts. The therapist continues with the same type of question until an irrational belief, a "must," an awfulizing statement, an "I can't stand it," or a global evaluation is uncovered. Inference chains will keep clients emotionally aroused, because you are getting closer to their real core issue. De-spite the increase in emotional arousal, clients feel relieved to get their core beliefs out in the open. And this is usually a bonding experience between the therapist and client.

**Table 8.5.   The thirteen steps of rational emotive behavior therapy in session note format**

REBT Session Note and Guide

Client: _____   Session #: _____   Date: _____

Persons Present: _____

Step 1:  Ask client for the problem. _____
_____

Step 2:  Define and agree on the goals of therapy. _____
_____

Step 3:  Assess the emotional and behavioral "C." _____
_____

Step 4:  Assess the "A." _____
_____

Step 5:  Assess the existence of any secondary emotional problems. _____
_____

Step 6:  Teach the B → C connection. _____
_____

Step 7:  Assess the irrational beliefs. _____
_____

Step 8:  Connect the irrational beliefs to the disturbed emotions, and connect the rational beliefs to the nondisturbed emotion. _____
_____

Step 9:  Dispute irrational beliefs: Circle all that you have done: *logical, empirical, heuristic, design new rational alternative beliefs, didactic, Socratic, metaphorical, humorous.* _____
_____

Step 10:  Prepare your client to deepen his or her conviction in the rational belief. _____
_____

Step 11:  Encourage your client to put new learning into practice with homework. _____
_____

Step 12:  Check homework assignments. _____
_____

Step 13:  Facilitate the working through process. _____
_____
_____

The second primary strategy is based on the awareness that not all clients are capable of putting their irrational beliefs into language because as tacit, schematic cognitions they are not stored in verbal memory. DiGiuseppe (1990, 1991a) suggests that all therapists develop hypotheses about their clients' irrational beliefs. Rather than let clients struggle to try and become aware of their core irrational beliefs, therapists can offer hypotheses to clients. To do this effectively, therapists should (a) be sure to use suppositional language, (b) ask the client for feedback on the correctness of the hypotheses, (c) be prepared to be wrong, (d) revise the hypotheses based on the responses of the client.

The next steps in the sequence are to link the irrational beliefs with the clients' emotional disturbance (Step 8), and to begin disputing the irrational beliefs (Step 9). Disputing irrational beliefs is the most difficult task in REBT. DiGiuseppe (1991b) has presented a detailed explanation of the disputing process by dissecting many hours of Ellis's videotapes doing therapy. One can dispute an irrational belief by challenging its logic, by testing its empirical accuracy, and by evaluating the functionality of the consequences that follow from holding it. Also, one needs to propose an alternative rational idea, and challenge it with the same arguments to assess whether it fares any better. In addition to adjusting the type of argument, DiGiuseppe (1991b) suggests that therapists can vary the rhetorical style of their disputing. One can use didactic (direct teaching) strategies, Socratic strategies, metaphors, or humor. Kopec, Beal, and DiGiuseppe, (1994) have created a grid with each cell representing a type of argument and a type of rhetorical style. They recommend that therapists generate the disputing statements for each cell in the grid before each therapy session. Their data suggest that this activity increases trainees' self-efficacy in disputing. To better learn disputing techniques, the reader can try this activity for several weeks across several clients. Another important component of disputing is the use of imagery. Therapists and clients can construct scenes of the client approaching the activating event and rehearsing the new rational coping statement, experiencing adaptive emotions, and behaving appropriately.

Step 10 in the model involves deepening clients' conviction in their rational beliefs. This is accomplished through continued disputing, and also by defining how they would behave differently if they actually held the new rational belief (Step 11), and agreeing to actual homework between sessions to achieve their goals (Step 12). Although REBT uses the term *homework* with adults, it is best to use a term like practice or rehearsal for school-age clients, since homework is something they naturally resist. Homework could include having them complete REBT homework sheets that guide clients through disputing an irrational belief, the rehearsing of imagery, or engaging in a behavioral activity. Step 13, the final, is to review other examples of activating events the client has been upset about to promote generalization.

## INDIVIDUAL PSYCHOTHERAPY WITH CHILDREN AND ADOLESCENTS

Early in his career, Ellis adapted REBT to children in The Living School, an educational program within the Institute. To many people's surprise, REBT can be used with children from as early as age 5, with a variety of emotional problems. Techniques differ for children between the ages of 5 and 11, and adolescents 12 to 18 years old. The most common objection to using such a cognitively oriented therapy with children and adolescents is that children are not cognitively mature enough to engage in this type of discourse. Developmental considerations are important. Several authors have independently suggested (Bernard & Joyce, 1984; DiGiuseppe & Bernard, 1983; Vernon, 1989a) that children who have reached Piaget's (1963) concrete operations stage will be able to benefit from disputing. Research (Casey & Berman, 1985) has confirmed that cognitive interventions are more efficacious for children over 8 years old than under age 8, the approximate age when children enter this stage. It is important to remember that children who have not yet reached the concrete operations phase (those under 8 years old), will have difficulty with the logic of disputing and with thinking about their thinking. For these children, therapists are recommended to use treatments that focus on concrete skills, such as problem-solving (Spivack, Platt, & Shure, 1976; Spivack & Shure, 1974) and rehearsing rational coping statements (DiGiuseppe, 1977; Meichenbaum, 1971).

Children are referred because they are disturbing not because they are disturbed. As a result, most children attend therapy against their will. As a result, children often have not yet decided that they want to change. Therefore, discussing the goals and tasks of therapy is more critical to the establishment of a therapeutic alliance with children than with adults. It is particularly important to consider the concepts of stages of change and processes of change outlined by Prochaska and DiClemente (1981). They propose that people pass through a series of stages of attitudes about change. These include the precontemplative stage, where the person does not want to change; the contemplative stage, where the person is thinking he or she might change; the action stage, where a person tries to change; and the maintenance stage where a person consolidates gains and attempts to keep the new behaviors. Prochaska and DiClemente (1981) proposed that the type of therapy needs to match clients' stage of change. REBT is an action-oriented therapy, designed for people in the action stage of change. Since most children and adolescents arrive in the precontemplative stage, the therapists must establish the agreement on the goals and tasks of therapy to build the therapeutic alliance, before using such an active approach.

DiGiuseppe (1995; DiGiuseppe & Bernard, 1983; DiGiuseppe & Jilton, 1996; Walen et al., 1992) has presented a cognitive behavioral approach to establish the therapeutic alliance in children and adolescents or adults who arrive in therapy in the precontemplative stage (see Table 8.6). Identifying and challenging one's irrational beliefs only makes sense if one holds some prerequisite beliefs. The elements of this motivational syllogism are as follows: My present emotion is dysfunctional. There is an alternative acceptable emotional script for this type of activating event. It is better for me to give up the dysfunction emotion and work toward feeling the alternative one. My beliefs cause my emotions, therefore I will work at changing my beliefs to change my emotions. Establishing all these beliefs will help motivate a child or adolescent to engage in the REBT process. This model facilitates agreement on the goals of therapy and moving clients to the action stage of change. Therapists need to assess each child's and

**Table 8.6.    The motivational syllogism to establish agreement on the goals and tasks of therapy**

Prerequisite beliefs to disputing irrational beliefs

1. *Insight 1.* My present emotion is dysfunctional. *Technique:* Through Socratic questions, get the client to see how the present emotional reaction is dysfunctional.

2. *Insight 2.* There is an alternative acceptable emotional goal. *Technique:* Through reviewing acceptable models, help the client see that there are alternative, and more adaptive, emotional scripts.

3. *Insight 3.* It is better for me to give up my dysfunctional emotional reaction and replace it with the alternative emotional script. *Technique:* Use Socratic questions to get the client to imagine feeling the new emotional script and review the possible consequences of experiencing the new emotion. This should accomplish agreement on the goals of therapy.

4. *Insight 4.* My beliefs influence my emotions; therefore, it is appropriate to examine and change my thinking. *Techniques:* Teach the B → C connection. This should accomplish agreement on the tasks of therapy.

adolescent's stage of change and agreement on the goals of therapy before proceeding with any REBT interventions. If the child or adolescent has not reached the action stage and does not desire to change, techniques outlined by DiGiuseppe, and Jilton or other similar techniques like motivational interviewing (Miller & Rollnick, 1991) could be used to accomplish this task.

The models proposed by DiGiuseppe and Jilton (1996) involve asking clients to assess the consequences of their emotional and behavioral responses in a Socratic fashion. This helps them identify the negative consequences for their emotional disturbance and behavior. Next, the therapists presents alternative emotional reactions that are culturally acceptable to each client. Because people learn emotional scripts from their families, and learn that some emotional scripts are acceptable to their cultural group, it is possible that the disturbed child or adolescent has not changed because he or she cannot conceptualize an acceptable emotional script to experience in place of the disturbed emotion. Therapists need to explore with the client alternative emotional reactions that are culturally acceptable. Next, therapists need to help clients make the connection that the alternative script is more advantageous to the client.

## Individual Therapy with Children

A typical therapy session with a preadolescent child might involve some variations on the 13-step model and could be organized as follows:

1. Since children do not always remember what has happened during the week, the session may start by meeting with the parents and child to talk about the progress of the past week.

2. Together, the therapist and child plan the session agenda.

3. The therapist reviews the homework assignment from the past week, sets session goals, discusses activities to be used to reach session goals, and discusses the consequences of modifying disturbed behaviors and emotions.

4. The client is helped to generate alternate emotional scripts, that include new ways to feel and act.

5. Next the therapist will teach the B→C; and explore the beliefs that lead to the disturbed emotion.

6. The client and therapist challenge the irrational beliefs and explore rational alternative beliefs.

7. The client and therapist agree on homework assignment for the coming week and review the homework assignment with the parents (DiGiuseppe, 1994).

Therapists explain and demonstrate how thoughts can cause feelings, and that certain thoughts (irrational beliefs) produce disturbed emotions, whereas other thoughts (rational beliefs) lead to nondisturbed emotions. Some children may have difficulty distinguishing between disturbed and nondisturbed emotions, and therefore, the therapist may need to teach them to identify and label various emotions and then to be able to distinguish between those that are helpful and those that are hurtful. Further, the therapist teaches that thoughts can be changed to produce nondisturbed feelings. The therapist helps the child practice distinguishing between disturbed and nondisturbed cognitions and emotions. Additionally, the child practices disputing irrational beliefs and replacing them with more rational thoughts. Specific techniques used to help the client practice these skills include modeling, role-playing, and imagery, as well as homework involving the parents.

REBT with preadolescent children is concrete and usually involves activities and hands-on materials that teach the concepts. Many of these activities are presented in Bernard and Joyce (1984), Knaus (1974), and Vernon (1989a). With younger children, not yet capable of disputing, the therapist teaches them to use rational self-talk to deal with the problem situation whenever it arises. The child practices rational coping statements, based on Meichenbaum's self-instructional guidelines. (See DiGiuseppe, 1977, for a case study.)

## Individual Psychotherapy with Adolescents

Developmentally, adolescents are very concerned with forming their identities. They can often be oppositional and refuse to heed the advice of people from a different generation. They are somewhat egocentric and believe that their problems are unique to themselves or their generation. They are also often sent to therapy against their will, and arrive in the preoperational stage of change. With adolescents, it is particularly important to ensure that the therapist has agreement on the goals and tasks of therapy, and to explain to the client how the tasks will improve their current situation. Therefore, we recommend therapists go through the steps of the motivational syllogism before the discussion of each new problem and before the use of any intervention.

Compared to working with children, the therapist can focus more on providing insight, and can expect to engage in both elegant and inelegant disputing. It is important though, not to assume that the adolescent will necessarily follow a logical argument and therefore can engage in disputing irrational beliefs. Although adolescents have achieved greater cognitive development, some research suggests that REBT is more effective with preadolescent children (DiGiuseppe & Kassinove, 1977). Adolescents are developmentally mature enough that the therapist can use all the strategies and cognitions that have been proposed with adults. However, adolescents know it all. Therefore, they appear to do better with Socratic disputing than with didactic interventions. Clinical experience suggests they respond best to functional disputes of their irrational beliefs rather than logical ones. Adolescents, as a whole, are idealistic. They often believe that what is good or righteous must be. Empirical disputes aimed at demonstrating that reality is not as it should be also seem not as helpful. Again functional disputes appear to work best. Time will eventually teach adolescents to distinguish between the real and ideal world. Also, adolescents overvalue peer acceptance. It is helpful to have an adolescent recall rational beliefs that have been endorsed by a peer, or to search the lyrics of popular songs for rational messages. These techniques increase the likelihood the idea will be adopted.

## GROUP PROCEDURES WITH CHILDREN AND ADOLESCENTS

Ellis has long advocated Rational Emotive Behavior Group Therapy (REBGT). The group process, or focusing on how group members relate to each other, is not the primary focus of REBGT. However, conflicts between members that develop are important topics for discussion because they often reflect the child's ability to relate to peers, which is often a reason for referral.

Group therapy is usually recommended for financial reasons. Administrators like therapists to provide group therapy because more clients are treated for the same hour of therapist times. It is important that therapists use group therapy for clinical rather than economic reasons. REBGT appears most helpful for people with social difficulties. The group forces them to confront their social fears and the exposure to others helps build social skills. It is also helpful to place clients in groups after a brief period of individual therapy. The group experiences help them overlearn the skills of controlling their emotions, after they have gotten a good start from individual therapy. Clinical experience suggests that children with disruptive behavior problems do poorly in groups. They are primarily reinforced for their disruptive behavior by peer attention that the therapist cannot control. Therefore, the group can become uncontrollable. Younger children with disruptive behavior problems, 7 years and below, can be treated in groups if the therapist has a reinforcement system for cooperation and has access to rewards that are of interest to that age level.

Two formats can be used in REBGT. With the open-ended format, each group member takes a turn presenting a problem on which he or she wants to receive help. Therapists and group members help that client solve the problem using REBT principle. As the group continues, each client learns from the problems he or she presents, from the advice and comments of the therapist and the other group members, and from observing how the other group members are helped. With this format, therapists need to be aware of the clock to ensure that one client does not take too much time in any session, and that all clients get equal opportunity to present their problems. Clients tend to offer more practical solutions than emotional solutions in the group. A discussion of philosophical solutions is unlikely to occur unless therapists steer the discussions in that direction.

A second format is the homogeneous group. Here all the group members have a similar problem. Therapists can present a series of discussions and exercises related to the problem. In each session, the therapist leads the members in a discussion and/or exercises, and makes sure that all members participate and learn to apply the new skills to their individualized problem.

With adults, REBGT has been practiced with members with homogeneous and heterogeneous problems. However, with children it appears best to group the members by the presenting problem and by the child's age. Mixing children with too many different problems may make it difficult for them to focus on issues that do not relate to them. REBGT employs a psychoeducational model. Having children who differ in age by more than three years also presents too great a range of developmental skills for the therapist to address all the members' issues and to keep the attention of all the members. Much of the material that has been developed for classroom applications of REBT can and is used by psychotherapists in REBGT.

## CLASSROOM AND EDUCATIONAL APPLICATIONS

From its inception, Ellis considered REBT to be a psychoeducational procedure that could be taught to people in workshops, classrooms, and groups. From 1971 to 1975, the Institute for Advanced Study in Rational Psychotherapy ran an elementary school in the building with a curriculum that taught rational thinking as a preventive mental health program along with the standard academic subjects. During this time, the Institute staff developed exercises and classroom activities to teach various thinking skills. These activities resulted in several syllabi (Knaus, 1974) which included well-specified activities that teachers, guidance counselors or therapists could use to educate children in the ABC's. These original materials served as models for further generations of such manuals including the more detailed *Thinking, Feeling and Behaving* classroom/group manuals by Dr. Ann Vernon (1989a, 1989b). These syllabi focus on specific emotional problems children have and lessons that teach the following skills: (a) developing critical thinking skills; (b) distinguishing between thoughts and feelings; (c) distinguishing between opinions, facts, and hypotheses; (d) linking thoughts and feelings, the B→C connection; (e) identifying ideas that lead to emotional upset; (f) distinguishing between rational and irrational beliefs; (g) challenging irrational beliefs; and (h) specific modules on self-worth versus self-esteem, low frustration tolerance, demandingness, and catastrophizing. Although these materials were designed for educational purposes, they make excellent activities to use in groups.

The most comprehensive educational REBT program is Dr. Michael Bernard's *You Can Do It*. This multimedia presentation includes an excellent, professionally produced video that focuses on the cognitive skills and attitudes necessary to succeed academically, and the irrational beliefs that block achievement. In addition to these videos, the *You Can Do It* series includes student workbooks, teachers' manuals to guide discussions, and accompanying visual overheads. All the materials are designed with appealing cartoon characters.

Dr. Bernard (1990) developed an REBT stress management program group for teachers. The program includes a teachers' irrational belief scale that can be used as a pretest to identify each teacher's irrational beliefs. The scale has been shown to discriminate between teachers who are on disability because of emotional stress and well-functioning teachers. His REBT stress management syllabus helps the participants learn the ABC's and identify the beliefs that led to their job stress. It also teaches strategies to dispute irrational beliefs, and how to develop rational alternative beliefs.

Bernard and DiGiuseppe (1993) have attempted to adapt REBT to consultation activities in the school. Most models of psychological consultation assume that the consultant may have some expert knowledge that the consultee can use. By building a collaborative relationship and problem-solving set, the consultant is able to suggest information or strategies that the consultee is free to accept or reject. Most models of organizational, educational, behavioral, and instructional consultation assume that the consultee only needs new information. Like mental health consultation, REBT theory suggests that teachers, parents, principals, and administers can be blocked from seeing or implementing solutions to problems by their own emotional disturbance. Bernard and DiGiuseppe suggest that consultants evaluate the consultees emotional responses to the problems and their thinking. Often consultees are stuck because they rigidly adhere to ideas about how things must be done and respond emotionally to problems instead of seeking solutions. The REBT-oriented consultant will look for such reactions in consultees and Socratically explore the consultees' emotional reactions and rigid thinking. The first task of the consultant is to help consultees become aware of their emotional reactions and have them agree to discuss their feelings and thinking. Chapters in Bernard and DiGiuseppe apply this model to working with teachers, parents, and administrators around instructional and organizational issues.

## PARENTAL AND FAMILY INVOLVEMENT IN THERAPY

Parents can become involved in REBT sessions in several ways. First, they can be the primary targets of intervention to overcome their own emotional disturbance that interferes with their parenting. Research has shown that parents' emotional disturbance is the primary reason adults fail to engage in correct parenting practices (Dix, 1991) and fail to benefit from behavioral parent training programs (Dadds & McHugh, 1992). Although behavioral parent training appears to be the most successful intervention with children with externalized disorders (Kazdin, 1994), parents are unlikely to follow therapists' recommendations if their emotional disturbance about their child's behavior interferes. DiGiuseppe (1988) has proposed a sequential family therapy

**Table 8.7.    Sequence of family therapy for treatment of externalized disorders**

*Stage 1: Assessment.* Assess (a) the nature of psychopathology, (b) the developmental level of functioning, and the discriminative stimulus that elicit the problems and its reinforcers, (c) the structure of the family, (d) roles of individual members (e) who will resist? (f) emotions, skills, and cognitions of each member.

*Stage 2: Engaging parents in the therapeutic alliance.* If one parent is resistant to change use motivational interviewing or problem-solving with the motivated parent to engage the resistant parent.

*Stage 3: Behavioral Intervention.* Choosing a target behavior and reinforcers.

*Stage 4: Assessing parents' ability to carry out agreed intervention.* Assess the parents' emotions, and cognitions that may stop them from carrying out the agreed-on intervention. Possible parental interfering emotions: guilt, anger, anxiety, discomfort, anxiety. Parents' irrational beliefs: demandingness, catastrophizing, frustration intolerance, self-downing, projected frustration intolerance, condemnation of the child.

*Stage 5: Therapy on the parents.* Cognitive restructuring of the parents' irrational beliefs. Use all the techniques that one would in adult REBT to focus on the emotions and cognitions identified in the previous stage.

*Stage 6: Predict resistance.* What do the parents believe the child or others will do to sabotage their efforts? Problem-solve how they can respond to those attempts at sabotage. This will help them do it on their own after termination.

*Stage 7: Assessment of the parents' ability to follow intervention.* Imagine themselves following through. What emotions and beliefs will they have about this new action? What do they believe their emotional reactions will be to these interventions? Assess emotions and cognitions that will get in their way of following through on the intervention chosen to counteract the sabotage.

*Stage 8: Intervention with parents.* Dispute the irrational beliefs that they will experience and that could encourage them to give into the resistance.

*Stage 9: How will child respond to new action.* (a) Repeat assessment, (b) redesign interventions through collaborative problem-solving, (c) continue to assess parents' ability to carry out the new interventions, (d) continue to use cognitive restructuring to help them follow through on the planned interventions.

*Stage 10: Individual therapy for the child or adolescent.* At the beginning of each session, assess the progress the child and parents have made. If parents have followed their interventions, remain in this stage. If they have not, return to Stage 8. Use motivational syllogism to help child internalize the desirability of change and cooperation with the therapists. Use all REBT and CBT methods to reduce the undesirable target behaviors and support the desired positive changes.

model for the treatment of externalized disordered children who are unwilling to participate in individual therapy (see Table 8.7). It focuses on the following steps:

1. A thorough assessment of the child's pathology, a behavioral analysis of the eliciting stimuli and reinforcers, consequences, and family functioning.
2. Forming a therapeutic alliance with the parents.

3. Choosing a target behavior and consequences collaboratively with the parents.

4. Assessing parents' ability to carry out the interventions, including their emotional reactions and irrational beliefs.

5. Changing parents' irrational beliefs and emotions that would interfere with performing the new parenting strategies.

6. Have parents predict what resistence they expect to occur to their new parenting strategies from the identified patient or other family members, and generate solutions to confront these attempts at resistance.

7. Assess the parents' ability to follow the strategies they choose to handle the resistance, again focusing on their emotions and irrational beliefs.

8. Intervening with parents again at changing the irrational beliefs and schemata that would prevent them from handling the resistance.

9. Continuing to assess the children's progress and the parents' compliance with the behavioral skills, and modify behavior treatment plan as needed.

10. Start individual therapy with the child to internalize gains made by the behavioral intervention.

In DiGiuseppe's (1988) model, changing the parents' irrational cognitions and emotional disturbance is done to get the parents to adopt more effective parenting skills, which is necessary to accomplish the primary goal of changing the child's symptomatic behavior. However, the parents' disturbance is a crucial target of the interventions.

Huber and Baruth (1989) have integrated REBT with family systems therapy. They maintain that family systems theories require some individual psychological variables to explain how the family members maintain dysfunctional homeostasis. Huber and Baruth believe that irrational beliefs and their resulting emotional arousal lead to avoidance of change and thereby maintain the homeostasis. This model hypothesizes that family members share common irrational beliefs such as rigid rules about the roles family members must play, beliefs that certain topics must not to be discussed, beliefs that certain or all family members must behave in certain ways, or rules about how family members must react to the outside world. Many family systems therapists present similar cognitive constructs, which they call "family myths." Huber and Baruth believe that acknowledging the role of shared family cognitions and integrating systems therapy with cognitive interventions such as REBT can provide therapists with a set of skills to accomplish the cognitive elements in family disturbance. Huber and Baruth see families as a unit and work at identifying the family structure, assessing the irrational family beliefs or myths that maintain the dysfunctional family structure. They then help all family members challenge and replace the irrational family myths, and conceptualize new ways of behavior based on alternative rational family beliefs.

Parents can play a role in treatment even when the focus of therapy is changing the child. In individual therapy, parents are often unaware of the issues discussed by the therapist and child. Parents often want to be involved in their children's therapy because of their natural concern for their children's well-being. If the child agrees, if the problem does not necessarily involve a family matter the child would feel inhibited to discuss in front of the parents, and if the parents are willing, parents can play a helpful role in the child's individual therapy. Bernard and DiGiuseppe (1990) recommend four different ways that parents can become involved to improve the effectiveness of individual therapy. First, children can be given the homework assignment of describing the important points of a session to their parents, such as the B→C connection or disputes to irrational beliefs or the rational coping statements they will use when they become upset. This technique provides children with opportunities to rehearse the principle therapists want to teach, and allows the parents to feel involved with their children's treatment.

Second, parents join the therapy session. When problematic activating events or emotional upsets occur between sessions, parents usually attempt to help their children and provide advice. Sometimes parents' comments are inconsistent with the therapists' goals, or they reinforce their children's irrational thinking or are just not helpful. If parents have been present during the sessions, they can remind their children of the rational coping statements that were provided in the session or they can use the principles of REBT that they learned in session to guide their responses to their children when the child experiences problems. Again, parents who participate in this way feel good about being part of the solution and report learning how to talk to their children in ways that are helpful to their children. Some parents even report that it has helped them with their own emotional problems.

Third, parents can provide information that children often forget. Weekly therapy sessions were designed for adults. Children often fail to remember significant events that happen between sessions, thus denying therapists important information on problems children have had between sessions. When parents are present, they often remind the children of successful coping experiences that they have had that therapists can reinforce. The parents also report important activating events that children do not handle well that could be the focus of the session.

Fourth, therapists can often design homework assignments that include the parents. For example, children with social anxieties who withdraw when they are teased need to learn disputes to their fear-provoking beliefs and to learn new rational coping statements to verbal attacks by peers. Often therapists can role-play the verbal attacks in the session and the children learn to rehearse their disputes and coping statements. Therapists can enlist the parents to role-play their children's tormentors between sessions. The parent can call out a barb to the child and the child will rehearse the new cognitions as well as new social skills. Here the parent prompts rehearsal of a new response and can coach the child because of what he or she has learned in the session. Whenever and however possible, involve parents in the child's treatment.

## THE EFFICACY OF REBT

Lambert and Bergin (1994) have concluded that substantial research exists to indicate that psychotherapy is generally effective, and the effects of therapy tend to be lasting. They also believe "The differences in outcome between various forms of therapy are not as pronounced as might have been expected" (p. 181). Research in psychotherapy has evolved considerably in the past four decades. Presently, few researchers are interested in the "horse race" of determining which therapy is the most efficacious. Today, researchers are exploring the integration of different therapies to find the most efficacious mix of treatments, the number of sessions needed to achieve clinical significance, which therapist variables contribute to efficacy, and testing the role of the mediational variables assumed to cause change (Lambert & Bergin). Before committing oneself to practicing a form of therapy, a professional had better review the outcome literature to evaluate its efficacy. This should be true of REBT, because Ellis has placed such a value on the scientific method.

Smith and Glass (1977) in their original meta-analytic review of psychotherapy outcome studies, concluded that RET (as it was called then) was the second most effective psychotherapy, after systematic desensitization. Successive meta-analytic reviews failed to distinguish between narrowly defined types of therapies and categorized therapies into broader classes of cognitive-behavioral, behavioral, and psychodynamic. REBT studies have been categorized with cognitive behavior therapies. Despite its early showing by Smith and Glass, REBT has maintained a reputation of having insufficient empirical support. This view probably evolved because Ellis's career has focused on theory and practice rather than research.

DiGiuseppe, Goodman, and Nevas (1996) explored the REBT outcome research and discovered 14 previous reviews (DiGiuseppe, Miller, & Trexler, 1977; Engels, Garnefski, & Diekstra, 1993; Gossette & O'Brien, 1992, 1993; Haaga & Davison, 1989; Hajzler & Bernard, 1990; Jorm, 1989; Lyons & Woods, 1991; Mahoney, 1974; McGovern & Silverman, 1984; Oei, Hansen, & Miller, 1993; Polder, 1986; Silverman, McCarthy, & McGovern, 1992; Zettle & Hayes, 1980). Most of these have been narrative reviews; three have been meta-analyses (i.e., Engels et al., 1993; Lyons & Woods, 1991; Polder, 1986). Most have included studies of adults and children, others have focused only on adults (Gossette & O'Brien, 1992; Zettle & Hayes, 1980), and two have focused only on research with children and adolescents (Gossette & O'Brien, 1993; Hajzler & Bernard, 1990). Most reviewers have included published reviewed articles and unpublished dissertations. Others have included a majority of unpublished dissertations in their review (Gossette & O'Brien, 1992, 1993). Most have been favorable, although some others have been critical. Table 8.8 lists the reviews alphabetically by author, the year published, the range of years of the studies included, the populations reviewed, and their general conclusions.

Each review employed a different selection criterion. Over 280 studies are mentioned in these 14 reviews. However, the reviews rarely included the same studies. Only 13 studies were mentioned in 5 reviews; 3 studies were included in 6 reviews; and 124 studies were mentioned in just 1 review. DiGiuseppe et al. (1996) calculated *Kappa* coefficients for all of the possible pairs of reviews to determine the degree of agreement between any two studies to include a study from the population of available studies that covered the same time periods and other criteria used by the reviews. Reviews had very low agreement on which studies to include. Each of the 14 reviews ignored, excluded, or failed to uncover a sizable number of studies from the time period they

**Table 8.8.  Reviews of the REBT outcome literature**

| Authors | Year Published | Range of Years of Studies | Number of Studies | Focus | Conclusions |
|---|---|---|---|---|---|
| DiGiuseppe, Miller, & Trexler | 1977 | 1970–1977 | 26 | Published and unpublished studies of children and adults. | Support for RET, " . . . appear(s) generally positive 7 promising, but far from conclusive" p. 70. |
| Engels, Garnefski, & Diekstra | 1993 | 1970–1988 | 32 | Published and unpublished studies of children and adults. | "RET on the whole was effective, compared with placebo and no treatment. Its effects were maintained over time, and it produced a delayed treatment effect with regard to behavioral outcome criteria" p. 1088. |
| Gossette & O'Brien | 1992 | 1970–1990 | 85 | Published and unpublished studies of adults. | "RET was effective in 25% of comparisons" p. 9 RET results in " . . . a decreased score on scales of irrationality. . . . a parallel decrease in self reported emotional distress. Other measures, noticeably behavior, were insensitive to RET. . . .RET has little or no practical benefit" p. 20. |
| Gossette & O'Brien | 1993 | 1974–1992 | 36 | Published and unpublished studies of children and adolescents. | RET has little or no practical benefit. The most distinctive outcome of RET is a decrease in the endorsement of irrational beliefs p. 21. We can conclude that continued use of RET in the classroom is unjustified, in fact, contraindicated p. 23. |
| Haaga & Davison | 1989 | 1970–1987 | 69 | Published and unpublished studies of children and adults. | |
| Hajzler & Bernard | 1990 | 1970–1982 | 45 | Published and unpublished studies of children and adolescents. | " . . . support for the notion that changes in irrationality and changes in other dimension of psychological functioning." " . . . changes have been maintained at follow up periods" p. 31. |
| Jorm | 1989 | 1971–1986 | 16 | Studies of any type of theory that included a measure of trait anxiety or neuroticism. | "While RET and related therapies proved superior in the present meta-analysis (to other therapies), this conclusion is limited by the breadth of studies available" p. 25. |
| Lyons & Woods | 1991 | 1970–1988 | 70 | Published and unpublished studies of children and adults. | "The results demonstrated that RET is an effective form of therapy. The efficacy was most clearly demonstrated when RET was compared to baseline or other forms of controls. Effect sizes were largest for dependent measures low in reactivity (i.e., low reactivity = behavioral or physiological measures; high reactivity = measures of irrational thinking)" p. 68. |

*(continued)*

**Table 8.8.**   *(Continued)*

| Authors | Year Published | Range of Years of Studies | Number of Studies | Focus | Conclusions |
|---|---|---|---|---|---|
| Mahoney | 1974 | 1963–1974 | 10 | Published and unpublished studies of cognitive restructuring and RET. | RET " . . . has yet to be adequately demonstrated" and " . . . may be viewed as tentatively promising" p. 182. |
| McGovern & Silverman | 1984 | 1977–1982 | 47 | Published and unpublished studies of children and adults. | " . . . there were 31 studies favoring RET. In the remaining studies, the RET treatment groups all showed improvement and in no study was another treatment method significantly better than RET" p. 16. |
| Oei, Hansen, & Miller | 1993 | 1982–1988 | 9 | Studies designed to assess whether irrational beliefs mediate change in other psychological constructs. | "This review demonstrates that while RET has been demonstrated to be an effective therapeutic intervention for a variety of target problems, there is no evidence to show that improvement in RET is due to changing irrational beliefs to rational beliefs" p. 99. |
| Polder | 1986 | | | | REBT yielded higher effect sizes than other forms of CBT. |
| Silverman, McCarthy, & McGovern | 1992 | 1982–1989 | 89 | Published and unpublished studies with children, adolescents and adults. | " . . . 49 studies resulted in positive findings for RET." When compared to other treatments, " . . . no other treatments were found to be significantly better than RET" p. 166. |
| Zettle & Hayes | 1980 | 1957–1979 | 20 | Published and unpublished studies with college students and adults. | " . . . the clinical efficacy has yet to be adequately demonstrated" p. 161. |

selected from. The most inclusive reviews were the two by Silverman and colleagues (McGovern & Silverman, 1984; Silverman et al., 1992).

DiGiuseppe et al. (1996) found over 70 REBT outcome studies not reported by the reviews. Although some of these were published after the reviews were published, many appeared during the period the reviews sampled studies. A total of 350 REBT outcome studies have been found. A substantial number of studies exist that compare REBT to no treatment, waiting lists, or placebo controls, and support the efficacy of REBT across a wide range of problems including: social, testing, math, performance, and public speaking anxiety, agoraphobia, neuroticism, stress, depression, anger, teacher burnout, personality disorder, obsessive compulsive disorder, marriage and relationship problems, alcohol abuse, poor dating skills, overweight/obesity, school discipline problems, unassertiveness, Type A behavior, parenting problems, emotional reactions to learning disabilities, school underachievement, sexual fears and dysfunction, and bulimia.

Despite the larger number of investigations of REBT, research has failed to advance our knowledge. The overwhelming majority of studies compared REBT with a no contact, waiting list, or placebo condition. Few studies compare REBT with a viable, alternative treatment. Although REBT is better than no treatment or placebo treatments for many problems, there is no evidence that it is more efficacious than alternative treatments or that there is one condition for which it is the treatment of choice.

Also, the research has done little to advance our knowledge concerning the best way to practice REBT. Does the inclusion of imagery, written homework forms, bibliotherapy, or the style of disputation make a difference in the outcome? How many sessions of REBT are necessary for clinical improvement? Researchers have failed to explore which are the critical components of REBT. However, considerable research by Mersch and Emmelkamp (Mersch, Emmelkamp, Bogels, & Van der Sleen, 1989; Mersch, Emmelkamp, & Lipps, 1991; Mersch, Hildebrand, Lavy, Wessel, & van de Hout, 1992) indicates that in vivo exposure exercises are a critical component to REBT with social phobia. Also, no studies have addressed the issues of whether the positive effects of REBT are obtained by changing clients' irrational beliefs before change occurs in other dependent measures (Oei, Hansen, & Miller, 1993). The meta-analysis by Lyons and Woods (1991) suggested that more therapy sessions produced greater effect size and that more experienced therapists produced larger effect sizes than less experienced therapists. They concluded that dependent measures low in reactivity produced higher effect sizes than measures high in reactivity. These findings are the opposite of those reported by Gossette and O'Brien (1992, 1993). Several reviews indicated that no alternative treatment was more efficacious than REBT.

Generally, psychotherapy research with children and adolescents has lagged behind research with adults (Kazdin, 1994). This has also been true of research in REBT. Sixty-nine studies mentioned by the reviewer had been done with children and adolescents. However, the majority of these studies could be considered analogue studies or tests of REBT as a preventive intervention because they focused on using REBT with normal children in groups or in classrooms. Studies of clinically diagnosed children and adolescents are lacking.

Meta-analytic reviews of psychotherapy with children and adolescents have demonstrated that behavioral and cognitive therapies produce more change than nonbehavioral or traditional, nondirective, or play therapies (Weisz, Weiss, Alicke, & Klotz, 1987; see Kazdin, 1994, for a review). Since REBT shares many similarities with other behavioral and cognitive therapies, there is good reason to suspect that research in REBT with children and adolescents will continue to support its effectiveness. However, there are many unanswered questions. Is REBT better than other forms of therapy? Is REBT more efficacious than other CBT or behavioral interventions? Is there a problem for which REBT is the treatment of choice? It is important for research to addresses the effectiveness of specific techniques in REBT with children and adolescents. Do all children benefit from logical disputing, or can rehearsing rational coping skills without disputing be as effective? Although there is some evidence to indicate that children can benefit from REBT written homework forms (Miller & Kassinove, 1978), do all children benefit from the bibliotherapy and written homework sheets frequently used in REBT?

A series of recent studies, not mentioned by any of the reviews, suggests that REBT can be useful for practitioners working in clinics or school settings. Sapp used an

REBT program with African American children to improve their academic performance (Sapp, 1994, 1996; Sapp & Farrell, 1994; Sapp, Farrell, & Durand, 1995). Joyce (1988) designed an REBT parent training program and demonstrated it improved parents' emotional reactions to their children. Graves (1996) expanded on Joyce's program and demonstrated that the program could reduce stress and improve parenting skills in parents of Down syndrome children. Bernard (1990) demonstrated that an REBT program decreased teacher stress. Although more research is needed, these studies suggest that psychologists may find REBT useful in educational settings.

## CONCLUSION

Although REBT was one of the original cognitive behavior therapies, it has changed significantly since it was introduced by Ellis over 40 years ago. The theory focuses on the role of irrational, dogmatic, and rigid thinking in causing psychopathology. Irrational beliefs are tacit, pervasive, rigid schematic representations of the way the world is and ought to be. These beliefs are both factual and evaluative. Beliefs are irrational when they are rigidly held in the face of evidence that they are logically inconsistent, antiempirical, and self-defeating. The theory discriminates between adaptive and maladaptive emotions. Its goal is not to eliminate negative emotion, but to replace maladaptive negative emotions with more adaptive negative emotions, and to help people better their lives when they are free of emotional disturbance.

The primary techniques of REBT involve challenging and replacing dysfunctional irrational beliefs. Many logical, empirical, and functional strategies for challenging beliefs are recommended. In addition, REBT employs a wide range of behavioral, imaginal, and emotive exercises to bring about change. The theory stresses the importance of rehearsal of new ways of thinking, and almost any technique that accomplishes this purpose is appropriate.

Although REBT was originally designed for neurotic adults, it has been used with children and adolescents for over 25 years. It follows a psychoeducational model that allows it to be used in groups, workshops, and classrooms as a preventive procedure. Because of its psychoeducational format, REBT can easily be integrated into educational settings. It can be used in an educational format to teach students, parents, and teachers how to reduce their emotional disturbance and improve their productivity. REBT provides a model for school mental health services including direct service and consultation.

REBT can be integrated with family systems notions to work with parents. The theory helps identify clients' thinking that reinforces dysfunctional family homeostasis. The use of REBT techniques can eliminate parents' emotional disturbance freeing them to explore and follow more productive models of relating and parenting.

There is a substantial body of research supporting the efficacy of REBT. However, this research has employed too few designs and been limited to comparing REBT with no contact or placebo controls. Future research could focus on identifying the crucial techniques of REBT, the problems and populations for which it is best suited, and more efficient ways of helping clients.

## CASE STUDY

Michele M. was a 10-year-old, fifth grader, referred in February by her mother because of social problems. Michele had few friends in her neighborhood, and was teased by her classroom peers. She had one good friend in class for the past several years, Sangitha. Michele had had difficulty making friends for several years. Her mother believed that her social difficulties resulted because she was rigid, did not share well, and wanted things her way. In September of this school year, a new girl entered Michele's class and became friendly with her only friend. The newcomer set up a competition between herself and Michele for Sangitha's friendship. The newcomer teased Michele and encouraged the other girls to do the same. Michele frequently came home upset and crying about her peers teasing her.

The mother revealed a history of academic difficulties in reading and spelling. Michele had been evaluated by the school psychologist and a phonetic learning disability was uncovered. Michele received resource room services during Grades 3 and 4. Her mother believed that Michele lacked confidence as a result of embarrassment over her reading and spelling difficulties. This past September, Michele was declassified and was no longer receiving any special services. Michele had an enmeshed relationship with both of her parents. They both responded to her social difficulties by engaging in play activities with her to compensate when she was lonely. Because her parents rescued her, Michele had few opportunities to develop social skills. An interview with Michele's teacher confirmed all the things Michele reported, and revealed that her peers were reinforced by Michele's behavior. Her classmates enjoyed seeing Michele upset and her immature behavior and emotional outbursts reinforced their negative view of her. The teacher felt sorry for Michele and gave her extra attention when she became upset.

An interview with Michele revealed that she became despondent when she saw the newcomer talking to Sangitha. She had automatic thoughts such as, "She will never be my friend now." "No one will ever like me." "There must be something wrong with me." When teased, Michele became noticeably upset and would cry, go to the teacher to report how she was teased, or go to her seat and pout. When she encountered her tormentors between these torturous events, she either held her head down, so as not to make contact, or made nasty remarks to them. Her behavior appeared to keep the cycle of strife going. Michele was not good at sharing or making reciprocal arrangements with peers. When asked if she knew how to make friends with other girls in the class or how to respond to neutralize the fights when teased, she reported that she had ". . . no idea." The therapist pursued the technique of inference chaining and uncovered the following core irrational beliefs: "Others *should* come to me and be my friend." "I *must* be liked by the other kids, or it means I am *no good*." "It's too hard to make friends and I *should not* have to do it on my own."

Michele did not play well with other children and was described as selfish. She did not share the joystick on electric computer games with peers and always put on the TV program that she wanted to watch. When her mother was discussing an example of Michele's failure to share, she burst out, "But they *should* let me have my way, I *shouldn't* have to share to have them be my friends." She also reported thinking, "I *can't stand* to take turns and *should not* have to do it."

A case conceptualization was developed using REBT, behavioral, and systemic principles. Michele had two major problems. Coping with the teasing by the girls in her class, and making and maintaining new friends. Michele was prepared to perceive any indifference to her, any criticism of her, or any noninvolvement with her as rejection. Such activating events elicited the negative thoughts that she would never have any friends and was worthless. She felt either anxiety and/or depression. These emotions resulted in the behaviors of crying, pouting, and seeking attention and support from adults. These behaviors had the cyclical effect of reducing her desirability as a friend to her peers. Besides changing these core irrational schemata, Michele needed help in improving her inadequate social skills to make friends. Her teacher's and parents' attention reinforced her cognitive processes, her emotional upset, and the behaviors. Michele's parents' behaviors also had the effects of preventing her from developing new social skills. In addition, Michele had problems with frustration intolerance that interfered with her social skills and discouraged children from playing with her.

Since REBT is a multimodal form of therapy, a comprehensive treatment plan was developed that included emotional and practical solutions, and used cognitive, behavioral, and systemic interventions. The following nine goals were identified:

1. Change Mr. & Mrs. M's emotional response to Michele's emotional upset from guilt and anxiety to concern.
2. Change Mr. & Mrs. M's behavior from rescuing Michele, and have them reinforce prosocial behavior and teach her coping rather than isolation and histrionics.
3. Change Michele's emotional reaction when she is teased by her peers from depression to sadness and coping.
4. Change Michele's anxiety about making friends to concern.
5. Teach Michele strategies to cope with the teasing and defuse these events.
6. Teach Michele social skills to make new friends and maintain the ones she has.
7. Change the teacher's behavior from reinforcing emotional upset to reinforcing prosocial behavior.
8. Teach Michele to share, and to make joint decisions and reciprocal arrangements with peers.
9. Increase Michele's frustration tolerance to allow sharing and reciprocal relationships with peers.

The first phase of therapy was to work with Michele's parents. The therapists elicited reports of their behavior toward Michele when she became upset. They were asked to consider how their reaction helped Michele learn to cope with the problem or how it would help her make friends in the future. They reported that they were aware that their behavior was not solving the long-term problem but that they felt so upset when she became upset, they thought they had to do something. The therapist identified the goal of changing their emotional reaction to Michele's problem. Then the therapist taught them the B→C connection and engaged then to look for the beliefs they had that made them upset. They reported thinking, "It is terrible to watch your child experience pain and I must do something to rescue her." The therapist led them in a discussion of this idea and helped them replace it with the rational alternative, "It is uncomfortable to watch your child have problems; but sometimes children have to learn to solve problems even if it is hard." "Rescuing fails to teach" "I can only teach her that she is strong and can cope by showing her that I believe that she can be strong and can cope." These interventions accomplished Goal 1. They would step up a reward system to reinforce Michele for not being upset and discussing her social interactions calmly, for focusing on how to cope, and for engaging in social activities with children in or out of school. They still did not know what to say to Michele about the other children teasing her. They and Michele agreed that one or both parents could be present in Michele's sessions. Usually the mother attended and we agreed that the parent present would discuss the session's proceedings with the absent parent. This partially accomplished Goal 2.

The next group of sessions focused on Michele and her experiences of being teased. The therapist explored the factual nature of Michele's automatic thoughts. She was teased by a number of the most popular girls in her class. The therapist challenged Michele's demand that she had to be liked by these girls to be a worthwhile person.

Therapist:   Do these girls like everyone in the class?

Michele:   Of course not.

Therapist:   You mean there are other girls who are not their friends?

Michele:   Yes!

Therapist:   Well, what do you think of these other girls who are not friends with the girls club (our term for the band of tormentors)? Are they worthless as well?

Michele:   I never thought of that. . . Of course they are not worthless!

Therapist:   Well, why not? If you are worthless because you are not their friend, shouldn't all girls who are not their friend be just as worthless as you?

Michele:   No, some of them are nice kids.

Therapist:   Even though they do not hang around with the girls club?

Michele:   I guess so.

Therapist:   Can you tell me who these other girls are and what you think is good about them?

(Michele described the other kids who were not liked by the girls who teased her and what their good qualities were.)

Therapist:   Well, if these other girls can be good even though they are not members of the girls club, why can't you?

Michele:   Well, maybe.

Therapist:   You don't sound convinced. Maybe you have some good qualities even though you are not a member?

Michele:   Well, I never thought about it like that.

Therapist:   Let's think about it. Do you have any good traits?

Michele:   I suppose I do.

Therapist:   What would anyone find that is good about you?

(Michele reported on friends she had over the years and why they may have liked her. Her mother reported positive things that other cousins and friends of the family had said about Michele.)

Therapist:   Well, I guess you're not all bad?

Michele:   I guess not, but that does not make them like me.

Therapist:   You are right, but do they have to like everybody?

Michele:   Of course not, they can't like everybody. There are only eight of them and there are more girls than that in my class. So I guess they can't be friends with everyone.

Therapist:   And there are other classes too, and other grades too. Are all those girls who are not friendly with the club just "NO GOOD"?

Michele:   I guess not.

Therapist:   Then why are you no good? What makes you different from the other girls that they do not behave friendly with?

Michele:   I guess there is no difference. But I just think it about myself, not about the others.

Therapist:   Does that make sense?

Michele:   No.

Therapist:   Why not? Why does it not make sense?

Michele:   I am not sure. I just believe it about me, not about them.

Therapist:   Well, if they can be okay even if they are not liked by the girls club, why can't you?

Michele:   I never thought about it that way.

Therapist:   Well try it. Just say the words out loud. "I am just as good as all the other kids. And I don't need to liked by the girls club to be okay!"

Michele:   I can't remember all that. (Therapist repeats the statement, and Michele repeats it after three tries.)

Therapist:   Well, how do you think you would feel if you really thought that way?

Michele:   I guess I might feel better.

Therapist:     Okay, let's practice getting you to think that way. What can we do to
         practice it?

After 3 sessions of similar dialogue, Michele felt much better about being teased.
At Session 7, we enlisted her mother to tease her as the girls did and Michele would
rehearse the coping statement that we had used in the above session. This accomplished Goal 3.

Once Michele had better control over her depression, the third phase of therapy
focused on learning new responses to the girls who teased her. Each session, she,
her mother, and I discussed what the girls had done, continued to analyze her
ABC's, and discussed what she could have said differently to the girls. We agreed
that she would say nice things to them in between upsetting events, such as giving
them compliments. When they teased her, she would ignore the content of their
statements and assertively say, "I guess you are still trying to get me upset." We
practiced these responses and had Michele role-play them with her mother between
sessions. We agreed that each day Michele and her mother would review the events
of the day and discuss how Michele was using the ABC's to keep herself calm, what
the other girls actually did and how Michele could have responded, and what opportunities Michele could have had to say nice or neutral things to the girls. This
occurred for 4 weeks. Each session, Michele and her mother reported on their meetings, and the therapist reviewed their progress and added information when needed.
The role here was to be a coach. During this time, the therapist also consulted with
the teacher to try and ignore emotional outbursts by Michele, and reinforce her with
praise for coping or giving a prosocial response. After 12 sessions, we accomplished
most of Goals 2, 3, and 5.

The next series of 8 sessions followed the same process but focused on reducing
Michele's anxiety over approaching new friends in her class and teaching her what
to say to make friends. We reviewed the automatic thoughts that occurred when she
became upset and used inference changing to uncover her irrational beliefs. The
therapist challenged her irrational beliefs and discussed rational alternatives. We
discussed homework, which involved approaching other children. Mrs. M continued
attending the sessions and having her daily debriefing sessions with Michele. These
sessions accomplished Goals 4, 6, and 7.

Once Michele had established some emerging friendships, the therapy switched
focus to Michele's behavior with peers. The target of the interventions was her irrational beliefs that she had to have her way and should not have to share. Again,
Mrs. M continued attending most sessions with Michele, and continued her daily
debriefing with Michele. In 10 sessions, we made significant progress on improving
her social skills and accomplished Goal 8. Throughout the last three stages of therapy, the parents maintained and adjusted the reinforcement system set up to reward
prosocial behavior.

Michele made considerable progress in therapy. She was no longer depressed
when teased. She handled herself well in social confrontations. She was always a little reluctant to make new friends, but pushed herself. She had new friends in class

and in her neighborhood. She had also developed a new closeness with her mother. She enjoyed her debriefing sessions where she got another person's impressions of her behavior. She later transferred this behavior to close friends. Mr. and Mrs. M felt more confident in their ability to deal with their daughter, and they were more likely to let her try new activities. As of this writing, Michele is a sophomore in high school and has maintained all these treatment gains.

## ANNOTATED BIBLIOGRAPHY

A complete list of books, pamphlets, and audiotapes describing the theory and practice of REBT and video demonstrations of actual REBT psychotherapy sessions can be obtained from the Albert Ellis Institute, 45 East 65th Street, New York, NY, 10021. You can reach the Institute by E-mail at info@rebt.org or by phone at 212-535-0822. The following annotated list includes the most important works in REBT for those who want to learn more about the theory and practice of REBT in general and children, adolescents, and families in particular.

Bernard, M., & DiGiuseppe, R. (Eds.). (1993). *Rational emotive models of consultation in applied settings.* Hillside, NJ: Lawrence Erlbaum Associates.

> The contributors to this edited work focus on adapting REBT principles to consultation activities in schools and other agencies.

Bernard, M., & Joyce, M. (1984). *Rational emotive therapy with children and adolescents.* New York: Wiley.

> This comprehensive discussion of REBT with children and adolescents reviews the research support for the theory and provides detailed descriptions of assessment and intervention techniques.

Borcherdt, B. (1996). *Making families work and what to do when they don't: Thirty guides for imperfect parents of imperfect children.* New York: The Haworth Press.

> Borcherdt discusses irrational beliefs commonly held by parents and how they lead to ineffectual parenting. This self-help book is valuable for both parents and professionals.

DiGiuseppe, R. (1991). Comprehensive cognitive disputing in RET. In M. E. Bernard (Ed.), *Doing rational emotive therapy effectively* (pp. 173–195). New York: Plenum.

> Disputing irrational beliefs is the most difficult part of REBT. This chapter outlines a systematic approach to help therapist learn these difficult skills.

DiGiuseppe, R. (1993). Comprehensive cognitive behavior therapy with a socially withdrawn child. In K. Kuehlwein & H. Rosen (Eds.), *Cognitive therapy in action: Evolving innovative practice.* San Francisco, CA: Jossey Bass.

This book chapter presents a detailed case description of the comprehensive, multimodal REBT treatment of a socially anxious boy.

Dryden, W. (1995). *Rational emotive behavior therapy: A reader*. London: Sage.

The selections consist of classic articles by Ellis and other REBT thinkers and practitioners.

Dryden, W., & DiGiuseppe, R. (1990). *A rational emotive therapy primer*. Champaign, IL: Research Press.

This book provides a basic step-by-step description of the tasks of an REBT therapy session.

Ellis, A. (1985). *Overcoming resistance: Rational emotive therapy with difficult clients*. New York: Springer.

We think this is Ellis's best professional book. It provides great clinical strategies for dealing with difficult clients and with difficult situations in therapy.

Ellis, A. (1994). *Reason and emotional in psychotherapy: A comprehensive method of treating human disturbance—Revised and updated*. New York: Birch Lane Press.

This revised edition of Ellis's first professional book on REBT is a classic and contains a detailed discussion of theory and practice.

Ellis, A., & Dryden, W. (Eds.). (1990). *The essential Albert Ellis*. New York: Springer.

Classic papers by Dr. Ellis are in this collection.

Ellis, A., McInerny, J., DiGiuseppe, R., & Yeager, R. (1988). *Rational emotive therapy with alcoholics and substance abusers*. Needham, MA: Allyn & Bacon.

Professionals working with adolescent substance abusers will find this book is useful.

Walen, S., DiGiuseppe, R., & Dryden, W. (1992). *A practitioner's guide to rational emotive therapy (2nd ed.)*. New York: Oxford University Press.

This book is the closest thing to an REBT treatment manual.

# REBT Self-Help Form

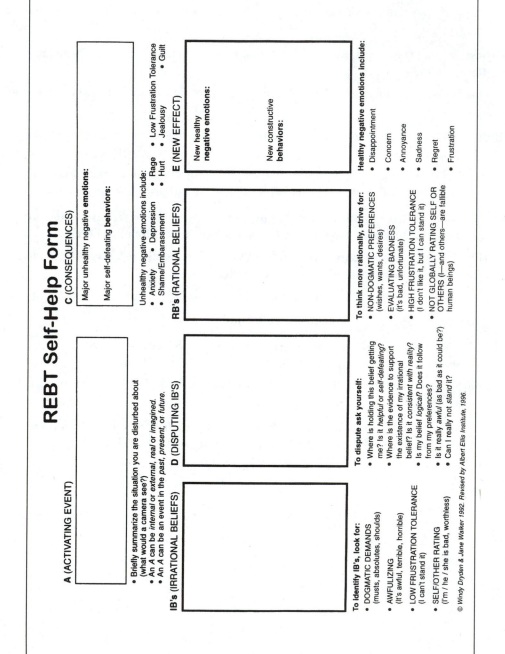

**A (ACTIVATING EVENT)**

- Briefly summarize the situation you are disturbed about (what would a camera see?)
- An A can be internal or external, real or imagined.
- An A can be an event in the past, present, or future.

**IB's (IRRATIONAL BELIEFS)**

**To identify IB's, look for:**

- DOGMATIC DEMANDS (musts, absolutes, shoulds)
- AWFULIZING (It's awful, terrible, horrible)
- LOW FRUSTRATION TOLERANCE (I can't stand it)
- SELF/OTHER RATING (I'm / he / she is bad, worthless)

**D (DISPUTING IB'S)**

**To dispute ask yourself:**

- Where is holding this belief getting me? Is it helpful or self-defeating?
- Where is the evidence to support the existence of my irrational belief? Is it consistent with reality?
- Is my belief logical? Does it follow from my preferences?
- Is it really awful (as bad as it could be?)
- Can I really not stand it?

**C (CONSEQUENCES)**

Major unhealthy negative **emotions:**

Major self-defeating **behaviors:**

Unhealthy negative emotions include:
- Anxiety
- Depression
- Shame/Embarrassment
- Rage
- Hurt
- Low Frustration Tolerance
- Jealousy
- Guilt

**RB's (RATIONAL BELIEFS)**

**To think more rationally, strive for:**

- NON-DOGMATIC PREFERENCES (wishes, wants, desires)
- EVALUATING BADNESS (It's bad, unfortunate)
- HIGH FRUSTRATION TOLERANCE (I don't like it, but I can stand it)
- NOT GLOBALLY RATING SELF OR OTHERS (I—and others—are fallible human beings)

**E (NEW EFFECT)**

New healthy **negative emotions:**

New constructive **behaviors:**

Healthy negative emotions include:
- Disappointment
- Concern
- Annoyance
- Sadness
- Regret
- Frustration

© Windy Dryden & Jane Walker 1992. Revised by Albert Ellis Institute, 1996.

# REFERENCES

Bandura, A. (1986). *Social foundations of thought and action: A social cognitive theory.* Englewood Cliffs, NJ: Prentice-Hall.

Barlow, D. H. (1991). Disorders of emotion. *Psychological Inquiry, 2*(1), 58–71.

Bartley, W. W. (1987). In defense of self applied critical rationalism. In G. Radnitzky & W. W. Bartley (Eds.), *Evolutionary epistemology, theory of rationality and sociology of knowledge* (pp. 279–312). LaSalle, IL: Open Court.

Beck, A. T. (1972). *Cognitive therapy and the emotional disorders.* New York: International Universities Press.

Beck, A. T., & Freeman, A. (1990). *Cognitive therapy of personality disorders.* New York: Guilford Press.

Bernard, M. E. (1990). *Taking the stress out of teaching.* North Blackburn, Victoria, Australia: Collins/Dove.

Bernard, M. E. (1995). It's prime time for REBT: Current theory, practice, research recommendations, and predictions. *Journal of Rational Emotive and Cognitive Behavioral Therapies, 13*(1), 9–27.

Bernard, M. E., & DiGiuseppe, R. (1990). Rational emotive therapy and school psychology. *School Psychology Review, 19*(3), 267.

Bernard, M. E., & DiGiuseppe, R. (Eds.). (1993). *Rational emotive models of consultation in applied settings.* Hillside, NJ: Erlbaum.

Bernard, M. E., & Joyce, M. (1984). *Rational emotive therapy with children and adolescents.* New York: Wiley.

Casey, R. J., & Berman, J. S. (1985). The outcome of psychotherapy with children. *Psychological Bulletin, 98,* 388–400.

Dadds, M. R., & McHugh, T. A. (1992). Social support and treatment outcome in behavioral family therapy for child conduct problems. *Journal of Consulting and Clinical Psychology, 60,* 252–259.

DiGiuseppe, R. (1977). Using behavior modification to teach rational self-statements to children. In A. Ellis & R. Grieger (Eds.), *Rational emotive psychotherapy: A handbook of theory and practice.* New York: Springer.

DiGiuseppe, R. (1983). Rational emotive therapy and the treatment of conduct disorders. In A. Ellis & M. E. Bernard (Eds.), *Rational emotive approaches to the problems of childhood.* New York: Plenum Press.

DiGiuseppe, R. (1986). The implications of the philosophy of science for rational emotive theory and therapy. *Psychotherapy, 23*(4), 634–639.

DiGiuseppe, R. (1988). A cognitive behavioral approach to the treatment of conduct disorder children and adolescents. In N. Epstein, S. Schlesinger, & W. Dryden (Eds.), *Cognitive behavioral therapy with families* (pp. 183–214). New York: Brunner/Mazel.

DiGiuseppe, R. (1989). Cognitive therapy with children. In A. Freeman, K. Simon, L. Buetler, & H. Arkowitz (Eds.), *Comprehensive handbook of cognitive therapy.* New York: Plenum Press.

DiGiuseppe, R. (1990). Assessment. *School Psychology Review, 19*(3), 268–269.

DiGiuseppe, R. (1991a). A rational emotive model of assessment. In M. E. Bernard (Ed.), *Doing rational emotive therapy effectively.* New York: Plenum Press.

DiGiuseppe, R. (1991b). Comprehensive disputing in rational emotive therapy. In M. E. Bernard (Ed.), *Doing rational emotive therapy effectively.* New York: Plenum Press.

DiGiuseppe, R. (1994). Rational emotive therapy with depressed children. In J. LeCroy (Ed.), *Handbook of child and adolescent treatment manuals.* New York: Plenum Press.

DiGiuseppe, R. (1995). Developing the therapeutic alliance with angry clients. In H. Kassinove (Ed.), *Anger disorders.* Washington, DC: Taylor & Francis.

DiGiuseppe, R. (1996). The nature of irrational beliefs: Progress in rational emotive behavior therapy. *Journal of Rational Emotive & Cognitive Behavior Therapy, 14*(1), 5–28.

DiGiuseppe, R., & Bernard, M. E. (1983). Principles of assessment and methods of treatment with children: Special considerations. In A. Ellis & M. E. Bernard (Eds.), *Rational emotive approaches to the problems of childhood.* New York: Plenum Press.

DiGiuseppe, R., Goodman, R., & Nevas, S. (1996). *Selective abstraction errors in reviewing the REBT outcome literature.* Manuscript in preparation, St. John's University.

DiGiuseppe, R., & Jilton, R. (1996). The therapeutic alliance in adolescent psychotherapy. *Applied and Preventive Psychology.*

DiGiuseppe, R., & Leaf, R. (1993). The therapeutic relationship in rational emotive therapy. *Journal of Rational Emotive and Cognitive Behavior Therapy, 11*(4), 223–234.

DiGiuseppe, R., Miller, N. J., & Trexler, L. D. (1977). A review of rational emotive psychotherapy outcome studies. *The Counseling Psychologist, 7,* 64–72.

DiGiuseppe, R., Robin, M., & Dryden, W. (1991). Rational emotive therapy and the Judeo-Christian philosophy: Complimentary clinical strategies. *Journal of Cognitive Psychotherapies: An International Quarterly, 4*(4), 355–368.

Dix, T. (1991). The affective organization of parenting: Adaptive and maladaptive processes. *Psychological Bulletin, 110*(1), 3–25.

Dryden, W., & DiGiuseppe, R. (1990). *A rational emotive therapy primer.* Champaign, IL: Research Press.

Ellis, A. (1959). Requisite conditions for basic personality change. *Journal of Consulting Psychology, 23,* 538–540.

Ellis, A. (1962). *Reason and emotion in psychotherapy.* Secacus, NJ: Lyle Stuart.

Ellis, A. (1976). RET abolishes most of the human ego. *Psychotherapy, 13,* 343–348.

Ellis, A. (1977). Skills training in counseling and psychotherapy. *Canadian Counselor, 12*(1), 30–35.

Ellis, A. (1979). Discomfort anxiety: A new cognitive behavioral construct. Part I. *Rational Living, 14*(2), 3–8.

Ellis, A. (1980a). Discomfort anxiety: A new cognitive behavioral construct. Part II. *Rational Living, 15*(1), 25–30.

Ellis, A. (1980b). Rational emotive therapy and cognitive behavior therapy: Similarities and differences. *Cognitive Therapy and Research, 4,* 325–340.

Ellis, A. (1985). *Overcoming resistance: Rational emotive therapy with difficult clients.* New York: Springer.

Ellis, A. (1994a). Rational emotive behavior therapy. In R. Corsini & D. Wedding (Eds.), *Current psychotherapies.* Itasca, IL: Peacock.

Ellis, A. (1994b). *Reason and emotional in psychotherapy: A comprehensive method of treating human disturbance* (Revised and updated). New York: Birch Lane Press.

Ellis, A. (1996). Responses to criticisms of rational emotive behavior therapy by Ray DiGiuseppe, Frank Boyd, Windy Dryden, Steven Weinrach, and Richard Wessler. *Journal of Rational Emotive & Cognitive Behavior Therapy, 14*(2), 97–122.

Ellis, A., & DiGiuseppe, R. (1993). Appropriate and Inappropriate emotions in rational emotive therapy: A response to Craemer & Fong. *Cognitive Therapy and Research, 17*(5), 471–477.

Ellis, A., & Dryden, W. (1997). *The practice of rational emotive therapy* (2nd ed.). New York: Springer.

Ellis, A., & Harper, R. (1961). *A new guide to rational living.* Englewood Cliffs, NJ: Prentice-Hall.

Engels, G. I., Garnefski, N., & Diekstra, R. F. W. (1993). Efficacy of rational emotive therapy: A quantitative analysis. *Journal of Consulting and Clinical Psychology, 61,* 1083–1090.

Gossette, R. L., & O'Brien, R. M. (1992). The efficacy of rational emotive therapy in adults: Clinical fact or psychometric artifact. *Journal of Behavior Therapy & Experimental Psychiatry, 23,* 9–24.

Gossette, R. L., & O'Brien, R. M. (1993). Efficacy of rational emotive therapy with children: A critical re-appraisal. *Journal of Behavior Therapy & Experimental Psychiatry, 24,* 15–25.

Graves, D. (1996). *The effect of rational emotive parent education on the stress of mothers of young children with Downs syndrome.* Dissertation, University of Melbourne, Australia.

Griger, R. M., & Boyd, J. D. (1989). Rational emotive approaches. In D. T. Brown & H. T. Prout (Eds.), *Counseling and psychotherapy with children and adolescents: Theory and practice in school and clinical settings* (2nd ed., pp. 303–362). Brandon, VT: Clinical Psychology.

Haaga, D. A., & Davison, G. C. (1989). Outcome studies of rational emotive therapy. In M. E. Bernard & R. DiGiuseppe (Eds.), *Inside rational emotive therapy: A critical appraisal of the theory and therapy of Albert Ellis* (pp. 155–197). San Diego, CA: Academic Press.

Haaga, D. A., & Davison, G. C. (1993). An appraisal of rational emotive therapy. *Journal of Consulting and Clinical Psychology, 61*(2), 215–220.

Hajzler, D. J., & Bernard, M. E. (1990). A review of rational emotive education outcome studies. *School Psychology Quarterly, 6,* 27–49.

Hayes, S. C., McCurry, S. M., Afan, N., & Wilson, K. (1991). *Acceptance and commitment therapy (ACT).* Reno: University of Nevada Press.

Huber, C. H., & Baruth, L. G. (1989). *Rational emotive systems family therapy.* New York: Springer.

Jacobson, N. (1992). Behavioral couples therapy: A new beginning. *Behavior Therapy, 23,* 491–506.

Johnson, B. (1996). *REBT with Christian clients.* Paper presented at the 104th annual convention of the American Psychological Association, Toronto, Ontario.

Johnson, B., Devries, R., Ridley, C., Pettorini, D., & Peterson, D. (1994). The comparative efficacy of Christian and secular RET with Christian clients. *Journal of Psychology and Theology, 22*(2), 130–140.

Johnson, B., & Ridley, C. R. (1992). Brief Christian and non-Christian RET with depressed Christian client: An exploratory study. *Counseling and Values, 36,* 220–229.

Jorm, A. F. (1989). Modifiability of trait anxiety and neuroticism: A meta-analysis of the literature. *Australian and New Zealand Journal of Psychiatry, 23,* 21–29.

Joyce, M. (1988). Unpublished doctoral dissertation, University of Melbourne, Australia.

Kazdin, A. (1994). Psychotherapy for children and adolescents. In A. E. Bergin & S. L. Garfield (Eds.), *Handbook of psychotherapy and behavior change* (4th ed., pp. 543–594). New York: Wiley.

Kelly, G. (1955). *The psychology of personal constructs* (Vol. 1). New York: Norton.

Kendall, P. C., Haaga, D. A. F., Ellis, A., Bernard, M. E., DiGiuseppe, R. A., & Kassinove, H. (1995). Rational emotive therapy in the 1990's and beyond: Current status, recent revisions, and research questions. *Clinical Psychology Review, 15*(3), 169–185.

Knaus, W. (1974). *Rational emotive education.* New York: Institute for Rational Living.

Kopec, A. M., Beal, D., & DiGiuseppe, R. (1994). Training in rational emotive therapy: Disputation strategies. *Journal of Rational Emotive and Cognitive Behavior Therapies, 12*(2).

Kuhn, T. (1970). *The structure of scientific revolutions.* Chicago: University of Chicago Press.

Lamber, M., & Bergin, A. E. (1994). In A. E. Bergin & S. L. Garfield (Eds.), *Handbook of psychotherapy and behavior change* (4th ed., pp. 143–189). New York: Wiley.

Lazarus, A. A. (1976). *Multimodal behavior therapy.* New York: Springer.

Lyons, L. C., & Woods, P. J. (1991). The efficacy of rational emotive therapy: A quantitative review of the outcome research. *Clinical Psychology Review, 11,* 357–369.

Mahoney, M. (1974). *Cognition and behavior and behavior modification.* Cambridge, MA: Ballinger.

Mahoney, M. (1991). *Human change processes: The scientific foundations of psychotherapy.* New York: Basic Books.

McGovern, T. E., & Silverman, M. S. (1984). A review of outcome studies of rational emotive therapy from 1977 to 1982. *Journal of Rational Emotive Therapy, 2*(1), 7–18.

Meichenbaum, D. (1971). *Cognitive-behavior modification.* New York: Plenum Press.

Meichenbaum, D. (1993). Changing conceptions of cognitive behavior modification: Retrospective and prospective. *Journal of Consulting and Clinical Psychology, 61*(2), 202–204.

Mersch, P. P., Emmelkamp, P. M., Bogels, S. M., & Van der Sleen, J. (1989). Social phobia: Individual response patterns and the effects of behavioral and cognitive interventions. *Behaviour Research and Therapy, 27*(4), 421–434.

Mersch, P. P., Emmelkamp, P. M., & Lipps, C. (1991). Social phobia: Individual response patterns and the long term effects of behavioral and cognitive interventions: A follow up study. *Behavior Research and Therapy, 29*(4), 357–362.

Mersch, P. P., Hildebrand, M., Lavy, E. H., Wessel, I., & van de Hout, W. J. (1992). Somatic symptoms in social phobia: A treatment method based on rational emotive therapy and paradoxical interventions. *Journal of Behavior Therapy and Experimental Psychiatry, 23,* 199–211.

Miller, N. J., & Kassinove, H. (1978). Effects of lecture, rehearsal, written homework, and the IQ on the efficacy of a rational emotive school mental health program. *Journal of Community Psychology, 6,* 366–373.

Miller, W. R., & Rollnick, S. (1991). *Motivational interviewing: Preparing people to change addictive behavior.* New York: Guilford Press.

Neimeyer, R. (1993). An appraisal of constructivist psychotherapies. *Journal of Consulting and Clinical Psychology, 61*(2), 221–234.

Nielsen, S. (1996). *REBT and Christian values.* Paper presented at the 104th annual convention of the American Psychological Association, Toronto, Ontario.

Oei, T. P. S., Hansen, J., & Miller, S. (1993). The empirical status of irrational beliefs in rational emotive therapy. *Australian Psychologist, 28,* 195–200.

Persons, J. (1989). *Cognitive therapy in practice: A case formulation approach.* New York: Norton.

Piaget, J. (1963). *The origins of intelligence in children.* New York: Norton.

Polder, S. K. (1986). A meta-analysis of cognitive behavior therapy. *Dissertation Abstracts International, B47,* 1736.

Popper, K. (1962). *Conjecture and refutation.* New York: Harper.

Prochaska, J., & DiClemente, C. (1981). *The transtheoretical approach to therapy.* Chicago: Dorsey Press.

Prochaska, J., DiClemente, C., & Norcross, J. (1992). In search of how people change: Applications to addictive behavior. *American Psychologists, 47*(9), 1102–1115.

Rogers, C. (1957). The necessary and sufficient conditions of therapeutic personality change. *Journal of Consulting Psychology, 21,* 95–103.

Rorer, L. (1989). Rational emotive theory: II. Explication and evaluation. *Cognitive Therapy and Research, 13,* 531–548.

Silverman, M. S., McCarthy, M., & McGovern, T. (1992). A review of outcome studies of rational emotive therapy from 1982–1989. *Journal of Rational Emotive & Cognitive-Behavior Therapy, 10,* 111–175.

Sapp, M. (1994). Cognitive behavioral counseling: Applications for African American middle-school students who are academically at risk. *Journal of Instructional Psychology, 21*(2), 161–171.

Sapp, M. (1996). Irrational beliefs that can lead to academic failure for African American middle-school students who are at-risk. *Journal of Rational Emotive & Cognitive Behavior Therapy, 14*(2), 123–134.

Sapp, M., & Farrell, W. (1994). Cognitive behavioral interventions: Applications for academically at risk special education students. *Preventing School Failure, 38*(2), 19–24.

Sapp, M., Farrell, W., & Durand, H. (1995). Cognitive behavior therapy: Applications for African American middle-school at risk students. *Journal of Instructional Psychology, 22*(2), 169–177.

Seligman, M. E. P. (1991). *Learned optimism.* New York: Knopf.

Sherwood, V. (1990). The first stage of treatment with the conduct disordered adolescent: Overcoming narcissistic resistance. *Psychotherapy, 27,* 380–387.

Smith, M. L., & Glass, G. V. (1977). Meta-analysis of psychotherapy outcome studies. *American Psychologist, 32,* 752–760.

Spivack, G., Platt, J., & Shure, M. (1976). *The social problem solving approach to adjustment.* San Francisco: Jossey-Bass.

Spivack, G., & Shure, M. (1974). *Social adjustment of young children: A cognitive approach to solving real-life problems.* San Francisco: Jossey-Bass.

Vernon, A. (1989a). *Thinking, feeling, behaving: An emotional education curriculum for children grades 1–6.* Champaign, IL: Research Press.

Vernon, A. (1989b). *Thinking, feeling, behaving: An emotional education curriculum for children grades 7–12.* Champaign, IL: Research Press.

Walen, S., DiGiuseppe, R., & Dryden, W. (1992). *A practitioners' guide to rational emotive therapy* (2nd ed.). New York: Oxford University Press.

Walen, S., DiGiuseppe, R., & Wessler, R. (1980). *A practitioners' guide to rational emotive therapy* (2nd ed.). New York: Oxford University Press.

Weisz, J. R., Weiss, B., Alicke, M. D., & Klotz, M. L. (1987). Effectiveness of psychotherapy with children and adolescents: Meta-analytic findings for clinicians. *Journal of Consulting and Clinical Psychology, 55,* 542–549.

Wessler, R. A., & Wessler, R. L. (1980). *The principles and practice of rational emotive therapy.* San Francisco: Jossey-Bass.

Wolpe, J. (1990). *The practice of behavior therapy.* Needham Heights, MA: Allyn & Bacon.

Zajonc, R. B. (1980). Thinking and feeling: Preferences need no inferences. *American Psychologist, 35,* 151–175.

Zettle, R., & Hayes, S. (1980). Conceptual and empirical status of rational emotive therapy. *Progress in Behavior Modification, 9,* 125–166.

# Chapter 9

# *REALITY THERAPY APPROACHES*

Gerald B. Fuller and Diane L. Fuller

Reality therapy was developed by William Glasser (1965, 1972, 1976a, 1976b, 1981) when he recognized that existing therapeutic systems did not produce rapid and durable change. The essence of reality therapy is the acceptance of responsibility by individuals for their own behavior, thus helping them to achieve success and happiness. Concomitant with this responsibility is the importance of personal involvement in all the therapeutic and growth processes. Reality therapy teaches better ways of fulfilling needs. It stresses the idea that, given an atmosphere of human involvement and supportive confrontation, an individual can learn how to behave in a more responsible and productive manner.

## HISTORY AND STATUS

Dr. Glasser, in conjunction with Dr. G. L. Harrington, began the development of reality therapy in 1962 while working at a Veterans Administration hospital in California. During this same period he was the chief psychiatrist at the Ventura School for Girls, which housed 14- to 16-year-old female "incorrigibles." Here the principles of reality therapy were used in developing specific programs for the girls and for the school as a whole. These young women had, understandably, poor self-esteem, and one of Glasser's immediate goals was to build success into their experiences. The school became a place where honest praise was given freely. The girls were put in charge of themselves, thus giving them the responsibility for their own behavior. Rules were clearly defined, as were the consequences for breaking them. The praise and personal responsibility helped shift the girls' attention away from the authority figures against whom they had rebelled.

The title "reality therapy" was officially introduced in an article dealing with juvenile delinquency (W. Glasser, 1964). The following year, his book *Reality Therapy* (W. Glasser, 1965) appeared. At approximately the same time, Dr. Glasser founded the Institute for Reality Therapy. Here therapists do both individual and group counseling and teach the concepts of reality therapy to both laypersons and professionals.

In 1966, Glasser began consulting in the California school system. His experience in the schools led to the publication of *Schools without Failure* (W. Glasser, 1969). Here he applied the concepts of reality therapy to contemporary education. He described the inadequacies of current educational procedures and suggested techniques aimed at reducing school failure. Again, these techniques aimed at the children's involvement in their schooling, giving them a sense of self-esteem and a successful identity. He felt this whole process could best be accomplished by making education interesting and relevant, by retiring the grading system, by showing true concern, and by allowing the children to progress at their own speed. A good classroom, he asserted, should incorporate praise, active listening, and relevant helpfulness.

In 1969, as a result of the popularity of *Schools without Failure,* the Educator Training Center (ETC) was opened to handle the flood of requests for information and teaching materials. By offering materials such as films, cassettes, and books that emphasized the principles of reality therapy, the Center helped teachers and other school personnel create these *schools without failure.* So many children who appeared to have had adequate advantages (e.g., comfortable homes, security, attention) were responding by failing in school, using drugs, and demonstrating an unwillingness to work for reasonable goals. Glasser's search for an explanation for this phenomenon led to his concept of *role versus goal.* This theory was the impetus for *The Identity Society* (W. Glasser, 1972). Here he discussed the replacement of a "survival society," where behavior is directed toward keeping people fed, clothed, and comfortable, by an "identity society," where emphasis is placed on caring, involvement, respect, and satisfaction. Children gain strength and successful identities through involvement with others, and with this strength children can do what is necessary to reap the benefits available in the identity society. Glasser proposed that a person, in looking for ways to gain personal strength or confidence, could become addicted to positive behavior. These positive addictions, the antithesis of negative addictions such as drugs and alcohol, which make one weaker, help to make one stronger. Jogging, tennis, or reading could thus become positively addictive. These ideas were set forth in *Positive Addiction* (W. Glasser, 1976b).

In an attempt to fill the gap that often exists between theory and practice, a case study compilation entitled *What Are You Doing? How People Are Helped through Reality Therapy* was edited by N. Glasser (1980). A solid neurological and psychological base was added to the clinical approach of reality therapy with the publication of *Stations of the Mind* (W. Glasser, 1981). Its thesis is that people are internally motivated and, thus, behavior is purposeful. Each individual may perceive a different reality, however, and this idea must be kept in mind when interpreting others' behaviors. What is motivating a particular child and what others think is motivating him or her may be very different indeed.

In *Take Effective Control of Your Life* (W. Glasser, 1984), Glasser describes his new "control theory," which proposes that people can better their lives through conscious control of their emotions and actions. This is based on his theory that everything a person does, thinks, and feels comes from inside an individual and is not, as most people believe, a response to external circumstances.

In his most recent book, *Control Theory in the Classroom* (W. Glasser, 1986a), Glasser addressed the need for schools to restructure the classroom environment to keep students interested and involved in learning. He contends that students are currently not successful in school because school is not part of the picture in their heads that fulfills their basic needs. Glasser proposed the use of a cooperative learning approach which would satisfy students' basic needs for fun, belonging, power, and freedom. Thus, students would be provided with mental pictures of learning in school that would be "need fulfilling."

To demonstrate the role of Control Theory in the practice of Reality Therapy, a case study book titled *Control Theory in the practice of Reality Therapy: Case Studies* was edited by N. Glasser (1989). These case studies provide interesting examples of ways that Control Therapy can be translated into the practice of Reality Therapy.

W. Glasser (1990) in *The Quality School: Managing Students without Coercion* continued his thinking about schools by combining the work of Edward Deming with his own experience with education and control theory. He presents an effective management style for school based on many years of research. Glasser suggests that traditional management is the problem in school as it has turned students and staff into adversaries. He proposes a system that brings them together to produce quality schoolwork and quality teaching. Control theory is expanded by W. Glasser (1993) in *The Quality School Teacher*. He explains how a working knowledge of control theory can improve the relationship between teacher and student. Specific guidelines are given for teachers as they help their students achieve better. This was followed by *The Control Theory Manager* (W. Glasser, 1994) which provides insight to management on control theory, and discusses how focusing on leadership and rejecting coercion produce quality. His latest book, *Staying Together: A Control Theory Guide to Lasting Relationships* (W. Glasser, 1996), provides substantial examination of intimate relationships, focusing on what characteristics make them last.

The Institute for Reality Therapy teaches the practice and concepts of reality therapy to professional people, interested groups, and organizations. Individuals are taught in one-week sessions which include lectures, discussions, demonstrations, and role-playing situations. To become certified as a reality therapist one must complete a one-week basic intensive seminar followed by a supervised practicum which is arranged, a second intensive week, followed by a second practicum. The basic and advanced practicums each entail a minimum of 30 hours over at least a 6-month period.

The *Journal of Reality Therapy* was first published in the fall of 1981. This semi-annual publication focuses on theoretical, research-based, and specific descriptions of the successful applications of reality therapy principles in field settings. An edited book by Litwack (1994) contains a selection of articles from the first 13 years of the *Journal of Reality Therapy*. The articles present an overview of the development of the concepts and practice of reality therapy.

## OVERVIEW OF THEORY

### Basic Theory and Assumptions

*Components of a Successful Identity*

Reality therapy purports that the driving force for all behavior is the basic, intrinsic goal of having a different, distinct, and unique identity. Each child wants to believe there is no other person quite like him or her anywhere on earth. To attain and maintain this identity, *regardless* of whether it is centered on success or failure is critical.

Failure-identity children are those who believe "I can't do it. I'm no good. I'm not successful. I'm worthless." Believing they have little chance to succeed or to be happy, these children appear to have a distressing or negative attitude toward school and life. For them, the real world is uncomfortable. These children have given up and, for the most part, have resigned themselves to failure. They often see themselves as losers and lonely and do not care about themselves or others. They are self-critical, irrational, and irresponsible and have little to look forward to. "Apathetic," "indifferent," "uninvolved," and "unconcerned" are some of the terms that are used to describe these children. School failure is personalized and so these children come to view themselves as worthless.

For children to acquire the feeling that they are basically successful or good, they must fulfill the following general or basic needs:

1. *Love.* Belonging, friendship, caring, and involvement.
2. *Power.* Importance, recognition, worth, and skill.
3. *Fun.* Pleasure, enjoyment, laughter, and learning.
4. *Freedom.* Independence, choice, and autonomy.

All people need to be loved and cared for from birth to old age. To love and be loved are necessary ingredients for successful growth and development. The child must learn both to give love and to receive it in return. This necessitates that there must be at least one person who cares for the child and for whom the child cares. The child's need for love and belonging can be seen in the interaction with the members of his or her family and with others in school. In school, this might be reflected in social responsibility. Children must learn to care for, to be responsible for, and to help one another. To the extent that the child becomes involved with others, the child who belongs or is involved is more successful than the uninvolved child who may well be lonely and suffering.

In addition to love, children also need power or a sense of importance. There are ways to satisfy this need for power that are positive and do not interfere with other people's needs. One positive way to meet the need for power is to receive recognition. It is important to remember that it is children's perception of what they do, helped by recognition from others, that gives them that ultimate sense of worth. To feel worthwhile and successful, children must maintain a satisfactory standard of behavior; that is, they must behave in ways that will gain the love and respect of others. It is also necessary for them to behave in a way and to perform so that what they do is worthwhile to themselves as well. To do this, they must learn to evaluate and correct behavior that is wrong, and, most important, to give themselves credit when it is right. Children's being attuned to morals, standards, and values of right and wrong as well as to school behavior, then, is linked to fulfillment of their need for self-worth.

Although belonging and self-worth are separate, children who love and are loved will usually think they are worthwhile. The overindulged child can be the exception.

These children are loved too much. Their parents mistake the total acceptance of good or bad behavior for good discipline. Love does not mean blanket approval. When children receive love for behavior that they know is wrong, they do not feel worthwhile and, thus, may act out as a way of asking for limits. A child needs to learn that being the subject of someone's love does not in and of itself give him or her self-worth.

Children need time for fun and time to enjoy themselves and others. This must involve active participation in contrast to passive participation such as is inherent in watching television. Children who do not know how to enjoy life actively, who do not know how to engage in having fun, are often too serious. As such, they tend to stress the aversiveness of a problem and to exaggerate the significance of things. They may also be people who construct their time poorly; the delinquent child often has nothing better to do than to get into trouble. How much fun the child has at home and school is an important variable to evaluate.

Freedom is important to everyone. Reality therapy defines freedom as being able to do and say what you want within the limits of the laws of society and being able to express yourself without discount. Reality therapy encourages the client to look at the range of freedom they do have along with the responsibilities of this freedom. Discounts among family members and teachers and children are most destructive. Freedom from criticism does not imply no correction or a laissez-faire attitude. It means refraining from the little extra comments that teachers and parents so often make that chip away at the child's self-concept: "How dumb can you be?" "Don't you ever care about anybody but yourself?" Criticism of this kind tells children that they are not good people and pushes them toward failure identities. *Criticism should always be directed at the behavior and not at the child or the person.*

When children are not fulfilling their needs, they are unhappy and must do something to reduce their pain and hurt. Often the means they devise are ineffective, and, try as they might to succeed, they view themselves as failures. The concomitant loneliness, pain, and discomfort are often dealt with in four ways: depression and withdrawal, acting out, thinking disturbances, and sickness.

## Control Theory

Since 1984, Glasser has integrated reality therapy with control theory, which suggests that the preceding basic needs are part of our genetic structure. Built into our brains are these fixed needs which, if not satisfied, result in stress, tension, and suffering. At the survival level, these needs include food, shelter, and safety; while at the psychological level, they include the needs discussed earlier. Consequently, all our behavior is a constant attempt to satisfy one or more of the basic needs that are written into our genetic structure. When there is a difference between what we want (as perceived in our head) and what we are perceiving in the external or real world, the mismatch results in dissatisfaction. Often the child in need of therapy has chosen unsatisfactory behavior that attempts to meet, but does not alleviate, those needs which remain unfulfilled.

From one's general or basic needs, there is a world of specific needs that are not genetic but learned. We usually function at the level of these specific needs although we are also aware of basic needs. We refer to these specific needs as wants—specific perceptions related to a basic need. For example, swimming is a *want* related to the basic *need* for fun.

The mechanism through which needs are met is the inner world of wants, which is described by W. Glasser (1984) as a "picture album." Exploring the needs and perceptions in this album is a means of working with a child in therapy. This is also the first procedure that lends itself to change.

In a theory that explains how we live our lives on a daily basis, the brain is seen as a "control system" that seeks to control, maneuver, and mold the external world to satisfy an internal goal. Recently, Glasser has brought the theory to a clinical level with practical application (W. Glasser, 1984).

## VIEW OF PSYCHOPATHOLOGY

### ("The Fruits of a Failure Identity")

*Depression and Withdrawal*

Unable to reduce the pain of failure and loneliness through acceptable and realistic means, the child withdraws into the self-involvement of unhappiness and depression. The child behaves in a way that causes him or her to feel depressed and then uses that feeling as an excuse for an inability to handle problems. In reality therapy terms, a feeling such as depression is called *depressing* because it is viewed as a feeling *behavior*. Depression is not something that comes over children, but rather is something they actively choose and help create. The child would rather depress than admit to an inability to figure out better behaviors for belonging and getting along. In the child's view, it is better to use depression as an excuse than to admit to not knowing what to do. Depressing provides a rationalization for continuing uninvolved behavior. After all, how can anyone expect a depressed child to become involved with others when he or she feels so bad? The successful child when feeling depressed, realizes that something must be done, whereas the unsuccessful child fights to maintain the depressing behavior because it provides some temporary relief. To give up the depressed state would be to expose oneself to the pain of feeling like a failure—unloved and worthless. To experience this is more than the child wants to do. Depressive behavior may have some value, however, if it can be seen as a child's request for help.

*Acting Out*

Another way to relieve the pain of failure and worthlessness is to act out. Many children strike out in an effort to get rid of pain by hurting people they believe are denying their needs. They are often indifferent to social rules and reinforce their lack of regard for others by putting the blame on someone else. These children are not afraid of punishment; they often expect it. Having identified and reinforced themselves as failures, they often become antagonistic, breaking home and school rules. Because they feel they will fail anyway, they attempt to gain what they want while expending as little energy as possible. Needing to fulfill this identity, they assert that they are someone—a failure; and they use this as a rationale for their capricious behavior. Consequently, when they are punished, these children often feel victimized or persecuted. The punishment they receive can serve as a source of involvement because they obtain attention through their acting-out behavior. Punishment is painful, but it is better than being alone.

*Thinking Disturbances*

Some children, either unable to figure out a satisfying behavior or having tried and failed, attempt to meet their needs by living in a world of their own. They deny reality in an effort to reduce pain. Once self-involved, they do not have to deal with the pain of failing and not being involved. For these children, their own world becomes the real world. All their seemingly crazy thoughts and behaviors make sense; it is an attempt to avoid a world that they fear they will be unable to control.

*Sickness*

Some children manifest somatic complaints such as headaches, stomachaches, nausea, or dizziness with no physical causes present. It may be better to stay in bed than to face a hectic day at school. If one is too sick, one cannot possibly do schoolwork. For these children, the ache and physical pain are very real, making it impossible to carry on a normal day. By causing the child to be sick and helpless, the behaviors keep anger in check and allow the child to be offered help or to seek it. Probably more than most other behaviors this one allows for sympathy and attention. Somatic illness has the added attractiveness of reassuring the child and his or her teacher and parents that the problem is physical rather than social or psychological.

## General Therapeutic Goals and Techniques

Although reality therapy places some emphasis on behavioral change, more importance is given to goals that are concerned with values and concepts of individual responsibility. A strong focus is placed on helping individuals understand and accept themselves as they are. An individual's achievements, within the limits of inherited endowment and environment, are what the individual makes of him- or herself. Decisions, not conditions, determine the way a person behaves and whether the person acts responsibly or irresponsibly. Other goals might include developing the ability to express mature and responsible love, and the ability to give and take. Self-awareness should move toward increasing the client's ability to focus on present concerns and to avoid rehashing the past, particularly mistakes, and dwelling on the distant future. Soon clients will be able to act out more responsibly to solve personal crises more effectively and to fulfill their own needs without hurting others or themselves (W. Glasser & Zunin, 1979).

Reality therapy is a verbally active psychotherapy. A conversational exchange occurs between therapist and client that may include agreements and disagreements. Clients are confronted with their irresponsible behavior. Constructive arguing will focus on showing the client more responsible ways of behaving. The therapist may attempt to "pin down" the client in terms of what the client intends to do about his or her current life situation. A statement such as "I might look for a job" will be met with questions such as "How?" and "When?" with the therapist not accepting excuses. Throughout the therapy process, the therapist directs the client to focus on real-life issues and is concerned with what the client does and what the client plans to do.

The steps for child and adolescent therapy outlined in the next section are essentially similar to the principles (e.g., see W. Glasser & Zunin, 1979) that guide all reality therapy. Reality therapy begins with the therapist communicating a caring, personal involvement to the client. The focus is on present behaviors and concerns, helping the client make his or her own value judgments on whether the behavior is responsible, and assisting the client in making plans to change "failure behavior" to "success behavior." Then the therapist strongly encourages the client to make the commitment to act out on the value judgments and to carry out the specific plans formulated. The therapist does not accept excuses for failure, yet does not punish the client when failure occurs. Throughout, the therapist takes an encouraging, client-advocate stance.

## INDIVIDUAL PSYCHOTHERAPY WITH CHILDREN AND ADOLESCENTS

Because the basic approach of reality therapy in working with children and adolescents is essentially the same, no distinction will be made between techniques for these age groups.

### Step 1. Involvement

This step has also been referred to as "Be personal" or "Make friends." Because the child who is acting irresponsibly and has a failure identity is lonely and alienated, it follows that an important technique to use is to become involved with him or her. Involvement is a therapeutic prerequisite for anyone who hopes to be helped. Often this step is not given the importance it should have in the therapeutic process. Beginning therapists hear this and agree in principle but are often overly anxious to move on to the "action" of therapy. However, a therapist's skill in dealing with a child depends heavily on this first step.

A child must be made to believe that the person working with him or her is concerned. The therapist needs to be warm, supportive, interested, and genuine in the relationship. Unless this can be done from the beginning to the end, the therapy will seldom be successful. Convincing the child that you want to be involved is demanding, requiring a good sense of humor, patience, and acceptance. The child needs to be convinced that another person cares and is willing to talk about anything that is of interest to the child rather than just focusing on what has gone wrong. This makes it essential that one have a good grasp of child or developmental psychology. It is important to know about the current television programs, movies, records, or books in which children at different ages are interested. In addition, hobbies, recreational activities, and peer relationships should be explored.

What the child says must be respected, although one does not have to agree with it all. If the child makes contradictory statements or is unclear, the therapist should strive for clarification by saying, for example, "I don't understand" or "I'm confused." The therapist should be open and honest with the child. It should be made clear that the therapist is willing to talk about almost anything the child wishes to discuss. Initially, as little emphasis as possible should be placed on the child's present symptoms or behaviors; this has been done enough in the past. The therapist should not focus on problems or misery first. This only reinforces behavior by giving value to the failure and self-involvement. The less the therapist discusses the problem and instead stresses the possibilities open to the child, the better.

The question of how much time to give the child in therapy often arises. To a child who is lonely and uninvolved, the friendly therapist becomes a much-desired source of needed gratification. It is impossible to be extensively involved with every child in a time-consuming relationship, especially within a school setting. The therapist should never promise more time than can be given. Most children can accept honest statements from the therapist about time commitments once involvement is established. Whatever the amount, it is usually more productive and rewarding that what the child has had previously.

During this first step, it is important to ascertain what the child wants. The therapist should begin where the child is, not where the therapist thinks the child is. Suggesting what the child might want is counterproductive. Helping the child to examine wants and to establish priorities demonstrates early on that the child needs to begin taking responsibility for his or her actions. A brief summary by the therapist during or at the end of the session helps the child know that the therapist is paying attention. It also gives the child a chance to hear his or her wants, something the child may never have listened to before. In addition, it gives the child an opportunity to correct any misinterpretation. This summarizing technique continues to be valuable throughout therapy.

## Step 2. Focus on Present Behavior

Here the therapist asks the child, "What are you doing?" This question is used in place of the "why" question of conventional therapy. The emphasis is on the present—what the child is doing now and what is planned for the future. Reality therapy sees focusing on the past to be of little use. Dwelling on the past only reinforces the apparent importance of past experiences and their association with the child's present problems. The only way a child can work toward a successful identity is to become aware of his or her current behavior. This approach does not deny that problems can be rooted in the past. But we can basically only deal with current behavior in order to plan a better strategy for the future; we cannot undo what has already occurred. Acknowledge the child's past, believe in it, but focus on the present.

This does not mean that one never asks about the past. If the therapist thinks that knowing something about the past will help plan for more suitable behavior now or in the future, such information should be pursued. However, one should look for the past successes to use as building blocks for a better now and tomorrow. Talking about past failures often reinforces the child's use of them as an excuse for present behavior: "My brother was this way and so am I," or "I have a temper like my mother's and that's just the way I am."

Reality therapy purports that a child's behaviors are a combination of his or her actions, thoughts, and feelings. To the child who is upset, it may seem, however, that these feelings are most important. The therapist should not ask the child how he or she feels unless the feeling is associated strongly with what the child is doing now or plans to do in the future. Talking about a feeling may temporarily make the child feel better, but it doesn't change anything and is worthless in the long run. *Feelings should be tied to the behavior that evokes them.* This helps the child to understand that one can and must change what one is doing to find relief from this present misery. In essence, behavior is readily observed and responded to; feelings are not. If changes are to occur, it is easier to start with behavior than with feelings. This doesn't mean that the therapist rejects the feelings but tries to point out that the way the child feels may not be as important as the way the child behaves. The therapist might respond, "I believe you; you are upset, you are angry, but what are you doing?" It is hoped that this will redirect the child's attention to his or her responsibility for the behavior. If the child is depressed and is complaining about sitting at home all the time on weekends feeling miserable and thinking unhappy thoughts, the therapist can listen to the upset feelings but stress the sitting-at-home behavior. The therapist might ask, "Is that what you are choosing to do?" The idea is to focus more and more on the activity or the lack of it rather than on the misery and upset conditions. It is easier to change the sitting-at-home behavior than the depressed feelings or miserable thoughts.

Asking the angry, acting-out child about feelings is counterproductive and may produce more anger and hostility. Focusing on what the child is doing and putting less emphasis on feelings may actually reduce frustration. The anger is not the cause of the problem, but rather the result of an inability on the part of the child to satisfy his or her needs.

It is a basic premise that the behavior the child exhibits is chosen. The therapist must keep in mind that children very seldom see their behavior as having anything to do with the problem. Children usually see the world—not themselves—as needing to change. This has often been referred to as an external locus of control. Also, children may see themselves as victims of things over which they have no control.

### Step 3. Value Judgment

The important question to be asked here is: "Is what you are doing helping you?" or "Is what you are doing against the rules?" The child must determine if the behavior is good for him or her and for those the child cares for and if it is socially acceptable. Because the child acts by choice, he or she must make the judgment whether to continue the behavior. This is the child's responsibility. Here the child begins to answer the question "Is it helping?" The child will not change until he or she determines that the behavior does not help accomplish what is wanted. What is actually being asked of the child is, "Are you doing what will help you fulfill your needs? The therapist should be very careful here to remain nonjudgmental about the child's behavior; the child is being asked to make the judgment. The therapist prepares the child to make this judgment by using what was established in the preceding steps—the examination of the present behavior and the trust that comes with involvement. The value judgment may include a decision about what the child wants. "So you really want to quit school? Can a boy of sixteen find a good job? Are you willing to live with the hassle of school?"

Often there is no clear choice about which behavior is the best or most responsible. In some cases, such as obtaining independence from parents, it is difficult for the child to make a choice. If the child is unwilling to make the judgment that what is being done is not helping or that it is against the rules, nothing can be planned or accomplished. No one can make anyone do anything as long as that person is unwilling to accept the consequences of his or her behavior. The most the therapist can do is to continue to strive for increased involvement that will encourage a move away from failure.

## Step 4. Planning Responsible Behavior

Once the child has judged that his or her behavior is not helping and wants to change, it is the responsibility of the therapist to help the child make a plan to do better. This is the time to examine the possible alternatives to the child's present behavior. Both the positive and negative alternatives should be discussed. Children often have a limited repertoire of behavioral responses, making it difficult for them to suggest many alternative. Initially, the therapist may have to generate some ideas. More than one idea or alternative should be presented so that the child can choose the one most acceptable to him or her. In some cases where the therapist must make a plan for the child, it is important to establish that the child thinks he or she can carry it out. Actually, it does not matter who makes the plan as long as it is accepted and becomes the child's plan. It is hoped that the child will learn new behaviors via the plan of action developed. Sometimes, planning proceeds by trial and error; that is, a plan is developed, attempted, and perhaps modified until one is found that fits the situation.

The therapist should be aware that making plans takes skill and that critical components must be considered:

- A plan must be *small* and *manageable,* in terms of both time and what the child is going to do. For example, a child might do 15 minutes of homework for each of 4 days. If the plan is too large, it will only reinforce failure. The child needs to feel successful. To allow the child to say, "I will not fight from now on" is setting the child up for future failure. It would be better for the child to say, "I won't fight in the next 2 hours." Only after initial successes can the time be prolonged.

- The plan must be *specific,* definite, and detailed. It should be something the child can visualize doing, like completing a math assignment. Key words for the therapist to use here include *what, where, how, when, with whom,* and *how many.* The plan should also depend on what the child does rather than what others do: "I will clean my room every Monday if you let me stay up and watch TV" is an unsatisfactory plan; "I will clean my room every week" is better.
- A plan should be *reasonable.* It should make sense, and the child and therapist should see the value in doing it.
- The plan should be *positive.* The focus should be on what the child is going to do rather than on what he or she is not going to do.
- The plan should begin as soon as *possible.* The longer a child waits to put a plan into effect, the less likely he or she is to do it.
- The plan should be *repetitive.* It should be something that can be done often or something that can be easily repeated each day. This helps form daily patterns of the new behavior.

If the plan fails, the therapist must have the ability to think of another one or to help the child replan. If, in the attempt to make a new plan, a problem comes up that seems unresolvable, rather than force the issue, it is better for the therapist to relax and just chat with the child about an interesting subject. In time, it is hoped, child and therapist will be able to return to the difficulty during the session and resolve it.

After a plan has been made, it is often wise to return to the value judgment step. The therapist should ask the child if the plan is workable. The therapist might ask the child, for example, "Is the plan reasonable or is it asking for too much?" It is also beneficial to have the child repeat the plan to be sure that the child understands it. This clarification again points out the potential value of summarizing.

If the child carries out the plan, this accomplishment is the beginning of his or her becoming more responsible; this concept cannot be overly stressed. The therapist will have to emphasize over and over again that the child must take the responsibility, that things in life cannot always be done for him or her, and that one must live one's own life. The child must recognize that the therapist will be of help for a while but that all the therapist can do is to get this process started. The child must come to the realization that eventually all people must assume responsibility for their behavior and live in a world much larger than the restricted world of therapy.

## Step 5. Commitment to the Plan

After the child makes the reasonable, workable plan, a commitment must be obtained that the plan will be carried out. The child is being asked, "Will you do it?" This is an important stage in plan making because it shifts the responsibility to the child. Commitment is both motivating and binding. It means that the child is no longer alone. What the child does now is not only for him- or herself but also for someone else. This helps provide a sense of strength and purpose.

Getting the failure-identity child to make a commitment is not always an easy task. Having already failed on a number of occasions, these children are often reluctant to commit themselves again for fear of exposing themselves to more painful rejection and consequent feelings of worthlessness. Commitment is also involvement, which may be met with resistance. However, until the child is willing to make a commitment to something or someone else, it is likely that the child will remain self-involved and unable to develop a success identity.

The commitment is made either verbally or in writing. A written commitment is preferred because it is stronger, more binding, and more clear. There is little doubt about the conditions of a commitment when they are written out and signed by the child. It is a good idea for the therapist to sign it also, thus demonstrating involvement. Two copies of the agreement are made, one for the child and one for the therapist as a backup in case the child loses the copy. This approach may sound too businesslike and legal, but it is a fact that a person is more hesitant to escape from a written commitment than from a verbal one. It also avoids disagreements over the terms of the plan.

## Step 6. Accept No Excuses

Plans do fail sometimes, and the therapist must make it clear that excuses are unacceptable because they break the involvement and allow the child an opportunity to avoid responsibility. Excuses, if allowed, do provide temporary relief; they reduce the child's tension and improve feelings on a short-term basis. The excuse undermines the need for action because momentarily the child is off the hook. Too frequently, teachers and parents accept apologies such as "I'm sorry" because it is easier to accept the apology than to go through the time-consuming process of assessing responsibility and present behavior. It is also very possible that the child could interpret the acceptance of excuses as a lack of concern. The accepting of an excuse also implies that the child's inadequacy and inability are also accepted.

When the child does not follow through on the commitment to the plan, the therapist asks, "When will you do it?" or "When will it happen?" or "I'm glad you are sorry, but what are you planning to do so that this same thing doesn't happen again?" It may be necessary to alter the plan. The child is not discounted or punished for failing. Actually, without punishment or rejection, there are no good reasons for excuses.

When the commitment fails, the plan must be reevaluated. If the plan is still reasonable, the child must decide whether to commit to it again. At this point, a value judgment must again be obtained from the child, and a new plan and commitment formulated. A good way to reduce excuses is to ask for a value judgment every time the child gives an excuse. Often, the making of an excuse is evidence that the child has not fully understood the value judgment that was made. The therapist might say, "Do you want to work at getting along with your teacher or do you want to give up?" Returning to the value judgment often helps put the therapy back on the right track.

A teacher faced with excuses might say, "If you don't do your assignment, I will not punish you, but I do insist we work out a better solution. I don't care why you didn't do the assignment; I will accept your thinking that you have a valid reason. However, we have to solve the problem. We have to find a better way for you to follow the rules and get your schoolwork done."

## Step 7. Do Not Punish

This step probably elicits the most controversy. Many successful people regard the fear of punishment as the prod toward achievement. As a result, punishment has enjoyed a solid reputation in our society. Punishment, while never good, can serve as a deterrent to the success-oriented child who may have strayed momentarily from the path of responsibility. With the child who is a failure, however, punishment often reinforces the failure identity; the punishment only confirms the child's low self-esteem and can even sanction other reckless behavior.

The goal here is not to put more pressure on the child than is now being experienced. This step recognizes and accepts that a child does not function well when he or she is hurting. It proposes that although there is not to be any punishment administered, minimally painful, reasonable consequences (i.e., appropriate discipline) have value.

Criticism is also unacceptable. Many children who fail actually expect the therapist to be critical and hard on them and may attempt to provoke this attitude. If the therapist succumbs, the child will use the therapist's behavior to continue excusing inadequacies. This is a popular game played by failing children. A nonpunitive, noncritical therapist will not become involved in the child's inadequate lifestyle.

Reality therapy defines punishment as any treatment that is intended to cause a child mental or physical pain. Punishment is to be distinguished from natural consequences or discipline. A comprehensive list of the differences (Table 9.1) between the two is given by Dreikurs, Grunwald, and Pepper (1971).

This step does not imply that reality therapy is passive, permissive therapy. Discipline is an essential part of reality therapy for children. Reasonable, agreed-on consequences for irresponsible behaviors are not punishment but discipline. Logical consequences set out the reality of social responsibility. In any given situation, it is necessary that the rules be learned. The establishment of consequences and the understanding of rules help to eliminate the element of the unexpected. Children should suffer reasonable consequences when they break the rules. Yelling at children adds nothing to the learning process and only makes things worse. The child might now suffer what is perceived as the loss of parental or teacher approval and is burdened additionally with the work of reconciliation.

If the child breaks the rules at school or at home, reasonable consequences must follow. The most reasonable of these is deprivation of either a *freedom* or a *privilege*. The child might be asked to sit in a chair at home or school until a plan is worked out. A quiet place to sit, to do schoolwork, to think, provides the child with the opportunity to get over the upset and to think about a plan. After an appropriate length of time, the teacher or parent should approach the child in a mild manner offering an opportunity for problem solving. If the child is ready, they then return to Step 4 and continue planning from there.

**Table 9.1.   Differences between punishment and discipline**

| Punishment | Discipline |
|---|---|
| 1. Not appropriate for (related to) the action. Too severe. | 1. Appropriate for the action. Not too severe or meaningless. |
| 2. Unexpected because the punisher has reacted on the spur of the moment. | 2. Expected because the individual has been informed of the rules and results of infringement. |
| 3. Often delayed. | 3. Immediate consequences. |
| 4. Expresses power of a personal authority. | 4. Based on logical consequences expressing the reality of the social order. |
| 5. Punishment imposed. Responsibility is that of the punisher (no choices). | 5. Discipline assumed. Responsibility is that of the individual (choices offered). |
| 6. Focuses on stopping past negative behavior. | 6. Focuses on teaching present and future positive behavior (e.g., mistakes are seen as chances to learn). Solution orientation. |
| 7. Focuses on external control of behavior. | 7. Focuses on reinforcing internal control of behavior. |
| 8. Reinforces failure identity (confirms low self-esteem and may increase rebellion and hostility or withdrawal). | 8. Emphasizes teaching ways that will result in a more successful identity. |
| 9. Often is, or is seen as, an expression of anger and hostility. | 9. Should be friendly—a partnership. |
| 10. Easy, expedient, and requires little skill. | 10. Difficult, time-consuming, requires much patience. |
| 11. Often alienates the individual. | 11. Strengthens the relationship over time as consistency demonstrates caring. |
| 12. Expression of moral judgment by punisher. | 12. Individual's own value judgement of his or her behavior. |
| 13. Often seen as linked to the punishee rather than to the act (doer is wrong). | 13. Linked to the act (emphasis is on the deed). |
| 14. Only recognizes results. | 14. Recognizes effort as well as results. |
| 15. No opportunity for individual to redress wrong. | 15. Opportunity for individual's retribution or repair. |

Children should not be allowed to criticize themselves unless it is part of a value judgment or is tied to a plan to correct the problem. Even under these circumstances, such criticism should not be accepted but rather dealt with. If the child says, "I'm no good; I never do right," the therapist might reply, "I don't think I can go along with that. You go to school every day on time, and some of the time, from what you say, you do well. You are also here which shows a willingness not seen in everyone. You are doing some things right."

It is also important that the therapist refrain from criticizing the child. Instead, the therapist might say, "Is what you are doing helping you or anyone else?" or "I think I can suggest a better way; let's discuss it." The child has an option in the second state-ment and is assured of help in doing better. During all of this, the child is learning a better way to handle problems and to cooperate with another person.

## Step 8. Never Give Up

This step is a reminder to the therapist. No matter what the child does or says, the ther-apist should continue to convey the attitude of persistence long after the child wants the therapist to give up. Not giving up will, it is hoped, solidify the idea for the child that someone does care. Often the child begins to work only after receiving this assurance.

## REALITY THERAPY AND CONTROL THEORY

W. Glasser (1984) has asserted that the methods of reality therapy are consistent with the concepts of control theory.

The goal of reality therapy in counseling or teaching is to help the child and adoles-cent gain more effective control over his or her life. In the classroom, teachers can use these same ideas to help the student become aware that it is beneficial to work hard and succeed academically. In either case, the goal is to help the child to become more re-sponsible. To accomplish this, the child is asked to look honestly in the direction the behavior is heading and to determine whether this direction is satisfactory both imme-diately and in the long run. If either the direction of his or her life or the behavior he or she is choosing in order to move in this direction is not as satisfying or effective as desired, the goal of reality therapy is to help find a more effective behavior, a better direction, or both.

To do this, the steps of reality therapy have been expanded and reworked into two major components of reality therapy counseling (W. Glasser, 1986b): the *counseling en-vironment* and the *procedures that lead to change*. These components should be used together if counseling is to be effective.

## Counseling Environment

The counselor must attempt to develop an environment in which the client feels secure enough to make an adequate evaluation of the effectiveness of his or her present behav-iors. The client is then helped both to learn and to attempt different behaviors in an effort to find more effective ways to meet his or her needs. The success of therapy de-pends on maintaining this environment throughout the counseling relationship.

The counseling environment needs to be perceived by the child as safe and positive. The child comes or is brought to counseling when some aspect of his or her life is not in effective control. It is critical for the child to see the therapist as a person who is capa-ble and interested in assisting him or her to find better choices for behavior. Therapists need to present themselves as persons who are not overwhelmed by the problems of the child and his or her family. To do this, the therapist should avow confidence in the child's ability to learn to live life more responsibly and effectively.

The therapist must remember that a client behaves according to the perceptions of his or her own world (as held in the mind). One must realize that what the client perceives may be very different from what the therapist and others close to the client might perceive. Early in therapy, time is directed toward helping the client understand that these differences exist. Learning to deal with these differences becomes the next step in therapy. Unless the client can learn to get along better with those who perceive the world differently, it will be difficult to satisfy needs effectively.

A client is more successful when he or she recognizes and accepts the responsibility for chosen behavior. The role of the therapist is to maintain a relationship with the child that accomplishes the following:

- Helps the child avoid excuses and accept responsibility.
- Emphasizes the child's assets and strengths.
- Provides the child with the chance to learn and to try new and more effective behaviors.

## Procedures That Lead to Change

First, the therapist needs to focus on the child's total behaviors; that is, how the child is *acting, thinking,* and *feeling* at the present time. Next, a child must learn that these total behaviors are chosen.

To effect this, ask the client what is wanted now. If the client does not know, continue to focus on the choices and the resultant direction in which those choices are taking the client. The critical question to ask here is, "Does your present behavior have a chance of getting you what you want now and will it take you in the direction you want to go?"

If the answer is no, this implies that the client's direction is reasonable, but that the present behaviors will not get him or her there. At this point, the therapist should help the client plan new behaviors. For example, "I want to improve my grades but to do so I will have to study more."

At times, the client is unable to move in the right direction regardless of how much effort he or she puts forth. If this occurs, the therapist should ask the client to consider changing directions. For example, "No matter how hard I study, my grades do not improve. I may have to consider a tutor." In this case, the plan now focuses more on changing the direction of the behavior than on the behavior itself.

If the answer to the critical question is yes, the behavior will get the client what is wanted now and will achieve the desired direction. Such an answer indicates that the client sees nothing wrong with this current behavior or the direction it is taking.

Before a plan is attempted, both client and therapist should agree that it has a reasonable chance of success, and a commitment should be given for follow-through. Usually the client who makes commitments tends to work harder. With younger children, a written commitment is generally more effective than a verbal one.

The therapist should remember that clients choose their behavior and that the best behavior is always that which the client believes can be accomplished. To this extent, the behaviors are "effective" for the client. One must also be aware that a client will not change a behavior until it appears that the present behavior will either not result in what is wanted or will not take the appropriate direction. Change becomes possible only when the client believes that another available behavior will allow him or her to satisfy needs in a more acceptable way.

## Reality Therapy Techniques

The following techniques are used in the application of these steps of reality therapy:

- *Humor:* The therapist may use humor to help the child understand that things are not as serious as they appear. It can be used confronting issues such as irrational behavior or lack of responsibility. It also helps the client develop the healthy ability to laugh at him- or herself. The message in humor is that life can be better, that there is hope, and that laughter is good medicine.
- *Confrontation:* Facing the child with a here-and-now, no-excuses stance is definitely confrontational. Most confrontations require client action: A value is pushed, and the client is challenged to look for alternatives and is encouraged to formulate a new plan. This technique is often used when a child is unable to shake the mistaken ideas or beliefs behind his or her behavior.
- *Contracts:* A written contract is often used in therapy. A signed contract serves as evidence of the client's intent to change behavior. It also specifies those changes in written form. Completion of a contract, like the fulfillment of needs, promotes feelings of self-worth within an individual. Here is evidence that the child *can* work responsibly toward a goal and succeed. Contracts may be one-sentence agreements such as, "Jack will speak to one new friend by Friday," or they may be quite detailed. The therapist and client each should sign the contract and keep a copy of it.
- *Instruction:* When a specific skill is needed to formulate a new course of action, instruction may be needed. This can be part of the therapy session if the therapist has the needed competence or, if not, the child can be referred elsewhere for skill instruction. If at all possible, the client should be encouraged to assume responsibility for the instruction/learning process.
- *Information:* The child often needs specific and new information for a plan of action and the therapist should be ready to provide it. If the therapist does not have the information the client requires, the therapist should assist the client in finding it. It is the therapist's responsibility to have available a list of probable and reliable sources.
- *Role Playing:* Role playing is often used when a child is experiencing difficulties in interpersonal relationships or needs to practice a new behavior. Role playing is frequently followed with a feedback session—a discussion of what the client and therapist experienced while playing the roles of others. The session often affords the therapist the opportunity to encourage clients by emphasizing what they did

well. Role playing also offers an opportunity to focus on nonverbal behaviors that are part of successful behavioral interactions.

- *Support:* Support is used to increase the child's awareness, anticipation, and expectation of a positive outcome. Children with a failure identity need much support, especially when putting their plans into action. They have learned to expect failure and do not want to take any further risks. Encouragement and support are paramount if children are to commit to a new or different behavior. Support can be given by the following means: asking the child's opinion, requesting the child's evaluation of his or her present behavior, providing praise for successfully completing a plan, and expressing confidence in the child's ability to change. If successful, this approach will usually increase the child's motivation and serve to communicate feelings of worth.

- *Homework Assignments:* Homework is used to build continuity between sessions and to facilitate counseling by encouraging the child to work on problems between sessions. Typical assignments include trying a new behavior, reducing or stopping a present behavior, keeping a record of current behavior, or researching solutions to a specific problem.

- *Bibliotherapy:* The goals of bibliotherapy include (a) allowing the child to see the similarity between his or her problems and those of others; (b) encouraging free expression concerning problems; (c) looking at alternative solutions; (d) helping the child to analyze attitudes and behaviors. When using bibliotherapy, be sure to discuss the readings with the child. Discussion should be focused on feelings, thoughts, behaviors, and consequences. Make certain that the child sees the relationship between the reading and his or her own life. Bibliotherapy can be viewed as a form of cognitive restructuring directed toward educating the child about certain areas of concern such as sex, divorce, or death. Suggested books for bibliotherapy can be found without difficulty.

- *Self-Disclosure:* Some self-disclosure by the therapist is usually needed to obtain involvement with the client. Because reality therapy calls for active and equal participation of both the client and therapist, there may be times when the therapist is asked how he or she deals with certain problems. In such circumstances, relevant to therapeutic goals, the therapist can share personal experiences.

- *Summarizing and Reviewing:* Because clients often give the impression that they are listening when they are not, it is advisable to have the child summarize what was said or discussed in the therapy session. This can be done halfway through the session and/or at the end of it.

- *Restitution:* It is better to help the student make restitution for a behavior than to apply punishment. The goal of this technique is to assist the student in developing self-discipline. The child is helped to understand that he or she can learn to remedy his or her mistakes. One does not focus on the fault or the mistake. The focus is on making things right. The therapist's job is to offer information and examples—to answer questions, to demonstrate, to question. Some restitution options are to fix it, pay back, say several positive things about another child or give time in lieu.

- *Questioning:* Use questioning to gather information, especially to clarify what was said. Well-timed questions help clients think about what they want and evaluate whether their behavior is leading them in the right direction.
- *Paradox:* This technique was introduced into reality therapy by Wubbolding (1988). It is designed to counter strong resistance to a plan that is not carried out. The usual approach is to ask the client not to continue the plan, to go slowly in carrying it out, or to keep breaking it. Sometimes the best way to make desired changes is to do so indirectly. This involves looking at the subject's behavior in an inverse way.

## GROUP PROCEDURES WITH CHILDREN AND ADOLESCENTS

Once the therapist has established involvement and a relationship with the child, it is still necessary to convince the child that such relationships are also available with others. Reality therapy can be used with groups as well as with individuals. At this point in treatment, the advantages of group therapy become apparent. The group offers the opportunity for involvement and provides more support, need satisfaction, and assurance than any one individual can provide. There is also more opportunity for safety in risking or trying new behaviors. Often, too, when the child listens to and becomes involved with other children, he or she becomes less self-involved. The group also allows a wide range of feelings and thoughts to be expressed. Instead of having only the therapist who cares for and approves of the child, there is now the potential for the child to experience approval from the whole group. Being part of the group means that the child has an opportunity to get personal, to be warm, to show concern, and to develop more responsible behavior. This gives the child a taste of success and the chance to feel better about him- or herself.

### Become Involved

In the initial stages of the group, the therapist takes an active role. Responsibility and caring must be molded while getting the group members involved with one another. The therapist becomes involved with each member of the group, asking questions, requesting information, and encouraging comments. It is advisable to use games, value clarification, or group projects during the beginning sessions rather than to focus on problems. As in the first step of reality therapy with individuals, being friendly is important to involvement; it may take five or six sessions to get the group running smoothly.

### Focus on Reality

The therapist must help the groups to focus on reality. After involvement has been established, the attention is focused on present behaviors and problems. Events discussed in the group should be kept to a minimum. The children are encouraged to evaluate and analyze, with the therapist asking such questions as: "What are you doing?" "What do you want?" "Is it doing you any good?" "Is it against the rules?" These questions help the children focus on the reality of the situation. The therapist does not evaluate the behavior but helps the children to become more aware of the behavior and to reach a decision about it. The children, however, may evaluate behavior and can also offer specific suggestions concerning how they would handle certain problems.

## Make a Plan

Initially, the therapist will be very active in plan making. It will more than likely be up to him or her to develop alternative plans or different choices. However, the therapist must always be encouraging the children to become actively involved in this process. The therapist is cautioned to help make a reasonable plan that will have the best opportunity for success. After a plan has been decided on, a commitment is obtained from the child or children involved. If the plan does not work, the therapist must firmly refuse to accept excuses; no one should be let off the hook. The therapist should be supportive and encouraging by asking, "Are you going to carry it out?" but the therapist must not punish or allow the other children to punish.

## Establish Rules

The therapist, together with the children, must see that rules are established and consequences are set up if the rules are broken. For example, it might be established that one must raise a hand to speak to the group. The first time a child does not follow this rule, a warning is given; the second time the rule is broken, the child must leave the group until he or she feels able to follow the rule; the third time, the child must leave the group and may not come back until he or she presents a plan for following the rule.

## Group Makeup

Many therapists, because of time demands, put all their problem children in one group. A group made up solely of children with acting-out behaviors, history of truancy, or academic difficulties is destined to fail. If one purpose of the group is to help children with failure identities, it makes sense that they should be involved with or come into contact with children who have successful identities. For the most part, children with failure identities learn very little that is responsible from other children with failure identities. A truant child has little that is constructive to offer another truant—if anything, he or she may reinforce and support the truant behavior. A child with a good attendance record may be more likely to help the truant as this child is already living more responsibly and can offer strength, encouragement, and support of the failing child. The successful child may be able to think of several alternatives or different choices for the problem situation and may also help in the development of a plan. It is important to include successful children in the group whenever possible.

## Group Size and Duration

The size of the group will depend on the purpose of the group and the setting in which it occurs. However, 8 to 10 children are more than enough to work with at one time. With younger children, the therapist may want to begin with a smaller number. The group must meet regularly, thus giving the children the opportunity to plan to attend and to assume responsibility for being on time. Age becomes an important variable when considering a time frame. W. Glasser (1969) recommends that primary school children begin by meeting for 10 to 15 minutes per session, increasing to 30 minutes per session. Fourth, fifth, and sixth graders can easily meet for 30 to 45 minutes, and high schoolers for 45 minutes to an hour. The minimum number of meetings for all age groups is once a week; two or three times a week is more desirable.

## Time of Day

A morning time is preferable when the children are fresh. Meetings should not be scheduled before recess or lunch.

## CLASSROOM AND EDUCATIONAL APPLICATIONS

If one were to poll junior and senior high school-age children concerning their objections to school, many would reply that school has no relevance to the real world and that, although they are forced to go, they simply put in their class time, waiting for the 10 minutes of socialization between classes and the half hour at lunch. Those who comply with the system often complain that they are learning to memorize, not to think. Or those who have gotten on the memorization railroad, ride it all the way to the perfect "A" report card, the graduation with honors, and the scholarships waiting at the end of the line. Either way, there are prevailing feelings among these students that school is something to which one submits, that apathy serves better than taking on the system, and that teachers and the administration don't care as long as they get paid. Although it may be harder to elicit these feelings from the elementary school children, they are there, expressed in the child who reaches over and crumples a classmate's paper, or who wanders aimlessly around the room, or who bullies on the playground.

## The Classroom Meeting

Fun, freedom, self-esteem, and belonging—the four components of a successful identity if one follows the thinking of reality therapy—are for the most part missing from our educational system where an "If you want to pass, you'll do it my way" attitude prevails. It is possible, however, at any level to begin to help students become involved in developing goals of their own, to help them form better relationships with one another and with their teachers, and to help them experience success, gain confidence in their control over their education, and enjoy the process.

The vehicle that has offered students a feeling of belonging and of social responsibility, that has given them an opportunity to both give and receive concern, is the *classroom meeting*. Basically, there are three types: open-ended, education-diagnostic, and social-problem solving. These meetings allow the teacher to apply some principles of reality therapy in the classroom.

The *open-ended meeting* centers around thought-provoking questions related to the children's lives. The teacher presents hypothetical questions designed to enable the children to become involved. The discussion that follows is aimed at stimulating and developing intellectual curiosity. Any topic of interest to the class can be used. There are no right or wrong answers, only alternatives. Topics might include any number of relevant issues (depending, to an extent, on the age of the children) such as war, politics, taxes, or abortion. At no time should the teacher or leader of the group make value judgments.

*Education-diagnostic meetings* are directly related to what the class is studying. The teacher may use this meeting to evaluate his or her teaching techniques and the current curriculum. This kind of class meeting provides an alternative to objective testing and helps determine whether the children are learning the material being taught. The meeting is informational—"How much have my students learned?"—and is not used for grading. It is seen as an efficient method for determining the children's strengths and weaknesses in a given subject. The discussion should provoke individual thinking and allow the children to correct false or misguided information.

The *social-problem-solving meeting* deals with any individual or group problems of the class or school. Problem-solving is the major thrust here. Solutions, it should be pointed out, never include punishment or faultfinding. This type of meeting gives the children some feeling of control over their lives. Loneliness, attendance, grades, and individual behavior problems are legitimate issues for discussion. The meetings should not strive for perfect answers but should at least work toward clarification of problems that may very well not have solutions. The child learns that it is beneficial to discuss problems and learns to recognize that there is more than one way of dealing with a problem.

All these meetings should be conducted with everyone seated in a circle. The circle provides the children with a feeling of acceptance because they have been allotted an equal amount of space with one another and the teacher.

The initial role of the teacher is to generate questions that will arouse the children's interest. A basic technique to help stimulate interaction among the children is what has been called a *floater*. This is a statement that does not call for an answer; it is simply a comment sent out for response. The teacher should not feel a need to fill voids or silence; instead, he or she can offer another nondirective comment or can simply wait for a response. It is critical that the teacher respond to early statements by the children in a way that will not turn them off. This is best accomplished by remaining relatively value free. For example, even a very good response should not be praised because such praise may inhibit some of the other children from offering what they then believe is a comment of less importance. The teacher should, however, indicate an appreciation for the contribution. Children who fail to volunteer might be brought into the discussion by saying, "You are paying attention; would you like to comment?" or "Think about it and let me know if you come up with an idea or answer." It is important that the teacher be supportive of any child's effort and discourage any attempt to criticize a child. If one child is dominating the group's time, the teacher can handle this situation by saying, "Thanks for your comments; let's hear from someone else now."

When a student behaves in a way that is disruptive to the other students in the class, this student needs to be confronted and helped by the entire class. For this type of situation, the social-problem-solving meeting is held. Here the so-called problem child hears what the other children think of his or her behavior. The teacher needs to be more in control of this type of meeting to ensure that it does not become a free-for-all. The reason for the meeting should be explained to the class (e.g., to discuss that a child has been stealing from other children). It is suggested that the group might be able to help the child to act in a more responsible manner. The children are asked to state what this child has been doing that interferes with them personally. The children are encouraged to tell the child directly what the behaviors are and the effects that these behaviors have had on them. After each person in the group, including the teacher, has had a chance to speak, the child with the irresponsible behavior is given a chance to explain what others have done to interfere with him or her. At this point, the meeting moves quickly from getting all the facts out on the table to doing something with the information that has been obtained. It might be suggested that the class and the child involved offer some possible solution to the problem that would be acceptable to everyone. The teacher listens to all the solutions and then tells the group to narrow down the alternative plans and solutions. Last, the child is asked to pick a plan and commit to it. The class members are also asked to commit themselves to doing anything that will help the child carry out the plan. The conclusion of the meeting is an agreed-on, manageable plan.

These class meetings are basically techniques used by individual teachers in their respective classrooms. A schoolwide approach to discipline or problem-solving has been formulated by W. Glasser (1974) and is presented in the next section.

## A 10-Step Discipline Program

Reality therapy is a common sense, nonpunitive approach that helps the children figure out what to do when their behavior is displeasing to themselves or interfering with the rights or needs of others. It focuses mainly on personal involvement and is structured toward helping the children plan and commit themselves to a plan that will make their lives better. Reality therapy helps children gain a sense of belonging and personal worth.

Based on the principles of reality therapy, a 10-step, schoolwide approach for dealing with problem children has been developed. The approach deals with problems by means of a constructive, no-nonsense but nonpunitive method built on a positive teacher-student involvement, but it does not accept excuses in place of results. Built into the program are alternatives to consider when something does not work.

For example, Jack has behavior problems in school. It is now February, and despite several conferences with the principal, the school psychologist, and Jack's parents, nothing seems to be working. Perhaps Jack comes from a poor home background or is an only child or is the last child of a large family. He has barely learned to read and may have had few good school experiences. Whatever his problems, the teacher now has Jack in the classroom for an entire school year; and if the teacher cannot get him to cooperate, Jack will suffer and the teacher's life will be miserable.

If the following 10 steps to better control are followed by the teacher, Jack may be helped to change. His behavior can become, though not perfect, improved enough to reward all the efforts. No miracles will occur; it is hard, slow work. A period of several months is probably a good minimum time commitment.

This program is divided into three parts. The first 3 steps look realistically at how the child is dealing with his or her problems and are concerned with what can be done to decrease or reduce these problems. Steps 4 through 6 give the teacher a simple, practical approach for working with the child and getting the child to identify, evaluate, and plan alternatives to his or her unacceptable behavior. Steps 7 through 10 consider resources within the school and/or community that can be used if the child refuses to change the behavior or continues to break the rules.

## Steps 1–3: What Am I Doing Here?

### Step 1. What Am I Doing That Isn't Working?

Set aside some time and make a list of the things you currently do when Jack upsets you. Ask yourself the questions, "What am I doing? Do I yell at him . . . threaten him . . . ignore him?" Be honest and look at the efforts you have made to help the child. For the next few weeks refrain from doing the things you have on the list that have not been working. When you are tempted to use old methods, look at the list and ask yourself: "If they didn't work before, what chances do they have of working now?"

### Step 2. A New Start

If you have decided that your present techniques are not working, consider stopping these behaviors. Promise yourself that tomorrow, if Jack manifests a problem, you will attempt to act as though this is the first time it is occurring. Stay away from such statements to him as, "You are doing it again," or "I have told you a thousand times, stop it." Do not remind him that his behavior is repetitive behavior. If, on the other hand, he does something right or good, even though he has done it before, reinforce him: "Jack, it's really neat when you sit still," or "I appreciate that." A pat on the head, verbal recognition, or an approving nod is helpful in telling him he is okay. A fresh start for him, if not for you, may make a big difference.

### Step 3. A New Strategy

Plan at least one thing you could do for Jack that might help him have a better day *tomorrow*. It doesn't have to be a big deal. This step is based on the adage, "An ounce of prevention is worth a pound of cure." Whatever you do should have a positive aspect, such as a pat on the back as soon as he comes in, a special errand, or a "Good to see you, Jack." It can be anything helps that shows your personal concern for him. Fifteen seconds of unexpected recognition can mean a great deal. Commit yourself to these little plans for several weeks. The hope is that Jack will get the idea that he has some value in your class. Don't expect to be repaid with changed behavior immediately. Jack didn't develop his problems overnight nor will he become a pillar of responsibility in just a few days. Initially, he may reject you even more than before. You must stay calm and be persistent. Remember, these first three steps are aimed at changing *your* attitude and strategy.

## Steps 4–6: Who's in Control Here?

### Step 4. Calm Direction

Even if you have some success with the first three steps, at some point Jack is going to demonstrate the problems again. Perhaps when you ask him to pay attention, he will daydream and not respond. Act as if this is the first time he has ever done this (Step 2), and ask him to pay attention and begin his assignment. You might also say, "Please stop it." It is hoped that your improved relationship with him through the first three steps will now help him to do as you ask and he will focus on the task. If he does not respond, walk over to him and help him get started. Do this in a quiet manner, possibly putting your hand gently on his shoulder at the same time. At this point, you might say, "Can you now do your work?" If he doesn't agree to do his work, don't give up; you still have six steps left. You are trying to establish that although he must take responsibility for not doing his work, you are willing to help him get started. If he accepts this, that ends it. You are not blaming, yelling, or threatening. If this step works, say nothing more accept to give him some reinforcement such as, "Jack, I knew you could do it."

### Step 5. Question Time

If Step 4 does not work, ask the child one or both of the following two questions: "Is what you are doing against the rules?" and "What are you doing?" Often the child will say nothing or refuse to answer. If this happens, say, "This is what I say you are doing and it is against the rules." In essence, you are saying that Jack should be doing his work. You will have to be insistent. You are telling him that he is breaking a rule. Although he might try to evade the issue, you should continue focusing on the rule. These questions may be all you need to ask to help him begin working. You may also continue by asking, "Can you make a plan to follow the rules?" or "Are you willing to do your work?"

### Step 6. Develop a Plan

Go through Step 5 briefly, and, if it does not work, tell the child in a very firm voice, "We have to work this out. We have to make a plan that will help you follow the rules or change your behavior." What you are looking for here is more responsible behavior. It will be necessary to make some time available to talk with him about making a plan. If it cannot be done immediately, you might say, "We will work it out later." The time it takes to do this is usually much less than the time you spent with procedures that didn't work. The plan has to be more than "I'm sorry" or "I'll stop it." It has to be a *doing* plan that will help the child move toward more responsible behavior. You might say, "I am glad you are sorry, but what are you going to do so it won't happen again?" The plan should be short, specific, and concrete. At first, you may have to put many of your ideas into the plan. Gradually, as he does better, the child may make more contributions to the plan. In Jack's case, you might say, "You do not want to do your work, but there are rules. Can you make a plan with me so you can get your work done? Let's try to work it out. Why don't we take some time and talk this over. It doesn't appear you are having much fun and maybe I can help you." Jack may be quite cautious at first, believing that this will just delay his ultimate punishment. Tell him he won't be punished and that you'd like to help him work it out. Listen to his complaints; talk with him; get to know him better. Try not to bring up old behaviors or faults but instead stress that rules are important and you believe he can follow them. You may want to put the plan in writing; such a contract helps keep the commitment. You are saying to Jack that he has the power to make a good plan. Developing a plan does take some time, but it is a lot better than the techniques that have failed in the past.

## Steps 7–10: Hope at the End of the Rope

### Step 7. Someplace Close

Assume that Jack still manifests a problem or disrupts again and you are convinced that the previous steps will not work. Now it is time for the child to be isolated, or "timed out." The decision for time-out may be made by you or it could have been established as a natural consequence at the planning level in Step 6. This isolation is done right in the classroom. You need to create a place where the child can sit that is comfortable but separate from the class. If this is impossible to do, a desk could be set up in the hallway within viewing distance from the door. This conveys to the child that he is no longer involved in active participation in the class. The child can listen but cannot take part in classroom activities until a plan to follow the rules is worked out with the child. The child needs to inform you of the plan and make a commitment to carry it out. This plan should be mutually agreed on. If Jack continues his behavior, then say, "Go sit over there." Try not to say anything else. Be firm and quick and send him without discussion. Don't be upset if he spends hours or most of the day there. Isolation has a way of making the everyday class routines look more attractive. It is important that the child learn that rules cannot be broken, and the best way to learn this is through experience. You might, when you think Jack has had enough, ask him if he is ready to return to his seat and participate. If the answer is yes, at your next break, go over the rules and ask him if he has a plan to follow. Remember you are trying to teach him something in a few months that he has not learned over a period of many years. If the child continues the behavior in isolation, the child's only alternative is to be excluded, and yours is to move to Step 8.

### Step 8. Someplace Farther

In-school suspension is involved in this step. You have tried, you have been patient, but now you have had enough. At this step, there are no questions to be asked. You can make this statement, "Jack, things did not work out for you here. We have both tried hard to work out the problems but now it is time for you to spend time outside the class and maybe talk with some other people. Please report to the Counselor's office [or the Principal's office, or the in-school suspension room]." The room or place should be staffed by a person who can get the following idea across to the child: "We want you in school and class but we expect you to follow the rules. When you have a plan as to how you can return to class and follow the rules, let me know. If you need help carrying out the plan, let me know and I will help you." What you want to get across to the child is that the plan will be different and better than what was used in the past. To get Jack to change his behavior is the task for which a new environment as well as new approaches are necessary. Don't be concerned if he sits there for a time. The whole idea is used to reduce the alternatives to two choices: to be in class and behave, or to be out of class and sit. It is hoped that the class will begin to look better. The point that needs to be communicated to the child is, "Follow reasonable rules, or you are out." However, while he is out, you are not going to hurt or reject the child, which would let the child rationalize his behavior on the basis of his dislike for you. This kind of nonpunitive place may be hard for the school and you, the teacher, to accept, but review Step 1 again—you can see the child has been in the "old" place a long time with no results. Be ready for a lot of excuses from the child; follow them up with, "But you cannot go back to class until you have a plan." When more than one day is required, you should notify Jack's parents that their child is not in class. It may well be that 3 days to a week or more will be required. Perhaps the child's schoolwork will suffer (although he could do schoolwork while in in-school suspension). It is hoped that the child will learn one of the most important things that can be learned: One must be responsible for one's own behavior and one does have the choice to behave in a way helpful to oneself and others.

### Step 9. A Day Off

If Jack cannot be handled in an in-school suspension, the parents should be notified and asked to take the child home. The child will now be put on "a day off" with the idea that he can return the following day. One could say, "We would like your child to return, but we must maintain reasonable behavior. If his behavior goes beyond the rules, he will have to go home again." This means that Jack starts again at Step 8, or at in-school suspension, and can stay until his behavior changes for the better or until he reaches Step 9 again. If the child cannot be helped in school at all, then he will have to stay home, which means either having a tutor at home or the school's proceeding to Step 10.

### Step 10. Someplace Else

If Jack is continually unsuccessful in Step 9, he should stay home and be referred to some other community agency. This may sound tough, but it may take something like this to jolt the child into taking some responsibility for his behavior. If the child is in jail or juvenile detention, perhaps he could return to school for a day to see if he can make it, but not unless a specific plan and commitment have been made to follow the rules.

## PARENTING SKILLS

A Parent Involvement Program (PIP) has been designed to help parents gain the necessary reality therapy skills (McGuiness, 1977). Many of the activities demonstrate ways to facilitate increased involvement with one's children. Other aspects of the program attempt to teach parents better listening skills and to reflect to their children the good they see in them.

**Table 9.2.   Parent involvement program**

| Lesson Objectives | Topics Covered |
| --- | --- |
| 1. To build trust and support among group members. To help parents understand the cultural shift that has occurred since World War II. To help parents understand how these cultural changes are affecting their relationship with their children. | Group involvement. The Identity Society role versus goal-activities. |
| 2. To help parents realize the importance of building warm, personal, friendly relationships with their children. To help parents understand a problem-solving approach (reality therapy) to helping children become responsible. | Importance of involvement. Successful versus failing identities. Principles of reality therapy. |
| 3. To give parents insights that will help them reflect to their children the goodness and beauty which they see in them. To share with parents ideas that enhance total family involvement and help create a successfilled atmosphere for the home. To develop with the parents a personal plan that incorporates the concepts basic to reality therapy. | Practice in using steps of reality therapy. Total family involvement. How to increase involvement at home. |
| 4. To share successes and concerns based on the activities developed from each parent's personal plan. | Successful experiences. Communication. Components of good listening. |
| 5. To help parents improve their communication skills. To clarify any misconceptions concerning the understanding and use of the basic steps of reality therapy. To expose parents to current authors who have written significant articles in the area of parent-child relationships. | Nonverbal communication. One-way versus two-way communication. Discipline techniques. |
| 6. To help parents gain insights in working with their children, based on articles read and shared with each other. To help parents clarify for themselves the basic concepts introduced and to share with their families the spirit of the workshop. | Review and feedback. |

The program is accomplished in six 3-hour sessions, which can be conducted on weekends or evenings during the week. Each of the sessions has a definite content to provide parents with knowledge about a skill to be used in dealing with their children. The sessions are based on practice after they receive the theory. The sessions are structured to allow the parents to personalize the ideas, share their concerns, and develop a plan to improve things at home.

The objectives of the program for each session contained in the *Idea Book for the Parent Involvement Program* (McGuiness, 1977) are outlined in Table 9.2.

The parents are involved in a number of activities including some of the following:

1. Viewing films and listening to tapes that include:
   a. Identity Society.
   b. Reality of Success.
2. Using worksheets that include:
   a. Reality therapy planning form.
   b. Questions to accompany "Success-Oriented Home Exercises."
3. Reading articles such as:
   a. "Basic Principles in Dealing with Children."
   b. "How to Drive Your Child Sane."
   c. "Rules, Goals, and Failure."
   d. "Your Child and Discipline."
4. Discussing ideas in small and large groups.
5. Making personal plans to meet the needs of the family.
6. Participating in role playing to allow for practice of what is being presented.

## FAMILY INTERVENTIONS

Reality therapy does not at present offer a framework for family therapy in the traditional sense. Family therapies usually identify the family as the client and do not focus on an individual, identified client. In family therapies, the focus is on systems, relationships, structures, and interdependencies. Reality therapy emphasizes developing the individual's successful identity and encouraging personal responsibility.

The family therapy focus on environmental influences on behavior is somewhat at odds with reality therapy. Family therapy views individual problems as stemming from a dysfunctional family system or structure, whereas reality therapy views individual problems as resulting more from individual identity and choices. Thus, the two approaches are not entirely compatible.

The reality therapist, however, does have some tools to use with problems that have family components. The first is the Parent Involvement Program, previously described. This allows work with families where problems seem centered around a need for more parental involvement with children and a need for the parents to provide more positive feedback to their children. The second tool is marital therapy or conjoint marital counseling (W. Glasser & Zunin, 1979), to be used when the family problems seem to be a result of marital discord. This type of therapy is often time-limited, usually 5 to 15 sessions. This marriage counseling begins by clarifying the couple's goals in seeking counseling. Questions would be directed at determining whether the goal is, on the one hand, to continue in the marriage or, on the other hand, to attempt a last-ditch effort to save the marriage even though a decision to end it has already been made. Attention would also be focused on defining the couple's similarities and differences in opinion and interest, on how the couple seeks friends and other activities, and how much the couple actually knows, as opposed to assumes, about each other. The overall goal is intimacy, not simply familiarity.

## EFFICACY

There are numerous favorable case reports in Glasser's writings, two published casebooks (N. Glasser, 1980, 1989), a survey of Glasser's work (Bassin, Bratter, & Rachin, 1976), and a compendium of articles on reality therapy (Litwack, 1994). In addition, seven books have been written by Ford and others (Ford, 1974, 1987, 1989, 1994; Ford & Englund, 1977, 1979; Ford & Zorn, 1975) that discuss the techniques and principles of reality therapy as applied to discipline, raising children, marriage, loneliness, and stress. A book by Robert (1973) discusses the use of reality therapy in the school situation to deal with loneliness. Wobbolding (1988), 1991) has written two very useful books demonstrating the practical uses of control theory. Gossen (1992) presents in detail, how restitution, a key approach to discipline, is used in reality therapy.

The methods and techniques of reality therapy and their justification appear reasonable and have been accepted by many professionals in the field. Reality therapy follows certain tenets in attaining involvement and influencing responsible, realistic behavior:

- Personalization—becoming involved.
- Concentrating on the here-and-now.
- Emphasizing behavior.
- Refraining from asking why.
- Helping the client evaluate behavior.
- Developing a different or better plan of behavior.
- Refusing to accept excuses.
- Never punishing—only disciplining.
- Offering little sympathy.
- Approving and praising responsible behavior.
- Never giving up.

There certainly is no lack of testimony concerning the efficacy of reality therapy. However, in these books there is no adequate statistical evidence or support for reliability and validity. W. Glasser and Zunin (1973) reported there had been no long-term research on the effectiveness of reality therapy with outpatients. Follow-up work at the Ventura School for Girls, however, indicated that the use of reality therapy in the treatment program had the recidivism rate for that environment (Glasser & Zunin).

Some studies have focused on classroom meetings and their effect on self-concept, social adjustment, locus of control, and achievement. Matthews (1972) studied the effect of class meetings on the discipline, self-concept, social adjustment, and reading achievement of 221 fourth and fifth graders. Treatment consisted of 16 weeks of a language arts program in the control group and reality therapy in the experimental group. Pretreatment and posttreatment data were collected on three tests. His findings indicated that both treatments increased self-concept scores but neither change was significant. It was also found that neither treatment was significantly better in improving social adjustment. However, reality therapy was found to be significantly more effective in lowering the incidence of discipline problems in the experimental group compared with the control group.

Hunter (1973) reported nonsignificant findings when studying the effects of reality therapy and Rogerian group sessions on math achievement, self-concept, and behavior of 40 fifth-grade students. The students were matched on sex and randomly assigned to a math remediation, a Rogerian discussion, a reality therapy, or a control group. Six weeks of treatment (twelve 40-minute sessions per group) resulted in no significant change in math achievement, self-esteem, or behavior in any of the groups.

Tangeman (1973) investigated the effects of a reality therapy program on the achievement and self-esteem of 93 third graders. Four classrooms were randomly assigned to two treatment approaches—reality therapy class meetings and Developing Understanding of Self and Others (DUSO)—and two control groups. Twenty 30-minute meetings were held for each group over a 10-week period. Pretest and posttest data from two tests were analyzed. The results indicated no significant changes for any of the groups on self-concept or achievement.

Hawes (1971) evaluated the use of reality therapy on the locus of control, self-concept, and classroom behavior of 340 third- and sixth-grade Black students. Three tests were administered for pretest and posttest evaluation. Reality therapy class meetings were employed for a 16-week period, with a control group receiving no treatment. The results showed that the reality therapy program did significantly shift the children's belief system toward an internal orientation. A significant change in behavior was also found, as the reality therapy group demonstrated more appropriate changes on the self-concept measure.

Shearn and Randolph (1978) evaluated the effect of reality therapy class meetings on self-concept and on-task behavior for fourth-grade children. In an attempt to construct a "true placebo control" design, the authors randomly assigned four intact classes (27 students in each) into four treatment conditions: pretested reality therapy, unpretested reality therapy, pretested placebo (career education activities), and unpretested placebo (career education). Several tests were administered to all the groups. Pretest and posttest scores were collected for one experimental and one placebo group, while only posttest scores were collected for the other experimental and control group. The results indicated that neither treatment, pretesting, nor the interaction of treatment and pretesting for posttest scores had any significant effect on self-concept or on-task behavior. The authors concluded that their findings do not support using reality therapy in the classroom. They did caution that the inability to measure the effects of reality therapy empirically in the classroom is a factor that confounds interpretation of research in this area.

Quinn (1979) used seventh- and eighth-grade children to investigate the effects of class meetings on self-concept and attitude toward school. Three seventh- and eighth-grade classes were randomly assigned, each to one of the following groups: class meetings, a quasi-experimental group (performing plays), or a control group (no treatment). Pretest and posttest scores were collected on self-concept and school attitudinal scales. The results failed to demonstrate any significant changes in self-concept or improved attitude toward school. Here nonsignificant results may have been a function of insufficient time for behavioral changes to occur.

A study by Grant (1972) used open-ended class meetings to investigate possible changes in self-concept and locus of control of 163 fourth-grade pupils. Classrooms were randomly assigned as open-ended classroom meetings. Each treatment group met in twenty-nine 30-minute meetings over a 6-week period. All children were rated by their teachers prior to the treatment on a rating scale as either Normal ($N = 78$) or Deviant ($N = 85$). Results of the study demonstrated that the class meetings influenced self-concept somewhat, but had little influence on locus of control. The only significant changes in locus of control occurred in experimental students who had been rated as "deviants" by their teachers. Students in the normal group accepted responsibility for failure much more than did the deviant-rated control students. The author concluded that, in general, the open-ended class meetings were of little value in effecting change in self-concept or locus of control.

Rosario (1973) measured the effects of reality therapy group counseling on college students by means of the Nowicki-Strickland Internal-External Scale. The author predicted that extremely external students would show very little change of control orientation, extremely internal students would become slightly less internal, and moderately internal-external students would benefit most from class meetings. A pretest and posttest model, with a follow-up testing 5 months after completion of treatment, was used. Results of the analysis of data for the initial posttest indicated that no significant shift was found for high internals, high externals, or those rated moderately internal-external. After the 5-month follow-up, results indicated that extremely external students did shift toward a more internal stance. The author thought that the change in locus of control for the external males may have been the result of attitude change based on the practice of the behaviors. The study had a number of shortcomings, including the absence of quasi-experimental and control groups. In addition, the use of 10 therapists allowed for uncontrolled variability in application of reality therapy techniques.

English (1970) also focused on the use of reality therapy (counseling) in various school environments. He demonstrated that reality therapy was an effective method for reducing disciplinary problems, increasing school achievement, and improving teacher-teacher and teacher-student interactions.

Marandola and Imber (1979) evaluated the effects of classroom meetings on the argumentative behavior (verbal and physical) of 10 preadolescent, inner city, learning-disabled children. Both open-ended and problem-solving classroom meetings were used. During the intervention period, classroom meetings were used daily for 8 days with the focus always related to argumentative behavior in the classroom. Three types of behavior were used for analysis: verbal argument between two classmates, verbal argument involving two or more classmates, and physical confrontation between two classmates. The results of the study provided strong support for the classroom meeting and its role in behavior change. Appropriate behaviors for positive interactions were maintained, and inappropriate argumentative behaviors were sharply decreased as a result of the class meetings. The study had some limitations: Nine of the 10 children had been with the teacher for 2 years, and strong rapport had been established between teacher and students. The children were also accustomed to having discussions, although they were not the same as Glasser's class meetings.

Poppen and Welch (1976) utilized reality therapy with 16 overweight adolescent girls who volunteered to participate in a weight-loss program. The subjects were evaluated by pretesting and posttesting with a self-concept scale. The treatment program lasted for 6 weeks. The results of the study indicated that reality therapy was effective in producing a significant weight loss; however, no significant changes in self-concept were detected.

Hough-Waite (1980) compared the effectiveness of the Parent Involvement Program with a behavioral program entitled the "Art of Parenting." A group of untreated controls was also included. Participants in treatment groups were 19 randomly assigned parents who volunteered to participate in a parent education group. Eight were assigned to the Art of Parenting Program, and 11 to the Parent Involvement Program. The control group consisted of 14 parents randomly selected from a large population. A Child-Rearing Practices Questionnaire was administered before and after training, which lasted 6 weeks. The results indicated that neither treatment group differed significantly from the controls or from each other. Some factors could have confounded the results, including small sample size, lack of a sensitive outcome measure, and the use of volunteers as subjects.

Bigelow and Thorne (1979) compared client-centered and reality therapy techniques in group counseling at the elementary school level. One group contained six children and the other eight. All children were volunteers for a summer remedial reading program. Six group counseling sessions were conducted with both groups. The Hill Interaction Matrix was administered before and after the six sessions. The results indicated that the reality therapy group performed more efficiently than did the client-centered group in that significantly more therapeutic group member interactions were elicited by reality therapy techniques. It was also concluded that a counselor can direct an elementary-school age group into defined work areas and maintain it there more rapidly using a reality-oriented counseling approach.

Baskin and Hess (1980) conducted a review of seven affective education programs, one of which was Schools without Failure. In the area of self-esteem, the authors cited a two-year evaluation of Schools without Failure in Grades 1 through 6, which found no significant impact on self-esteem but did find that the frequency of discipline referrals to the principal decreased with the implementation of the Schools without Failure program. It was also reported that no differences were found between treatment and control group achievement levels. The authors also discussed the methodological difficulties inherent to evaluating a program such as Schools without Failure and reality therapy.

Omizo and Cubberly (1983) studied 60 learning-disabled students, aged 12–24, who were assigned to experimental and control conditions. The students in the experimental group were exposed to discussions (e.g., obstacles to academic success) by teachers trained in reality therapy. Multivariate analysis revealed that the students in the experimental group attained higher academic aspirations and lower anxiety levels than those in the control group.

Yarish (1986) studied 45 male juvenile offenders (aged 12–16 years) to determine whether positive perceptual changes could be brought about by the application of reality therapy. The Nowicki-Strickland Locus of Control Scale for Children was administered to subjects during their first and last week in a treatment facility. A significant difference was found between the treatment and control groups. The subjects who received reality therapy moved in an internal direction and chose to behave better with control of their fate in their own hands. Subjects were treated for an average of 4 months.

Hart-Hester (1986) studied 5 fourth-grade students who exhibited behavioral problems such as noncompliance, aggressiveness, off-task behavior, and absenteeism. She tried to improve several targeted behaviors (i.e., on-task behavior, peer interactions, and student-teacher interactions) through the use of reality therapy. Using anecdotal reports from the school principal, classroom teacher, and independent observation by investigation, the data indicated that reality therapy increased on-task behavior but not peer interactions or student-teacher interaction.

Tamborella (1987) investigated how "troubled" adolescents responded to the use of reality therapy procedures in a structured alternative school environment. Twenty students and six staff members were involved in the study. Evaluation was accomplished by using in-depth interview schedules, student permanent records, student attendance reports, student suspension reports, and the Statements about Schools Inventory. The results indicated that the use of reality therapy techniques that govern the types of student-teacher interactions in the alternative school program is effective in producing increased attendance and decreased rates of suspension. Students and staff experienced positive changes in self-perception, and students had positive perceptions regarding personal and academic needs satisfaction. It was demonstrated that significant and positive change in students and staff can be brought about through the impact of reality therapy.

Gorter-Cass (1988) evaluated an alternative school for disruptive junior high school youth. Program staff were trained in reality therapy techniques. The results indicated that the initial steps of reality therapy were successfully delivered. Significant changes were found in identity, personal self-worth, family-self, and total self-concept. The later and more specific steps of reality therapy dealing with assuming responsibility and planning and carrying out behaviors were not successfully carried out. The behavioral outcome goals established by the steps of reality therapy were not achieved. However, a trend toward less severe behavior was demonstrated.

Bean (1988) investigated whether reality therapy could produce significant positive outcomes with community-based, male juvenile offenders. Changes were measured by recidivism rates and locus of control. The Nawicki-Strickland Locus of Control for Children was used to measure locus of control. Seventy-two offenders, aged 14–17, were randomly assigned to reality therapy, community service, Crossroads, or probation conditions. The recidivism rate for reality therapy was significantly lower than the recidivism rate of the Crossroads condition. There were no overall significant differences between groups or pretest or posttest locus of control measures. However, the reality therapy group demonstrated significantly more internal locus of control than the Crossroads group on an individual posttest pairwise comparison. The study concluded that reality therapy was the most effective in reducing recidivism rates. Reality therapy also appeared to affect locus of control significantly.

A study by Allen (1990) examined the efficacy of group counseling using reality therapy and a study skills program with at-risk students in the fifth and sixth grades. The children were evaluated on general self-esteem, behavioral academic self-esteem, grades, and attendance. Ninety children from two elementary schools were assigned randomly to one of three groups; reality therapy ($N = 30$), study skill ($N = 30$), and no treatment ($N = 30$). The groups were seen for 45 minutes twice a week over a 6-week period. Pretest and posttest measures included the Coopersmith Self-Esteem Inventory, Behavioral Academic Self-Esteem Rating Scale, academic grades, and attendance rates. There were no significant results for general self-esteem, academic grades, and attendance between reality therapy and study skill treatment groups. There was also no significant difference in the outcome of the four measures between the treatment groups and the control group. The reality therapy group failed to demonstrate a significant effect at the end of the 6-week treatment period.

Coats (1991) studied the impact of reality therapy on teacher attitudes and the behavior of emotionally disturbed children. Thirty-three students (aged 5–14 years) with severe emotional and behavioral disabilities, who were attending a special school, were used in this study. The children's behavior was measured by using staff interviews and examination of student behavior logs for the 1991–1992 school year. The findings indicated that reality therapy contributed in reducing the frequency of severe student behaviors. The majority of teachers interviewed perceived reality therapy as having a positive impact on student behavior. For example, seclusionary time-outs showed a marked reduction over the school year.

Harris (1992) assessed the use of reality therapy as part of an adolescent pregnancy prevention program. Two groups of 27 students were randomly selected to participate in the study. One group received reality therapy-based instruction while the other group served as the control. Measures of self-esteem, locus of control, and decision-making skills were used as predictors of responsible behavior. There was a significant increase on self-esteem for both groups with no significant difference on locus of control. Students who participated in the reality therapy group were able to distinguish between responsible and irresponsible behaviors. Most of the students reported that the reality therapy approach was beneficial in helping them choose responsible behaviors.

The purpose of a study by Kunze (1992) was to determine whether or not group counseling would improve the achievement (grade-point average), self-concept, and locus of control of students in an alternative educational program. Sixty-six 9th-grade students were assigned on a random basis to a treatment or control group. Subjects in the treatment group participated in ten 45-minute group counseling sessions over a 4-month period. Reality therapy techniques were used with an emphasis on goal setting, decision making, and problem-solving skills. There were no significant findings to support group counseling.

Block (1995) studied the use of reality therapy in small group sessions to improve the self-concept of fifth- and sixth-grade students. The students were placed in two treatment groups each led by a different group leader. There were seven students in each group. The groups met for six 45-minute sessions over a 6-week period. The basic principles and techniques of reality therapy were used to enhance self-concept. A control group was also included in the study. The Piers-Harris Children's Self-Concept Scale was given before and after treatment to all three groups. The results indicated reality therapy, when applied in small group sessions, was effective in increasing the overall self-concept of upper elementary aged students. It was also found that using different group leaders had no significant effect on the outcome for the two experimental groups.

The results discussed in this section that dealt with actual research studies included 25 articles or theses. In fact, the majority were doctoral dissertations. Most of this research has been done with group or class meetings. These findings indicated mixed results for self-concept, achievement, and locus of control. However, a number of the studies showed significant decreases in discipline problems.

There were 11 studies that used reality therapy in a counseling situation rather than as part of a class meeting. These studies demonstrated that the therapy process significantly decreased behavioral problems, aided weight loss, increased attendance, lowered recidivism, and decreased rate of suspension. The findings were contradictory for self-concept, locus of control, and achievement.

The preceding studies share the usual methodological problems encountered when the effectiveness of therapeutic approaches is evaluated. It is very difficult to measure items such as involvement, happiness, fulfillment, and successful identity.

The four greatest problems in evaluating reality therapy, class meetings, and other therapies are the following, as discussed by Baskin and Hess (1980):

1. The use of more than one teacher or therapist in either the program or control groups.
2. Difficulty in assessing goals because of the complexity of the behaviors to be evaluated. The measures used to evaluate outcomes are not sensitive enough to detect changes that occur as a result of treatment. Bernal and North (1978) suggest that multiple outcome measures, including objective measures of changes,

should be used. In addition, the construct validity of self-concept and of locus of control have not been established.

3. The use of testers who do not know the purpose of the evaluation and identity of treatment and control groups.

4. The usual problems of self-evaluation research, including both the tendency of some subjects to answer questions in a socially desirable manner and the amount of self-disclosure a subject is willing to give to a self-report inventory.

In addition, most of the studies reviewed here utilized small sample size and relatively brief training periods. Also, the amount of time available for actual behavior change to take place is a limitation, because usually several weeks or more need to be spent developing student-teacher or therapist involvement and group cohesiveness. How much experience one has had in the therapeutic technique used is also a variable.

There is little question that reality therapy has directly or indirectly inspired many individuals and schools. Numerous testimonies and endorsements have been made, but, most applications of the therapy have not been subjected to any kind of formal research program.

The limited research with class meeting and reality therapy counseling does lend some support to its effectiveness in areas such as discipline and lends little support in other areas such as self-concept. Additional research to deal with some of the evaluation problems raised in this discussion is necessary for substantiating the validity and usefulness of the reality therapy concepts and principles.

## CONCLUSION

Reality therapy is based on a common sense philosophy that can be used by trained persons in many situations. These persons include the teacher in the average classroom, those involved in corrections and mental institutions, clinicians, and parents.

Responsibility is a basic tenet of reality therapy. It is thought that an assuming of responsibility will lead to a heightened sense of self-worth or self-respect and a greater sense of freedom, both of which may, at the same time, help the person experience more fun in life.

Reality therapy emphasizes the rational and the cognitive. A client is asked to describe his or her behavior specifically and to make a value judgment concerning its effectiveness. A specific plan to alter a concrete behavior is then drawn up, and a commitment to follow that plan is elicited from the client. Praise is given for success; no excuses are accepted nor is punishment given for failure. Although this approach appears almost simplistic, its success is dependent on an honest and thorough commitment on the part of the therapist to maintain concern and effort in the face of continued failure. As W. Glasser (1965) wrote: "[the] practice [of] reality therapy takes strength; not only the strength of the therapist to lead a responsible life himself, but also the added strength both to stand up steadily to patients who wish him to accede to their irresponsibility, and to continue to point out reality to them no matter how hard they struggle against it" (p. 23).

Testimonials and informal surveys indicate that reality therapy has a positive effect on clients and situations, but new and better approaches to definitive research must be sought. Future research designs must include explicitly defined control and experimental groups and the use of reliable and valid criterion measures.

Reality therapy requires time to be effective. Future research should be oriented toward longitudinal studies of a year or more, and the shorter term studies must include more sessions and subjects if one hopes to measure impact. Use of a formal behavior rating scale, test, or coding instrument to measure the actual behavior change of the client from pretreatment to posttreatment is recommended. It may also prove fruitful to develop an empirical observation system that could help validate the degree to which reality therapy techniques are actually being implemented in the classroom.

Reality therapy focuses on freedom, not license. With loving firmness and respect, the child is led away from irresponsibility toward the responsibility and concomitant self-respect that come with true freedom and a successful identity.

## CASE STUDY

John, age 10, was referred by his parents at the request of the public school system because of his continued refusal to talk. The difficulty manifested itself in kindergarten, and by the end of third grade, he had become a legend in the school system with a multitude of school personnel eager to take on the challenge of making him talk. The previous year he had been diagnosed as having elective mutism and as manifesting anxiety, social withdrawal, and depression both at school and at home. He was passive and withdrawn when confronted with the usual sibling onslaughts from his two brothers and two sisters, and he did not play with the neighbor children. At age 10, he was still an occasional bed wetter. His mother characterized him as a good boy who was quiet and reserved, who entertained himself well, and who enjoyed playing alone.

Initially, John appeared tense, stiff, immature, and sensitive. He lowered his head to avoid eye contact, and if the situation became too stressful for him, he began scratching his arm and cheek. He was fearfully shy and refused to speak. A beginning relationship was formed with him through playing games, going for walks, or getting some candy at a nearby store. As he gradually relaxed, he began to smile and laugh a bit during the sessions, but when asked a question, he would only shake his head or occasionally write his answer on a piece of paper.

As the relationship became stronger, he was told that he and the therapist would no longer play for the entire hour. Instead, he was told they would talk or sit together for the first 15 minutes. When he came for the next session, this plan was initiated. He was questioned about his happiness and unhappiness and about events at home and at school. Although he didn't speak, he nodded yes that he was unhappy. The problem behaviors that his parents and the school said he was engaging in were stated, and he was asked for his opinion. These behaviors included not talking in school, having no friends, crying a lot, and receiving poor grades. These were written on a piece of paper, and he was asked to check the ones that he agreed with. He checked not talking in school and having no friends. With several of his problem behaviors out in the open, he was asked if they were making him unhappy and if he wanted to do something about them. He nodded. Although some behaviors were identified and a value judgment made by John, he was not yet ready to do something about them. Attempts to elicit a plan from him resulted only in a lowered head and a shrug of his shoulders. At this point, more strengthening of the relationship was needed, and the sessions continued with the initial 15 minutes reserved for conversation. Initially, the therapist talked and John nodded when possible or else they sat in silence. On occasion, the therapist would ask a question and then answer it for him in a manner he wouldn't like. This action made John uncomfortable but did not elicit any speech. The sessions began focusing on his refusal to speak at school. He indicated that he wanted to talk, that he understood that it was important to do so, that he realized his not talking might result in his failing for the year, and yet he refused to speak.

As the relationship grew stronger, it became more threatening to John. He had begun to initiate some silent mouthing that indicated at least some desire to talk. He was now faced with giving up his symptoms. An occasion when the therapist called John's home added to this pressure. Expecting the mother to answer, the therapist was surprised to be greeted by a loud male child's voice. It was John's. At the next session, John was confronted with the phone call. John smiled but did not respond. At this point, the therapist tested the relationship by pointing out that John had been coming for 2 months, but that he was contributing very little, and perhaps they should consider termination. He was told to think about these things and that they would pursue the subject at his next session. He agreed to this with a nod of his head.

On his next visit, John appeared more uneasy than usual. He started the session by indicating that he wanted to play. This proposal was countered by the therapist's saying that last week's problem had to be discussed. After a brief review of the problem and reconfirmation of John's value judgment, he was asked to talk. Again, he refused. In an attempt to force the issue, the therapist suggested that John's mother be called and told that they were terminating. John sat still for several minutes before nodding his head in consent. The therapist immediately said he decided against it, changed the subject, and took John to play. The rationale behind taking a chance was the risk that the involvement was great enough to keep John from terminating. Strong as it was, however, the involvement was not yet sufficient to help John replace his problem behavior. So with this in mind, the therapist backed off and continued to be friendly and interested in John. Therapy is based on a relationship, and there are times in every relationship when one loses face or gives ground. Frightening as it might have been for the therapist, his move demonstrated to John the important lesson that one can be strong without always being in control.

For the next month, John's presenting problem was avoided and the involvement was focused on. His nonverbal interaction increased and he was more relaxed, laughing, and appearing content. At the end of this month he was once again asked what he was doing and whether it was doing him any good. He seemed quicker to agree to his symptoms and to indicate that he was not pleased with them. While joking with him about hearing his voice on the phone, the therapist had the thought that John might talk into a tape recorder. John indicated he would not. He was asked if he would take the recorder home, talk into it there, and then bring it back the next time. He agreed to this, and they shook hands on the plan. He did not, however, follow through. Rather than preaching, the therapist indicated to John that he hadn't carried out the plan as agreed, and John was asked if he wanted to try again. He indicated that he did, and the following week, he arrived with the tape, gesturing to have it put on the recorder, which the therapist did. In a whispered tone came the word "Hello." John was praised a great deal for his feat. Over the next several sessions, John continued to make tapes at home and bring them to each following session. John's responses on tape were eventually enlarged into whispered sentences. Each of John's efforts was reinforced, and the therapist often asked him if it felt good to have accomplished this. Always John would smile and nod yes.

But it was time now to move on, and during the next session, it was again indicated to John that he would have to start talking aloud, that using the tapes was a good start and an indication that it wasn't so bad to talk. It was emphasized that it was time for John to demonstrate his contribution to the relationship and to talk because the therapist had been doing most of the work. "Please say 'Hi'," the therapist said. There were several minutes of silence and finally, with great effort and initial mouthing behavior, John said "Hi" in an audible whisper. This was a special moment for both of them, and it was followed by much praise. On leaving, John whispered, "Good-bye." This incident impressed again how necessary a strong involvement is in therapy and how critical it is in effecting change. How much it must have taken John to say those words!

Expectations for the next session were quickly lowered when John sat and said nothing during the beginning of the hour. Asked if he would talk aloud, he shook his head no. Reminding him of the progress from the last session and the triumph of his success, the therapist asked John whether he would talk if the therapist turned his back to him. He nodded yes and they shook on it. The therapist turned his back and looked out the window. About 5 minutes passed before John spoke loudly enough to be heard. The therapist, continuing to sit with his back to John, then asked him several simple questions and received the answers. Then they talked about John's success during his session, with a lot of praise being given. A plan was made to continue this approach for the next couple of sessions. A written commitment was made. The plan was carried out, with John talking to the therapist in a whisper while the therapist sat with his back to John.

After two sessions, a plan was made that they would talk face to face. When John arrived for the next session, he was more uneasy than usual. He sat down and the therapist said hello. About two minutes of silence followed before John whispered

"Hi." They talked about what he had watched on television and what he had done on the weekend and in school, with John responding in whispers. This continued for several sessions, and the therapist then asked him what could be done to help him talk in his normal voice. At first John shrugged his shoulders, but then he said, "Talk louder." This became his responsibility for the next session. At the next meeting, John fulfilled his commitment; he and the therapist talked for approximately 30 minutes.

After this meeting, each session lasted for about 45 minutes, and they were able to talk for the entire time. Up until this point John's not talking in school had not been discussed. It was important for him to get used to talking in his "loud" (normal) voice over a period of time in order to break his old habit of getting by without speaking. At a certain point, however, it was hoped that John might be able to generalize his success. Consequently, John was asked if the therapist could call his teacher to check on his school progress; John agreed. The therapist learned that John was not talking in the classroom.

At the next session, the therapist asked John if this was true and John said it was. When the subject was pursued, John said he did not want to continue not talking in school. He was asked what his plan would be, and he said he would talk to his teacher. The therapist indicated that the plan wasn't quite clear in terms of *how, when,* and *where.* After some discussion, it was decided that he would talk to the teacher on Tuesday and Friday mornings. When asked what he would say, he indicated that he would say hello and ask to go to the bathroom instead of just raising his hand. The plan was written up and signed, with each of them receiving a copy.

When John came back the following week, he indicated that he had carried out the plan. Over the next several sessions, they worked on increasing the number of days and the things he would say. Indeed, everything seemed to be progressing even better than expected. Each time a plan was formulated, a commitment was made and executed. A phone call from John's mother, however, changed all that.

John's mother called, saying that she had just returned from a parent-teacher conference and was told that John was not talking at school. This news was an eye-opener because previous contacts with her had been encouraging; she indicated earlier that John was talking more in the neighborhood and in the local stores. John, it turned out, had been telling both his mother and the therapist that he was talking in school when, in fact, he was not. The therapist had taken John's word, which on the surface seemed to be the thing to do because a good relationship existed. But John had learned to keep the therapist off his back by quickly setting up a plan and then indicating that he had carried it out.

The next time John came to therapy and indicated that he had executed his plan, he was asked if he had any objection to the therapist's calling his teacher to ask how he was doing. He said yes. When the therapist asked what the objection was, John replied that it wasn't necessary to call the teacher, that he was reporting everything that was happening. The therapist expressed doubt and told John about his mother's phone call. John admitted to not having talked in school and started to make excuses for his lack of success. He was immediately interrupted and asked if he wanted to

talk in school; he said he did. Plans similar to the ones used before were then for-
mulates, with the further stipulation that the therapist would call the teacher each
week to check on how John's plan was working. The therapist told John he was very
much interested in John's talking progress in school and also in knowing how the
teacher perceived the progress and whether this progress was the same as he, the
therapist, thought it was. John agreed to this additional plan.

To coordinate their efforts, the therapist saw the teacher before the next session.
She was cooperative and interested in helping in any was possible. She was informed
of John's progress to date and of some of the techniques that were being used with
him. She agreed to read some literature on reality therapy and carry out some suggestions. The need to praise John's talking and the consequences to be used if the
rules were not followed were particularly emphasized.

John was told that what took place at this meeting between the teacher and the
therapist and what could be expected. It became evident that John was much more
likely to talk if he went up to the teacher's desk. They started with this approach,
and soon he was doing this at least once a day. John would walk to the teacher's desk
when he had a question, and later, the teacher would also ask him questions. Eventually, plans were also made and carried out whereby John talked to his gym and
music teachers. Again, he was able to communicate with them in a whisper.

During this period, John was strongly regarded for his successes, and his feelings
of self-worth appeared to increase. He would now admit that school was a better
place than before and that he did enjoy it more. John and his therapist discussed
John's talking louder and also talking from his desk, but he was still not willing to
make a commitment to either of these actions. At this point the school year had
ended, and because of a number of scheduling problems and summer programs, it
was decided that there would be no more therapy sessions during the summer. It was
agreed that John's mother would contact the therapist in the fall if things were not
going well for him.

In the beginning of October, John's mother called and indicated that John had regressed in school and that he wanted to come for therapy. The mother attributed this
regression in part to his new teacher, who was older and more authoritarian than the
previous one. She reported that he had had a good summer, that he talked to others
outside the home, and that he was less shy and more outgoing.

The therapist and John were able to pick up and begin pretty much where they
ended in the spring. John was still talking in a loud voice to the therapist and, in no
time at all, in a whisper, one again, to the teachers. In a short time, the therapist was
able to elicit a value judgment and a commitment from John that he wanted to talk
out loud in school. It was agreed that John would speak with the teacher alone at her
desk. It was also established that if the plan was not carried out, John would have to
miss recess. Because he understood and agreed to the outcome before he engaged in
the activity, missing recess was seen as a logical consequence of his behavior, not as
punishment. When he did not talk out loud to his teacher at her desk for the first
time, he missed recess. At the same time, it was stipulated that he would have to
come up with a plan so that not talking aloud and missing recess would not happen

again. His plan was to try it once more with a specific sentence to say, which turned out to be, "Can I have my math assignment?" This time it worked for him. At this point, he and his teacher agreed to his doing this at least three times a week with the days being his choice. The plan was accomplished, and within a short time John was saying something out loud at least once a day. Because the teacher was working so well with him., John and the therapist agreed to meet only twice a month.

There were ups and downs during the school year, but overall John continued to improve. Toward the end of school, John was beginning to talk out loud from his desk, but this activity was still somewhat troublesome for him. The therapist agreed to continue to see him during the summer once a month to help him prepare for a new teacher and grade. In the last several sessions he talked "a blue streak." He was spontaneous, showing no shyness, and was much more confident of his own ability to perform. They went to a store to buy candy and there he asked the clerk several questions and responded to a question asked of him. John and the therapist also talked about alternative strategies and choices—he agreed to talk out loud from his desk when school began in the fall, and he appeared confident about doing so.

During the course of therapy, the therapist repeatedly emphasized that he was interested in John's dealing with the present, particularly in John's attempts to succeed and to deal with his problems in an effective and responsible manner. With John, it was necessary that he be assured that the therapist would stick with him until his problem was resolved. To this extent, the relationship played a major role. When John resorted to "I can't," in discussing certain situations, the therapist converted "I can't," to "You don't want to or you mean you won't—let's explore the choices you have." Until the two were involved and until John realized that he was responsible for his own behavior and that something could be done about his problem, little progress occurred. Through the involvement, he finally realized that he was responsible for his talking. In this way, he was helped to understand his capacity for more worthwhile behavior in his immediate environment. His decisions to become involved, to change his behavior, and to continue talking were the essence of therapy.

## ANNOTATED BIBLIOGRAPHY

Glasser, N. (Ed.). (1980). *What are you doing? How people are helped through reality therapy.* New York: Harper & Row.

In this book, 25 case histories by therapists who have received certification from the Institute of Reality Therapy are presented. The cases were selected to show as many different kinds of problems as possible. The cases are so varied that anyone using the steps of reality therapy should be helped toward a better understanding of how the steps work in practice. Eight of the cases deal with children and adolescents.

Glasser, N. (Ed.). (1989). *Control theory in the practice of reality therapy: Case studies.* New York: Harper & Row.

Glasser examines control theory's role in the practice of reality therapy through case studies. These case studies provide interesting examples of ways that control theory can be translated into the practice of reality therapy. The cases are detailed enough so professionals can learn more about how control theory and reality therapy can be applied together.

Glasser, W. (1969). *Schools without failure*. New York: Harper & Row.

The concepts of reality therapy as applied to the schools are presented here. Many school practiced are described that promote a sense of failure in the student, and suggestions are given for correcting these practices. The three types of class meetings are presented with numerous topics that could be used for each one.

Glasser, W. (1986). *Control theory in the classroom*. New York: Harper & Row.

The author provides a useful analysis of what is wrong with traditional schooling and what needs to be done. The book translates control theory into a classroom model of team learning in the schools. Numerous ideas are given that will contribute to the success of classroom teachers. The book discusses discipline problems and learning team models.

Gossen, D. (1992). *Restitution: Restructuring school discipline*. Chapel Hill, NC: New View Publications.

This book presents in detail how restitution, a key approach to discipline, is used in reality therapy. It focuses on how children and adolescents can correct mistakes and stresses positive solutions to problems instead of punishment.

Litwack, L. (Ed.). (1994). *Journal of Reality Therapy: A compendium of articles 1981–1993*. Chapel Hill, NC: New View Publications.

These articles, from the first 13 years of the *Journal of Reality Therapy,* present a thorough overview of the development of the concepts and practice of reality therapy.

Wubbolding, R. (1988). *Using reality therapy*. New York: Harper & Row.

The author demonstrates the practical uses of reality therapy and the principles of control theory. Case studies and exercises allow readers to apply specific reality therapy principles to their own behaviors. In addition, the book covers marriage and family counseling, the use of paradoxical techniques, supervision, and self-help.

Wubbolding, R. (1991). *Understanding reality therapy: A metaphorical approach*. New York: Harper & Row.

Professionals will find a detailed presentation of the principles behind control theory and the techniques of reality therapy. Metaphors, analogies, and anecdotes are used in a clear, concrete, and brief style that enables the professional to develop applications for clients. Also included are conversations with patients and questionnaires that help analyze feelings and how to take better control of one's actions.

# REFERENCES

Allen, J. M. (1990). Reality therapy with at-risk elementary students to enhance self-esteem and improve grades and attendance (Doctoral dissertation, University of San Francisco). *Dissertation Abstracts International, 51* AAC 9114834.

Baskin, E., & Hess, R. (1980). Does affective education work?: A review of seven programs, *Journal of School Psychology, 18,* 40–50.

Bassin, A., Bratter, T., & Rachin, R. (Eds.). (1976). *The reality therapy reader: A survey of the work of William Glasser.* New York: Harper & Row.

Bean, J. S. (1988). The effect of individualized reality therapy on the recidivism rates and locus-of-control orientation of male juvenile offenders (Doctoral dissertation, University of Mississippi). *Dissertation Abstracts International, 49,* AAC 8818138.

Bernal, M., & North, J. (1978). A survey of parent training materials. *Journal of Applied Behavior Analysis, 11,* 533–544.

Bigelow, G., & Thorne, J. (1979). Reality versus client-centered models in group counseling. *Group Counselor,* 191–194.

Block, M. A. (1995). A study to investigate the use of reality therapy in small group counseling sessions to enhance the self-concept levels of elementary students (Doctoral dissertation, Walden University). *Dissertation Abstracts International, 56,* AAC 9520590.

Coats, K. (1991). *The impact of reality therapy in a school for emotionally disturbed youth.* (ERIC Document Reproduction Service No. ED 355 690).

Dreikurs, R., Grunwald, B., & Pepper, R. (1971). *Maintaining sanity in the classroom.* New York: Harper & Row.

English, J. (1970, March). *The effects of reality therapy on elementary age children.* Paper presented at the meeting of the California Association of School Psychologists and Psychometrists, Los Angeles.

Ford, E. (1974). *Why marriage?* Niles, IL: Argus.

Ford, E. (1987). *Love guaranteed: A better marriage in 8 weeks.* New York: Harper & Row.

Ford, E. (1989). *Freedom from stress.* Scottsdale, AZ: Brandt Press.

Ford, E. (1994). *Discipline for home and school.* Scottsdale, AZ: Brandt Press.

Ford, E., & Englund, S. (1977). *For the love of children: A realistic approach to raising your child.* Garden City, NY: Anchor Press.

Ford, E., & Englund, S. (1979). *Permanent love: Practical steps to a lasting relationship: A reality therapy approach to caring.* Minneapolis, MN: Winston Press.

Ford, E., & Zorn, R. (1975). *Why be lonely?* Niles, IL: Argus.

Glasser, N. (Ed.). (1980). *What are you doing?: How people are helped through reality therapy.* New York: Harper & Row.

Glasser, N. (Ed.). (1989). *Control theory in the practice of reality therapy: Case studies*. New York: Harper & Row.

Glasser, W. (1964). Reality therapy: A realistic approach to the young offender. *Crime and Delinquency, 10,* 135–144.

Glasser, W. (1965). *Reality therapy*. New York: Harper & Row.

Glasser, W. (1969). *Schools without failure*. New York: Harper & Row.

Glasser, W. (1972). *The identity society*. New York: Harper & Row.

Glasser, W. (1974). A new look at discipline. *Learning: The Magazine for Creative Teaching, 3,* 6–11.

Glasser, W. (1976a). A new look at discipline. In A. Bassin, T. Bratter, & R. Rachin (Eds.), *The reality therapy reader: A survey of the work of William Glasser.* New York: Harper & Row.

Glasser, W. (1976b). *Positive addiction*. New York: Harper & Row.

Glasser, W. (1981). *Stations of the mind*. New York: Harper & Row.

Glasser, W. (1984). *Take effective control of your life*. New York: Harper & Row.

Glasser, W. (1986a). *Control theory in the classroom*. New York: Harper & Row.

Glasser, W. (1986b). *The control theory—reality therapy workbook*. Canoga Park, CA: Institute for Reality Therapy.

Glasser, W. (1990). *The quality school: Managing students without coercion*. New York: HarperCollins.

Glasser, W. (1993). *The quality school teacher: A companion volume to the quality school*. New York: HarperCollins.

Glasser, W. (1994). *The control theory manager*. New York: HarperCollins.

Glasser, W. (1996). *Staying together: A control theory guide to lasting relationships*. New York: HarperCollins.

Glasser, W., & Zunin, L. (1973). Reality therapy. In R. Corsini (Ed.), *Current psychotherapies*. Itasca, IL: Peacock.

Glasser, W., & Zunin, L. (1979). Reality therapy. In R. Corsini (Ed), *Current psychotherapies. Glasser's approach to discipline*. Itasca, IL: F. E. Peacock.

Good, E. (1987). *In pursuit of happiness*. Chapel Hill, NC: New View.

Good, P. (1992). *Helping kids help themselves*. Chapel Hill, NC: New View.

Gorter-Cass, S. E. (1988). Program evaluation of an alternative school using William Glasser's reality therapy model for disruptive youth (Doctoral dissertation, Temple University). *Dissertation Abstracts International, 49,* AAC 8818789.

Gossen, D. (1992). *Restitution: Restructuring school disciplines*. Chapel Hill, NC: New View.

Grant, F. (1972). A study of the effects of open-ended classroom meetings on social and academic self-concept and internal responsibility for academic successes and failures. *Dissertation Abstracts International, 33*(10-B), 1506-B.

Harris, M. A. (1992). Effect of reality therapy/control theory on predictors of responsible behavior of junior high school students in an adolescent pregnancy prevention program (Doctoral dissertation, University of North Carolina at Greensboro). *Dissertation Abstracts International, 54,* AAC 9314582.

Hart-Hester, S. (1986). The effects of reality therapy techniques on the behavior of elementary school students across setting. *Dissertation Abstracts International, 48,* DA 8715124.

Hawes, R. M. (1971). Reality therapy in the classroom. *Dissertation Abstracts International, 32*(5-A), 2483.

Hough-Waite, L. (1980). *A comparison of the art of parenting and parent involvement program.* Unpublished master's thesis, Central Michigan University, Mt. Pleasant.

Hunter, M. L. (1973). Group effect on self-concept and math performance. *Dissertation Abstracts International, 33*(10-B), 5169.

Kunze, K. S. (1992). The effects of group counseling on low-achieving and/or underachieving ninth graders participating in an alternative education program (Doctoral dissertation, Virginia Polytechnic Institute and State University). *Dissertation Abstracts International, 53,* AAC 9231483.

Litwack, L. (Ed.). (1994). *Journal of reality therapy: A compendium of articles 1981–1993.* Chapel Hill, NC: New View.

Marandola, P., & Imber, S. (1979). Glasser's classroom meeting: A humanistic approach to behavior change with preadolescent inner-city learning disabled children. *Journal of Learning Disabilities, 12,* 30–34.

Matthews, D. B. (1972). The effects of reality therapy on reported self-concept, social adjustment, reading achievement, and discipline of fourth and fifth graders in two elementary schools. *Dissertation Abstracts International, 33*(9-A), 4842.

McGuiness, T. (1977). *Idea book for the parent involvement program.* Los Angeles: Educator Training Center.

Omizo, M., & Cubberly, W. (1983). The effects of reality therapy classroom meetings on self-concept and locus of control among learning disabled children. *Exceptional Child, 30,* 201–209.

Poppen, W., & Welch, R. (1976). Work with overweight adolescent girls. In A. Bassin, T. Bratter, & R. Rachin (Eds.), *The reality therapy reader: A survey of the work of William Glasser.* New York: Harper & Row.

Quinn, B. (1979). *The efficacy of the open-ended classroom meetings with junior high children on self-concept and attitude toward school.* Unpublished manuscript, Central Michigan University, Mt. Pleasant.

Robert, M. (1973). *Loneliness in the schools.* Niles, IL: Argus.

Rosario, A. C. (1973). The interaction of counseling strategy and locus of control. *Dissertation Abstracts International. 33*(10-B), 5169.

Shearn, D., & Randolph, D. (1978). Effects of reality therapy methods applied in the classroom. *Psychology in the Schools, 15,* 79–83.

Tamborella, E. (1987). The perceptions of staff and students in an alternative high school program using RT behavior management. *Dissertation Abstracts International, 48,* DA 8727114.

Tangeman, J. A. (1973). An investigation of the effects of two classroom guidance programs on self-concept and achievement of third grade students. *Dissertation Abstracts International, 34*(8-A, pt. 1), 4764.

Wubbolding, R. (1988). *Using reality therapy.* New York: Harper & Row.

Wubbolding, R. (1991). *Understanding reality therapy.* New York: HarperCollins.

Yarish, P. (1986). Reality therapy and locus of control of juvenile offenders. *Journal of Reality Therapy, 6,* 3–10.

Zeaman, R., & Martucci, L. (1976). The application of classroom meetings to special education. *Exception Children, 42,* 461–462.

# Chapter 10

# SYSTEMIC APPROACHES— FAMILY THERAPY

William B. Gunn, Jr. and Barbara L. Fisher

The systemic theories of psychotherapy are unique in considering the dynamic relationship between symptomology and the interpersonal context in which the symptoms occur. Systems theorists believe that the system (e.g., a family) maintains the symptoms of its members and relationship patterns are maintained by the symptom(s). For example, Family A has a 7-year-old daughter who is depressed and withdrawn. In addition to considering the unique characteristics of the girl, a family therapist would view the family itself as a unit of focus. The depression and withdrawal are viewed as being maintained by the structure, patterns, and beliefs of the family. In turn, the depression and withdrawal permit the family to operate with the least amount of change and the most amount of predictability. This enables a maintenance of the family's structure, patterns, and beliefs. Systemic thinking represents a dramatic epistemological shift from other approaches to psychotherapy particularly with the premises that etiology and history are often less relevant than understandings of family structure, interaction patterns, and belief systems.

A number of theoretical perspectives have emerged that focus on slightly different dynamics of the general assumption just described. Our overview theory, which integrates three of the major schools of thought (structural, strategic, and systemic), is described in this chapter as an innovative approach to treating children and adolescents. Each of these early approaches has been developed and expanded over the past 20 years.

Family therapy is much more than an additional technique in the psychologist's bag of tricks. Family therapy represents a new frontier and worldview that encompasses the entire treatment process, including conceptualizing, assessing, and intervening.

## HISTORICAL PERSPECTIVE

Most family therapy historians agree that the decade following World War II was formative for the family therapy movement. Goldenberg and Goldenberg (1985) point to five "seemingly independent scientific and clinical developments that together set the stage for the emergence of family therapy" (p. 90). The first one was the adaptation of psychoanalytic formulations to the study of the family. Nathan Ackerman, a psycho-analyst and child psychiatrist is credited with extending this orientation beyond the inner life of the person to the person within his or her family, community, and social contexts. Second, general systems theory, proposed by Ludwig von Bertalanffy, was adapted to family systems. This theory created a unique perspective for understanding symptoms. The third scientific development was research into the area of schizophre-nia. During the 1950s, three independent research teams (led by Gregory Bateson at the Mental Research Institute in California, Ted Lidz at Yale, and Murray Bowen at the National Institute of Mental Health) all arrived at a similar conclusion: There is a strong relationship between family processes and the development of schizophrenia. Each team developed different explanations for this correlation, but the basic conclu-sion helped open the door to family therapy for the treatment of disorders previously believed to be "intrapsychic conflicts." Fourth, the areas of marriage counseling and child guidance emerged early in this century and provided a foundation for family therapy later in the 1950s. The fifth and final development was group therapy, which had emerged around 1910 as a new curative approach to intrapsychic conflicts. The ex-tension of group principles to families (a natural group) was a logical step.

Family therapy is approximately 40 years old. The first two decades (1950s, 1960s) could be characterized as the foundational years. Many "family therapists," beginning as physicians or researchers, started questioning traditional approaches at this time. Several treated families without interacting with other professionals for fear of ostra-cism. Researchers began to speculate about the nature of the relationship between fam-ily dynamics and intrapsychic pathology. During the 1970s, family therapy proliferated and diversity emerged. Several camps of theories and therapies developed including the intergenerational approaches (Bowen, Nagy, Framo, Paul, Williamson), Behavioral (Stuart, Jacobsen, Liberman), Structural (Minuchin, Aponte), Strategic (Watzlawick, Haley, Madanes), and Systemic (Selvini-Palazolli, Papp). The late 1970s and 1980s were characterized by divergence and specialization. Family therapists worked in many clinical settings, with a wide variety of problems, integrating family therapy with individual therapy, addictions recovery, and medicine. Family therapy became more integrated into the broader mental health culture. The most recent trend through the 1990s has been labeled post-modern or constructivist. These approaches include solution oriented (de Shazer, 1985), narrative (White & Epston, 1990), and compe-tency forward (Waters & Lawrence, 1993). These latest additions focus on engaging families to motivate their own internal resources and competencies to create unique solutions to difficult problems.

The field of family therapy has mushroomed, particularly in the past 15 years. The first journal in the field, *Family Process* was started in 1962. Today, there are well over a dozen journals and hundreds of books published on family therapy. A unique publi-cation, the *Family Therapy Networker*, provides discussion of topical issues and is an excellent resource for upcoming workshops and seminars. The American Association of Marriage and Family Therapy (AAMFT) publishes a clinical/research journal, the *Journal of Marriage and Family Therapy,* and a newspaper, the *Family Therapy News,* which keeps readers informed about national trends and legislative efforts in the field.

There are two professional associations for family therapists. AAMFT is the largest (about 15,000 members) and serves to promote the profession and the practice by credentialing practitioners and by accrediting graduate programs. AAMFT established the Commission on Accreditation for Marriage and Family Therapy Education (COA) in the 1970s. The COA is officially recognized by the Federal Department of Education as the accrediting organization for marriage and family therapy training programs. There are almost 50 programs accredited in North America to teach marriage and family therapy. The second organization, the American Family Therapy Association (AFTA) is an academy of advanced professionals. AFTA is a think tank composed of approximately 500 members who meet yearly to share ideas and develop common interests.

## OVERVIEW OF THEORY

### Basic Theory and Assumptions

In describing the theoretical differences between systemic or interpersonal therapies and intrapsychic therapies, the metaphor of a camera is often used. In individual therapies, the lens is focused on the thoughts, feelings, or experience of the client. In all approaches to family therapy, the lens is widened from the individual to the relevant context in that individual's life, usually the family. However, family approaches differ in terms of the specific focus of observations, hypotheses, and interventions. This section describes a comprehensive overview theory, which highlights the important theoretical components of four widely used systemic approaches. These correspond to three important aspects of family functioning: the structure/organization of the family, the patterns by which they interact, and the belief systems the family has developed.

Emphasis on the structure and organization of family systems is a crucial factor in the approach developed first by Minuchin (1974). Three key structural concepts are subsystems, hierarchy (guidance and leadership), and boundaries (closeness and distance).

Subsystems in a family are individuals, dyads, or larger groups who make up a subset of the family. While some subsystems are natural (e.g., the parental team or sibling group), there are others unique to a particular family. For example, a mother and youngest child can form a subsystem such that everyone else is excluded. From the formation of this coalition, problems may develop. A therapist evaluates the functionality of the family in terms of hierarchy and boundaries in these subsystems as well as in the family as a whole.

All systems, including families, need to maintain some hierarchy and leadership function to move through normal developmental stages as well as manage acute crises.

This usually involves the adults being able to make decisions that are in the best interests of the children and the family. A common problem described in adolescence is an inverted hierarchy (Haley, 1980) in which adolescents are directing the parents.

Boundaries are invisible barriers, often compared to cell membranes, that surround individuals and subsystems regulating the amount of closeness with other subsystems. If there are thin or diffused membranes, closeness is emphasized over autonomy. If the membranes are thick and rigid, the reverse is true. Boundaries can further be described as internal: between members or subsystems, or external: between neighbors, friends, school, society.

Minuchin (1974) described boundaries as being on a continuum between rigid and diffuse. Rigid boundaries are overly restrictive and permit little contact with other family subsystems or external systems. Families with rigid internal boundaries tend to be disengaged from each other. Children in such families often feel isolated or neglected. On the other end of the continuum, families with diffuse internal boundaries tend to be enmeshed (e.g., overly supportive; may learn to rely too heavily on each other). Families with rigid external boundaries tend to create overdependence on each other and isolation from others. In families with diffuse external boundaries it is difficult for family members to feel connected with each other. It is often hard to tell who is a family member and who is not. The important contribution of structural assessment to a unified theory is its focus on organization, particularly concepts of hierarchy (who is up—who is down) and boundaries (who is in—who is out). It enables a therapist to see strengths, to emphasize to a family ("You have developed a very close bond with your daughter"), as well as identify themes for therapy ("In addition, it will be important for her to develop some ability to handle disappointment on her own").

A second aspect of family functioning is the actual problem-maintaining sequences of behavior or patterns of interaction. If the sequences that maintain the symptoms can be changed, the symptom is no longer necessary. Thus, symptoms are viewed as maintained by repetitive cycles of interaction. Patterns of interaction are redundant sequences of behavior that may recur across many different content areas. For example, Mom is talking to oldest son when daughter interrupts. Dad criticizes daughter for interrupting and Mom criticizes Dad for being too harsh. Son gets upset about being ignored and leaves the room. This simple pattern may be repeated over and over in this family utilizing different topics to begin the sequence.

In addition to interactions, rules and roles become part of symptom maintenance. Rules govern power, division of labor, and patterns of interaction in a family. Some rules are overtly stated (e.g., a rotation of dishwashing or taking out the trash). However, many family rules are covert and not talked about openly. "Go to your room when Mom and Dad fight" or "If Mom has been drinking, don't talk to her," are examples of such covert rules. Roles are a natural extension of rules. For example, Mom may be "nurturer," Dad the "breadwinner," oldest son the "hero," second son the "troublemaker," and youngest daughter the "peacemaker."

When these patterns prevent the system from accomplishing its tasks, symptoms may develop. The symptomatic behavior (e.g., a child refusing to go to school) is dysfunctional from the school's point of view, but may be logical within the interpersonal network of the family. If the mother of such a child is depressed and suicidal, the child's "protective" behavior may serve to stabilize the system. Thus, the symptom is adaptive for the family system.

In their book *Change, Principles of Problem Formation and Problem Resolution,* Watzlawick, Weakland, and Fisch (1974) emphasize that families are always trying to adapt and adjust to changing circumstances while also trying to avoid change and its uncertainties. Thus, when confronted with normal life difficulties, families find solutions to resolve their often conflictual change/don't change position. It is these solutions that become the problems. If the system or individuals in them can discover new solutions that do not turn difficulties into problems, the symptom will no longer exist.

There are three types of solutions to difficulties that can result in problems and rigid problematic sequences. The first are those in which some action needs to be taken, but the family does not act. From this denial of a difficulty, any acknowledgment—let alone an attempted solution—runs the risk of being labeled as madness or badness. An example of this type of problem development would be failure to alter parenting style as a child becomes an adolescent. This can result in increased rebellion and power struggles. A second way problem sequences develop is when actions on a difficulty are taken when there is no need to do so. These are situations where the solution or "cure" is the problem. A couple who have the idea that they will always insist on strict obedience from their children may create a negative environment by their constant action and unwillingness to "pick their battles carefully." The third way problematic sequences develop is when there is a problem and action is taken, but it is at the wrong level of intervention. For example, parents may try to "cheer up" an adolescent who is depressed. When these attempts to do not meet with success, the parents may make more vigorous attempts with the result being an increasingly withdrawn and angry teenager who feels controlled and manipulated. Both parents and child can become engaged in a pattern that does not relieve the symptoms, but actually leads to their increase as a consequence of the misdirected solution.

The final area of this overview theory is the belief system of a particular family. This is the focus of the general systemic theorists from Milan, Italy (Selvini-Palazzoli, Boscolo, Cecchin, & Prata, 1978) and written about in this country by the therapists at the Ackerman Institute and in Canada by Karl Tomm (1984).

The basic theoretical premise of this view is that family members attribute meaning to behavior within a context and the meaning becomes more important than the behavior. For example, one family may define a child's behavior as cute and amusing while another family may define similar behavior as unacceptable. Behavior is far less significant than the meaning attached to it. Behavior is also analyzed through the context in which it occurs. Similar behavior may take on different meaning in different contexts. A child interrupting a parent at a social gathering may draw a punishment, whereas a child interrupting a parent to warn of an approaching danger may be praised. The interpersonal context in which behaviors occur is crucial to a systemic therapist. A child may behave very differently at home when one parent is present compared with when both parents are present. School behaviors may be totally different than those at home, and certainly behavior with peers may be even more diverse. An analysis of as many settings as possible to discover what happens when and who is involved is important in developing hypotheses about the problem and designing interventions.

Family beliefs are constantly evolving. Problems develop when old ways of thinking (beliefs) do not fit the current situation. Moreover, problems develop because of the "meaning" families attribute to themselves. If new information can be given to family members to help them understand their behavior in a new way, change can occur.

The belief systems of family members are usually linear, that is they explain events as cause-effect phenomena. Steve did this, then Jenny did that. However, to understand the nature and impact of a family's belief system, a circular view of events must be employed. Circularity is the concept that problems are maintained by patterns of interaction between people that have no clear beginning or end. Circularity maintains a focus on present patterns and emphasizes the reciprocal nature of behavior, thus including all family members in a problem. Behavior problems in a child are not thought of as being "caused" by poor self-esteem or divorcing parents. Circular thinking does not permit individuals in the family to be identified as villains or heroes. There is no extensive search for the cause of a child's misbehavior, only a clear description of what maintains it in the present. In fact, there is a search for positive intention and competency to assist family members in seeing the "story" in a more positive light. A circular hypothesis examines the relationship between the system and the symptom and provides for interventions that impact the entire system.

Beliefs define the rules, roles, interaction patterns, and structure of the family, while these in turn, define the family's belief. The interdependence of these relationships are graphically depicted in Figure 10.1. For example, if a parent believes her child cannot be trusted, she may overcontrol the child's behavior thus making it difficult for the child to learn how to respond to different situations. If the child is given some freedom and acts in a way that displeases the parent, her belief that the child is not trustworthy will be reinforced.

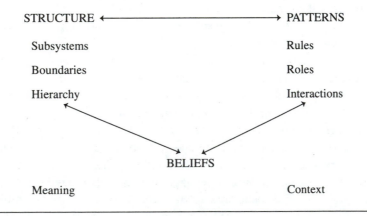

**Figure 10.1.   Important components of overview theory.**

## Family Development—Health and Pathology

A cornerstone of this overview theory is the concept that families generally develop through a series of predictable stages requiring the completion of sequential and cumulative developmental tasks. Carter and McGoldrick (1988) suggest there are six stages of the Family Life Cycle. These are outlined in Table 10.1.

Adjustments are required as the family becomes more complex and matures. The view of family development through stages is helpful in understanding what is expected or normal for a family at particular stages as well as understanding why a family may be struggling. It is known that disruptions in development or inability to effectively complete the tasks of one stage interferes with the ability of the family to complete the tasks of a later stage. However, it has important limitations. It can present a "normal" model that other types of families (e.g., divorce/remarriage, childless couples, gay and lesbian) can feel "needlessly abnormal." It also does not reflect the wide cultural diversity in terms of tasks required to complete stages.

Only in the past 10 to 15 years have family therapists/researchers focused on normal/healthy family processes. As previously shown, one of the foundational areas of family therapy was research into family pathology. Three research studies of the 1970s found very similar characteristics of healthy families. Lewis, Beavers, Gossett, and Phillips (1976) completed an extensive study of families and developed a rating scale to distinguish healthy from disturbed families. They concluded that no single quality identified the healthy family, but that healthy families have the following qualities:

- Strong parental coalition.
- An affiliative attitude toward encounters.
- Respect for the subjectivity of others.
- Open and direct communication.
- An understanding of varied and complex human needs and motivations.
- Spontaneity.
- High levels of initiative.
- Enjoyment of the uniqueness of each individual.

Stinnett (1979) studied "strong" families and found the following common characteristics:

- Appreciation for one another.
- Time together that is genuinely enjoyed.
- Good communication patterns.
- Commitment to promoting the happiness and welfare of others in the family.
- High degree of religious orientation.
- Ability to deal with crises in a positive manner.

**Table 10.1.   The stages of the family life cycle**

| Stage | Emotional Process | Tasks Required |
|---|---|---|
| 1. Between Families: The Unattached Young Adult | Accepting parent-offspring separation. | a. Differentiation of self in relation to family of origin.<br>b. Development of intimate peer relationships.<br>c. Establishment of self in work. |
| 2. The Joining of Families through Marriage: The newly married couple. | Commitment to new system. | a. Formation of marital system.<br>b. Realignment of relationships with extended families and friends to include spouse. |
| 3. The Family with Young Children | Accepting new members into the system. | a. Adjusting marital system to make space for child(ren).<br>b. Taking on parenting roles.<br>c. Realignment of relationships with extended family to include parenting and grandparenting roles. |
| 4. The Family with Adolescents | Increasing flexibility of family boundaries to include children's independence. | a. Shifting of parent-child relationships to permit adolescent to move in and out of system.<br>b. Refocus on mid-life marital and career issues.<br>c. Beginning shift toward concerns for older generation. |
| 5. Launching Children and Moving On | Accepting a multitude of exits from and entries into the family system. | a. Renegotiation of marital system as a dyad.<br>b. Development of adult-to-adult relationships between grown children and their parents.<br>c. Realignment of relationships to include in-laws and grandchildren.<br>d. Dealing with disabilities and death of parents (grandparents). |
| 6. The Family in Later Life | Accepting the shifting of generational roles. | a. Maintaining own and/or couple functioning and interests in face of physiological decline; exploration of new familial and social role options.<br>b. Support for a more central role for middle generation.<br>c. Making room in the system for the wisdom and experience of the elderly; supporting the older generation without overfunctioning for them.<br>d. Dealing with loss of spouse, siblings, and other peers and preparation for own death. Life review and integration. |

Fisher, Giblin, and Hoopes (1982) identified the following aspects as important to health family functioning:

- A sense of belonging to the family.
- Communication that attends to feelings and content.
- Attentively listening.
- Expressing feelings and thoughts openly.
- Enjoyment of one another—doing things that are fun.
- Acceptance and support for each other's needs.
- Feeling safe and trust with one another.
- Ability to depend on one another.

These empirical studies shed light on healthy family dynamics but "there is a paucity of theoretical and empirical information about normal families" (Gantman, 1980, p. 106).

Likewise, a number of concepts have been elaborated in the literature on dysfunction in families. An attempt to list or catalog these concepts would result in a confusing laundry list of qualifying characteristics. There is no single qualifying criterion that justifies labeling a family as pathological. "Pathology" is viewed as functional or adaptive. Pathological behavior "makes sense" when viewed in its context.

Thus, family health is context-specific and stage-specific. A family must continue to grow, and rules, roles, structure, beliefs, and interaction patterns must be moderately flexible for its members to stay healthy. Too much or too little flexibility can create problems in a family. Families that change too rapidly encounter confusion and chaos. Families that change too little may be viewed as "stuck" or unable to modify roles, rules, structures, beliefs, and/or interactions. Family therapy seeks to break through the "stuckness" or stabilize the chaos so the family can regenerate healthier patterns.

## BASIC TECHNIQUES AND INTERVENTIONS IN FAMILY THERAPY

It would be impossible in this kind of overview chapter to describe all the techniques developed from systemic theory. In this section, we briefly outline a few of them that correspond to the theories of family functioning described earlier. We also provide references for a more complete review of techniques.

To a large extent, the interventions a therapist chooses depend on which aspect of the overview theory is in focus. With a structural emphasis, a therapist joins with the family, maps structural dynamics such as hierarchy and boundaries, and has the family enact patterns that give them new possibilities for alternative relationships. Minuchin and Fishman's (1981) book *Family Therapy Techniques* provides detailed descriptions of interventions into the structure/organization of the family. *Joining* is a technique by which a therapist works to understand and accept each person's position in the family.

The family often approaches therapy with some anxiety and guilt, and it is important to connect with each member. Failure to join and accommodate to the way things are may produce resistance to therapeutic interventions. Joining includes but is not limited to the initial session. It occurs throughout therapy and does not always mean listening and "being nice." Often it involves saying something that is painful, but real in the experience of one or more family members. *Mapping the family structure* involves two stages. In planning for sessions, the therapist makes some hypotheses about structure. This occurs even before the first session. Questions such as, "Who seems most powerful?" "What relationships might be disengaged from each other?" or "Is the hierarchy functional?" can be asked. These questions or hypotheses continue to be generated throughout therapy. The second stage of mapping involves testing these hypotheses by watching the family interact as well as by asking them to talk to each other. This latter intervention, creating enactments, is a powerful way of allowing the therapist to actually see what happens in the family.

*Enactments* can also be used to highlight or modify interactions. The therapist encourages family members to behave in new, competent ways. For example, a mother and a daughter who are in a constant battle for control may be asked to engage in a different kind of interaction. In a soft tone, sitting in close proximity to the mother, the therapist may ask the mother to talk in a soft tone, sit next to her daughter and talk to her about her concerns for the daughter's safety.

An emphasis on changing the patterns of interaction involves different kinds of interventions. The therapist is more interested in changing the symptom maintaining sequences than on changing the structure. *Precise questioning* about the process occurring around the problem and attempted problem solutions is important. Tasks, either direct or paradoxical, are assigned to alter these sequences.

The questions asked in the initial interviews revolve around who does what, how, and when the problem occurs. This not only provides information about the process, but also about the possible functionality of the symptom for the overall system. Haley (1987) provides an excellent description of such an initial interview.

In these initial sessions, each family member presents his or her view of the problem and of the solutions that have been tried. It is these solutions that often are addressed by therapeutic interventions. After a clear problem definition is agreed on, the family and therapist set goals for therapy. This is often the most difficult phase of therapy. Presenting problems such as "we want to communicate more," tend to be vague, and families have more ideas about what they don't want than what they do want. However, for the strategically designed interventions that follow to be effective, this problem definition/goal setting is crucial.

*Assignment of tasks* to be completed outside the sessions is a primary intervention utilized by therapists focused on altering patterns. These can be direct or paradoxical. Straightforward directives are given with a rationale designed to correspond to the goals agreed on in the initial sessions. If therapeutic rapport is developed and resistance to change is low, the family will be able to carry these out. Attention is paid to the way in which families carry out the assigned tasks. Their level of resistance to change can be gauged by whether they carry out the task exactly, modify the task, or fail to do it at all.

*Paradoxical interventions* are designed to counter strong resistance to change (Watzlawick et al., 1974). The usual method is to ask the family not to change, to go slow in changing, or to continue the symptom. These directives are given with the intent that the family will be placed in a bind. If they follow the directives, they are exercising control over these symptoms. If they don't comply, the symptoms change. These interventions have been extremely controversial with proponents arguing they are congruent and respectful of the family's fear of change while others argue that they are tricky and manipulative. The key variable seems to be the rationale that accompanies the directive and the degree to which the therapist believes it to be true. If paradoxical interventions become routine statements used in every case, they are not likely to be as effective as if they come out of the family's efforts in therapy, and are designed to have unique meaning to the family.

Cloe Madanes (1981) describes another type of paradoxical intervention. She advocates the use of "pretend" techniques to playfully confront destructive patterns. For example, a symptomatic child is asked to pretend to have the symptom and the parents are encouraged to pretend to help. The child can give up the actual symptom; pretending to have it is enough. One cannot pretend to have a phobia or throw a tantrum and have a real one at the same time. The intervention can turn a deadly serious struggle that would not respond to a direct approach at change into a playful make-believe game.

The third area of family functioning in the overview theory is in the belief systems of the family. While the focus on structure and patterns emphasizes behavior change first with a belief change to follow, the systemic therapists emphasize belief or meaning change as the primary target. Three interventions from this approach are reframing (Watzlawick et al., 1974), circular questioning (Nelson, Fleuridas, & Rosenthal, 1986; Selvini-Palazzoli, Boscolo, Cecchin, & Prata, 1977; Tomm, 1984), family rituals (Selvini-Palazzoli et al.), and narrative story telling (White & Epston, 1993).

*Reframing* is an intervention used often by family therapists. The therapists hears the situation as presented by the family and then restates it in a new way. The goal is to change the way reality is perceived so that new behaviors will follow. For example, an anorexic girl who is seen as "sick" by her parents and in need of a great deal of tender loving care can be reframed as being "disobedient" and in a power struggle with her parents. A delinquent boy can be viewed alternatively as sad and insecure who is in need of firm structure and guidance to feel secure. As with the paradoxical directive, these restatements of the problem must be unique to the particular situation and not seen as standard to be used in every case.

*Positive connotation* (Selvini-Palazzoli et al., 1977), a form of reframing, always defines symptomatic behavior in terms of its helpfulness to the system. For example, a child's misbehavior may be redefined as helpful to her parents' communication.

*Circular questioning* is a technique that has received increasing attention in the clinical literature. This form of questioning serves as an efficient process for soliciting information from each member of the family regarding his or her opinion and experience of (a) the family's presenting concern; (b) in what context the behaviors occur; (c) sequences of interactions, usually related to the problem; and (d) differences in family members' relationships over time. Questions such as "Who is the most upset when John throws a temper tantrum?" or "Who feels the most helpless when it happens?" are asked of all family members. The answers are used to generate additional hypotheses about family functioning or additional questions. The questions themselves are seen as interventions in that they may provide the family with new information about the way things are now and they way they could be in the future. New belief systems can be created that necessitate new behaviors by family members.

A therapist can prescribe *family rituals,* which are usually a complex, elaborate task involving all family members. The therapist asks the family to complete an action or series of actions sometimes accompanied by verbal expressions. The ritual is prescribed in every detail: the place it must be carried out, who must say and do what action, and the number of times the ritual is to be completed. Often, the instructions are given in writing and the session is ended without further discussion about the assignment. A particular ritual is designed for a family after careful consideration of the unique rules that maintain their problems. The ritual breaks these rules in some way and the family can experience an alternative belief about themselves.

The narrative story-telling approach advocated by White and Epston (1993) is a wonderful way of looking at dysfunctional beliefs with an emphasis on their susceptibility to being changed. After clarifying what the problem is and how much harm it has done, the authors work to help a client become aware of how much he or she knows and does already to ensure functioning and lead to better actions. They then work to build awareness of how much control already exists and help by practicing it in a variety of ways. In a direct way, they enhance a client's sense of control over their own outcome without ignoring the dysfunctional patterns.

## GROUP PROCEDURES

The family is a small group with a shared history. In some respects, family therapy may be considered similar to group therapy. However, an additional dimension of family therapy is multiple families in group programs. Three models of family-group facilitation are described by Hoopes, Fisher, and Barlow (1984). Family education programs are primarily instructional in focus, with the expressed intent of imparting information and skills to family members. Parent education courses are a common type of family education program. One well-developed parent education program is Bavolek and Comstack's (1985) Nurturing Parent Program. This is a 15-week structured program designed to enhance parental self-esteem, parenting skills, social support, and overall healthy family functioning.

Family enrichment programs are designed to enhance skills and healthy family interactions through instructional and experiential activities. Two well-known programs, Understanding Us (Carnes, 1981) and Family Cluster (Sawin, 1979), bring groups of families together to share experiences, learn new skills, and develop healthier interactions. Enrichment and education programs provide knowledge and skills in a preventive spirit. They assist families in sidestepping or effectively coping with potentially difficult situations and, therefore, maintaining family integrity and cohesion.

Family treatment groups are designed to resolve problems encountered and developed by families and, therefore, are remedial in nature. Multiple family group therapy involves the treatment of several families together with regularly scheduled sessions. A common use of multiple family treatment is in chronic illnesses and in addiction recovery (e.g., substance abuse) and eating disorders. Steinglass and colleagues have developed a comprehensive protocol for running these groups and have conducted research on their efficacy (Gonzalez, Steinglass, & Reiss, 1989).

In all three models, family members learn from the facilitator(s) and other families. All models offer a supportive context for the development of new roles and behaviors. In Hoopes et al. (1984), several tested enrichment, education, and treatment programs for families with children and adolescents are actually provided.

## CLASSROOM AND EDUCATIONAL APPLICATIONS

Systemic theory applies as well to a classroom, a school, or an entire school system as it does to a family. Broadening the lens of analysis to include subsystems such as teacher-student, student-student, principal-staff, teacher-parents-student can help to provide a more organized way of approaching the problem as well as provide more options for intervention. Once this lens is widened, the choices for intervention can be on the structure/organization of the family, the patterns of interaction, or the meaning/belief system.

Children who are exhibiting behavior problems are often afraid of the power these symptoms have over adults. They may even escalate the problems to encourage adults to take charge. Teachers, concerned about this escalation, may call the parents in to a conference. After these meetings become adversarial, each looks to blame the other for the child's problem. Principals are sometimes present at these meetings, but either are forced to support the teacher's position or try to play a mediating role.

This school-family conference is an excellent example of a technique that focuses on the organization or structure of that system. The purpose of these conferences is to "join" with all family members and establish a clear leadership team between the adults. Joining would involve displaying a keen interest in knowing whether problems seen at school are observed in the home context and vice versa. This is done with curiosity about the differences between the two settings rather than projection of blame. One of the important benefits of these meetings is that the child is given a clear role to play. This depends somewhat on the age of the child, but generally, he or she is asked to observe the discussion and to provide input in a structured way when it is requested. The child thus observes the important adults in his or her life working together. More detailed descriptions of the possible structure of these interviews can be found in Fine and Holt (1983), Molnar and Lindquist (1984), or Friedman (1969).

A classroom can be thought of in much the same way as a family with the teacher playing the same role as a therapist. In most therapeutic approaches, a child's misbehavior would lead to a focus on the child and an intervention designed to change the child's behavior. A systemic approach would enable the teacher to focus on his or her part in maintaining the problem behaviors. Outside consultants such as psychologists, social workers, or principals can help teachers to have that perspective and use systemic techniques in the problem.

Intervention can be made by focusing on the patterns of interactions that occur in a classroom. When teachers are able to look at their students and classrooms as systems, they are able to look at their own beliefs and behavior as part of that system. Instead of looking at the sequence of "teacher yells→child disrupts" or "child disrupts→teacher yells" in a cause-effect manner, both are seen as mutually determining each other. To the extent that the teacher yells, the child disrupts. To the extent the child disrupts, the teacher yells. This dyadic example could be expanded to include complex interactions between groups of students and teachers or administrators.

Another example is as follows: A typical sequence at recess involves one child consistently being scapegoated into trouble by two other students with the teacher having to enforce punishment on the scapegoat. If the teacher were to change her part of the pattern by intervening in a positive manner with all three before recess, she might prevent her negative involvement later. This example enlarges the context to include the teacher and would require the teacher to embrace firmly the belief that he or she helps to define roles played by the students. This is an alternative to the traditional belief that students are totally responsible for their own behavior.

Reframing or positive connotation is a technique described earlier. It involves a focus on the belief system or meaning of the problem, or some aspect of it. Teachers can also use reframing. An "angry, defiant" child can be seen as "extremely sad and desperately seeking to provide structure in his environment." Two children "constantly fighting" can be seen as attempting to "work problems out" in the only way they know how. An "annoying" child who is constantly sharpening her pencil can be seen as "anxious to please and perform well on schoolwork." A teacher's response to a child will depend in large measure on his or her belief about the child's behavior. A teacher who sees a behavior as annoying is likely to become easily irritated and yell at the child. If the same behavior is seen as "anxious to please," the teacher may feel more compassionate and help shape the behavior in a more positive way.

## PARENTING SKILLS

An awareness and careful assessment of family systems dynamics is extremely important for counselors and therapists who utilize parent educational approaches. Often parent education is begun individually or in groups where each of the parents has a child exhibiting behavior problems in school or in the community. Interactional patterns in the family that might contribute to maintaining these problems need to be explored. Three of these issues are discussed in a recent article by Getz and Gunn (1988).

The first issue is that most current parent education approaches present a one-sided view of the parent-child relationship: That is, parents from a systemic perspective cause their children's behavior. Parents and children are involved in a process of mutual influence. One program, Student Effectiveness Training (Getz & Morrill, 1978), was an attempt to balance the skewedness of Parent Effectiveness Training by teaching the same communication skills to adolescents and parents.

A second issue is the reality that often mothers are the only ones involved in learning new parenting strategies. Levant and Doyle (1981) conducted a review of the literature on parent training and did not find any study that focused on the training of fathers or indicated whether fathers were ever involved in the training. If one member of a family system is changing attitudes and behaviors, there is the danger that the other parent may have difficulty adjusting. A key concept in systemic theory is the parental hierarchy that functions in making decisions for the children. Thus, parent education only to the mother may contribute to the disruption of that hierarchy.

Finally and most important, the same parenting skills are typically taught regardless of the specific characteristics of each of the families. This may aggravate preexisting patterns. Gunn (1983) developed a training program for parents of children identified as emotionally disturbed and currently receiving special education in the public schools. He interviewed each family separately to assess their strengths and weaknesses in handling positive as well as conflictual situations. He then organized a parent training group that used individualized instruction to focus on those weaker areas which could be enhanced with better child-rearing skills. In addition, parents with strengths in certain skill areas served as models for other parents.

Table 10.2 provides examples of family system issues and parent education approaches that would be important to emphasize.


## EFFICACY

As noted earlier, clinical research was one of the key movements that launched the field of family therapy. Since that time, several hundred outcome and process studies have been completed on a broad range of family problems, treatment approaches, therapist factors, and the effectiveness of family therapy. According to Gurman, Kniskern,

**Table 10.2.    Parent education strategies for different family dynamics**

| Family System Issues | Parent Education Approaches |
|---|---|
| 1. Family communication<br>   Dysfunctional communication patterns | Active listening<br>Confrontation and problem-solving skills<br>Examination of irrational beliefs |
| 2. Emotional distance between family members<br>   Enmeshed families (too little distance) messages<br>   Disengaged families (too much distance) | Analysis of children's mistaken goals<br>Use of logical consequences<br>Confrontation skills and "I"<br>Communication skills<br>Family meetings |
| 3. Family role structuring<br>   Inverted hierarchy (lack of parental authority)<br>   Split parental team | Assertive discipline<br>Behavior modification<br>Use of logical consequences<br>Parental communication and negotiation |

and Pinsof (1986) "By the 1980s, research had come to occupy a truly significant and undoubtedly permanent place in the field of family and marital therapy" (p. 567).

Family therapy is inherently complex. While seeking to illuminate answers to "what therapy is most effective for what problems, treated by what therapists, according to what criteria, in what setting" (Paul, 1967, p. 11), perplexing issues of target outcome variables, measurement, design, control groups, random selection, subject population, integration of research and practice are complicated by a systemic theoretical foundation. For example, targeted outcome variables may consist of increased healthy family functioning, increased individual functioning, and reaching the client's goal for treatment. With regard to increased healthy family functioning, how will this be defined, by whom, and how measured? If increased individual functioning is the target variable, which individual(s) in the family is(are) measured? Studies in which client goals are the outcome criteria, what about those families in which the members do not agree to a common goal? Despite these and other difficulties, researchers have provided studies that conclusively demonstrate the efficacy of family therapy. These studies have been notably reviewed by Gurman and Kniskern (1978, 1981), Gurman et al. (1986), and Todd and Stanton (1983). In general, the following conclusions are some of those that may be drawn from family therapy research:

- Family therapy is as effective or more effective than individual and other treatment approaches. Gurman and Kniskern (1978) examined 14 comparative studies (family therapy compared with other modalities) and found that family therapy was superior in 10 and equal in the remaining studies. Family therapy produces beneficial effects in about two-thirds of cases. In fact, Gurman and Kniskern estimated the overall improvement rate for family therapy cases at 73%.

- Family therapy can produce positive results in treatment of short duration (1–20 sessions). Short-term or time-limited family therapy is as effective as longer term therapy (Gurman et al., 1986; Todd & Stanton, 1983).

- The involvement of the father in family therapy substantially increases the probability of successful outcome (Todd & Stanton, 1983).

- There is little evidence that one marriage and family therapy approach is superior to another. No systematic comparison of the various "schools" has been completed (Todd & Stanton, 1983).

- Marriage and family therapy can also cause deterioration in individuals and relationships. Deterioration rates (5%–10%) for marriage and family therapy is roughly comparable to those reported for individual and group therapy. Gurman and Kniskern (1978) isolated certain therapist behaviors that were related to poor outcomes, including poor relationship skills, the confronting of emotionally loaded issues and defenses early in treatment, and little structuring of early sessions. More refined therapist skills seem necessary to yield positive outcomes. The age/developmental level of the "identified parent" (child, adolescent, adult) is not associated with treatment outcomes (Gurman & Kniskern, 1978).

With regard to specific disorders of childhood and adolescence, family therapy research has focused on psychosomatic disorders, juvenile delinquency and conduct disorders, and mixed emotional/behavioral disorders.

Structural family therapy has been studied for the treatment of anorexia, diabetes mellitus, and chronic asthma. Minuchin, Rosman, and Baker (1978) reported on 86% improvement/recovery rate for 53 anorexics and their families. Minuchin et al. (1975) reported a 90% improvement rate for diabetes and chronic asthma. All three populations were treated with a structural approach.

Juvenile delinquency and family therapy have been extensively studied at the University of Utah by James Alexander and associates (Alexander & Parsons, 1973; Klein, Alexander, & Parsons, 1977; Parsons & Alexander, 1973) applying "functional" family therapy. Families treated with this approach significantly improved in communication and showed a lower rate of recidivism (26%) than other treatment modalities (47% for client centered; 50% for untreated persons; and 73% for dynamic-eclectic therapy approaches).

Patterson (1982) studied conduct disorders involving aggressive (e.g., physically violent) and nonaggressive (e.g., stealing, lying) behaviors utilizing "parent management training." This approach has been demonstrated to change child classroom and at-home behaviors.

No meaningful conclusions may be drawn for mixed childhood and adolescent disorders, due to sampling techniques of every study (Gurman et al., 1986).

Family therapy research has continued into such areas as adult schizophrenia, psychosomatic symptoms, addictions, depressions, anxiety, marital distress, and sexual dysfunction. While the field has experienced conceptual and methodological problems, the outcome of well-designed studies indicates the effectiveness of family therapy.

## CONCLUSION

Family therapy is the clinical application of systems theory in working therapeutically with children and adolescents. It has added to the therapist's options of looking at problems and methods of effecting change. The primary orientation is toward evaluating the relevant context in which behaviors occur and what factors within that context maintain the presenting problem(s). Interventions are designed to increase family members' ability to function in that context. Family therapists are not particularly interested in the historical etiology of problems, but on the factors that allow the problem behaviors to continue.

Within the field of family therapy, discussion continues about the aspects of family functioning that are most salient for therapeutic focus. This chapter has described three of these in terms of theory, interventions, group procedures, and educational applications. Assessment covers structure and organization of family hierarchy and boundaries, patterns of interaction, and the belief system of individual members or of the family as a whole.

There are several new directions for family therapy. Research will continue to measure outcomes and demonstrate the effectiveness of interventions. These studies will need to state more specific questions such as which theory/technique is effective with what kinds of problems on what kinds of families. Questions such as "When should structural interventions be applied?" or "Are tasks given to complete within the session more effective than those given outside the session?" will be asked in future research studies.

While family theorists may argue about the correctness of a given approach, clinical practitioners do not seem to be as concerned. In fact, there has been much more of an integration of approaches in the past few years. The overview theory described in this chapter is an example of this trend. Systems therapists are beginning to apply contextual theories in new areas. One example is the training of family medicinal physicians. Family therapists have begun to work closely with these physicians in cases involving physical, behavioral, and emotional difficulties (Doherty & Baird, 1983). Another application is in the area of organizational consultation. Schools, businesses, and work teams are systems to which these principles have been applied.

Finally, family therapy has been criticized for losing the "tree for the forest." Intrapsychic dynamics have largely been ignored. The return of the "self in the system" has broadened the thinking of family therapists to consider intrapsychic theories within the systemic perspective.

## CASE STUDY

Susan, aged 8 years, was identified by her mother, Cathy, and her teacher as having significant emotional, behavioral, and learning problems. She was attending a small, rural school and engaging in frequent physical fights with peers. She was often defiant and verbally abusive to her teacher. Cathy reported that while these behaviors were not new, negative school reports had escalated this year. In addition, Susan would throw two or three weekly tantrums at home usually in response to her mother's request to complete a task.

### Relevant Background Information/Family History

Susan was the younger of two girls. Her sister, Elaine, who was 11, had never been in any trouble. Elaine was reported to have been a model child both at home and at school. Susan's father, Tom, had been a long distance truck driver during his entire 15-year marriage to Cathy. He was home on an irregular and unpredictable basis. Cathy had not been employed outside the home.

Susan began to experience respiratory problems when she was 1-year-old. In the following 3 years, the family had her evaluated by a number of medical specialists and she was hospitalized several times. A diagnosis of atypical asthma was not confirmed until the end of that time. Both parents agreed that this was an extremely difficult time for everyone. They lived in almost constant fear their daughter would stop breathing so she was never left alone. Although Susan had not been sick for several years, the parents admitted to a fair degree of watchfulness due to fear of relapse. Cathy felt that she worried more since Tom was away a large part of the time. Cathy expressed a great deal of anger and mistrust toward the school system. She moved Susan three times due to her perception of the teacher's lack of understanding of what her daughter needed. She felt the teacher was only interested in making Susan obey and did not allow her to express her opinions.

## Assessment

There were two relevant interactional systems to consider in understanding what maintained (not what caused) Susan's problems; the family and family-school systems. During three family interviews and consultation with the school, an assessment was made of the (a) structure/organization of these systems, (b) patterns of interaction, and (c) the beliefs held about Susan's problems. Beliefs about the implicit rules for interaction between those involved were also explored. This assessment resulted in the following four hypotheses:

1. There were poorly defined boundaries within the family, particularly around Cathy and both girls. It was difficult for Cathy to know what level of responsibility Susan should be given. To the extent that Cathy did things for her, Susan sensed her mother's concern, and acted in ways to justify it. The subsystem of mother-daughter could be described as enmeshed. It was difficult to know where "one stopped and the other began."

2. There seemed to be a coalition between the females that, to some extent, excluded Tom. Tom's job requirements were such that he was gone for long periods of time and this helped to maintain the coalition.

3. The following patterns of interaction around the problem were described by the family. If Susan strongly refused to comply with the teacher, she was removed from the classroom and usually Cathy was called. Cathy described feeling threatened by the school and usually responded angrily and defensively to the school, but acted helpless and hopeless in front of Susan. Cathy and Elaine, as well as Susan, expressed the same bewilderment saying frequently everything had been tried. The school had developed a role in which they were only the bearer of bad news and had become increasingly frustrated by Cathy's nonsupport and anger toward them. They began to resist calling Cathy except in extreme circumstances. When Tom came home, he was told about the incidents in which Susan had been involved at school. He offered counseling and advice as well as established consequences for future misbehavior. These were rarely carried out in his absence, and it seemed that Susan had the worst times when he was away. Mother and daughters felt that Tom was extremely helpful when he came home suggesting this pattern had a possible function for the system.

4. The family maintained some strong belief systems that were relevant for designing interventions. The first was a certainty on the part of the parents that Susan could get very sick again if she and they were not watchful. Second, was the view that Cathy was the leader and the glue that held the family together. Her moods set the tone for the rest of the family and strong fear was expressed about her becoming depressed. Third, the overt view about Tom was that he did the best he could do although covertly there was a great deal of resentment about his erratic work schedule. Finally, Elaine was seen as perfect and needing little attention, guidance, and nurturance to do well. The only problem was a concern that she ate very little and was 15 pounds underweight.

## Interventions

Using the assessment data about structure, patterns, and belief systems, the following interventions were among those implemented during the course of therapy:

1. A family-school conference was held with the therapist in charge. The teacher, principal, both parents, and Susan were present. The agenda of developing a unified plan for assisting Susan to succeed at home and school was presented. Susan was asked to leave the meeting for a while during which time a plan was developed for communication and positive and negative consequences of Susan's behaviors. The plan was presented to Susan at the end of the session. This plan involved Tom a great deal, and he expressed a willingness to be more directly involved. This gave Cathy a chance to have a "vacation" from the problem so she did not get overwhelmed.

2. Reframing was begun at the family-school conference and continued in family therapy. The early illness patterns of reframing involved protection. Susan was described as becoming stuck at about 4 years of age due to the uncertainty of her medical condition. The normal patterns that developed around the illness were still in place, but not necessary and were delaying Susan's emotional growth.

3. A concern was raised about Elaine having an eating disorder in the future. Several therapy sessions focused on this possibility (i.e., why she might be at risk and some possible preventive strategies, all of which involved paying more attention to her normal development). Cathy was given several assignments to encourage and teach Elaine how to socialize effectively with her peers.

## Analysis

The family-school conference was an intervention designed to establish a clear hierarchy and appropriate boundaries between the adults and children in the system. Susan was included in a way that presented the message as clearly as possible. She was put in a student/child role and the discussion was in the language of teaching and learning new skills rather than control or punishment of past behavior.

Reframing was used to present an alternative reality/belief system to all involved. Susan was presented as a girl with important developmental tasks to learn rather than an emotionally disturbed or delinquent child. This intervention served to shut the door on guilt for the parents and open the door to embrace and practice new, more competent behaviors. The structural move to increase Tom's involvement was designed to break up the coalition between Cathy and Susan, give him a more responsible role, and disengage Cathy. Tom found out earlier about any problems and dealt with them more effectively. This replaced the mother's helpless "dance" and may have helped to break the pattern that maintained Susan's problematic behavior.

The focus on Elaine was not used solely to take the spotlight away from Susan although that was one benefit. It also provided a different role and alternative belief system for Elaine and added a more active nurturant dimension to the relationship between her and her parents.

### Results

There were dramatic and significant improvements immediately between home and school in the areas of collaboration, support, and communication between the adults. Susan's behavior at school also improved. Tom was able to negotiate his work schedule a month ahead, which made family events more predictable. He reported being happy with being in charge of the school-home program and felt successful.

## ANNOTATED BIBLIOGRAPHY

Boscolo, L., Cecchin, G., Hoffman, L., & Penn, P. (1987). *Milan systemic family therapy.* New York: Basic Books.

The authors are two members of the original Milan team and two American Milan therapists. In the Introduction, the authors report the evolution of this approach. The remainder of the book is dedicated to case studies of family therapy from a Milan perspective.

Goldenberg, I., & Goldenberg, H. (1985). *Family therapy: An overview* (2nd ed.). Monterey, CA: Brooks/Cole.

This excellent overview for the uninitiated covers family systems and family dysfunction, several major theoretical perspectives, techniques of family therapy, and training. It is frequently used as an introductory text at the master's level in marriage and family therapy courses.

Gurman, A. S., & Kniskern, D. P. (1981). *Handbook of family therapy.* New York: Brunner/Mazel.

This is considered one of the major texts in family therapy today. Under one cover, first-generation theorists (for the most part) in family therapy have written about their theories in a manner that allows for comparison. Also included are excellent chapters on the history of marriage and family therapy and research into this field.

Haley, J. (1987). *Problemsolving therapy (2nd ed.).* San Francisco: Jossey Bass.

This is the second edition of a classic book in which Haley first coined the term "strategic therapy." It is a clear exposition of the basic tenets underlying Haley's approach to family therapy, a combination of structural and strategic concepts. His chapter on conducting the initial interview is particularly good for new therapists who are desirous of a structured way to conduct a family interview. His chapter on ethical issues attempts to address charges that strategic practices are deceptive or manipulative.

Madanes, C. (1981). *Strategic family therapy.* San Francisco: Jossey-Bass.

Madanes, C. (1984). *Behind the one-way mirror.* San Francisco: Jossey-Bass.

These well-written books have been useful additions to the scope of strategic family therapy. Madanes emphasizes planning ahead and discovering hidden metaphors in families. The majority of case examples in these books involve children and her unique "pretend" interventions describe ways for therapists to more gently change patterns in a family.

Minuchin, S. (1976). *Families and Family Therapy.* Cambridge, MA: Harvard University Press.

This seminal text in structural family therapy is an excellent place to begin reading. Minuchin clarified his theory through verbatim therapy transcripts and parallel commentary. Particularly helpful in this book is the description of family mapping, an assessment technique that allows a therapist to visually place family members or involved systems in space to design structural interventions.

Mirkin, M., & Koman, S. (Eds.). (1985). *A handbook of adolescents and family therapy.* Gardner Press, New York.

The contributions to this handbook cover many topics related to adolescence. The first section of the book covers theoretical issues, while authors of the second explore settings in which therapy occurs. Finally, the last two sections of the book address issues in treatment such as substance abuse and suicide. This book is highly recommended for professionals working with adolescents.

Papp, P. (1983). *The Process of Change.* New York: Guilford Press.

Peggy Papp, writing from a systemic perspective, provides a very clear approach to treating families. She describes systemic hypothesizing and innovative interventions in practical terms. This is an enjoyable book to read.

Watzlawick, P., Weakland, J., & Fisch, R. (1974). *Change.* New York: Norton.

Written by the early pioneers in family therapy and based on the work of Gregory Bateson and the Palo Alto project, these are the basic assumptions of one version of strategic brief therapy. Innovative interventions are presented that are consistent with these assumptions. Descriptions of how solutions can become problems and the concepts of first- and second-order change are presented.

# REFERENCES

Alexander, J. F., & Parsons, B. (1973). Short term behavioral intervention with delinquent families: Impact on family process and recidivism. *Journal of Abnormal Psychology, 81,* 219–225.

Alexander, J. F., & Parsons, B. (1982). *Functional family therapy.* Monterey, CA: Brooks/Cole.

Bevolek, S. J., & Comstack, C. (1985). *Nurturing program for parents and children: Parents handbook.* Eau Claire, WI: Family Development Resources.

Carnes, P. (1981). *Understanding us.* Minneapolis, MN: Interpersonal Communication Programs.

Carter, B., & McGoldrick, M. (1988). *The changing family life cycle: A framework for family therapy* (2nd ed.). New York: Gardner Press.

de Shazer, S. (1985). *Keys to solution in brief therapy.* New York: Norton.

Doherty, W. J., & Baird, M. A. (1983). *Family therapy and family medicine: Toward the primary care of families.* New York: Guilford Press.

Fine, M. E., & Holt, P. (1983). Intervening with school problems: A family systems perspective. *Psychology in the Schools, 20,* 59–66.

Fisher, B. L., Giblin, P. R., & Hoopes, M. H. (1982). Healthy family functioning. *Journal of Marital and Family Therapy, 8*(3), 273–284.

Friedman, R. (1969). A structured family interview in the assessment of school learning disorders. *Psychology in the Schools, 6,* 162–171.

Gantman, C. (1980). A closer look at families that work well. *International Journal of Family Therapy, 8,* 106–119.

Getz, H., & Gunn, W. B. (1988). Parent education from a family-systems perspective. *School Counselor, 35,* 331–336.

Getz, H. E., & Morrill, R. (1978). SET! Student effectiveness training. *Humanist Educator, 16,* 134–144.

Goldenberg, I., & Goldenberg, H. (1985). *Family therapy: An overview* (2nd ed.). Monterey, CA: Brooks/Cole.

Gonzalez, S., Steinglass, P., & Reiss, D. (1989). Putting the illness in its place: Discussion groups for families with chronic medical illness. *Family Process, 28,* 69–87.

Gunn, W. (1983). *The Pulaski project.* Unpublished manuscript.

Gurman, A. S., & Kniskern, D. P. (1978). Research on marital and family therapy: Progress, perspective and prospect. In S. L. Garfield & A. F. Bergin (Eds.), *Handbook of psychotherapy and behavior change* (2nd ed.). New York: Wiley.

Gurman, A. S., & Kniskern, D. P. (1981). *Handbook of family therapy.* New York: Brunner/Mazel.

Gurman, A. S., Kniskern, D. P., & Pinsof, W. (1986). Research on the process and outcome of marital and family therapy. In S. L. Garfield & A. E. Bergin (Eds.), *Handbook of psychotherapy and behavior change* (3rd ed.). New York: Wiley.

Haley, J. (1980). *Leaving home.* New York: McGraw-Hill.

Haley, J. (1987). *Problem-solving therapy.* San Francisco: Jossey-Bass.

Hoopes, M. H., Fisher, B. L., & Barlow, S. H. (1984). *Structured family facilitation programs.* Rockville, MD: Aspen Systems.

Klein, N. C., Alexander, J. F., & Parsons, B. V. (1977). Impact of family systems intervention on recidivism and sibling delinquency: A model of primary prevention and program evaluation. *Journal of Consulting and Clinical Psychology, 45,* 469–474.

Lacqueur, H. P. (1976). Multiple family therapy. In P. J. Guerin (Ed.), *Family therapy: Theory and practice.* New York: Gardner Press.

Levant, R. E., & Doyle, G. (1981). *Parent education for fathers: A personal developmental approach.* Unpublished manuscript, Boston University.

Lewis, J., Beavers, W. R., Gossett, J., & Phillips, V. (1976). *No single thread: Psychological health in family systems.* New York: Brunner/Mazel.

Madanes, C. (1981). *Strategic family therapy.* San Francisco: Jossey-Bass.

Madanes, C. (1984). *Behind the one-way mirror.* San Francisco: Jossey-Bass.

Minuchin, S. (1974). *Families and family therapy.* Cambridge, MA: Harvard University Press.

Minuchin, S., Baker, L., Rosman, B., Liebman, R., Milman, L., & Todd, T. (1975). A conceptual model of psychosomatic illness in children. *Archives of General Psychiatry, 32,* 1031–1038.

Minuchin, S., & Fishman, H. C. (1981). *Techniques of family therapy.* Cambridge, MA: Harvard University Press.

Minuchin, S., Rosman, B., & Baker, L. (1978). *Psychosomatic families: Anorexia nervosa in context.* Cambridge, MA: Harvard University Press.

Molnar, A. E., & Lindquist, B. (1984). Demons or angels? A lot depends on how you respond to misbehavior. *Learning, 13*(9), 22–26.

Nelson, T. S., Fleuridas, C., & Rosenthal, D. M. (1986). The evolution of circular questions: Training family therapists. *Journal of Marriage and Family Therapy, 12,* 113–127.

Parsons, B. V., & Alexander, J. F. (1973). Short term family intervention: A therapy outcome study. *Journal of Consulting and Clinical Psychology, 41,* 195–201.

Patterson, G. R. (1982). *Coercive family process.* Eugene, OR: Castalia Press.

Paul, G. L. (1967). Outcome research in psychotherapy. *Journal of Consulting Psychology, 31,* 109–188.

Sawin, M. (1979). *Family enrichment with family clusters.* Valley Forge, PA: Judson Press.

Selvini-Palazzoli, M., Boscolo, L., Cecchin, G., & Prata, G. (1978). *Paradox and counterparadox.* New York: Aronson.

Selvini-Palazzoli, M., Boscolo, L., Cecchin, G., & Prata, G. (1980). Hypothesizing-circularity-neutrality. *Family Process, 19,* 73–85.

Selvini-Palazzoli, M., Boscolo, L., Cecchin, G., & Prata, G. (1977). Family rituals: A powerful tool in family therapy. *Family Process, 16,* 445–453.

Stinnett, N. (1979). In search of strong families. In N. Stinnett, B. Chesser, & V. De-Grains (Eds.), *Building family strengths.* Lincoln: University of Nebraska Press.

Todd, T. C., & Stanton, M. D. (1983). Research on marital and family therapy: Answers, issues and recommendation for the future. In B. Wolman & G. Stricker (Eds.), *Handbook of family and marital therapy.* New York: Plenum Press.

Tomm, K. (1984). One perspective on the Milan systemic approach: Part 1. Overview of development, theory and practice. *Journal of Marital and Family Therapy, 10*(2) 113–125.

Waters, D., & Lawrence, E. (1993). *Competence, courage and change.* New York: Norton.

Watzlawick, P., Weakland, J., & Fisch, R. (1974). *Principles of problem formation and problem resolution.* New York: Norton.

White, M., & Epston, D. (1990). *Narrative means to therapeutic ends.* New York: Norton.

# Chapter 11 ———————————————————————————

# *OTHER APPROACHES, TECHNIQUES, AND SPECIAL SITUATIONS*

Anne P. Cituk, Leigh R. Graves, and H. Thompson Prout

The previous chapters in this book have dealt with theoretical approaches that have well-developed rationales and strategies for working with children and adolescents and with some of the broader issues in the area. Other literature exists dealing with somewhat narrower topics and issues. The purpose of this chapter is to discuss these other topics and issues. Although there are obviously some topics we will not cover, this chapter provides an overview of other theoretical approaches that have some application with children and adoeslcents, brief descriptions of several techniques that are not necessarily identified with a particular theoretical approach, and a discussion of treatment issues related to several special problems or situations encountered by children and adolescents.

## OTHER THEORETICAL APPROACHES

### Gestalt Therapy with Children

Gestalt therapy was developed by Fritz Perls (1969, 1973). This form of therapy was named after the learning theory proposed by the Gestalt psychologists (Korb, Gorrell, & Van De Riet, 1989). Gestalt therapy posits that people are unhappy because they live their lives isolated from part(s) of themselves. The goal of Gestalt therapy is to make people aware of themselves and integrate isolated parts into a whole and fully functioning person.

Gestalt therapy proposes that the individual is more than the sum of his or her parts. The goals of therapy are to help clients to develop an awareness of, and take responsibility for, their thoughts, feelings, and behavior and to experience and integrate the parts of themselves, in a variety of situations. To help accomplish this, the here-and-now is emphasized, as opposed to focusing on the past. The approach seeks to aid clients in learning to live in the present. Techniques are used to help clients experience feelings and emotions that they have had in the past, by bringing them into the present. Gestalt therapy also assumes that all individuals are continually adjusting to themselves and to the environment, so the process is never complete. Gestalt therapy utilizes numerous activities and techniques to help clients maintain their here-and-now orientation and access their feelings and emotions in the situations of their lives. These techniques and activities make Gestalt therapy especially suited for use with children. Some of the techniques highlighted here involve fantasy and imagination, language, and role playing or enactment (Korb et al., 1989).

The "Imaginary Fantasy Trip" is an activity that takes several forms and is designed to take the child to his or her own "special place." Fantasy activities are especially useful with children because they are not only fun, but also give us insight into the child's fantasy process. This is important because the fantasy processes are generally parallel to the child's actual life processes (Oaklander, 1978). Through fantasy we can better understand what is going on in the child's life, and how the child perceives it.

Drawing allows children to express themselves and their view of the world, on paper. Drawings may involve family situations, scribbles, expressing the world with curved lines, or group drawings. When appropriate, children may be encouraged to talk about their completed artwork (Thompson & Rudolph, 1992).

Thompson and Rudolph (1992) and Oaklander (1978) describe a range of other techniques for use with children. The use of "I" language encourages the client to use the word "I" instead of a generalized "you," in conversation. For example: "You know how it is when you can't get your homework finished, and you get in trouble." By personalizing this message and substituting "I" for "you" the message becomes, "I know how it is when I can't get my homework finished, and I get in trouble." This technique is especially useful for helping children take responsibility for how they are behaving and feeling.

Teaching children to substitute "won't" for "can't" is another useful technique in Gestalt therapy. Instead of saying, "I can't finish my homework," the child says "I won't finish my homework." Again, this aids children in accepting responsibility, and shows them that the choice is theirs.

"No gossiping" is another concept that is helpful in working with clients in Gestalt therapy. During the therapy session, if the child must talk about someone who is not present, then the talk must be in the present tense, and directed toward an empty chair. Children are encouraged by this technique to focus on themselves and their own behavior and feelings.

"Taking responsibility" is a technique especially suited for use with adolescents. The client is asked to fill in sentence blanks like the following, "Right now I'm feeling _____, and I take _____ percent of the responsibility for this feeling." This technique helps clients focus on the fact that their feelings are their own.

The "empty chair" technique is designed to help resolve feelings between the client and another person, or within the client. The client takes turns sitting in the chairs that represent the two poles of the situation, and speaking for that side. The opposing views confront each other until they can be merged into a new, balanced view.

"Role rehearsal" is another typical Gestalt technique. In role rehearsal, clients are asked to rehearse a role that they plan to engage in outside the counseling session. The client can become familiar with how it feels to be in this role, and deal with things that may occur as a result of their being in this role. In a companion technique to role rehearsal, the client can also engage in "role reversal." With this activity, the client may act out a behavior that is the opposite of the one they would normally engage in. Again, the client can experience how this role feels and begin to decide whether it might be appropriate for him or her.

Many of the children's activities that are traditional to Gestalt therapy are adaptations from the book *Windows to Our Children* by Violet Oaklander (1978). This book contains numerous activities to use in Gestalt therapy with children and adolescents, and is an excellent resource books for therapists, probably the best single source of Gestalt techniques with children.

Gestalt therapy represents an excellent approach to working with children. The many and varied activities provide a good foundation for helping children express their situations and their emotions. As a result of this expression, the therapist can work with children to correct faulty information or beliefs they have received, and help them develop more appropriate and healthy ways of interacting with others. Many of the techniques promote and facilitate expression and may have value in the context of other theoretical approaches.

## Hypnosis and Hypnotherapy with Children

While the phenomenon of hypnosis has been documented since the days of the ancient Egyptians and Greeks, increased interest occurred in the 1700s. Franz Anton Mesmer (1734–1835) is generally associated with the beginning of the modern history of hypnosis. Interest in the phenomenon of hypnosis continued throughout the 1700s and 1800s, primarily in France and England. During the late 1800s and the early 1900s, there was increased interest in hypnosis in the United States. World War II offered many opportunities for the use of hypnosis in veterans' medical facilities, both in the United States and abroad. After the war, societies for the study of hypnosis, and many journals on the topic, came into existence. These not only provided an outlet for the dissemination of information gleaned from research and therapeutic practice, but also helped build professionalism and legitimize the field. Following World War II, numerous university-based laboratories were established for the study of hypnosis. Topics studied included techniques of hypnotism; hypnotizability of subjects relative to age, sex, and personality characteristics; and the ability to reduce pain through suggestion. Hypnosis also found its way into textbooks of psychology, further legitimizing its use. Currently, hypnosis enjoys favor in the fields of psychology, dentistry, and medicine (Crasilneck & Hall, 1975; Gibson & Heap, 1991).

Essentially, hypnosis is a state of increased suggestibility, whereby the patient is open to suggestions and images introduced by the therapist. This state includes deeper forms of relaxation as well as complete hypnotic induction. It appears that hypnosis "involves a shift in concentration, executed in a passive manner (such as daydreaming or sleeping), resulting in a state of consciousness that is distinguishably different from alertness or ordinary sleep" (Matheson, 1985). There are several ways of inducing hypnosis. Some of the ways are direct and somewhat commanding. Other ways are less directive and are designed to break down resistance (Siegel, 1986).

Olness and Gardner (1988) and Olness and Kohen (1996) see the goal of hypnotherapy as being to teach the child/patient an attitude of hope in the context of mastery. The child/patient learns to be an active participant in his or her own behalf, to focus on creating a solution rather than on enduring a problem, and to discover and use resources for inner control as much as possible. Hypnosis is an intervention that requires specialized training from a professional. Before undertaking hypnosis in therapeutic counseling, therapists must receive this training and be competent in its practice.

Numerous techniques are commonly used in working with clients, ranging from deep relaxation to guided hypnotic imagery, to those that induce a deep hypnotic trance. The success of these techniques depends heavily on the suggestibility of the client, and any resistance that the person may have to the process. Olness and Gardner (1988) and Olness and Kohen (1996) survey hypnotic induction techniques that are appropriate for use with children. They group the techniques into the following categories: visual imagery techniques, auditory imagery, movement imagery, storytelling techniques, ideomotor techniques, progressive relaxation techniques, eye fixation techniques, distraction and utilization techniques, and machine-aided techniques. The age and cognitive level of the child are important considerations when choosing the most appropriate induction technique.

Currently, hypnosis has widespread applications, including behavior modification with pain management, control of addictive behaviors, and treatment of phobias. It has also been used for the enhancement of performance in areas such as athletics and cognitive activities. Some hypnotherapists use hypnosis as a catharsis and to help clients uncover repressed or restrained emotions (DePiano & Salzberg, 1986). Hypnosis has also been used to deal with habit problems that are often found in children such as enuresis, encopresis, habitual coughs and other tics, nail biting, hair pulling, thumb sucking, and sleep walking. Additionally, there is a growing body of research data on the use of hypnotherapy with children's medical problems. Specific uses include childhood asthma, recurring hives, dermatological problems, diabetes, hemophilia, gastrointestinal disorders, juvenile rheumatoid arthritis, malignancies, and neurological problems (Olness & Gardner, 1988; Olness & Kohen, 1996).

Hypnotherapy with children is a treatment modality that enjoys continued, and ever increasing, interest and research. Its documented uses are widespread and represent a broad area of needs for which children may enter therapy. Hypnotherapy remains a helpful form of intervention, in the hands of a well-trained professional. The most recent edition of the text *Hypnosis and Hypnotherapy with Children* by Olness and Kohen (1996) probably represents the best single resource on the application of hypnosis with children and adolescents.

## Transactional Analysis with Children

Transactional analysis (TA) is a counseling theory that was developed by Eric Berne (1961). TA focuses on the way people view themselves and their role, the interactions between people, and the games people play. TA is contractual and decisional, and actively involves the client in the therapeutic process. Berne asserts that people's behavior is determined by the roles they perceive themselves to have in their interactions with other people. TA emphasizes the person's ability to make decisions that change the habit patterns of their interactions, and choose new goals and behaviors that are in their own best interest.

Thompson and Rudolph (1992) outline six major points of TA that are most useful in counseling children:

1. Definition and explanation of ego states.
2. Analysis of transactions between ego states.
3. Positive and negative stroking (or "warm fuzzies" and "cold pricklies").
4. I'm OK, you're OK.
5. Games and rackets.
6. Scripts.

These six aspects of TA will be briefly explored.

Three separate patterns of behavior, or ego states are identified: Parent, Adult, and Child (P-A-C). The Parent ego state is usually a combination of a person's experiences with his or her own parents and parental substitutes. This ego state contains "oughts" and "shoulds," and has both a "nurturing parent" and a "critical parent." The Adult ego state is where information is processed. It is analytical, objective, and pragmatic. The Child ego state consists of a person's feelings and impulsive acts. Berne delineates several manifestations of the Child, the "Natural Child," the "Little Professor," and the "Adapted Child."

Three basic types of transactions that take place in communication are also prominent in the theory. They are parallel or complementary transactions; crossed transactions; and ulterior transactions. Complementary transactions occur when a message is sent from an ego state and it gets the expected response from the receiving ego state. A crossed transaction occurs when a message is sent from an ego state and it gets an unexpected response from the receiving ego state. Finally, ulterior transactions are the most complex, and involve disguised messages that involve more than two ego states.

Strokes are basic to TA theory. They are a form of recognition that people seek, and can be expressed both verbally and nonverbally. Strokes can be positive or negative, depending on their content. They can also be conditional or unconditional. People are constantly seeking recognition, or strokes. As undesired as they may be, negative strokes are better than no strokes at all.

TA identifies four life positions that children (or adults) develop. These positions are based on the child's concept of his or her own self-worth, and the worth of others. Harris (1969) has outlined these positions as follows:

1. I'm not OK—You're OK.
2. I'm not OK—You're not OK.
3. I'm OK—You're not OK.
4. I'm OK—You're OK.

Games are another key concept of TA theory. Games are a series of ulterior messages that progress to a predictable outcome. They lead to one of the two people in an interaction feeling bad, and they are designed to block intimacy. Rackets are the bad feelings that are felt at the end of the game.

Finally, TA introduces the concept of scripts. These scripts are each individual's personal life plan. These scripts are created early in life primarily through injunctions that are passed from the opposite sex parent's Child, to the child's Child. The script continues to influence and direct the individual's behavior in many important aspects of his or her life (Clarkson, 1992).

TA is especially suited for use with children because of its emphasis on reeducation and its active focus. Massey and Massey (1988) see TA as well suited for use with children and their families because of its functioning on both the experiential and interactional levels. Clarkson and Fish (1988) examine systemic assessment and treatment consideration in TA child psychotherapy, and offer a framework to aid counselors in selecting the most appropriate modality for intervention. Bala (1986) outlines a general treatment plan for using TA with autistic children, in a day-school setting. Clarkson (1992) explores the use of TA with children and their families in intervention formats including individual psychotherapy, psychotherapy with child and primary caretaker, and family therapy.

TA has been widely used in school settings by counselors doing individual or group work. TA's emphasis on communication and interactions between people makes it ideal for counseling in classrooms and groups. TA has been used with normal students to increase self-esteem and facilitate a greater understanding of self and others. Socially maladjusted high school students have shown improved behavior with TA instruction, and students with learning disabilities have shown increased self-esteem (Miller & Capuzzi, 1984). TA offers a viable intervention option for use with both children and their families. Its language is readily understood by children and the principles of TA are easily applied in their everyday lives.

## MISCELLANEOUS TECHNIQUES

### Art and Drawings in Therapy

Creative elements exist to some degree in everyone. Even more evident is the daily ebb and flow of emotional drives. Explanations about the relationship of these two forces to each other have taken several forms. Many view creative needs as providing the drive for constructive adaptations and adjustments to new situations. Torrance (1970) describes these creative needs in children as being curious, meeting challenges, attempting difficult tasks, becoming completely immersed in a task, being independent in judgment and convictions, having sensitivity and intuition, and being open to experience. In many respects, these represent the attributes of positive mental health. These characteristics, he notes, are summated in the basic need "to be oneself." It is this need, whatever explanations are given for its origin, that gives creative art expression its great value as a vehicle for the emergence of the self and concomitantly as a tool for therapy.

There are several significant interpretations of the ways art may be used in the therapeutic process. Ulman (1975) points out that in the broadest interpretations, art therapy is the use of any visual materials in some attempt to assist integration or reintegration of the personality. The forms that drawings and art therapy seem to take may in large part emerge from the setting in which they are practiced. For example, art in clinical settings has produced psychoanalytic and psychodynamic applications, whereas art in educational settings has emphasized the integration of cognitive and emotional processes to enhance development, motivation, behavior, and learning. Oster and Gould (1987) emphasize the role of art therapy in increasing expression and the capacity to relate, particularly for those children where direct verbal communication and insight are limited.

Rubin (1975) emphasizes the need for a psychological climate in the art experience where a child with a disability finds acceptance, openness, and empathy from the adult. She points out that there are many challenges in working with these children, and art can help to strengthen the bridge between therapist and child. Concern with breakdown in interpersonal communication has been expressed by numerous specialists who have worked extensively with children with disabilities. From her work with learning disabled and emotionally disturbed children, Gonick-Barris (1976) concludes that this population is in even greater need of creative art experiences than are children who do not have such disabilities. Since these children most often express themselves in unusual ways, they need alternative methods to express the same emotional impulses and attitudes they share with all children. Similarly, Carter and Miller (1975) have reflected these same concerns in their creative art program for minimally brain-injured children. Their experimental program for eight children between the ages of 7 and 10 years was designed with two basic guidelines. Art activities provide the incentive or motivation to learn and encourage the development of perceptual awareness and manipulative skills. Therefore, art activities should be an effective procedure for achievement of perceptual and motor skills by children with learning disabilities. The results of their 6-week experimental program showed significant gains made by each child on a visual-perception task.

It is important for professionals to listen to children and synthesize what they say about their art, for they can provide revealing clues about the children themselves, their feelings and their personalities. Dinkmeyer and Caldwell state that through artwork the child may be able to project meanings only dimly revealed in his or her verbal expression (Dinkmeyer & Caldwell, 1970). Drawings and art in therapy encourage personal expression of feelings, and through art a child can reveal hidden concerns more willingly and easily than may be possible through verbal communication (Liebmann, 1986). As mentioned, art therapy is a huge concept, encompassing the use of art expression for many purposes with several distinctive philosophical approaches. The three major theoretical orientations are (a) the psychoanalytic orientation, where art is used in conjunction with psychotherapy and takes into account many of its principles; (b) the creativity approach, which sees art as inherently therapeutic and applies it to allow the child to display and explore his or her talents; and (c) the humanistic orientation, in which art is a means of establishing one's identity.

Art as a form of communication can also facilitate communication even when children are not able or willing to interact with others. While many of them do not engage in art activity for its cathartic value, there are times when children are worried, and art can allow them to express their feelings. It can be used to help children feel better about themselves by promoting feelings of success, and the completion of the project can bring much joy to a child (Oster & Gould, 1987).

Some artistic methods used in therapy with children are automatic drawing, color exploration, and drawing completion (Fine & Fine, 1988). Automatic drawing is also known as the scribble technique. The individual is allowed to free draw and express him- or herself using any form of art media. In color exploration, the child may produce a piece of artwork using his or her least and most favorite colors. The child is then asked to discuss how the colors interact. Furthermore, this approach can be refined to incorporate exercises where a child can draw pictures expressing feelings. Each feeling is captured by incorporating a specific color. The final product is then discussed. With drawing completion, the child is presented with a few lines or shapes. The child is then requested to make a picture using all the elements. Denny (1975) suggests techniques that can be applied to increase the child's self-awareness. Children may be requested to paint and discuss the phrases "I feel" or "I am." They could also be asked to draw three figures, which would include the ideal self, the real self, and the way others perceive them.

Art therapy can also focus on more specific situations and issues. Oster and Gould (1987) describe many situations where art can be used in both individual and group treatment situations. They note that the art can be both free or open response or can be more focused with children guided to draw more specific situations. For example, family situations or members may be suggested foci for art. They also encourage the use of other art modalities, such as clay, painting, use of colors, and fingerpainting. Knoff and Prout (1985) developed an integrated system for kinetic drawings that includes depiction of settings and individuals in those settings, with the added component of action ("Draw everyone doing something"). Their system has assessment and treatment uses with drawings of family (Kinetic Family Drawing) and school (Kinetic School Drawing) situations.

Drawings and art therapy have been utilized for children with developmental and emotional problems and chronic illnesses. One of the advantages of art activities is that they are usually best initiated in groups, because children appear to inspire one another. Many types of supplies can be applied in art, and a therapist must be aware of what materials need to be selected with well-thought purpose and with the child's needs in mind (Robbins & Sibley, 1976). The book by Oster and Gould (1987) is an excellent resource for mental health professionals on the uses of drawings in child and adolescent therapy.

## The Use of Games in Therapy

Among the many techniques available for use with children, games offer an opportunity for children to deal with unacceptable urges in socially acceptable ways. Games also allow children to explore their feelings without threat. One of the first recognized pioneers of the therapeutic utilization of games was Loomis (1957). While using checkers in therapy, he recognized the potential application of the game as a vehicle for expression of resistance and unconscious conflict. The game was seen as a safe environment where the child lets loose of his or her defenses (Loomis). Others have noted that these games provide opportunities for social learning as well as help children to communicate, cooperate, learn to respect governing rules, and control anger while in competition. Finally, table games can be applied to help children learn how to deal with power and autonomy.

One therapeutic game currently available is the "Talking, Feeling, Doing Game" developed by Richard Gardner (1983). Gardner developed this board game with the intent of assisting uncooperative children in exploring their feelings, and it is similar in many ways to most board games. Within this game, according to Gardner, the Talking cards assist the child in making comments that are primarily intellectual, while the Feeling cards focus on emotional issues. Finally, the Doing cards require the child to engage in some sort of play activity or acting. Many cards are in each stack, and they range from nonthreatening to moderately anxiety-provoking questions (Gardner). This game has been shown to be useful with defensive children, as well as with resistant children. As an additional benefit, this game is very useful and appropriate for groups. Several other games have been formulated with a similar purpose in mind; they include the Changing Family Game, the Assertion Game, and the Classroom Survival Game (Fine & Fine, 1988).

While there are now many games solely developed for purposes of therapy, it has been suggested that several commercially available games are also suitable for prominent therapeutic goals (Schaeffer & Reed, 1986). Sutton-Smith and Roberts (1971) described three classifications of games that can be purchased in most retail stores:

1. Games applying physical skills, such as tiddlywinks, Pick Up Sticks, and Operation, can help children with their eye-hand coordination.
2. Games of strategy attempt to enhance cognitive skills and allow an observer to informally gather insight on a child's problem-solving abilities. Games such as backgammon, checkers, chess, word games, and Connect Four all fit into this category.
3. Finally, there are games of little strategy, which merely involve chance. These games are usually beneficial because they neutralize the adult's superiority in intellect and skill. Games that fit under this category are Chutes and Ladders and several card games, such as War (Sutton-Smith & Roberts).

Gardner has also adapted several existing table games for therapeutic use with children. He has modified Scrabble for Juniors, Campbell's Alphabet Soup Game, the Pick-A-Face Game, and the Make-a-Picture Story Cards successfully and has used them numerous times in his play therapy with his clients (Gardner, 1993).

## Puppet Therapy

Puppetry can be an effective therapeutic technique within a developmental therapy framework to help troubled children communicate feelings, resolve emotional conflict, solve interpersonal problems, and practice new communication and social skills. Because puppets are magical and expressive, they are fun to use and are motivational. Puppets are motivating because children credit them with real and believable personalities. Most importantly, puppets can be surrogates for the children themselves. For these reasons, puppetry, if used correctly, can be a pleasurable and significant experience for troubled children. By planning puppet activities that match a child's developmental needs, a therapist can ensure that each child will be successful and will respond with pleasure. This will enhance the children's trust in the environment, adults, and themselves. The children are then on their way to risking themselves in new situations (Woltman, 1971). As with other techniques, the use of puppets can facilitate expression and encourage safe outlets for both fantasy and impulses (Schaeffer & O'Connor, 1983).

Puppet activities should be experientially based. Because children are attracted to puppets and encounter pleasure in involvement with them, they are eager to express themselves through them. Giving children this opportunity stimulates "learning by doing." Puppetry has been effectively used with emotionally troubled and autistic children, and may be combined with other methods such as storytelling. Puppet therapy can be particularly effective with children for the following reasons (Schaefer & O'Connor, 1983; Woltman, 1971):

- A child identifies with a puppet, or projects the personality of one of his family members into it.
- Spontaneity, creativity, and emotional release are stimulated through puppetry.
- Puppetry provides an opportunity for group work fostering the sharing of ideas and fantasies.
- Puppetry offers the child an outlet for expression of fears, anxieties, and fantasies.
- Through a puppet, a child begins to express feelings more freely because he or she feels protected and cannot be held responsible for what the puppet says or does.
- Because puppets motivate children, they create incentives to participate in an activity.
- A puppet can be an attention getter because it arouses and stimulates the child.
- The puppet can be a positive intermediary between the child and the adult, which will produce responses that will help the child associate pleasure with adults.
- The entertainment element of puppetry enhances motivation for learning.

Woltmann (1940, 1971) was one of the first to write about his use of puppets in inpatient settings and as therapeutic techniques. Schaefer and O'Connor (1983) point out that it is important to have a range of puppets available, and that some structure is necessary to help children produce a spontaneous story. They suggest that "a range of puppet types can be spilled out on the floor in a pile, and the child invited to select whatever appeals to him or her. After the selection process is finished, the child is asked to go behind a small stage or table and begin the puppet story by "introducing" the selected characters. With any child, it often helps to lengthen the initial warm-up by engaging in friendly dialogue with the puppets (not the child) to help the child focus, pretend, and feel more comfortable. It is important, of course, not to "lead the witness" and thereby contaminate the data but to ask open-ended questions that can lead to ease of associations for the story to follow. Once the characters are introduced, the therapist can announce the beginning of the show and become the audience-observer. When the child is finished, the format of the show can be extended by interviewing puppets, puppeteer, or both to elicit further associations and thus help unravel the story's many meanings. In a sense, the enacted story is similar to the manifest content of a dream; it is full of distortions and disguises meant to protect and obscure. To decipher the story without the child's associations is to engage in wild analysis; both therapist and child need to work to understand the latent meanings of the story through the child's associations and elaborations.

## Storytelling Techniques

Storytelling as a formal therapy technique with children was first popularized by Richard Gardner (1971). However, it is unlikely that he was the first therapist working with children to use this technique. Storytelling appears to be a natural means of connecting and communicating with children, whether for therapeutic or other purposes. Children invent stories as part of their development in an attempt to deal with their environment more effectively.

Storytelling has been a vehicle for making sense of the environment and of transmitting information, knowledge, and wisdom from generation to generation among many ethnic groups across the world, including the North American continent. Fables, myths, fairy tales, and legends have been developed for the purposes of transmitting values and knowledge (Pellowski, 1977). Storytelling has also served families to transmit family lore and values from parents or grandparents to children, and to help children mature, learn about their ancestry, and to facilitate parent-child relationships (Godbole, 1982). Children, in turn, use storytelling to reveal information about themselves to family members, friends, teachers, and other significant individuals in their lives; to express affects and needs indirectly; and to engage in problem-solving. All three of these uses of storytelling are relevant to storytelling psychotherapy which combines the purposes of all, namely, the transmission of information and wisdom, the teaching of values and facilitation of relationships, uninhibited self-disclosure, and catharsis that results in psychological growth.

A story told by a child teaches the therapist about the child's functioning, approach to life, and beliefs about the family environment. Just as a parent can use stories to inform the child about family values and to enhance rapport with the child and development of values, so can the therapist use stories to facilitate a therapeutic relationship and the internalization of limits and guidelines. Finally, just as a child can use stories to communicate and express herself or himself to family, self, or friends, so can the same child use the story to reveal herself or himself to a therapist. The therapist can respond to the child based on the story, and a dialogue can be established that is based on the child's language.

The transmission of values, knowledge, and wisdom that has originally been an important aspect of storytelling in different cultures and families, is maintained in the therapy setting. The process, however, is altered somewhat. The child, in relating a story, transmits his or her knowledge and beliefs. The therapist does not merely receive this information, as does a listener in the traditional use of the story, but responds and provides information, thus also becoming a storyteller (Gardner, 1971, 1993). In the storytelling technique as applied to therapy, child and therapist switch roles being senders and receivers of information in completing an interaction. In the traditional use of stories, senders do not become receivers in the same interaction, nor do receivers become senders.

Two primary purposes make the storytelling technique useful in child therapy: the giving and receiving of information. Most commonly, children give information first, and then receive it (i.e., the child tells the first story). Therapists receive information first, and then respond (i.e., the therapist tells his or her own story *after* having listened to the child's story and only in response to the child's story). This process not only facilitates assessment, but also rapport-building and understanding of the child. It provides an environment in which therapeutic intervention can be implemented in a nonthreatening and culturally sensitive manner (Greenbaum & Holmes, 1983).

Children give information by using stories to express and master feelings, to communicate about themselves and their families, and so forth. Therapists receive information from children's stories, learning about children's problems and frustrations and gaining insight into children's defenses, conflicts, and family dynamics (Gardner, 1993). Stories used in this way are an excellent supplement to other assessment procedures and can be used to validate hypotheses about both child and family. Stories can provide a fuller understanding of the child in his or her surroundings, both cultural and familial. The advantage of the story used for this purpose is its nonintrusive and nonobvious nature. Most children are not aware of the vast self-disclosure they engage in while telling a story. In many ways, stories are projective techniques, much like free associations or dreams. They reveal information about the child innocuously, as the child does not need to provide explanations or commentary, does not have to defend or protect self or family, and can share information without needing to feel accountable for it.

The therapist merely has to listen carefully and has to be able to listen to the underlying message. There is no need to make the child's metacommunication overt or conscious. Instead, the therapist can understand the child based on the metaphor that was used and can respond using the same metaphor to communicate directly with the child without having to bring the problem up in direct or confrontational language. In Gardner's (1993) view, the therapist communicates directly with the child's unconscious and need not worry about making the unconscious conscious for the child. In this way, the therapist can give something to the child without an overt process of giving or advising. In fact, through the process of responding to the child's metaphor by telling a story back using the same characters and setting, with a slightly different outcome, the therapist can provide a corrective experience, can suggest solutions and coping strategies, can reinterpret or reframe events, and can give advice, without ever doing so overtly (Stiles & Kottman, 1990).

There are no formalized approaches in the literature to the actual procedure of the storytelling technique as outlined by Gardner (1993). However, clinical use of the procedure suggests and has demonstrated that some variation in implementation is indeed possible depending on the needs of individual children. Miller and Boe (1990) have used storytelling in conjunction with sandplay to assist children in telling their stories and to teach staff to respond to children through the metaphor. Gabel (1984) has adapted the technique by asking the child to draw, not merely tell, the story in order to solicit assessment information from reticent or oppositional children.

As Gardner (1971, 1993) demonstrated, storytelling provides an excellent means for metacommunication with children. The procedure uses the metaphors and symbolisms that are so natural for young children and can easily be fitted into any child therapy, regardless of theoretical background of the therapist. No technique in adult treatment is comparable to storytelling. Storytelling is uniquely applied to child clients and serves an excellent purpose in that realm. It is one of the techniques most conducive to the internalization of change without requiring the child to be able to verbalize insights or understanding of how changes occurred, making the technique appropriate for child therapy.

## SPECIAL PROBLEMS IN CHILDHOOD

### Crisis Intervention

Psychological crises in children and adolescents occur when the child and/or family cannot respond to a change in their lives with behaviors that yield successful adaptation. Children and families may be unable to deal with the change and integrate the new circumstances into their expected ways of thinking, feeling, and acting. These stressful changes include obviously painful issues such as the death or illness of a loved one, loss of a job, exposure to crime, or natural catastrophe. Other stresses that may induce a crisis include developmental issues such as the appearance of autonomous behavior in a toddler, a move to a new residence, starting school, and others. While these changes are normative experiences, they may be perceived by particular families in idiosyncratic ways, eliciting high levels of discomfort and upsetting normal patterns of behavior (Dattilio & Freeman, 1994; Gold, 1988).

Individuals and families are guided in their attempts at problem-solving by their learning histories and biological endowments. They are also influenced in their flexibility and success in problem-solving by their unique levels of vulnerability to stress, the grade of familiarity presented by the new stressor, and by their past successes and failures in adapting to new situations. When the family's level of discomfort can be limited to moderate levels by their coping efforts and/or adequate social resources, the period of disorganization is usually followed by the reorganization of familial functioning. Crises are resolved by reestablishing a level of harmony equal to, or surpassing the precrisis level. This adaptation will partially depend on choosing appropriate coping strategies. Possibly more importantly, it may also depend on the family's ability to assess the effectiveness of these solutions. These assessments can be used to decide rationally whether the solution should be continued and emphasized until the problem is solved, or whether the solution should be modified or abandoned because it is not helping or is even worsening the whole situation. Unfortunately, many people cannot operate in this way. Quite often, the number of potential solutions available to them is limited and none of these solutions, in fact, may be useful. Other people may have available a greater number of choices but do not have the flexibility or awareness to use the feedback from their unsuccessful attempts at coping to try other approaches. Both groups then enter a state in which one or a few unsuccessful solutions are applied to the problems in more and more emphatic ways, leading to a vicious circle of distress-failed solutions—more distress, more failed solutions—more distress and so on (Dattilio & Freeman, 1994).

Gold (1988) presents a model for crisis intervention with children and families in which the goal is prevention of further suffering of the child. The model integrates concepts and techniques drawn from family therapy, cognitive therapy, and short-term psychoanalytically oriented psychotherapy. This intervention is aimed at halting maladaptive, behavioral, cognitive, and affective patterns that contribute to the etiology of a crisis. The treatment approach is organized into three sequential phases. The first phase is the behavioral phase, during which the therapist's strategies and interventions are aimed at the management, resolution, or limitation of the behavioral manifestations or symptoms of the crises (e.g., psychosis, suicidal behavior, aggressive behavior) and altering the behavioral patterns that maintain and reinforce these symptoms. The second phase of the therapy is the cognitive phase, during which the therapeutic activity is directed at the elaboration and modification of individual and shared familial pathogenic beliefs, ideas, and assumptions. During the final phase of the crisis therapy, the central emotional and dynamic issues influencing motives, fantasies, and anxieties are identified, and interpreted, clarified, and confronted.

Increasingly often, professionals are asked to provide crisis counseling to children in group environments, such as churches and schools, and through other activities. Crises naturally stimulate feelings of helplessness, isolation, fear, loss, sadness, and shock, and children worry about the loss of their parents, their friends, and their security. In many cases, parents are coping with their own loss or grief, and are unable to help the child with his or her own feelings. Some parents may not realize their children are worried because most children are not able to successfully verbalize their pain. Those who work with children recognize that young people cannot learn or perform their daily activities with these fears and concerns. They become irritable and restless, have difficulty concentrating and sleeping, and may experience physical symptoms such as nausea or diarrhea. Someone has to help them cope, and this can be successfully and efficiently accomplished through group discussion and group counseling (Thompson & Rudolph, 1992).

Gilliland and James (1988) propose a series of steps for counseling children in a crisis situation that are similar to reality therapy models. These steps include identification of the facts about the crisis, examination of feelings about the crisis, delineation of the symptoms or effects of the crisis, and a teaching phase involving examination of potential responses to the crisis. In addition, they urge that counselors take steps to ensure the physical and emotional safety of the client, and to assist him or her in identifying additional support systems, coping mechanisms, and appropriate actions. There is a need for the crisis counselor to assess the severity of the crisis subjectively and objectively. They also caution that consideration should be given to the child's emotional state and his or her ability to cope with the problem. Crisis counseling is short term, and counselors should carefully consider the need for referrals for some children or other arrangements to ensure that each client successfully copes with the crisis in the days and weeks to follow.

Mental health professionals will encounter crisis situations that involve children, regardless of their specialization. Professionals need to know the signs of a child in crisis and possess the skills and knowledge to successfully cope with the child in his or her environment. Group counseling can be a highly effective method for changing children's lives as well as preventing excess stress and conflict in their lives. It is rewarding for children to find their place in a group and to help one another. It is rewarding for the group counselor to watch the children grow and develop into caring, functioning group members (Thompson & Rudolph, 1992).

## Divorce

The lives and relationships of children in a divorcing family are profoundly affected, socially, economically, psychologically, and even legally. Children must adjust to the separation from one parent and formation of a new and different relationship with the other. A change in the family's economic status, possibly a change in the home and school environment, different parenting styles, custody battles, and sometimes a totally different lifestyle bring about a variety of feelings that may be positive or negative. For many families, the separation and divorce brings stress, pressure, and overwhelming burdens (Wallerstein, 1989).

Most researchers have reported that children, especially boys, going through a divorce experience academic problems (Werner & Smith, 1980). School is usually the second most stable environment for the child, and when the home environment is disrupted, it is natural for a child to turn to the school and teachers for support and comfort. Guidubaldi, Cleminshaw, Perry, and McLoughlin (1983) found that an orderly, structured, and predictable school environment was related to the resumption of student achievement. Results of longitudinal research indicate that while many children do indeed suffer negative outcomes related to divorce, many also do quite well. For some, coping with these life transitions can have developmental benefits. Increased understanding of the protective variables and resiliencies of these children can contribute to interventions to reduce or eliminate the potential negative impact of divorce.

Several kinds of interventions seem promising for children of divorce (Stolberg, 1988). Divorce mediation involves bringing together divorcing adults to discuss with an impartial party the resolution of disputes. With respect to children, the intent is to develop cooperative coparenting and to lay the groundwork for resolving future conflicts. Other prevention programs intervene with single parents. By improving parenting skills and parent-child interactions, they can enhance child adjustment. School-based intervention programs have the advantage of working with children in a natural setting with similar peers. The Children of Divorce Intervention Project is an example of such a program that has proven successful (Alpert-Gillis, Pedro-Carroll, & Cowen, 1989). Children experiencing separation or divorce meet in groups that provide support, explore feelings, and examine perceptions of divorce.

Wallerstein (1989) describes "psychological tasks" children of divorce must successfully resolve. A knowledge and understanding of these tasks will help counselors choose effective methods for working with children experiencing family breakup. These tasks include acknowledging the reality of the marital rupture, disengaging from parental conflict and distress, and resuming customary pursuits, resolution of loss, resolving anger and self-blame, accepting the permanence of the divorce, and achieving realistic hope about relationships.

A primary intervention strategy for children of divorced parents is to provide honest information about the separation and divorce that is appropriate to the children's developmental level. Children can cope with honesty and truth, but secrets are not manageable. It is often hard for children to understand that other families or children have felt the way they do, or to believe that they will ever be happy again. The opportunity to talk with other children whose parents have separated, or to hear that other children have experienced separation, allows them to begin thinking creatively about their own situation and ways in which they can help themselves. Therapeutic groups that allow children to identify with peers have become a popular way to help mitigate the behavioral and emotional problems associated with separation and divorce (Stolberg, 1988; Wallerstein, 1989).

King and Kleemeier (1983) suggest a similar focus for individual treatment, with an emphasis on providing a safe and supportive environment for the child to grieve openly, express fears, feel free to express rage and anger at both parents, and then begin learning skills to cope with the situation. Bibliotherapy is another widely used intervention strategy; there are many children's books that identify divorce-related feelings, issues, and coping skills. Books can be used in a preventive way by parents to explain divorce to their children, or as resources for treatment.

Intervention with parents is also a role of the child's therapist. Parents often find that supportive groups can be a therapeutic way to share feelings and concerns, and to begin to cope with the realities of their situation. Cebollero, Cruise, and Stollak (1986) have described concurrent groups for mothers and children experiencing the long-term negative effects of divorce. The parents indicated that the groups were very supportive and gave them new problem-solving skills; in addition, serving as cotherapists for the children's group gave them a better view of the divorce from their children's perspective.

Yauman (1991) has found evidence for the efficacy of school-based group counseling for children of divorce. As mentioned, the school represents the second most important environment for children and also provides a venue for peer support. The provision of support in the school solidifies the child's feelings of stability in this setting. Groups also appear to be a good modality for dealing with issues that more and more children experience. Yauman describes strategies that can be integrated into groups including emphasizing the positive aspects of the divorce and changed situation at home, use of bibliotherapy, viewing of movies, enactment of role plays, and general discussion.

Familiar surroundings can help a child utilize established social support systems to begin coping with the breakup. Thus, if at all possible, the added stress of changing homes, schools, neighborhoods, caregivers, and so on should be avoided. Likewise, daily routines, activities, chores, and expectations should be kept as normal as possible. This allows the child to learn what parts of life will remain the same and what parts will be different. An emotionally supportive environment with clearly established rules sets the stage for children to become increasingly competent and independent. It is thus important for parents to maintain expectations for each child's behavior and to continue to set limits for inappropriate behavior. Children are likely to express a lot of their concerns and worries through inappropriate behavior or emotional lability. It is important for parents to acknowledge a child's feelings as they put limits on the behavior (Stolberg, 1988). Children whose parents are separating may have increased psychosomatic complaints. Although it is important to have medical professionals attend to these physical complaints, it is often the case that such children are worried or upset about what is happening in the family. These complaints will usually decrease if the children are helped to identify and communicate openly about their feelings and anxieties.

## Grief Therapy

Childhood grief at bereavement is often puzzling and misunderstood. Yet, it is very real and very painful for children. Those who work with and care for children often want to protect our children from pain, attempting to "make it right" and to "hug and kiss the pain away." Children have the capacity to respond to loss with deep grief and often have many questions about the deceased (Bertoia & Allan, 1988). This may yield uncomfortable feelings about a child in pain, frustration about the inability to remove the child's pain, and reluctance to deal with difficult questions. Acceptance that children have the capacity to experience the emotions of grief when a loved person dies allows the professional to show concern and openly communicate about the loss.

Helping the child through this adjustment period will enable that child to be better equipped to deal with future losses and sorrows in life (Lohnes & Kalter, 1994). A grieving child needs reassurance that he or she is loved and deep sorrow is a normal feeling when losing someone loved. Children, like adults, have a need to return to emotional equilibrium. As professionals, and as humans, we must give the child hope that once again, he or she will be happy. Also like adults, children react to grief as an intensely private experience. Each child is unique and will have a different level of thoughts, feelings, and needs. Each child will respond to the loss with different intensity depending on age, personality, and closeness to the deceased. Four general themes/guidelines emerge in dealing with grieving children:

1. A child, unlike an adult, will grieve intermittently over a longer period with normal activities in between.
2. Any child facing grief through death may regress.
3. A child's security is threatened by loss of a loved one through death. The younger the child, the more immediate the need to have security reestablished.
4. Communication does not always have to be verbal. Nonverbal communication such as touching, hugging, or sitting together is a powerful and direct way of telling a child you care (Bertoia & Allan, 1988; Segal, 1984). Adolescents often show symptoms of depression and feelings of abandonment that may be a focus of treatment (Freudenberger & Gallagher, 1995).

The younger the child, the more his or her world is made up of immediate feelings and reactions to these feelings. The young child's ability to feel develops far in advance of the ability to verbalize feelings. Young children generally communicate through their actions. Often because they lack communication as a way of handling grief, they will behave in ways that are certain to get attention. These behaviors include being uncooperative, aggressive, hostile, or destructive. The child may also express his or her feelings by noisy play which is usually annoying to adults. It is the child's way of feeling in action. Children will often work at playing out feelings. They may play funeral, death, and so on. Adults often become upset at this way of hearing a child work through grief. Parents and caregivers must be reminded that such play is not morbid or disrespectful. Children may also substitute feelings they can handle for those they cannot understand. Children may giggle or laugh when not appropriate. They may burst into a fit of anger over a small incident. Younger children will often have loud crying, sobbing spells that last 15 to 30 minutes. These spells may be set off by an incident related or totally unrelated to the deceased. Parents and mental health professionals need to remember that all of a child's responses will not be obvious or immediate. Often, all that an adult can do is to be patient and be available. It is important to understand that the younger the child, the less that he or she has developed resources for coping with intense feelings (Costa & Holliday, 1994; Segal, 1984).

Several writers in this area detail various stages or phases of the grieving process (Heikkinen, 1979; Kübler-Ross, 1969). Therapists and parents should be prepared to address these stages which are common to grief and affect children of all ages as well as adults. These feelings often cannot be separated out as they are intertwined and feed on each other. These stages can be described as denial, anger, fear, and guilt.

1. *Denial.* This is common in young children who do not understand death is final. It may be expressed in the young by a statement that the loved one did not actually die and is coming back. A young child may outwardly show little concern about the deceased. This child may be pretending death did not occur as the grief is too much to feel.

2. *Fear.* A child who has lost a loved one through death will face two specific fears: abandonment and death of self or others emotionally close. Often inappropriate comments from others such as "be brave," "be extra good for mommy," or "now you are the man of the family" increase these fears as they may suppress the child's grief. In older children, this fear may be expressed as panic or confusion about who will take care of them. They may take on characteristics of the deceased or idealize the deceased. They may also try to emotionally replace the deceased with a substitute to handle the fear and pain of abandonment.

3. *Anger.* Children who feel abandoned by the loved one usually experience intense anger. This anger is often directed at the survivors or at themselves. Children's anger upsets adults and is often expressed in destructive ways.

4. *Guilt.* The younger the child, the more likely he or she is to think that anything that happens in the world is his or her fault. What child has not wished at some time that a parent would die? The older the child, the more the guilt can be relieved by giving the child permission to have positive and negative feelings about the deceased.

A mental health professional will generally see grieving children under extreme stress, who tend to have the typical reactions of withdrawal and acting out or fighting. Parents and caregivers will report that these behaviors seem out of control and uncharacteristic for the child. In withdrawal, the bereaved child will be more submissive and dependent. Extreme silent, withdrawn behavior may be a cry for help. When acting out and fighting, the bereaved child may express distress in ways not closely associated with the loss, such as peer problems or problems in school. These actions may be interfering with the child's normal progress or well-being and may require the intervention of a professional. In addition, the loss of a sibling is a "double whammy" as the child has lost a loved one and often the emotional support of the parents as well (Bertoia & Allan, 1988). Issues related to unresolved grief will continue to surface throughout an individual's life, therefore, it is vital that professionals feel competent about their abilities to help a bereaved child. As with any counseling issue, an appropriate referral is warranted if it is out of the therapist's realm of competency.

Segal (1984) recommends a number of games and communication exercises to help children express feelings related to losses. He suggests passing out small blank cards and pencils to children in a group and asking them to write down a question about death or dying. Assurances should be given that the writer's name will not be revealed. The group leader reads the questions, and the children discuss their thoughts about the questions. Art techniques, including crayon drawings, clay, or hand puppets, may help children portray their conflicts. Children can be asked to sculpt or carve a figure representing someone for whom they have a great deal of love; usually the figure will be the person they have lost. These drawings, carvings, or hand puppets can express the pain of the loss more easily than the child can verbalize it. Segal also describes a technique for illustrating feelings with paper and music. The children draw "peaceful" views of death on one side of the paper while listening to soft music; they then draw "harsh" views of death on the other side of the sheet while listening to dissonant music. Phototherapy, having the child respond to different photographs of men, women, or children, may also be used to stimulate discussion concerning losses of loved ones. All nonverbal means of communication should be followed with a discussion of their meaning and of coping strategies for the problems revealed.

Although it may be difficult to form a group with children experiencing grief, there is evidence that both peer group counseling (Quarmby, 1993) and general psychotherapy bereavement groups (Tonkins & Lambert, 1996) can be effective for children and adolescents. Group experiences have been shown to reduce both the length and intensity of the grieving process, facilitating an adjustment to the loss. The nature of the group process and sharing with peers may help children understand their own reactions and diminish the common feelings of isolation that occur with loss.

## Sexual Abuse

Statistics have suggested that as many as 40 million people, about one in six Americans, may have been sexually victimized as children and as many as a quarter of these people may be suffering from psychological problems, ranging from guilt and poor self-esteem to sexual difficulties. Tennant (1988) presented a list of possible indicators of sexual abuse such as vaginal discharge, discomfort in the genital area, difficulty walking or sitting, and venereal disease or pregnancy in a child under age 13. Behavior changes may include sleep disturbances (fear, nightmares, bed-wetting), eating problems, changes in school behavior, performance, or attendance, unusual sexual behavior for the child's age, sudden dependency, and fear of losing a particular person (Tennant). Common issues that may need to be dealt with in treatment include the "traumagenic" factors of stigmatization, powerlessness, betrayal, and traumagenic sexualization (Zaidi & Gutierrez-Kovner, 1995).

Hollander (1989) believes that "an aware child is a safe child" (p. 184). She presents a preventive educational program that uses bibliotherapy. The program is used jointly by school personnel and parents. Local protective and enforcement agencies precede the books with a presentation. The materials should be readily available to the children, and they should be aware of professionals in the school able to answer questions that result from their reading.

Thompson and Rudolph (1992) offered specific counseling suggestions for use with abused children:

• Counseling abuse victims entails becoming completely involved with the child and being prepared for the child's repeated testing of their caring.

- To help children overcome the feelings of worthlessness and guilt associated with the abuse and to build self-esteem, Holtgraves (1986) suggests using visual imagery. This technique aids children in developing positive attitudes toward life. The imagery might include situations in which the children encounter and successfully resolve uncomfortable or dangerous circumstances. Emphasis should be placed on developing strengths and positive attributes.

- Many professionals prefer a playroom, rather than an office, for interviewing children suspected of experiencing abuse. The play media will assist children in their efforts to communicate their feelings, and the natural environment will help the child feel safe and in control.

- Specific techniques such as bibliotherapy, role plays, play therapy, or group counseling may be considered, depending on the child's maturity. However, therapists need to be cautious about placing sexually abused children in groups, especially if the trauma is very recent. The child may not be ready to share intense feelings with others.

- Be sure words used by the child are understood, and it is important that the adult uses developmentally appropriate language.

- "Good" and "bad" touching should be discussed. The child's rights with regard to his or her body or touching someone else's body should be discussed. It should be made clear to the child that "bad" touches can come from those close to us.

- Assertiveness training that focuses on how to say no or handle potentially abusive situations may be necessary. The child will need to be helped to determine the warning signs of abuse and to plan ways for coping with the situations. Role playing these strategies will prepare children to handle such situations more effectively.

- Issues of trust must be addressed with sexually abused children. They have learned how not to trust. Developmental theorists have emphasized the importance of children developing trust in people and their interactions in order to live effectively. Yet children receive many daily messages, designed to protect them, that imply that the world and the people in it are dangerous. Group discussions and activities to help children decide whom to trust and when to be cautious are recommended. Also, parent education programs with this theme are suggested because parental fears are extremely influential in children's lives.

Childhood abuse is a part of an overall pattern of abusive behavior, and the family network, as well as the personality of the abuser, must be considered. In addition, family reactions to the child who has been abused will enhance or interfere with counseling treatment and progress. Counselors may want to consider family therapy at an appropriate time in their treatment plans (Silovsky & Hembree-Kigin, 1994).

Group treatment may offer a suitable modality for treating childhood sexual abuse victims (Silovsky & Hembree-Kigin, 1994; Zaidi & Gutierrez-Kovner, 1995). The group format, as with other problems discussed here, provides peer support and understanding of similar experiences. Further, structured activities and focused discussions can deal with the emotional reactions and development of coping strategies. Whatever the modality, therapists working with sexually abused children must be prepared to provide understanding and support for all persons involved. It is a natural reaction to feel anger at anyone who hurts a child; however, the therapist must recognize and resolve these feelings to work effectively with the child and the family, particularly the abuser.

## REFERENCES

Alpert-Gillis, L., Pedro-Carroll, J., & Cowen, E. (1989). The children of divorce intervention program: Development, implementation, and evaluation of a program for young urban children. *Journal of Consulting and Clinical Psychology, 57*(5), 583–589.

Bala, J. (1986). Mama stop doing MMMMMMM: TA in the treatment of autistic children. *Transactional Analysis Journal, 16,* 234–239.

Berne, E. (1961). *Transactional analysis in psychotherapy.* New York: Grove Press.

Bertoia, J., & Allan, J. (1988). School management of the bereaved child. *Elementary School Guidance and Counseling, 23,* 30–38.

Carter, J. L., & Miller, P. K. (1975). Creative art for minimally brain-injured children. *Academic Therapy, 6,* 245–252.

Cebollero, A., Cruise, K., & Stollak, G. (1986). The long-term effects of divorce: Mothers and children in concurrent support groups. The divorce process: A handbook for clinicians [Special issue]. *Journal of Divorce, 10*(1/2), 219–228.

Clarkson, P. (1992). *Transactional analysis psychotherapy.* New York: Routledge & Kegan Paul.

Clarkson, P., & Fish, S. (1988). Systemic assessment and treatment considerations in TA child psychotherapy. *Transactional Analysis Journal, 18,* 123–132.

Costa, L., & Holliday, D. (1994). Helping children cope with the death of a parent. *Elementary School Guidance and Counseling, 28,* 206–213.

Crasilneck, H. B., & Hall, J. A. (1975). *Clinical hypnosis: Principles and applications.* New York: Grune and Stratton.

Dattilio, F. M., & Freeman, A. (1994). *Cognitive-behavioral strategies in crisis intervention.* New York: Guilford Press.

Denny, J. (1975). Techniques for individual and group art therapy. In E. Ulman & P. Dachinger (Eds.), *Art therapy in theory and practice.* New York: Schocken Books.

DePiano, F. A., & Salzberg, H. C. (Eds.). (1986). *Clinical applications of hypnosis.* Norwood, NJ: ABLEX.

Dinkmeyer, D., & Caldwell, E. (1970). *Developmental counseling and guidance.* New York: McGraw-Hill.

Fine, A. H., & Fine, N. M. (1988). *Therapeutic recreation for exceptional children.* Springfield, Ill: Thomas.

Freudenberger, H. J., & Gallagher, K. M. (1995). Emotional consequences of loss for our adolescents. *Psychotherapy, 32,* 150–153.

Gabel, S. (1984). The draw a story game: An aid in understanding and working with children. *Arts in Psychotherapy, 11*(3), 187–196.

Gardner, R. A. (1983). The talking, feeling, and doing game. In C. Schafer & K. O'Connor (Eds.), *Handbook of play therapy* (pp. 259–273). New York: Wiley.

Gardner, R. A. (1971). *Therapeutic communication with children: The mutual story-telling technique.* New York: Aronson.

Gardner, R. A. (1993). *Storytelling in psychotherapy with children.* Northvale, NJ: Aronson.

Gibson, H. B., & Heap, M. (1991). *Hypnosis in therapy.* Hillsdale, NJ: Erlbaum.

Gilliland, B., & James, R. (1988). *Crisis intervention strategies.* Pacific Grove, CA: Brooks/Cole.

Godbole, A. Y. (1982). Dyad as a technique of behavioural change. *Psycho–Lingua, 12,* 95–110.

Gold, J. R. (1988). An integrative psychotherapeutic approach to psychological crises of children and families. *Journal of Integrative and Eclectic Psychotherapy, 7,* 135–151.

Gonick-Barris, S. E. (1976). Art for children with minimal brain dysfunction. *American Journal of Art Therapy, 15,* 67–73.

Greenbaum, L., & Holmes, I. (1983). The use of folktales in social work practice. *Social Casework, 64*(7), 414–418.

Guidubaldi, J., Cleminshaw, H., Perry, J., & McLoughlin, C. (1983). The impact of parental divorce on children: Report of the nationwide NASP study. *School Psychology Review, 12*(3), 300–323.

Harris, T. (1969). *I'm OK, you're OK.* New York: Harper & Row.

Heikkinen, C. A. (1979). Counseling from personal loss. *Personnel and Guidance Journal, 58,* 47–56.

Hollander, S. (1989). Coping with child sexual abuse through children's books. *Elementary School Guidance and Counseling, 23,* 183–193.

Holtgraves, M. (1986). Help the victims of sexual abuse help themselves. *Elementary School Guidance and Counseling, 21,* 155–159.

Knoff, H. M., & Prout, H. T. (1985). *Kinetic drawing system for family and school: A handbook.* Los Angeles: Western Psychological Services.

Korb, M. P., Gorrell, J., & Van De Riet, V. (1989). *Gestalt therapy: Practice and theory* (2nd ed.). New York: Pergamon Press.

Kubler-Ross, E. (1969). *On death and dying.* New York: Macmillan.

Liebmann, M. (1986). *Art therapy for groups.* Cambridge, MA: Brookline Books.

Lohnes, K. L., & Kalter, N. (1994). Preventive intervention groups for parentally bereaved children. *American Journal of Orthopsychiatry, 64,* 594–603.

Loomis, E. (1957). The use of checkers in handling certain resistances in child therapy and child analysis. *Journal of the American Psychoanalytical Association, 5,* 130–135.

Massey, R. F., & Massey, S. D. (1988). A systemic approach to treating children with their families. *Transactional Analysis Journal, 18*(2), 110–122.

Matheson, G. (1985). Hypnosis. In D. G. Benner (Ed.), *Baker encyclopedia of psychology* (pp. 543–547). Grand Rapids, MI: Baker Book House.

Miller, C., & Boe, J. (1990). Tears into diamonds: Transformation of child psychic trauma through sandplay and storytelling. *Arts in Psychotherapy 17*(3), 247–257.

Miller, C. A., & Capuzzi, D. (1984). A review of transactional analysis outcome studies. *American Mental Health Counselors, 6,* 30–41.

Oaklander, V. (1978). *Windows to our children: A gestalt therapy approach to children and adolescents.* Moab, UT: Read People Press.

Olness, K., & Gardner, G. G. (1988). *Hypnosis and hypnotherapy with children* (2nd ed.). New York: Grune & Stratton.

Olness, K., & Kohen, D. P. (1996). *Hypnosis and hypnotherapy with children.* New York: Guilford Press.

Oster, G. D., & Gould, P. (1987). *Using drawings in assessment and therapy: A guide for mental health professionals.* New York: Brunner/Mazel.

Pellowski, A. (1977). *The world of storytelling.* New York: Bowker.

Perls, F. S. (1969). *Gestalt therapy verbatim.* Moab, UT: Real People Press.

Perls, F. S. (1973). *The Gestalt approach.* Palo Alto, CA: Science and Behavior Books.

Quarmby, D. (1993). Peer counseling with bereaved adolescents. *British Journal of Guidance and Counseling, 21,* 196–211.

Robbins, A., & Sibley, L. (1976). *Creative art therapy.* New York: Brunner/Mazel.

Rubin, J. A. (1975, December). Art is for all human beings especially the handicapped. *Art Education,* 5–10.

Schaefer, C., & O'Connor, K. (1983). *Handbook of play therapy.* New York: Wiley.

Schaefer, C., & Reed, S. (1986). *Game play.* New York: Wiley.

Segal, R. (1984). Helping children express grief through symbolic communication. *Social Casework: The Journal of Contemporary Social Work, 65,* 590–599.

Siegel, D. (1986). Trance induction: Methods and research. In F. A. DePiano & H. C. Salzberg (Eds.), *Clinical applications of hypnosis* (pp. 3–19). Norwood, NJ: ABLEX.

Silovsky, J. F., & Hembree-Kigin, T. L. (1994). Family and group treatment for sexually abused children: A review. *Journal of Child Sexual Abuse, 3,* 1–20.

Stiles, K., & Kottman, T. (1990). Mutual storytelling: An intervention for depressed and suicidal children. *School Counselor 37*, 337–342.

Stolberg, A. L. (1988). Families in transition: Primary prevention programs that work. *Primary prevention of psychopathology, 11*, 225–251.

Sutton-Smith, B., & Roberts, J. (1971). The cross-cultural and psychological study of games. *International Review of Sport Sociology, 6*, 79–87.

Tennant, C. (1988). Preventive sexual abuse programs: Problems and possibilities. *Elementary School Guidance and Counseling, 23*, 48–53.

Thompson, C. L., & Rudolph, L. B. (1992). *Counseling children* (3rd ed.). Pacific Grove, CA: Brook/Cole.

Tonkins, S. A. M., & Lambert, M. J. (1996). A treatment outcome study of bereavement groups for children. *Child and Adolescent Social Work Journal, 13*, 3–21.

Torrance, E. P. (1970). *Encouraging creativity in the classroom.* Dubuque, Iowa: Wm. C. Brown.

Ulman, E. (1975). Art therapy: Problems of definition. In E. Ulman & P. Dachinger (Eds.), *Art therapy in theory and practice* (pp. 3–13). New York: Schocken Books.

Wallerstein, J. S. (1989). *Second chances: Men, women, and children a decade after divorce.* New York: Ticknor & Fields.

Werner, E., & Smith, R. (1980). An epidemiologic perspective on some antecedents and consequences of childhood mental health problems and learning disabilities. *Annual Progress in Child Psychiatry & Child Development, 13*, 133–147.

Woltmann, A. G. (1940). The use of puppets in understanding children. *Mental Hygiene, 24*, 445–458.

Woltmann, A. G. (1971). Spontaneous puppetry by children as a projective technique. In A. I. Rubin & M. R. Haworth (Eds.), *Projective techniques with children* (pp. 188–202). New York: Grune & Stratton.

Yauman, B. E. (1991). School-based group counseling for children of divorce: A review of the literature. *Elementary School Guidance and Counseling, 26*, 130–138.

Zaidi, L. Y., & Gutierrez-Kovner, V. M. (1995). Group treatment of sexually abused latency-age girls. *Journal of Interpersonal Violence, 10*, 215–227.

# Chapter 12

# COUNSELING AND PSYCHOTHERAPY WITH CHILDREN AND ADOLESCENTS WITH DISABILITIES

Harriet C. Cobb and Patricia J. Warner

In providing therapeutic intervention for any child, with or without disabilities, the most important characteristics therapists and counselors must take into consideration are the child's thoughts, feelings, and unique attributes. Furthermore, taking a systems approach by working with the child's family and school is crucial to maximize efficacy. For children with exceptionalities, there are specific issues that the child therapist, to be effective, must keep in mind. These include the special cognitive, educational, emotional, and physical characteristics, as well as family dynamics that differentiate children with disabilities from their nondisabled peers.

Describing children on the basis of their disabilities is a difficult task. Each of the groupings under the rubric "exceptional" dealt with in this chapter (children with learning disabilities, children with mental retardation, children with physical disabilities, children with traumatic brain injury, and children with attention deficit disorder) is extremely heterogeneous. Children must be recognized as individuals, each with many facets, with their disability being only one aspect of their personalities. The reader is directed to the References at the end of the chapter for additional information regarding specific characteristics of each disability.

An important issue for clinicians working with children is their own attitudes and feelings regarding people with disabilities. Many studies have examined the perceptions of professionals toward individuals with disabilities (Chubon, 1982; Cook, Kunce, & Getsinger, 1976; Greer, 1975). These studies show a clear relationship between the attitudes a given therapist holds and the effectiveness of the therapy he or she provides with a given population. The therapist's thoughts and feelings about a particular disability have significant impact on the behavior of the client (Yuker, 1988). Nathanson (1979) describes several beliefs commonly held by professionals working with the disabled that can inhibit therapeutic intervention. For example, a problem may arise if the therapist views the child only in terms of the label (e.g., mentally retarded, learning disabled, or physically disabled) and provides treatment to the child based on preconceived notions related to that label. The counselor/therapist may tend to evaluate the child primarily on the basis of a unitary dimension related to a single aspect of the disability, such as lower intelligence. This perception may result in a disregard for other attributes of the child including interests, positive personality characteristics, social skills, and adaptive behavior. The uniqueness of the child as an individual may be undervalued, and stereotypes of what the child can and cannot do may be imposed. The child may be wrongly assumed to conform to limitations and potentials that have been imposed by the therapist as characteristic of a given label.

One of the most common feelings that many people, including professionals, have toward children with disabilities is pity. The therapist's attention may be directed only toward the negative aspects of the child's life instead of the positive. The counselor may see the child as a victim in a despairing situation, and this attitude may prevent the child from focusing on his or her strengths and capabilities as well. The well-intentioned therapist may assume that the child or adolescent is less able to cope with frustrations and crises than he or she really is. Such an assumption may subsequently foster dependency—something the counselor would not instigate with a child considered to be nondisabled. Goals in therapy may be set too low, with the counselor/therapist projecting the attitude, "If this were me, I don't know how I would manage."

Another common trap is that the therapist may unconsciously reject the child because of a feeling of revulsion toward the particular disability. These feelings may be manifested in avoidance or impatience and will interfere with establishing rapport. A therapist who has not had experience with children with disabilities previously may have feelings of anxiety and uncertainty despite being quite competent to deal with children in general.

It is not unusual, however, for the child therapist to experience feelings of anxiety or pity when first encountering a child with a disability. As has been indicated above, these feelings are the prevailing attitudes held by society toward persons with disabilities. Therefore, it is important for the therapist to examine his or her own attitudes about persons with a disability and to modify them accordingly. To work effectively with children, therapists must monitor their own behavior and prevent personal beliefs from interfering with therapeutic efficacy. A primary step in this direction is for the counselor/therapist to acquire a basic working knowledge of the various disabilities. It is also beneficial for therapists to undergo peer review of their therapeutic interventions for feedback about their projections of attitudes in the therapeutic setting.

Within the therapeutic process itself, providing basic information about the disability to the child may be the most important component of the counseling process. This includes comprehensive information on the disability itself—what it is *and* what it is not. Some children may be reluctant to voice their questions, and it is appropriate for the therapist to say something like, "Children who have a learning disability often ask . . ." This serves the dual purpose of helping the child put his or her thoughts into words, perhaps expressing the "worst fears," as well as letting him or her know that other children have similar questions and similar problems.

The conclusions that children with disabilities formulate about their impairment have a profound impact on their total self-concept. These conclusions are usually based on the reactions of parents, peers, teachers, or others to the disability—reactions that may vary from complete acceptance to total rejection. These children may experience feelings of unhappiness in relation to any limitations imposed by the disability. In addition, they may have unrealistic goals, and the process of assisting them in coming to terms with any real limitations may be slow and painful. In some children, the unhappiness about the disability may become so severe that the behaviors exhibited include manifestations of depression. As depression often occurs in children who experience a personal loss, recognition of the limitations imposed by their disability may constitute a severe loss of certain goals and opportunities for these children, and thereby result in depression.

While knowledge of the special needs condition, such as mental retardation or learning disabilities, is necessary, it is not sufficient for providing effective intervention. The learning, emotional, or behavioral characteristics accompanying the disability, in addition to the unique attributes of the individual child, are critical aspects in providing therapy. Knowledge of normal developmental changes experienced by children is crucial in working with children with disabilities as well as with the nondisabled. In addition, however, therapists must accommodate their own approaches to the special needs of children with disabilities.

As an example, let's consider how this accommodation would apply in the case of a child with mental retardation. This child will possess more limited cognitive ability, and therefore, will require a more concrete approach. Children with mental retardation learn at a slower rate, and their overall maturity level typically is lower than their non-retarded peers. The child's experiential background and vocabulary may be restricted, and thus the expressive vocabulary utilized by the therapist must be adjusted. For example, a 12-year-old child with mild mental retardation may be more similar to an average 8-year-old. Their attention span is often shorter, and this fact, in combination with distractibility, may limit the length of therapy sessions. In addition, the therapist may need to make a concerted effort to reinforce the child's attending behaviors and provide additional structure to manage other unwanted behaviors exhibited by the child.

With children with disabilities, the use of role playing and behavior rehearsal is often more appropriate than other forms of therapy to facilitate the attainment of goals such as the acquisition of social skills. Skill in social interaction may be the most important affective goal for some children with disabilities because perception by others of their overall level of impairment is directly influenced by the social skills they demonstrate.

Similar considerations must be made when the therapist is dealing with the learning disabled and physically disabled. Attention span, distractibility, physical stamina, neurological impairment, and perceptual disorganization are all factors that will require modification in the therapeutic process. The ability of the therapist to estimate the impact of these disabilities on personality functioning is a major aspect of the diagnostic process prior to therapeutic intervention. The remainder of this chapter is devoted to detailing specific considerations in providing therapy to children with disabilities and their families. A number of therapeutic interventions also are discussed.

## SPECIAL NEEDS OF DISABLED CHILDREN

Neely (1982) has listed four concerns that commonly arise in the counseling of children with disabilities: self-other relations, maladaptive behavior, self-conflict, and a need for vocational counseling. Nondisabled children may experience these problems as well, but they are particularly pertinent to the disabled. As DeBlassie and Cowan (1976) pointed out, children with disabilities face greater numbers of frustrations, are misunderstood and rejected more often, and have greater difficulty developing positive self-concepts.

Children with disabilities may be confronted with prejudice and stereotypes about their disability and may be subjected to excessive teasing by classmates. Counselors must be prepared to assist these children in learning to cope with attitudes that may be cruel or that impose unnecessary limitations on opportunities for certain experiences. Facilitating the development of a healthy self-concept in these children is a major task of the therapist. Helping them accept the disability and see themselves as capable human beings often allows them some immunity from ridicule or the results of stereotyping. Therapists may find it necessary to involve the parents and school in learning to accept these children's disabilities and in learning to communicate confidence in their capabilities. Whether or not these children have been included with nondisabled peers, the awareness of being "different" or of being perceived as different may take its toll on building positive relationships with others. Group counseling can provide the ideal situation for helping children with disabilities develop skills in relating to others as well as experiencing the feeling of not being alone. In some cases, including nondisabled children in the group can further the process of normalization since it exposes children without disabilities to the disabled and simultaneously provides a shared experience. Through social learning, children with disabilities acquire more normalized forms of behavior. This allows opportunities for friendships between children with disabilities and those without disabilities.

Group counseling can also offer the opportunity for learning appropriate social skills such as tact, assertiveness, and making conversation (Kish, 1991). Since maladaptive behaviors are often associated with certain disabilities, social skills training is a commonly used approach among counselors and others who work with children with retardation or learning disabilities (Brannigan & Young, 1978; LaGreca & Mesibov, 1979; Zigmond & Brownlee, 1980).

Maladaptive behaviors such as impulsivity and distractibility are not only characteristics of some children with attention deficit disorder, but also may be targets for modification and counseling. Meichenbaum (1977) described a cognitive behavioral method of decreasing impulsivity using verbal rehearsal and fading. These techniques are discussed in detail in Chapter 7.

Making the appropriate match between therapeutic method and the specific problem while taking into consideration the implication of the disability itself can be a challenge to the counselor. It is important for the therapist to keep in mind that any learning situation, even with a trusted adult, can be anxiety-producing for children who have experienced failure with academic or other tasks that involve learning something new. Furthermore, because of the special characteristics of children with disabilities, many situations will be new and unfamiliar to them (Schontz, 1980). Guaranteeing success by proceeding in small steps, along with keeping expectations for change realistic, are appropriate approaches, not only for teachers and parents but also for therapists.

Self-conflicts experienced by children with disabilities referred to by Neely (1982) include anxiety, frustration, lack of motivation, and depression. Often these problems are a result of feelings of inadequacy brought about by repeated failure experiences. Although children with disabilities have the same fears as other children, worries about being accepted by others or doing well in school are exacerbated. Therapists can draw from techniques found to be successful in coping with anxiety. These include relaxation training, rational emotive therapy (RET), and other behavioral techniques. Frustration is often experienced by children with disabilities who have repeatedly had their goals thwarted. Sometimes this frustration results from misinformation or lack of information provided by adults. It may also result from unrealistic expectations that these children may have for themselves. Although children respond differently to frustration—some with aggressiveness, others with depression or apathy—all need to acquire skills to cope with frustrating events. It is often in this context that therapists must provide basic information about disabilities to the children as well as to the parents. For example, in the case of the child with mental retardation or the physically disabled child, sexuality may be an issue avoided by well-meaning adults who feel uncomfortable with this topic. Specially written materials about sexuality can be used as part of the information-giving process (Gordon, 1975).

Children with disabilities may feel overwhelmed by the implications of their disabilities and will need help in removing barriers to success, as well as support in learning how to tolerate obstacles that cannot be removed. If children with disabilities feel that any goal is impossible to attain, this may be reflected in unmotivated behavior. Helping the child to formulate realistic goals (assuming the goals of parents and teachers are not unrealistic either) is the appropriate course to take.

Depression in children with disabilities may be manifested in feelings of unworthiness, apathy, and withdrawal or it may be masked, manifesting itself as aggressive behavior, just as it occurs in nondisabled children. Children who fail to come to terms with any limitations imposed by their disability may experience a sense of personal loss. The therapist can help these children through the stages of grief that may be associated with this sense of loss.

Once children have accepted their disabilities, the need for acquiring decision-making skills is usually apparent, particularly when the time for choosing a career approaches. The counselor should be aware of instruments specifically designed for individuals with disabilities to measure interests and abilities, such as the Reading Free Vocational Interest Inventory (Becker, 1975), the Occupational Aptitude Survey and Interest Schedule (Parker, 1991), or the Social and Prevocational Information Battery (Halpern, Raffield, Irvin, & Link, 1975). Vocational counseling and instruction in decision-making skills are important components of therapy with disabled adolescents.

Career satisfaction is a major part of emotional stability. For children with mental retardation, career choices are limited and must be examined carefully.

Children or adolescents with disabilities encounter the same developmental changes and life stressors that nondisabled individuals experience, such as the birth of a sibling, moving, a divorce, or a death in the family and may need extra assistance in understanding and coping with such crises. Deutsch (1985) reminds us that individuals with disabilities develop attachments and experience losses throughout their lives, too. Like other individuals, they may enter a period of mourning for which they are completely unprepared. Their poorer adaptive skills make it difficult enough to cope with everyday stress, let alone the loss of a significant interpersonal relationship. The therapist can be helpful in assisting them through the grief process with educative counseling, catharsis, and specific cognitive behavioral techniques (Deutsch).

## THE CHILD WITH LEARNING DISABILITIES

The current definition of a learning disability found in Public Law 101-476, is as follows:

> Specific Learning Disability means a disorder in one or more of the basic psychological processes involved in the understanding of language, spoken or written, which may manifest itself in an imperfect ability to listen, speak, read, write, spell, or to do mathematical calculations. The term includes such conditions as perceptual handicaps, brain injury, minimal brain dysfunction, dyslexia, and other developmentally caused disorders. The term does not include children who have learning problems which are primarily the result of visual, hearing, or motor handicaps, or mental retardation, emotional disturbance, or environmental, cultural, or economic disadvantage.

While there is some controversy over the exact nature and etiology of learning disabilities, a child is generally diagnosed on the basis of school performance as evidenced by a problem with academic achievement. If achievement level falls significantly below that which would be predicted by aptitude measures, a learning disability is suspected as being the cause. Incidence figures for learning-disabled children range from 1% to 15%, but most professionals consider 2% to 5% to be the most realistic estimate (Hallahan & Kauffman, 1997).

Children who are labeled learning disabled often demonstrate inconsistency in their performance marked by pronounced patterns of cognitive and academic strengths and weaknesses (Salvia & Ysseldyke, 1991). Associated characteristics according to *DSM-IV* (American Psychiatric Association, 1994) include: (a) demoralization, (b) low self-esteem, (c) deficits in social skills, (d) impulsivity, (e) attention deficits, (f) hyperactivity, (g) cognitive processing difficulties such as memory problems, (h) coordination difficulties, and (i) communication difficulties.

This group consists of children with specific learning difficulties that become apparent after they have entered school. These disabilities may coexist with emotional stress reactions such as separation anxiety, school phobia, and mild depression. According to the National Joint Committee on Learning Disabilities (1988), most learning disorders stem from information processing deficits of assumed neurological basis. Concomitant problems in self-regulation and social interaction may exist, yet do not constitute a learning disability. More recently, the focus of counseling/therapy intervention for children with learning difficulties has moved beyond remediation of their cognitive deficits to addressing the social and affective effects of learning disabilities.

For many older children and adolescents who may have experienced years of frustration in the classroom, their poor social skills and acting-out behavior may be the major concern of those working and living with them. Indeed, in terms of long-term success in life and the workplace, social skills deficits for the child with a learning disability are probably the biggest concerns. Later problems related to poor psychosocial adjustment include dropout of school, juvenile delinquency, marital problems, unemployment, and substance abuse (Kish, 1991). Group therapy has an advantage for helping these children as their difficulties with peers, teachers, and parents often are related to poor interpersonal skills. Group counseling can help them deal with their failure to recognize the cause-and-effect relationship between their own behavior and the responses of others (Kish).

While not all learning-disabled children will possess the preceding characteristics, most will exhibit at least one or more of these behaviors. The child therapist must make modifications in techniques to accommodate the special needs of clients with learning disabilities. As Morse (1977) pointed out, specialized knowledge of specific learning disabilities and the ability to be flexible and creative are essential skills for working with children with a learning disability. As with mental retardation, a shorter attention span and distractibility means that it may be necessary to hold briefer sessions. The sessions may also need to be more structured and to include a greater amount of "activity-oriented" material. Depending on the learning disability, the therapist may need to identify the best means of communicating with these children. For example, with a child who is distractible with auditory short-term memory deficits, it may be helpful to make notes or list in writing the major points covered in each session. These should be commensurate with the child's vocabulary level and reviewed with the child. If the child has difficulty reading, it is possible to use pictures of objects, rebus symbols, signs, and letters that suggest words or phrases in place of the usual written word. If, for example, the therapist is attempting to work with the child in meeting the goal of completion of household chores, it might be helpful to use a series of pictures representing those chores. For the child with memory or organizational problems, using a written list of chores may be helpful. This list can be attached to the child's desk or bedroom door as a visible reminder of his or her commitment.

Since children with learning disabilities are often emotionally labile and erratic in their behavior patterns, progress in therapy may be somewhat slower than with nondisabled children. Therapists may see gains made one day only to watch these children regress by the time the next session is held. While this seesawing can be true of all children in a therapy situation, it is especially common for a child with a learning disability. Children with learning disabilities have difficulty with attention span, concept formation, motor control, and communication skills and these deficits hinder many common therapeutic interventions. Often intervention must focus on these variables at the same time that counseling occurs.

## THE CHILD WITH MENTAL RETARDATION

The most recent definition of mental retardation given by the American Association on Mental Retardation (AAMR) is as follows:

> Mental retardation refers to substantial limitations in present functioning. It is characterized by significantly subaverage intellectual functioning, existing concurrently with related limitations in two or more of the following applicable adaptive skill areas: communication, self-care, home living, social skills, community use, self-direction, health and safety, functional academics, leisure and work. Mental retardation manifests before age 18. (Luckasson et al., 1992)

Within this general definition, the AAMR outlines four levels of classification based on level of support: intermittent, limited, extensive, and pervasive; educators have usually referred to the terms *educable, trainable,* and *severe/profound.* Approximately 2% of the U.S. population is considered mentally retarded. There are specific characteristics of children with mental retardation that have implications for counseling.

A primary characteristic of children with mental retardation is the reduced speed and efficiency with which they learn (Robinson & Robinson, 1965; MacMillan, 1982). Attention span and memory are two components of the learning process that may be particularly affected. In addition, the adaptive behavior of a child with mental impairment is significantly below that of comparable chronologically aged peers. This is particularly evident in the area of social interaction, self-help skills, motor development, and affective development. Furthermore, the acquisition of basic concepts is significantly slowed and may be totally absent in the more severely involved individuals. This lack of concept development limits the therapeutic interventions that may be utilized with this population.

Children with mental retardation often have difficulty focusing their attention on a given stimulus and may exhibit hyperdistractible behavior. Their memory processes tend to be limited and unpredictable. Short-term memory processes that fluctuate erratically may prevent or slow down the learning of new tasks and skills. The long-term memory of a child with mental retardation may be as good as that of their nondisabled peers, but the presence of short-term memory deficits results in much slower acquisition of new material.

Children with mental retardation experience the same emotional and social problems as other children. Parental pressure, peer conflicts, sibling rivalry, and other childhood stresses are common among children with mental retardation. However, the child's cognitive ability limits the responses to these situations. The level of formal operations characterized by abstract thinking which begins to manifest itself in adolescence may never be attained by children with mental retardation. Thus, complex cognitive solutions to social interaction problems are beyond their capability. Since their thinking is more concrete, problem-solving skills must concentrate on areas that can be easily remembered. Solutions that have a focus far into the future will not be easily acquired. This difficulty means that coping with developmental changes or unexpected crises is a much more difficult process for the child with mental retardation than for the normal child. The ability of these children to predict the future is severely limited by their lack of conceptual development.

Language deficits are much more common in this population than in children who are not retarded. Verbal expression in less elaborate, and repetitive or perseverative language is quite common. Frequently, receptive language is significantly better than expressive language. The social and emotional development of a child with mental retardation often lags behind his or her nonretarded peers. Although physical development may not differ, their ability to understand and cope with physiological changes or limitations may be limited. Adaptive behavior deficits are an integral part of the definition of mental retardation. Therefore, the child's level of independence for adults in the areas of self-help and vocational competence may be significantly delayed. The role of the parents in therapy is even more critical for children and adolescents with mental retardation than it is for other young clients.

Children with mental retardation are particularly vulnerable to sexual abuse and exploitation due to dependence on caregivers throughout their life span. Therapists must be on the alert for signs of abuse, provide information on sexuality, and protect them from abuse. Children who are mentally retarded frequently are not taught about sex or sexuality (Tharinger, Horton, & Millea, 1990). The sexual drive and development of persons with mild and moderate retardation usually are no different than for the nondisabled. Sexuality of the mentally retarded is still a difficult issue for parents and professionals to deal with, and thus sexuality information is often not provided to this population. Just as they often don't receive information about sexuality, these children often fail to receive sexual abuse prevention information either. Although there is limited research on the effects of sexual abuse on children with mental retardation, there is some indication that their reaction will be more severe than for individuals without disabilities (Varley, 1984). The type of intervention for victims of sexual abuse would depend on their age, cognitive and social development levels, gender, family, and living arrangements.

Selwa (1971) suggests several considerations for psychotherapy with children with mental retardation. Therapeutic interventions must be structured around concrete situations and elements and sessions may need to be shorter. The verbal comprehensive and expressive abilities of the child must define the parameters of the language used by the therapist. This means that the therapist must spend time in formally evaluating the expressive and receptive language skills of the child prior to therapeutic intervention. The use of materials and play media such as clay, painting, toys, and puppets may be appropriate even for adolescents to help them dramatize problems, fears, and anxieties that they feel.

A more directive approach is often recommended for clients with cognitive limitations. As Hurley and Hurley (1986) point out, the therapist sets the agenda and generally provides more structure than is necessary with a nondisabled child. During the initial interview, the therapist needs to take extra care in introducing him- or herself and explaining what counseling is in language the child will understand. The therapist must educate the client as concretely as possible regarding (a) how often the sessions will take place, (b) what generally will occur during the sessions, (c) what will be expected of the client between sessions, and (d) under what circumstances the child can request an emergency session. Since children with mental retardation usually learn more slowly, the frequency of sessions may need to be increased.

The therapist must be careful to ascertain how the child is conceptualizing his or her problem. This determination may involve actually teaching the child vocabulary words such as those related to emotional expression. Because of the child's attention and short-term memory deficits, the counselor may find it necessary to apply the principle of "overlearning." This means that complex tasks will need to be segmented and rehearsed over a long period of time before they are finally mastered. The use of repetition is critical in assisting the child in generalizing newly acquired coping skills to situations outside the therapy room.

A long-standing stereotype of mental retardation suggests that group counseling and therapy are not appropriate intervention techniques. Several studies have indicated, however, that children with mental retardation can benefit from this method of intervention. Humes, Adamszyk, and Myco (1969) found that group counseling resulted in better adjustment for educable mentally retarded adolescents, as seen in teacher ratings on a behavioral scale. Blohm (1978) found that self-concept can be as difficult to change in the mentally retarded as it is with other children. However, group counseling did improve 3 of 13 personality factors for elementary school children with moderate levels of retardation. Welch and Sigman (1980) also recommended using group therapy with adolescents with mental retardation. They specifically suggest that the therapist take an active role in structuring therapy and that this therapy include nonverbal activities. They cite the advantages of group therapy as providing the mentally retarded adolescent contact with peers and a sense of belonging to a peer group, the availability of behavioral models, greater opportunities for feedback, and improvement in participants' verbal skills. Selwa (1971) suggests using homogeneity in intellectual level in the grouping of children with mental retardation for therapy, since persons with retardation of the same chronological age may differ significantly in mental maturity. The therapy session should concentrate on a series of operationally defined objectives. In addition, the length of sessions should be shorter than those normally used with nonretarded children.

Group work should be concrete, focused in the present, and realistic (Wells & Allan, 1985). As with nondisabled clients, group counseling can teach members to express thoughts and feelings, understand themselves and others, and learn new behaviors. It affords the child or adolescent with disabilities the opportunity to feel a sense of "belongingness" to a group, reducing feelings of isolation and loneliness. Wells and Allan describe a group counseling program in a school setting for secondary-aged students with mental retardation. The program specifically addressed the issues of experiencing failure and how to cope with it. Activities were divided into two types:

listening and memory games, and discussions of memories around a set topic, such as "feeling embarrassed." These sharing-of-memories sessions were preceded by a discussion, with the leader always modeling the first response. At one point, students without disabilities were invited to share difficult experiences, which demonstrated the potential benefits of self-disclosure in a supportive setting.

Although most efficacy studies with the mildly retarded utilize behavioral and directive approaches, at least two studies (Davidson, 1975; Hayes, 1977) used a psychoanalytic approach in an effective manner with children with mental retardation. This approach was developed on the basis of Anna Freud's developmental theory rather than traditional Freudian therapy.

## CASE STUDY OF AN ADOLESCENT WITH MENTAL RETARDATION

Tracy was a 14-year-old girl identified as mildly mentally retarded, who was referred for counseling by the social services department. A number of incidents regarding sexual abuse had been brought to their attention. Tracy had become withdrawn in school, and her mother complained that Tracy didn't listen to her the way she used to.

Tracy was seen by the psychologist for a period of six months on a regular basis for individual counseling; she also participated in group counseling. Tracy was quite withdrawn at first, avoiding eye contact and rarely speaking. It became apparent that she was operating on a very concrete level and was extremely confused about the incidents of sexual abuse that had precipitated her referral. Although she had attained sexual maturity at the age of 12, her knowledge of sexuality and reproduction was almost nonexistent. Her verbal expressive skills were extremely deficient, and this deficit in combination with her reluctance to talk, made developing communication with her a very slow process. Because of her limited verbal skills, drawings were used extensively as a means of communicating. To elicit expression of feelings, it was easier to request that she draw a picture of "what was on her mind." Large portions of the early sessions were spent in attempting to expel some of the misperceptions Tracy had about sexual abuse. For example, she believed that since she was first molested at the age of 7, pregnancy could ensue at any time. She also believed that these incidents had caused one of her breasts to be larger than the other. A sex education booklet that was intended specifically for adolescents with mental retardation was used to aid in explaining relevant points about sexuality to Tracy. Role playing was also a frequently used technique in helping Tracy to acquire coping and social skills. Conflict resolution methods were role-played, and Tracy was encouraged to use them at home (a social worker was working closely with Tracy's parents during this time.) Coaching and social reinforcement were effective in facilitating the development of the skills in Tracy, although it took several months before any noticeable changes occurred. When Tracy appeared to be ready for further peer interaction, group counseling was initiated. Tracy and four other girls (with cognitive functioning in the mildly retarded to borderline range) met with the psychologist for eight sessions on a weekly basis. At least one of the other girls had been sexually abused; the others had not had this experience. However, as with other adolescents, the major issues dealt with in the sessions were parent conflicts and relationships with peers. Feelings of universality and cohesiveness developed rather quickly in the group. Tracy participated somewhat reluctantly at first but soon responded positively to the others and developed a close relationship with one of the other group members. Tracy maintained friendships with the girls in the group after the sessions had ended. For Tracy, a major turning point in her progress occurred when one of the girls invited Tracy to spend the night at her house. Although conflicts with her parents continued to exist from time to time, Tracy's mother reported that they were getting along better and Tracy had become more cooperative at home.

## THE CHILD WITH PHYSICAL DISABILITIES

The term *physically disabled* includes several different conditions that are congenital, accidental, or disease related, and result in the individual being physically limited. Children with physical disabilities are those whose nonsensory physical limitations or health problems interfere with their school attendance or learning to such an extent that special services, training, equipment, or materials are required. The incidence of physically disabled school-age children is approximately 0.5%, as estimated by the U.S. Department of Education. Causes may be prenatal, associated with perinatal or maternal factors, genetic factors, accidents, or infections; or in some cases, there may be an idiopathic etiology.

Persons with physical disabilities are such a heterogeneous group that generalizations are impossible to make. As Neely (1982) points out, these children may have normal intelligence or may be mentally disabled as well as having other sensory impairments. Some children with physical disabilities have adapted well to their disability while others experience considerable difficulty in this regard. Therefore, with this population, particular care must be taken by the counselor to view each child in relation to the specific condition and to generate the therapeutic approach that focuses on strengths and coping strategies commensurate with the disability.

Career exploration and counseling should be considered with these children, especially as it relates to their self-esteem. Seeing a wide array of career choices and potentials lays a solid foundation for their vocational development. Under the provisions of the Individuals with Disabilities Act (1990) (IDEA), educational plans in the schools should include preparation for their transition to further education or training or the world of work.

The developmental process of disengaging from the family may be especially difficult for the physically disabled adolescent, as the issue of dependence/independence becomes more complicated than for teenagers with no limitations. The therapist needs to be sensitized to the ambivalent feelings of the adolescent as well as of the parents. This is particularly important if the adolescent with a disability acquired his or her impairment adventitiously as opposed to congenitally. Family involvement may be crucial at this stage in the intervention process.

## THE CHILD WITH TRAUMATIC BRAIN INJURY

With the amendment of PL 94-142, via IDEA (*Federal Register,* 1990), a new category of exceptionality was established, traumatic brain injury (TBI). There will likely be an increase in the identification of these children in the schools and subsequent referral for counseling. Walker (1997) encourages all children with TBI to have counseling as part of their rehabilitation. Following a brain injury, children often experience behavior problems not seen before the injury as well as reactions to the injury that require intervention to promote a healthy adjustment. One in four children with TBI is described as impulsive.

The impact of TBI on the social-emotional functioning of the survivor is perhaps the least understood and most often overlooked of the potential effects of the injury, including physical and cognitive sequelae (Begali, 1992; Walker, 1997). The most common emotional symptoms associated with TBI include:

- Behavioral control problems—disinhibition/impulsivity.
- Poor self-worth.
- Mood disorders—apathy, lability, social withdrawal/indifference, depression.
- Denial of disability.
- Anxiety disorders.
- Inappropriate social or sexual behavior.
- Aggressive, agitated behavior.

One of the contributing factors to their social-behavioral difficulties stems from their comparison of self to premorbid functioning levels—what they could do before the injury. There is also pressure from family and friends to get back to their "old self." This is a major difference from disabilities that are lifelong and present from birth.

Before beginning counseling with a child with an acquired brain injury, the most important thing to know is how long it has been since the injury. Generally, the most gains are made 6 months to 2 years following the injury. Family factors must also be considered so that progress is not impeded. Since many children with TBI were high risk takers before their injury, parental supervision and monitoring of their safety is an important issue. As part of the early recovery process, children may move through stages of being hyperactive, depressed, belligerent, and impulsive, and their behavior may resemble many disabling conditions such as learning disabilities, mental retardation, and emotional disturbance.

Self-awareness of deficits needs to be addressed and is a long-term adjustment issue for these children. They typically lack an awareness, which can be viewed either as a coping mechanism to deal with their loss of ability or can result from poor reasoning due to the injury. Once acceptance begins to set in, frustration and depression often follow. This population differs from other disabilities in that they can remember being different prior to injury. Therefore, loss is often the biggest issue in coming to terms with the implications of their disability.

Following brain injury, children are frequently less able to interpret nonverbal cues and the emotions of others and therefore are often socially inappropriate. This interferes with their acceptance by peers, friends, and potential employers. Explaining their injury to others and asking others to slow down are good strategies for coping. Children with TBI need help understanding the injury, accepting the loss or change of abilities and devising ways to compensate for their weaknesses. Begali (1992) has suggested use of music, art, storytelling, and literature during counseling sessions to help children express themselves and facilitate communication. Play therapy is a good choice for children with limited verbal abilities. Videotherapy can be of value in modeling appropriate behaviors, developing effective interpersonal strategies, and practicing behaviors needed for social events and job interviews (Begali).

Counseling skills for a child with TBI will need to be modified by following the four basic principles of brain injury rehabilitation outlined by Walker (1997):

1. *Clarity.* Communication abilities may be compromised. To ensure a child with TBI understands you, have him or her repeat your question or instructions or paraphrase.
2. *Repetition.* Repeat instructions, activities, and goals, as well as your role in the therapy process. Frequent repetition of key concepts and use of oral and written summaries after each session can enhance learning and aid in remembering the content of sessions. Increase the frequency of sessions as well.
3. *Structure and Consistency.* Keep your routine and office environment the same throughout therapy sessions to help them make sense of what often seems to be a confusing, fast-paced world.
4. *Flexibility.* The rehabilitation process for children with TBI is new and constantly developing so monitoring of progress is crucial. What worked last week may not work this week due to the recovery process.

Play therapy is also an excellent milieu for helping children with disabilities develop a sense of strength and competency. The two main approaches are the "I am" emphasis, which focuses on their emotional adjustment and self-esteem, and the "I can" emphasis, which relates to feelings of competence and control of their environment. For children with physical and sensory disabilities, the focus of therapy can be physical development through learning new skills and testing limits. All traditional approaches to play therapy, directive and nondirective, have been successful with children with disabilities including TBI.

Play therapy accommodations necessary for these children may include adapting toys and altering the setting itself. Carmichael (1993) suggests adaptations such as taping paintbrushes to hands, using Velcro on gloves, and using beanbags instead of balls for children with motor impairments. The therapist may have to switch from the typical arrangement of toys on shelves to introducing toys one at a time and limiting the selection for children who may have difficulty exploring their environment due to visual, motor, or attentional impairments.

## CASE STUDY OF AN ADOLESCENT WITH TRAUMATIC BRAIN INJURY (TBI)

Danny was a 15-year-old boy who had been involved in an accident when the all-terrain vehicle he was driving crashed into a telephone pole. Although most cognitive functions remained intact, the accident resulted in significant speech and motor deficits. Danny had previously been active in sports and was very involved with his friends. He was referred by his mother, a single parent, for counseling. She described herself as at "wit's end" coping with her son's tendency to be oppositional at home and not working to his potential in school. When seen by this clinician, Danny had been in school for 6 months after completing a rehabilitation program at a residential facility. Danny was placed in a special educational program within a resource room model. While Danny's mother was caring and generally supportive, she had not come to terms with Danny's difficulty in expressing himself verbally. She had not followed through with obtaining a communication device that the rehabilitation specialists had recommended, assuming his speech would soon improve "well enough." It was apparent that a source of extreme frustration and depression for Danny was his limited ability in expressing himself clearly to others. He therefore gave up easily in class and became oppositional toward adults. Danny responded well to supportive counseling, which included two sessions with his mother present. Danny's mother agreed to pursue obtaining the communication board and to seeking some personal counseling for herself. A consultation session with Danny's teachers provided more detailed information about realistic expectations for Danny, resulting in greater willingness on Danny's part to sustain his effort. Additionally, some of Danny's friends were contacted and encouraged Danny to frequent some of his old "hangouts."

## THE CHILD WITH ATTENTION DEFICIT DISORDER

Attention deficit disorder (ADD), with or without hyperactivity, is an impairment in attention and regulating activity and impulse control that is one of the most common childhood disorders. In order to receive a diagnosis of Attention-Deficit/Hyperactivity Disorder, according to *DSM-IV*, some hyperactive, impulsive, or inattentive symptoms that cause impairment must have been present before age 7, and some impairment must be present in at least two settings. The subtypes include Attention-

Deficit/Hyperactivity Disorder, combined type, Attention-Deficit/Hyperactivity Disorder, predominantly inattentive type, and Attention-Deficit/Hyperactivity Disorder, predominantly hyperactive-impulsive type. Please refer to *DSM-IV* (APA, 1994) for specific diagnostic criteria. Of all children with ADD, something like one in four also have a learning disability. Since the diagnosis of ADD is often difficult to make, one must consider other possible causes for a child's symptoms of overactivity and restlessness such as frustration associated with a learning disability (often undiagnosed), anxiety, depression, or a significant life event such as a death in the family or divorce.

Children and adolescents with ADD respond well to treatment with psychopharmacological management in conjunction with therapy such as behavior modification and family therapy. Without treatment, these children are at increased risk for trauma, substance abuse, and conduct disorders, as well as family dysfunction, job failures, divorce, and incarceration in adulthood. ADD is now viewed as a lifelong condition, not disappearing at puberty as was the previously held belief. Children who have ADD may remain distractible, impulsive, inattentive, and disruptive throughout life.

The child with ADD has trouble controlling impulses, focusing attention, and following rules. Behavior management is most commonly used to address these behaviors by determining their acceptable and unacceptable behaviors and designing a program to increase the "good" behavior and reduce the "bad." These children lose interest quickly in rewards, so they need to be changed regularly. For adolescents, cognitive behavioral therapy can be attractive because it gives them an element of control in developing problem-solving techniques and monitoring their behavior, whereas typical behavior management programs may be seen as a threat to their independence, autonomy, and self-esteem. However, it seems no one approach is sufficient, and combined multimodal treatment over extending over long periods of time produces the greater gains (Faigel, Sznajderman, Tishby, Turel, & Pinus, 1995).

For children on medication, the therapist should be alert to the strong feelings that may arise in response to the changes in their behavior and attention span. Typical reactions include surprise at the effects of medication, fear of loss of autonomy and control, fear of not maintaining good results, and loss of identity. Keep in mind, the child may be in the process of shaping a new identity.

Social skills training is important for children with ADD, as they are frequently rejected by peers who see them as not following rules in games, interrupting, and getting them in trouble. Helping them keep track of appointments can be enhanced by memory and organizational aids such as electronic notebooks. When implementing ADD interventions for social skills, success will be more likely when the following six guidelines are considered:

1. Target specific skills rather than global ones such as problem solving.
2. Select behaviors relevant to social success with peers as well as adults.
3. Address other symptoms such as poor self-esteem that may result from peer rejection.
4. Focus on establishing and maintaining appropriate behavior as well as changing and reducing inappropriate behaviors.

5. Use multiple trainers in different settings.

6. Be aware that peer problems for girls may be different from those of boys.

## CASE STUDY OF A CHILD WITH
## ATTENTION DEFICIT DISORDER (ADD)

Timmy was a 9-year-old fourth grader who had been identified as having an attention deficit disorder. Timmy was very bright and creative, but his extreme distractibility and lack of organizational skills negatively affected his daily classroom performance. Furthermore, although family relationships were quite positive, Timmy was manipulative and had become a management problem at home. The school psychologist saw Timmy on a regular basis for 4 months. In addition, monthly sessions were held with his parents over that time period.

The goals of the intervention were to increase Timmy's on-task behavior in the classroom and to reduce some of the parent-child conflict that occurred in the home. A checklist for keeping track of acceptable behaviors was developed with the parents. In addition, the teacher's and Timmy's active participation were also solicited. Points for on-task behavior were accumulated and spent on extra art time, one of Timmy's favorite activities. A separate checklist was made for home that included jobs such as helping to set the table and going to bed without a fuss. The parents were also advised to participate in a STEP group (Systematic Training for Effective Parenting, described in Chapter 5), which they were able to join during the latter part of the intervention period.

Timmy began each session very excitedly, talking about whatever was on his mind (the subject usually did relate to the goals of the intervention). After a brief period set aside for "catch-up" talk, Timmy was then taught progressive relaxation to acquire calming behavior. He was encouraged to use this in the classroom when he was feeling particularly jumpy and restless. Like many children with an attention deficit disorder (and many children without disabilities), Timmy had difficulty remembering to use his new skill of relaxing, which he had learned quickly. The teacher agreed to give Timmy a discreet hand signal when it was time for him to "calm down." In addition, Timmy was taught self-talk strategies as described by Meichenbaum (1977), which he used with a worksheet to increase accuracy. After 3 months of weekly sessions practicing relaxation and self-talk, as well as setting new goals, Timmy had significantly increased his on-task behavior in the classroom. Participation in the STEP program enabled his parents to learn to avoid power struggles with Timmy, and he was able to reach his weekly goals by the third month fairly easily.

The intervention program with Timmy was implemented with full knowledge that his distractibility and lack of organization would interfere. Sessions were kept quite brief (20 minutes), although most 9-year-olds are capable of maintaining concentration for longer periods of time. Timmy's catch-up talk time was structured, and a timer was set so Timmy could see when it was time to work. The checklists at school also were displayed on the refrigerator door. Both his parents and teacher had additional copies, so losing a checklist did not interrupt the weekly goals nor cause time to be lost in looking for the list. Toward the end of the sessions, points were given to Timmy for not losing checklists. The teacher's hand signal for relaxation was needed throughout the intervention period. Although she used it less frequently as the school year progressed, it still continued to be needed occasionally.

The counseling sessions were held in the school psychologist's office, and it was necessary to remove materials from the office desk to minimize distractibility for Timmy. The long-term goal for the intervention was to gradually fade many of the cues utilized for calming behavior and, concurrently, to increase the level and quality of Timmy's attention span.

## PARENT AND FAMILY INVOLVEMENT

It has been pointed out elsewhere in this book that the child clinician must always acknowledge the parent/family role in therapeutic intervention. Regardless of theoretical orientation, the etiology of many childhood disorders involves parent-child and parent-parent interactions. The role of the parent may be even more significant for children with disabilities.

The birth or later acknowledgment of a child with a disability, particularly if the impairment is severe, has a significant impact on the entire family as well as the parents of the child. The degree to which it is seen as a crisis depends on whether family members perceive the event as changing their lives in an undesirable manner (Turner, 1980). Parents have been described as progressing through the stages of grieving for personal loss of a perfect child and of experiencing "chronic sorrow" (Olshansky, 1970). Parents usually need assistance in working through their reactions to their child's disability. Most agencies (especially the public schools) serving children with disabilities are primarily child-centered and may inadvertently neglect the needs of the parents. It is especially important for the professional involved to provide follow-up to the parents over an extended period. It is not realistic to expect the parents to go through the process of adjustment in one session or even several sessions in a brief time span. According to Blacher (1984), a review of the literature indicates there is a general pattern of parental reactions, but individual family differences do exist.

Parents want specific information about how to foster cognitive and/or social development in order to have their child's behavior approach that of other, nondisabled children. They often want to know the relationship of personality characteristics and cognitive abilities to the specific disability. Some parents want information about aiding their child in developing as much autonomy and independence as possible. They may desire information about realistic alternatives that may aid their child in making decisions about vocational training, careers, and other independent living concerns.

While families of the disabled are more similar than dissimilar to other families, there are special dimensions to routine parental tasks such as discipline, guidance, and nurturance. It is unrealistic to advise parents to treat their disabled child exactly like the other children in the family. Parents may need periodic counseling in relation to such issues as expectations, value conflicts, and life transitions. According to Gilbride (1993), professionals should particularly attend to the parents' attitudes about their ability to handle their child's needs. The parents' beliefs about themselves influence their expectations about the child's success.

In their initial shock, parents may experience a period of denial in which they seek advice from a multitude of sources and may move from professional to professional seeking a more hopeful diagnosis. Denial serves as a defense against the anxiety produced by the discrepancy between the desired healthy baby and the reality of the disabled child. It may be relatively easy to continue denial while the child is young and comparisons with other, normal children can be avoided. This denial may result in unrealistic expectations for achievement since there is "nothing wrong" with the child.

Anger usually follows denial, and this anger may be directed toward the child in the form of rejection or as envy of other parents who have normal children. Feelings of anger may also translate into guilt or resentment of one parent toward the other, which may lead to marital conflict.

Bargaining is often the next stage of the grief process in which the parents may believe that if they work hard enough and long enough in some special program, the child will be normal. When it becomes increasingly apparent that their child is still handicapped no matter what program they work at or which professional they consult, depression may result.

The grief may remain unresolved to a certain extent because of the recurring crises that center around the different stages in the life of the disabled child. These crises may include informing other family members and friends of the child's disability, coping with the educational needs of the child, dealing with special medical problems, and maintaining the child at home through adulthood. Attempts on the family's part to meet each new crisis may evoke the same feelings of sadness, anger, and grief (Turner, 1980).

To cope with overwhelming feelings of guilt and depression, parents either may become overprotective or may cause their child to avoid interaction with other children. Either move exacerbates the problem. The therapist can play a major role in aiding the family toward resolution of these issues.

Sometimes, parents attempt to cope with the stress caused by their child's disability in different ways. These differences may increase the conflict between the parents as a couple. One parent may become overinvolved and the other withdrawn and distant from the family. The family may become totally enmeshed in this process, resulting in confusion about roles and a failure on the part of the disabled child to develop appropriate self-concept and individuation.

Sibling rivalry is often exacerbated in families with a disabled child. Siblings may resent exemptions from rules given to the child with a disability. Or, a sibling may attempt to take over the parenting role and his or her own needs for attention and nurturing may be neglected. Professional intervention may focus on assisting the siblings in developing tolerance, educating them in how to adapt to their sister or brother with special needs, and reinforcing their ability to express their own needs to parents.

Fine (1991) proposes a collaborative model of parental involvement that has four primary objectives:

1. To include parents in the decision making regarding their child.
2. To educate parents for participation in the decision-making process regarding their child.
3. To assist parents therapeutically, as needed, to handle periodic crises.
4. To empower parents to work actively in behalf of their child.

This model has three dimensions: educational, which addresses the need for information and training; therapeutic, which addresses the need for parents to process and understand their emotions and experience; and organizational, which addresses the social support needs of parents.

Once rapport is established, a major component of the counseling relationship with parents of the disabled is that of anticipatory guidance (Fine, 1991). This refers to the giving of information at the optimal time regarding problems to expect. This information can be provided within the context of a group parent session or on an individual family basis. It is helpful to answer questions regarding the assessment process and current developmental functioning of the child, and to explain unfamiliar terminology. In addition, the procedures for gaining access to other resources such as advocacy groups is usually perceived as very useful by parents. This information can be incorporated into collaborative sessions intermittently to avoid overloading parents with too much data at one time. The therapist must be prepared for the ventilation of frustrations and complaints about other professionals and be able to handle such outpourings empathically. Comprehensive knowledge about disability conditions is essential for the therapist to work effectively with parents and families. Therefore, the therapist must have training and expertise in the etiology and psychoeducational implications of various disabilities. It is particularly helpful for the therapist to have a thorough knowledge of community resources and facilities for this population.

Parents of children with disabilities experience a number of unique problems. While no two experiences are exactly alike, some of the most common difficulties experienced by parents include (Cobb & Reeve, 1991):

- Accepting that the child has a disability.
- Coping with the increased financial responsibility associated with certain physical disabilities.
- Coping with stress built up by carrying a burden that cannot be adequately shared with others.
- Facing the conflict and ambivalence they may have regarding their child.
- Planning for the education and perhaps lifetime care of their child.

Training needs for the parents of the disabled are often more extensive for the preceding reasons.

Interventions can take the form of either primary parent education or family therapy. Turner (1980) proposed a list of five suggested interventions for families of children with mental retardation that are applicable to families of children with other disabilities:

1. An accurate assessment of family functioning is essential, including the strengths and weaknesses of the family system.

2. The family should be assisted in redirecting its focus from the handicapped child to examining the entire family's method of coping with change.

3. Attention should be directed to the communication network within the family and expression and acceptance of feelings encouraged.

4. The family should reinforce responsibility to supporting effective coping behaviors and encouraging their use.

5. The family should be provided with basic information about the child's disability and on how to locate additional resources as they are needed.

Multiple-family sessions may be helpful in facilitating the individual family's ability to cope. These sessions would provide the opportunity to families for sharing feelings, modeling effective coping skills, exchanging possible solutions to common problems, and increasing the knowledge base and awareness of future developmental crises. Depending on the disability, the child can be included in family therapy. If the child is moderately to severely retarded, the role may be quite limited, as is usually the case with children under the age of three.

As with families without a disabled member, some families with a disabled child may be dysfunctional and require significant professional assistance. This may occur for a number of reasons, such as the psychopathology of individual family members. Munro (1985) cites several characteristics of these dysfunctional families:

- *Chronic Complaining.* Any minor problem is perceived as a major crisis.
- *Program Sabotage.* Attempts to assist the family are blocked.
- *Extreme Overprotectiveness.* Attempts for individuation of any family member are thwarted.

In some families, the child with a disability may be actively avoided, either by both parents, or by one (Cobb & Gunn 1994). Therapists are advised to focus on specific here-and-now strategies, while working on developing a trust relationship with the family. In a study comparing three family treatment programs for family conflicts with adolescents who have ADHD, Barkley, Gueuremont, Anastopoulous, and Fletcher (1992) found that behavior management training, problem-solving/communication training, and structural family therapy were all effective in reducing conflicts. Furthermore, after treatment, mothers reported themselves as less depressed in all three approaches.

The "Families Program," developed by the University of Kansas Institute for Research in Learning Disabilities, described by Walter, Thomas, Hazel, Schumacher,

Vernon and Deshler, cited in Fine (1991), provides training for parents of learning-disabled children. The program includes relationship building, teaching, problem-solving, and goal achievement in an effort to prepare and support the family of a child with a learning disability. An evaluation of the program was quite favorable, with parents reporting increased feelings of effectiveness with their children, and children noticed positive changes in the ways their parents helped them with such things as homework and making friends.

Because of the unique stresses placed on the families of children with disabilities, the teaching of coping mechanisms is an important aspect of therapy and can aid families in a better understanding of their child's needs. If developmental factors are taken into account, family therapy can be a successful intervention.

## CONCLUSION

While children with disabilities have the same fundamental needs as their nondisabled peers, the techniques for therapeutic intervention must be modified for the therapy to be effective. Consideration must be given to the child's learning style, including cognitive abilities, length of attention span, and memory processes. Language and communication skills must also be considered; the level of language development is a key factor in the designing of interventions. In addition, the presence of any physical limitation must also be taken into account. The setting of objectives must be tempered by knowledge of the child's developmental level relative to his or her chronological age. When dealing with the disabled, therapeutic interventions are generally more concrete and involve the family.

Other special problems occur in the designing of interventions for the disabled:

- The child's acceptance of the disability.
- The child's relationship with his or her peer group.
- The degree of parental acceptance or rejection of the disability.
- The level of knowledge about the disability expressed by both parents and child.
- The level of dependency experienced by the child as a result of the disability.

A key goal for therapy is to provide detailed information to both the child and parents. A psychoeducational approach often aids in acceptance of the disability and dispels myths generally surrounding the perception of the disability. The therapist must also concentrate efforts on determining the dynamics of the family as a result of having a child with a disability. The early rearing strategies employed by parents with their child may be the key variable in explaining current modes of behavior. The intervention process must concentrate on the entire ecosystem, cutting across individual, family, and institutional settings. The current intervention literature on the disabled tends to stress the need for the clinician to have an awareness of the special characteristics of children and adolescents with disabilities within a systems context. This means implementing integrated interventions that involve the child, the family, and the school.

## ANNOTATED BIBLIOGRAPHY

Fine, M. (Ed.). (1991). *Collaboration with parents of exceptional children.* Brandon, VT: Clinical Psychology Publishing Co.

This book provides an excellent model for working with parents of exceptional children. The reader will find specific information regarding education and interventions, as well as common issues faced by families of the disabled.

Hallahan, D., & Kauffman, J. (1997). *7th Exceptional Learners: Introduction to special education* (7th ed.). Englewood Cliffs, NJ: Prentice-Hall.

This comprehensive text on exceptionality covers disabilities in-depth. It includes characteristics, interventions, and issues related to legislation, diversity, and resources for children and families.

Neely, M. A. (1982). *Counseling and guidance practices with special education students.* Homewood, IL: Dorsey Press.

Counseling techniques for use with the disabled receive comprehensive coverage in this book. The author discusses both individual and group interventions in a wide variety of settings including the schools. Parent counseling is also reviewed in depth.

Strohmer, D. C., & Prout, H. T. (Eds.). (1993). *Counseling and Psychotherapy with Persons with Mental Retardation and Boarderline Intelligence.* Brandon, VT: Clinical Psychology Publishing.

This thorough overview of counseling with the mildly mentally retarded includes sections on psychopathology, assessment, individual therapy, behavior therapy, group therapy, family therapy, and vocational counseling. It is an excellent resource for the practitioner.

## REFERENCES

American Psychiatric Association. (1994). *Diagnostic and statistical manual of mental disorders* (4th ed.). Washington, DC: Author.

Barkley, R. A., Gueuremont, D. C., Anastopoulos, A. D., & Fletcher, K. E. (1992). A comparison of three family therapy programs for treating family conflicts in adolescents with attention deficit hyperactivity disorder. *Journal of Consulting and Clinical Psychology, 60*(3), 450–462.

Becker, R. L. (1975). *The reading free vocational interest inventory.* Washington, DC: American Association of Mental Deficiency.

Begali, V. (1992). *Head injury in children and adolescents: A resource and review for school and allied professionals* (2nd ed.). Brandon, VT: Clinical Psychology.

Blacker, J. (1984). Sequential stages of parental adjustment to the birth of a child with handicaps: Fact or artifact? *Mental Retardation, 22,* 55–68.

Blohm, A. L. (1978). Group counseling with moderately mentally retarded and learning disabled elementary children (Doctoral dissertation, East Texas State University, 1978). *Dissertation Abstracts International, 39,* 3362A. (University Microfilms No. 7824128)

Brannigan, G. G., & Young, R. C. (1978). Social skills training with the MBD adolescent: A case study. *Academic Therapy, 13,* 214–222.

Carmichael, K. D. (1993). Play therapy for children with disabilities. *Issues in Comprehensive Pediatric Nursing, 16*(3), 165–173.

Chubon, R. (1982). An analysis of research dealing with the attitudes of professionals toward disability. *Journal of Rehabilitation, 48*(1), 25–30.

Cobb, H., & Gunn, W. (1994). Family intervention. In D. Strohmer & H. T. Prout (Eds.), *Counseling and psychotherapy with persons with mental retardation and borderline intelligence* (pp. 237–255). Brandon, VT: Clinical Psychology.

Cobb, H., & Reeve, R. (1991). Counseling approaches with parents and families. In M. Fine (Ed.), *Collaboration with parents of exceptional children.* Brandon, VT: Clinical Psychology.

Cook, P., Kunce, J., & Getsinger, S. (1976). Perception of the disabled and counseling effectiveness. *Rehabilitation Counseling Bulletin, 19,* 470–475.

Davidson, C. D. (1975). Psychotherapy with mentally handicapped children in a day school. *Psychotherapy: Theory, Research and Practice, 19,* 470–475.

DeBlassie, R. R., & Cowan, M. A. (1976). Counseling with the mentally handicapped child. *Elementary School Guidance and Counseling, 10*(4), 246–253.

Deutsch, H. (1985). Grief counseling with mentally retarded clients. *Psychiatric Aspects of Mental Retardation Reviews, 4*(5), 17–20.

Faigel, H. C., Sznajderman, S., Tishby, O., Turel, M., & Pinus, U. (1995). Attention deficit disorder during adolescence. *Journal of Adolescent Health, 16,* 174–184.

Fine, M. (Ed.). (1991a). *Collaboration with parents of exceptional children.* Brandon, VT: Clinical Psychology.

Fine, M. (1991b). The handicapped child and the family: Implications for professionals. In M. Fine (Ed.), *Collaboration with parents of exceptional children* (pp. 3–24). Brandon, VT: Clinical Psychology.

Gilbride, D. (1993). Parental attitudes toward their child with a disability: Implications for rehabilitation counselors. *Rehabilitation Counseling Bulletin, 36*(3), 139–150.

Gordon, S. (1975). The disabled are also sexual. In L. Buscaglia (Ed.), *The disabled and their parents: A counseling challenge.* Thorofare, NJ: Slack.

Greer, B. G. (1975). Attitudes of special education personnel toward different types of deviant persons. *Rehabilitation Literature, 36,* 182–184.

Halpern, A., Raffield, R., Irvin, L. K., & Link, R. (1975). *Social and prevocational information battery: Textbook user's guide, examiner's manual, technical report, answer key, class record.* Eugene: University of Oregon Rehabilitation Research Training Center in Mental Retardation.

Hayes, M. (1977). The responsiveness of mentally retarded children to psychotherapy. *Smith College Studies in Social Work, 47,* 112–153.

Humes, C. W., Adamszyk, J. S., & Myco, R. W. (1969). A school study of group counseling with educable retarded adolescents. *American Journal of Mental Deficiency, 74,* 191–195.

Hurley, A. D., & Hurley, F. J. (1986). Counseling and psychotherapy with mentally retarded clients: The initial interview. *Psychiatric Aspects of Mental Retardation Reviews, 5*(5), 22–26.

Kish, M. (1991). Counseling adolescents with L.D. *Intervention in School and Clinic, 27*(1), 20–24.

LaGreca, A. M., & Mesibov, G. B. (1979). Social skills intervention with learning disabled children: Selecting skills and implementing training. *Journal of Clinical Child Psychology, 8,* 234–241.

MacMillan, D. L. (1982). *Mental retardation in school and society* (2nd ed.). Glenview, IL: Scott & Foresman.

Meichenbaum, D. (1977). *Cognitive-behavior modification: An integrative approach.* New York: Plenum Press.

Morse, D. (1977). Counseling the young adolescent with learning disabilities. *School Counselor, 77,* 8–15.

Munro, J. D. (1985). Counseling severely dysfunctional families of mentally and physically disabled persons. *Clinical Social Work Journal, 13*(1), 18–31.

Nathanson, R. (1979). Counseling persons with disabilities: Are the feelings, thoughts, and behaviors of helping professionals helpful? *Personnel and Guidance Journal, 58,* 233–237.

National Joint Committee on Learning Disabilities. (1991). In J. K. Torgeson (Ed.), *Learning disabilities: Historical and conceptual issues.* San Diego, CA: Academic Press.

Neely, M. A. (1982). *Counseling and guidance practices with special education students.* Homewood, IL: Dorsey Press.

Olshansky, S. (1970). Chronic sorrow: A response to having a mentally defective child. In R. L. Noland (Ed.), *Counseling parents of the mentally retarded: A sourcebook.* Springfield, IL: Thomas.

Parker, R. M. (1991). *Occupational aptitude survey & interest schedule: Examiner's manual* (2nd ed.). Austin, TX: PRO.ED.

Parker, R. M. (1992). *The occupational aptitude survey and interest schedule: Interest survey* (2nd ed.). Austin, TX: PRO.ED.

Robinson, H. B., & Robinson, N. M. (1965). *The mentally retarded child: A psychological approach.* New York: McGraw-Hill.

Salvia, J., & Ysseldyke, J. M. (1991). *Assessment* (5th ed.). Boston: Houghton Mifflin.

Schontz, F. C. (1980). Theories about the adjustment to having a disability. In W. M. Cruickshank (Ed.), *Psychology of exceptional children and youth.* Englewood, NJ: Prentice-Hall.

Selwa, B. T. (1971). Preliminary considerations in psychotherapy with retarded children. *Journal of School Psychology, 9,* 12–15.

Tharinger, D., Horton, C. B., & Millea, S. (1990). Sexual abuse and exploitation of children and adults with mental retardation and other handicaps. *Child Abuse & Neglect, 14,* 301–312.

Turner, A. (1980). Therapy with families of a mentally retarded child. *Journal of Marital and Family Therapy, 6*(2), 167–170.

Varley, C. K. (1984). Schizophreniform psychoses in mentally retarded girls following sexual assault. *American Journal of Psychiatry, 141,* 593–595.

Walker, N. W. (1997). *Best practices in assessment and programming for students with TBI.* Raleigh: North Carolina State Department of Instruction.

Welch, V. O., & Sigman, M. (1980). Group psychotherapy with mildly retarded, emotionally disturbed adolescents. *Journal of Clinical Child Psychology, 9,* 209–212.

Wells, L., & Allan, J. (1985). Counseling the mentally handicapped students. *Guidance and Counseling, 1*(2), 13–21.

Yuker, H. (Ed.). (1988). *Attitudes toward persons with disabilities.* New York: Springer.

Zigmond, N., & Brownlee, J. (1980). Social skills training for adolescents with learning disabilities. *Exceptional Education Quarterly, 2,* 77–83.

# Index